D0771134

COLLECTIVE BEHAVIOR AND SOCIAL MOVEMENTS

COLLECTIVE BEHAVIOR AND SOCIAL MOVEMENTS

Edited by

RUSSELL L. CURTIS, JR.
University of Houston

BENIGNO E. AGUIRRE
Texas A&M University

ALLYN AND BACON
Boston London Toronto Sydney Tokyo Singapore

Senior Editor: Karen Hanson
Editor-in-Chief of Social Sciences: Susan Badger
Production Administrator: Annette Joseph
Production Coordinator: Holly Crawford
Editorial-Production Service: Lynda Griffiths, TKM Productions
Cover Administrator: Linda K. Dickinson
Cover Designer: Suzanne Harbison
Manufacturing Buyer: Louise Richardson

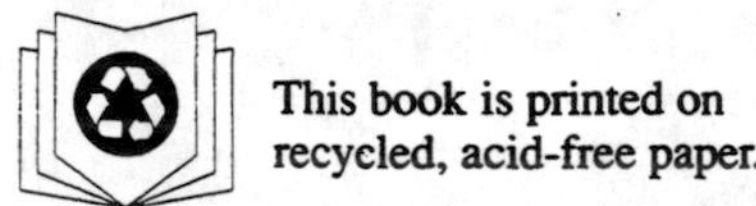

This book is printed on
recycled, acid-free paper.

Library of Congress Cataloging-in-Publication Data

Curtis, Russell L.
Collective behavior and social movements / Russell L. Curtis, Jr., and Benigno E. Aguirre.
p. cm.
Includes bibliographical references.
ISBN 0-205-14533-7
1. Collective behavior. 2. Social movements. 3. Social movements—United States. I. Aguirre, Benigno E. II. Title.
HM281.C87 1992
303.48'4—dc20 92-17669
CIP

Printed in the United States of America
10 9 8 7 6 5 4 3 2 97 96 95 94 93 92

CONTENTS

PART FOUR
Organizational Arrangements of Collective Behavior and Social Movements 227

Preface

Our long and sustained interest in collective behavior and social movements, and the rejuvenation of interest in the field by social scientists, prompted the publication of this book. The belief that social organization and culture cannot be understood without a comprehension of noninstitutionalized social change has been strengthened by recent events such as the legitimation revolution of Iran and the radical transformation of Eastern Europe and the former Soviet Union. This view has been further underscored by the appearance of new religions, the continued pursuit of environmental and moral questions through citizen groups, and the rapid legal and political acceptance of such groups as Mothers Against Drunk Drivers (MADD).

Near the completion of this volume in April 1992, riots were occurring in Los Angeles following the acquittal of police officers on most counts of brutality by a California jury. According to subsequent interviews with anonymous jurors, the jury's deliberations had centered on the meaning of *brutality* and led to a "definition of a situation." The national viewing audience, having seen a videotape of Rodney King's beating by police officers, had already formed its own interpretation. The unanticipated decision for acquittal on most counts resulted in violence and rioting. After the riots, members of the media and politicians offered editorial definitions of the collective behavior.

Post-riot analyses of the Los Angeles events included the suggestion that protests may accompany the presidential nomination conventions, pointing to widespread public dissatisfaction with the economy, including the unemployment rate and the national debt, as well as the health care delivery system, public education, and domestic affairs in general. If rumors prove valid, the two national conventions will face the collective dissatisfaction of pro-life and pro-choice groups, environmentalists, labor representatives, and advocates for the homeless and for children, among others. In essence, there promises to be informal, collective effort to gain the formal, institutional support of the presidential nominees and their parties.

There were several considerations in undertaking this project. First, despite the large number of radical social changes in the United States and throughout the world, and despite the evident growth in interest and productive research in the field of collective behavior and social movements, there have been no new anthologies on the topic for over a decade.

Second, this text represents an effort to address an academic imbalance between the increasing emphasis on formal movement structures and decreasing attention to episodic and seemingly chaotic behaviors (crowds, riots, etc.) and between an increasing focus on supposedly rational movement elements (e.g., planned protests, professional protest leadership) and a deemphasis on the so-called emotional components (e.g., crowds, crazes, fads, riots) that are part of the same process. The readings present and synthesize the interplay of the emergent and informal, as collective action begins, and the structured and formal, as it *may* become institutionalized.

Third, the book contains a blend of both classic and contemporary material. The articles have been carefully selected to depict the current, central issues in methodology and theory as well as fundamental intellectual statements and perspectives by outstanding scholars.

As the research and publications have grown, so, too, have the subfields and the "camps" within the area of collective behavior and social movements. Thus, a fourth purpose is to examine the reliability of research findings and the consistency of conceptual and theoretical interpretations that are prevalent in the literature. The selections embrace the content of conflict and controversy, yet avoid symbolic and stylistic disagreement.

Finally, this text fits our purpose to continue our commitment to the moral, ethical, and social implications of collective protests and social movements. The extraordinary increases in protest and revolutionary events now appear to be *non*exceptional in Latin America, Eastern Europe, the former USSR, the Middle East, and South Africa. Although the extent to which social movement organizations have planned and led the recent collective behavior events in the former USSR, China, Eastern Europe, and the West Bank and Gaza is unknown, the reports we have show that these momentous events were brought about in large part by the collective action of millions of people who shared a perceived sense of national destiny and a desire to resolve their widespread discontent. Factors such as long-repressed national aspirations, old symbols of religion and motherland, felt needs to pay homage to national martyrs, the weakening of official ideology and organs of social control, the exuberance of youth long constrained by rigid doctrine and practice, the transformation of information fields brought about by the new organs of the electronic world culture, as well as the action of social movement organizations, structured these events.

This book is organized into six parts. The first is structured around definitions of the field of collective behavior and the importance of technology, resources, rewards, norms, and emotions. The second part discusses the precipitating episodes of collective behavior and social movements, including existing power arrangements, absolute and relative deprivation, social change, and the setting of collective action. Part Three presents works on mobilization for collective action dealing with networks, rumors, emergent norms, crowd emergence, and organization. Part Four explores the organizational arrangements of formal movement goals, leadership and membership control, recruitment and socialization, and resources. The next part centers on movement environment and response. It considers the interorganizational field and the strategies and tactics of movements and collective action. Part Six presents works on the outcomes of collective behavior and social movements at the individual, organizational, institutional, and societal levels.

Undoubtedly, much worthwhile research and theorizing in the specialty of collective behavior and social movements could not be included in this text. Nevertheless, we are confident that the excellent scholarship presented here will convince our readers to read more in what is perhaps one of the most exciting and relevant areas of investigation in the social sciences. Much remains to be learned, and this book is our invitation to you, our readers, to participate in the process of discovery.

ACKNOWLEDGMENTS

The risks and difficulties of this type of book were well known to us in the beginning. Yet, we believed that the fact that no general anthologies, to our knowledge, had appeared in the area of collective behavior and social movements during the past decade demanded our continued commitment and investment.

Karen Hanson of Allyn and Bacon was enthusiastic and encouraging throughout the project. Her attentive suggestions kept us going during some doubtful moments.

The Department of Sociology at the University of Houston supplied funds for the production of copies and made other resources available. We thank Gary Dworkin, Chair of the Department, for this assistance.

Other colleagues made important contributions. Especially helpful were the critical reactions to the general project by Helen Ebaugh and the detailed and extensive contributions of Joe Kotarba to selected articles. They responded quickly and graciously to some of our emergency requests. We would also like to thank Elisa Tyler, who helped keep the project in motion during one hot summer in Houston. She prepared letters, made copies of articles, made more copies of the same articles, helped with permissions, and kept things in order. More, she was instrumental in keeping us on schedule. Mary Jo Duncan and Lonnie Anderson helped us at the end in an emergency attempt to meet deadlines. They did so at a moment's notice, adding enthusiasm, efficiency, and grace to our efforts. Finally, we thank the authors and journals for their permission to reprint the material.

COLLECTIVE BEHAVIOR AND SOCIAL MOVEMENTS

PART ONE

Introductory Overview

Part One begins with Ralph H. Turner and Lewis M. Killian's conceptualization of the field of collective behavior. Turner and Killian's classic text is *Collective Behavior,* now in its third edition, from which we present their introduction to the field of collective behavior. Their book and their many other publications have had enormous impact on the development of the specialty. The authors utilize a symbolic interactionist conception of social organization. They define *collective behavior* as "those forms of social behavior in which usual conventions cease to guide social action and people collectively transcend, bypass, or subvert established institutional patterns and structures." Faced with an urgent shared problem that cannot be solved by the established institutions, people interact and consider alternative solutions; out of this meaning-creating social process, a new norm emerges to guide the actions of the collectivity. The occurrence of collective behavior depends on the feasibility and timeliness of the acts, the extent of preexisting social networks and other support available to people considering acting collectively, and their normative justification.

Article 2 consists of excerpts from Neil J. Smelser's *Theory of Collective Behavior*. Almost three decades after publication, this work continues to be the most elegant theory in the specialty. According to this theory, collective behavior occurs under situations of structural strain among values, norms, motivational systems, and situational facilities—what are termed the *components of social action*. Collective behavior is characterized by the shortcircuiting of the appropriate relationships among these components under the influence of a generalized belief that is akin to a magical belief. The theory is also important because of its detailed specifications of the necessary and sufficient conditions that must exist for the occurrence of the various forms of collective behavior it models. It is unfortunate that consideration of the indisputable LeBonian undertones of Smelser's definition of *collective behavior* has distracted attention from the other (in our view, more solid) elements of the theory, such as its placement of collective behavior within a general structural explanation of social organization, the demarcation of collective behavior forms, and the identification of unique sets of explanatory factors associated with each. Quarantelli and Hundley (see Article 19) offer what for many is the most definitive test of this theory at present.

The next reading, Richard A. Berk's gaming approach to collective behavior (Article 3), presents an examination of the microdynamics of crowd behavior. Its focus is on the person having to decide what to do in a social situation in flux. The gaming approach conceives participants as trying to maximize benefits and minimize costs of interaction. It also recognizes that the actor must attend to the behavior of the collectivity, for such collective behavior is an important determinant of individual utilities. Another important contribution of the gaming approach, also used in research by David Snow and colleagues (see Article 17), among others, is the importance it gives to the ecological context in which collective behavior occurs: its time and space coordinates. As Berk indicates, the gaming approach can be understood within the symbolic interactionist tradition represented by emergent norms (see Article 1), although its emphasis on the effects of time and space on processes of communication and collective symbolism, reminiscent of Erving Goffman's ideas, is distinctly its own.

Article 4 is John D. McCarthy and Mayer N. Zald's influential article on the resource mobilization approach to the study of social movement. Its focus on the complex organizational components of social movements fills an important gap in understanding social movements. Among the worthwhile contributions of the approach is a new vocabulary to understand social movements, the realization that social movements are often planned affairs in which the organization creates the discontent, the linkage of the emergence of social movement organizations with career interests of social movement entrepreneurs, and the exploration of the variegated sources of potential support that may be operating in specific movements and countermovements. The approach generates many testable hypotheses, perhaps one reason for its popularity at present. For example, McCarthy and Zald hypothesize that the resources available to the social movement sector are a function of the extent of discretionary resources of elites and masses in a society. They also hypothesize that the relative level of resources of the social movement sector facilitates the emergence of social movement industries and organizations, and that the type of resources available to an organization will impact its strategy and tactics. (A number of the articles included in this text reflect the influence of this ascendant theoretical perspective.)

The next reading is Herbert Blumer's conceptualization of social problems as collective behavior (Article 5). It is an influential reinterpretation of the nature of social problems. Its focus is on the process of social construction through which a collectively shared definition and solution to a social problem emerges. According to Blumer, the creation of social problems involves their legitimation, mobilization of action, formation of an official plan of action, and implementation of the official plan. At each of these stages, Blumer emphasizes their importance on the eventual fate of the proposed problem, the organizational acts for and against it, and the weight of established interests, planning, and compromise on the claims. Although Blumer does not explicitly use the concepts of the resource mobilization approach (see Article 5), his article is couched at the interorganizational level, focusing on the strategy and tactics of organized collectivities. Blumer's linkage of collective behavior and social movement phenomena, as well as his acknowledgment of the importance of collective behavior processes within institutions such as the legislature, is a refreshing reaffirmation of the value of a holistic vision of sociology.

Article 6, by Jack M. Weller and E. L. Quarantelli, is one of the most influential criticisms and expansions of Turner and Killian's emergent norm formulation (see Article 1). Its typology of collective behavior and institutionalized social organizational forms, built around the general concepts of norms and social relations, adds to the understanding of collective behavior. Among its contributions is maintaining the separation between collective behavior and institutionalized behavior, and acknowledging that at times collective behavior does not involve emergent norms and social relationships but instead results from the "confluence of previously dissociated norms and relationships." This insight finds fuller expression in Zald and Berger's reading (Article 9).

Finally, Part One concludes with Article 7, John Lofland's typology of collective behavior forms constructed through the use of dominant emotion and organizational forms. Three dominant emotions are employed: fear, hostility, and joy. Two organizational forms intersect them: the crowd and the mass. Within each of the resulting cells, the author identifies collective behavior forms in accordance with the strength of the dominant emotion that characterizes them. Thus, for example, Lofland develops eight subtypologies of joyful crowds, diminishing in levels of joy, from the ecstatic upheaval to the excited crowd. The reading presents an extraordinary synthesis of a vast body of literature. Also laudable is Lofland's unique and valuable attempt to reclaim a place of theoretical import for the concept of dominant emotion without recourse to by now devalued collective behavior explanations centered on the irrationality of participants. Because of the striking differences among them, this typology should be compared to the typology presented by Weller and Quarantelli (Article 6).

ARTICLE 1

The Field of Collective Behavior

RALPH H. TURNER
LEWIS M. KILLIAN

In the year 1096, in the square before the cathedral at Clermont, Pope Urban II issued his call for a crusade to free the Holy Land. Within a short time the whole of Europe was in a state of unprecedented excitement and feverish activity.

The Crusades

For several months after the Council of Clermont, France and Germany presented a singular spectacle. The pious, the fanatic, the needy, the dissolute, the young and the old, even women and children, and the halt and lame, enrolled themselves by hundreds. In every village the clergy were busied in keeping up the excitement, promising eternal rewards to those who assumed the red cross, and fulminating the most awful denunciations against all the worldly-minded who refused or even hesitated.... All those who had property of any description rushed to the mart to change it into hard cash. Lands and houses could be had for a quarter of their value, while arms and accoutrements of war rose in the same proportion. ... During the spring and summer of this year (1096) the roads teemed with crusaders, all hastening to the towns and villages appointed as the rendezvous of the district. Some were on horseback, some in carts, and some came down the rivers in boats and rafts, bringing their wives and children, all eager to go to Jerusalem. Very few knew where Jerusalem was. Some thought it fifty miles away, and others imagined that it was but a month's journey; while at sight of every town or castle the children exclaimed, "Is that Jerusalem? Is that the city?"

Nearly a thousand years later, in the United States, hundreds of "crusaders" converged at the call of a modern spiritual leader, Martin Luther King, Jr., to march the fifty miles from Selma to Montgomery, Alabama.

The Selma March

In a growing stream, the marchers assembled in Selma. The men, women, and children who followed King into the streets and into jail all through the campaign were ready to walk again. And outsiders flocked to his call; clerics and nuns, pert coeds and hot-eyed student rebels; VIP's like the U.N.'s Ralph Bunche and anonymous farmhands from the southwest Alabama cattle, corn and cotton country. A blind man came from Atlanta, a one-legged man from Saginaw, Michigan. An Episcopal minister from Minneapolis got plane fare from a parishioner and took the gift to be a sign from God that he should make the pilgrimage. And a little Selma Negro girl tagged along "for freedom and justice and so the troopers can't hit us no more."

Both of these crusades, as far separated in history as they were, raised the same sorts of questions and doubts in the minds of observers. Were the goals as simple and noble as the leaders

Ralph H. Turner and Lewis M. Killian, *Collective Behavior*, 3rd ed., © 1987, pp. 1–14, 16. Reprinted by permission of Prentice Hall, Englewood Cliffs, New Jersey.

represented them to be? Were the leaders really devout men of God seeking to overcome the forces of evil, or were they cynical schemers seeking fame, treasure, or power? Were the rank and file of the crusaders, ancient and modern, motivated by sincere religious conviction, or were they, wittingly or unwittingly, really seeking adventure, loot, or publicity? What did these events, which social scientists call social movements, accomplish? After all the sacrifices made by the participants in a social movement, is the course of history significantly altered, and if it is, to what extent is the change in the direction envisioned by the leaders and followers?

Robert E. Park, the sociologist who founded the field called *collective behavior*, believed such actions played a central part in social change. He used the term *crowd* in a broad sense that seems strange today, writing, "The great classic examples of crowds are the last vast migration of peoples, the Crusades, and the French Revolution."

Although he described the mechanisms of collective behavior in language which carried what today we consider misleading implications—"the social epidemic" and "the influence of a collective stimulus"—he did not regard the crowd as merely a bizarre, destructive, pathological collectivity. Rather, he said of the Crusades and the French Revolution, "Crowd movements played a double role here—they were the forces which dealt the final blow to old existing institutions, and they introduced the spirit of the new ones."

A few years before Park coined the term *collective behavior*, some European scholars, including Gustave LeBon in France, Scipio Sighele and Pasquale Rossi in Italy, and Sigmund Freud in Vienna, had begun writing about what they called "crowd psychology," "collective psychology," or "group psychology." All of them emphasized the irrationality and abnormality of the crowd. Freud said of the mobs which he saw in Paris as a young man, "I believe they are all possessed of a thousand demons. . . . They are the people of psychical epidemics, of historical mass convulsions." Nearly a hundred years later many observers, both laypeople and "experts," still invoke such notions to explain what they regard as unusual and undesirable group behavior. After 11 people were killed in a crowd trying to get into an auditorium for a rock concert in Cincinnati, the mayor of the city said that the crowd "lost all sense of rationality." Psychologists and psychiatrists told a reporter that "mob psychology" was operating—"the tendency of individuals to be carried away by the excitement of the groups, a contagious flow of energy, a situation in which emotion outweighs rational thinking. . . ."

Although most sociologists now reject such explanations, they still find that such behavior stimulates novel questions about human group action. Accustomed to studying the regularities of group life made predictable by stable social structures and traditional norms, they ask questions about the social and psychological forces that come into play in situations where established institutional patterns cease to guide human activities. The sociologist asks questions related primarily to the interaction among the individuals who make up a crowd or social movement. How do they influence one another? Are the processes of interpersonal influence and the operation of social control similar to those found in ordinary group behavior or are different ones brought into play? How are the actions of different members coordinated? What is the relative importance of common predispositions, imitation, role-taking, and conformity to social norms in producing coordinated action? Do norms exist in a collectivity? If so, how do they develop, what is their relationship to the preexisting norms of the society, and what leads people to conform to them? A common view of collective behavior implies that it consists simply of the violation of usual norms by a large number of people at the same time—that it is disorganized, deviant behavior. The sociologist asks whether there may not be some sort of social organization present and conformity to some norms, no matter how deviant the behavior may seem as measured by usual standards.

Since a collectivity is made up of individuals, the sociologist is also concerned with the relationship of the characteristics that these people bring with them to the situation. How do such individual properties as age, education, and socioeconomic status affect the propensity of persons to become involved in collective behavior and the types they will engage in? How much does knowledge of the preexisting attitudes and the personality characteristics of participants help to predict and explain both the emergence and the nature of collective behavior?

It is the fact that people do, at times, collectively engage in behavior that seems to contrast with normal social and institutional behavior that leads the sociologist to define a special field of study. That this behavior appears to be not simply a large number of deviant acts by individuals that happen to occur at the same time, but rather seems to reflect some common influence on the participants or some interaction between them, leads the sociologist to look for the sources of coordination that make the behavior truly collective despite its contrast to conventional group behavior. Three general types of theory have emerged during this quest, each emphasizing a different possible source of coordination. *Convergence* theories focus on the characteristics and predispositions which individuals bring to the situation, suggesting that the simultaneous presence of people who are already similar in some way explains the emergence and the course of action of a collectivity. *Contagion* theories emphasize special psychological mechanisms whereby moods, attitudes, and behavior are communicated rapidly and accepted uncritically. *Emergent norm* theories emphasize the definition of the situation which arises under out-of-the-ordinary circumstances. This definition of emergent norm serves to guide and coordinate behavior by providing for the actors both *meaning*, an interpretation of what is going on, and *rules* about what sorts of behavior are consistent with this definition.

DEFINITION OF COLLECTIVE BEHAVIOR

While Park and later students of collective behavior had much to say about the excitement, the emotion, and sometimes the destructiveness of crowds and social movements, these were never their central interests. They have not regarded the various forms as sideshows to history, freakish but inconsequential; rather, they have viewed them as central to the drama of social change. Park never regarded the crowd as the only significant form of collectivity. His doctoral dissertation, written at Heidelberg in 1903, was entitled *Masse und Publikum*—"The Crowd and the Public." While he believed that the public, in contrast to the crowd, was controlled by the norms of logic, he still argued that both "serve to bring individuals out of old ties and into new ones." Similarly, current popular interest in the sometimes exciting, sometimes horrifying behavior of crowds is matched by interest in publics and public opinion. Many people would readily agree with Park that many social changes begin with slow, cumulative shifts in public opinion. Of equal interest to both laypeople and social scientists are the activities of social movements. Much of the daily news and of the content of history books consists of accounts of the challenges offered by social movements.

In line with both popular preoccupations and the classic definitions advanced by Park and his student, Herbert Blumer, we included as the major forms of collectivities the *crowd*, the *public* and the *social movement*. These are the types of human groupings in which what we call collective behavior usually takes place. As Blumer points out, all social behavior is "collective," so the use of the term to refer to a particular kind is arbitrary and conventional. As he put it, however, "The student of collective behavior seeks to understand the way in which a new social order arises, for the appearance of a new social order is equivalent to the emergence of new forms of collective behavior."

Not all the collective behavior studied by social scientists is so momentous as the phrase "the appearance of a new social order" suggests. Often episodes of crowd behavior constitute mere interludes of revelry, flight, acquisitiveness or destructiveness. Not all social movements are of profound political or religious significance. Even the less significant instances of collective behavior are worthy of study, however, because in them we may be able to observe the dynamics which operate in all types of collectivities and perhaps in all human groups.

Collective behavior may be defined as those forms of social behavior in which usual conventions cease to guide social action and people collectively transcend, bypass, or subvert established institutional patterns and structures. The field thus defined is clearly a division of sociology, not of social psychology. Collective behavior refers to the actions of collectivities, not to a type of individual behavior.

As a group, a collectivity is more than simply a number of individuals. A group always consists of people who are in interaction and whose interaction is affected by some sense that they constitute a unit. This latter sense is most universally expressed in the members' concern to define the group's opinions and what the group expects of its members.

But collective behavior is not merely identical with the study of groups. A contrast is generally drawn between collective behavior and organizational behavior. Organizational behavior is the behavior of groups that are governed by established rules of procedure, which have the force of tradition behind them. Even in the case of a new organization, there is generally a concern to find operating rules that have sanction in the larger culture, such as Robert's *Rules of Order*, and any action once taken becomes an incipient tradition through the principle of observing precedent. Collectivities, or the groups within which collective behavior takes place, are not guided in a straightforward fashion by the culture of the society, however. Although a collectivity has members, it lacks defined procedures for selecting and identifying members. Although it has leaders, it lacks defined procedures for selecting and identifying them. The members are those who happen to be participating, and the leaders are those who are being followed by the members. The collectivity is oriented toward an object of attention and arrives at some shared objective, but these are not defined in advance, and there are no formal procedures for reaching decisions.

There is coordination of at least an elementary sort between the individual members' actions. In some instances, such as panic flight, the behavior of each individual is similar and parallel to that of the others, and the behavior of all is directed toward the same objective. In other cases, a division of labor may be discerned in the collectivity, giving the impression of a more complex coordination of the members. Yet the coordination and direction do not seem amenable to explanation in terms of established norms, preexisting social organization, or primary-group integration. There exists, nevertheless, a sense of constraint that forces individuals into certain types of behavior and leads to punishment of nonconformity. The task of studying collective behavior involves identification of the sources of this coordination and exploration of the relationship to ordinary social behavior.

Collective behavior contrasts even more sharply with institutional behavior, which characterizes groups that are envisaged in and guided by the culture of the larger society. Yet the continuity between all these ideal types of human interaction must be emphasized. Although in some cases, as in short-lived crowds, collective behavior may involve people who are essentially strangers to each other, in most instances it develops between people who are already related to each other in organizations or informal groups. The emergence of both new norms and new social relationships must thus be considered. Jack Weller and E. L. Quarantelli underscored this when they observed, "Phenomena need not involve the emergence of both social norms and relationships to be usefully regarded as collective behavior." They suggested a threefold typology. In one type the normal social relationships endure but norms emerge, as when a hospital staff has to operate in an extraordinary fashion during a disaster. In a second type enduring norms are followed but an emergent, ephemeral collectivity carries out the action—this we have called "conventionalized" collective behavior. It is of the type that occurs week after week in football crowds in the United States, or at rock concerts. Collective behavior involving both emergent norms and emergent structure or social relationships constitutes only one of these three ideal types. It is of particular importance in the analysis of social movements, for an important element of this sort of collectivity is the action of one or more pre-existing "social movement organizations" around which is formed a new coalition with a somewhat novel program of action.

THE HISTORY OF THE FIELD

Although we identify Robert E. Park as the founder of the field of study called collective behavior, interest in the phenomenon goes back much earlier and has never been confined to sociologists. An example of such an early interest was the book published in 1841 by an English scholar, Charles Mackay, entitled *Memoirs of Extraordinary Delusions and the Madness of Crowds*. Gustave LeBon, writing a half-century later, was representative of a number of writers who held a predominantly negative view of the behavior of what they called "the crowd." LeBon, for example, believed that when the "mind of the crowd" took over—whether in a mob, in the French Chamber of Deputies, or in an entire nation—people acted destructively, under the influence of instincts which are ordinarily inhibited.

Such views have since been reflected in what became a very popular explanation of collective behavior, although not among sociologists—the pathological approach. This often represented an application of some version of psychoanalytic theory to the analysis of social movements as well as of crowds. One of the earliest examples was *The Behavior of Crowds*, written in 1920 by Everett Dean Martin. Martin regarded the crowd not as a particular kind of collectivity but as a mental condition resulting from simultaneous release of repressed, socially forbidden impulses. Thus, he coined the memorable saying that the crowd consists of "people going crazy together." A more recent view of collective behavior as irrational and socially undesirable is to be found in the widely read paperback book by the longshoreman-philosopher, Eric Hoffer—*The True Believer*.

So widespread was the influence of what Lang and Lang have called the "pathological view" of the crowd and social movements that critics have mistaken it for the dominant theme in sociological theories of collective behavior. In 1970 Currie and Skolnick asserted:

> *Collective behavior theory has its roots in the antidemocratic theorists of nineteenth-century Europe, best represented by LeBon. In being transferred to American social science, the antidemocratic biases in "crowd" theory were modified but not abolished.*
>
> *Perhaps the most fundamental of these biases is the implication that collective behavior is in some sense "irrational" behavior.*

But a conscientious reading of the work of such sociologists as Robert E. Park, Herbert Blumer, Ralph Turner, Kurt and Gladys Lang, and Joseph Gusfield shows that all have rejected the assumption that collective behavior is necessarily less rational than institutional behavior. A possible exception is Neil Smelser, who developed a social-structural explanation derived from Talcott Parsons' general theory of social action. In Smelser's "value-added" approach, the major determinant of collective behavior is some sort of strain in the social structure, demanding action to relieve the strain and reorganize the structure. The social-psychological mechanism involved, however, is mobilization under a generalized belief, and Smelser's "generalized belief" does sound very much like some of LeBon's ideas. It is held to be both generalized and "short-circuited," leading to action that bypasses many of the specifications and controls required for effective, realistic social action. So, Smelser says, "Collective behavior is the action of the impatient."

The widespread social movements and the many instances of anti-establishment crowd action which swept the cities and campuses of the United States during the 1960s aroused an unprecedented interest in the topic. If "classical" collective behavior theory did indeed portray collective behavior as irrational, irresponsible, and destructive, then it could be charged with reflecting a political bias in favor of law and order and of sympathy with official perspectives on social problems and how to solve them. Thus there developed what may be called a "politico-rational" approach to collective behavior rejecting the stereotype of irrationality and substituting one which, in the words of Gary Marx, tended to "see all violent outbursts as 'rational,' 'intrinsically political,' and 'instrumental and purposive.'" Rather than rejecting the utility of the concepts "rational" and "irrational" as applied to group behavior, many sociologists merely reversed what they perceived as the traditional emphasis.

While the impassioned defense of any kind of anti-establishment social action as "rational" subsided during the 1970s, the emphasis on rationality in collective behavior did not. Widespread interest developed in theories emphasizing the rationality of decision making in collective behavior. The "gaming approach" advocated by Richard Berk seeks to apply decision theory to crowds, attempting to develop methods for discovering how each individual tries to maximize rewards and minimize costs as he or she considers various courses of action. Even more widely applied has been the approach to social movements called by its advocates "resource mobilization theory." It, too, emphasizes "the importance of costs and rewards in explaining individual and organizational involvement in social movement activity." Charles Perrow has described two variants of this theoretical approach. What he calls "RM I" has been formulated mainly by Anthony Oberschall, Charles Tilly, and William Gamson. RM I, Perrow says, "is Clausewitzian in character; protest is the continuation of orderly politics by other (disorderly) means. Because protest grows out of the ongoing political process and is a part of it, it need not be irrational nor discontinuous. . . ." The RM II version has been formulated by Mayer Zald and John McCarthy. It is even more rationalistic that RM I theory, and is based on an economic-organizational, input-output model.

None of these approaches is derived from the tradition based on the attempt of Robert E. Park to delineate a field of study in sociology which he termed collective behavior. Although many of Park's characterizations of crowd behavior seem to reflect a pathological approach, it is clear that he did not regard collective behavior as abnormal or undesirable. Impressed by the powerful hold of culture and social control on the members of a society, he was intrigued by the question of how they could ever break out of their established routines and establish a new social order. The alternation between the old and the new—in other words, social change—was to him as normal a part of social life as was order, tradition, and continuity. Although he placed undue emphasis on "impulse" as the dynamic element in collective behavior, he emphasized that the "common and collective impulse was always the result of social interaction." That he did not believe the crowd to be driven by repressed, instinctive forces to act blindly and irrationally is indicated by his assertion that, "the organized crowd is controlled by a common purpose and acts to achieve, no matter how vaguely it is defined, a common end." He added that in contrast to the animal herd, "the crowd . . . responds to collective representations."

In 1939, Park's student, Herbert Blumer, wrote what has become a classic statement on the nature of collective behavior. He was asked to contribute a section on the topic to a volume called *Principles of Sociology* which Park was editing. Blumer's contribution consisted of five chapters. In the first three, he outlined the mechanisms of elementary collective groupings—the crowd, the mass, and the public. In a separate chapter, he dealt with social movements which he regarded as differing from elementary forms in that "as a social movement develops, it takes on the character of a society," developing a culture, a social organization, and a new scheme of life.

Like Park, Blumer did not regard collective behavior as pathological, destructive behavior. It was to be, rather, that part of sociology devoted to the study of social action which was not under the influence of custom, tradition, conventions, rules, or institutional regulations—behavior which "arises spontaneously and is not due to pre-established understandings or traditions." Its importance lay in the fact that

> *while the student of sociology in general is interested in studying the social order and its constituents (customs, rules, institutions, etc.) as they are, collective behavior is concerned with studying ways by which the social order comes into existence, in the sense of the emergence and solidification of new forms of collective behavior.*

Blumer was also a student of the philosopher and social psychologist, George Herbert Mead, whose ideas became the basis of what is known as the symbolic interactionist approach in sociology. This includes important conceptions of the nature of society and of individual action. One is that "society," the social order of which Park and Blumer wrote, is not a static system or structure but a process of ongoing activity in which human beings construct and share their social worlds. Hence the approach to collective behavior derived from Park through Blumer has never been compatible with concepts of structural determinism. A second important feature is that the individual is viewed primarily as an actor, constructing his or her line of behavior by making symbolic representations to the self as to what the situation is and what other people expect—hence "symbolic interactionism." Therefore the "collective behavior" approach has historically incorporated the notion that people act on conceptions rather than on objective reality, even though these conceptions may have to be revised as they are tested by encounters with reality. This emphasis on consciousness as the most salient characteristic of human social action makes the approach incompatible with theories of biological or psychological determinism which view human behavior as merely the release of impulses in overt action.

Many of the concepts used by Blumer in his early, tentative treatment of the "mechanisms of elementary collective behavior," such as "circular reaction," "social contagion," and "homogeneity" seem to later writers in the collective behavior tradition to be inappropriate or misleading. In his own subsequent writings, he used them less and less and used more concepts derived from the symbolic interactionist approach which he pioneered and named. What has endured to characterize the "collective behavior" approach has been the emphasis on the centrality of interaction, the emergent nature of social order, and the normality of collective behavior as the vehicle through which social change comes about.

QUESTIONS ABOUT COLLECTIVE BEHAVIOR

This conception of collective behavior treats it as normal, not pathological or irrational, but still distinguishes it from the relatively stable and predictable forms of group behavior guided by traditional norms. If we are to understand collective behavior we must begin by singling out its distinctive features for explanation. First, we must explain how it is that people come to transcend, bypass, or subvert established institutional patterns and structures. Dissatisfied with their spiritual life, people may participate more actively in an established church or they may form a cult or sect that operates on the margins of established society. Annoyed when the California Transportation Authority reserved one Los Angeles freeway lane for car-pooling and buses only, commuters might have called or written their elected representatives. Instead, for several days, hundreds of single-occupant vehicles took over the reserved lane each morning by prearranged schedule in defiance of the new regulations. Restive when gates are not opened on time, concert-goers may "gripe" but wait and enter in orderly fashion when the gates finally open, or they may storm the gates and trample over fallen individuals in their haste to reach seats.

Second, we must explain behavior or action as contrasted with attitudes. Many more people sympathize with the antinuclear movement or the protest against federal income taxes than send in contributions, demonstrate at construction sites, or withhold payment of their taxes. Discontent was widespread in the black ghettos of the United States for years before the mass eruptions of the 1960s occurred. An adequate approach to collective behavior must analyze how perceptions, ideas, and feelings get translated into action.

Third, we must explain the fact that people act collectively rather than singly. The rhythmic stamping of feet by hundreds of concert-goers in unison is different from isolated, individual cries of "bravo." Coordinated defiance of highway regulations is different from the frequent individual violation of traffic laws. A mass panic in which people engage in mutual shoving and even trampling is different from individual "queue-jumping."

Some Assumptions. In formulating an approach to deal with these three characteristics of collective behavior, we shall proceed on the basis of several fundamental assumptions. First, there is no single explanation for any of the features of collective behavior. Second, the three features of collective behavior singled out for special attention are interactive rather than independent in their effects. Third, these features are all matters of degree and not attributes that are merely present or absent. Fourth, the development and interaction of these key features of collective behavior are continuous and cumulative. Collective behavior is distinctively changeable and unstable, and outcomes reflect the sequence in which events occur as much as the simple combination of circumstances. Fifth, the conceptions that people act on are constantly tested, leading to revisions of conceptions and actions. Sixth, people ultimately act on conceptions rather than on objective reality.

In saying that we must explain extra-institutionalism, action, and collectivity, we have identified questions but not answers. The development of a general theory for collective behavior begins with the specification of answers to these questions.

Extra-institutionalism. Extra-institutionalism has been explained in various ways. Early theories generally contrasted ordinary or institutional behavior in which people were governed by social norms, including folkways, mores, and laws, to collective behavior, in which these social norms were cast aside while people acted on the basis of emotion or suggestibility or unsocialized impulse. Another group of more recent theorists have downplayed the significance of social norms as guiding behavior in both institutional and collective behavior, stressing rational calculation that takes into account the possibilities for successful action and self-interest.

In contrast to both these approaches, we propose that collective behavior takes place under the governance of *emergent norms*. Some shared redefinition of right and wrong in a situation supplies the justification and coordinates the action in collective behavior. People do what they would not otherwise have done when they panic collectively, when they riot, when they engage in civil disobedience, or when they launch terroristic campaigns, because they find social support for the view that what they are doing is the right thing to do in the situation.

The redefinition of right and wrong that we identify by the term emergent norm can range from permissive to obligatory. The simplest forms of collective behavior are permissive. Mass panic requires the shared conviction that participants are justified in disregarding ordinary rules such as taking turns and treating each other courteously. Mass looting is viewed by looters as taking what rightfully belongs to them or punishing those who have exploited them. Panic always involves a sense of necessity and mass looting a sense of opportunity. But according to emergent norm theory these conditions are not enough. Opportunity for theft often exists without leading to mass looting and the "honorable" behavior of passengers aboard the sinking Titanic illustrates the conclusion that necessity is insufficient to provoke mass panic.

The more complex and sustained forms of collective behavior that require commitment and sacrifice depend on emergent norms that define extra-institutional behavior as obligatory, as well as permissible. Something *must* be done about war, about environmental desecration, about racial and ethnic discrimination, about Godlessness in the public schools, about drunken drivers on the highways, about the miserable quality of life in the cities, about increased fees and tuition for students. The activist is driven by a sense of mission, of social duty.

Social norms are invariably linked with the idea of social sanctions. Those who violate norms *ought* to be punished. Punishment is *deserved* if it follows violation of norms, and unjustified if no legitimate norms have been violated. Because of the linkage, the failure of the larger community or authorities to impose sanctions for normally proscribed behavior may contribute to the emergence of a permissive norm. Furthermore, all social norms depend ultimately on an impression of group consensus among those who understand the situation and are morally qualified. But the group normally delegates considerable moral authority to people in positions of authority and to organizations. Consequently, perceived attitudes of authorities often help to trigger collective behavior. For example, eyewitness accounts of American race riots during the three decades immediately following the First World War quite consistently feature conspicuous participation by police, military personnel, or other uniformed individuals. Their participation seems to have contributed substantially to the conviction by rioters that what they were doing was justified.

Norms are never simply out-of-context rules of behavior. Norms are always connected to conceptions of the situation. Automobile drivers are obligated to exercise unusual caution near a pedestrian carrying a white cane because the pedestrian is assumed to be blind and unable to exercise normal caution. Similarly, the emergent norms in collective behavior are inseparable from conceptions that define the situation as exceptional or define a long-standing situation in new terms.

Because emergent norms do not have the support of tradition and institutionalization, the supporting conceptions of situations must also be normative if the behavioral norms are to have effect. The looters in civil disorders cannot tolerate public expression of the view that their victims are not exploiters, since the view would undermine justification for looting. Hence emergent norms are first and foremost revised conceptions of reality that people feel righteous about.

We have already mentioned that permissiveness is increasingly supplemented with obligatoriness in behavioral emergent norms as we move from simpler and more transitory forms of collective behavior to more complex and enduring forms. Similarly, emergent normative conceptions range from fleeting images of depersonalized actors in a dog-eat-dog relationship to highly elaborated ideologies such as the environmentalist's view of the consequences of ecological imbalance and the Marxist's view of class struggle.

From Feelings to Actions. The translation of conceptions and feelings into actions has been explained in several ways. Perhaps the most common explanation is on the basis of intensified feelings. As the intensity of fear mounts, for example, it is postulated that a threshold is reached after which people panic. As indignation mounts over a media-reported crime wave, a threshold is said to be passed after which a save-the-children movement is formed.

While a movement can hardly develop when concern about a problem is insufficient and panic could hardly occur without sufficient fear, there is abundant evidence that escalating emotions do not necessarily lead to action and are often conducive to paralysis and inaction. We shall stress instead that translation of feelings and conceptions into action depends principally upon *feasi-*

bility and *timeliness,* as well as upon *justification* by an emergent norm.

Feasibility is usually a vague impression about the possibilities inherent in a situation, the facilities or resources needed for carrying out the action, and the ability of the potential actors to carry out the action successfully. Impressions of feasibility derive from past experience, from current perceptions, from interpretations by associates and the media, and from experience with ongoing activity. While people act on impressions, their impressions are constantly tested in action. The failure or success of initial actions may produce a sense of hopelessness that discourages further action or the increased assurance that fosters more courageous action. Action is facilitated by new ideas that identify new possibilities in a situation, by apparent weakness of the opposition or evidence of social support for a course of action, by the availability of new resources such as money or weapons, and by experiences that strengthen confidence in the constituency.

Timeliness can be a matter of fleeting opportunity and "last chance," or it can be based on the appropriateness of action to the cultural meaning of some occasion. So-called triggering events like an assassination, an oil spill, a nuclear near-disaster, or an "outrageous" action by authorities often provoke the shift from discontent to action. But even without renewed provocation, St. Bartholemew's night was for many years the religious occasion for collective attacks on Protestants in Europe, as May Day now produces labor demonstrations, and significant anniversaries are occasions for escalated violence in Northern Ireland.

Feasibility and timeliness are different for different kinds of collective behavior. The time span for social movements is much longer than the time span for demonstrations and riots, and shortest for mass panics. The feasibility requirements for symbolic actions are much less than for more instrumental actions. Feasibility requirements for disruptive actions are much less than for constructive actions. Hence not only the incidence but also the type of action are affected by levels of feasibility and timeliness.

Both the conditions that make action feasible and the threshold for normative redefinition vary according to complexity of the situation. In the simplest situation an event occurs for which the social organization offers insufficient directives or means for action. The normative implications are slightly complicated when the necessity to replace a temporarily inoperative social organization is added to the absence of directives. Successively greater complications occur when the operative social order must be set aside and when it must be actively opposed as a condition for carrying out the indicated action.

Forming and Sustaining Collectivities. Why do people act collectively? How do people come together to form collectivities? How do people in collectivities develop collective understandings in the form of emergent norms? And how do people come to act together or collaborate in action?

In answering these questions, we shall stress the combined effect of (1) a condition or event that is sufficiently outside the range of "ordinary" happenings that people turn to their fellow human beings for help and support in interpreting and responding to the situation, and (2) the availability of pre-existing social groupings through which intercommunication can be initiated fairly easily. An automobile accident, a conflagration or a police arrest in a public place draws spectators, and the extraordinary nature of the event moves people to attend to the reactions of others at the scene and initiate a limited exchange of comments. But many of the people at a typical scene of this kind have assembled as pairs and in small groups of friends or family members. Discussion typically begins within these groups, then overflows into intergroup discussions. When such groups are not present, and among detached individuals when they are present, people tend to form *ad hoc* groups on the basis of membership in some recognizable "nominal" grouping. For example, in the case of a residential fire, gardeners near the scene will talk to each other, members of a distinctive racial or ethnic group will talk together, age- and sex-similar groupings will often form. An extramundane event helps to overcome many normal barriers. But the communication within pre-existing groupings primes the pump for more widespread communication, and is seldom totally displaced as the critical channel through which communication is sustained and the translation into action is monitored.

How the extramundane circumstances and pre-existing groupings function depends upon the kind and complexity of collective behavior. The preceding illustration describes only the simplest form of collective behavior, one we call the casual crowd. We shall stress three distinctions concerning the nature of the collectivity. First, solidaristic behavior requires more complex decision-making and communication systems than individualistic collective behavior, to facilitate cooperation and to develop and maintain the division of labor. Second, in diffuse, in contrast to compact, collective behavior, some combination of pre-existing communication networks in the community and use of the mass media are essential, though even then communications are eventually sifted through discussion in small groups of family members, neighbors, friends, and coworkers. Finally, the problems of communication and collaborative action are much greater for sustained than for transitory action.

A MODEL OF COLLECTIVE BEHAVIOR

To complete our model, we must incorporate process. Collective behavior is constantly being formed and reformed. In the beginning it is about events—extraordinary conditions or a precipitating incident—that a norm justifying extra-institutional action emerges. At the same time it is the event which stimulates interaction in pre-existing groups or ad hoc formations. It is in this interaction that a keynote is selected and a norm develops. The interaction does not consist merely of detached, theoretical discussion, however. During the preliminary stages of collective behavior tentative actions, "trials," are undertaken, obstacles are encountered, and both resources and resistance are weighed. Hence an impression of the feasibility of action itself and of different types of action is formed. If action appears justified and feasible in the definition of the situation developed by the collectivity, collective behavior follows. The process continues, however—changing events continuously affect all three basic features of collective behavior. Emergent norms develop and change through the keynoting process. Trials and encounters affect perceptions of feasibility and timeliness. Continuous group and solidarity formation modifies the scope and character of collectivities throughout their careers.

Figure 1.1 is a simplified schematic representation of this model, incorporating both the three components with their interaction and the continuous process of forming and reforming collective behavior.

RECURRING ISSUES IN COLLECTIVE BEHAVIOR

Collective behavior is still not an area in which generalization can be presented in precise form with the backing of experimental or quantitative evidence. There is no dearth of ideas derived from historical analysis and from the impressionistic examination of cases, but few steps have been taken toward the verification of these ideas through more rigorous procedures. Consequently, collective behavior abounds with many as yet unresolved issues. Among the issues, however, there are some that rest on semantic confusion, obvious oversimplification, or sheer dogmatism. Often these pseudo-issues recur because they are used to assign scholars to "schools of thought" or "traditions" which can be dealt with by namecalling.

By eliminating certain major pseudo-issues and by trying to state other issues in their essential terms, it may be possible to avoid some of the

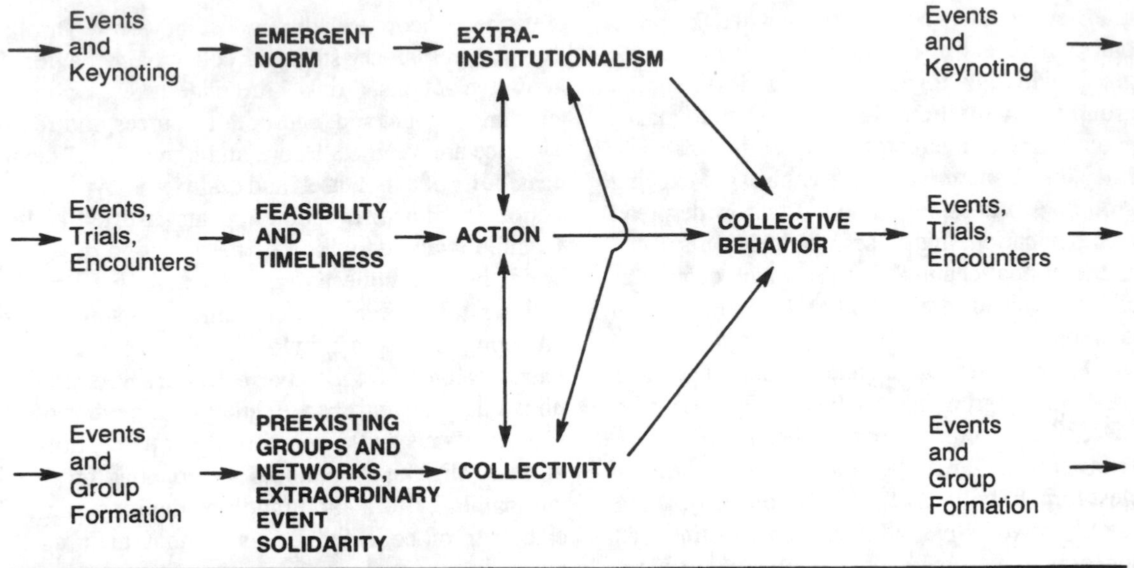

FIGURE 1.1 Model for Collective Behavior

false leads found in the literature on collective behavior, particularly that part dealing with social movements. With this objective in mind we shall briefly examine two groups of issues. First, we shall attempt to separate semantic from empirical questions in the so-called "group mind" problem, the issue of individualistic versus group explanations of behavior. Second, we shall discuss the fruitless but persistent argument as to whether collective behavior is "rational " or "irrational," along with the related question of the importance of emotion in this and other types of behavior.

The Group Mind Issue. A great deal of heat has been generated as to whether there is a group mind, whether the group is something other than the sum of individual responses, and similar questions. These issues have received unusual attention in the area of collective behavior, where the studies of individual and group behavior tend to merge. Accusations of "group mind fallacy" and "individualistic fallacy" have been freely hurled. Some of the confusion lies in the fact that not one but several questions are actually involved. By looking at some of these questions separately, we may be able to eliminate spurious issues and clarify the legitimate points of disagreement.

The first question is how to describe group activity. A group is both many individuals and a totality. Groups tend to impress observers more strongly as wholes, with the result that descriptions usually are cast in terms of the group's acting and reacting, rather than the separate member's. We hear that "the mob attacked its victim" or "the public favored a particular course of action." There are dangers in this prevalent way of describing group behavior. In the first place, it is often a serious oversimplification. By thinking in these terms we may be blinded to any diversity of individual behavior or differing degree of individual conviction backing up the apparent behavior of the group.

In the second place, the description of group behavior as the actions of a total unit often leads us to think of the group through analogies derived from individual behavior. Here we find the tendency to attribute to the group a mind, a conscience, a sense of responsibility, a lack of self-control, or a sense of self-esteem. A shift in crowd behavior is the crowd "changing its mind," as if a group could change its mind in the same sense as an individual does. These tendencies to personify the group are accentuated in those spectacular instances of crowd behavior that arouse our indignation and make us seek something that can be an object of moral blame.

In order to escape these fallacies, some investigators insist that only the behavior of individuals can be described. But this solution is not without danger. In its most naive form it becomes a mere semantic sleight of hand whereby the action of the group is restated as though applying to each of its members. Thus we may be told that the members of the crowd attacked their victim. The same danger of overlooking complexity applies here as in group description. And the danger of thinking in terms of analogy between the individual and group remains but in changed form. The tendency is to impute to the individual members of the group the motives and attitudes that would explain the action of the total group—if it had been the action of an individual. Thus the explanation of war is sought by attributing hostile attitudes to the members of the warring nations. Because individuals usually fight each other only when they feel hatred toward one another, it is assumed that war eventuates from the hatred that members of the warring nations feel toward one another. Modern research on war has demonstrated clearly that this is not so, but the pattern of thinking continues to be applied to group behavior in many ways.

Even when these fallacies are assiduously avoided, simple description of individual actions is likely to be both inefficient and incomplete. Where something more than an aggregation exists, some division of labor inevitably arises, and individual behavior is patterned into roles that in some way complement one another in furthering a group objective. When crowds of demonstrators have clashed with the police some crowd members have actually grappled with the officers, sometimes simply because they were in the front ranks. Others have hurled missiles while yet others have merely shouted deprecations. These different forms of behavior need not reflect different orientations toward government or police but instead constitute a division of labor influenced by location in the crowd, age, sex, physical strength, courage, and a host of other variables. Specifying the general end and pattern of behavior in the group may be more useful than detailed accounts of individual behavior, and will most certainly provide a necessary framework for interpreting the individual behavior.

There is a place for both group and individual types of description, when the respective sets of fallacies can be avoided. Neither the group nor the individual descriptive approach is inherently more error-free than the other. Each type of description completes the other. Which will be given priority depends on the purpose at hand. Groups as wholes have effects on society, and they tend to be perceived as wholes. To the degree to which we are interested in society, then individual description will be subordinated to group description. When groups are of interest only as contexts for the study of individual psychological processes, group description will be subordinated but not omitted.

A second question involved in the group-versus-individual issue concerns whether the individual in the group acts differently from the way he would act if not in the group. Answers have ranged from one extreme view—that the group suffuses its members with attitudes and motives that have no counterparts in their individual psyches—to the opposing view—that the group is no more than several individuals with common purposes doing what each as an individual would be doing anyway. Actually, neither extreme answer has often been given. The individualists have admitted that division of labor takes place and that the intensity of behavior may be heightened by the presence of like-minded persons, while contending that the behavior remains an expression of attitudes that were present in the individual originally. The group mind advocates have often meant only that there is a decision-making process, which takes place on a group basis, reaching conclusions that would not have eventuated from individual decision making.

Many of the discrepancies between these points of view vanish when certain observations are made. First, a person seldom has a single, clear-cut attitude on any given matter. The typical law-abiding citizen is often quite ambivalent about the police, as this story by a London newspaper columnist illustrates:

> *Herewith two snatches of conversation I had, yesterday, with a neighbour, a bustling matron of unassailable virtue. "Do you know," she said, "this young policeman came up and stopped me as I was walking down the street and asked would I show him the contents of my shopping bag? Well, of course, I refused point blank. I mean, really. Are we living in a police state or what?"*
>
> *And, later on, sandwiched between the appalling price of everything and a blow-by-blow description of her recent dental work, "Do you know, that repairman stole a silver bowl? I am sure it was him. I telephoned the police. I described him and I said I expected them to find him and search for my bowl. Well, of course, with their usual inefficiency . . ."*

Not all attitudes on a given question are equally well recognized by the individual. In the extreme case of repression actors possess attitudes that affect behavior but that they would vigorously disclaim. Consequently, any individual can find attitudinal support for a variety of actions regarding any particular objects. In a group situation certain attitudes are elicited and reinforced, so that individuals act in accordance with attitudes that would not necessarily have become dominant had they been acting as individuals.

Second, action is a consequence not merely of attitudes toward the object in question but of attitudes toward the group, toward the self, and toward many others. Those who fear a crowd may conform to a course of action that is not in accordance with any of their attitudes toward the object in question. Those who conceive of themselves as leaders may sense the direction in which the group decision is going and actively espouse it in order to retain leadership. Their private attitudes toward that course of action may be different.

For these reasons it is entirely appropriate and not in the least mystical to speak of collective decision making. Group decisions and group actions could never have been predicted simply by summing up individual attitudes. At the same time, the attitudes of the individuals, both toward the object in question and toward matters that become indirectly involved, do make decisions in certain directions easier to obtain than decisions in other directions, and will render other potential decisions impossible. Thus both the processes of group decision making and individual attitudes must be taken into account. Individuals in the group do indeed act differently from the way in which they would if alone, though not without some basis for this action in their own attitudes.

Answers to these two questions indicate the answer to the final question. Some have argued that since the only real actions are the actions of individuals, there can be no special set of principles governing group action but merely the application of the psychology of individual behavior to action in a group context. Experience has demonstrated that at the group level regularities can be observed and generalizations formulated quite apart from the understanding of individual psychological principles underlying them. Best documented are the regularities of economic behavior. Study of the individual processes, which culminate in these observed regularities of economic functioning, is a useful type of investigation but does not take the place of generalizations at the collective level. Animals and plants are made of chemicals, but generalizations at the chemical level do not take the place of generalizations about the characteristics of plants or animals. Similarly, generalizations at the group level are needed and can be made, whether the individual psychological processes underlying the group are understood or not. Each level of investigation can benefit by cues from the other, so investigators at one level keep informed of developments at the other. Each benefits from advances at the other level, but each level has its own generalizations to develop.

Irrationality and Emotionality. Another recurring problem in collective behavior is the tendency to single out for study only those collective phenomena of which the observer disapproves and to depict the processes of collective behavior in value-laden terms. Alarm about destructive mobs, panics, and revolutionary or totalitarian social movements is reflected in this tendency. On this basis collective behavior is often erroneously contrasted to rational behavior by being designated irrational or emotional. There are two important errors involved in approaching collective behavior in this way.

In the first place, the terms *irrational* and *emotional* have reference to individual behavior. In accordance with our discussion of the group mind problems, the application of these terms to the group means one of two things. Either it is a shorthand way of saying that each of the members in the collectivity is acting irrationally, or it is reasoning by analogy that a group, like an individual, can be emotional or irrational. The latter procedure we recognize as fallacious, and the former assumption of homogeneity among members of collectivities is not supported by our knowledge.

In the second place, the very distinctions themselves are difficult to make. Emotion and reason are not today regarded as irreconcilables. Emotion may accompany the execution of a well-reasoned plan, and the execution of an inadequately reasoned plan may be accompanied by no arousal of emotions.

Despite the inappropriateness of applying to groups terms which have reference to individual behavior, some theorists have described crowds and social movements as rational. This corresponds to a popular image of rational action as weighing the possible costs and rewards of a course of action and choosing the way which will maximize chances of success and minimize losses. Richard Berk, in his "gaming approach" to collective behavior, suggests that the gathering of a crowd should be viewed "as an opportunity in which individuals can experience certain rewards and certain costs. Each individual tries to maximize rewards and minimize costs." The approach to social movements called "resource mobilization theory" by its proponents uses an economic model. It emphasizes the importance of costs and rewards in explaining individual and organizational involvement in social movement activity.

The use of such models overlooks the variety of ways in which individuals, particularly as they are influenced by a collectivity such as a crowd or social movement, may conceive of "rewards" or "success." The belief that death in the service of one's religion is the highest value inspired the followers of the Ayatollah Khomeini during and after the Iranian revolution to risk death without consideration of what their martyrdom might accomplish. To many western observers their behavior appeared not just reckless but fanatical and "irrational," but losing their lives was not a "cost" to them. In every situation what may be a cost to one actor may be a gain for another—one's rationality may be madness to the other!

Other connotations of "rational" refer not so much to the type of goal pursued but to the means chosen to achieve the end. Sometimes behavior is termed rational on the basis of the external criterion of efficiency in achieving the goal. Using an internal criterion, action might be termed irrational if individuals do not weigh all the possible alternatives of which they might be aware in deciding their course of action. Yet neither type of criterion serves to distinguish collective behavior from institutional or traditional behavior. In the light of the widespread and increasing use of drugs in the United States one might argue that the passage of existing drug-control laws constituted irrational action, even though it was done after parliamentary deliberation within the institutional framework. In contrast, the spontaneous but destructive ghetto insurrections of the 1960s might be viewed as rational because they had the consequence of focusing attention on certain problems and evoking some relief measures which more deliberative and institutionalized approaches had not secured.

If we rely on the internal criterion of consideration of all alternatives, no behavior could be called rational, for tradition makes some solutions "unthinkable" and formal norms reduce the options of actors within a system. Thus collective behavior is not different from other types of behavior in restricting attention within the range of theoretically possible alternatives. Usually the judgment that someone has acted irrationally is made in hindsight or by someone who is not in the situation of the actor and thus has a different perspective. When people attempting to escape from a burning building pile up at what appears to them to be the only exit, they are often described as having acted irrationally and in panic by people who learn afterwards that there were other exits available. To the actor in the situation who does not know of the existence of these alternatives, fighting to reach the only exit in sight may seem a very logical choice as opposed to burning to death.

One basis for these errors lies in the fact that in folk usage we tend to confuse rationality with behavior in conformity with the dictates of culture. When an individual uncritically follows the courses of action sanctioned in our society we tend to think of this person as reasonable because he or she is (1) like us and (2) predictable and easy to deal with. When a person challenges the established dictates or is forced to act when cultural guidelines are nonexistent, vague, or contradictory the behavior appears unpredictable, bizarre and hard to deal with. Thus when some oppressed people have felt that ordinary, legitimate avenues of redress were not open to them and have resorted to terrorism they have been characterized as "irrational" or as "mad dogs." Some of the activists in the Peace Movement in the United States in the 1960s who felt that "civil" means of protest were ineffective were called "the crazies" even by their ideological allies. On the other hand, the fact that they approve of the goals of non-conformist behavior has led some observers to classify it as "rational" in contrast to the actions of "the Establishment."

In summary, all conscious human behavior involves some sort of cognitive process or reason no matter how "unreasonable" other people's "reason" may seem to us. At the same time, some sort of feelings, influenced by the operation of the nervous and endocrine systems of the body, accompanies any behavior. To attempt to divide the actions of individuals into "rational" versus "emotional" or "irrational" types is to deny the complexity of human behavior. To attempt to do so for the actions of groups or collectivities is to use an analogy which is not only inappropriate but is also based on a false model of individual behavior. . . .

ARTICLE 2

The Nature of Collective Behavior

NEIL J. SMELSER

INTRODUCTION

Having identified several components of action and sources of strain, we now ask: What is the nature of collective behavior in general? How does it differ from conventional behavior? Our answers will be framed in terms of the components of social action.

THE GENERAL NATURE OF STRUCTURAL REORGANIZATION

When strain exists, we might say that the components of social action are out of order and require fixing. How, *in general,* is strain overcome? How is social action repaired? By outlining the general character of the process of reorganizing the components of action, we shall be able to specify the nature of collective behavior. To facilitate our discussion we have reproduced Table 5—the components of social action in full detail. . . .

The general principle for reconstituting social action is this: when strain exists attention shifts to the higher levels of the components to seek resources to overcome this strain. We may characterize this process in the language of Table 5 by saying that, in the search for solutions to conditions of strain, people turn their attention either *upward* or *to the left,* or *both.*

To illustrate the *upward* movement we shall consider a situation of strain in American society which was particularly acute during the first two years or so following the launching of the first Russian Sputnik in the fall of 1957. Because Americans judged that progress in the conquest of space was important for our international prestige, the pressure to produce successful space vehicles was great. Yet we could not assemble the facilities to put even a modest capsule into orbit. We were uncertain whether a military or civilian agency was better suited to develop a space program, and how resources should be allocated to develop the best space equipment in the shortest time. Thus serious strains began to build up at the operative levels of the Facilities Series (Levels 5–7 of Table 5).

How might these strains have been overcome? We could have encouraged the space program by increasing its budget and by giving political authorization to various space agencies to move ahead quickly. Such action would have invested greater financial and political resources in the space effort. Formally, this kind of action can be described as a movement *up* the Facilities Scale to Level 4 in order to overcome the strains at the lower levels.

This movement to Level 4, however, would have been satisfactory *only if* we had already

TABLE 5 Levels of Specificity of the Components of Social Action

LEVEL	VALUES	NORMS	MOBILIZATION OF MOTIVATION FOR ORGANIZED ACTION	SITUATIONAL FACILITIES
1	Societal values	General conformity	Socialized motivation	Preconceptions concerning causality
2	Legitimization of values for institutionalized sectors	Specification of norms according to institutional sectors	Generalized performance capacity	Codification of knowledge
3	Legitimization of rewards	Specification of norms according to types of roles and organizations	Trained capacity	Technology, or specification of knowledge in situational terms
4	Legitimization of individual commitment	Specification of requirements for individual observation of norms	Transition to adult role-assumption	Procurement of wealth, power, or prestige to activate Level 3
5	Legitimization of competing values	Specification of norms of competing institutional sectors	Allocation to sector of society	Allocation of effective technology to sector of society
6	Legitimization of values for realizing organizational goals	Specification of rules of cooperation and coordination within organization	Allocation to specific roles or organizations	Allocation of effective technology to roles or organizations
7	Legitimization of values for expenditure of effort	Specification of schedules and programs to regulate activity	Allocation to roles and tasks within organization	Allocation of facilities within organization to attain concrete goals

More specific (down levels) → More specific (across columns)

possessed an adequate technology for producing the appropriate kinds of space vehicles. In fact, we did not. Merely to allocate more funds and greater authority to space agencies would not have been enough. It was necessary to move higher in the Facilities Scale in an attempt to improve our technology (Level 3).

Yet technology alone might not have been enough. Some persons felt that without "basic research" we were inherently limited in our ability to develop an effective space program. What is basic research? It is the production of *scientific knowledge itself*, on which new technology can be built. Formally, basic research means activity at Level 2 of the Facilities Series; this activity is more generalized than the production of technology. The principle of moving up the levels of generality, then, is that when any given level (e.g., technology) reaches a limit and becomes inadequate to deal with the condition of strain, it is necessary to move to the next higher level (e.g., basic research) in order to broaden the facilities for attacking the strain.

One more level of generality goes beyond Level 2. In the flurry of excitement, dismay, and self-criticism after the Russians launched their first Sputnik, some persons felt that American society has the wrong "approach" to scientific endeavor. American society, it was felt, is too pragmatic. Historically we have had to rely on European scientists for high-level theory in mathematics and physics; we, as technicians, have applied this theory, not created it. To develop a really advanced space program it is necessary to *go beyond* the basic research possible in our system; it is necessary to create a new outlook, perhaps even a new philosophy (Level 1). Only then would we generate fundamental scientific knowledge (Level 2) and apply it down the line through technology (Level 3) and investment (Level 4) to the world of operations (Levels 5–7).

The reduction of strains such as the unfulfilled demand for an adequate space program frequently lies in the *generalization* of facilities. If facilities at one level are inadequate, attention turns to the next higher level. After reconstitution occurs at the higher level, moreover, the new higher-level facilities must be reapplied back down the line to the lower levels. New basic research must be converted into new technology; new investment and authorization must be given this new technology; new agencies must be set up or old ones modified, and so on. For any given empirical case of strain, the exact level of generality which must be reconstituted to overcome the strain depends on two things: (a) the seriousness of the initial conditions of strain, and (b) the adequacy of the existing facilities at each level to meet the conditions of strain.

To illustrate the process of generalization *to the left* in Table 5, we shall consider the strains occasioned by a major financial crisis and business depression. Many persons lose their jobs, others their fortunes. Strain concentrates on the deprivation of rewards (Mobilization Series) and on the disorganization of norms governing market behavior (Normative Series). How can such conditions of strain be attacked? The first line of attack would be to punish those individuals—e.g., financiers or government officials—who behaved irresponsibly. This reaction concentrates on the Mobilization Series. It is not too drastic from the standpoint of the total system, for it merely withholds rewards from *particular* agents who presumably behaved imprudently or dishonestly enough to bring on an economic crisis.

A more general solution would be to pass laws and regulations which affect not only those who behaved irresponsibly in the past, but also all others who might do so in the future. An example would be to place restrictions on those speculative practices that were to blame for the financial collapse. Thus the slogan "there ought to be a law" is more drastic than the slogan "throw the rascals out" because it is more general in its applicability. The former deals with the Normative Series rather than with particular agents.

Even more general is a solution that brings the values of the economic system itself into question. The most drastic attack on the system that produces economic crises and business depressions would be to do away with the system itself and bring some sort of socialistic values to bear. This solution is more far-reaching than merely passing laws and regulations, for it means reorganizing the values by which the laws and regulations are legitimized.

What happens, then, to social action when strain exists? Attempts are made to move to higher-level components, reconstitute them, then incorporate the new principles back into the more concrete, operative levels of social action. In the event of failure at one level of generality, moreover, the tendency is to "appeal to an even higher court" in an attempt to understand and control the action that is under strain at the lower levels. This process of generalization moves toward the higher levels of each individual component, toward the higher-level components (norms, values) or both. Having generalized to higher levels, attempts are then made to work "back down the line." Attempts are made to generalize, then respecify; the components of action are first *de*structured, then *re*structured. Many instances of social change can be interpreted according to this scheme.

COLLECTIVE BEHAVIOR AS GENERALIZED BEHAVIOR

Collective behavior involves a generalization to a high-level component of action. Like many other kinds of behavior, it is a search for solutions to conditions of strain by moving to a more generalized level of resources. Once the generalization has taken place, attempts are made to reconstitute the meaning of the high-level component. At this point, however, the critical feature of collective behavior appears. Having redefined the high-level component, people do not proceed to respecify, step by step, down the line to reconstitute social action. Rather, they develop a belief which "short-circuits" from a very generalized component *directly* to the focus of strain. The accompanying expectation is that the strain can be relieved by a direct application of a generalized component. From a slightly different perspective, collective behavior is a *compressed* way of attacking problems created by strain. It compresses several levels of the components of action into a single belief, from which *specific operative solutions* are expected to flow. An episode of collective behavior itself occurs when people are mobilized for action on the basis of such a belief. Thus our formal characterization of collective behavior is this: *an uninstitutionalized mobilization for action in order to modify one or more kinds of strain on the basis of a generalized reconstitution of a component of action.*

In the following chapter we shall discuss hysterical and wish-fulfillment beliefs. Both beliefs arise in a situation of strain (for example, danger to life, threat of loss of funds). Both beliefs also constitute redefinitions of the situation of strain. In these redefinitions some aspect of the situation is selected and attributed a *power* or *force* (Facilities Level 1) that is sufficiently generalized to *guarantee the outcome* of the situation at hand. This outcome may be a catastrophe (produced by the negative forces envisioned in a hysterical belief) or a blessing (produced by the positive forces envisioned in a wish-fulfillment belief). The force may be felt to reside in any object, event, action, or verbal formula. The defining characteristic of such a force is that it will guarantee the outcome of an ambiguous situation of strain. Such a force operates, moreover, without reference to the many steps of respecification that must intervene between generalized force and concrete situation to make the force genuinely operative.

Take the space example again. We would consider it a wish-fulfillment belief if a body of persons subscribed to the following: *If only* we concerned ourselves with purifying and reaffirming the American way of life, we would not be experiencing frustrations in the development of operative space vehicles. This assumes that generalized facilities—"the American way"—will guarantee a specific solution and that the intervening steps of scientific codification, technological specification, investment, and so on, will follow. In reality each of these steps contributes in transforming the American way into particular successes. The hypothetical faith in the American way alone, however, short-circuits many of these necessary steps, and thus constitutes a compressed solution to the problem of facilities.

We shall find this "if only" mentality in the beliefs associated with all forms of collective behavior. For instance, in the norm-oriented movement, we shall find extraordinary results promised if only certain reforms are adopted, and (on the negative side) gloomy predictions of decay and collapse if the sources of strain are not attacked quickly and vigorously. Adherents to such movements exaggerate reality because their action is based on beliefs which are both *generalized and short-circuited.*

In the detailed expositions that comprise the rest of the volume we shall expand and document our characterization of collective behavior. We can suggest already, however, why collective behavior displays some of the crudeness, excess, and eccentricity that it does. By short-circuiting from high-level to low-level components of social action, collective episodes by-pass many of the specifications, contingencies, and controls that are required to make the generalized components operative. This gives collective behavior its clumsy or primitive character. Furthermore, "solutions" to situations of strain that are produced by the riot and craze are sometimes "irresponsible" because the headlong attempt to apply generalized beliefs to specific situations disregards many existing moral and legal restrictions and violates the interests and integrity of many individuals and groups.

Collective behavior, then, is the action of the impatient. It contrasts with the processes of social readjustment that do not short-circuit the journey from generalized belief to specific situation. Historically, collective behavior is closely associated with processes of structural reorganization of the components of action. In fact, episodes of collective behavior often constitute an early stage of social change; they occur when conditions of strain have arisen, but before social resources have been mobilized for a specific and possibly effective attack on the sources of strain. this is one reason for defining collective behavior as uninstitutionalized; it occurs when structured social action is under strain and when institutionalized means of overcoming the strain are inadequate. We might note that certain types of social control operate as an intermediary between these short-circuited collective episodes and orderly social change. Social control blocks the headlong attempts of collective episodes to bring quick results; if social control is effective, moreover, it channels the energy of collective outbursts into more modest kinds of behavior.

EXCLUSION OF OTHER PHENOMENA FROM THE FIELD OF COLLECTIVE BEHAVIOR

According to our definition, any instance of collective behavior must contain the following: (a) uninstitutionalized (b) collective action, (c) taken to modify a condition of strain (d) on the basis of a generalized reconstitution of a component of action. The term "collective behavior" has in the past been applied to many types of behavior which have one or several, but not all, of these characteristics. For this and other reasons, "collective behavior . . . is obviously a catchall for various phenomena that do not readily fit into conceptions of institutional order." We shall now mention several types of behavior—some of which have been called collective behavior—which we do not intend to encompass by our technical definition:

1. Collective reaffirmations of values, rituals, festivals, ceremonials, and rites of passage. By these we mean, for example, the homecoming, the alumni rally, the salute to the flag, the patriotic demonstration on holidays, the ritual rebellion, and the revelry which frequently accompanies such occasions. Even though these celebrations may provide the setting for genuine collective outbursts—e.g., the patriotic demonstration that turns into a riot—they are not in themselves examples of collective behavior. True, they are based often on generalized values such as the divine, the nation, the monarchy, or the *alma mater*. True, they are collective. True, they may release tensions generated by conditions of structural strain. The basic difference between such ceremonials and collective behavior—and the reason for excluding them—is that the former are institutionalized in form and context. The index of their institutionalization is that such events are often scheduled for definite times, places, and occasions, and are shrouded in formal rituals such as chants, or semi-formal "ways of celebrating," such as drinking, whooping, marching, and so on. Such celebrative activities are well described by the phrase "conventionalization of the crowd." The beliefs on which they are based are not assembled as quick solutions for problems arising out of structural strain. Ceremonial activities are occasions for periodic reaffirmation of existing generalized components of action rather than the creation of new components.

We may illustrate the difference between ceremonial behavior and collective behavior further by reference to two aspects of the same episode of behavior. The worker-socialist movements that have developed in the history of American labor are episodes of collective behavior, since they involve unprecedented and uninstitutionalized mobilization of action to abolish many institutional norms (and even values) of industrial capitalism, and to establish corresponding social forms envisioned in the socialist ideology. We must exclude from our definition, however, their collective songs, pledges to solidarity, initiation rites, and so on, because they are significant primarily as regularized reaffirmations of the established values and symbols of the movement itself. Thus, even though we include such social movements as instances of collective behavior, we do not include the ceremonies that build up within movements.

Empirically some types of behavior are on the borderline between collective behavior and ceremonial behavior. Let us examine lynching, for instance. In some cases it is a genuine hostile outburst closely related to economic and status deprivation. As such it would fit the definition of collective behavior. Lynching also has been both in the West and the South, a quasi-institutionalized form of justice to replace weak civil regulations or general conditions of political disorganization. Furthermore, some evidence indicates that lynching was in part a ritual to reaffirm old southern values and to defy the North during Reconstruction and post-Reconstruction times. Finally, as the term "lynching bee" connotes, it is possible that lynching was a kind of periodic, partially organized entertainment or release of tension for people who "crave some excitement, some interest, some passionate outburst." The multiple significance of lynching should remind us that in many cases history does not always produce instances that fit neatly into our analytic definition of collective behavior. We must examine carefully the context of the event in question before we decide upon its relevance for study.

2. The audience. Let us consider both the casual and the intentional audiences. An example of the first is a gathering of passers-by to watch construction crews at work, the second an audience at a symphony. We would exclude the "watchers" as an instance of collective behavior on several grounds: (a) The common object on which they focus is not generalized in a technical sense. It is simply men and machinery at work. (b) In all likelihood structural strain does not underlie the gathering. (c) No modification of any component of action is envisioned. In the case of the symphony audience, they may gather on the basis of generalized esthetic symbols; in addition, the music may have certain tension-release functions. Still, the audience is an institutionalized form. Persons gather at fixed times and places, even evoke enthusiastic "bravos" at selected moments. Both the street throng and the audience provide common settings for genuine collective episodes such as the panic or the riot. This is true, however, not because the audience itself is an instance of collective behavior, but rather because the audience situation provides geographical proximity and ease of communication and mobilization (as contrasted with other more dispersed situations).

3. Public opinion. In general the term "public opinion" refers to a body of significant ideas and sentiments about controversial issues. This kind of opinion is related to our definition of collective behavior in two ways: (a) Collective episodes may constitute a part of total "public opinion." In the 1880's and 1890's, for instance, a significant part of American public opinion was a product of collective movements—the Farmers' Alliance, the Grange, and the Populists—which gripped many parts of the agricultural population. (b) Public discussion of an issue may contribute to the rise of episodes of collective behavior. For instance, the spread and discussion of information on the danger of radioactive fall-out may produce widespread fears and perhaps a number of movements to prevent testing. Despite these links between public opinion and our definition of collective behavior, we do not treat public opinion as a type of collective behavior; it lies on a different conceptual level.

4. Propaganda is the "expression of opinion or action . . . deliberately designed to influence opinions or actions of . . . individuals or groups with reference to predetermined ends." Propaganda is related to collective behavior in several ways: (a) It may be an attempt to create attitudes that will inspire collective outbursts. An example is the broadcasts to enemy populations in wartime with the intention of aggravating the dissatisfactions and discomforts from which they are suffering already. (b) Propaganda may attempt to prevent the rise of beliefs which could produce collective outbursts. Government propaganda that exaggerates the prosperous condition of a starving population is an example. (c) Reform and revolutionary movements themselves may use propaganda to gain adherents. Thus, propaganda may be a discouragement to, an encouragement to, or an adjunct of collective behavior. Propaganda does not, however, qualify as a type of collective behavior as we define the term. Often it is institutionalized—as in advertizing, political campaigning, or political control—even though its aim may be to stir uninstitutionalized behavior. Even when it is the adjunct of a reform or revolutionary movement, propaganda is not the act of collective mobilization; it is one instrument by which participants in the movement hope to convince others and mobilize them for action.

5. Crime. Individual crime poses no problems for classification, since it is not collective. What about organized crime? In many cases it flatly violates institutionalized property and personal rights. In addition, crime often springs from conditions of social strain such as poverty and broken families.

Why, then, is organized crime not a form of collective behavior? In criminal activity no attempt is made to *reconstitute* a component of action on the basis of a generalized belief. Organized robbery, for instance, differs from a reform movement to change property laws in two senses: (a) In one sense criminals *accept* the existing social arrangements more than do adherents of the reform movement. They do not attempt to redefine or modify the general definition of property. Rather, crime feeds on existing property arrangements by stealing, pilfering, extorting, and blackmailing. Criminals attempt to subvert or avoid authority rather than change its form. Furthermore, a band of criminals offers no institutional "solutions" for the social problems created by the conditions of strain underlying criminal activity. (b) In another sense, criminals *reject* the social order more than adherents of the reform movement. The former wish to break the law as such. Reformers are not interested in illegality for its own sake; they desire to reject *but also to substitute* new institutional definitions. Participants in collective episodes may break the law—as in the riot or revolutionary outburst—but the aim of the outburst is not simply to profit from defiance. In collective behavior, law-breaking is generally a concomitant of a headlong attempt to modify some component of social action. Criminal activity, then, may be an aspect of collective behavior, but crime alone does not constitute collective behavior. The criminal act of robbery, for instance, differs radically from the prison riot of convicted criminals. The latter is generally a protest against the conditions of prison life with the implication that these conditions should be modified.

6. Individual deviance such as hoboism, addiction, or alcoholism. Although such behavior has social and psychological origins similar to those of collective behavior, much deviance poses no problem of classification because it is individual, not collective. Furthermore, such behavior—like crime—does not involve any envisioned change in the components of social action. On occasion the use of drugs is an aspect of a collective movement—as in the Peyote cults among the American Indians—but it is not the use of the drug which makes the movement an instance of collective behavior. Rather it is the belief in the regeneration of a social order that gives the movement its distinctive character as a collective episode.

ARTICLE 3

A Gaming Approach to Crowd Behavior

RICHARD A. BERK

This paper argues that emphasis on the irrationality of crowd participants is at best misplaced. Building on a detailed examination of a particular instance of crowd behavior and a blend of several different theoretical perspectives, I propose a new approach to crowds, in which participants exercise considerable cognitive skill while consciously trying to produce concerted rewarding actions.

. . . The paper will build on Decision Theory applications to crowd behavior. First, I will present a detailed case study of a particular instance of crowd behavior to illustrate the need for a revised theoretical approach and to lay the groundwork for such a revision. Second, with some additional insights of applied game theorists, I will develop a new theoretical perspective. Finally, I will discuss some implications of this perspective.

RESEARCH METHODS

Even in this microsociological case study one cannot avoid epistemological problems in learning about psychological events. Where possible, inference generating behavior and statements are detailed. Unless one wishes to exclude mental process from theory, these difficulties are inevitable.

The data come from five sources. First, a research assistant and I used participant observation techniques in a particular instance of crowd behavior. Hundreds of verbal statements (many solicited), gestures, and actions were observed and recorded. These field notes form one crucial source of the data. Second, additional field notes were taken by twelve undergraduate sociology majors who observed the crowd. They had been encouraged to focus on the issue of "irrationality" in crowds, and their data reflect important inferences about mental processes. Third, after the crowd behavior, I conducted thirty-seven informal interviews with people who had participated in the events. My purpose was to gather retrospective accounts that might elaborate the statements and actions recorded in field notes. Fourth, additional detail was gathered from a report prepared by the campus police in which a chronology of events was constructed. Finally, press accounts, especially those appearing in the

Berk, Richard A. (1974, June). A gaming approach to crowd behavior. *American Sociological Review, 39*, 335–373. Reprinted by permission of the American Sociological Association.

campus newspaper, were scrutinized for additional detail and potential contradictions. All five sources of data essentially supported one another. There were no glaring differences in the sequence of activities or their quality.

CHRONOLOGY OF EVENTS

The setting is Northwestern University in Evanston, Illinois. At about 12:45 p.m., Tuesday, May 9, 1972, students and faculty began gathering at Rebecca Crown Plaza, a paved open area about half the size of a football field, surrounded on three sides by buildings which house University administration offices. (Fisher, 1972, would call this the "arena.") A meeting, publicized for about a week, had been called to foster "dialogue" between students and the University President about increased dormitory fees. While much talk had been heard for several days of this upcoming "confrontation" between administrators and students, the meeting's agenda was abruptly amended when President Nixon announced the mining of Haiphong Harbor. Though there were no official announcements or circulars, large numbers of students and some faculty believed that individuals would pressure the University President for an anti-war strike. The nature and source of such pressure were unclear. In fact, several small student factions had quietly planned to call for a strike; however, their aims were not publicized, and there was clearly little campus consensus on what to expect.

Informal conversations with students and faculty before the gathering indicated a wide variety of projections. Some anticipated a physical confrontation around a strike. Others expected rhetoric from all sides, but little actual activity. Still others anticipated a discussion of the student housing issue but no talk of the war. Finally, some, moved largely by curiosity, had no clear expectations.

The wide range of expectations produced a wide range of verbalized motives. Some wanted a strike under any conditions. Some would accept only a democratically mandated strike. Some were hoping to prevent any strike. Some were hoping to prevent any strike attempt. The verbalized motives on the housing question were also mixed. Since the issue had been visible for many months and had been discussed at numerous meetings, several opposing views existed based on relatively subtle distinctions. In addition to considerable discord among people active on the housing issue and between administrators and students, there was conflict with the anti-war advocates who seemed to be subverting the meeting's original agenda. Finally, large numbers saw the gathering as a chance to observe something of interest, socialize with friends, and spend some time in the sun.

Apparently feelings and thoughts also varied widely. Some wanted a strike to protest the war escalation, others to pressure the University President into taking an institutional position against the war. Some wanted a strike to cut classes. Others doubtless viewed a strike as a chance to be a leader. Still others hoped a strike would enliven the campus. Further, each individual typically held several and sometimes conflicting views. In short, neither individuals nor groups planning to go to the meeting appeared single-minded.

People typically arrived at Crown Plaza in small groups and drifted towards the southwest corner where a microphone was set up. Those closest to this spot sat very close to one another establishing a relatively impermeable and expanding circular boundary. The student body president, three security guards, two lower level administrators and several students were standing near the microphone conversing amiably. About three-quarters of the crowd milled around the seated students, their density decreasing with distance from the microphone. Seated students were within a foot of one another, while near the fringes people stood from two to ten feet apart.

As more people arrived the number, but not proportion, of seated students increased. Conversations shifted somewhat to the upcoming "confrontation" with the University President. People apparently interpreted the turnout of about four hundred, made impressive by the small arena, as indicating wide campus involvement. Since the university was reputed to be politically apathetic, the turnout suggested unusual concern. Some assumed this to be anger about the war, some anger about housing, while others assumed that many students simply wanted to "get it on." In short, something important seemed to be occurring.

The presence of a television camera and technical crew heightened the sense of seriousness. Though most thought the television coverage was in response to the housing crisis (apparently it was), some took it as a sign of violence to come. This view was reinforced by the presence of campus police and others who looked like law enforcement personnel. (The presence of undercover city policemen was never confirmed.)

At 1:15 the student body president began to speak from the microphone. At that point about three-quarters of the crowd sat down, partly due to urgings from others, and formed a dense circle about sixty feet across. The student body president said the meeting would be divided into two parts, the first on housing, the second or "main issue" on the war. The crowd cheered showing strong anti-war sentiment. The cheering also suggested less enthusiasm for the housing issue.

The University President was introduced and made a speech that seemed to anger many in the audience. First, he spoke far too long: over twenty-five minutes. This was taken as another lecture masquerading as dialogue and of the tendency of faculty and administrators to talk too much. Second, he was clearly playing to the media; using phrases understandable and acceptable to other audiences. Third, though announcing that the increase in board rates would only be 15% (rather than the expected 20%), he denied that the reduction was in response to student pressure. He acknowledged the legitimacy of student concerns but refused to grant that students had exercised any power or that "negotiation " with students was legitimate.

As the speech progressed, heckling from the crowd began. Besides the usual profanity, some accused him of lying, of not knowing the facts, and of trying to give them the run-around. However, many of the approximately twenty hecklers were shouted down, and student discord reigned. Some agreed with the President's position and saw the hecklers as rowdies. Others disagreed with the President but felt it best to sit quietly rather than show public disrespect (especially with T.V. cameras present). Others agreed with the hecklers and their actions but did not have the courage to join them. Further, there was apparently strong support for "free speech" and strong opposition to violent, undemocratic and "uncivilized" actions.

The President's "lecture" was followed by ten minutes of questions and answers. Some questions were clearly disrespectful, and many of the President's rejoinders drew loud protests. After the first few exchanges, many people apparently concluded that a "real dialogue" was impossible and some demanded that the meeting move to the second agenda topic. Further, the absence of audience microphones made it nearly impossible to hear questions; and many foci of attention had developed that could not be dealt with. The President probably sensed the rising tension and confusion, thanked the audience for its attention, and gave the microphone back to the student body president.

The student body president then introduced a graduate student from the Philosophy Department to talk about the recent war escalation, and attention again focused on a single speaker. People's expectations seemed somewhat unclear. Most had heard anti-war talks for several years and were probably hoping for some fresh insights. Many wanted to consider only appropriate anti-war activity. In contrast, for some this was a first exposure and for sophomores and freshmen a first chance to participate in a "heavy" college action. In any case, crowd members seemed more agitated than when they arrived, but no closer to a consensus. The wide range of motives that drew people to the meeting apparently still existed.

Several characteristics of the speech stand out. First, the speaker had a southern accent. He was not another "New York Radical" and was not hindered by the cynicism with which students often greeted speeches from big-city types. Second, he did not tell people "facts," but "reminded" them of what they already knew. "We all know," he said, "that the war reflects business interests." His style minimized the lecturing flavor so common in anti-war speeches, while still allowing "uninformed" people to get the message. Third, he used a soft plaintive tone; a low-key almost weary delivery. He appealed quietly for thoughtfulness, never speaking above conversational level. Fourth, his message linked the frustration and emptiness of individuals, the American economic and political structure, and the war in Southeast Asia. It was a very personal message about feelings and thoughts. To most he seemed a humane radical; sensible, intelligent, and probably most important, non-violent. A few more experienced activists thought him naive, too emotional, a "liberal," and a damper to "serious" political activity. Fifth, his ideas were so general that few could disagree. For example, "the war is tragic," and being drafted is "a curtailment of individual freedom." Sixth, he did not propose specific action. He suggested that the campus "get itself together," unite to foster change. But he did not call for a strike, further rallies, or demonstrations.

Frustrations generated during the President's speech were not less in evidence. There were no hecklers, though a few people shouted "shut it down." People sat quietly listening. When his talk ended, there was no visible crowd reaction.

The next four speakers advocated a wide range of potential activity; most were moderately militant. They suggested blocking rush hour traffic, teach-ins, demonstrations, marches to Nixon election headquarters and, of course, a student strike. No one mentioned writing congressmen or supporting peace candidates. The greatest impact was produced by a student from the seminary who told of militant actions seminarians had undertaken and of their strike already in progress. Students muttered, "If they can get it together, why can't we?"

The crowd cheered popular proposals, and these reactions were an important gauge of crowd sentiment. However, many said nothing, and crowd noise may have inaccurately reflected the majority. Furthermore, the open "voting" probably mitigated against the expression of unpopular positions. Nevertheless, it seemed that a strike proposal was clearly endorsed. Cries of "shut it down" drew widespread, enthusiastic cheers.

Crowd noise now began to increase and many foci of attention appeared. There seemed strong strike support, and people were much more animated in speech and movement than ten minutes earlier. The student body president then seized the microphone. He said that although he favored a strike, it could not occur without majority student support. He urged them to be "democratic" and not force their wishes on others. He argued that those present were not numerous enough for a strike. Rather, he proposed a student referendum on the strike saying that only if a majority of undergraduates voted for it, would the student government endorse a strike. Though he spoke coherently, his delivery was strained and shining. Compared to the graduate students, he seemed panicky.

Reactions were mixed. Some ignored him, choosing instead to talk to neighbors. People in front were laughing, apparently in scorn. Others tried to shout him down, unsuccessfully. Yet, there seemed strong sentiment for democratic procedures. And those demanding a strike gave no directions on how to begin. Hence, students wanting to strike had no program to implement.

The student body president finished his pleas with a request that everyone return to their dormitories and encourage their friends to vote that evening in a student referendum. He explained where to vote, indicating that the results would be announced that night.

The crowd dispersed with a wide range of verbal reactions. Even those pleased with the outcome expressed many different views. Some were pleased because they thought a majority would support it. Still others were pleased that a democratic procedure would be used whatever the outcome. Grumbling persons were also divided. Some wanted an immediate strike. Others were upset that a strike was even being considered. Many were ambivalent, confused by the events and unsure of where they stood.

To go from the plaza to the dormitories, many had to travel north. The most direct route led to Sheridan Road, a large city thoroughfare running the length of the campus. Rather than use the sidewalk, about half chose to take the middle of the street. This act was unnecessary and clearly defiant. Though the traffic was light, the students were a potential inconvenience to drivers.

During the strike of 1970, Sheridan Road had been a center of activity. Blockades were erected which seriously disrupted rush hour traffic, and students remembered the blockades as the strike's most effective and exciting activities. Earlier that day, when talk of a student strike first appeared, some students discussed blocking Sheridan Road. They noted its symbolic value in relation to Nixon's blockade of Haiphong Harbor.

From where students spilled out onto Sheridan Road to about three hundred yards north, there were about 250 "jaywalkers." They walked in groups of five or six, and their talk reflected diverse motives. The student clusters could not accurately be characterized as a march, since there was no organization, no interlocking of arms, no parallel lines of marchers, and no slogans, banners or chants. Small groups were simply strolling down the middle of a main street about twenty feet apart.

The "jaywalking" continued about five minutes until one student ran to a wooden fence (near some construction), and tried to break off a section to move onto the street. He called to two friends for help, and together they dragged enough fencing across the road to block it completely. They yelled to students behind them and ahead of them to return and erect a barricade. Sheridan Road became the new arena and attention focused on the activity around the fence.

About two hundred students (the majority) responded; the rest continued north. People were still in clusters of three to ten with those closest to the fence the most aware of what was happening. Groups of people converged rapidly to within a half block but only about thirty actually approached the fence. Most remained on the sidewalks and grass areas on either side of the road.

At first, many opposed the barricade. They said it would "turn people off," that nothing would be gained and that it misrepresented popular sentiment. Those in favor argued they were "bringing the war home," that there was no time for democratic decision-making, and that disruption was needed to arouse anti-war sentiment. At this point, the students who felt most keenly about the issues, seemed to be around the fence. Their movements were animated, their voices loud, their speech rapid. The less intense students stood on sidewalks and nearby grass areas talking calmly. By the fence, arguments developed and many clear and cogent points were made.

The next three minutes were especially critical for the evolving crowd behavior. Three students had "seized the time" when they began to construct a barricade. It seemed clear to everyone that the three probably could not finish the job alone. (At the very least the crowd would have to remain passive.) Hence, the act of tearing the fence and dragging it across the road was primarily a symbolic call for action, and students at the barricade responded by beginning many simultaneous "negotiations." Various proposals were made and debated: "This barricade stuff is stupid and risky because it is destruction of property. Why don't we just stage a sit-down here in the street instead?" "What you guys are doing is too risky. You'll be arrested or suspended. I know it's just not worth that much to me. Why don't we just go along with the strike." "A barricade will just turn people off. I don't want any part of it. I'm going back to the dormitory." Observers on the sidewalks engaged in similar discussions, in a lower key. Much talk seemed almost academic, as if what they did would have no consequences.

This talk led to various decisions. Some finding the barricade alien to their values and suspecting that moderation was impossible, simply left. Some argued for more "constructive" activities, but departed when it became clear that many intended militant action. Among those in sympathy with the barricade who remained, many disagreed about the degree of disruptiveness that should be encouraged. Some favored a temporary human barricade, while others suggested that Sheridan Road be "liberated" until the Haiphong blockade was lifted. A few preferred "trashing" of downtown stores. Nevertheless, the idea of a barricade soon gathered enough support that increasing numbers of people moved from the sidewalks to the road; while others began to collect more building materials.

Within minutes it was clear that those wanting to erect a barricade would do so, while those opposed would not intervene. With about fifty people following in the street and fifty more supporting the fence, the barricade was moved a block and a half south to a main intersection. More material was added: parts of another fence, boards from a nearby construction site, and large trash receptacles. In ten minutes a substantial structure was built and about 250 students were milling around, many still arguing. An active minority strongly endorsed the barricade. A smaller though equally active minority opposed it. Most students seemed undecided but eventually chose temporarily to support the barricade, or at least to let it stand.

Despite many differences of opinion there were no longer two distinct crowds. the physical boundaries which had earlier separated the apathetic from the concerned, now gave way. Some spectators could be observed at the barricade, while some activists were on the sidewalks. In short, the crowd was permeable, and location in the gathering was no longer a good indicator of role.

Later, when students were asked what they had been thinking at this critical time, their answers differed. Even those most committed to the barricade (including persons later arrested trying to maintain it) were weighing many considerations. Should they make a "public anti-war statement," "bring the war home," generate a 1970-style strike, stimulate the militancy of 1970, embarrass the University President, and/or "train" political activists? Should they risk "turning off" the public, punishment from police or the University? Some felt cynically that no action would work and others wanted only to relax in the sun. Then too, many considered how friends and parents would react if he/she participated. Some were concerned by their desire to be leaders, and for others the actions meant a break from their life-style. The militants differed primarily in their tallying of costs and benefits. Though ambivalent, they saw the barricade as useful. Others believed it cost too much. Many could not decide.

In the hours that followed, the divisions of opinion did not change. The street was blocked and used as a forum for many speakers. Police were called, but did not move against the students or their barricade. Traffic was rerouted.

Students remained into the night, and fires were built for warmth. People brought guitars, and small groups fathered in friendly fashion. The police stood by, and interacted cordially with students. There was no name-calling from either camp. Some students knew a few of the police, and it was made clear that the actions were not anti-police.

By 1:00 a.m., seventy-four students remained. By 4:00 a.m., thirty remained. At 5:15 a.m., the police told the remaining twenty-four that the barricade would be torn down at 5:30, and they could disperse or be arrested. Seven chose to stay. Morning rush hour traffic moved normally down Sheridan Road.

That morning, in response to the referendum's endorsement a two-day strike was called. The administration did not support the strike, but did not take action against the strikers. Faculty were told by a University vice president to meet with their classes and most did. Attendance was about twenty-five percent.

DISCUSSION AND ANALYSIS

Despite muddy definitions, few would dispute that the events on Sheridan Road could be called crowd behavior. A large group of people in close proximity participated in an unplanned activity. In addition, the people on Sheridan Road were clearly trying to interpret the situation, trying to give meaning to their perceptions. Thus, they were exercising some form of thought. The dominant theories of crowd behavior do not effectively provide for such cognitive processes.

First, each student held varied beliefs about the situation; and rarely did one belief predominate. The data showed that even the fifty students who built the barricade were complexly motivated and often ambivalent.

Second, one would be hard pressed to categorically call the students' beliefs "short-circuits" of reality or the product of uncritical suggestion. While many hoped the action might help end the war, few were optimistic. In short, their beliefs seemed well grounded in reality. Even those intensely involved noted options, estimated the likelihood of various events, projected sequences of events, ranked outcomes, and made decisions consistent with these preparations. The solutions acted on were not "best" in any absolute game theory sense, but Raiffa's Decision Theory explicitly excludes this criterion. Rather, the gauge of rationality is the *degree* to which the *processes* in individual decision-making approximate Raiffa's proposed strategy. Dominant sociological views would seem either to ignore these complexities or define them away a priori, and hence, do not account for significant aspects of the action and dialogue around the barricade.

Third, the behavior of the group was also multiply determined. Participants brought mixed motives and beliefs to the action, and the group activity reflected a series of compromises. Those who wanted to "trash" had to cooperate with those who favored "non-violence" if they wanted a major action. In short, there was little evidence of the homogeneity of motive many theories assume.

Fourth, while some beliefs may have been childish, magical, and simplistic, and some apparently well-grounded views later proved inaccurate, the beliefs in this crowd seem no more uncritical, magical, or simplistic than those in many human groups. Careful attention to a faculty meeting, a TV talk show, a political convention, and perhaps even a court hearing (Mayer, 1969), would likely yield similar proportions of sophisticated and naive understandings. One must not be unduly influenced by customary hierarchies of credibility which prejudge vital empirical questions.

In summary, the dominant sociological perspectives seem inadequate for this instance of crowd behavior. Theories which assume attitudinal homogeneity in crowds (whatever its nature) ignore essential interpersonal processes. Such notions cannot explain the richness of thought, action, and interaction, apparent on Sheridan Road. These processes are of intrinsic interest and important for any theoretical understanding of crowd behavior. In short, current approaches seem weak in at least two ways: a) some may misrepresent the cognitive processes of crowd members; and b) those which emphasize a common homogeneous belief skirt the impact of important individual differences and ignore certain vital interpersonal processes at the scene . . . .

APPLICATIONS AND CONCLUSIONS

The revised collective decision-making approach to crowd behavior can be usefully applied to our data. However, since the theoretical perspective did not crystalize until the analysis was begin, the sample of applications will necessarily be *post hoc* and best understood as illustrations of potential utility.

1. The earlier speeches appeared to have altered the payoff matrices of potential crowd participants. For example a conciliatory stance by the university president might have undermined a variety of motivations for disruption. Or, had the seminarians seemed less militant, other students might have felt less need to take a visible stand. Among other things, the seminarians were implicitly challenging the crowd to take risks for their principles.

2. The group interactions in Crown Plaza were vital to the eventual crowd behavior. People had time to talk to one another and gauge the degree and type of anti-war sentiment. This was also a period when many potential anti-war responses were proposed and discussed. People had a chance to formulate their views and think about the issues in detail, and reactions to the speeches provided a means by which central tendencies in crowd sentiment might be roughly gauged. For example, had the cries of "shut it down" not drawn such cheers, the existence of widespread militancy would have been less evident. In short, had the crowd been moving along Sheridan Road after a football game (all other factors being the same) a barricade would probably not have been built.

3. The rapid mobilization of the crowd was aided by the following features of the environment. First, the barricade was begun in a level area in plain view of most students. Had the first actions occurred around a bend in Sheridan Road, the crowd would probably have grown more slowly. Second, the three students who dragged the fence across the road were located in about the middle of the people moving north. Had they been on the fringes of the crowd, most people might not have seen what was happening and the mobilization might have been hindered. In addition, the central location facilitated rapid communication of the events because the outward diffusion process could proceed in all directions. Had the fence incident occurred on the crowd's edge, people would have been on the average farther away and the lines of communication would have been longer. Third, since the action of initiating the barricade actually blocked the northward progress of many "jaywalkers," it necessarily drew immediate attention and demanded an immediate response. Had the three students sat down in the road, their protest would have been invisible to all but their closest neighbors and would have had little impact on the flow of the crowd. Fourth, the initiation of a single incident (rather than many) simplified the decisional environment. If several different groups of students had begun several different actions, there would have been much more data to assimilate, leading to a more confusing and complex series of negotiations. Picture the confusion if in addition to the fence incident, some students staged a "sit in" and others started trashing nearby buildings.

4. The actual building of the barricade rather than a verbal proposal to that effect had an important impact on people's assessments of support. Dragging the fence across Sheridan Road communicated effectively that some people were committed to a street blockade. By taking risks, the three students had greatly enhanced their credibility which then strengthened the belief that some support for this kind of militant action was likely. A cry of "to the barricades" or a similar suggestion at conversation level would have been far less potent. Further, no one could chide the three "to put up or shut up." They had already put up.

5. The fence incident was also effective because by directly altering the crowd's environment it altered the range of potential costs and benefits. First, once the fence was in the road, the costs for those who would have tended to support a barricade were reduced. Someone had already taken the risk of beginning action; others would not have to. Second, the costs for many other kinds of activity were raised. For example, to leave the scene would have appeared to some as deserting the three students who "put themselves on the line." Or, to oppose the three physically and try to remove the fence from the road may well have generated a serious confrontation. In

short, given that the mix of motives in the crowd was consistent with some kind of anti-war action, the three students effectively seized the initiative by tilting the potential costs and benefits in favor of their tactics.

This interpretation has a different emphasis than the concept of "keynoting" (Turner, 1964:406). Keynoting involves the "crystallization of sentiment" in which attitudes are adjusted to be consistent with a particular utterance or action or in which some previously latent views are highlighted at the expense of others. While these processes may well have been triggered by the fence incident, they seem an incomplete explanation for its potent effects.

6. The moderate density on Sheridan Road permitted the actions of the three who initiated the barricade to be easily seen and still understood in terms of potential group action. Much higher or much lower density may have substantially lessened the chance of generating support.

7. The interactions around the barricade can be understood not as "contagion," but as attempts to communicate and influence individual payoff matrices while proposing alternatives for action. Hence, the emphasis on rational interpersonal processes generating the crowd behavior and the various roles played by different individuals. With better data, one could have studied in detail the development of support for the barricade.

8. The generation of support for the barricade did not occur evenly over time. Rather, the increase in size of the supporting crowd appeared to grow exponentially and then taper off, a pattern which suggests the "S" shaped effect of number of participants on probability of support. This was probably not a ceiling effect (the rate of increase must taper off as the percentage of total potential participants approach 100%) because at least a third of those present did not participate in building and holding the barricade.

9. The barricade generated support quickly in part because its symbolic content was clear. The previous strike and obvious analogy to Nixon's Haiphong blockade provided vehicles for interpreting the actions. This clarity may have been one of the factors making leaders for the action unnecessary. Little explanation was required. Further, Smelser's generalized belief seems both unnecessary and inaccurate as a factor in the rapid mobilization. There developed a common base of understanding about the barricade, but this had little to do with short-circuited thinking or magical expectations for the outcome. One must not confuse the occurrence of *some* common emergent interpretations of events with a distorted world view. In addition, the common perspectives were but one of the many factors operations, *not the defining characteristic.*

The above applications of gaming perspectives should begin to indicate how these views differ from more traditional collective decision-making approaches. While there is insufficient space here to detail these differences, a few final observations may be made.

First, there need be no contradiction between gaming perspectives and emergent norm theory. It is apparent that some collective definitions evolve and that group pressures somewhat constrain crowd members. However, it seems misleading to assume that the "suggestion" fostered by emergent norms cripples the cognitive abilities of participants or that people in crowds are somehow less able than people in other circumstances to examine their situation critically. If there are important differences (probably in degree) in the ways individual judgments are made, it would seem to be more a function of the problematic environments in which crowds operate than any fundamental change in the capacity to reason.

Second, the gaming perspective fills important gaps in emergent norm theory. Close reading of Turner (1964) and Turner and Killian (1972) suggest that they never address systematically or in depth where the norms came from. Crowds seem to exist in an almost featureless pain where the physical environment and the motives of individual crowd members are nearly irrelevant.

The theoretical emphasis is on the role of evolving norms in shaping crowd behavior to why a particular norm, or set of norms, is originally considered. In other words, their analysis begins after certain interpretations and proposals have been introduced. By failing to address motives or responses to the environment, they leave the impression that almost *any* set of norms can be superimposed. The only reality for crowd members is the normative reality.

Third, gaming perspectives and emergent norm approaches imply very different, though probably complementary psychological mechanisms. The former involve a conscious calculus in which the best anticipated outcomes are selected. Concerted action develops in crowds because of apparent mutual benefit. The latter rests on the unconscious tendency to accede to group norms. Concerted action involves a kind of self-fulfilling prophecy in which norms shape behavior because they reflect underlying shared understandings, which are in turn further supported by behavioral conformity.

In conclusion, perhaps the most fruitful way to conceptualize crowd behavior is through a notion of collective innovation. As Weller and Quarantelli (1973) suggest, collective behavior can be characterized by concerted group activity when previous norms and/or social relationships fail to meet immediate needs. This paper describes one set of mechanisms through which such coordination might occur. However, while Turner and Killian focus on normative issues, and the gaming perspective emphasizes rational attempts to gain optimal outcomes, ultimately the relative salience of these and other factors is an empirical question. Equally important will be how these processes interact. An inclusive theory of collective behavior will have to address such complexity.

REFERENCES

Allport, F. H. 1924. Social Psychology, Boston: Houghton.

Becker, Howard S. 1967. "Whose side are we on?" Social Problems 14 (March):239–47.

Berk, Richard A. 1972a. "The controversy surrounding analyses of collective violence: some methodological notes." Pp. 112–18 in James F. Short, Jr. and Marvin E. Wolfgang, Collective Violence. Chicago: Aldine.

Berk, Richard A. 1972b. "The emergence of muted violence in crowd behavior: a case study of an almost race riot." Pp. 309–28 in James F. Short, Jr. and Marvin E. Wolfgang, Collective Violence. Chicago: Aldine.

Berk, Richard A. 1974. Collective Behavior. Dubuque: W. C. Brown.

Berk, Richard A. and Howard E. Aldrich. 1972. "Patterns of vandalism during civil disorders as an indicator of selection of targets." American Sociological. Review 37 (October): 533–47.

Blumer, H. 1946. "Collective behavior." Pp. 170–93 in A. M. Lee, New Outline of the Principles of Sociology. New York: Barnes and Noble.

Brown, Roger. 1965. Social Psychology. New York: Free Press.

Canetti, Elias. 1966. Crowds and Power. New York: Viking Press. Chernoff, Herman and Lincoln E. Moses. 1959. Elementary Decision Theory. New York: John Wiley.

Cofer, Charles N. and Mortimer Appley. 1964. Motivation: Theory and Research. New York: John Wiley.

Cohen, Jerry and William S. Murphy. 1966. Burn Baby Burn! New York: Avon Books.

Currie, Elliot and Jerome Skolnick. 1972. "A critical note on conceptions of collective behavior." Pp. 60–71 in James F. Short, Jr. and Marvin E. Wolfgang, Collective Violence. Chicago: Aldine.

Fisher, Charles S. 1972. "Observing a crowd: the structure and description of protest demonstrations." Pp. 187–212 in Jack D. Douglas. Research on Deviance. New York: Random House.

Fleisher, Belton M. 1966. The Economics of Delinquency. Chicago: Quandrangle Books.

Fogelson, Robert M. 1971. Violence in Protest. New York: Doubleday.

Freud, Sigmund. 1957. "Group psychology and the analysis of the ego." Pp. 169–209 in A General Selection of the Works of Sigmund Freud. New York: Anchor Books.

Goffman, Erving. 1959. The Presentation of Self in Everyday Life. Garden City: Doubleday Anchor Books.

Goffman, Erving. 1969. Strategic Interaction. New York: Ballantine Books.

Hayden, Tom. 1967. Rebellion in Newark. New York: Random House.

Hook, Sidney. Dimension of the Mind. New York: New York University Press.

Iverson, Gudmund R. 1970. "Statistics according to Bayes." Pp. 185–99 in Edgar Borgatta, Sociological Methodology. San Francisco: Jossey-Bass.

Klapp, Orrin. 1972. Currents of Unrest. New York: Holt, Rinehart and Winston.

LeBon, Gustave. 1960. The Crowd. New York: Viking Press.

Lemert, Edwin M. 1962. "Paranoia and the dynamics of exclusion." Sociometry 25 (March): 2–20.

Luce, R. Duncan. 1964. Individual Choice Behavior: A Theoretical Analysis. New York: Wiley.

Luce, R. Duncan and Howard Raiffa. 1957. Games and Decisions. New York: John Wiley.

McPhail, Clark. 1971. "Civil disorder participation: a critical examination of recent research." American Sociological Review 36 (December): 1058–73.

Marx, Gary. 1972. "Issueless riots." Pp. 47–59 in James F. Short, Jr. and Marvin E. Wolfgang, Collective Violence. Chicago: Aldine.

Mayer, Milton. 1969. Man vs. the State. Center for the Study of Democratic Institutions: Santa Barbara, California.

Milgram, Stanley and Hans Toch. 1969. "Collective behavior: crowds and social movements." Pp. 507–610 in Gardner Lindzey and Elliot Aronson (eds.). The Handbook of Social Psychology, Vol. 4. Reading, Mass.: Addison-Wesley.

Nardin, Terry. 1971. "Theories of conflict management." Peace Research Reviews 4 (April): 1–87.

Nieburg, H. L. 1972. "Agonistics—ritual of conflict." Pp. 82– 99 in James F. Short, Jr. and Marvin E. Wolfgang (eds.), Collective Violence. Chicago: Aldine.

Raiffa, Howard. 1970. Decision Analysis. Reading, Mass.: Addison- Wesley.

Savage, Richard I. 1968. Statistics: Uncertainty and Behavior. Boston: Houghton Mifflin.

Schelling, Thomas C. 1963. The Strategy of Conflict. New York: Oxford Press.

Schmitt, Samuel A. 1969. Measuring Uncertainty. Reading, Mass.: Addison-Wesley.

Shibutani, Tomatsu. 1944. "The circulation of rumors as a form of collective behavior." Unpublished doctoral dissertation. University of Chicago.

Shibutani, Tomatsu. 1966. Improvised News. New York: Bobbs-Merrill.

Sjoquist, David Lawrence. 1973. "Property crime and economic behavior: some empirical results." American Economics Review 63 (June): 439–46.

Smelser, Neil J. 1962. Theory of Collective Behavior. New York: Free Press.

Smelser, Neil J. 1972a. "Two critics in search of a bias: a response to Currie and Skolnick." Pp. 72–81 in James F. Short, Jr. and Marvin E. Wolfgang (eds.), Collective Violence. Chicago: Aldine.

Stroktbeck, Fred and James F. Short, J. 1964. "Aleatory risks versus short-run hedonism in explanation of gang action." Social Problems 12 (Fall): 127–40.

Sykes, Gresham M. 1970. "The society of captives." New York: Atheneum.

Turner, Ralph H. 1964. "Collective behavior." Pp. 382–425 in Robert E. L. Faris (ed.). Handbook of Modern Sociology. Chicago: Rand McNally.

Turner, Ralph H. and L. M. Killian. 1957. Collective Behavior. Englewood Cliffs. New Jersey: Prentice Hall.

Weller, Jack M. and E. L. Quarantelli. 1973. "Neglected characteristics of collective behavior." American Journal of Sociology 9 (March): 665–85.

ARTICLE 4

Resource Mobilization and Social Movements: A Partial Theory

JOHN D. MCCARTHY
MAYER N. ZALD

For quite some time a hiatus existed in the study of social movements in the United States. In the course of activism leaders of movements here and abroad attempted to enunciate general principles concerning movement tactics and strategy and the dilemmas that arise in overcoming hostile environments. Such leaders as Mao, Lenin, Saul Alinsky, and Martin Luther King attempted in turn to develop principles and guidelines for action. The theories of activists stress problems of mobilization, the manufacture of discontent, tactical choices, and the infrastructure of society and movements necessary for success. At the same time sociologists, with their emphasis upon structural strain, generalized belief, and deprivation, largely have ignored the ongoing problems and strategic dilemmas of social movements. . . .

The resource mobilization approach emphasizes both societal support and constraint of social movement phenomena. It examines the variety of resources that must be mobilized, the linkages of social movements to other groups, the dependence of movements upon external support for success, and the tactics used by authorities to control or incorporate movements. The shift in emphasis is evident in much of the work published recently in this area (J. Wilson 1973; Tilly 1973, 1975; Tilly, Tilly, and Tilly 1975; Gamson 1975; Oberschall 1973; Lipsky 1968; Downs 1972; McCarthy and Zald 1973). The new approach depends more upon political sociological and economic theories than upon the social psychology of collective behavior.

This paper presents a set of concepts and propositions that articulate the resource mobilization approach. It is a partial theory because it takes as given, as constants, certain components of a complete theory. The propositions are heavily based upon the American case, so that the impact of societal differences in development and political structure on social movements is unexplored, as are differences in levels and types of mass communication. Further, we rely heavily upon case material concerning organizations of the left, ignoring, for the most part, organizations of the right.

The main body of the paper defines our central concepts and presents illustrative hypotheses about the social movement sector (SMS), social movement industries (SMI), and social movement organizations (SMO). However, since we

McCarthy, John D., & Zald, Mayer N. (1977, May). Resource mobilization and social movements: A partial theory. *American Journal of Sociology, 82* (6), 1212–1241. Reprinted with permission of The University of Chicago Press.

view this approach as a departure from the main tradition in social movement analysis, it will be useful first to clarify what we see as the limits of that tradition.

PERSPECTIVES EMPHASIZING DEPRIVATION AND BELIEFS

Without question the three most influential approaches to an understanding of social movement phenomena for American sociologists during the past decade are those of Gurr (1970), Turner and Killian (1972), and Smelser (1963). They differ in a number of respects. But, most important, they have in common strong assumptions that shared grievances and generalized beliefs (loose ideologies) about the causes and possible means of reducing grievances are important preconditions for the emergence of a social movement in a collectivity. An increase in the extent or intensity of grievances or deprivation and the development of ideology occur prior to the emergence of social movement phenomena. Each of these perspectives holds that discontent produced by some combination of structural conditions is a necessary if not sufficient condition to an account of the rise of any specific social movement phenomenon. Each, as well, holds that before collective action is possible within a collectivity a generalized belief (or ideological justification) is necessary concerning at least the causes of the discontent and, under certain conditions, the modes of redress. Much of the empirical work which has followed and drawn upon these perspectives has emphasized even more heavily the importance of understanding the grievances and deprivation of participants. (Indeed, scholars following Gurr, Smelser, and Turner and Killian often ignore structural factors, even though the authors mentioned have been sensitive to broader structural and societal influences, as have some others.)

Recent empirical work, however, has led us to doubt the assumption of a close link between preexisting discontent and generalized beliefs in the rise of social movement phenomena. A number of studies have shown little or no support for expected relationships between objective or subjective deprivation and the outbreak of movement phenomena and willingness to participate in collective action (Snyder and Tilly 1972; Mueller 1972; Bowen et al. 1968; Crawford and Naditch 1970). Other studies have failed to support the expectation of a generalized belief prior to outbreaks of collective behavior episodes or initial movement involvement (Quarantelli and Hundley 1975; Marx 1970; Stallings 1973). Partially as a result of such evidence, in discussing revolution and collective violence Charles Tilly is led to argue that these phenomena flow directly out of a population's central political processes instead of expressing momentarily heightened diffuse strains and discontents within a population (Tilly 1973).

Moreover, the heavy focus upon the psychological state of the mass of potential movement supporters within a collectivity has been accompanied by a lack of emphasis upon the processes by which persons and institutions from outside of the collectivity under consideration become involved; for instance, Northern white liberals in the Southern civil rights movement, or Russians and Cubans in Angola. Although earlier perspectives do not exclude the possibilities of such involvement on the part of outsiders, they do not include such processes as central and enduring phenomena to be used in accounting for social movement behavior.

The ambiguous evidence of some of the research on deprivation, relative deprivation, and generalized belief has led us to search for a perspective and a set of assumptions that lessen the prevailing emphasis upon grievances. We want to move from a strong assumption about the centrality of deprivation and grievances to a weak one, which makes them a component, indeed, sometimes a secondary component in the generation of social movements.

We are willing to assume (Turner and Killian [1972] call the assumption extreme) ". . . that there is always enough discontent in any society to supply the grass-roots support for a movement if the movement is effectively organized and has at its disposal the power and resources of some established elite group" (p. 251). For some purposes we go even further: grievances and discontent may be defined, created, and manipulated by issue entrepreneurs and organizations.

We adopt a weak assumption not only because of the negative evidence (already mentioned) concerning the stronger one but also because in some cases recent experience supports the weaker one. For instance, the senior citizens who were mobilized into groups to lobby for Medicare were brought into groups only after legislation was before Congress and the American Medical Association had claimed that senior citizens were not complaining about the medical care available to them (Rose 1967). Senior citizens were organized into groups through the efforts of a lobbying group created by the AFL-CIO. No doubt the elderly needed money for medical care. However, what is important is that the organization did not develop directly from that grievance but very indirectly through the moves of actors in the political system. Entertaining a weak assumption leads directly to an emphasis upon mobilization processes. Our concern is the search for analytic tools to account adequately for the processes.

RESOURCE MOBILIZATION

The resource mobilization perspective adopts as one of its underlying problems Olson's (1965) challenge: since social movements deliver collective goods, few individuals will "on their own" bear the costs of working to obtain them. Explaining collective behavior requires detailed attention to the selection of incentives, cost-reducing mechanisms or structures, and career benefits that lead to collective behavior (see, especially, Oberschall 1973).

Several emphases are central to the perspective as it has developed. First, study of the aggregation of resources (money and labor) is crucial to an understanding of social movement activity. Because resources are necessary for engagement in social conflict, they must be aggregated for collective purposes. Second, resource aggregation requires some minimal form of organization, and hence, implicitly or explicitly, we focus more directly upon social movement organizations than do those working within the traditional perspective. Third, in accounting for a movement's successes and failures there is an explicit recognition of the crucial importance of involvement on the part of individuals and organizations from outside the collectivity which a social movement represents. Fourth, an explicit, if crude, supply and demand model is sometimes applied to the flow of resources toward and away from specific social movements. Finally, there is a sensitivity to the importance of costs and rewards in explaining individual and organizational involvement in social movement activity. Costs and rewards are centrally affected by the structure of society and the activities of authorities.

We can summarize the emerging perspective by contrasting it with the traditional one as follows:

1. Support base
   a. Traditional. Social movements are based upon aggrieved populations which provide the necessary resources and labor. Although case studies may mention external supports, they are not incorporated as central analytic components.
   b. Resource mobilization. Social movements may or may not be based upon the grievances of the presumed beneficiaries. Conscience constituents, individual and organizational, may provide major sources of support. And in some cases supporters—those who provide money, facilities, and even labor—may have no commitment to the values that underlie specific movements.
2. Strategy and tactics
   a. Traditional. Social movement leaders use bargaining, persuasion, or violence to influence authorities to change. Choices of tactics depend upon prior history of relations with authorities, relative success

of previous encounters, and ideology. Tactics are also influenced by the oligarchization and institutionalization of organization life.

b. Resource mobilization. The concern with interaction between movements and authorities is accepted, but it is also noted that social movement organizations have a number of strategic tasks. These include mobilizing supporters, neutralizing and/or transforming mass and elite publics into sympathizers, achieving change in targets. Dilemmas occur in the choice of tactics, since what may achieve one aim may conflict with behavior aimed at achieving another. Moreover, tactics are influenced by interorganizational competition and cooperation.

3. Relation to larger society

a. Traditional. Case studies have emphasized the effects of the environment upon movement organizations, especially with respect to goal change, but have ignored, for the most part, ways in which such movement organizations can utilize the environment for their own purposes (see Perrow 1972). This has probably been largely a result of the lack of comparative organizational focus inherent in case studies. In analytical studies emphasis is upon the extent of hostility or toleration in the larger society. Society and culture are treated as descriptive, historical context.

b. Resource mobilization. Society provides the infrastructure which social movement industries and other industries utilize. The aspects utilized include communication media and expense, levels of affluence, degree of access to institutional centers, preexisting networks, and occupational structure and growth.

THEORETICAL ELEMENTS

Having sketched the emerging perspective, our task now is to present a more precise statement of it. In this section we offer our most general concepts and definitions. Concepts of narrower range are presented in following sections.

A *social movement* is a set of opinions and beliefs in a population which represents preferences for changing some elements of the social structure and/or reward distribution of a society. A *countermovement* is a set of opinions and beliefs in a population opposed to a social movement. As is clear, we view social movements as nothing more than preference structures directed toward social change, very similar to what political sociologists would term issue cleavages. (Indeed, the process we are exploring resembles what political scientists term interest aggregation, except that we are concerned with the margins of the political system rather than with existing party structures.)

The distribution of preference structures can be approached in several ways. Who holds the beliefs? How intensely are they held? In order to predict the likelihood of preferences being translated into collective action, the mobilization perspective focuses upon the preexisting organization and integration of those segments of a population which share preferences. Oberschall (1973) has presented an important synthesis of past work on the preexisting organization of preference structures, emphasizing the opportunities and costs for expression of preferences for movement leaders and followers. Social movements whose related populations are highly organized internally (either communally or associationally) are more likely than are others to spawn organized forms.

A *social movement organization* (SMO) is a complex, or formal, organization which identifies its goals with the preferences of a social movement or a countermovement and attempts to implement those goals. If we think of the recent civil rights movement in these terms, the social movement contained a large portion of the population which held preferences for change aimed at "justice for black Americans" and a number of SMOs such as the Student Non-Violent Coordinating Committee (SNCC), the Congress of Racial Equality (CORE), the National Association for the Advancement of Colored People (NAACP), and Southern Christian Leadership Conference (SCLC). These SMOs represented and shaped the broadly held preferences and diverse subpreferences of the social movement.

All SMOs that have as their goal the attainment of the broadest preferences of a social movement constitute a *social movement industry* (SMI)—the organizational analogue of a social movement. A conception paralleling that of SMI, used by Von Eschen, Kirk, and Pinard (1971), the "organizational substructure of disorderly politics," has aided them in analyzing the civil rights movement in Baltimore. They demonstrate that many of the participants in a 1961 demonstration sponsored by the local chapter of CORE were also involved in NAACP, SCLC, the Americans for Democratic Action (ADA), or the Young People's Socialist Alliance (YPSA). These organizations either were primarily concerned with goals similar to those of CORE or included such goals as subsets of broader ranges of social change goals. (The concept employed by Von Eschen et al. is somewhat broader than ours, however, as will be seen below.)

Definitions of the central term, social movement (SM), typically have included both elements of preference and organized action for change. Analytically separating these components by distinguishing between an SM and an SMI has several advantages. First, it emphasizes that SMs are never fully mobilized. Second, it focuses explicitly upon the organizational component of activity. Third, it recognizes explicitly that SMs are typically represented by more than one SMO. Finally, the distinction allows the possibility of an account of the rise and fall of SMIs that is not fully dependent on the size of an SM or the intensity of the preferences within it.

Our definitions of SM, SMI, and SMO are intended to be inclusive of the phenomena which analysts have included in the past. The SMs can encompass narrow or broad preferences, millenarian and evangelistic preferences, and withdrawal preferences. Organizations may represent any of these preferences.

The definition of SMI parallels the concept of industry in economics. Note that economists, too, are confronted with the difficulty of selecting broader or narrower criteria for including firms (SMOs) within an industry (SMI). For example, one may define a furniture industry, a sitting-furniture industry, or a chair industry. Close substitutability of product usage and, therefore, demand interdependence is the theoretical basis for defining industry boundaries. Economists use the *Census of Manufacturers* classifications, which are not strictly based on demand interdependence. For instance, on the one hand various types of steel are treated as one industry, though the types (rolled, flat, wire) are not substitutable. On the other hand, some products are classified separately (e.g., beet sugar, cane sugar) when they are almost completely substitutable (Bain 1959, pp. 111–18).

Given our task, the question becomes how to group SMOs into SMIs. This is a difficult problem because particular SMOs may be broad or narrow in stated target goals. In any set of empirical circumstances the analyst must decide how narrowly to define industry boundaries. For instance, one may speak of the SMI which aims at liberalized alterations in laws, practices, and public opinion concerning abortion. This SMI would include a number of SMOs. But these SMOs may also be considered part of the broader SMI which is commonly referred to as the "women's liberation movement" or they could be part of the "population control movement." In the same way, the pre-1965 civil rights movement could be considered part of the broader civil liberties movement.

Economists have dealt with this difficulty by developing categories of broader inclusiveness, sometimes called sectors. Even this convention, however, does not confront the difficulties of allocating firms (SMOs) which are conglomerates, those which produce products across industries and even across sectors. In modern America there are a number of SMOs which may be thought of as conglomerates in that they span, in their goals, more narrowly defined SMIs. Common Cause, the American Friends Service Committee (AFSC), and the Fellowship of Reconciliation (FOR) are best treated in these terms as each pursues a wide variety of organizational goals which can only with difficulty be contained within even broadly defined SMIs. The *social movement sector* (SMS) consists of all SMIs in a society no matter to which SM they are attached. (The importance of this distinction will become apparent below.)

Let us now return to the resource mobilization task of an SMO. Each SMO has a set of *target goals,* a set of preferred changes toward which it claims to be working. Such goals may be broad or narrow, and they are the characteristics of SMOs which link them conceptually with particular SMs and SMIs. The SMOs must possess resources, however few and of whatever type, in order to work toward goal achievement. Individuals and other organizations control resources, which can include legitimacy, money, facilities, and labor.

Although similar organizations vary tremendously in the efficiency with which they translate resources into action (see Katz 1974), the amount of activity directed toward goal accomplishment is crudely a function of the resources controlled by an organization. Some organizations may depend heavily upon volunteer labor, while others may depend upon purchased labor. In any case, resources must be controlled or mobilized before action is possible.

From the point of view of a SMO the individuals and organizations which exist in a society may be categorized along a number of dimensions. For the appropriate SM there are adherents and nonadherents. *Adherents* are those individuals and organizations that believe in the goals of the movement. The *constituents* of a SMO are those providing resources for it.

At one level the resource mobilization task is primarily that of converting adherents into constituents and maintaining constituent involvement. However, at another level the task may be seen as turning nonadherents into adherents. Ralph Turner (1970) uses the term bystander public to denote those nonadherents who are not opponents of the SM and its SMOs but who merely witness social movement activity. It is useful to distinguish constituents, adherents, bystander publics, and opponents along several other dimensions. One refers to the size of the resource pool controlled, and we shall use the terms mass and elite to describe crudely this dimension. Mass constituents, adherents, bystander publics, and opponents are those individuals and groups controlling very limited resource pools. The most limited resource pool which individuals can control is their own time and labor. Elites are those who control larger resource pools.

Each of these groups may also be distinguished by whether or not they will benefit directly from the accomplishment of SMO goals. Some bystander publics, for instance, may benefit directly from the accomplishment of organizational goals, even though they are not adherents of the appropriate SM. To mention a specific example, women who oppose the preferences of the women's liberation movement or have no relevant preferences might benefit from expanded job opportunities for women pursued by women's groups. Those who would benefit directly from SMO goal accomplishment we shall call *potential beneficiaries.*

In approaching the task of mobilizing resources a SMO may focus its attention upon adherents who are potential beneficiaries and/or attempt to convert bystander publics who are potential beneficiaries into adherents. It may also expand its target goals in order to enlarge its potential beneficiary group. Many SMOs attempt to present their goal accomplishments in terms of broader potential benefits for ever-wider groupings of citizens through notions of a better society, etc. (secondary benefits). Finally, a SMO may attempt to mobilize as adherents those who are not potential beneficiaries. *Conscience adherents* are individuals and groups who are part of the appropriate SM but do not stand to benefit directly from SMO goal accomplishment. *Con-*

science constituents are direct supporters of a SMO who do not stand to benefit directly from its success in goal accomplishment.

William Gamson (1975) makes essentially the same distinction, calling groups with goals aimed at helping nonconstituents universalistic and those whose beneficiaries and constituents are identical, nonuniversalistic. Gamson concludes, however, that this distinction is not theoretically important, since SMOs with either type of constituents have identical problems in binding them to the organization. It is not more "irrational," in Olson's sense, to seek change in someone else's behalf than in one's own, and in both cases commitment must be gained by other means than purposive incentives. The evidence presented by Gamson suggests that this dimension does not bear much relationship to SMO success in goal accomplishment or in the attainment of legitimacy. We argue below, however, that the distinction should be maintained: it summarizes important attachments and social characteristics of constituents. The problems of SMOs with regard to binding beneficiary and conscience constituents to the organization are different, not with regard to the stakes of individual involvement relative to goal accomplishment (the Olson problem) but with regard to the way constituents are linked to each other and to other SMOs, organizations, and social institutions (see also J. Q. Wilson 1973).

A SMOs potential for resource mobilization is also affected by authorities and the delegated agents of social control (e.g., police). While authorities and agents of control groups do not typically become constituents of SMOs, their ability to frustrate (normally termed social control) or to enable resource mobilization are of crucial importance. Their action affects the readiness of bystanders, adherents, and constituents to alter their own status and commitment. And they themselves may become adherents and constituents. Because they do not always act in concert, Marx (1974) makes a strong case that authorities and delegated agents of control need to be analyzed separately.

The partitioning of groups into mass or elite and conscience or beneficiary bystander publics, adherents, constituents, and opponents allows us to describe more systematically the resource mobilization styles and dilemmas of specific SMOs. It may be, of course, to the advantage of a SMO to turn bystander publics into adherents. But since SMO resources are normally quite limited, decisions must be made concerning the allocation of these resources, and converting bystander publics may not aid in the development of additional resources. Such choices have implications for the internal organization of a SMO and the potential size of the resource pool which can be ultimately mobilized. For instance, a SMO which has a mass beneficiary base and concentrates its resource mobilization efforts toward mass beneficiary adherents is likely to restrict severely the amount of resources it can raise. Elsewhere (McCarthy and Zald 1973) we have termed a SMO focusing upon beneficiary adherents for resources a classical SMO. Organizations which direct resource appeals primarily toward conscience adherents tend to utilize few constituents for organizational labor, and we have termed such organizations professional SMOs.

Another pattern of resource mobilization and goal accomplishment can be identified from the writings of Lipsky (1968) and Bailis (1974). It depends upon the interactions among beneficiary constituency, conscience adherents, and authorities. Typical of this pattern is a SMO with a mass beneficiary constituency which would profit from goal accomplishment (for instance, the Massachusetts Welfare Rights Organization) but which has few resources. Protest strategies draw attention and resources from conscience adherents to the SMO fighting on behalf of such mass groups and may also lead conscience elites to legitimate the SMO to authorities. As a result of a similar pattern, migrant farmworkers benefited from the transformation of authorities into adherents (Jenkins and Perrow, forthcoming).

But a SMO does not have complete freedom of choice in making the sorts of decisions to which we have alluded. Such choices are constrained by a number of factors including the preexisting organization of various segments of the SM, the size and diversity of the SMI of which it is a part, and the competitive position of the SMS (McCarthy and Zald 1974; Zald and McCarthy 1974). Also, of course, the ability of any SMO to garner resources is shaped by important events such as war, broad economic trends, and natural disasters. . . .

REFERENCES

Bailis, L. 1974. *Bread or Justice*. Springfield, Mass.: Heath-Lexington.

Bain, J. S. 1959. *Industrial Organization*. New York: Wiley.

Blumer, H. 1946. "Collective Behavior." Pp. 167–219 in *A New Outline of the Principles of Sociology*, edited by A. M. Lee. New York: Barnes & Noble.

Bowen, D., E. Bowen, S. Gawiser, and L. Masotti. 1968. "Deprivation, Mobility, and Orientation toward Protest of the Urban Poor." Pp. 187–200 in *Riots and Rebellion: Civil Violence in the Urban Community*, edited by L. Masotti and D. Bowen. Beverly Hills, Calif.: Sage.

Bradburn, N., and D. Caplovitz. 1964. *Reports on Happiness*. Chicago: Aldine.

Breton, A., and R. Breton. 1969. "An Economic Theory of Social Movements." *American Economic Review. Papers and Proceedings of the American Economic Association*, vol. 59, no. 2 (May).

Brown, L. 1970. "Hunger U.S.A.: The Public Pushes Congress." *Journal of Health and Social Behavior* 11 (June): 115–25.

Campbell, A., P. E. Converse, W. E. Miller, and D. E. Stokes. 1960. *The American Voter*. New York: Wiley.

Cantril, H. 1941. *The Psychology of Social Movements*. New York: Wiley.

———. 1965. *The Pattern of Human Concern*. New Brunswick, N.J.: Rutgers University Press.

Cicchetti, C. J., A. M. Freeman III, R. H. Haveman, and J. L. Knetsch. 1971. "On the Economics of Mass Demonstrations: A Case Study of the November 1969 March on Washington." *American Economic Review* 61, no. 4 (September): 719–24.

Clark, P. B., and J. Q. Wilson. 1961. "Incentive Systems: A Theory of Organizations." *Administrative Science Quarterly* 6 (September): 129–66.

Connolly, W. E. 1969. *The Bias of Pluralism*. New York: Atherton.

Converse, P. E. 1969. "Of Time and Partisan Stability." *Comparative Political Studies* 2, no. 2 (July): 139–71.

Crawford, T. J., and M. Naditch. 1970. "Relative Deprivation, Powerlessness and Militancy: The Psychology of Social Protest." *Psychiatry* 33 (May): 208–23.

Critical Mass Bulletin. 1973–74. Vol. 1. University of Tennessee.

Downs, A. 1972. "Up and Down with Ecology—the Issue Attention Cycle." *Public Interest* 28 (Summer): 38–50.

Etzioni, A. 1968. *The Active Society*. New York: Free Press.

Freeman, J. 1975. *The Politics of Women's Liberation*. New York: McKay.

Gamson, W. A. 1968. *Power and Discontent*. Homewood, Ill.: Dorsey.

———. 1975. *The Strategy of Protest*. Homewood, Ill.: Dorsey.

Gerlach, L., and V. Hines. 1970. *People, Power and Change: Movements of Social Transformation*. Indianapolis: Bobbs-Merrill.

Gurr, T. R. 1970. *Why Men Rebel*. Princeton, N.J.: Princeton University Press.

———. 1972. *Politimetrics: An Introduction to Quantitative Macropolitics*. Englewood Cliffs, N.J.: Prentice-Hall.

Halloron, R. 1971. "The Idea that Politics Is Everybody's Business." *New York Times*. (March 7), sec. 4, p. 3.

Harrington, M. 1968. *Toward a Democratic Left: A Radical Program for a New Majority*. New York: Macmillan.

Heberle, R. 1951. *Social Movements: An Introduction to Political Sociology*. New York: Appleton-Century.

———. 1968. "Types and Functions of Social Movements." Pp. 438–44 in *International Encyclopedia of the Social Sciences*, vol. 14, edited by David Sills. New York: Macmillan.

Hentoff, N. 1963. *Peace Agitator: The Story of A. J. Muste*. New York: Macmillan.

Hubbard, H. 1968. "Five Long Hot Summers and How They Grew." *Public Interest* 12 (Summer): 3–24.

Jenkins, C., and C. Perrow. 1977. "Insurgency of the Powerless: Farm Workers Movements (1946–72)." *American Sociological Review* (forthcoming).

Jonas, G. 1971. *On Doing Good: The Quaker Experiment*. New York: Scribner's.

Kahn, S. 1970. *How People Get Power: Organizing Oppressed Communities for Action*. New York: McGraw-Hill.

Kanter, R. M. 1972. *Commitment and Community: Communes and Utopias in Sociological Perspective*. Cambridge, Mass.: Harvard University Press.

Katz, H. 1974. *Give/Who Gets Your Charity Dollar?* Garden City, N.Y.: Doubleday.

Killian, L. 1972. "The Significance of Extremism in the Black Revolution." *Social Problems* 20 (Summer): 41–48.

Leites, N., and C. Wolf, Jr. 1970. *Rebellion and Authority*. Chicago: Markham.

Levy, S. 1970. "The Psychology of Political Activity." *Annals* 391 (September): 83–96.

Lin, N. 1974–75. "The McIntire March: A Study of Recruitment and Commitment." *Public Opinion Quarterly* 38 (Winter): 562–73.

Lipset, S. M., and E. Raab. 1970. *The Politics of Unreason: Right-Wing Extremism in America*, 1790–1970. New York: Harper & Row.

Lipsky, M. 1968. "Protest as a Political Resource." *American Political Science Review* 62: 1144–58.

Lowi, T. J. 1971. *The Politics of Disorder*. New York: Basic.

McCarthy, J. D., and M. N. Zald. 1973. *The Trend of Social Movements in America: Professionalization and Resource Mobilization*. Morristown, N.J.: General Learning Press.

———. 1974. "Tactical Considerations in Social Movement Organizations." Paper delivered at the meeting of the American Sociological Association, August, Montreal.

Martin, G. T. 1971. "Organizing the Underclass: Findings on Welfare Rights." Working Paper no. 17. Human Side of Poverty Project, Department of Sociology, State University of New York at Stony Brook.

———. 1974. "Welfare Recipient Activism: Some Findings on the National Welfare Rights Organization." Paper presented at the annual meeting of the Midwest Political Science Association, Chicago, April 26.

Marx, G. T. 1970. "Issueless Riots." *Annals* 391 (September): 21–33.

———. 1974. "Thoughts on a Neglected Category of Social Movement Participant: The Agent Provocateur and the Informant." *American Journal of Sociology* 80 (September): 402–42.

Marx, G. T., and M. Useem. 1971. "Majority Involvement in Minority Movements: Civil Rights, Abolition, Untouchability." *Journal of Social Issues* 27 (January): 81–104.

Marx, G. T., and J. Wood. 1975. "Strands of Theory and Research in Collective Behavior." *Annual Review of Sociology* 1: 363– 428.

Meier, A., and E. Rudwick. 1973. *CORE: A Study in the Civil Rights Movement, 1942–1968*. New York: Oxford University Press.

———. 1976. "Attorneys Black and White. A Case Study of Race Relations within the NAACP." *Journal of American History* 62 (March): 913–46.

Miller, W. E., and T. E. Levitin. 1976. *Leadership and Change: The New Politics and the American Electorate*. Cambridge, Mass.: Winthrop.

Morgan, J. N., R. F. Dye, and J. H. Hybels. 1975. *A Survey of Giving Behavior and Attitudes: A Report to Respondents*. Ann Arbor, Mich.: Institute for Social Research.

Morris, B. 1975. "Consumerism Is Now a Luxury Item." *Washington Star* (October 28), pp. 1, 7.

Morrison, D. E. 1971. "Some Notes toward Theory on Relative Deprivation, Social Movements, and Social Change." *American Behavioral Scientist* 14 (May/June): 675–90.

Mueller, E. 1972. "A Test of a Partial Theory of Potential for Political Violence." *American Political Science Review* 66 (September): 928–59.

New York Times. 1974. "Social Action Hit by Financial Woes." (November 8), sec. 1, p. 20.

Oberschall, A. 1973. *Social Conflict and Social Movements*. Englewood Cliffs, N. J.: Prentice-Hall.

Olson, M., Jr. 1965. *The Logic of Collective Action*. Cambridge, Mass.: Harvard University Press.

Organizer's Manual Collective. 1971. *The Organizer's Manual*. New York: Bantam.

Orum, A. M., and K. L. Wilson. 1975. "Toward a Theoretical Model of Participation in Political Movements. I. Leftist Movements." Unpublished paper. Department of Sociology, University of Texas at Austin.

Perrow, C. 1970. "Members as Resources in Voluntary Organizations." Pp. 93–116 in *Organizations and Clients,* edited by W. R. Rosengren and M. Lefton. Columbus, Ohio: Merrill.

———. 1972. *Complex Organizations: A Critical Essay*. Glenview, Ill.: Scott, Foresman.

Pombeiro, B. G. 1975. "Recession Cripples Social Aid Groups." *Philadelphia Inquirer*. (October 12), pp. 1–2.

Quarantelli, E. L., and J. R. Hundley. 1975. "A Test of Some Propositions about Crowd Formation and Behavior." Pp. 317–86 in *Readings in Collective Behavior,* edited by R. R. Evans. 2d ed. Chicago: Rand McNally.

Rose, A. 1967. *The Power Structure*. New York: Oxford University Press.

Ross, D. K. 1973. *A Public Citizen's Action Manual*. New York: Grossman.

Ross, R. 1975. "Generational Change and Primary Groups in a Social Movement." Unpublished paper. Clark University, Worcester, Mass.

Sale, K. 1973. *SDS*. New York: Random House.

Salisbury, R. H. 1969. "An Exchange Theory of Interest Groups." *Midwest Journal of Political Science* 13 (February): 1–32.

Samuelson, P. 1964. *Economics: An Introductory Analysis*. New York: McGraw-Hill.

Smelser, N. 1963. *Theory of Collective Behavior*. New York: Free Press.

Snyder, D., and C. Tilly. 1972. "Hardship and Collective Violence in France." *American Sociological Review* 37 (October): 520– 32.

Stallings, R. A. 1973. "Patterns of Belief in Social Movements: Clarifications from Analysis of Environmental Groups." *Sociological Quarterly* 14 (Autumn): 465–80.

Stinchcombe, A. L. 1965. "Social Structure and Organizations." Pp. 142–93 in *Handbook of Organizations,* edited by James March. Chicago: Rand-McNally.

Stouffer, S. 1955. *Communism, Conformity and Civil Liberties*. Garden City, N.Y.: Doubleday.

Strickland, D. A., and A. E. Johnston. 1970. "Issue Elasticity in Political Systems." *Journal of Political Economy* 78 (September/October): 1069–92.

Tilly, C. 1973. "Does Modernization Breed Revolution?" *Comparative Politics* 5 (April): 425–47.

———. 1975. "Revolution and Collective Violence." Pp. 483–555 in *Handbook of Political Science,* edited by G. Greenstein and N. Polsky. Vol. 3. *Macro Political Theory*. Reading, Mass.: Addison-Wesley.

Tilly, C., L. Tilly, and R. Tilly. 1975. *The Rebellious Century: 1830–1930*. Cambridge, Mass.: Harvard University Press.

Tullock, G. 1966. "Information without Profit." Pp. 141–60. In *Papers on Non-Market Decision Making,* edited by G. Tullock. Charlottesville: University of Virginia, Thomas Jefferson Center for Political Economy.

Turner, R. H. 1969. "The Public Perception of Protest." *American Sociological Review* 34 (December): 815–31.

———. 1970. "Determinants of Social Movement Strategies." Pp. 145– 64 in *Human Nature and Collective Behavior: Papers in Honor of Herbert Blumer,* edited by Tamotsu Shibutani. Englewood Cliffs, N.J.: Prentice-Hall.

Turner, R. N., and L. Killian. 1972. *Collective Behavior*. 2d ed. Englewood Cliffs, N.J.: Prentice-Hall.

U.S. Treasury Department. 1965. *Report on Private Foundations*. Washington, D.C.: Government Printing Office.

Von Eschen, D., J. Kirk, and M. Pinard. 1969. "The Disintegration of the Negro Nonviolent Movement." *Journal of Peace Research* 3: 216–34.

———. 1971. "The Organizational Sub-Structure of Disorderly Politics." *Social Forces* 49 (June): 529-43.

Walzer, M. 1971. *Political Action: A Practical Guide to Movement Politics*. Chicago: Quadrangle.

Wilkinson, P. 1971. *Social Movements*. New York: Praeger.

Wilson, J. 1973. *Introduction to Social Movements*. New York: Basic.

Wilson, J. Q. 1973. *Political Organizations*. New York: Basic.

Wolfe, B. 1955. *Three Who Made a Revolution*. Boston: Beacon.

Wootton, G. 1970. *Interest Groups*. Englewood Cliffs, N.J.: Prentice-Hall.

Zald, M. N., and R. Ash. 1966. "Social Movement Organizations: Growth, Decline and Change." *Social Forces* 44 (March): 327–40.

Zald, M. N., and D. Jacobs. 1976. "Symbols into Plowshares: Underlying Dimensions of Incentive Analysis." Unpublished paper. Vanderbilt University, Nashville, Tenn.

Zald, M. N., and J. D. McCarthy. 1974. "Notes on Cooperation and Competition amongst Social Movement Organizations." Unpublished paper. Vanderbilt University, Nashville, Tenn.

———. 1975. "Organizational Intellectuals and the Criticism of Society." *Social Service Review* 49 (September): 344–62.

ARTICLE 5

Social Problems as Collective Behavior

HERBERT BLUMER

My thesis is that social problems are fundamentally products of a process of collective definition instead of existing independently as a set of objective social arrangements with an intrinsic makeup. This thesis challenges the premise underlying the typical sociological study of social problems. The thesis, if true, would call for a drastic reorientation of sociological theory and research in the case of social problems.

Let me begin with a brief account of the typical way in which sociologists approach the study and analysis of social problems. The approach presumes that a social problem exists as an objective condition or arrangement in the texture of a society. The objective condition or arrangement is seen as having an intrinsically harmful or malignant nature standing in contrast to a normal or socially healthful society. In sociological jargon it is a state of dysfunction, pathology, disorganization, or deviance. The task of the sociologist is to identify the harmful condition or arrangement and to resolve it into its essential elements or parts. this analysis of the objective makeup of the social problem is usually accompanied by an identification of the conditions which cause the problem and by proposals as to how the problem might be handled. In having analyzed the objective nature of the social problem, identified its causes, and pointed out how the problem could be handled or solved the sociologist believes that he has accomplished his scientific mission. The knowledge and information which he has gathered can, on the one hand, be added to the store of scholarly knowledge and, on the other hand, be placed at the disposal of policy makers and the general citizenry.

This typical sociological approach seems on its face to be logical, reasonable, and justifiable. Yet, in my judgment, it reflects a gross misunderstanding of the nature of social problems and, accordingly, is very ineffectual in providing for their control. To give an initial indication of the deficiency of the approach, let me indicate briefly the falsity or unproven character of several of its key assumptions or claims.

First, current sociological theory and knowledge, in themselves, just do not enable the detection or identification of social problems. Instead, sociologists discern social problems only after they are recognized as social problems by and in a society. Sociological recognition follows in the wake of societal recognition, veering with the winds of the public identification of social problems. Illustrations are legion—I cite only a few of recent memory. Poverty was a conspicuous social problem for sociologists a half-century ago, only to practically disappear from the sociological scene in the 1940's and early 1950's, and then to reappear in our current time. Racial injustice and exploitation in our society were far greater in

the 1920's and 1930's than they are today; yet the sociological concern they evoked was little until the chain of happenings following the Supreme Court decision on school desegregation and the riot in Watts. Environmental pollution and ecological destruction are social problems of very late vintage for sociologists although their presence and manifestation date back over many decades. The problem of the inequality of women's status, emerging so vigorously on our current scene, was of peripheral sociological concern a few years back. Without drawing on other illustrations, I merely assert that in identifying social problems sociologists have consistently taken their cue from what happens to be in the focus of public concern. This conclusion is supported further by the indifference of sociologists and the public, alike, to many questionable and harmful dimensions of modern life. Such injurious dimensions may be casually noted but despite their gravity are given the status of social problems by sociologists. A few instances that come to mind are: the vast overorganization that is developing in modern society, the unearned increment in land values which Henry George campaigned against three-quarters of a century ago, the injurious social effects of our national highway system, the pernicious social consequences of an ideology of "growth," the unsavory side of established business codes; and may I add for my State of California, a state water plan with hidden social consequences of a repelling character. I think that the empirical record is clear that the designation of social problems by sociologists is derived from the public designation of social problems.

Let me add that, contrary to the pretensions of sociologists, sociological theory, *by itself*, has been conspicuously impotent to detect or identify social problems. This can be seen in the case of the three most prestigeful sociological concepts currently used to explain the emergence of social problems, namely, the concepts of "deviance," "dysfunction," and "structural strain." These concepts are useless as means of identifying social problems. For one thing, none of them has a set of benchmarks that enable the scholar to identify in the empirical world the so-called instances of deviance, dysfunction, or structural strain. Lacking such clear identifying characteristics, the scholar cannot take up each and every social condition or arrangement in society and establish that it is or is not an instance of deviance, dysfunction, or structural strain. But this deficiency, however serious, is of lesser importance in the matter I am considering. Of far greater significance is the inability of the scholar to explain why some of the instances of deviance, dysfunction, or structural strain noted by him fail to achieve the status of social problems whereas other instances do reach this status. There are all kinds of deviance that do not gain recognition as social problems; we are never told how or when deviance becomes a social problem. Similarly, there are many alleged dysfunctions or structural strains that never come to be seen as social problems; we are not told how and when so-called dysfunctions or structural strains become social problems. Obviously, deviance, dysfunction, and structural strain on one side and social problems on the other side are not equivalent.

If conventional sociological theory is so decisively incapable of detecting social problems and if sociologists make this detection by following and using the public recognition of social problems, it would seem logical that students of social problems ought to study the process by which a society comes to recognize its social problems. Sociologists have conspicuously failed to do this.

A *second* deficiency of the conventional sociological approach is the assumption that a social problem exists basically in the form of an identifiable objective condition in a society. Sociologists treat a social problem as if its being consisted of a series of objective items, such as rates of incidence, the kind of people involved in the problem, their number, their types, their social characteristics, and the relation of their condition to various selected societal factors. Is it assumed that the reduction of a social problem into such objective elements catches the problem in its central character and constitutes its scientific analysis. In my judgment this assumption is erroneous. As I will show much clearer later, a social problem exists primarily in terms of how it is defined and conceived in a society instead of being an objective condition with a definitive objective makeup. The societal definition, and not the objective makeup of a given social condition, determines whether the condition exists as a social problem. The societal definition gives the social problem its nature, lays out how it is to be approached, and shapes what is done about it. Alongside these decisive influences, the so-called objective existence or makeup of the social problem is very secondary indeed. A sociologist may note what he believes to be a malignant condition in a society, but the society may ignore completely its presence, in which event the condition will not exist as a social problem for that society regardless of its asserted objective being. Or, the objective breakdown made by a sociologist of a societally recognized social problem may differ widely from how the problem is seen and approached in the society. The objective analysis made by him may have no influence on what is done with the problem and consequently have no realistic relation to the problem. These few observations suggest a clear need to study the process by which a society comes to see, to define, and to handle their social problems. Students of social problems notoriously ignore their process; and it scarcely enters into sociological theory.

There is a third highly questionable assumption underlying the typical orientation of sociologists in the study of social problems. It is that the findings resulting from their study of the objective makeup of a social problem provide society with the solid and effective means for remedial treatment of that problem. All that society has to do, or should do, is to take heed of the findings and to respect the lines of treatment to which the findings point. This assumption is largely nonsense. It ignores or misrepresents how a society acts in the case of its social problems. A social problem is always a focal point for the operation of divergent and conflicting interests, intentions, and objectives. It is the interplay of these interests and objectives that constitutes the way in which a society deals with any one of its social problems. The sociological account of the objective makeup of the problem stands far outside of such interplay— indeed, may be inconsequential to it. This distant removal of the sociological study from the real process through which a society acts towards its social problems is a major explanation of the ineffectiveness of sociological studies of social problems.

The three central deficiencies that I have mentioned are only a sketch of a needed full fledged criticism of the typical sociological treatment of social problems. But they serve as a clue and hence as an introduction to the development of my thesis that social problems lie in and are products of a process of collective definition. The process of collective definition is responsible for the emergence of social problems, for the way in which they are seen, for the way in which they are approached and considered, for the kind of official remedial plan that is laid out, and for the transformation of the remedial plan in its application. In short, the process of collective definition determines the career and fate of social problems, from the initial point of their appearance to whatever may be the terminal point in their course. They have their being fundamentally in this process of collective definition, instead of in some alleged objective area of social malignancy. The failure to recognize and respect this act constitutes, in my opinion, the fundamental weakness in the sociological study of social problems and in sociological knowledge of social problems. Let me proceed to develop my thesis.

To lodge the emergence, the career, and the fate of social problem in a process of collective definition calls for an analysis of the course of this process. I find that the process passes through five stages. I shall label these: (1) the emergence of a social problem, (2) the legitimation of the problem, (3) the mobilization of action with regard to the problem, (4) the formation of an official plan of action, and (5) the transformation of the official plan in its empirical implementation. I propose to discuss briefly each of these five stages.

THE EMERGENCE OF SOCIAL PROBLEMS

Social problems are not the result of an intrinsic malfunctioning of a society but are the result of a process of definition in which a given condition is picked out and identified as a social problem. A social problem does not exist for a society unless it is recognized by that society to exist. In not being aware of a social problem, a society does not perceive it, address it, discuss it, or do anything about it. The problem is just not there. It is necessary, consequently, to consider the question of how social problems arise. Despite its crucial importance this question has been essentially ignored by sociologists.

It is a gross mistake to assume that any kind of malignant or harmful social condition or arrangement in a society becomes automatically a social problem for that society. The pages of history are replete with instances of dire social conditions unnoticed and unattended in the societies in which they occurred. Intelligent observers, using the standards of one society, may perceive abiding harmful conditions in another society that just do not appear as problems to the membership of the latter society. Further, individuals with keen perceptions of their own society, or who as a result of distressing experience may perceive given social conditions in their society as harmful, may be impotent in awakening any concern with the conditions. Also, given social conditions may be ignored at one time yet, without change in their makeup, become matters of grave concern at another time. All of these kinds of instances are so drearily repetitive as not to require documentation. The most casual observation and reflection shows clearly that the recognition by a society of its social problems is a highly selective process, with many harmful social conditions and arrangements not even making a bid for attention and with others falling by the wayside in what is frequently a fierce competitive struggle. Many push for societal recognition but only a few come out of the end of the funnels. . . .

LEGITIMATION OF SOCIAL PROBLEMS

Societal recognition gives birth to a social problem. But if the social problem is to move along on its course and not die aborning, it must acquire social legitimacy. It may seem strange to speak of social problems having to become legitimated. Yet after gaining initial recognition, a social problem must acquire social endorsement if it is to be taken seriously and move forward in its career. It must acquire a necessary degree of respectability which entitles it to consideration in the recognized arenas of public discussion. In our society such arenas are the press, other media of communication, the church, the school, civic organizations, legislative chambers, and the assembly places of officialdom. If a social problem does not carry the credential of respectability necessary for entrance into these arenas, it is doomed. Do not think because a given social condition or arrangement is recognized as grave by some people in a society—by people who indeed attract attention to it by their agitation—that this means that the problem will break through into the arena of public consideration. To the contrary, the asserted problem may be regarded as insignificant, as not worthy of consideration, as in the accepted order of things and thus not to be tampered with, as distasteful to codes of propriety, or as merely the shouting of questionable or subversive elements in a society. Any of these conditions can block a recognized problem from gaining legitimacy. If the social problem fails to get legitimacy it flounders and languishes outside of the arena of public action.

I want to stress that among the wide variety of social conditions or arrangements that are recognized as harmful by differing sets of people, there are relatively few that achieve legitimacy. Here again we are confronted with a selective process in which, so to speak, many budding social problems are choked off, others are ignored, others are avoided, others have to fight their way to a respectable status, and others are rushed along to legitimacy by a strong and influential backing. We know very little of this selective process through which social problems have to pass in order to reach the stage of legitimacy. Certainly such passage is not due merely to the intrinsic gravity of the social problem. Nor is it due to merely the prior state of public interest or knowledge; nor to the so-called ideologies of the public. The selective process is far more complicated than is suggested by these simple, commonplace ideas. Obviously, many of the factors which operate to affect the recognition of social problems continue to play a part in the legitimation of social problems. But it seems evident that there are other contributing factors through which the elusive quality of social respectability comes to be attached to social problems. We just do not have much knowledge about this process, since it is scarcely studied. It is certainly a cardinal matter that should be engaging the concern of students of social problems.

MOBILIZATION OF ACTION

If a social problem manages to pass through the stages of societal recognition and of social legitimation, it enters a new stage in its career. The problem now becomes the object of discussion, of controversy, of differing depictions, and of diverse claims. Those who seek changes in the area of the problem clash with those who endeavor to protect vested interests in the area. Exaggerated claims and distorted depictions, subserving vested interests, become commonplace. Outsiders, less involved, bring their sentiments and images to bear on their framing of the problem. Discussion, advocacy, evaluation, falsification, diversionary tactics, and advancing of proposals take place in the media of communication, in casual meetings, organized meetings, legislative chambers, and committee hearings. All of this constitutes a mobilization of the society for action on the social problem. It seems scarcely necessary to point out that the fate of the social problem depends greatly on what happens in this process of mobilization. How the problem comes to be defined, how it is bent in response to awakened sentiment, how it is depicted to protect vested interests, and how it reflects the play of strategic position and power—all are appropriate questions that suggest the importance of the process of mobilization for actions. . . .

FORMATION OF AN OFFICIAL PLAN OF ACTION

This stage in the career of social problems represents the decision of a society as to how it will act with regard to the given problem. It consists of the hammering together of an official plan of action, such as takes place in legislative committees, legislative chambers, and executive boards. The official plan is almost always a product of bargaining, in which diverse views and interests are accommodated. Compromises, concessions, tradeoffs, deference to influence, response to power, and judgments of what may be workable—all play a part in the final formulation. This is a defining and redefining process in a concentrated form—the forming, the re-working and the re-casting of a collective picture of the social problem, so that what emerges may be a far cry from how the problem was viewed in the earlier stage of its career. The official plan that is enacted constitutes, in itself, the official definition of the problem; it represents how the society through its official apparatus perceives the problem and intends to act toward the problem. These observations are commonplace. Yet, they point to the operation of a defining process that has telling significance for the fate of the problem. Surely, effective and relevant study of social problems should embrace what happens to the problem in the process of agreeing on official action.

IMPLEMENTATION OF THE OFFICIAL PLAN

To assume that an official plan and its implementation in practice are the same is to fly in the face of facts. Invariably to some degree, frequently to a large degree, the plan as put into practice is modified, twisted and reshaped, and takes on unforeseen accretions. This is to be expected. The implementation of the plan ushers in a new process of collective definition. It sets the stage for the formation of new lines of action on the part of those involved in the social problem and those touched by the plan. The people who are in danger of losing advantages strive to restrict the plan or bend its operation to new directions. Those who stand to benefit from the plan may seek to exploit new opportunities. Or both groups may work out new accommodative arrangements unforeseen in the plan. The administration and the operating personnel are prone to substitute their policies for the official policy underlying the plan. Frequently, various kinds of subterranean adjustments are developed which leave intact central areas of the social problem or transform other of its areas in ways that were never officially intended. The kind of accommodations, blockages, unanticipated accretions, and unintended transformations of which I am speaking can be seen abundantly in the case of many past attempts to put official plans into actual practice. Such consequences were conspicuous in the implementation of the prohibition amendment. They are notorious in the case of the regulatory agencies in our country. They are to be seen in the case of most new law enforcement programs designed to combat the problem of crime. I scarcely know of any facet of the general area of social problems that is more important, less understood, and less studied than that of the unforeseen and unintended restructuring of the area of a social problem that arises from the implementation of an official plan of treatment. I am unable to understand why students of social problems, in both their studies and their formulation of theory, can afford to ignore this crucial step in the life-being of social problems. . . .

ARTICLE 6

Neglected Characteristics of Collective Behavior

JACK M. WELLER
E. L. QUARANTELLI

... Our discussion begins by developing three basic ideas. First, we identify an omission in recent efforts in the literature to develop a social-level theory of collective behavior. Next, we express in opinion, contrary to some recent critics, that important developments in collective behavior can be built upon contemporary work in this area. Third, we note the type of social phenomena that have been the empirical pattern against which we have assessed both collective behavior theory and our own thoughts.

The early Italian and French writers (LeBon 1887; Tarde 1903; Sighele 1895; Rossi 1907) described collective behavior in individualistic and psychological terms. Early scholars writing in English maintained a similar orientation (see the discussions of Ross, McDougall, Conway, Trotter, Sidis, and Martin in Manning 1970). Even the "Americanization" of the study of collective behavior (Bramson 1961, pp. 47–72) and its establishment as a sociological specialty did not alter this basic stance. Individual liberation rather than alienation was the theme of Park and his University of Chicago students (see Elsner 1972), but they still located the essence of collective behavior in the characteristics of its participants or their atypical reactions to each other.

In the last 15 years, several writers have contributed to the development of a more distinctly sociological approach to collective behavior. Central aspects of the analyses of such writers as Turner (1964*a*, 1964*b*), Killian (1964), and Smelser (1963, 1968) are explicitly expressed in social terms. However, the advantages of a fully sociological analysis of collective behavior have not been exploited. Smelser (1963) does indicate conditions at a social level which explain collective behavior; so do Gusfield (1968), Tiryakian (1967), and Turner (1968). Consequences of collective behavior are carefully depicted by Turner and Killian (1972), as well as by Killian's (1964) discussion of social movements' contribution to social change. But, the social nature of collective behavior itself has not been adequately conceptualized. This behavior is still described in terms of psychological states of participants or atypical forms of interaction among them.

Failure to identify the social properties of collective behavior is one of the major barriers to development of a fully sociological theory of collective behavior and, consequently, is a primary factor in promoting the gap between collective behavior and general sociological perspectives. We suggest that not only the search for social conditions and social consequences of collective

Weller, Jack M., & Quarantelli, E. L. (1973, November). Neglected characteristics of collective behavior. *American Journal of Sociology, 79*(3), 665–685. Reprinted with permission of The University of Chicago Press.

behavior, but also all problems of its analysis be defined at a social level. Once the distinctive social characteristics of collective behavior have been specified, it will be possible to view the behavior itself as enacted by distinctive types of collectivities, with some significant social-level differences from those collectivities that enact institutionalized patterns of behavior. Such a definite social-level conception will provide symmetry to the analysis of collective behavior: the conditions explaining collective behavior, the collectivities enacting it, and its consequences for participating and encompassing social systems can all be conceptualized and related at a social level.

Some recent critics call for a rather sharp break with contemporary efforts of collective behavior theorists (for example, see Skolnick 1969, and Currie and Skolnick 1970). Without dismissing some worthwhile criticisms, we take exception to these conclusions. This is no time to begin again in the analysis of collective behavior. Both classic and contemporary writers have laid a foundation that can bear many useful theoretical and empirical extensions. According to Brissett (1968), the theoretical tradition of collective behavior has already played an important, if negative, role by challenging, and thereby leading to modifications in theories of, social psychology. Recent developments in the specialty also point the way to equally fruitful (and positive) contributions to social-level theories.

This tradition points to the sociological problem we wish to define and emphasize. The problem, while neglected, has not gone unmentioned (Blumer 1957; Tilly 1963). Furthermore, the materials from which we construct an initial step in developing the question are implicit in that tradition. For example, Durkheim in his treatment of the emergence of collective representations (1915, pp. 87–88 and 205–39) touches on matters which we emphasize. So does Summer's (1906) sketchy analysis of the creation of folkways. Our conviction is that the tradition of collective behavior theorists is a fruitful one, kept from even more fruitful cross-fertilization with other sociological perspectives by the neglect of a central problem: what are the social properties of the collectivities that engage in collective behavior, and how do they conceptually compare and, contrast with the complexes of social action engaged in institutionalized behavior?

Our third point of departure provides an empirical reference point for our conceptual enterprise. The arguments we detail later were not developed systematically from empirical studies. However, when examining existing views about collective behavior, we did use a series of research observations and a body of empirical data seldom discussed so far in the collective behavior literature. For, at the same time we were developing these critiques and extensions of collective behavior theory, we were engaged in the study of organizational and community responses to natural disasters and civil disturbances. The diverse social responses that emerge to cope with the exigencies of such community crises provide a much more fruitful prototype for the area of collective behavior than the commonly accepted prototype of the crowd with which LeBon launched the specialty three-quarters of a century ago.

Crowds are amorphous and fleeting. Systematic observations of them are difficult. Because of this and the fact that they have been relatively little studied, a number of incorrect views about their nature and behavior have developed leading to a serious question about using them as a prototype for all collective behavior. Couch (1968) points out several erroneous stereotypes of collective behavior that can be seen to be misconceptions of the crowd that have been projected upon the entire class of phenomena. Furthermore, from what we do know about the crowd, we can see that it has some features less likely to appear in other types of collective behavior. For example, the rapid turnover in leadership, the continuous but short-lived patterns of participation, and the tendency of crowds to draw the direct attention of social control agencies are important crowd characteristics not equally shared with many other forms of collective behavior.

Collectivities that can be observed in sudden and unexpected community crises provide an alternative prototype of collective behavior. We have in mind the heterogeneous array of organized responses that are elicited by two different kinds of crises, natural disasters, and civil disturbances (Quarantelli 1970*a*). This behavior ranges from the emergence of entirely new groups to the adjustments of existing groups in a suddenly changed context. Furthermore, these social responses reflect the conflict stance of a civil disturbance crisis or the cooperative orientation of the consensus context of natural disasters. Empirically, the range of groups involved is broad. In natural disasters, for example, there is often the concurrent appearance of many new or reorganized collectivities such as search and rescue groups, informal communication and coordination centers, committees of distant outsiders organized to assist victims, expanded welfare groups, highly elaborate and unplanned systems for handling intense medical problems, and the switching of organizations from predisaster to disaster-relevant domains of action. In civil disturbances, not only groups of looters appear, but also rioting police units, informal youth patrols, ad hoc committees of community leaders, counterrioter groups, and extensive adjustments on the part of social control and public safety organizations. Many of these examples do not fit the pattern of collective behavior extrapolated from stereotypes of the crowd. Nor, for that matter, do most fit within other standard types of collective behavior such as hostile outbursts, panics, crazes, social movements, and cults. But they are undeniably not institutionalized behavior. Furthermore, they do exhibit the dynamic and ephemeral qualities associated with almost all types of collective behavior. They take a variety of forms and follow several patterns of development. This variety presents conceptual and explanatory problems much more representative of the range of collective behavior than does the typical example of the crowd. These organized social patterns require a social level of conceptualization. We want to suggest such a conception of collective behavior, but first the next section illustrates the neglect of such social characteristics by influential writers on collective behavior.

NEGLECT OF SOCIAL CHARACTERISTICS

For a long time collective behavior was regarded as psychologically abnormal. Even now, it is so regarded by many sociologists who are not specialists in the area (for example, see Broom and Selznick 1968, pp. 221–54). However, viewpoints that find collective behavior irrational, essentially emotional, or nonsocial have been almost totally rejected by collective behavior specialists. For example, Turner and Killian (1972), Turner (1964*a,b*), Smelser (1963), Skolnick (1960), Marx (1970), and especially Couch (1968) have pointed out various ways these conceptions neither adequately distinguish collective behavior from other behavior, nor capture its essential characteristics. Nevertheless, a more subtle but similar tendency remains. Many writers still locate the essence of collective behavior in the makeup of participants or their reactions to each other. Sociologists seem concerned with providing a psychological account of the nature of collective behavior.

This can be seen in the writings of such distinguished contributors to the field as Blumer, the Langs, and Smelser. In many respects their works differ significantly. However, they do share and exemplify a tendency to view collective behavior in terms of individual participants. Although they refer to existing patterns of social organization in defining what collective behavior is not, and rely in varying degrees on social factors to explain collective behavior, their conceptions of the behavior itself are couched in social-psychological terms. In discussing the behavior, they attempt to depict what is happening to and within individual participants.

Consistent with Park from whom he drew his substantive focus. Herbert Blumer eschewed earlier pejorative views o collective behavior. Yet, in work spanning three decades, Blumer (1939, 1969*a*) uses Mead's interaction framework to describe the nature of collective behavior. He suggests that participants in the behavior respond to others by circular reaction rather than symbolic interpretation (1951, pp. 170–177). As Smelser notes (1963, p. 10; 1964, p. 117), blumer locates the distinguishing characteristic of collective behavior in the interaction of participants. In fact, the distinguishing characteristic ultimately reduces to the individual's mode of response to others' gestures. Such a view invites us to conceptualize collective behavior as a characteristic of participants' responses to social cues and to search for its explanation in conditions that influence individuals to abandon symbolic interpretation. In other work in the area, Blumer (see especially 1957) does not so restrict his analysis. His classic discussions of publics (1948) and fashion (1969*b*), for example, are not totally restricted to this level of analysis. However, because the crowd is offered as a prototype, the implication is often taken that this conception applies to all collective behavior.

A rough parallel is found in Lang and Lang (1961, 1968). They suggest that participants in collective behavior act without guidance of social structure. In their terms this means that participants act without the benefit of patterned generalized expectations associated with social statuses. Thus, defining the nature of collective behavior, they focus in detail upon collective dynamics by which individuals acquire the social definitions usually supplied by traditional patterns. As Turner (1964*b*, p. 128) suggests, the resulting theory uses a sophisticated contagion approach. The problem for analysis is to discover how individuals are caught up in collective episodes, rather than the forms collective behavior takes (Manning 1970, p. 150).

Neil Smelser (1963) presents the most consistently sociological analysis of the range of social conditions that must be examined to explain collective behavior episodes. But, even though his early work (1963) is an avowedly sociological theory of collective behavior, it provides a third major example of an individualistic conception of collective behavior. He views the behavior itself as based upon participants commonly holding a "generalized belief." Despite his sociological conception of many of the determinants of collective behavior, these conditions are ultimately reduced to the beliefs of the participants. that generalized beliefs are central to Smelser's conception of the nature of collective behavior can be seen in two aspects of his analysis. First, it is the major way he distinguishes between collective behavior and institutionalized behavior and, second, it is the only way he distinguishes subtypes of collective behavior. Smelser (1970, p. 48), of course, explicitly claims this conception is quite sociological. However, as Milgram and Toch note, "Smelser's theory employs as its central postulate the notion of generalized belief, implying a unitary outlook at the root of collective action" (1969, p. 561; see also Quarantelli and Hundley 1969 and Currie and Skolnick 1970, although the latter critique is inaccurate in several respects). Smelser's more recent work (1972) seems to move even more explicitly in a psychological direction.

Each of these major theorists and others that could be mentioned rely on psychological and social-psychological terms to discuss the nature of collective behavior. This tendency is partially a consequence of the idea that individuals "normally behave according to institutionalized patterns (for explicit statements on this, see Blumer 1957, p. 130; Lang and Lang 1961, p. 6; and Smelser 1964, p. 117). Because collective behavior is not routine, recurring activity for its participants, theorists have attempted to explain the mechanisms of individual behavior during collective behavior episodes. They ask how the individual is different in these situations as opposed to those in which he engages in institutionalized behavior. This concern with having an adequate model of the individual has absorbed much of the effort expended to develop conceptions of collective behavior. Most sociological treatments of collective behavior have consequently been side-tracked from proceeding to define their initial problem as one requiring conceptual elaboration at a social level.

The consequences of this concentration of theoretical attention can be illustrated by comparing treatments of individual social actors by institutional and collective behavior theories. In accounting for the social characteristics of institutional behavior, individual behavior is taken as unproblematic. That is, for most purposes of studying institutional behavior, a simple model of the individual has been assumed. Distorted for brevity, this model holds that individuals come to act according to social norms through a variety of social mechanisms, for example, socialization, anticipation of sanctions, exchanges of valued commodities, and asymmetrical power relations. The benefits of this model are not in its "realism." It can easily be criticized as an inadequate representation of the reality of individual behavior (see, for example, the criticisms of Wrong 1961 and Blumer 1969*c*). However, the assumptions of this model of the individual allow us to suspend the consideration of individuals in favor of social patterns. The model does not solve the problem of individual behavior. It merely expedites a focus upon other interesting sociological problems, for example: how do patterns of action in different group contexts compare? What are the effects of the interplay between environments and the groups they encompass? How do the characteristics of groups change? The model permits an uncomplicated view of the relationship between individual and social behavior. It frees sociologists to concentrate on the social characteristics of the social action they study.

Unfortunately, approaches to collective behavior are not based on an equally uncomplicated model of the individual that also allows concentration on problems defined at a social level. Instead, development of a model of the individual engaging in behavior so unusual for him and so unsupported by the norms that guide his routine behavior is taken as the problem to be solved by a theory of collective behavior. Models as widely varying as Lang and Lang's (1961) and Smelser's (1963) share the fault of not emphatically dealing with the social characteristics of the collectivities engaging in collective behavior. Collective behavior is identified or conceptualized in terms that can most clearly be seen as properties of individuals, not collectivities. In many cases, the social actions of these collectivities are regarded as the aggregate responses of individuals converging along similar lines or spreading through contagion-like processes (see Klapp 1972). Thus, collective behavior is assumed to be described and explained adequately by accounting for how a single individual in a given situation could pursue the course of action observed of the collectivity as a whole (see Turner 1964*a* , pp. 384–97).

Turner's (1964*a*) development of the emergent norm perspective (from its inception in Turner and Killian 1957) responds to this problem. He provides an improved view of the social psychology of collective behavior by suggesting that it should be analyzed with the same model of individual and interactive behavior as institutionalized behavior. This is a far more satisfactory perspective on collective behavior participants than those posited by other theories. At the same time, however, the distinction between institutionalized and collective behavior is obliterated. The strength of the emergent norm perspective is that it rules out looking at atypical characteristics of individuals and their reactions to each other to identify and explain collective behavior. But it does not then provide alternative criteria for conceptualizing the differences this behavior has from institutionalized behavior. While we are eager to accept the argument that there are no fundamental psychological differences between participants in institutionalized and collective behavior, this does not mean that there are no differences at all. There are obvious differences, and if they are not social psychological, then we are almost forced to look for them in the social properties of the collectives that enact them. Couch makes a similar point when he observes that it is not enough to point to the lesser importance of cultural factors in crowd behavior. He feels that attention also needs to be directed to the crowd as a social system "with social processes and social relationships" (1968, p. 321). Elsewhere he adds, "relatively few studies have attended to structures of social units engaged in collective behavior" (1970, p. 457). It is to questions at this level that the social-psychological postulates of the emergent norm perspective lead us . . . .

The foundations of the social action of any collectivity are social norms and social relationships. Sometimes the latter is seen as subordinate to the former. Too often, the social bases of social action are merely equated with a system of social norms. Blake and Davis persuasively state that at times it seems sociologists "adopt the extreme view by treating normative systems as the sole object of analysis or as the sole determinant of social phenomena" (1964, p. 461). However, many sociologists have noted that social relationships are conceptually distinct from norms (for especially effective discussions of this distinction, see Burns 1958 and Blau and Scott 1962, pp. 4–6). As a basis for behavior either may predominate. For example, the relationship between mother and child is a social basis of their behavior through a variety of changing normative contexts. Both social relationships and social norms are necessary elements of collectivities. The conceptual dimensions of social relationships and social norms both can be fruitfully imposed to organize the study of any acting collectivity. It is along these two dimensions that we can make a positive, generic identification of collective behavior that parallels standard sociological descriptions of institutionalized behavior.

Blumer has said that "social organization is a framework inside of which acting units develop their actions" (1969*c*, p. 87). Social organization not only "contains" social action, it also provides a foundation of social norms and relationships upon which action is built. Both institutionalized and collective behavior are contained within and predicated upon social organization. However, for institutionalized behavior, social organization bears a relatively permanent or traditional relationship to the social setting in which the behavior takes place, while in collective behavior the substructure of social organization is at least in part new to that setting. That is, the collectivities engaging in collective behavior are in some sense new. Collectivities make possible the interdependent and coordinated interaction of people. In collective behavior they are new in that some major aspect of this social foundation is created at the time the social behavior in enacted. Institutionalized behavior is based on enduring systems of social norms and social relationships, but collective behavior upon similar systems in part created concurrently with their implementation as social action.

Furthermore, phenomena need not involve the emergence of both social norms and relationships to be usefully regarded as collective behavior. In fact, some examples of collective behavior appear not to involve the emergence of norms or relationships at all. We can see at least four types of collectivities, each of which differs from an ideal type conception of those enacting institutionalized behavior. Each of these four has an aspect of its social-organizational foundation for behavior created concurrently with the behavior it enacts, and each seems to fit the social-organizational nature of phenomena usually regarded as collective behavior.

TYPES OF NEW COLLECTIVITIES

Figure 1 represents three types of collectivities that contrast with those engaged in institutionalized behavior. These ideal types are obtained by dichotomizing and cross-classifying variations in the collectivity's source of social norms and social relationships as to whether they are enduring or emergent with respect to the social setting in which behavior takes place. (This dichotomization is illustrative. Actually both of these dimensions are quite likely continuous. For example, a range of mixtures between completely emergent and completely enduring social norms is likely.) The collectivities of institutionalized behavior

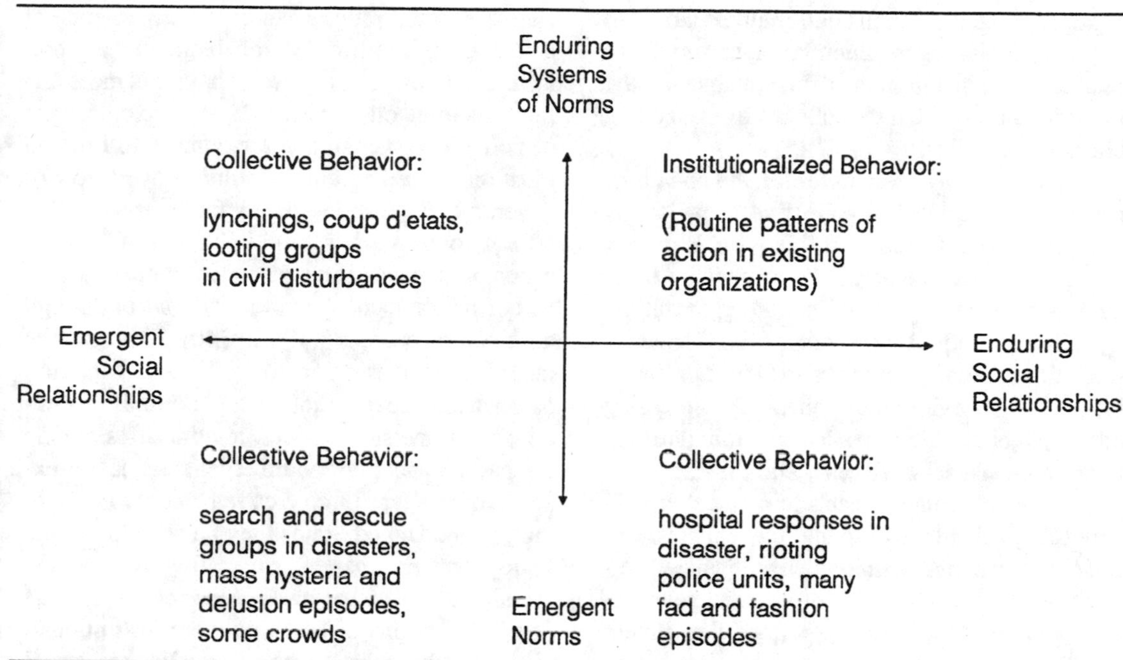

FIGURE 1 Institutional and Collective Behavior Collectivities

have both enduring systems of norms and relationships. Three types of collectivities engaging in collective behavior are either entirely emergent or emergent on only one of these dimensions. A fourth type (not depicted in the figure) involves emergence in neither dimension, but occurs when previously dissociated systems of norms and relationships are integrated with each other into a collectivity.

First, we want to stress that social organizational conceptions of collective behavior should not be confined to collectivities with both emergent norms and relationships. Existing systems of social relationships are often combined with emergent norms as a basis of social action that is not institutionalized and that can be fruitfully classified as collective behavior. for example, adjustments in a disaster situation may lead to the assumption of entirely new tasks by an ostensibly old, preexisting community agency—a formal group responding to the crisis with its preemergency identity, membership, and authority relationships, while nevertheless operating often with a substantially different set of norms. Hospitals in the immediate aftermath of a sudden major disaster impact frequently exhibit this pattern (Quarantelli 1970*b*). The same situation can be seen when changes in song fads or dress fashion are examined. Well-established formal social entities such as fashion houses, large circulation magazines, department store chains (Lang and Lang 1961, pp. 465–88), music companies, radio stations, and music stores (Hirsch 1970) maintain their names, personnel, internal leadership roles, and communication channels at the same time that new normative patterns emerge. Perhaps even more important, the innovations are typically taken over and then discarded by group members in relatively fixed peer relationships to one another (see, for example, Johnstone and Katz 1957).

In both examples, new norms emerge while social relationships endure. Any strict limitations of the scope of collective behavior to totally new collectivities with both new systems of norms and social relationships misses such cases that cannot be treated by an institutionalized model of behavior. Social organization involves two major dimensions, and emergence in any one of the dimensions means that the collectivity is enacting collective behavior.

This view may seem to stretch the bounds of phenomena classified as collective behavior beyond previous definitions. If this is so, it merely responds to a need clearly demonstrated by those with dynamic conceptions of social organization. Thus, Strauss and his co-workers (1963) have for some time been pointing out that normative guides to behavior are constantly emerging within established groups. They particularly illustrate this in a study (Bucher and Strauss 1961) in which developing segments in medical professions are analyzed as having the character of social movements within institutionalized arrangements. The emergence of a partial new normative pattern in a public works department during a flood threat illustrates the same point (Brouillette and Quarantelli 1971).

On the other hand, collective behavior cannot be defined solely in terms of the emergence of norms. In fact, to do so would only duplicate the emergent norm formulations already developed by Turner (1964*a*). Social relationships are an integral and necessary aspect of collectivities, and they too emerge in many cases of social action that can be adequately captured neither by an institutionalized model of behavior nor by the emergent norm model of collective behavior. In the agency response to disaster and fashion examples noted above, it is social relationships that endure, while norms emerge. But the converse can also be the case.

Norms guiding collective behavior may be rather firmly institutionalized. For example, the recent urban disorders in the United States have shown consistency in some of their behavior patterns. Looting, for example, appears to be normative (Quarantelli and Dynes 1970*b*). In such cases, the norms guiding the behavior can be regarded as institutionalized. The occurrence of collective behavior depends on the emergence of a system of social relationships before the norms can be enacted rather than on the emergence of new norms. The problem of distinguishing collective and institutionalized behavior is more difficult in some other cases. For example, transfer of political power in some countries follows an institutionalized pattern of military overthrow of governments. Huntington in fact observes that reform coups d'etat should be viewed as mechanisms of change, "the non-constitutional equivalent of periodic changes in party control through the electoral process" (1962, p. 40). This could be regarded as dissimilar to collective behavior. Nevertheless, even though the norm is institutionalized, the set of social relationships among the participants may be emergent. A clearer example of this type of collective behavior is lynchings. In the United States they have followed the same normative pattern time after time. In the social settings of the early American West and South, the norms of lynching were institutionalized, and the question as to whether the social action would occur depended on the emergence of a system of social relationships, including a division of labor in the lynch mob itself (Raper 1933). This seems to be particularly true for Western vigilante groups (Brown 1969, pp. 154–225).

Of course, there are situations where there are both emergent norms and relationships. For research these are the most easily identifiable because in a sense they are the purest forms of collective behavior. Collectivities engaged in a crowd behavior, for instance, clearly involve in many cases, although not all, the emergence of new social relationships as well as norms. This is why there is much less confusion in the literature as to the placement of crowds in collective behavior taxonomies compared with the location of fashion (see, for example, Turner and Killian 1972, pp. 152–54) or publics (see Smelser 1963, p. 172) where only one social organizational dimension may often be involved. We, however, are not equating crowds with collectivities having both emergent norms and relationships, since, for example, an established audience assembled for traditional purposes may maintain its prior set of relationships as its normative behavior develops new forms. (A classic case is described in Douglas [1939], where a funeral procession became a very expressive social collectivity.) Established social groups maintaining some of their old relationships as their members develop mob actions can also be seen in some police behavior in recent urban disturbances. Marx, for instance, notes that in some cases the same application of a collective behavior perspective to the rioters "might equally be applied to the police" (1970, pp. 48–50). Grimshaw (1963) documents the same for earlier historic periods.

A liberal interpretation of the scope of collective behavior can thus include at least three types of collectivities that are alternatives to established groups. New collectivities can exhibit emergent norms, or emergent social relationships, or both. To single out only emergence on one dimension, as implied by the emergent norm formulation, leaves out two other possibilities for the organization of new collectivities. Similarly, to characterize, as Swanson (1971, pp. 75–110) does, crowds and social movements as "transitional organization"—while perhaps an improvement over the term "collectivity"—seems to exclude emergent phenomena in enduring groups that seem best conceptualized as collective behavior.

A fourth type of collectivity does not seem well conceived of as institutionalized behavior, nor does it seem to involve emergence, but it also might be fruitfully conceived of as collective behavior. So far we have looked at collectivities that create some aspect of their social organization. In other cases, it seems borrowing is more salient than creation. There are cases where it is very difficult to understand the behavior as institutionalized for the collectivity engaging in it, even though it is quite traditional for other groups. For example, when an existing peer group becomes a cult by copying norms of witches' behavior (Quarantelli and Wenger 1973), or a long-established teachers' professional association becomes a militant social movement by adopting the norms of collective bargaining, we have no emergence, but instead the confluence of previously dissociated norms and relationships. What appears to have been created in this type of collectivity is the integration of these dissociated dimensions of social organization.

We feel that this typology and the arguments on which it is based can be useful for examining several problems. It is derived in a systematic fashion and works toward describing collective behavior in terms that are comparable with those of a social-organizational perspective on institutionalized behavior. In addition to this contribution, the formulation has both theoretical and research implications for the specialty of collective behavior.

First, the typology serves as a definition of collective behavior. In its terms, collective behavior is social action engaged in by one of four types of collectivities. The identification, furthermore, is a positive one. The types and collective behavior as a whole are defined in terms of characteristics they do possess, rather than by the absence of certain qualities or features. This positive approach to definition may also be helpful in identifying empirical instances of collective behavior, especially more marginal ones such as emergent gangs (Yablonski 1959; Pfautz 1961), "conventional" assemblages (Concepcion 1962), and nonviolent accommodation groups (Quarantelli 1970*a*; Marx and Archer 1971). This may overcome what appears to be a common tendency to label research cases as collective behavior because of their surface similarity to past cases reported in the literature, rather than because they exhibit required characteristics. Also, the use of positive characteristics to identify collective behavior improves its conceptual separation from institutionalized behavior.

Second, the typology avoids collapsing of dimensions that delineate types with factors that are used to explain the behavior or record its consequences. For example, Smelser (1963) uses his five types of generalized beliefs both to delineate a typology and as a major explanatory factor in his value-added scheme. Also, it is parsimonious in the number of dimensions it employs. In contrast, as Smelser notes (1963, p. 7), Blumer uses at least four disparate criteria to distinguish four elementary collective behavior groupings.

Third, our arguments undermine the place of the crowd as a prototype of collective behavior (for example, as is typified in the uncritical view of Fisher [1972, p. 187]). Collectivities traditionally classified as crowds fall into at least the first three types of our typology. Seen from this vantage point, the crowd has no special place as a preeminent example of collective behavior. Instead, we should recognize that the processes and problems of forging out new social relationships might be quite different from those in the emergence of norms. Furthermore, how previously dissociated norms became part of the social organization of a group differs significantly from the processes by which norms and social relationships emerge together (for examples, see Forrest 1968). Instead of using the crowd as a prototype of all collective behavior, a view that emphasizes the emergence or borrowing of both norms and relationships should be more useful.

Finally, while the major purpose of this paper is to account neither for conditions nor consequences of collective behavior, but rather to delineate its characteristics, the typology suggested could contribute to these other two aspects. For example, including emergent social relationships as a quality of some collectivities indicates that collective behavior may occur in situations other than where traditional norms are absent or inoperative. Where norms are clear but the social relationships necessary to implement them are lacking, collective behavior may occur to create them. An implication here is that institutionalized social relationships are not always one end product of the crystallization of norms. The reverse is true in some cases: established relationships may help crystallize norms. This is consistent with observations such as by Turner (1964*b*, p. 132), Couch (1968, p. 320), Quarantelli and Hundley (1969, p. 547), and others about crowd development. They note that it is not the supposed anonymity of participants that is crucial in crowd formation, but that crowd norms emerge from the nuclear cores provided by preexisting social relationships among members. A similar point is made by Freeman (1973) in her analysis of the more successful emergent groups involved in the women's liberation movement.

At a more fundamental level, since the typologies allow for partial institutionalized patterns intermixed with emergent patterns, there is an encouragement of the convergence of the two perspectives involved. The earlier cited quotation from Turner is but a more explicit and forceful statement of a view increasingly being expressed. Thus, Zald and Ash (1966, p. 328) state in their discussion of social movements that "the sociological approach to organization utilized . . . helps to bridge the gap between organizational analysis and collective behavior." Merton, in his preface, favorably observes that Barton's (1969, p. xxii) book on community disasters attempts to make a connection between collective behavior and the behavior of organizations. Other recent statements (Dynes and Quarantelli 1968; Denzin 1968; Lammers 1969; Landsberger 1969, pp. 1–62; McPhail 1969, p. 443; Oberschall 1973) on the historical gap between the sociology of organizations and collective behavior consistently note the handicap it creates for theory and research in both areas. . . .

REFERENCES

Barton, Allen. 1969. *Communities in Disaster*. New York: Doubleday.

Berk, Richard. 1972. "The Controversy Surrounding Collective Violence: Some Methodological Notes." In *Collective Violence,* edited by James Short and Marvin Wolfgang. Chicago: Aldine-Atherton.

Blau, Peter M., and W. Richard Scott. 1962. *Formal Organizations*. San Francisco: Chandler.

Blumer, Herbert. 1939. "Collective Behavior." In *An Outline of the Principles of Sociology,* edited by Robert E. Park. New York: Barnes & Noble.

———. 1948. "Public Opinion and Public Opinion Polling." *American Sociological Review* 13 (October): 542–49.

———. 1951. "Collective Behavior." In *New Outline of the Principles of Sociology,* edited by A. M. Lee. New York: Barnes & Noble.

———. 1957. "Collective Behavior." In *Review of Sociology,* edited by Joseph Gittler. New York: Wiley.

———. 1969*a* "Collective Behavior." In *Principles of Sociology,* edited by A. M. Lee. New York: Barnes & Noble.

———. 1969*b* "Fashion: From Class Differentiation to Collective Behavior." *Sociological Quarterly* 10 (Winter): 275–91.

———. 1969*c Symbolic Interactionism: Perspective and Method* Englewood Cliffs, N.J.: Prentice-Hall.

Bramson, Leon. 1961. *The Political Context of Sociology*. Princeton, M.J.: Princeton University Press.

Brissett, Dennis. 1968. "Collective Behavior: The Sense of a Rubric." *American Journal of Sociology 74* (July): 70–78.

Broom, Leonard, and Philip Selznick. 1968. *Sociology*. 4th ed. New York: Harper & Row.

Brouillette, John, and E. L. Quarantelli. 1971. "Types of Patterned Variation in Bureaucratic Adaptions to Organizational Stress." *Sociological Inquiry* 41 (Winter): 39–46.

Brown, Richard Maxwell. 1969. "The American Vigilante Tradition" In *Violence in America,* edited by Hugh Graham and Ted Gurr. New York: Bantam.

Bucher, Rue, and Anselm Strauss. 1961. "Professions in Process." *American Journal of Sociology* 66 (January): 325–34.

Buckley, Walter. 1967. *Sociology and Modern Systems Theory*. Englewood Cliffs, N.J.: Prentice-Hall.

Burns, Tom. 1958. "The Idea of Structure in Sociology." *Human Relations* 11 (3): 217–27.

Coleman, James S. 1969. "The Methods of Sociology." In *A Design for Sociology: Scope, Objectives, and Methods,* edited by Robert Bierstedt. Philadelphia: Academy of Political and Social Science.

Concepcion, Mercedes. 1962. "Ritual Mourning: Culturally Specified Crowd Behavior." *Anthropological Quarterly* 35 (January): 1–9.

Couch, Carl. 1968. "Collective Behavior; An Examination of Some Stereotypes." *Social Problems* 15 (Winter): 310–22.

———. 1970. "Dimensions of Association in Collective Behavior Episodes." *Sociometry* 33 (December): 457–60.

Currie, Elliot, and Jerome Skolnick. 1970. "A Critical Note on Conceptions of Collective Behavior." *Annals of the American Academy of Political and Social Sciences* 391 (September): 34–45.

Davis, Judith Blake, and Kingsley Davis. 1964. "Norms, Values, and Sanctions." In *Handbook of Modern Sociology,* edited by R.E.L. Faris. Chicago: Rand McNally

Denzin, Norman K. 1968. "Collective Behavior in Total Institutions." *Social Problems* 15 (Winter): 353–65.

Douglas, J. J. 1939. "The Funeral of 'Sister President.'" *Journal of Abnormal and Social Psychology* 44 (April): 217–23.

Drabek, Thomas, and E. L. Quarantelli. 1967. "Scapegoats, Villains and Disaster" *Transaction* 4 (March): 12–17.

Durkheim, Emile. 915. *Elementary Forms of Religious Life*. New York: Macmillan.

Dynes, Russell R., and E. L. Quarantelli. 1968. "Group Behavior under Stress: A Required Convergence of Organizational and Collective Behavior Perspectives." *Sociology and Social Research* 52 (July): 416–29.

———. 1973. "Editors' Introduction: Urban Civil Disturbance: Organizational Change and Group emergence." *American Behavioral Scientist* 16 (January/February) 305–11.

Elsner, Henry, 1972. "Introduction." In *Robert E. Park: The Crowd and the Public and Other Essays,* edited by Henry Eisner, Jr. Chicago: University of Chicago Press.

Fisher, Charles. 1972. "Observing a Crowd." In *Research on Deviance,* edited by Jack Douglas. New York: Random House.

Forrest, Thomas. 1968. "Emergent Organizations: A new Approach for Study." Ph.D. thesis, Ohio State University.

Freeman, Jo. 1973. "Origins of the Women's Liberation Movement." *American Journal of Sociology* 78, no. 4 (January): 792–811.

Grimshaw, Allen. 1963. "Actions of Police and Military in American Race Riots." *Phylon* 24 (Fall): 271–89.

Gusfield, Joseph 1968. "The Study of Social Movements." In *The International Encyclopedia of the Social Sciences,* edited by David Sills, New York: Free Press.

Heberle, Rudolf. 1951. *Social Movements*. New York: Appleton- Century-Crofts.

Hirsch, Paul 1970 *The Structure of the Popular music Industry*. Ann Arbor: Institute for Social Research, University of Michigan.

Huntington, Samuel. 1962. "Patterns of Violence in World Politics." In *Changing Patterns of Military Politics,* edited by Samuel Huntington. New York: Free Press.

Janowitz, Morris. 1964. "Converging theoretical Perspectives." *Sociological Quarterly* 5 (Spring): 113–32.

Johnstone, John, and Elihu Katz. 1957. "Youth and Popular Music: A Study in the Sociology of Taste." *American Journal of Sociology* 62 (May): 563–68.

Kerckhoff, Alan. 1970. "A Theory of Hysterical Contagion." In *Human Nature and Collective Behavior: Papers in Honor of Herbert Blumer,* edited by Tamotsu Shibutani. Englewood Cliffs, N.J.: Prentice-Hall.

Killian, Lewis M. 1964. "Social Movements." In *Handbook of modern Sociology,* edited by R.E. L. Faris. Chicago: Rand McNally.

Klapp, Orrin. 1969. *Collective Search for Identity*. New York: Holt, Rinehart & Winston.

———. 1972. *Currents of Unrest; An Introduction to Collective Behavior*. New York: Holt, Rinehart & Winston.

Lammers, C.J. 1969. "Strikes and Mutinies." *Administrative Science Quarterly* 14 (April): 558–72.

Landsberger, Henry. 1969. *Latin American Peasant Movements*. Ithaca, N.Y.: Cornell University.

Lang, Kurt, and Gladys Lang. 1961. *Collective Dynamics*. New York: Cromwell.

———. 1968. "Collective Behavior." In *The International Encyclopedia of the Social Sciences,* edited by David Sills. New York: Free Press.

LeBon, Gustav. 1897. *The Crowd*. London: Unwin.

McPhail, Clark. 1969. "Student Walkout: A Fortuitous Examination of Elementary Collective Behavior." *Social Problems* 16 (Spring): 441–55.

Manning, Roy. 1970. "Sociological and Non-sociological Collective Behavior." Ph.D. dissertation, New York University.

Marx, Gary. 1970. "Civil Disorders and the Agents of Social Control." *Journal of Social Issues* 26:19–57.

Marx, Gary, and Dane Archer. 1971. "Citizen Involvement in the Law Enforcement Process." *American Behavioral Scientist* 14 (October): 52–72.

Milgram, Stanley, and Hans Toch. 1969. "Collective Behavior: Crowds and Social Movements." In *The Handbook of Social Psychology,* edited by Gardner Lindzey and Elliot Aronson. Vol. 4. Reading, Mass.: Addison-Wesley.

Oberschall, Anthony, 1973. *Social Conflict and Social Movements*. Englewood Cliffs, N.J.: Prentice-Hall.

Pfautz, Harold. 1961. "Near-Group Theory and Collective Behavior: A Critical Reformulation." *Social Problems* 9 (Fall): 167– 74.

Quarantelli, E. L. 1970*a* "Emergent Accommodation Groups: Beyond Current Collective Behavior Typologies." In *Human Nature and Collective Behavior: Papers in Honor of Herbert Blumer,* edited by Tamotsu Shibutani. Englewood Cliffs, N.J.: Prentice- Hall.

———. 1970*b* "The Community General Hospital: Its Immediate Problems in Disasters." *American Behavioral Scientist* 13 (January/February): 380–91.

Quarantelli, E. L. and Russell R. Dynes. 1970*a* "Editors' Introduction: Organizational and Group Behavior in Disasters." *American Behavioral Scientist* 13 (January/February): 325–30.

———. 1970*b* "Property Norms and Looting: Their Patterns in Community Crises." *Phylon* 31 (Summer): 168–82.

Quarantelli, E. L., and James Hundley. 1969. "A Test of Some Propositions about Crowd Formation and Behavior." In *Readings in Collective Behavior,* edited by Robert R. Evans. Chicago: Rand McNally.

Quarantelli, E. L., and Dennis Wenger. 1973. "A Voice from the Thirteenth Century: The Characteristics and Conditions for the Emergence of a Ouija Board Cult." *Urban Life and Culture* 1:379–400.

Raper, A. 1933. *The Tragedy of Lynching*. Chapel Hill: University of North Carolina Press.

Rossi, Pasquale. 1907. *Sociologia e psicologia collettiva*. Milan: Rimo Sandron.

Rush, Gary, and R. Serge Denisoff. 1971. *Social and Political Movements*. New York: Appleton-Century-Crofts.

Sighele, Scipio. 1895. *La folla delinquente*. Turin: Bocca.

Skolnick, Jerome. 1969. *The Politics of Protest*. Washington, D.C.: Government Printing Office.

Smelser, Neil. 1963. *Theory of Collective Behavior*. New York: Free Press.

———. 1964. "Theoretical Issues of Scope and Problems." *Sociological Quarterly* 5 (Spring): 116–22.

———. 1968. *Essays in Sociological Explanation*. Englewood Cliffs, N.J.: Prentice-Hall.

———. 1970. "Two Critics in Search of a Bias." *Annals of the American Academy of Political and Social Science* 391 (September): 46–55.

———. 1972. "Some Additional Thoughts on Collective Behavior." *Sociological Inquiry* 42 (Spring): 97–103.

Smith, Thomas S. 1968. "Conventionalization and Control: An Examination of Adolescent Crowds." *American Journal of Sociology 74:172–83*.

Snyder, David, Charles Tilly, 1972. "Hardship and Collective Violence in France, 1830 to 1960." *American Sociological Review* 37 (October): 520–32.

Strauss, Anselm, Leonard Schatzman, Danuta Ehrlich, Rue Bucher, and Melvin Sobshin. 1963. "The Hospital and Its Negotiated Order." In *The Hospital in Modern Society*, edited by Eliot Freidson. New York: Free Press.

Sumner, William Graham. 1906. *Folkways*. Boston: Ginn.

Swanson, Guy E. 1971. *Social Change*. Glenview, Ill.: Scott Foresman.

Tarde, G. 1903. *The Laws of Imitation*. New York: Holt.

Tilly, Charles. 1963. "The Analysis of a Counter-Revolution." *History and Theory* 3 (1): 30–58.

Tiryakian, Edward. 1967. "A Model of Societal Change and Its Lead Indicators." In *The Study of Total Societies*, edited by Samuel Klausner. New York: Doubleday.

Turner, Ralph. 1964*a* "Collective Behavior." In *Handbook of Modern Sociology*, edited by R.E.L. Faris. Chicago: Rand McNally.

———. 1964*b* "New Theoretical Frameworks." *Sociological Quarterly* 5 (Spring): 122–32.

———. 1968. "The Theme of Contemporary Social Movements." *British Journal of Sociology* 20 (December): 390–405.

Turner, Ralph, and Lewis Killian. 1957. *Collective Behavior*. Englewood Cliffs, N.J.: Prentice-Hall.

———. 1972. *Collective Behavior*. 2d ed. Englewood Cliffs, N.J.: Prentice-Hall.

Weller, Jack M. 1971. "Current Sociological Approaches to Collective Behavior." Paper presented at the annual meeting of the American Sociological Association, Denver, Colorado.

Wrong, Dennis. 1961. "The Oversocialized Conception of Man in Modern Society." *American Sociological Review* 26 (April): 184–93.

Yablonski, Lewis. 1959. "The Delinquent Gang as a Near-Group." *Social Problems* 7. (Fall): 108–17.

Young, Frank W. 1970. "Reactive Subsystems." *American Sociological Review* 35 (April): 297–307.

Zald, Mayer, and Roberta Ash. 1966. "Social Movement Organizations: Growth, Decay and Change." *Social Forces* 44 (March): 327–41.

ARTICLE 7

Collective Behavior: The Elementary Forms

JOHN LOFLAND

QUESTIONS AND EMPHASIS

As used by sociologists, the term *collective behavior* refers roughly to "emergent and extra-institutional social forms and behavior," panic-stricken, riotous, and ecstatic crowds being among the more dramatic of its myriad expressions.

In a manner logically identical to other fields of inquiry, students of this subject seek to isolate *forms* and *causes* of collective behavior; *processes* of its operation; the functions it performs or the *consequences* it has for other social forms and for participants; and *strategies* people employ toward and in the context of it, among other concerns.

Each of these and still other foci are valid and indispensable moments in the full round of analysis in all fields of inquiry. But for reasons we may reserve for the scrutiny of the sociologists of knowledge and science, not all are accorded equal attention by investigators at each point in the history of a specialty, and such an imbalance is particularly noticeable in the field of collective behavior. Specifically, in more recent decades, collective behaviorists have displayed a marked preoccupation with questions of causes and some aspects of questions of process to the relative neglect of other questions, especially the question of form (Marx and Wood 1975; Aguirre and Quarantelli 1979; Marx 1979). I believe that this pronounced neglect of forms is having a critically retarding effect on the development of the field of collective behavior, and I attempt in this chapter to begin to redress the imbalance.

One can, of course, challenge the assertion that lack of attention to forms critically retards the study of collective behavior. In its favor, let me point to several matters. First, without articulate taxonomy, there is little guidance for cumulating relevant empirical inquiries. Important studies suffer inattention because no scheme, by its logic, directs attention to them. Among other forms described below, I refer, for example, to lynching and the more abstract pattern it exemplifies, a pattern that goes virtually unconsidered in recent treatments of collective behavior. Indeed, an important mission of this chapter is *genetic rescue* or, more accurately, *generic rescue*, an effort to save the varieties of collective behavior from death by citation neglect in the midst of publication overkill. I try to construct a metaphorical Noah's ark in which to keep the creatures safe in an ocean of informational glut swept by waves of selective attention. Second, without a strong sense of context provided by articulate taxonomy, study of process becomes highly indefinite and prone to loggerheaded and even sterile debate. I fear this has happened, specifically, in debates over the relative merits of the conta-

Lofland, John. (1981). Collective behavior: The elementary forms. In Rosenberg and Turner (Eds.), *Social psychology: Sociological perspectives*. New York: Basic Books.

gion, convergence, emergent norm, and rational calculus views of processes in crowd behavior (Turner 1964; Perry and Pugh 1978; Tierney 1980). I suggest that the next large step in that debate will take the form of specifying the taxonomical (and temporal) location of the operation of each of those four processes. The traditional topics of *milling* and *rumor* are also likely to advance in that manner. Third, I expect that a more complex and variegated rendering of forms will also have a salubrious effect on the study of causes. Undisciplined by taxonomy, causal statements tend either to be extremely general and virtually vacuous or, on the other side, situationally idiosyncratic ("historic"). Stronger efforts at midrange types and causal treatments so geared are likely to stimulate attention to new kinds of variables. I think, in particular, of Albert Bergesen's (1976 and 1980) excellent work on "official riots" and his attendant innovations in causal thinking (see below). (It is for such contextualizing purposes that I, in what follows, sometimes depart rom a strict form-focus, especially as regards study of process.)

For these reasons, then, my treatment is quite selective and somewhat different from most recent efforts. Because it is, I fear that many scholars of collective behavior who have focused on other questions, and who have made outstanding contributions to answering those questions, will be offended by my relative neglect of their achievements. I want to stress that my admitted neglect in this chapter proceeds not from ignorance or cavalier dismissal, but from a belief that expanding initiatives are in order. Expanding initiatives are not necessarily incompatible with existing concerns—at least not in this case—and my larger aim is to enrich the study of collective behavior rather than to displace or ignore what exists. My selectivity arises, instead, from the constraints of space and time and an assessment of priorities within such limits.

THE NATURE OF COLLECTIVE BEHAVIOR

The most basic question of "form" is, of course, that of collective behavior itself as a form relative to other social forms. Employing the "ideal type" or "idealization" (Lopreato and Alston 1970) strategy of theorizing, I think it is helpful to conceive the "pure" case of collective behavior as a limiting instance. Such a case may never (or rarely) be encountered in the empirical world, but the ideal typical model provides a bench mark in terms of which we can gauge the empirical cases we do see. In ideal-type logic, the features of the model are in fact variables—aspects that are more or less present in specific cases. Five such aspects may be pointed to in providing a definition of collective behavior.

Adhering to the spirit of historic ideas and sensitized by a decade of reality constructionist and related thought, a first component is cognitive and concerns how people are defining a situation. As the phenomenologically inclined have urged us to see, ordinary actors go about their ordinary lives within something these analysts call "the attitude of everyday life" (Berger and Luckmann 1966). Within such an attitude, the emerging events of experience are labeled "nothing unusual is happening" (Emerson 1970). For whatever reasons and with whatever consequences, certain actors at times label an emergent situation as to some degree outside "everyday life." They begin to label a situation as "something *un* usual is happening." The attitude of everyday life is to some degree suspended; the frame of ordinary reality, the taken-for-granted world, is made consciously problematic. A situation is to some extent defined as unordinary, extra-ordinary, and perhaps, as unreal. Such a suspension is the beginning point of the possibility of collective behavior, but it is not yet collective behavior. The attitude of everyday life is probably suspended most frequently by individuals or by very small groups rather than by collectivities of significant size. Episodes of robbery, mugging, interpersonal violence, grave financial loss, illness, and dying are typical situations of suspending the attitude of everyday life, but their private and individual character make of them scenes of deviance, crime, or mere personal crisis rather than of collective behavior. Second, collective behavior requires suspension of the attitude of everyday life by relatively large numbers of people—by crowds and masses. What is a relatively large number of people? We are speaking of a continuum, of course, and there are, therefore, a set of ambiguous cases between mere personal crises on the one side and full collective behavior on the other. Suspension of the attitude of everyday life is accompanied by increased levels of emotional arousal in participants. This level is highly variable in the same individual over time and from individual to individual at the same time and over time. In their strongest form, states of emotional arousal may approach what we ordinarily label panic, rage, or ecstasy. There are obviously also many states that fall short of these. Completing the ancient trinity of intellectual, emotional, and physical, in collective behavior episodes the emerging definition and affective arousal is accompanied by action defined by participants and observers as outside the ordinary. The degree to which action is extra-ordinary is itself a variable and at the extremes we can conceivably point to such behavior as uncontrolled flight, indiscriminate violence, and complete loss of voluntary control during states of exaltation. Finally, the proportion of a collectivity suspending the attitude of everyday life in varying degrees, and experiencing emotional arousal in varying degrees differs over time. In the ideal-typical case, the proportion and degree of suspension and the proportion and degree of arousal is maximum and sustained.

The idealized profile of collective behavior, then, is unanimous, and maximum suspension of the attitude of everyday life in a collectivity combined with uniform and maximal emotional arousal and universally adopted extraordinary activities. Obviously, this ideal-typical situation rarely, if ever, occurs. It is useful as a domain-marking approach exactly because it is so rare, and, as formulated, turns collective behavior into a variable, something that is measured across participants and is a matter of degree in concrete instances.

In so constitutionally incorporating the idea of diversity within and between collective behavior episodes, one of the major contributions of the emergent norm approach is elevated to a preeminent consideration. As pioneered by Ralph Turner (1964), that approach stresses the lack of unanimity in collective behavior episodes. By stressing that fact at the outset, we are better prepared to develop a more systematic intra- and inter-episode comparative perspective. Although I elect to treat forms, below, in terms of level of dominant emotional arousal, other reasonable directions include scales for measuring the presence of collective behavior that encompass a wider array of relevant indicators (cf. McPhail and Pickens 1975).

PRIMARY VARIATIONS

Attuned simultaneously to the received literature in collective behavior (my "generic rescue" concern) and the emerging logic of the field (just treated), three primary variations may be employed as vehicles for preserving the former while hopefully advancing the latter, albeit with some tension between the two.

Dominant Emotion. From among the several basic features of collective behavior just described, I am impressed with the usefulness of employing an episode's dominant emotion as the most basic classifying variation. The notion of *dominant emotion* refers to the publicly expressed feeling perceived by participants and observers as most prominent in an episode of collective behavior. For an emotion to be publicly most dominant—to have become the reigning definition of the emotional situation—is not to say that an especially large portion of that collectivity feels that emotion. Indeed, following the lead of Ralph Turner's formulation of emergent norm theory (1964), the dominant emotion is almost always far from a matter of uniform, unanimous, or even majority inner feeling. In so referring to what is publicly communicated and socially shared, the idea of dominant emotion has much the same logical status as that of the emergent norm. The shift here is simply away from the cognitive (that is, the notion of form) to the affective.

If we are to focus on dominant emotion, there is then the question of what emotions are to be employed. There are at least two approaches to deciding this. First, we can scrutinize the accumulated literature on collective behavior, asking what emotions appear dominant. Second, we can ask what emotions theorists of emotions per se would offer us. Happily, there is a reasonable accord between these two rather independently developed bodies of theory and research.

Without anyone making a strongly conscious effort, collective behavior studies have moved—haltingly and inarticulately—toward organization around three fundamental emotions: fear, hostility, and joy. This half-century trend is signaled most clearly in Neil Smelser's monumental *Theory of Collective Behavior* (1963), which organizes the field in terms of types of "generalized beliefs" and the quite special topics of the "panic", "hostile outburst," and "craze." Ostensibly about belief, the titles of the forms themselves are also clearly suggestive of dominant emotions. In codifying a vast literature around those three kinds of beliefs, Smelser was being responsive to the long-standing and wide use of something similar to such a trinity in collective behavior studies. Considered the single most important work in collective behavior for many years after its publication in 1963, Smelser's demarcation of the field has persisted, albeit revolving around matters more cognitive than emotive.

Turning to students of emotions per se, we discover several competing schemes of fundamental emotions, but virtually complete agreement that these three are among the most fundamental and even, moreover, transspecific (for example, Izard 1977; Plutchik 1962). Irrespective of these two sources of wisdom, only a modest amount of reflection on social life is required to recognize that these are ubiquitous and central emotions, and emotions that are especially entailed in collective behavior.

But why these three, and why only three? A fully appropriate answer would require an excursus into the sociology of knowledge, because, for better or worse, the historic concerns of the received literature have run largely along these lines. To the degree we take the literature seriously, our actions are constrained.

There are, nonetheless, other basic emotions that can become dominant in collective behavior. Among them are grief, disgust, surprise (Plutchik 1962), and shame (Izard 1977). Although there are some studies relevant to these emotions, they are so few that I will not attempt to treat them, save briefly to mention grief as an uneasy variation on fear (see below). One future task is expansion of the basic divisions of collective behavior in terms of other basic and dominant emotions.

Last, there is the question of the use of dominant emotion as a means of classifying forms of collective behavior. Indeed, some people would observe, the most recent movement in the field is quite explicitly away from concern with emotion because such a stress asserts or implies unusual or peculiar psychic state or mechanisms such as "contagion," "circular reaction," (Blumer 1969a:70–71; Turner 1964), cognitive "short-circuits" and "compressed" ways of acting (Smelser 1963:71). Imputations of "crudeness, excess and eccentricity" arise along with characterizations of collective behavior as ". . . the action of the impatient" (Smelser 1963:72).

I have no quarrel with those who reject such images of collective behavior and fear that they are a consequence of a stress on emotions. My concern, instead, is that stress on the cognitive (and behavioral) commits the opposite error, that of reducing the field to exercises in cognitive theory or, even more extremely, to a species of behaviorism in which the study of collective behavior is merely the study of human coordination (for example, Cough 1970; McPhail 1978). At bottom, though, it is probably impossible to decide rationally which course to take because the longer term consequences of the cognitive, affective, or behavioral stresses are impossible to assess beforehand and the fruitfulness of each changes as each emergently takes account of the others. And in the end, certainly, effort to integrate all three must be made.

Organizational Form. Cross-cutting each of the dominant emotions are questions of the organizational form in which collective behavior arises. Historically, the field stressed distinctions among the *crowd,* the *mass,* the *public,* and the *social movement.* Over recent decades the latter two have come increasingly to be treated as separate specialties, especially so in the case of the public and public opinion. (Virtually alone, Turner and Killian's text [1972] continues to treat public opinion.) It is indicative that the present volume provides each its own chapter.

In many recent treatments, even the distinction between the crowd and the mass has been deemphasized in favor of addressing collective behavior per se (for example, Perry and Pugh 1978). Neil Smelser's (1963) grand synthesis appears to have started this trend by defining its main dependent variables—the panic, craze, and hostile outburst—in a way that rendered crowd and mass forms irrelevant.

Nonetheless, the distinction is critical to understanding forms of collective behavior in relation to dominant emotions. A crowd may be thought of as a relatively large number of persons who are in one another's immediate face-to-face presence. A crowd is a special kind of *encounter* as that term has been defined and analyzed by Erving Goffman (1961b) and others (Lofland 1976:chapter 8). A crowd is an "over-populated" encounter in the sense that it presents an exceedingly complex array of mutual monitoring possibilities and constraints. Informed by the new sensitivities that scholars such as Erving Goffman have provided us about encounters, it is to be hoped that we can again begin to take crowds seriously. Features of the mass are less clear than those of the crowd, and it tends to be defined residually, that is, as whatever is left over after we have looked at crowds. More positively, the term refers to a set of people who attend to a common object, but who are not in one another's immediate physical vicinity.

The two dimensions of dominant emotion and organizational form provide a framework for organizing detailed types of collective behavior. The intersection of these two dimensions is shown in figure 14.1, "Elementary Forms of Collective Behavior," a figure that also provides a synoptic overview of the patterns treated in the sections that follow.

Level/Form. Pursuant to conceiving collective behavior as a variable, more specific forms within each of the six master types (so to speak) ought to be arrayed in terms of level of dominant emotional arousal. And pursuing ideal-type logic, the highest level dominant emotions ought to be presented first, moving through successive and lesser degrees or forms of dominant emotions. On the assumption that, overall, crowd situations possess a potential for dominant emotional arousal exceeding those of mass situations, crowd forms need to be treated prior to mass ones.

These principles lead us to envision three pure anchor points to which the paler empirical instances of real world crowds and masses can be contrasted. These may be labeled, in order, *crowd panic, rage,* and *ecstasy,* terms taken to be, by definition, the highest levels of fear, hostility, and joy, respectively. By bearing the pure possibilities in mind, we will have a clearer conception of how far we are straying from the center in our analytic travels. In accordance with this conception, explication within each of the three main domains will proceed, insofar as the materials make this feasible, from the strongest dominant emotions to the weakest, from forms and behavior that are consensually collective behavior to phenomena that probably ought not be discussed in the context of collective behavior.

Having outlined principles from which ideally to proceed, I must now demur and report that the obdurate world of existing materials has not always allowed me to execute these principles. I

		DOMINANT EMOTION		
		Fear	*Hostility*	*Joy*
Organizational Form	Crowd	Panic Terror Dread Horror Dismay	Political C→I, e.g., mob attacks C→C, e.g., political clashes C→E, e.g., protests E→I, e.g., bourbon lynchings E→C, e.g., official riots Leisure C→C, e.g., intrafan violence C→E, e.g., resort disorders Emergent C→I, e.g., proletarian lynchings C→C, e.g., communal riots C→E, e.g., ghetto riots Captive C→C, e.g., inmate clashes C→E, e.g., pre-planned bids	Ecstatic upheavals Ecstatic conventions Ecstatic congregations Euphoric moods Revivalist crowds Reverent crowds Revelous crowds Excited crowds

FIGURE 14.1 Elementary Forms of Collective Behavior

often need to revert to the prior and more primitive task of simply sorting important forms without judging the level of dominant emotion. This reversion is seen most clearly in the treatment of mass fears and crowd hostilities. When forced to a choice between the dual aims of this chapter (generic rescue and expanding initiative) I have preferred generic rescue. One consequence is that, in order to rescue forms irrespective of dominant emotion, I invoke classificatory principles in an ad hoc fashion. In one instance I even switch from emotion to behavior in ordering forms. In this I subscribe to Erving Goffman's admonition that we treat sociological concepts "with affection," tracing each in its own terms, sensitive to the materials themselves and not merely to logical consistency. As Goffman has put it: "Better, perhaps, different coats to clothe the children well than a single splendid tent in which they all shiver" (Goffman 1961:xiv). . . .

PART TWO

Precipitating Conditions

As in any other field of scientific investigation, scholars have felt the need to understand and predict the occurrence of collective behavior and social movement emergence. This means that a great deal of research and theorizing, some of which is included in this book, has been devoted to the identification of precipitating social and cultural conditions associated with greater likelihood of occurrence of these events, on the social arrangements and settings that are more conducive to the appearance of collective behavior and social movements.

Neil J. Smelser's value-added approach to collective behavior and social movement (Article 2) is perhaps the best known and most ambitious attempt to systematize the problem. He groups the precipitating conditions into five categories: the emergence of structural strain among the components of social action (situational facilities, motivational structures, norms, societal values), the growth of a shared generalized belief, the occurrence of a precipitating event that confirms the generalized belief, the mobilization of the collectivity for action on the basis of the generalized belief, and the relative effectiveness of social control measures and agencies prior to and after the mobilization of the participants. He uses these dimensions to argue that each of the emergent collective behavior and social movement forms identified in the theory have their own distinct etiology. It is unnecessary to agree with the larger tenets of the theory to appreciate the value of the synthesis of the preconditions of collective behavior and social movements advanced in the work.

Ralph H. Turner and Lewis M. Killian also develop their own multidimensional approach to the problem of identification from the perspective of symbolic interactionism. They argue that the occurrence of collective behavior depends on the feasibility and timeliness of the acts, the extent of preexisting social networks and other support available to people considering acting collectively, and their normative justification. E. L. Quarantelli emphasizes the dimensions of social organization and culture, arguing that there is greater probability of occurrence of collective behavior and social movements in social organizations that are more differentiated and stratified, and in cultural systems that are more heterogenous in their norms, values, and beliefs.

Recent debate in the specialty on the topic of the preconditions of collective behavior and social movement phenomena centers in part on the relative importance of grievance when compared to the presence of change agents such as social movement organizers. This perspective is elaborated by John D. McCarthy and Mayer N. Zald

(Article 4). By and large, in spite of these claims, the current agreement is that the emphasis on the latter is a valuable corrective to the older grievance tradition, although it cannot substitute it in its entirety. There has also been considerable attention given to the idea that a person's decision to participate in collective action and social movement organizational activities is largely determined by the context formed by the summed mobilization propensities or proclivities of potential participants in the mobilization episode. From this perspective, it is possible for an aggrieved person to decide not to participate in the collective behavior episode because his or her mobilization threshold is not met by the unfolding event; the person perceives that an insufficient number of people have mobilized and decides not to participate. Also couched at the level of the individual is what has come to be known as the free-rider problem: According to this line of thinking, in situations in which collective action goals are public goods for large categories of people—goods from which potential participants will benefit irrespective of whether or not they participate—they will choose not to participate.

A preliminary categorization of precipitating conditions must include the realm of personality, social organization, and culture, as well as the substratum of the biological and physical spheres and the facts of population. Research on preconditions is illustrated at the individual level of analysis by Anthony M. Orum's article (Article 12) in which he presents a very useful summary, evaluation, and synthesis of literature centered on five explanations of individual participation in organized attempts to change political systems: status inconsistency, cumulative deprivation, relative deprivation, rising expectations, and isolation. A causal model of the antecedents of participation is presented; it includes political trust, sense of efficacy, opportunity to participate, subjective dissatisfaction, group loyalty or identification, and self-esteem. Orum's model should be considered as a partial list of the factors that increase the probality that people will join in collective action and social movement mobilization.

We also include Joan Neff Gurney and Kathleen J. Tierney's review of relative deprivation explanations of participation in social movements. (Article 3). This article presents arguably the most thorough evaluation of the relative deprivation explanation of participation in social movements available to date. Among its important contributions is its assessment of the different definitions of relative deprivation in use, the problems attending the use of relative deprivation, an individual-level explanation (to make sense of the acts of collectivities), and the chronic lack of adequate empirical bases of the published tests of the hypothesis. Complicating the proper use of the concept of relative deprivation is the larger problem of individual motivation. No single explanation, be it rational or otherwise, can be assumed, a priori, to capture appropriately *the* reason for a collective behavior event, or subsume the multiple subjectivities involved in it. George Rude, among others, showed that economic, ideological, religious, and political ideas played their part in popular preindustrial disturbances in England and elsewhere on the continent, and their relative explanatory importance could be weighed only through the use of a historical, comparative framework of analysis. In spite of current intellectual fads, Rude's basic understanding is as valid today as when it was enunciated more than 30 years ago.

This section also includes Norris R. Johnson's work on panic (Article 10), the most thoroughly documented analysis of panic available in the extant literature. Panic is assumed by many people to be dominated by manifestations of antisocial, irrational, and ineffective behavior. E. L. Quarantelli challenged this view of panic and dispelled many myths surrounding panic behavior. He pointed out that the behavior of panic participants was not characterized by psychological regression but rather was an attempt to deal with a sudden, unexpected, urgent, and threatening event by nonrational and nonsocial individualistic flight. Johnson's empirical examination of panic supports many of the generalizations offered by Quarantelli and corrects his emphasis on nonsocial interaction. It shows that panic involves a great deal of cooperative behavior. An important finding, replicated in other studies of collective behavior, is that people participated in the gathering as members of small groups rather than as isolated individuals. Johnson shows that people did not stampede over others in their rush to enter the Coliseum. Instead, they helped each other throughout most of the incident, although competitive, ego-centered behavior did in fact take place during the final stages of the panic, as people tried to escape the deadly crush. This reading offers a stark proof of the point raised by Richard A. Berk (see Article 3), among others, about the importance of ecological factors in structuring the flow of communications in instances of collective behavior and the resulting multiple, and at times conflicting, tragic definitions of the situation in separate segments of the gathering.

Mayer N. Zald and Michael A. Berger's study of social movements in complex organizations is also included in this section (Article 9) because of its careful treatment of the conditions that make these emergent phenomena more likely. This imaginative article describes three types of emergent organized phenomena in complex organizations that bring about rapid social change in them: the coup d'etat, insurgency, and mass movements. It also identifies some of the conditions that make these emergent phenomena more likely, their outcomes, and a number of testable hypotheses. Its emphasis on the analysis of social emergence in institutionalized contexts in reminiscent of Herbert Blumer's and Jack M. Weller and E. L. Quarantelli's emphases (see Articles 5 and 6), among others. A careful assessment of the article will show the logical and empirical difficulties that come about from identifying collective behavior as the polar opposite of institutionalized social organization.

The section also includes another example of social movements in complex organizations—James R. Hayes's analysis of the GI movement in the U.S. Army (Article 11). This article shows the importance of social control mechanisms in the dynamics and strategies of social movements. The protests associated with this movement had characteristics of both insurgency and mass movement phenomena. In fact, the article should be read as a partial albeit unintended test of many of the hypotheses offered by Mayer N. Zald and Michael A. Berger (Article 9).

Conditions facilitating movements at the societal level are elaborated by Larry J. Griffin, Michael E. Wallace, and Beth A. Rubin's historical analysis of class dynamics in the marketplace (Article 8). This article shows the handsome payoffs that can be realized, for our understanding of social movement dynamics, from the study of complex organizations active in social movements (see Article 4). Written in part from the perspective of the resource mobilization approach, the article documents the countermovement organizations that emerged and were active in the United States during the first three decades of this century to fight against the U.S. labor movement. The reading identifies the various antilabor tactics used by capitalist organizations. It illustrates the dependence of sociological analysis on historical materials as well as the unique contributions that the sociological framework of interpretation can bring to our general understanding of social life.

ARTICLE 8

Capitalist Resistance to the Organization of Labor Before the New Deal: Why? How? Success?

LARRY J. GRIFFIN
MICHAEL E. WALLACE
BETH A. RUBIN

Class conflict engendered by the proletarianization of formerly self-sufficient and autonomous producers historically has taken place in the two institutions characterizing the political economy of a capitalist democracy, the commodity production system, including the exchange of commodified labor power for wages in a labor market, and the electoral-representative political system. In capitalist countries which have never spawned successful political parties committed to and dependent predominantly on the working class for their electoral victories (e.g., the U.S., Reich and Edwards, 1978), the market has remained the core arena within which workers have mobilized their collective resources both to resist the power of capital and to organize to preserve or to enhance their material well-being and control over shop-floor conditions. The American bourgeoisie, too, has created new markets or tailored existing ones to further its economic, political, or ideological objectives (Edwards, 1979; Gordon et al., 1982).

Labor markets therefore do more than simply distribute the fruits of production; they also generate class-specific interests and capacities, especially between the main actors engaged in

Griffin, Larry J., Wallace, Michael E., & Rubin, Beth A. (1986, April). Capitalist resistance to the organization of labor before the New Deal: Why? How? Success? *American Sociological Review, 51,* 147–167. Reprinted by permission of the American Sociological Association.

Address all correspondence to Larry J. Griffin. Department of Sociology. University of Minnesota. Minneapolis, MN, 55455.

This is a substantially revised version of a paper first presented at the 1982 Social Science History Association meetings. We would like to thank a number of our colleagues for their comments on an earlier and much longer version of this article, especially Ed Amenta, Frank Burleigh, Bill Corsaro, Neil Fligstein, Bill Form, Mike Goldfield, Rick King, David James and Whitney Pope. Participants in the History and Society Workshop at the University of Minnesota forced us to think more deeply about the relationship between quantitative social science and historical inquiry and offered a number of cogent remarks. Three anonymous ASR reviewers subjected the paper to a thorough critique. Space limitations and our own stubbornness precluded incorporation of some of the suggestions we received, so all readers are excused from our willful folly. We also acknowledge the support of the Division of Research and Graduate Development of Indiana University market relations, capitalists and workers, and structure relations, conflictual or harmonious or some mix of each, both between and among class agents (Mandel, 1968; Therborn, 1983; Wright, 1978). In a word, markets both forge classes and are used by men and women as they attempt to forge themselves into classes. Neither markets nor the competition or cooperation induced by them, however, exist in a political vacuum. States tolerate markets, occasionally regulate or shut them down, but always partially shape the realm of possibilities—to exploit, to organize, to struggle—available to actors in markets. By selectively encouraging the organization or disorganization of particular classes, or by facilitating or repressing the mobilization of class-linked resources, states and their policies, then, are also entangled in the process of class formation.

Classes are not static entities, fixed once and for all in time. Nor are they completely determined by "objective" economic "facts," such as the social relations of production (Prezworski, 1977). Rather, the process of class formation is the effect of the totality of ideological, political, and economic conflicts, themselves limited by the relations of production and often motivated precisely by the struggles of actors to define themselves and their adversaries as organized collectivities with perceptible boundaries and some degree of consciousness of collective interests (Prezworski, 1977; Therborn, 1983). Boundaries, interests, and mobilization, however, are always shifting; interests change, coalitions are formed and break up, positions in the economy are created or destroyed, demobilization occurs (Tilly, 1978). Classes are continually organized, disorganized, and reorganized (Prezworski, 1977). Indeed, an interest of any one class is usually to disorganize, either directly or indirectly via manipulation of the state or market, its (real or perceived) adversarial class, to render it ineffective as an organized collectivity pursuing its often different, occasionally antagonistic, interests. This, too, tends to generate conflict as the contending groups mobilize resources to press or fend off the attack (Tilly, 1978). "The very right to organize is an effect of struggles that in turn shapes the form of class organization." (Prezworski, 1977:372). To understand class formation, then, one must also understand how and why classes are disorganized by the conscious actions of agents of other classes or by the state. This is our general objective in this paper.

Our rather abstract concerns are addressed by examining, in the pre-New Deal period, why and how an increasingly organized capitalist class tried so assiduously to disorganize American workers-as-a-class. We emphasize the legal, social, organizational, and technological mechanisms used by capital to repress, fragment, "buy-off," and deskill labor and, in so doing, forestall its organizational efforts and mobilization. Our analyses pertain to the years 1902–28, from the beginning of capital's first organized mass offensive against labor, the "open shop drive" (Perlman and Taft, 1935; Foner, 1964), to the onset of the Great Depression. In general, the structure of labor-management relations and collective bargaining and the relationships among organized labor, capital and the state were so different in the pre- and post-Depression/New Deal years that the two epochs represent distinct regimes of industrial relations (Rubin et al., 1983; Snyder, 1975; Brody, 1980; Shelfin et al., 1981; Fiorito, 1982).

Our reading of the historical record, to be reviewed below, convinces us that much of the variation in unionization during this period—and the relatively low level of organization during the entire pre-New Deal era (see Wolman's 1923 and 1936 discussions of the waxing and waning of the labor movement during this period)– can be partially attributed to efforts of capitalists to defeat labor organization. The first question to be answered, then, is what were capital's interests vis-a-vis labor, i.e., the "gains or losses resulting from . . . interaction . . ." (Tilly, 1978:7). . . .

HOW DID CAPITAL RESIST? ORGANIZATION AND MOBILIZATION

Capital launched two major "counter-movements" (McCarthy and Zald, 1977) against trade unions during the pre-Depression years, the "open shop drive," which began around 1903 and lasted for a decade or so, and the "American Plan," which characterized the 1920s. While the movements differed to a degree tactically, and involved additional actors (e.g., the American Plan drew in, especially, the Chamber of Commerce as an extremely active participant, but also the National Grange, the American Bankers Association, and other business organizations; Perlman and Taft, 1935), they pursued essentially identical strategies and, excepting the time period were often indistinguishable. For purposes of brevity, we treat them as a single continuous movement, displaying different "moments" historically.

Two peak capitalist organizations were primarily responsible for the attacks on or attempts at the subornation of trade unions: the National Association of Manufacturers (NAM) and the National Civic Foundation (NCF). Employer resistance to unionism existed throughout the 19th century (Perlman and Taft, 1935), but it lacked national leadership and organization. The new president of the NAM, David Parry, supplied these in 1903, when accusing organized labor of having "exactly the same end and aim as Socialism," he urged the Association to organize a "crusadc against unionism" (quoted in Foner, 1964:37). The open-shop drive, the "employers mass offensive" (Perlman and Taft, 1935:129), had begun.

Two points of the NAM's newly adopted hostile policy toward labor were emphatically enunciated (Steigerwalt, 1964). First, the association should "inform" the public about the true nature of unionism. Second, the NAM should take the lead in encouraging and organizing the anti-union, open-shop efforts of the numerous but unorganized trade and employers associations which existed throughout the county. In effect, the NAM was to organize the capitalist class and mobilize its resources of money, access to the political center, and moral suasion. It sponsored, financed, or otherwise cooperated with a number of newly formed or extant anti-union associations or fronts many of which like the NAM, were formed for reasons other than anti-unionism (see, in particular, Bonnett, 1922:361–72). Here we see an example of how a newly mobilizing conflict group reduces its organizing costs by building on pre-existing organizational resources (Oberschall, 1973. See also Morris 1981 analysis of the black sit-in movement in the late 1950s).

In 1907, most of these associations coalesced, under the tutelage of the NAM to form the National Council of Industrial Defense, the purpose of which was to coordinate political pressure to defeat candidates and legislation (especially that pertaining to wages, hours and working conditions and exempting unions from the restrictions of the Sherman Anti-Trust Act) favorable to labor (Bernstein, 1960a; Foner, 1964; Steigerwalt, 1964). All in all, then, the NAM's line on the necessity of union-busting was followed faithfully by much of the business community, and most of its suggestions about how to disorganize the working class were in fact, adopted by a large number of industrialists, especially those in heavily organized states and industries (Steigerwalt, 1964:152).

The National Civic Foundation was organized in 1900 to work for specific reforms to stabilize the emergent corporate order and to check the rapidly spreading influence of the Socialist movement (Foner, 1964: Weinstein, 1968, 1970). It included among its officials eminent representatives of business, labor, and the public, including the more influential capitalists of the day (e.g., Mark Hanna, Samuel Insull, Andrew Carnegie). Samuel Gompers, who was the original First Vice President of the NCF, John Mitchell (president of the United Mine Workers), and the "heads of the major railroad brotherhoods and many AFL international unions" (Weinstein, 1970:8). Unlike those associations openly pushing open-shop ideology, the NCF espoused acceptance of conservative and "responsible" unionism (as represented by the AFL leadership) and support for workmen's compensation and for federal legislation to curb the rapacious competition among business enterprises (Weinstein, 1970: Foner, 1964).

The NCF's composition and "enlightened" stance towards the trade unions and progressive legislation have led some revisionist historians, notably Weinstein (1968) and Radosh (1970) to conclude that the NAM and the NCF proposed genuinely different solutions to the "labor problem," with the former urging cruder, war-like tactics and the latter offering labor an olive branch. Some factual support for this view exists. First, as we discussed above, is the representation of labor leaders in the higher echelons of the NCF. Second, competition existed between the NCF and the NAM and the two did exchange sharp verbal criticisms and insults (Foner, 1964). Third, the NCF did attempt to bridge the gulf between capital and labor and promote industrial peace of a certain sort (Weinstein, 1970; Radosh, 1970).

The Weinstein-Radosh interpretation is nevertheless overdrawn. Despite the ostensible hostility between the Foundation and the Association, "the top leaders of the most important employers' associations in the country belonged to both organizations" (Foner, 1970:116; see also Foner, 1964:69–70 and Montgomery, 1979:60–61). Big business, moreover, dominated the NCF and its policies. The NCF's lofty ideology of tolerance and conciliation was seldom matched in practice: Ralph Easley, the Secretary of the NCF, "sought to persuade the big industrialists that there was no basic difference between the Parrite [referring to the NAM's president, David Parry] and the NCF approach to organized labor" (quoted in Foner, 1964:69). Furthermore, the type of unions tolerated by the NCF were those craft unions organized by and for a privileged minority, unions which were "not [to] make trouble," and which were to "keep politics out of the union" (Easley to Gompers, as quoted in Foner, 1964:70–71). Radicals and the unskilled were to be excluded from these conservative unions; "responsible" union leaders were to police their own ranks; one open shop, where desirable, was not to be challenged, or in the words of Seth Low, the president of the NCF: "the right of other workingmen to forego collective bargaining if they wish to do so, will be equally unchallenged" (quoted in Foner, 1964:70). Whatever the degree of class collaboration between AFL bureaucrats and "civic-minded" and "progressive" members of the NCF, the Foundation's real purpose was to co-opt the labor movement and to channel its energies in ways acceptable to this faction of capital.

The total number of firms belonging to one or another open-shop or trade association adoption open-shop principles is not know. Two rough estimates of the size of the countermovement can be inferred from data presented in Bernstein (1960b) and Bonnett (1922). A recalculation of Bernstein's (p. 83) data suggests that 80 employers associations belligerent to unions were formed in the years 1897–1932. An additional 57 associations espousing "negotiation" with organized labor were formed in this period. In all likelihood, however, the majority of these "negotiated" in a manner similar to the NCF; that is, were conciliatory toward unions if the leadership delivered the labor peace and "cooperation" wanted by "liberal" business. Thus, unionized labor was faced, at one time or another in the pre-New Deal period, with up to 137 employers associations, the majority of which were openly hostile and the remainder covertly so. Based on data presented in Bonnett (1922), we calculate that between 1910 and 1920 at least 15,000 firms were represented by only 10 of these peak associations.

HOW DID CAPITAL RESIST? COLLECTIVE ACTION

The open-shop movement was, as we have seen, unified in its interests, extremely well organized and had mobilized considerable clout. But generally these must be put to use before one movement or class can inflict damage on another movement or class (Tilly, 1978). To do damage to an adversarial movement—to demobilize it, for example, or to raise the costs of its collective action to near-prohibitive levels—requires collective action. What were the "repertoires" (Tilly, 1978) of collective action used by the bourgeoisie during the open shop and the American Plan years?

Employers' tactics took a variety of often temporally specific forms, all experimental and frequently running at cross-currents with each other and all deriving from organization and coordination, either tight or loose. Most of these represented explicit policies undertaken by agents of the open shop/American Plan (OS/AP) associations and can be rather straightforwardly grouped into categories similar to those developed by Tilly (1978) to study the general consequences of resource mobilization.

I. *Capitalists attempted to diminish the unity of working-class interest and its "intrinsic class strength"* (Therborn, 1983:40) *that is, its "extent of common identity and unifying structure" and social cohesion on and off the job* (Tilly, 1978:54) in a variety of ways, but the most important appear to have been the use of immigrant labor, the reorganization of the labor process via mechanization and the implementation of new systems of factory administration, especially "systematic" and "scientific" management techniques, and corporate paternalism as embodied in "welfare capitalism" and company unions.

A. Immigrants supplied much of the raw labor power needed by an industrializing America: about one-fifth of the aggregate increase in the work force between 1870 and 1910 can be attributed to immigration (Vittoz, 1978). Ample evidence exists that employers on a very wide basis consciously exploited the massive influx and heterogeneity of immigrant labor. The sheer number of immigrants (which totaled over 21 million from 1891 to 1931), about 80 percent of whom were unskilled (Foner, 1964:257; Montgomery, 1979:34) and employed in unorganized industries, served as a "floating supply of labor" (quoted from the trade journal *Iron Age* by Brody, 1960:109), regulating employment and possibly (but see Vittoz, 1978:57) wages. Moreover, immigrants were occasionally used as strike breakers (though perhaps proportionally no greater than other workers; Vittoz, 1978), arousing the hostility of organized labor and exciting nativist sentiments in the working class generally (Gordon et al., 1982; Brody, 1960; Foner, 1964). The unionization and skill differentials between immigrant and native labor provided further ammunition for the bourgeoisie's "divide-and-conquer" strategy, which played on ethnic and associated differences by selectively hiring or firing particular groups or employing many ethnicities with no common tongue, or by segregating ethnic groups by departments or job categories within the firm (Montgomery, 1979; Perlman and Taft, 1935; Gordon et al., 1982). Here the explicit motivation of the capitalists was to disorganize workers and to breed hostility between native workers and immigrants and among the different immigrant nationalities and ethnicities.

Employers apparently had a sound understanding of the economics of immigrant labor. Until the early twenties, representatives of a number of trade associations, including the National Founders Association and the NAM, both testified before and lobbied Congress on the necessity of keeping immigrant streams open (Bonnett, 1922).

B. The mechanization and subsequent reorganization of the labor process was the prime mechanism used in the "transfer of skill"—discussed above as necessary for the rationalization of production—from craftsman to manager. Coupled with new management techniques, it freed the employer from reliance on expensive skilled workers, who were now increasingly replaced by semi-skilled machine operatives. (See the data on the changing skill composition of Detroit's metal industries workers presented in Gordon et al., 1982:133.) Craftsmen lost the single most important resource they possessed—their monopoly over production knowledge (Gordon et al., 1982; Brody, 1980; Montgomery, 1979)—and hence the very basis of their union organization and subsequent collective action. As Tilly (1978:79) notes, one of the most effective ways to demobilize an adversary is to appropriate its salient resources. With skilled workers and their organization on the defensive, capital often did rationalize production, with subsequent output gains and wage decreases. Brody (1960) and Stone (1975), for example, report drastic reductions in the wages of skilled union steel workers after their union was broken and the labor process reorganized.

By subdividing tasks into specialized operations and by erecting job hierarchies, management effectively countered, at least in the short run, the possibility that a now deskilled and homogeneous work force laboring in comparable work conditions for similar pay would organize. Performance in this elaborate division of labor, moreover, was rewarded through the use of "incentive pay," which individualized wages, rather than through the "old-fashioned" negotiations between the employer and the craft union. This restructuring of the labor process clearly fragmented the interests, and even objective relations, vis-a-vis managers, of workers; the "collective worker" (Wright, 1978:99) was partially destroyed; cohesion was replaced by segmentation. Managerial domination of the workplace, designed to increase output and reduce labor costs, became more of a reality. Bendix's (1956) analysis of open-shop literature led him to conclude that scientific management was one tool perceived by managers to enable them to exercise "absolute authority" (p. 274) in the workplace. This desire is also unapologetically presented in the charters of some of the trades associations. It is not surprising, then, that the NAM and the Council for Industrial Defense lobbied Congress in 1916 to table an "anti-efficiency in industry" bill (Nadworny, 1955:102; Bonnett, 1922:89).

C. The harshness of the mechanization of production, the prevalence of 'technical control," which entailed the conscious embedding of control in the technical structure of the firm (Edwards, 1979), and the atomization accompanying the new forms of management provoked tremendous resistance from labor in the form of greater strike activity and an unacceptably high level of turnover (Nelson, 1982; Brody, 1980; Montgomery, 1979; Gordon et al., 1982). The final set of anti-union strategies to be discussed in this section were attempts to ease this harshness by paternalism. In exchange for loyalty and commitment to the firm, capital was willing to extend to labor a "voice" was to be exercised through company unions known initially as "works councils" or "employee representation" plans; the well-being of the worker was to be achieved through "welfare capitalism."

Company unions, which enrolled about a million and a half workers in 1928 (National Industrial Conference Board, 1933), were evident as early as 1898, but began to be established extensively only in the early 1920s as an outgrowth of President Wilson's charge to the newly-formed National War Labor Board (NWLB) to keep labor peace (Brandes, 1976; Bernstein, 1960a). They were essentially formal grievance committees formed and controlled by management and after the wartime gains of organized labor, were increasingly established as a "safety valve" (National Industrial Conference Board, 1933:39) to counter labor's self-organization, often during an organizing drive or strike (McKelvey, 1952; Bernstein, 1960a:86–87; Brody, 1980; Brandes, 1976).

Company unions were supported throughout much of the 1920s by the NAM, the American Management Association, and the National Industrial Conference Board (NICB), another employer-sponsored "civic" organization (Bernstein, 1960a:171). They were used to cement the innovations in factory reorganization and managerial practices initiated during the earlier "systematic management" period (Nelson, 1982). Productivity gains were registered by those firms adopting works councils (Bernstein, 1960a; McKelvey, 1952), as were increases in job security and wages, at least in some plants (Brandes, 1976:130–1; results not presented also suggest that company unions may have stimulated hourly compensation). While the specifics of employee representation plans varied by firm, some generalities seemed to exist: managerial prerogative to organize the labor process remained intact, including "specifically the right to set the pace of work and pay rates" (Edwards, 1979:106); membership was often open only to non-union members (Bernstein, 1960a); individual grievances were heard, but no mechanism existed for workers to press for collective interests (Edwards, 1979); strikes were prohibited (Bernstein, 1960a; Foner, 1964); councils' decisions were subject to managerial approval—they had little, if any, independent power (Edwards, 1979); Brandes, 1976); and "employee representatives had no contact with other company or trade unions in the industry" (Bernstein, 1960a:172).

The following statement by the vice president of a copper company makes as clear as possible capital's intent in establishing company unions:

> *Employee representation has come from management and therefore is to be regarded as a vehicle to assist management leadership. . . . It is a great mistake to consider this device as a means of balancing the power of management by the power of another group. It should rather be regarded as a mechanism which the management officials utilize to assist them in their function of leadership (quoted in Lescohier and Brandeis, 1935:355).*

Employees representation was an anti-union tool of management, pure and simple.

Much the same can be said of welfare capitalism. Having its roots in the 19th century it flourished in the 1920s, giving workers in "large prosperous firms" (Brody, 1960:59) a variety of extrinsic job benefits, including recreational services, health care, group insurance, retirement pensions, stock options, profit-sharing, accident benefits, housing, educational services, and even attempts at employment stability (Bernstein, 1960a; Edwards, 1979; Lescohier and Brandeis, 1935; Brandes, 1976). By the end of the twenties, a non-trivial percentage of American workers in the economically dominant firms received some sort of corporate welfare benefit.

Corporate provision of services did reflect, to a degree, the philanthropic impulse; nevertheless, private welfare spending was also an attempt to "buy" the workers' loyalty and commitment to the firm. An immediate concern of the capitalists of the time was to find a solution to high turnover, which in some industries was as high as 348 percent and averaged, over 105 manufacturing firms, 100 percent in 1912–15 (Lescohier and Brandeis, 1935:331). Job benefits tied to the worker's stability seemed one answer, both to turnover and to the perennial problem of productivity. The NICB, in a 1929 report, suggested that firms with employee savings plans could expect "good feeling" [by employees] toward the company . . . [and] workers to remain with the company" (quoted in McKelvey, 1952:55). Likewise, Charles Schwab, the head of Bethlehem steel, argued that "A sense of proprietorship affords a powerful incentive to arouse interest in the performance of work" (quoted in Brody, 1980:54).

Welfare schemes were more than bonds cementing workers to their employers, though; they were also tactics used to woo employees away from unions. One International Harvester executive argued that accident insurance was "a weapon [which] would be much stronger than any profit-sharing proposition toward breaking up unionism" (quoted in Edwards, 1979:93). Employee ownership of stock, suggested the NICB in 1928, might generate "a more loyal and interested labor force . . . ," and as a result "unrest would be allayed and . . . there would be less incentive for response to outside organizations which might seek to divide the allegiance of the workers" (quoted in McKelvey, 1952:55). Employers put teeth into their anti-union rhetoric by withholding some services from striking employees and from union members (Foner, 1964; said Harold McCormick, then President of International Harvester: "As you know our Pension Plan is a purely voluntaristic expression of the company's desire to stand by men who have stood by it." Quoted in Edwards, 1979:93). It is therefore not coincidental that welfare capitalism was pushed most vigorously by the NCF (Weinstein, 1970; Edwards, 1979; Nelson, 1975; Brandes, 1976) and supported by the NAM (Steigerwalt, 1964; Brandes, 1976).

Debate endures as to the real successes of welfare capitalism and company unions in disorganizing American workers. Nevertheless, by rewarding loyalty to the firm, objectively linking the interests of capital and labor, and inculcating habits of dependence and subservience, corporate paternalism stunted the awareness and consciousness of "class" in an important segment of labor.

II. *The second set of tactics employers used was aimed at weakening directly the organizational capacity or mobilization of organized labor.* They represent explicit, "official" OS/AP movement actions and include: (a) boycotting union goods, (b) hiring labor spies and agents provocateurs (over 200,000 in 1928; Bernstein, 1960a:149), whose purpose was to "obtain the names of employees who were members of the union, advance strike plans . . . the precipitation of a strike before the union was prepared, and the discrediting of union leadership with the membership" (Bernstein, 1960a:150–1); (c) bribing union officials into quietude; (d) blacklisting union workers; (e) forcing workers to sign binding oaths and "yellow dog contracts" (i.e., a written agreement in which the worker promised to be non-union and remain that way and to refrain from organizing drives) before they could work in an open shop; (f) moving production facilities from unionized to non-unionized plants in "industrial satellites" and in the South (Gordon et al., 1982) and even some entire industries (e.g., textiles) to the South, where there were few unions; (g) organizing national lobbies against proposed legislation excluding unions from the Sherman Act and against pro-labor legislation generally; and (h) promoting and sponsoring trade schools, industrial education, and employer apprenticeship programs (culminating in 1913 in the National Association of Corporation Schools) to increase the supply of non-union skilled workers (Bonnett, 1922:26; Brandes, 1976:Ch. 6; Nelson, 1975:99).

III. *Efforts to decrease the efficacy of the collective actions of unions to deepen their organization constitute the third category of employer actions.* These, too, were official OS/AP movement policies. Here the employer associations (a) furnished employers with strike breakers (often, as we noted above, unskilled immigrants or blacks from the South), (b) subsidized and policed firms engaged in open-shop battles, harassed those businesses not fully committed to the OS/AP, and even imposed "severe sanctions" (Bernstein, 1960a:155) on firms violating "rules which required that members obtain the approval of the [National Metal Trades Association] for agreements with their employees . . ."; and (c) used the local police, state militia, and private agents to harass union leaders, suppress the free speech of strikers and organizers, break strikes, and generally repress with force the movement.

IV. *The final set of employer actions limited the structure of political "opportunities" (Tilly, 1978) available to the working class by delegitimating unionism, hindering mobilization, and raising the costs of collective actions of unions.* Concretely, OS/AP organizations elicited the aid of influential third parties through (a) an intensive propaganda effort intended both to educate the public as to the "true meaning" of unionism (Steigerwalt, 1964; Perlman and Taft, 1935) and to legitimate their repressive anti-union tactics and (b) the use of local, state, and federal legislation to cripple unions. To get their message across, OS/AP employers and associations boycotted unfriendly newspapers, enrolled friendly editors and journalists into the cause, and published and distributed to civic organizations and libraries millions of pamphlets extolling the virtues of the open shop, and painting unions (or their leaders) as "unprincipled," "radical," "corrupt," "murderous," "unconstitutional," "unholy," "lazy," and so on (Foner, 1964:49; Steigerwalt, 1964).

Vastly more important than propaganda, however, were employer maneuvers bringing the courts fully into labor-capital struggles. Some laws were explicitly enacted to ban revolutionary unions; other laws or statutes were interpreted by the courts to suppress the activities of non-revolutionary unions. Among the former the most important were the antisyndicalism laws, still on the books of twenty-two states and territories in 1931, which were used to decimate the Industrial Workers of the World by imprisoning or deporting its members (Perlman and Taft, 1935; Witte, 1932). Among the latter appear to have been (a) state laws prohibiting restraint of trade, conspiracy, and malice and (b) the federal Sherman Anti-Trust and Clayton Acts of 1890 and 1914, respectively, interstate commerce laws, and the "conspiracy statute" (Witte, 1932; Bernstein, 1960a).

The courts used either state laws or federal statutes to outlaw the following actions by legal non-revolutionary unions: (a) sympathy strikes, (b) strikes to obtain closed shops, (c) strikes to force employers to rescind "yellow-dog" contracts, (d) picketing, and (e) boycotts and secondary boycotts (Witte, 1932; Berman, 1930; Frankfurter and Greene, 1930; Bernstein, 1960a). Additionally, the legality of the "yellow-dog" contract was upheld by the U.S. Supreme Court in 1917 (Bernstein, 1960a). Thus, the OS/AP movement consciously capitalized on extant legislation or court rulings to demobilize labor's self-organization and limit its collective action. The very *right* of organized labor to exist was jeopardized by these rulings.

Perhaps the most effective anti-union legislation were the various anti-trust laws, especially the Sherman Act (Bernstein, 1960a:206), because the courts could issue an injunction restraining organized labor from pursuing certain acts if those acts could be interpreted as illegal restraint of trade. Injunctions were ordered in massive numbers during the pre-New Deal years; indeed, the period was characterized as "Government by injunction" (Frankfurter and Greene, 1930:1). Witte (1932:84) counted "definite references" to the issuance of 1872 injunctions during the years 1880–1931, half of which—921—were directed against labor in the 1920s. (Only 223 injunctions were sought but not granted.) The consequences of defying injunctions, moreover, were quite severe; unions were subject to damage suits and union leaders and members were fined, prosecuted, and if convicted, imprisoned. In a period when many work stoppages occurred over the issue of union organizing, "a union calculating a strike call contended with the strong possibility, if not probability, that a restraining order would issue" (Bernstein, 1960a:201). This, of course, was precisely why employers asked for injunctions and why the NCF and the NAM, the latter both directly and indirectly through its networks of open-shop associations, mobilized their organizational and financial resources to persuade Congress, until 1932, to shelve or table *all* anti-injunction bills and legislation exempting organized labor from the Sherman Act (Foner, 1964:76, 299–301, 338; Steigerwalt, 1964:128–38).

By acts of commission and omission, the state was therefore a very active participant in union-busting in the first third of the 20th century. Supreme Court Justice Louis Brandeis, in a dissenting opinion in the Bedford Cut Stone Co. case (1927) involving the right of organized labor to refrain from working on stone cut by unorganized labor, perhaps best expressed the consequences for unionism of the courts' interpretations: "If on the undisputed facts of this case, refusal to work can be enjoined, Congress created by the Sherman Act an instrument for imposing restraints upon labor which reminds of involuntary servitude" (quoted in Witte, 1932:72). . . .

CONCLUSION

Trade union organizing shares with most political and economic movements attributes common to any collective action. Some inferences we draw from this investigation therefore have broad relevance for studies of social movements more generally, especially those employing one variant or another of resource mobilization theory. We emphasize, in particular, the importance of "countermovements" (McCarthy and Zald, 1977), their organization and collective action. Repression, counter-organization, and the intervention of powerful third parties have received some attention in recent resource-mobilization literature, both conceptual (Tilly, 1978; Marx, 1974) and empirical (Gamson, 1975; Schwartz, 1976; McAdam, 1983). Barken's (1984) analysis of the use by dominant whites of the southern legal system to stymie the civil rights movement provides but one example of the explanatory power of this approach. Our analyses are another, and they further support the commonsensical, but under-researched view that investigations of the organization and collective action of movement participants must also consider the reaction of movement adversaries. It is literally impossible to understand why trade unionists behaved as they did, or how they came to define movement "success" as they did (see Gamson, 1975), without also understanding the actions of capital.

This point is nevertheless quite salient for future studies of unionization. The current research paradigm guiding scholarship on working-class organization and collective action is that of the "rational worker" using "utilitarian logic" to calculate the relative costs and benefits of union membership. (See Fireman and Gamson, 1979, for a general critique of this logic, and Roemer, 1978, for an attempt to circumvent Olson, 1965, by appeals to "collective rationality.") Our knowledge of collective action and collective bargaining has been advanced substantially by this research. However useful for some purposes, though, its application has been exceedingly narrow: most of the studies in this tradition assume that research on working class movements and organizations can somehow safely ignore the behaviors and reactions of employers, the very group that must bear at least some of the ideological, political, and economic "costs" of successful organizing drives by *"their"* employees. This assumption is simply too tenuous to sustain the rather strong inferences of most previous analysts (Bain and Elsheikh, 1976; Fiorito, 1982; Shelfin et al., 1981). Ashenfelter and Pencavel (1969:434) claim, for example, to have formulated and estimated a formal model demonstrating that "a single behavioral relationship can explain the progress of the American labor movement in the twentieth century." That relationship, at least as treated empirically, is entirely innocent of notions of employer counter-mobilization or state repression, and in light of the results presented here, appears statistically and substantively naive.

We have thus far pointed to the general implications of our analyses for both resource mobilization theory and unionization studies. But there is nonetheless something somewhat rare, if not singular, about trade unionism. In addition to being a "social" movement, it is also a class movement, a confrontation between, in this case at least, two classes opposed in their interests and in their visions of a proper way to organize productive activity. (That capital and labor appear to have reconciled their most grievous differences is acknowledged, but the "marriage" is of the "shotgun" sort, partly for the reasons elaborated in this paper and partly for reasons pertaining to a now crumbling "capital-labor" accord reached shortly after World War II; Bowles and Gintis, 1982.) A steady structural tension, however, latent it may be at any point in time, necessarily continues to exist between capital and labor because in our view, it is rooted in the very fabric of capitalism.

Unlike the movements for civil rights, for example (McAdam, 1983; Barken, 1984) or agrarian reform (Schwartz, 1976), or, indeed, most social movements, attempts at labor's self-organization call into question one of the organizing principles of a capitalist democracy. (Some segments of the populist movement did render problematic the fundamental fact of southern commodified agriculture, the crop-lien and tenancy system; Schwartz, 1976.) And, as such, it poses both opportunities and problems for social movement research not so clearly observed in investigations of most other movements. In particular, its *class* dimension must be acknowledged. We would argue that studies of what may be considered movements with "displacement" objectives (Gamson, 1975), such as unionization (at least in certain periods or social formations) or the more radical wing of the southern agrarian revolt, would be better understood if movement analysts were to employ more explicitly the perspectives and theories of class analysis more generally. It is also equally clear, however, that class analysts should more forcefully use concepts and strategies developed in, or at least associated with, the social movement literature. Classes, after all, are organized (or disorganized) entities acting (or not acting) in what they perceive to be their own interests (or they either do not perceive their interests to be obtainable, or they misperceive them). Attention to the dynamics of class struggle or class formation as *movements* should prove fruitful toward reaching an understanding of what classes do or do not do (c.f., Aminzade, 1984; Schwartz, 1976). Research on "displacement" movements may, therefore, both require and facilitate a merging of the sort attempted here of class-analytic and resource-mobilization approaches to social protest.

Our final point: though a utilitarian logic of "cost-benefit" analysis may indeed be an important component of a worker's decision to join a union, it presupposes that union membership was an existing right of the working class, to be embraced or rejected voluntarily by a worker properly imbued with the calculus of economic rationality. In fact it was not. That labor had to struggle—infrequently with the aid of the state but more often against it—for years with a highly organized and determined foe, corporate capital, to obtain that right and to obtain legal protection to exercise that right is often slighted in the social science literature which attempts to develop rather general and formal models of collective action without situating in any serious fashion the conflict within its *class* context. (Labor and social historians are quite sensitive to these matters.) This is social science largely devoid of the people—the Carnegies, the Rockefellers, the Morgans—who procured injunctions and convictions, broke strikes, and busted unions and, in so doing, shaped the course of the labor movement. It is social science which is, at best, incomplete, or at worst, misleading.

Capital's success in disorganizing labor cost the working class dearly: its future mobilization and collective action were hindered; its economic advancement in the market was visibly slowed; and its understanding of itself as a collectivity engaged in common struggle for common objectives was partially shattered, to the degree and where it existed, and stillborn, where it had existed only as an idea, as possibility. Resignation and the fragmentation of interests and organization of a working class already so fraught with internal cleavages and rivalries—a class, at one level, in name only, without common "objective" interests in opposing capital—seriously impeded the process of class formation and generally reduced "the salience of class as the basis of collective identification" (Prezworski, 1977:383). It is worth remembering that the mass insurgency and extraordinarily rapid mobilization of industrial workers in the 1930s were nonetheless centered around that "wholly conventional trade-union objective—a collective bargaining contract" (Brody, 1980:128). This, the "New Deal formula," (Montgomery, 1979), perceptibly exhausted as it appears today, still remains one of the enduring legacies of capital's disorganization of American workers-as-a-class in the first three decades of the twentieth century. . . .

REFERENCES

Aminzade, Ronald. 1984. "Capitalist Industrialization and Patterns of Industrial Protest: A Comparative Urban Study of Nineteenth-Century France." *American Sociological Review* 49:437–53.

Allen, Steven, 1984. "Trade Unions, Absenteeism, and Exit-Voice." *Industrial and Labor Review* 37:331–45.

Ashenfelter, Orley, George Johnson, and John Pencavel. 1972, "Trade Unions and the Rate of

Change of Money Wages in United States Manufacturing Industry." *Review of Economic Studies* 39:27–54.

Ashenfelter, Orley and John Pencavel. 1969. "American Trade Union Growth, 1900–1960." *Quarterly Journal of Economics* 83:434–48.

Bain, George and Farouk Elsheikh. 1976. *Union Growth and the Business Cycle: An Econometric Analysis*. Oxford: Basil Blackwell.

Barken, Steven, 1984. "Legal Control of the Southern Civil Rights Movement." *American Sociological Review* 49:552–65.

Bendix, Reinhard. 1956. *Work and Authority in Industry: Ideologies of Management in the Course of Industrialization*. Berkeley and Los Angeles: University of California Press.

Berman, Edward, 1930. *Labor and the Sherman Act*. New York: Harper and Brothers.

Bernstein. Irving. 1960a. *The Lean Years: A History of the American Worker*. 1920–1933. Boston: Houghton Mifflin.

———. 1960b. "Union Growth and Structural Cycles." Pp. 73–101 in *Labor and Trade Unionism: An Interdisciplinary Reader,* edited by S. M. Lipset. New York: Wiley.

Bonnett, Clarence. 1922. *Employers Associations in the United States: A Study of Typical Associations*. New York: MacMillian.

Bowles, Samuel, and Herbert Gintis. 1982. "The Crisis of Liberal Democratic Capitalism: The Case of the United States." *Politics and Society* 11:51–93.

Brandes, Stuart. 1976. *American Welfare Capitalism,* 1880–1940. Chicago: University of Chicago Press.

Brody, David. 1960. *Steelworkers in America: The Nonunion Era*. Cambridge: Harvard University Press.

———. 1980. *Workers in Industrial America: Essays on 20th Century Struggles*. New York: Oxford.

Douglas, Paul. 1930. *Real Wages in the United States. 1890–1926*. Boston: Houghton Mifflin.

Edwards, P. K. 1981. *Strikes in the United States. 1881–1974*. New York: St. Martin's Press.

Edwards, Richard. 1979. *Contested Terrain: The Transformation of the Workplace in the Twentieth Century*. New York: Basic Books.

Faulkner, Harold. 1951. *The Decline of Laissez Faire. 1897–1917*. White Plains, NY: M. E. Sharpe.

Fireman, Bruce and William Gamson. 1979. "Utilitarian Logic in the Resource Mobilization Perspective." Pp. 8–44 in *The Dynamics of Social Movements: Resource Mobilizaton, Social Control, and Tactics,* edited by J. McCarthy and M. Zald. Cambridge: Winthrop.

Fiorito, Jack. 1982. "American Trade Union Growth: An Alternative Model." *Industrial Relations* 21:123–27.

Fiorito, Jack and Charles Greer. 1982. "Determinates of U.S. Unionism: Past Research and Future Needs." Industrial Relations 21:1–32.

Foner, Philip. 1964. *History of the Labor Movement: Volume III: The Politics and Practices of the American Federation of Labor. 1900–1906*. New York: International Publishers.

———. 1970. "Historical Materialism and Labor History." Pp. 115–20 in *For a New America,* edited by D. Eakins. New York: Vintage Books.

———. 1980. *History of the Labor Movement in the United States: Volume V: The AFL in the Progressive Era. 1910–1915*. New York: International Publishers.

Frankfuter, Felix and Nathan Greene, 1930. *The Labor Injunction*. New York: MacMillian.

Gable, Richard. 1950. *A Political Analysis of an Employers Association: The National Association of Manufacturers*. Chicago: Unpublished Ph.D. Dissertation, The University of Chicago.

Gamson, William. 1975. *The Strategy of Social Protest*. Homewood, IL: Dorsey Press.

Goldfield, Michael. 1982. "The Decline of Organized Labor: NLRB Union Certification Election Results." *Politics and Society* 11:167–209.

———. 1984. "The Causes of U.S. Trade Union Decline and Their Future Prospects." *Research in Political Economy* 7:81–158.

Gordon, David, Richard Edwards, and Michael Reich. 1982. *Segmented Work, Divided Workers: The Historical Transformation of Labor in the United States*. Cambridge: Cambridge University Press.

Lescohier, Don and Elizabeth Brandeis. 1935. *History of Labor in the United States. 1896–1932: Volume III, Working Conditions and Labor Legislation*. New York: MacMillian.

Lewis, Gregg H. 1963. *Unionism and the Relative Wage in the United States*. Chicago: University of Chicago Press.

Mandel, Ernest. 1968. *Marxist Economic Theory, Volume I*. New York: Monthly Review Press.

Marx, Gary. 1974. "Thoughts on a Neglected Category of Social Movement Participant: The Agent Provocateur and the Informant." *American Journal of Sociology* 80:402–42.

McAdam, Doug. 1983. "Tactical Innovation and the Pace of Insurgency." *American Sociological Review* 48:735–53.

McCarthy, John and Mayer Zald. 1977. "Resource Mobilization and Social Movements: A Partial Theory." *American Journal of Sociology* 82:1212–41.

McKelvey, Jean. 1952. *AFL Attitudes Toward Production: 1900–1932*. Ithaca, NY: The New York State School of Industrial and Labor Relations, Cornell University.

Montgomery, David. 1979. *Worker's Control in America: Studies in the History of Work, Technology, and Labor Struggles*. Cambridge: Cambridge University Press.

Morris, Aldon. 1981. "Black Southern Sit-In Movement: An Analysis of Internal Organization." *American Sociological Review* 46:744–67.

Nadworny, Milton. 1955. *Scientific Management and the Unions, 1900–1932: An Historical Analysis*. Cambridge, MA: Harvard University Press.

National Industrial Conference Board. 1933. *Collective Bargaining Through Employee Representation*. New York: NICB.

Nelson, Daniel. 1975. *Managers and Workers: Origins of the New Factory System in the United States. 1880–1920*. Madison: University of Wisconsin Press.

———. 1982. "The Company Union Movement. 1900–1937: A Reexamination." *Business History Review* 56:335–57.

Neumann, George and Ellen Rissman. 1984. "Where Have All the Union Members Gone?" *Journal of Labor Economics* 2:175–93.

Oberschall, Anthony. 1973. *Social Conflict and Social Movements*. Englewood Cliffs, NJ: Prentice-Hall.

Offe, Claus and Helmut Wiesenthal. 1980. "Two Logics on Collective Action: Theoretical Notes on Social Class and Organizational Form." *Political Power and Social Theory* 1:67–115.

Olson, Mancur. 1965. *The Logic of Collective Action: Public Goods and the Theory of Groups*. Cambridge, MA: Harvard University Press.

Orloff, Ann. 1983. "Labor and the State: Labor Legislation in America, 1897–1898: A Time Series Analysis." Paper presented before the Annual Meetings of the American Sociological Association.

Perlman, Selig and Philip Taft. 1935. *History of Labor in the United States. 1896–1932. Volume IV: Labor Movements*. New York: MacMillan.

Przeworski, Adam. 1977. "Proletariat Into a Class: The Process of Class Formation from Karl Kautsky's 'The Class Struggle' to Recent Controversies." *Politics and Society* 7:373–401.

Radosh, Ronald. 1970. "The Corporate Ideology of American Labor Leaders from Gompers to Hillman." Pp. 125–52 in *For a New America*, edited by D. Eakins. New York: Vintage.

Reich, Michael and R. Edwards. 1978. "Political Parties and Class Conflict in the United States." *Socialist Review* 8:37–57.

Roemer, John. 1978. "Neoclassicism, Marxism, and Collective Action." *Journal of Economic Issues* 12:147–61.

Rubin, Beth, Larry J. Griffin, and Michael Wallace. 1983. "Provided Only That Their Voice Was Strong: Insurgency and Organization of American Labor from NRA to Taft-Hartley." *Work and Occupations* 10:325–47.

Schwartz, Michael. 1976. *Radical Protest and Social Structure: The Southern Farmers' Alliance and Cotton Tenancy. 1880–1890*. New York: Academic.

Shelfin, Neil, Leo Troy, and C. Timothy Koeller. 1981. "Structural Stability in Models of American Trade Union Growth." *Quarterly Journal of Economics* 96:77–88.

Snyder, David. 1975. "Institutional Setting and Industrial Conflict: A Comparative Analysis of France, Italy, and the United States." *American Sociological Review* 40:259–78.

Steigerwalt, Albert. 1964. *The National Association of Manufacturers. 1895–1914: A Study in Business Leadership*. Ann Arbor, MI: Bureau of Business Research, Graduate School of Business Administration.

Stone, Katherine. 1975. "The Origins of Job Structures in the Steel Industry." Pp. 27–84 in *Labor Market Segmentation*, edited by D. Gordon. Lexington, MA: Heath.

Taylor, Frederick. [1911] 1947. *Scientific Management*. New York: Harper and Row.

Therborn, Goran. 1983. "Why are Some Classes More Successful Than Others." *New Left Review* 138:37–56.

Tilly, Charles. 1978. *From Mobilization to Revolution*. Reading, MA: Addison-Wesley.

Troy, Leo. 1965. "Trade Union Membership. 1897–1962." *Review of Economics and Statistics* 47:93–113.

Vittoz, Stan. 1978. "World War I and the Political Accommodation of Transitional Market Forces: The Case of Immigration Restriction." *Politics and Society* 8:49–78.

Walter, Pam and Richard Rubinson. 1983. "Educational Expansion and Economic Output in the United States. 1890–1960: A Production Function Analysis." *American Sociological Review* 48:480–93.

Weinstein, James. 1968. "Gompers and the New Liberalism. 1900–1909." Pp. 101–104 in *For a New America,* edited by D. Eakins. New York: Vintage Books.

———. 1970. *The Decline of Socialism in America. 1912–1925*. New York: Monthly Review Press.

Weisskopf, Thomas, Samuel Bowles, and David Gordon. 1983. *Hearts and Minds: A Social Model of U.S. Productivity Growth*. Brookings Papers on Economic Activity.

Witte, Edwin. 1932. *The Government in Labor Disputes*. New York: McGraw-Hill.

Wolman, Leo. 1923. *The Growth of American Trade Unions. 1880–1923*. New York: National Bureau of Economic Research.

———. 1936. *Ebb and Flow in Trade Unionism*. New York: National Bureau of Economic Research.

Wright, Erik. 1978. *Class, Crisis, and the State*. LOndon: New Left Books.

ARTICLE 9

Social Movements in Organizations: Coup d'Etat, Insurgency, and Mass Movements

MAYER N. ZALD
MICHAEL A. BERGER

SOCIAL MOVEMENTS IN CORPORATE HIERARCHICAL ORGANIZATIONS

... Corporate organizations are those in which the units and facilities are "owned" by the group legitimated as the corporate office. That is, legitimate authority resides in the center (e.g., with board of directors or chief executive officers). Among themselves corporate organizations may vary in the extent of decentralization-centralization of this legitimate authority. Federated organizations, on the other hand, are those types in which the units (locals, departments, chapters, or partners) have clear property rights and discretion which is established in the constitution of the focal organization (and possibly backed up by force of law). Moreover, they may have legitimate rights in the selection of executives and the establishment of policy. Voluntary membership associations, in contrast, can be either corporate or federated, but their distinguishing characteristic is that the members contribute resources upon which the central authorities depend. Thus authorities of voluntary associations have less discretion vis-à-vis organizational policy and are often in a precarious position vis-à-vis members (Clark and Wilson 1961). Federated and voluntary organizations might therefore be called "upside down" organizations, for the flow of dependence is inverted from our conception of hierarchically arranged organizations.

All of these organizations may experience social movements. Hierarchical organizations differ from others in two major regards which have consequences for their political life. First, concentration of authority and power in a hierarchic structure means that there are higher costs of dissent and departures from organizational policy. Second, in such organizations subordinates have less normal access to the choices of major policy and of successors to executive offices. Conversely, in federated and voluntary organizations, units and members control both the resources that can be devoted to combating policies and legitimate access to organizational choice. This leads to two general and interrelated propositions: (1) federated and voluntary organizations are likely to have more open politics take place in corporate hierarchical organizations; (2) when unconventional politics take place in corporate hierarchical organizations, conspiratorial forms are likely to be more prominent.

The argument is not that conspiracies are absent from federated organizations or voluntary associations. Where the stakes are high, a minority may reject the well-institutionalized channels

Zald, Mayer N., & Berger, Michael A. (1971, January). Social movements in organizations: Coup d'etat, insurgency, and mass movements. *American Journal of Sociology, 83,* 823–861. Reprinted with permission of The University of Chicago Press.

of a federated organization in attempting change. Nor are we arguing that corporate organizations are likely to have more phenomena resembling social movements. By raising the probability of success or lowering the costs of participation, open political systems may encourage unconventional political behavior. The major thrust of our argument is that there is a push to conspiracy in corporate hierarchical forms. Let us discuss three types of social movements in corporate organizations: coups, insurgencies, and mass movements. For each type we define the phenomena, specify determinants, discuss process, and describe likely outcomes. Illustrative hypotheses are given.

Organizational Coup d'Etat

In his book *Coup d'Etat*, Luttwak (1969) argues that a coup is not an assault from the outside; it is a seizure of power from within. Second, he points out that a coup is usually politically neutral, with no immediate goal other than succession. Whatever policy emerges is a matter for the postcoup regime. Finally, he asserts that the technique used in a coup is not to confront, overwhelm, or smash down the adversary through sheer weight of power. On the contrary, it is a technique of judo in which the opponent's own advantages of weight and balance are turned into weapons against him. Luttwak therefore defines a coup in a nation-state as "the infiltration of a small but critical segment of the state's apparatus which is used to displace the government from the control of the remainder" (p. 12). Many coups involve subalterns, but a coup may involve one segment of a ruling junta ousting the current head of state.

By analogy, an organizational coup can be defined as the infiltration of a small but critical group from within the organization's structure to effect an unexpected succession. The term "infiltration" is used to denote the secrecy with which the plan is carried out. The small but critical group includes the palace guard of the chief executive officer (CEO) or some combination of inside and outside directors. The primary goal is succession, though less proximal goals of policy and change are implied in the political action.

Organizational coups can be contrasted with expected replacements (such as limited terms in office or retirement) and sudden successions which result from death. In the former, the succession is expected and conducted with a high degree of public awareness. In the latter, the succession is unexpected, yet once the initial shock of death wears off, replacement activities follow the regular institutionalized procedures. Organizational coups, on the other hand, are unexpected and deviate substantially from routinized procedures. That is to say, they are planned and executed without the CEO's knowledge or public awareness; otherwise the CEO would be able to retaliate. In addition, they involve the quick appointment of a new successor, which is at variance with the more usual procedure of search, trial, interviews, and selection. Five examples of organizational coups have been uncovered; here are brief illustrations of the climactic events in three of them.

> *[Interpublic:] For Marion Harper, Jr., the sky fell shortly after 10:00* A.M. *on Thursday, November 9, 1967. The setting was the windowless boardroom of the Interpublic Group, the world's largest advertising business, on the forty-fourth floor of Manhattan's Time-Life building. The occasion was a special meeting of Interpublic's board of directors with Harper presiding as chairman and chief executive officer. . . .*
>
> *. . . For nineteen years Harper, now fifty-one, had been in charge of the burgeoning organization. His energy, his ideas, his ambitions had pushed, dragged, bulled Interpublic into a $700 million business. . . .*
>
> *A twelve page agenda had been prepared and distributed in advance. . . . When Harper brought the first item before the board, one of the directors interrupted and requested permission to question Taggart, the chief financial officer, on the group's current financial situation. . . . Harper, suspecting nothing, allowed the question. . . . Another director spoke. Taking note of the gravity of the situation he moved that the first order of business be the replacement of the chief*

executive officer. The motion was immediately seconded. The vote: six ayes, one abstention. [Wise 1968, p. 136]

[Ford Motor Company] It was a press conference compounded of equal parts of vinegar and butter. The scene was a Detroit gathering called by auto mogul Henry Ford II last week to announce that the Ford Motor Company board of directors had voted to relieve President Semon E. Knudsen of his duties.

The bitter taste stemmed from Knudsen's calling of his own press conference an hour and a half earlier to say he was "puzzled by this sudden and unexpected action." Beaten to the punch, Chairman Ford was maneuvered out of the standard references in such situations to "a mutual understanding" and was forced to fall back on . . . "Sometimes these things just don't work out."

The butter, on the other hand, was what wouldn't melt in the mouth of Knudsen's arch-rival, ambitious Lido A. Iacocca, whose satisfied smile was in sharp contrast to the sober expressions on the other Ford executives present. ["Behind the Palace Revolt at Ford" 1969, p. 138]

[RCA] Robert W. Sarnoff always had a tough act to follow. His father, David, a one-time wireless operator who rose to brigadier general, had taken a relatively small company in the fledgling electronics business and, over four decades, built it into the giant RCA Corporation. Bobby—he was never able to shake either the nickname or the label of "the general's boy"—had ideas of his own, and after his father left the top spot at RCA, he pursued them vigorously. But two recessions and one gross miscalculation took their toll—last week, in a move that shocked Wall Street and company officials, RCA's board of directors ousted Bobby Sarnoff, 57, as chairman and chief executive officer. ["His Master's New Voice" 1975, p. 79]

In the Ford Motor case and the RCA case, the stories relate how senior executives organized and presented a bill of particulars to outside board members and key stockholders and pushed for the coup. In the most recent case we have found, that of the firing of Franklin Jarman of Genesco, a similar conspiracy from below is reported (Mullaney 1977).

Determinants. What are some of the conditions that make coups more likely in one kind of hierarchic corporate structure than in another? First, the subalterns must be quite dependent on the executives for their positions. The ethos of business corporations is to stress executive loyalty at the same time senior executives serve on the sufferance of the CEOs (Kanter 1977). If they did not serve on the sufferance of the CEO, they could criticize him. On the other hand, in universities deans and professors have tenure and can call for the resignation of the president. While there might be some negative consequences, they cannot be fired. We have not found any cases of coups in universities. We have found several cases in which deans and/or professors have openly called for the resignation of the president or the circumscription of his role.

Second, a coup, in which subordinates want one of their own to be the CEO, cannot work in organizations in which the CEO is often or usually brought in from the outside. One could conspire to have a university president forced out, but the conspirators would not have a guarantee that the successor would come from inside. The same argument applies to metropolitan school systems. In contrast, in business corporations, especially large ones, the CEO is rarely brought in from the outside. Third, the conspirators need access to those board members who control the key resources, votes. And some board members may be more important than others. They may control large blocks of shares or major lines of credit or contrast. Fourth, corporations often have officer-directors. Unlike almost any other corporate form, there is often continuing interaction between the CEO's subalterns and his employers (indeed some subalterns may even serve as "employers" if they are internal directors).

Finally, when are coups d'etat most likely to occur? Chief executive officers with recent records of bad decisions and poor performance are more likely to be faced with coup attempts than others. Yet even CEOs who have decent records of profit performance are not immune if they have created enemies. We have found several cases in which interpersonal hostilities and power battles led to the coup. For instance, if the CEO has recently taken steps leading to the demotion or lowered power of subalterns, it is likely that he has incurred their enmity. Until the demotion is fixed and they are isolated from power, the potential for a coup attempt is very high.

Processes of Interaction. Regardless of the sources of their grievances, once a conspiratorial group has agreed to attempt to force out an executive, it must gain access to key board members or stockholders to carry the battle. Two authority processes must be considered. First, the CEO must be neutralized. Otherwise he can counterattack either by mounting a persuasive argument or by isolating and dismissing the conspirators. Second, board members and stockholders must be convinced. They must see the high cost of maintaining the current CEO arrangement. In two of the cases we have examined, board members had been contacted at earlier times but took no action then. The second time around, a more persuasive case was made. Moreover, it is clear that the CEOs were always surprised by the action and were often out of touch with their offices. In the RCA case described above, Sarnoff was visiting plants in Australia when the conspiracy took place. In the Genesco case, Franklin Jarman was on his honeymoon in Jamaica.

In other cases a coup attempt may occur when the CEO is sick, and a sick CEO may recognize that a force out is coming. For instance, recently Donald Kircher was replaced as head of the Singer Manufacturing Company (Hough 1975). He had warned subalterns and the board a year or two earlier that any attempt to use an interim management arrangement to replace him while he was sick would be fought. But when he became sick again and realized that he would not be able to resume the mantle, he easily gave up the office.

Outcomes. What are the outcomes of a coup? At least two types must be distinguished: the consequences or results for the participants and the consequences for the structural operation of the organization. The coup attempt may fail, as when conspirators marshal support but board members dismiss the attempt as self-serving for the conspirators, and the CEO isolates or dismisses them. If successful, the coup may lead to a change in personnel, a change in the system, but have few other consequences, little change of the system. Students of coups in nation-states have remarked that coups often have little impact upon the larger society because they are not related to any underlying structural change. Coups in organizations may have relatively few consequences below the elite level. The coup leads to a change in the chief executive and possible to a few shifts down to the assistant vice-president level. Beyond that there is no necessary change. Product lines and company policy may be only tangentially at stake. Whether a coup leads to change other than personnel shifts depends upon the connection of the coup to any underlying trends in the organization and its environment. The coup is very important to the immediate participants, but the irony is that a company's long-range profitability is heavily dependent upon industry profitability and the position of the company in the industry. Within the normal range of company performance, who becomes CEO is unlikely to have great impact upon the company (see Lieberson and O'Connor 1972).

In the cases we have examined, organizational coups do not relate to political issues in the larger society, but they do relate to societal or industrial change. First, the CEO's stance on major strategies may have been found to be in error (e.g., the RCA case). Second, a coup may relate to hostile merger or takeover bids. Takeover and merger bids may lead to conversations between the company that expects to take over and factions in the executive office. Thus forcing out a CEO may be partially related to political factions within the organization more or less favorable to the company buying it out. The parallel at the nation-state level occurs when the coup anticipates loss of a war. The coup puts in office a CEO and ruling group more favorable to the potential occupying power or prepares for continuation of the war.

The main themes of our analysis of coups can be expressed as a set of hypotheses (one each for occurrence, process, and outcome).

Hypothesis 1: In corporate hierarchical organizations that (a) do not protect the positions of senior executives and (b) do promote within, (c) provide senior officers acces to board members, and (d) experience poor performance or other undesired situations attributable to the CEO, coup d'etat attempts are more likely to occur than in other types of corporate organizations.

Hypothesis 2: Successful coups are facilitated by surprise CEO neutralization and by the support of the more powerful board members and shareholders.

Hypothesis 3: The first-order effects of a coup are the reshuffling of executive positions; larger changes in the organizational system are rare.

Bureaucratic Insurgency

Bureaucratic insurgency differs from a coup in its target: its aim is not to replace the chief executive but to change some aspect of organizational function. It differs from a mass movement in extent of support and number of adherents. It resembles a coup in that for much of its duration it may be conspiratorial. It resembles some mass movements in that its goals are limited to change in specific aspects of the organization. In nation-states insurgency, as we are defining it, is analogous to the action of a pressure group or professional movement (McCarthy and Zald 1973). It typically involves a limited mobilization of personnel. At the organizational level, bureaucratic insurgency in corporate organizations is an attempt by members to implement goals, programs, or policy choices which have been explicitly denied (or considered but not acted upon) by the legitimate authority of the focal organization. The activity of the insurgents therefore takes place outside the conventional channels of politics of the organization.

Determinants. Bureaucratic insurgency is most likely to be found in organizations or organizational units which have strong normative elements or organizations which are dependent upon staff who have strong professional-ideological and moral commitments. These normative commitments provide personnel with reference bases to evaluate organizational products, priorities, and procedures. (On normative, coercive, and utilitarian compliance bases, see Etzioni [1961]; see also Clark and Wilson [1961] and Zald and Jacobs, in press.) The participants in bureaucratic insurgency may also includc thc subalterns of executives, but usually they range deeply into the organization, throughout middle management and, in organizations using professionals on the line, down to the line staff.

When the desired activity or change has been explicitly denied, bureaucratic insurgency may take the form of conspiracy. Here, the insurgents know they are pursuing disapproved lines of action (i.e., using organizational time and resources in ways which have been countermanded by authority). If the insurgency is reformist or narrow, discovery of the conspiracy may lead to repression, not necessarily expulsion.

Often, however, insurgency operates in gray areas where organizational behavior has not been explicitly prescribed. Thus insurgents attempt to establish their own definition of the situation or shift the weighting of priorities. Bureaucratic insurgency is also aided by factionalism or sympathetic support from the organization elite. For example, members of the control apparatus may overlook information which would suggest that a conspiratorial insurgency is actually taking place. The well-known phrase "You can do it, but I don't want to know about it" is a case in point.

A conspiratorial bureaucratic insurgency is thus facilitated by a low capacity for surveillance on the part of the central authorities. The effect of limited surveillance is compounded by organizational complexity; the larger the organization, the more diverse its structure, the more autonomous the units, and the more imprecise the reporting system, the more likely it is that an insurgency can continue for long periods of time.

We can delineate three major subtypes of insurgency: program or product development, whistle blowing, and policy choice. In program- or product-development insurgency, the insurgents accept the overall structure of authority in goal setting but attempt to introduce new techniques for accomplishing goals or refinements of organizational programs. Middle-level officials or line professionals with discretion in allocating organizational resources, the insurgents pursue their own concept of organizational programs or product development while watching over their shoulder for elite interference. Social workers running group programs or allocating welfare funds, army officers developing the armed helicopter, engineers developing the air-cooled engine at General Motors, or HUD bureaucrats attempting to push cities to have more racially integrated housing may all operate and be involved in this first type of bureaucratic insurgency.

Whistle blowing is a form of insurgency in which an insurgent deviates from loyalty norms to describe the disjunction between organizational functioning and public expectations. Whistle blowing may require only one insurgent. For instance, A. Ernest Fitzgerald, a systems analyst for the Defense Department, testified to the Senate on the massive cost overruns in building the Lockheed C-A5 cargo plane ("Defense: Ernest Fitzgerald RIF" 1969). Fitzgerald acted by himself, but more organized whistle blowing is feasible. Underground newspapers can serve as outlets for private information that will discredit the elites.

A third type of bureaucratic insurgency focuses upon the main goals and policy choice of the organization. In 1949 the "admirals' revolt" questioned policies of the Defense Department that seemed to lead to a diminished role for the navy ("Revolt of the Admirals" 1949). Once the insurgency came out in the open, it began to resemble a mass movement. The difference between mass movement and insurgency lies in the greater openness of the former, the number of people involved. The admirals' revolt was an insurgency at the top that was taken to higher authorities, Congress and the public. (The route was to Congress because the Defense Department was controlled by the executive.) One suspects that this form of large-scale and open insurgency at the top occurs only in corporate situations in which the insurgents have some degree of protection (e.g., good retirement plans or high job mobility) or in which the issue, the reward, the prize, is vital to the interests of the contesting elite.

External Support and Authority Response. Whereas the organizational coup d'etat requires the involvement of key board members, a wider range of external supports is necessary in insurgency. For instance, whistle blowing is fully dependent upon external support, for by definition organizational authorities have been unresponsive and typically have attempted to quash complaints. The insurgency may also be aided by explicit material support. Army officers developing the armed helicopter cooperated with small machine-tool companies which helped the officers machine and construct weapon supports and modify the helicopters. Bureaucratic insurgents may also arrange for client groups to request procedures or programs which ultimately serve the insurgent's *and* the client's ends.

If monetary or technical resources are not required, the major support is likely to come through professional and movement perspectives. That is, the insurgency is fueled by societal social movements and a professional ideology which has been previously learned or is currently fashionable. The social and ideological support of a radical caucus or an association of radical urban planners provides such reference support (see Ross 1975).

The response of authorities to insurgency depends at least in part upon their perceptions of the opportunity costs of compliance and the extent to which the insurgency is defined as compatible or incompatible with elite preferences and priorities. Thus some insurgent may be aided by some members of the elite; others may be seen as so removed from elite operative goals that the elite's aim is to quash the insurgency.

Outcomes. Outcomes of insurgency include failure and repression, continued segmental operation, enclave support, and total incorporation.

1. Failure and repression: when authorities discover insurgency and find it opposed to their definition of organizational priorities, they may suppress or disband the insurgency. Members may be expelled from the organization or punished. Officers and priests can be sent to undesirable posts; they can be forbidden to pursue their line of action. However, authorities must calculate not only the degree of threat presented by the insurgents but also the consequences for relevant others, both in and out of the organization, of taking a given line of punishment against the insurgents. To the extent that the insurgents are in fact moral exemplars in the organization, overreaction leads to the possibility that the authorities themselves will be discredited.

Even if the insurgent group is disbanded, however, it can still bring about changes in an organization. If the authorities or other members of the organization take over the decision premises and orientations of the insurgents, over time the organization may change. (Such a paradox parallels the impact of social movements in society: for instance, the Populist movement in the United States gained many of its goals even though many of its leaders never attained power.)

2. Segmental operation is the maintenance of the insurgency over long periods of time with no formal recognition from the center and without change in organizational products or goals. It occurs most often in organizations with multiple goals where there are continuing ambiguities and dilemmas in elite control.

3. Enclave support is likely when external pressures lead the executives to recognize and tolerate the insurgency. This outcome (as in demonstration projects or the setting up of separate departments or units) is likely if organizational goals are multiple and units are only partially interdependent with each other. The formal recognition of an insurgency is similar to Leeds's (1964) process of "protest absorption," but she addressed a much narrower range of phenomena.

4. Total incorporation of the insurgency depends upon the ability of the insurgents to get executive compliance or agreement. If over time the developed program or product can be shown to be consonant with the executive goals, the organization may fully incorporate insurgents' perspectives, and the insurgents may be promoted. Such total incorporation eliminates the raison d'être of the insurgency. The adoption of the armed helicopter and related strategies of mobile infantry as a major component of warfare is an example of a totally incorporated insurgency.

Three hypotheses summarize our argument about insurgency:

> *Hypothesis 4:* Insurgencies are most likely to occur where professional and normative commitments provide an independent base for perspectives on goals, products, and policies.
>
> *Hypothesis 5:* The more complex the organization and the more difficult the surveillance, the longer the duration of the insurgency.
>
> *Hypothesis 6:* The outcome of insurgency depends upon the extent to which the insurgents threaten authority and the costs to authorities of suppression.

Mass Movements: From Protest to Rebellion

As noted earlier, bureaucratic insurgencies may span many levels in an organization. They range from small cabals at the top to the concrete and concerted efforts of middle-level managers and professionals. When small, they may have a conspiratorial cast. On the other hand, as they become more organized, they may develop coordinating committees or caucuses which begin to resemble mass-action movements. As their numbers grow and their tactics move toward withdrawal of labor, petitions, and boycotts, they begin to resemble mass movements.

Mass movements at the nation-state level range from movements of protest to rebellion. They are defined as collective attempts to express grievances and discontent and/or to promote or resist change. They vary in goals from those aimed at melioristic change of specific practices or rights to those aimed at redefining the distribution of power, constitution of rules, and norms of society. By analogy, mass movements in organizations range from the expression of minor grievances (not previously acted upon by authorities) to major attempts to seize control of the organization.

Mass movements differ from insurgencies and coups in number of participants and the visibility of their actions. Coups and insurgencies may be restricted to face-to-face groups and become visible only toward the end of their histories. Mass movements, on the other hand, may be initiated by a small group, but larger numbers must be mobilized if the initiators are to gain their ends. Example of mass movements are work slowdowns, wildcat strikes, mutinies and secessions, mass desertions, and prison riots.

It is important to note that, while the proximal goal of the movement is to change the behavior and goals of organizational authorities and the structure of organizations, the real goal may be changes in the larger society. Thus the student movement disrupted the University of California at Berkeley, Columbia, Harvard, Michigan, and Wisconsin and had as proximal targets changes in administrative behavior. But the real goals were to change the behavior of Lyndon Johnson and Richard Nixon, or in more radical form, the structure of American society. Similarly, a plant seizure or strike may occur to achieve concrete gains, but it also may be a weapon for changing governmental policies or the governmentitself.

A paradox confronts us in thinking about mass movements in organizations. In discussion coups and insurgency, we drew on sparse evidence; on the other hand, when one turns to the study of mass movements, the literature appears rich, systematic, and quantitative. After all, economists and sociologists have been studying the factors related to strikes, industrial conflict, and unionization for two generations. And more recently quite sophisticated quantitative analyses have decomposed the determinants of the numbers, breadth, and duration of strike activity (Britt and Galle 1972). Yet the first glance is deceiving. For strikes need not represent the social movement-like phenomenon of unconventional politics. They may represent a fully institutionalized aspect of the collective-bargaining process. As such the are part of the normal and institutionalized political system of organizations.

Winning union recognition and the legitimation of strikes is part of a social movement process in society and in specific organizations. Yet the union has now become one of the political mechanisms for aggregating preferences and resolving conflicts in the organization. Snyder (1975) has shown that one can predict aggregate strike behavior from aggregate economic variables *after* a collective bargaining system has been institutionalized. From our point of view, institutionalized unions that engage in action are part of normal politics.

Of course there are some parallels between industrial strikes and mass movements in organizations. Both involve mobilization of workers and the calculation of costs and benefits. Yet the mechanisms for mobilization, the costs of organizing for collective action, and the extent of organization and societal support are different enough so that we cannot incorporate wholesale the literature on industrial conflict in our explanation of organizational mass movements.

Determinants of Mass Movements in Organizations. Olson (1965) has taught us that mass movements aim to provide collective goals. The provision of collective goods entails free-rider effects; since the goods will be provided to all, individuals have little incentive to work for their provision. Free-rider problems are overcome in coups and insurgencies: in both forms the benefits accrue to a small group of participants, and in insurgency social control and solidary incentives, coupled with career incentives and normative commitments, suffice to sustain the insurgents.

The question becomes, What organizational conditions facilitate mass action? Our perspective on resource mobilization and the interplay between organizations and their societal environment leads us to five hypotheses about the relations of size, homogeneity, vertical segmentation, exit options, and associational density. All of these hypotheses assume grievances or a gap between the current situation and desired alternatives. (Since our analysis here is more detailed than our earlier discussion, we couple hypothesis and analysis rather than presenting the hypotheses in summary form.)

> *Hypothesis 7:* The larger the size of the subordinate group, the greater the probability of organizational mass movements.

Classical theory and recent studies of riots in cities lead us to expect that larger subordinate groups in organizations are more likely than smaller groups to develop into social movements. There are several reasons for this. Larger groups are more likely to be cut off from superordinates (see below). Larger groups can hide dissidents from authorities; they are more impervious to social control. Moreover, larger subordinate groups are more likely to generate associations within them. In a study of prison riots and confrontations in the largest prisons, Wilsnack (in press) finds that the very largest (over 1,000 inmates) were more likely than the smaller ones in his sample to have experienced nonriot resistance (confrontation, refusal to work). Similarly, Peterson (1968) finds that large campuses were more likely than small ones to have been involved in antiwar protests. For most industries we would expect that large establishments are more easily organized than smaller ones.

> *Hypothesis 8:* The greater the homogeneity within the subordinate group, the more likely that subordinates will challenge superordinates.

On one hand, group consciousness is facilitated by homogeneity and shared values. On the other hand, heterogeneity may facilitate conflict within a subordinate group and the possibility of alliances between subclasses of subordinates and superordinates. This hypothesis follows Kerr and Siegel (1954). Thus we would expect that organizations with little occupational differentiation would be more likely to have superordinate-subordinate conflicts.

> *Hypothesis 9:* The greater the vertical segmentation, the more likely that grievance channels, mobility channels, and communication channels in general are blocked.

This hypothesis has been proposed in the social movement literature (see Oberschall 1973) and offered as an explanation for strike proneness (see Kerr and Seigel 1954). Of course it dates back at least to Pareto. In organizations in which occupational status and ethnic class status are overlaid, we would expect segmentation to be especially strong and both within-group solidarity and the chances for resentment to be high.

> *Hypothesis 10:* The more difficult or costly it is to exit and the greater the commitment to the incentives of the organization, the more likely social movements are to form.

In some ways this hypothesis, which just restates Hirschman's (1970) exit-voice thesis, parallels Thibaut and Kelley's (1959) analysis of "comparison-level alternatives." Thibaut and Kelley, of course, were interested in whether people continued their line of action within a social interchange or moved outside that interchange. It is apparent that different personnel in organizations and positions are confronted with differences in comparison-level alternatives. The value of the comparison-level alternatives can be broken into two components—the cost of exit and the value, negative or positive, of the perceived option once attained. Comparison level is the net value of the current situation or line of action minus the cost of exit and the value of the goal, once obtained. Some organizations have extremely costly exits. Military institutions raise the costs of exit very high. Nevertheless, it is apparent that exit is less costly in the army than in the navy at sea. Under relatively similar levels of disaffection and grievance, we would expect soldiers to mix use of desertion and protest, whereas sailors at sea use only mutiny. Blake's (1976) study of military resistance to the Vietnam war reports cases of mutinies in military prisons and among troops on the line (refusals to move into combat), but it is our impression that the number of actual mutinies on the line is much lower than in the more contained prison situation. All of the mutinies that Lammers (1969) studied were naval ones. There are, of course, cases of whole units of armies deserting; these should probably be seen as secessions. They are not protests of the bottom against the top; instead, they are led by dissident officers who disagree with either the treatment of their units by the authorities or the policies of authorities in prosecuting the war and in relation to subject populations (see Solzhenitsyn 1973).

Earlier we noted that strike rates do not necessarily reflect social movements in organizations; they do, however, reflect disagreements with management offers or existing conditions. With regard to the hypothesis under consideration, Stern (n.d.) finds a negative correlation, over communities, between quit rates and strike rates.

A final derivation from the exit-voice hypothesis can be suggested. The classical situation for exits is free markets with low costs for information and transportation. There buyers or sellers easily compare options, and consumers switch from seller to seller with no protest. However, our hypothesis suggests that consumer protests increase as monopoly increases—a relationship amply confirmed by American history—and monopoly can be defined as the opposite of exit choice. Monopoly exists when a single seller controls the sale of a good and there are no close substitutes for it.

The exit-voice hypothesis has a strategic role in accounting for the structural conditions of mass movements in organizations. First, it allows us to account for variation within an industry (defined as a set of organizations offering somewhat similar products) of two forms of expressing dissatisfaction, exit and voice. Second, it helps to provide an answer to Olson's question: Why collective action, when collective action is accompanied by free riders? The implication of Hirschman's argument is that, if one option for individuals, exit, is removed, an individual must weight taking no action against taking some action that will promise a surplus of benefits. Stated differently, the removal of the exit option raises the comparative discounted benefits of the voice option. But Olson's challenge still remains. Our next hypothesis treats it more directly.

> *Hypothesis 11:* The greater the associational density and the higher the proportion of organizational participants who are members of associations, the easier it is to mobilize.

A major part of the critique of the mass-society theory of social movement has been that people who are most involved in voluntary associations and political organizations are also more likely to be involved in social movement action (see Oberschall 1973). There is supporting evidence in organizations. Although not dealing with social movement participation, Lipset, Trow, and Coleman's (1956) study of the International Typographical Union makes it clear that the associationally dense culture of the ITU facilitated political involvement. Similarly, studies of the student protests find that antiwar protest was correlated with the proportion of students in left organizations (Peterson 1968). And Von Eschen,

Kirk, and Pinard (1971) found that early participants in the civil-rights-movement sit-ins were likely to be part of established, politically oriented organizations, often student based. But if the hypothesis said only that members of ideologically committed associations were more likely to take action than members of uncommitted associations or ideologically committed individuals, it would not say much. Its real thrust is to argue that belonging to associations and networks eases the cost of information flow and mobilization. In relation to Olson's question, it suggests that, even if the associations are not formed to pursue the specific target of collective action, a dense associational field within a hierarchical organization facilitates internal social movements.

Our last hypothesis in this series relates to organizational recruitment of participants.

> *Hypothesis 12:* The more an organization recruits members critical of existing conditions, the more likely it is to generate internal mass movement.

Although obvious, Hypothesis 12 reminds us that issues and grievances within organizations are developed in the larger society. Since organizations may draw upon different segments of society for subordinates, "exactly similar" internal conditions may be responded to and redefined by recruitment of members from varying backgrounds. The issues of the multiversity and the war in Vietnam could have been defined as grievances in South Dakota and Alabama as well as at Wisconsin and Berkeley. That they were responded to differently in academic communities is probably as much a result of self-selection as the internal organization of universities. A similar argument about differential recruitment applies to the locus of social movements in prisons and in manufacturing industries.

The hypotheses about mass movements presented above deal with the factors facilitating mobilization within organizations, but they do not deal with the goals of mass movements. Nor do they deal with the support and control of movements from both within and without the organization.

Goals, Facilitation, and Control. Mass movements in organizations range from narrow protests against specific organizational practices (e.g., the quality of food in the cafeteria) to shopping lists of practices, calls for the restructuring of authority or changes in the relationship of the organization to other elements of the society, and, at the broadest level, the restructuring of society itself. Let us examine the interaction among the goals of the movement, indirect and direct support, and the response of authorities.

When goals are narrow, the movement and the response of authorities are usually only weakly linked to external factors, either ideologically or materially. (To be sure, the standards for judging conditions internal to the organization may relate to the conception of adequate conditions in the society; e.g., what is adequate food in a prison in Turkey will not be seen as adequate in an American prison.) Indirectly, however, even narrow issues implicate the relationship of the organization to society. For example, the quality of food is related to the budget of the organization, and addressing specific grievances may be constrained by organizational resources and resource dependencies.

When the goals of the movement are broader, encompassing change in the authority structure of the organization in the larger society, we find the movement deeply dependent upon the larger society for the ideological acceptability of the goals; such dependency reshapes the response to the movement of external actors. In recent years, for instance, workers in England and France have seized plants which were about to be closed or have massive layoffs. Given the much more extensive nationalization of industry in these countries than in the United States and given ideologies of worker participation in management and socialism, such attempts at worker control have received both financial and political support. Similar moves to close plants in the United States are met with stoicism, some union bargaining, some community protest, but little governmental intervention or attempts to shift the criterion of authority or ownership.

External material and coercive resources may be mobilized by either the movement or authorities. Strikers are dependent upon several kinds of external resources—in particular, money for food and the honoring of the strike by other potential employees. Indirectly, the society supports or constrains the movement by its general provision of resources. For instance, Thieblot and Cowin (1972) have shown that the length of strikes in American communities is affected by ease of access to welfare payments. The easier the access, the longer the strikes. More directly, strikers may be funded by individuals and organizational contributions to maintain them. Coercive resources are provided or withdrawn by the police, military, and courts, who facilitate or inhibit authorities' and protestors' tactics of reprisal, boycotts, lockouts, etc. The provisional withholding of these coercive resources is based upon the general laws and attitudes governing their deployment and on the specific behavior and linkages between the movement and authorities and external groups.

The response of authorities to mass movements is affected by the goals and tactics of the movement, the autonomy of organizational authorities, and their own ideological predisposition.

Note first that authorities may have little discretion to respond. For instance, prison administrators are not autonomous; they can rarely respond positively to the demands of rioters or protestors. Indeed if the list of demands is long, the protestors recognize this dependency, and their first moves are to ask for the involvement of political authorities. Similarly, in many countries (most Latin American countries, France, etc.) the universities are not autonomous of the ministry of education. A mass movement in the university, especially if it moves into the streets, is responded to by political administrators, not university officials. Where officials do have discretion, several strategic policies may be adapted. Lammers (in press), in a comparative study of the response of university authorities to student movements, lists four general combinations of strategies, tactics, and goals:

Strategies	**Tactics**	**Goals**
Repressive	Fight off	Elimination
Concessive	Buy off	Appeasement
Preventive	Stand off	Nonemergence and dissolution
Experimental	Join in	Copartnership

In the first, the authorities attempt to eliminate the movement and its leaders. They suspend students and use heavy sanctions. In the fourth, the authorities appear to buy in to the goals of the movement and move to align the organization with the goals of the movement. Lammers goes on to assess how different types of tactics will work in different types of universities. For instance, he is skeptical about the viability of the experimental strategy and the tactics of joining in in large universities, and he believes that preventive strategy allows universities to continue to carry out their educational and research missions with less disruption than the use of either concessive or repressive strategies (He does not consider in detail the interaction of opposition and authority strategies.)

Outcomes. In mass movements, immediate outcomes depend upon the ability of partisans and authorities to sustain conflict and the extent to which there are viable options for bargaining. If situations are defined in zero-sum terms, a sheer power calculus can be used. But in open-conflict situations, a variety of symbolic and partial solutions may permit both parties to win. Mass movements with specific and narrow goals may accomplish a change in the system of a specific organization, with little impact upon society: On the other hand, movements with broad goals are likely to fail unless they are part of a broader movement in the society at large.

The ability of partisans and authorities to maintain a conflict depends on their ability to mobilize resources and on the continuous availability of resources. This is especially important in understanding the difference between mass movements in such organizations as universities, with high turnovers of personnel, and those occurring in such organizations as factories, with greater continuity of personnel and organization. Thus, although in a university the movement may be at high tide in the spring, the lack of continuity of student generations and the departure of student leaders at the end of their senior year lead to a high cost of remobilizing resources. On the other hand, workers in continuous organizations with a longer career span of leaders have fewer problems in maintaining continuity. In universities with off-campus student enclaves, however, developing a culture of activism which lasts longer than a student generation might lead to more movement continuity. Similarly, when student politics is more entwined in national politics, professional staff members from national political organizations (e.g., SDS, NAACP, CORE) may supply needed continuity.

As the continuation of the mass movement raises the costs to both members and authorities, search for settlement options takes place, much as in protracted conflict in society at large. Authorities may grant concessions, symbolic or material, or they may legitimate the movement and incorporate it in the decision structure. These would be considered successful outcomes.

The outcome of organizational rebellions may be failure. The reasons are straightforward: organizations are encapsulated in society, and an attempt to change an organization radically may strike at the heart of the authority relations of the larger society as well as in the organization. Such broad-ranging movements can succeed only where they are joined with existing mass rebellions in organizations gives them a life beyond their immediate outcome. For instance, the Soledad Brothers and the events at Kent State live in the symbolic history of American social movements. They recall an ideology and conflict which reminds all adherents of the defined inequities and injustices in society. Therefore, to the extent that mass movements occur and have some continuity, they can lead to the enshrinement and reliving of dramatic events in the future.

Three hypotheses summarize our discussion of mass movements in hierarchical organizations:

Hypothesis 13: Exit-voice options, subordinate homogeneity, vertical segmentation, selective recruitment, size, and associational density affect the costs and extent of solidarity, cleavage, and mobilization.

Hypothesis 14: The goals and duration of mass movements depend upon ideological and material supports in the larger society.

Hypothesis 15: Outcomes of the movement are dependent upon authority responses, continuity of movement participants, and relationship of the movement to movements in the larger society.

Comparative Summary

Earlier we mentioned several dimensions of social movements: breadth of support, goals, tactics, location in the social structure, relation to external support, and duration. Let us compare coups, insurgencies, and mass movement in corporate organizations along these dimensions (table 1 presents the comparison in brief form).

Breadth of Support. Social movements may vary in number of adherents (believers) and number of constituents (individuals or organizations who act in support). As the previous analysis suggests, an organizational coup d'etat involves a small group (the palace guard). Bureaucratic insurgency and mass movement, on the other hand, may include a department in the case of the former and/or significant segments of the organizational population in case of the latter. Breadth is important, for it implies the amount of mobilization costs. In a coup, mobilization is restricted to a small cabal; therefore organization costs may be low. In contrast, insurgency may require the cooperation of a larger group of organizational

TABLE 1 Dimensions of Social Movements in Organizations

DIMENSIONS	MOVEMENT TYPE		
	Organization Coups	*Bureaucratic Insurgency*	*Mass Movements*
Breadth	Small conspiratorial group	Medium-sized enclave or one whistle blower	Large group
Goal	Succession which may or may not lead to future change	Challenging the efficacy of existing norms to effect moderate organizational change	Expressing discontent and promoting or resisting narrow or broad goals
Main tactics	Infiltration and persuasion (e.g., using CEO's own record against him)	Violating rules and procedures without violence	Direct confrontation and possible violence
Activists' location in the organization's social structure	Organization elite	Middle managers and professionals	Lower-level participants
Linkage with external elements	A few key supporters, usually banking interests or key board members	Several important supporters beyond financial interests alone	Elaborate linkages of ideological and material support from society
Duration of over conflict	Conspiracy may brew over long period; very brief actual coup	Varies; can last several years, depending on how long the organization can stand the nonconformity	Varies, from a day to several months, depending on how long the organization can stand the disruption and on the extent to which the movement's members can mobilize for the conflict

participants, some of whom might not evaluate benefits to be worth potential risks. In mass movements, increasing breadth heightens the mobilization problem considerably, thereby leading to increased costs in organizing for collective action.

Goals. Goals can be evaluated in terms of the amount of change desired, the extent to which it involves personnel or distribution of goods, and the extent to which it is a change in the system of authority and relationship to the society. In a coup d'etat, personnel changes are usually the only goal. Structural or policy changes may follow the unexpected succession, but these are not the primary aim of the movement. Furthermore, the goals of personnel replacement is concrete. Bureaucratic insurgency and mass movements, on the other hand, may involve objectives aimed at transforming the basic structure, policy, and resource distribution of the organization itself. As insurgency or a mass movement becomes more involved in the structure and policy of the organization, goals tend to reflect larger abstract values such as mission, justice, and equitable treatment.

Choice of Tactics. Choice of tactics (e.g., violence or nonviolence) depends on a calculus which includes legitimate resource, degree of access to or exclusion from legitimate channels, the cost of using violent tactics, and the perceived utility of tactics in accomplishing strategic goals. In coups the palace guard is likely to have considerable legitimate resources available in terms of their knowledge of internal affairs and their authority to direct large segments of the organization. In addition, their access to board members, years of experience, and cohesion lead one to hypothesize a relatively peaceful choice of tactics, though they may include the threat of resignations.

Bureaucratic insurgents possess fewer legitimate resources, are more excluded from authority, and experience greater risks (e.g., being fired) in the use of violent tactics. In this case, tactics are also likely to be secret and nonviolent. Mass rebellions, on the other hand, represent the farthest extreme. With few legitimate resources for bargaining and limited or no access to authority, tactics may include the use of violence and disruption of the normal functioning of the organization.

Location in the Social Structure. Social movements differ in their location along vertical, horizontal, and sociodemographic dimensions. The vertical dimension refers to the location of adherents in the hierarchical system of the organization. The horizontal dimension includes both the spatial and functional differentiation of the organization. These differentiations provide the basis for the development of within-group solidarity and differentiated concepts of organizational mission, problems, and priorities. The sociodemographic dimension refers to the age-sex-social background of groups that combine to shape orientations and perspectives within the organization.

In an organizational coup, the palace guard is located close to the authorities. That is, the guard actually will be the elite in the status hierarchy and therefore experience very little spatial or functional differentiation. This lack of differentiation should lead to high within-group solidarity and congruence with the board concerning organization mission, problems and priorities. Such congruence is bolstered by similar social backgrounds, age, and sex. In contrast, the orientation of the insurgent department is likely to diverge from that of the authorities and be predicated on the distance from them, on spatial and functional differentiation vis-à-vis other parts of the system, and on wider variations in age, sex, and social background. Finally, rebels will probably be most detached in their orientation from authorities due to high vertical separation, extreme spatial and functional differentiation, and wide variations in age, sex, and social background.

Linkage with External Elements. Coups require linkages with key stockholders, outside board members, or key financial supporters. Insurgencies, on the other hand, are fueled by ideological and professional support. Mass movements with broad goals are heavily dependent upon support from outside the organization. These include the cooperation of agents of control (police), material resources, and political and ideological support.

Duration. Finally, the duration of conflicts varies considerably. The coup, though possibly brewing for a long period, is over in a few short hours; mass movement and insurgency, on the other hand, can continue for long periods of time.

In every case we have been considering in this section, there is a central legitimate authority and a relatively clear hierarchic distribution of power. We now describe social movements in organizations in which the central authority is usually weaker vis-à-vis the units or members. . . .

REFERENCES

Adams, Robert L. 1970. "Conflict over Charges of Heresy in American Protestant Seminaries." *Social Compass* 17 (2): 243–60.

"Behind the Palace Revolt at Ford." 1969. *Business Week* (September 20), pp. 138–41.

Benson, J. Kenneth. 1977. "Organizations: A Dialectical View." *Administrative Science Quarterly* 22 (1): 1–21.

Berg, Ivar. 1962. "The Nice Kind of Union Democracy." *Columbia Forum* 5 (Spring): 18–23.

Berger, Michael. 1975. "Organization Coup d'Etat: The Unexpected Social Movement for Succession." Xeroxed. Nashville, Tenn.: Vanderbilt University, Department of Sociology.

Bergerson, Frederick A. 1976. "The Army Gets an Airforce: The Tactics and Process of Insurgent Bureaucratic Politics." Ph.D dissertation, Vanderbilt University.

"The Big Board's New Mr. Big." 1976. *Newsweek* (May 10), pp. 85–86.

Blake, Joseph A. 1976. "A Case Study of Resistance in 'Total Institutions': The American Military during the War in Vietnam." Paper presented at the meeting of the Southern Sociological Society, Miami, April 9.

Britt, David, and Omer Galle. 1972. "Industrial Conflict and Unionization." *American Sociological Review* 37 (1): 46–57.

Bucher, Rue, and Anselm Strauss. 1961. "Professions in Process." *American Journal of Sociology* 66 (December): 325–34.

Burns, Tom. 1955. "The Reference of Conduct in Small Groups: Cliques and Cabals in Occupational Milieux." *Human Relations* 8 (November): 467–86.

———. 1961. "Micro-politics: Mechanisms of Institutional Change." *Administrative Science Quarterly* 3 (December): 257–81.

Clark, Peter B., and James Q. Wilson. 1961. "Incentive Systems: A Theory of Organizations." *Administrative Science Quarterly* 6 (September): 129–66.

Crozier, Michel. 1964. *The Bureaucratic Phenomenon.* Chicago: University of Chicago Press.

Cyert, Richard, and James March. 1963. *A Behavioral Theory of the Firm.* Englewood Cliffs, N.J.: Prentice-Hall.

Daniels, Arlene Kaplan, and Rachel Kahn-Hut, eds. 1970. *Academics on the Line.* San Francisco: Jossey-Bass.

"Defense: Ernest Fitzgerald RIF." 1969. *Newsweek* (November 17), pp. 106–8.

Edelstein, J. David, and M. Warner. 1975. *Comparative Union Democracy: Organizations and Opposition in British and American Unions.* New York: Halsted.

Epstein, Irwin. 1970. "Specialization, Professionalization and Social Worker Radicalism: A Test of the Process Model of the Professions." *Applied Social Studies* 2 (3): 155–63.

Etzioni, Amitai. 1961. *A Comparative Analysis of Complex Organizations: On Power, Involvement nad Their Correlates.* Glencoe, Ill.: Free Press.

Evan, William. 1965. "Superior-Subordinate Conflict in Research Organizations." *Administrative Science Quarterly* 10 (1): 52–64.

Gamson, William. 1968. *Power and Discontent.* Homewood, Ill.: Dorsey.

Gerstl, Joel, and Glenn Jacobs. 1976. *Professions for the People: The Politics of Skill.* New York: Wiley.

Heirich, Max. 1971. *The Spiral of Conflict: Berkeley 1964*. New York: Columbia University Press.

Hickson, David J., C. R. Hinings. C. A. Lee, R. E. Smeck, and J. M. Pennings. 1971. "A Strategic Contingencies Theory of Intraorganizational Power." *Administrative Science Quarterly* 16 (June): 216–29.

Hirschman, Albert O. 1970. *Exit, Voice and Loyalty: Responses to Decline in Firms, Organizations and States*. Cambridge, Mass.: Harvard University Press.

"His Master's New Voice." 1975. *Newsweek* (November 17), pp. 79–81.

Hough, Patricia. 1975. "How the Directors Kept Singer Stitched Together." *Fortune* (December), p. 100.

Kanter, Rosabeth Moss. 1977. *Men and Women of the Corporation*. New York: Basic.

Kelman, Steven. 1970. *Push Comes to Shove: The Escalation of Student Protest*. Boston: Houghton Mifflin.

Kerr, Clark, and Siegel. 1954. "The Interindustry Propensity to Strike: An International Comparison." Pp. 189–212 in *Industrial Conflict*, edited by Arthur W. Kornhauser, Robert Dubin, and Arthur M. Ross. New York: McGraw-Hill.

Kuhn, James W. 1962. *Bargaining and the Grievance Process*. New York: Columbia University Press.

Lammers, Cornelius J. 1969. "Strikes and Mutinies: A Comparative Study of Organizational Conflicts between Rulers and Ruled." *Administrative Science Quarterly* 14 (December): 558–72.

———. In press. "Tactics and Strategies Adopted by University Authorities to Counter Student Opposition." In *The Dynamics of University Protest*, edited by Donald W. Light. Chicago: Nelson Hall.

Leeds, Ruth. 1964. "The Absorption of Protest: A Working Paper." Pp. 115–35 in *New Perspective in Organizational Research*, edited by W. W. Cooper, H. J. Leavitt, and M. W. Shelly II. New York: Wiley.

Lieberson, Stanley, and James F. O'Connor. 1972. "A Study of Large Corporations." *American Sociological Review* 37 (April): 117–240.

Lipset, Seymour Martin, and Philip G. Altbach, eds. 1969. *Students in Revolt*. Boston: Houghton Mifflin.

Lipset, S. M., Martin Trow, and James Coleman. 1956. *Union Democracy: The Inside Politics of the International Typographical Union*. Glencoe, Ill.: Free Press.

Lipsky, Michael. 1968. "Protest as a Political Resource." *American Political Science Review* 62 (December): 1144–58.

Luttwak, Edward. 1969. *Coup d'Etat: A Practical Handbook*. New York: Knopf.

McCarthy, John, and Mayer N. Zald. 1973. *The Trend of Social Movements in America: Professionalization and Resource Mobilization*. Morristown, N.J.: General Learning.

———. 1977. "Resource Mobilization in Social Movements: A Partial Theory." *American Journal of Sociology* 82 (May): 1212–39.

McNeil, Kenneth, and James D. Thompson. 1971. "The Regeneration of Social Organizations." *American Sociological Review* 36 (August): 24–37.

Martin, John Bartlow. 1954. *Break down the Walls—American Prisons: Present, Past and Future*. New York: Ballantine.

Mullaney, Thomas E. 1977. "6 on Genesco Board Plan Action Today to Oust Chairman." *New York Times* (January 3).

Nagel, Ernest. 1961. *The Structure of Science: Problems in the Logic of Scientific Explanation*. New York: Harcourt, Brace & World.

Needleman, Martin, and Carolyn E. Needleman. 1974. *Guerrillas in the Bureaucracy: The Community Planning Experiment in the United States*. New York: Wiley.

Oberschall, Anthony. 1973. *Social Conflict and Social Movements*. Englewood Cliffs, N.J.: Prentice-Hall.

Olson, Mancur. 1965. *The Logic of Collective Action. Public Goods and the Theory of Groups*. Cambridge, Mass.: Harvard University Press.

Perrow, Charles. 1961. "Goals in Complex Organizations." *American Sociological Review* 26 (October): 859–66.

———. 1970. "Departmental Power and Perspectives in Industrial Firms." Pp. 58–59 in *Power in Organizations*, edited by Mayer N. Zald. Nashville, Tenn.: Vanderbilt University Press.

Peterson, Richard E. 1968. *The Scope of Organized Student Protest in 1967–68. Princeton, N.J.: Educational Testing Service.*

Pettigrew, Andrew. 1973. *The Politics of Organizational Decision-Making*. London: Harper & Row.

Pfeffer, Jeffrey, and Gerald Salancik. 1974. "Organizational Decision Making as a Political Process: The Case of the University Budget." *Administrative Science Quarterly* 19 (June): 135–51.

Pondy, Louis R. 1964. "Budgeting and Intergroup Conflict in Organizations." *Pittsburgh Business Review* 34 (April): 1–8.

"Revolt of the Admirals." 1949. *Time* (October 17), pp. 21–23.

Ross, Robert J. S. 1975. "Advocate Planners and Urban Reforms." Ph.D. dissertation, University of Chicago.

Selznick, Phillip. 1943. "An Approach to a Theory of Bureaucracy." *American Sociological Review* 8 (1): 47–54.

Serrin, William. 1973. *The Company and the Union. The "Civilized Relationship" of the General Motors Corporation and the United Automobile Workers*. New York: Knopf.

Sills, David. 1957. *The Volunteers*. New York: Free Press.

Snyder, David. 1975. "Institutional Settings and Industrial Conflict: Comparative Analyses of France, Italy, and the United States." *American Sociological Review* 40 (June): 259–78.

Snyder, David, and William Kelly. In press. "Strategies for Studying Violence and Social Change: Illustrations from Analyses of Racial Disorders and Implications for Mobilization Research." *In the Dynamics of Mobilization: Resource Mobilization, Tactics and Social Control,* edited by Mayer N. Zald and John D. McCarthy. Los Angeles: Sage.

Social Science Information. 1974. Vol. 13.

———. 1975. Vol. 14.

Solzhenitsyn, Alexander I. 1973. *The Gulag Archipelago,* 1918–1956: An Experiment in Literary Investigation. 2 vols. New York: Harper & Row.

Stern, Robert. n.d. "Fighters and Switchers: Alternating Forms of Industrial Protest." Mimeographed. Ithaca: New York State School of Industrial and Labor Relations, Cornell University.

Swanson, Guy E. 1971. "An Organizational Analysis of Collectivities." *American Sociological Review* 36 (August): 607–24.

———. 1967. *Religion and Regime: A Sociological Account of the Reformation*. Ann Arbor: University of Michigan Press.

Tannenbaum, Arnold. 1962. "Control in Organizations: Individual Adjustment and Organizational Performance." *Administrative Science Quarterly* 7 (2): 236–57.

Thibaut, John and Harold Kelley. 1959. *The Social Psychology of Groups*. New York: Wiley.

Thieblot, Armand J., Jr., and Ronald M. Cowin. 1972. *Welfare and Strikes: The Use of Public Funds to Support Strikers*. Philadelphia: Industrial Research Unit, Wharton School.

Thompson, James D. 1967. *Organizations in Action*. New York: McGraw-Hill.

Von Eschen, Donald, Jerome Kirk, and Maurice Pinard. 1971. "The Organizational Sub-Structure of Disorderly Politics." *Social Forces* 49 (June): 529–43.

Wicker, Tom. 1975. *A Time to Die*. New York: Quadrangle/New York Times.

Willer, David. 1967. *Scientific Sociology: Theory and Method*. Englewood Cliffs, N.J.: Prentice-Hall.

Wilsnack, Richard. In press. "Explaining Collective Violence in Prisons: Problems and Possibilities." In *Prison Violence,* edited by Albert K. Cohen, George F. Cole, and Robert Bailey. Lexington, Mass.: Lexington/Heath.

Wilson, James Q. 1966. *The Amateur Democrat*. Chicago: University of Chicago Press.

Wise, J. A. 1968. "The Coup d'Etat at Interpublic." *Fortune* (February), p. 134.

Wood, James R., and Mayer N. Zald. 1966. "Aspects of Racial Integration in the Methodist Church: Sources of Resistance to Organizational Policy." *Social Forces* 45 (December): 255–65.

Zald, Mayer N. 1962. "Organizational Control Structures in Five Correctional Institutions." *American Journal of Sociology* 68 (November): 335–45.

———. 1965. "Who Shall Rule: A Political Analysis of Succession in a Large Welfare Organization." *Pacific Sociological Review* 8 (1): 52–60.

———. 1970a. *Organizational Change: The Political Economy of the YMCA*. Chicago: University of Chicago Press.

———. 1970b. *Power in Organizations*. Nashville, Tenn.: Vanderbilt University Press.

Zald, Mayer N., and David Jacobs. In press. "Compliance/Incentive Classifications of Organizations: Underlying Dimensions." *Administration and Society*.

ARTICLE 10

Panic at "The Who Concert Stampede": An Empirical Assessment

NORRIS R. JOHNSON

On December 3, 1979, eleven young people were killed in a crush entering Riverfront Coliseum in Cincinnati, Ohio for a concert by the British rock group, The Who. The incident was immediately labeled as a "stampede" by the local media, and commentators were quick to condemn the "mob psychology" which precipitated the seemingly selfish, ruthless behavior of participants. Crowd members were thought to have stormed over others in their rush for good seats within the arena, leading a national columnist (Royko, 1979) to refer to the crowd of young people as barbarians who "stomped 11 persons to death [after] having numbed their brains on weeds, chemicals, and Southern Comfort . . . ," and a local editor to write of the "uncaring tread of the surging crowd" (Burleigh, 1979). . . .

PREVIOUS RESEARCH AND THEORIES OF PANIC

Many social scientists would categorize the crowd behavior described above as a special form of panic—usually termed an "acquisitive panic" (Brown, 1965) or "craze" (Smelser, 1963). Smelser distinguishes it from the classic panics of escape, e.g., flight from a burning building, in that the latter is a "headlong rush *away* from something" while the craze is a rush "toward something [the participants] believe to be gratifying . . ." (1963:170; also see Brown, 1965). In this form, the competition that arises is not to escape possible entrapment, but to acquire some valued commodity. The special group investigating the event for the city preferred the term "craze" to the "stampede" label affixed by the media (City of Cincinnati, 1980).

The several sociological and social psychological theories of collective behavior which consider panic (Brown, 1965; Kelley et al., 1965; Quarantelli, 1957; Smelser, 1963; Turner and Killian, 1987) generally agree that behavior in either form involves selfish competition uncontrolled by social and cultural constraints—i.e., it is unregulated. Yet, they make very different assumptions about the process producing the competition, variously attributing it to irrational behavior produced by fear and social contagion (LeBon, [1985] 1960; Smelser, 1963), rational calculation of potential rewards and costs (Brown, 1965; Kelley, et al., 1965; Mintz, 1951), or the emergence of normative support for selfish behavior (Turner and Killian, 1987).

Although many collective behavior theorists discuss the phenomenon, systematic studies of panic are uncommon. Researchers conducting such studies generally conclude that panic is a rare form of crowd behavior. Quarantelli and Dynes (1972) report that they have found few instances of panic after years of disaster research.

They indicate that even within the famous Coconut Grove fire most people did not panic. Smith (1976), a participant observer in a flight from the Tower of London after a 1976 bomb explosion, reported that panic responses were few, and that primary group bonds and roles were crucial in maintaining order in the situation. In fact, primary group ties were important in the minimal panic that did occur.

The particular form of panic represented by the surge at the rock concert is even less frequently studied. In systematic study of a bank run in Australia, Mann et al. (1976) concluded that the behavior in the situation did not match the description of panic. They found that people acted "in a cooperative manner, rather than a stampede" and did not exhibit the "selfish, disordered and uncoordinated behavior" (1976:233) described in discussions of panic.

The core of my analysis is an examination of the Cincinnati Police Division's file on The Who Concert incident. First, I describe the data source and then present a description of the surge based on that evidence. I then use material from the taped transcriptions of interviews with people present at the concert to assess the extent of unregulated competition, breakdown of group ties, and other behaviors characteristic of panic. Finally, I discuss the theoretical implications of this case study.

DATA AND METHODS

My analysis is based on data contained in a file created and kept by the Cincinnati Police Division, supplemented by accounts in daily newspapers. The police file includes 46 statements taken by officers investigating the event—22 from patrons, 13 from police officers present, and 11 from Coliseum employees or private security guards. The file also includes 10 statements presented by patrons at hearings conducted by a committee of the Cincinnati City Council. My primary data source is transcribed patron interviews and statements that I coded for analysis. I also coded and analyzed six interviews or statements from patrons which appeared in news articles reporting the incident.

I analyzed these materials by developing a questionnaire with which to "interview" each transcript. The questionnaire called for information relevant to theories of panic, particularly evidence of unregulated competition. For example, one question asked whether the "respondent" observed crowd members showing a "lack of concern for others," and another specifically asked, "Did the person report receiving help from others?" Coded responses to the latter question indicated whether, and from whom, help was received. A similar question concerned giving help to others. Other questions pertained to potential control variables such as age and sex of respondent, size and type of group with which the person arrived, time of arrival, and physical location relative to the doors.

I base most of my interpretations on vivid descriptions of the event by those present, particularly those most directly involved, and on the interviews with policemen, security guards, and Coliseum employees. In addition, I present quantitative results from the 38 questionnaires I coded. Of course, these data represent only those persons selected by others for interview (often because they were injured or had accompanied an injured person) or who came forward to write to newspapers or appear before a public hearing.

ANALYSIS

I will focus mainly on the issue of whether the observed behavior involved unregulated competition. I assume that competition in crowds awaiting entry into a concert is regulated by appropriate situational norms. I also assume that such crowds are characterized by a rudimentary social structure, reflecting at least the ties of crowd members to others with whom they arrived. Aveni (1977) has shown that crowd members typically arrive in small, primary groups. Accordingly, all of the persons whose transcripts contain relevant information reported that they arrived at the Coliseum with at least one other person, most often primary group members such as their spouse or other family member. An important research question, then, is whether these elements of social organization constrained behavior. A second question, which emerged during the research, is whether the conventional distinction between panics of escape and of acquisition (i.e., crazes) is a useful one.

Description of the Event

A useful and reasonably reliable account of the event can be constructed from the police file, which is the source of the description that follows. Transcripts of police radio transmissions provided the exact time of certain occurrences and an approximation of others. For instance, the radio log shows that at 1920:29 (i.e., just after 7:20 P.M. local time) an officer's response to a report of a broken door was that "there is little we can do . . . they haven't let this crowd in yet. There must be 8,000 people standing on the outside trying to get in." And at 1954:17 an officer called. "Emergency . . . we need a life squad. Coliseum on the concourse level. We have a man down, a possible heart attack" (Police Division, I, F).

The concert crowd began to arrive at least six hours before the scheduled 8 P.M. performance. The crowd was tightly packed within the space outside the arena doors (See Figure 1) with the greatest crush near the doors to the right (south) of the lobby (Location A, Figure 1). The crowd density became so great that one person reported that he could not raise his arm to scratch his head (Police Division, I, YZ), and another said he could not reach to his pocket for his wallet (Police Division, III, M). Others referred to being lifted from the pavement and carried along by the crowd's movement, unable to get

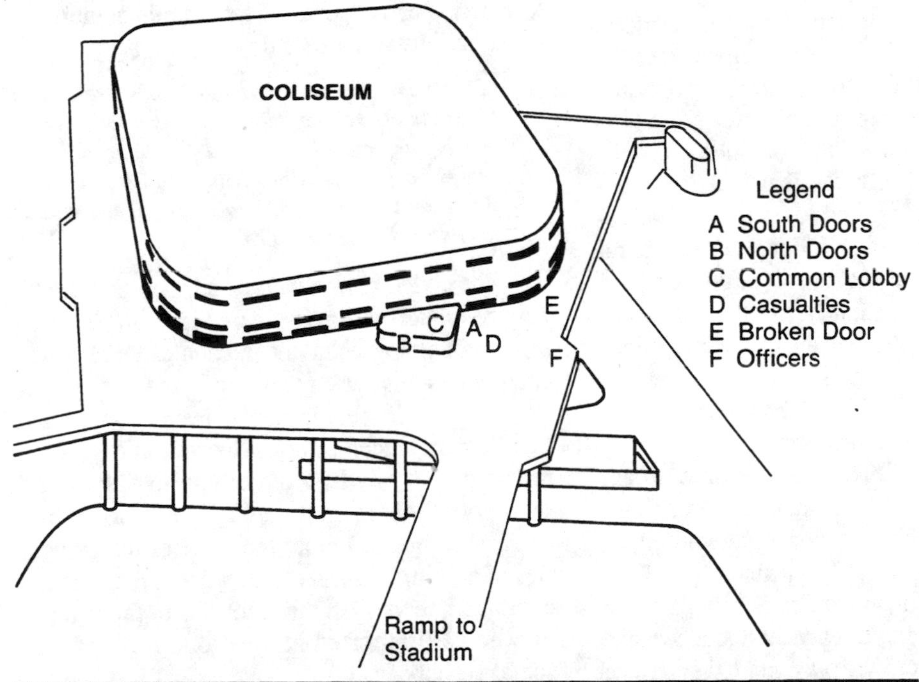

FIGURE 1 Diagram of Cincinnati's Riverfront Coliseum and Surrounding Plaza, Site of "The Who Concert Stampede," with Area of Densest Occupancy Shaded and Referenced Locations Marked

their feet back on the concrete surface (Police Division, I, YZ).

When the doors opened and the surge to enter began, approximately 25 people fell (at location D, Figure 1), some lying on the concrete for as long as 30 minutes (Police Division, Summary). Those immediately behind the first persons to fall were then pushed by the surge onto the growing pile of the fallen, which at its worse was three to five people deep. Many patrons tried to form a protective cordon around those who fell, but they were often forced by the surge to either walk over or to fall atop them. Those further from the doors were unaware that others had fallen and continued to surge forward. Some of the fallen were helped to their feet or were dragged into the arena. Others who would have otherwise fallen were also pulled inside by other patrons, security guards, or arena employees.

Entry through the few open exterior doors (Locations A and B, Figure 1) was into a lobby (Location C) separated from the seating area by a set of turnstiles. As the crowds surged through the doors, the lobby was quickly filled; thus, to regulate flow into the lobby, security guards tried to close and reopen exterior doors as space was available within the lobby. Those still outside could only see that the doors before which they had waited for hours were closing. At the same time, sounds of the band warming up added to their perception that they needed to enter immediately.

An expert consulted by the city's investigating group estimated that a ticket checker can process from 1,800 to 3,000 people per hour, depending on the procedure used (City of Cincinnati, 1980: Appendix). Therefore, in order to accommodate the expected crowd of 18,000, either more time than 30 minutes would be required, or more doors would have to be opened.

Most policemen and security guards were unaware of the growing threat near doors because the density of the crowd prevented them from circulating, and the similarity of the crowd situation to those at previous concerts made it seem "normal." By the time policemen located on the crowd fringe (Location F, Figure 1) became aware of the danger and worked their way through the crowd to those still down, the deaths and injuries had already occurred.

Helping Behavior

Since most theoretical explanations of panic focus on unregulated competition, the first research question is whether such competition existed in this case. That many people were killed and injured in a crowd of pushing people is not in dispute; the key issue is whether this was the result of callous competition for a seat at the concert at the expense of the lives of others.

However, evidence from the transcripts does not provide support for the theoretical models of panic and is in clear conflict with interpretations reported in the newspapers. One witness before the City Council committee specifically objected to newspaper accounts of the people as animals or barbarians and asserted:

> *[T]he people in our area were the most helpful people that I've ever known. . . . Everybody I saw was helping everybody else. At some point in the crowd people could not help them. It's not that they didn't want to. They were physically unable to (Police Division, I, YZ).*

The coded interview data support this claim. Approximately 40 percent of those interviewed reported helping behavior in each of three coded categories—giving, receiving, and observing help. Of the 38 people interviewed, 17 reported that they had received some help from others, 16 reported that they had given help to others, and 16 reported observing helping behavior by others. Some reported more than one of the categories of helping activities, and when indicators are combined, more than three-fourths of those interviewed (29) reported at least one form of prosocial activity.

Helping behavior possibly was even more common than indicated by those results. It is likely that additional respondents observed, but did not report, helping activity since interviewers did not ask a direct question concerning helping. In fact, only seven respondents reported action by others that was coded as showing a lack of concern for others, and six of these also reported helping behavior. Thus, just one of the 38 respondents reported *only* self-interested, competitive behavior. Although we cannot infer from this selective sample that a comparably large proportion of the entire crowd continued to behave in a cooperative manner, this evidence does suggest that many of those centrally located within the crowd, at just the location where persons were in most danger, demonstrated concern for others.

Helping behavior began during the early crush, long before the surge, and continued throughout the episode. People first simply tried to get people to step back and relieve the pressure, but others around them either could not hear or could not move. One young man noticed that the girl next to him could not breathe and "turned to ask people to back up, but soon realized that the only people who could hear me shouting couldn't move either." (Police Division, III, M). A small 17-year-old girl near the doors away from the worst crush (Location B, Figure 1) reported having problems nearly an hour before the "stampede." She pleaded with people to let her out, but neither she nor they could move. She told the police detective interviewing her:

> *I lost my footing an' slowly but surely began doing down. People behind me could do nothing to stop the pushing. I was saying "No. No. Please help me..." Some of the people around didn't even hear me.... So then I grabbed someone's leg an' whoever that was told three other guys about me. They all pushed me up, pulled me up, but it was hard.... At about 7 o'clock I passed out. The four guys who pulled me off the ground helped me to stay up until we got through the door (Police Division, II, V).*

Another person reported a similar observation from the view of the person trying to give help:

> *Smaller people began passing out I attempted to lift one girl up and above to be passed back.... After several tries I was unsuccessful and near exhaustion (Police Division, III, M).*

A few were successful in extricating themselves and helping others out of the crush. One man reported that he and friends picked up and carried from the crowd two nearly unconscious girls who had fallen (Police Division, III, M). These particular young men knew the girls they helped, but many helped others with whom they had no social ties. Thirteen of the 17 mentioned above as having received help were aided by others they did not know, and 12 of those 16 giving help gave it to strangers. As one person reported in a letter to a newspaper, "Total strangers probably saved my life" (*Cincinnati Enquirer*, 1979).

Helping became increasingly difficult after the first persons fell near the doors at the entrance and the pile of people (Location D, Figure 1), which was described as being 10 to 12 feet in diameter, began to form. Persons not in the immediate area were unaware that others had fallen, and those nearest the fallen who might have helped were themselves in danger of being pushed onto the pile. For instance, one person who, with his wife, was pushed atop the fallen described the situation in this way:

> *At that point everyone around the perimeter of the circle, of course, was trying to back off and trying to help the people get up onto their feet, but the people in the back of the crowd, of course, could not see this and continued to push forward (Police Division, II, L).*

Those who helped others to their feet were not alarmed at first, but then they began to fall. The press forward was impossible to stall, and those on the ground could not be protected because, in the words of another patron,

> *People in the crowd 10 feet back didn't know it was happening. Their cries were impossible to hear above the roar of the crowd.... I screamed with all my strength that I was standing on some-*

one. I couldn't move. I could only scream (Police Division, III, M).

Although most of the evidence leads to a conclusion that acts of ruthless competition were rare, there *were* such reports. For instance, one patron, who from a position just inside the arena doors was pulling people inside to safety, reported being angry with the mob:

> *People were climbin' over people ta get in . . . an' at one point I almost started hittin' 'em, because I could not believe the animal, animalistic ways the people, you know, nobody cared (Police Division, II, A).*

But both the analysis of the coded transcripts and the impressionistic accounts indicate that, even in the face of the throng, most persons tried to help others as long as possible. If a total disregard for others developed—and there is hardly any evidence that it did—it was only after cooperation was no longer possible.

Sex Differences in Helping Behavior

Normative expectations dictate generally that the stronger should help the weaker; specifically, men are expected to help women. The evidence indicates that such sex-role expectations continued to be an important influence on behavior during the event. Nine of the 13 females received help while only one reported giving help. On the other hand, almost twice as many men gave as received help. A few (three) reported helping their wives or members of their group, but, as noted above, most gave help to those around them, either friends or strangers. Thus, the sex-role norms of men helping women did not collapse when confronted with a threat.

Altruistic behavior, either generally or specifically toward women, was not universal; there *was* selfish competition. For instance, a young woman, interviewed in her hospital room late on the evening of the concert with the horror still fresh in her memory, complained that no one would move back:

> *They just kept pushin' forward and they would just walk right on top of you, just trample over ya like you were a piece of the ground. They wouldn't even help ya; people were just screamin' "help me" and nobody cared (Police Division, II, MC).*

And referring to another person who fell alongside her, she said,

> *I knew she was unconscious or something. And then everybody just trampled her like she wasn't even there; they just standin' on her (Police Division, II, MC).*

Another hospitalized woman reported a similar experience:

> *And there was a big group of people in front of me that had fallen down and people just went mad. They kept, you know, shovin' over me; they wouldn't help them get up; they wanted inside. . . . I fell down with them and no one helped me up and I—there was no way I could get up—and they just kept—there was people fallin' on me and then people walkin' over my legs tryin' ta get through the door (Police Division, II, P).*

Similar reports are included in the interviews with arena employees. But both women quoted above as having been trampled also reported receiving help. That they recognized the difficulty of helping is evident in the second woman's remark that "there was really no way they could help me because there were so many people tryin' to shove over the top of me that they would have to clear all them out just even to see me" (Police Division, II, P).

Overall, these data seem to confirm the continuing importance of normative expectations. Even with the possibility of self-serving statements and the possibility that men are likely to *say* they gave help to women, the evidence is compelling.

Distinctions between Panics of Acquisition and of Escape

Popular accounts of The Who Concert incident have generally characterized it as an acquisitive panic, implying that persons were competing for the most desirable locations in the arena in total disregard of others. Analysis of the transcripts reveals that the competition that did develop—recalling the extent of cooperative behavior—was for an escape from the crush rather than access to the concert.

A letter to the editor of a local newspaper presented this position in the assertion that, "To us, the door to the Coliseum was no longer to a concert, but to survival and safety" (*Cincinnati Post*, 1979). That interpretation was also evident in most of the interviews coded for this research. Only four of the 38 did not make some statement indicating that either they or others around them were trying to get "out" of the crush. A preferred location within the arena disappeared as a motive for those in the area where the crush was most severe. No interviews were available for those more distant from the entrances, but it is likely that the pushing in the rear was still to gain entry. Thus, there apparently were two forms of competition existing simultaneously—efforts to escape near the entrances and competition among those in the rear for entry into the concert.

For people nearest the doors, entering the Coliseum was the only likely escape from the danger. According to one of the transcripts, "everyone was scared for their own lives [and] the only way to go was in the doors, an' there was just that one door on the side where we were at" (Police Division, II, T). In the words of another, "It was a hysterical scene. People upon people trying to escape" (Police Division, III, M). Some reported unsuccessful efforts to escape by moving out toward the rear (see, e.g., Police Division, III, M; II, V).

People were struggling to avoid falling, recognizing the danger; but, according to one interview, those who did walk over other people to avoid falling "weren't animals just trying to get in to see the show [but] were fighting for their lives and trying to get on the inside. . . . They were fighting to stay alive together" (Police Division, II, U). This statement came from a person who saw someone die lying alongside him on the concrete and who was himself revived only after rescue workers arrived.

Those who continued to push forward from the rear were unaware of events near the front. A typical report stated: "A major problem was that except for those right on the perimeter, nobody knew what was happening, and they just kept pressing forward still only wanting to see the concert" (*Louisville Courier-Journal*, 1979).

Difficulty of communication within the crowd, a typical contributing factor in panic, was compounded by its high density. Patrons faced an additional communication problem in redefining the crowd situation for the police and other officials. Although most patrons who were interviewed defined the efforts to get through the doors as flights to safety, police officers and security guards continued to see them as gate-crashing efforts after the surge had begun. For instance, two officers reported trying to secure a door (Location E, Figure 1) forced open by gate-crashers (Police Division, I, N; I, O), but a 27-year-old male patron described in detail how the door was opened from the inside by two men trying to prevent injury to "two young girls [who] had been banging on that door for 20 minutes" (Police Division, II, M). Similarly, a couple referred to a friend who, once inside,

> *tried to shove open some more doors with his foot and immediately two ushers came up, one of them grabbed him, shoved him back in line and told him to either get in line or get back out. He then began to beg and plead with the usher, he said, "people are getting hurt, people were down" (Police I, YZ).*

The actual motives of those trying to open the doors are not as relevant as the fact that definitions of the situation differed markedly among patrons, police, and Coliseum workers.

If the crowd was in fact, a panic of escape, while police continued to see it as an "acquisitive mob," officers' experiences at other concerts surely influenced their interpretations and actions. A patron who said she was pleading with the ushers to let her enter recognized this. She understood that the officials might not believe her pleas because they "might have heard it before at other concerts and figured it was just people pretending or whatever, just to try to get in early, but this is one time . . ." (Police Division, I, YZ).

DISCUSSION

In sum, these data provide little support for the collective behavior theories which postulate undifferentiated competitive responses in their treatment of panic. Unregulated competition, which is crucial to most explanations of panic, did not occur; on the contrary, cooperative behavior continued throughout the course of the event. Behavior within the crowd continued to reflect both a social structure comprising the small groups in which people arrived and to conform to sex-role norms. Neither is it accurate to characterize the surge as an acquisitive panic created by competition for a scarce resource—seats at the concert. While those near the rear of the crowd did continue to push forward in order to enter the concert, the only behavior that resembled panic occurred nearer the front among those who were trying to escape an entrapping situation.

The lack of unanimity in crowd responses also reflects the absence of a common definition of the situation. All participants initially viewed the situation in essentially the same way. To patrons and policemen like, the situation was not unusual prior to a rock concert. The young people expected generally uninhibited behavior, including pushing (Radel, 1979; Stevens, 1979). Even the crowd density, almost unbelievable to the uninitiated, was routine for the aficionado. One unbelieving patron was told by others around him that the crush was to be expected, and that "if you think this is bad, you should have been at the Led Zeppelin concert; this is nothing" (Police Division, III, M). A security guard said of the crush, "we always have that. . . . [W]e have handled a lot of shows, concerts, and I thought that some of them was worse than this one" (Police Division, II, H). At an earlier concert at the same location, an "angry mob" threw rocks and bottles at police and windows (Chute, 1979).

The making of waves by pushing into the crowd also was routine. An entertainment reporter in the back of the crowd reported, "Five boys next to me . . . kept yelling 'shove, shove'" and pushing on the crowd (Stevens, 1979), unaware that people were dying just ahead, and a patron saw people going to the back of the crowd to shove into it just to see the waves (Police Division, II, L). At the same time, the police—some of whom thought that "hard rock" groups drew particularly threatening crowds (see, e.g., Police Division, II, R)—saw it as the usual rowdy concert crowd, potentially troublesome because of drinking and drugs, but not life-threatening. Even when nearly unconscious people stumbled into the Coliseum, security guards were not unduly concerned ". . . 'cause a lot of times they come in and they pass out from drinking or drugs or whatever" (Police Division, II, K). Consistent with this situational definition, police officers continued to carry out their rule-enforcement roles in a routine fashion, arresting patrons for shouting obscenities and attempting to open a door almost simultaneously with the deaths (Police Division, I, Q; I, R).

Those patrons nearest the doors were the first to redefine the situation as life-threatening, and then began to fight for entry into the Coliseum, trying to escape the crush. The policemen who were arresting gate-crashers and barring the broken doors and the ushers who were demanding tickets of those entering and insisting that they stay in line did so because they held to their initial interpretations of the crowd's behavior. Those nearer the crowd fringes also continued to define the situation as routine for the concert and to press forward to obtain choice seats.

The concept "definition of the situation" is central to Turner and Killian's (1987) emergent norm approach to collective behavior, and to symbolic interactionist theories generally. Social psychologists use this concept to refer to the fact that individuals organize in some coherent way their perception of the context in which activities take place (e.g., Hewitt, 1979). Specifically, Turner and Killian refer to panics, or the individualistic tendencies in crowds, as resulting from a definition of the situation in which norms of cooperation no longer apply and selfish pursuit of individual ends is viewed as legitimate. Their model captures more of the complexity of such situations than do other theories of panic. However, their emergent norm approach fails to give adequate consideration to differing or conflicting definitions of the situation which emerge within different segments of the crowd. And, like other approaches to panic, their model fails to recognize the strength and endurance of the social bonds which inhibit individualistic behavior.

CONCLUSION

We cannot conclude from one study that there are *no* situations in which competition for some valued commodity occurs without regard for social obligations. Perhaps there are situations such as a fire in a crowded theater in which people totally ignore others as they try to escape from danger. However, documented cases of either form of panic are surprisingly scarce in the literature.

One possible reason for the lack of evidence of unregulated competition in The Who concert incident is that the appropriate conditions did not exist. Perhaps the people in this situation did not place such a high value on a preferred location for the concert that they would do harm to others in order to get inside; perhaps those trying to escape the crush did not actually perceive a serious threat to their lives. Kelley et al. (1965) have noted that panic-like responses are less likely when there is variation in perception of the danger; those who define the situation as less urgent are more willing to wait their turns. In this case, those who placed less value on their concert location would be less likely to compete with others. Many did try to leave the crush, giving up their valued locations nearer the entrance. Mann et al. (1976) reached a similar conclusion in their study of the bank run.

But the repeated failure of researchers to find examples of ruthless competition suggests another conclusion. Most crowds are comprised not of unattached individuals but of small, often primary, groups (Aveni, 1977; Smith, 1976). Group bonds constrain totally selfish behavior, even when the situation seems life threatening; thus, the type of unregulated competition generally labeled as panic occurs very infrequently. More case studies of such infrequent and irregularly occurring social forms must accumulate before general conclusions can be drawn with confidence. However, the evidence from this study is more than sufficient to discount popular interpretations of "The Who Concert Stampede" which focus on the hedonistic attributes of young people and the hypnotic effects of rock music.

REFERENCES

Aveni, Adrian. 1977. "The not-so-lonely crowd: friendship groups in collective behavior." Sociometry 49:96–99.

Brown, Roger. 1965. Social Psychology. New York: Free Press.

Burleigh, William R. 1979. "Editors notebook: at death's door." *Cincinnati Post* (December 8).

Chute, James. 1979. "Rowdy crowds have rocked coliseum many times before." Cincinnati Post (December 4).

Courier Journal (Louisville). 1979. "I'm not sure how many people were under me. But none of them were moving." December 17:B6.

Enquirer (Cincinnati). 1979. "Readers' views: A dear price has been paid to learn an obvious lesson." December 10:A14.

Gamson, William A. 1975. The Strategy of Social Protest. Homewood, IL: Dorsey.

Garloch, Karen. 1979. "Crowds capable of developing own personalities, expert says." Cincinnati Enquirer (December 5).

Hewitt, John P. 1976. Self and Society. Boston: Allyn and Bacon.

Kelley, Harold H., J. Condry, Jr., A. Dahlke, and A. Hill. 1965. "Collective behavior in a simulated panic situation." Journal of Experimental and Social Psychology 1:20–54.

LeBon, Gustave. 1960. The Crowd. New York: Viking Press.

Mann, Leon, Trevor Nagel and Peter Dowling. 1976. "A study of an economic panic: the 'run' on the Hindmarsh Building Society." Sociometry 39:223–35.

McPhail, Clark. 1985. "The social organization of demonstrations." Paper presented at the annual meeting of the American Sociological Association, Washington, DC.

McPhail, Clark and R. Ronald Wohlstein. 1983. "Individual and collective behaviors within gatherings, demonstrations, and riots." Annual Review of Sociology 9:579–600.

Miller, David L. 1985. Introduction to Collective Behavior. Belmont, CA: Wadsworth.

Mintz, Alexander. 1951. "Non-adaptive group behavior." Journal of Abnormal and Social Psychology 46:1550–59.

Police Division, City of Cincinnati. No Final Report Concerning the Eleven Deaths Which Preceded the "Who" Rock Concert Held date at Riverfront Coliseum. Cincinnati: City of Cincinnati.

Post (Cincinnati). 1979. "Letters: about rock and barbarians." December 14:A8.

Quarantelli, Enrico. 1957. "The behavior of panic participants." Sociology and Social Research 41:187–94.

Quarantelli, Enrico and Russell R. Dynes. 1972. "When disaster strikes." Psychology Today 5:66–70.

Radel, Cliff. 1979. "Concertgoers leave manners 'back home'." Cincinnati Enquirer (December 5).

Royko, Mike. 1979. "The new barbarians: a glimpse of the future." Cincinnati Post (December 4).

Smelser, Neil J. 1963. Theory of Collective Behavior. New York: The Free Press.

Smith, Don. 1976. "Primary group interaction in panic behavior: a test of theories." Paper presented at the annual meeting of Southern Sociological Society, Miami Beach.

Stevens, Dale. 1979. "Concert a funeral in disguise." Cincinnati Post (December 4).

Task Force of Crowd Control and Safety. 1980. Report to the City Manager. Cincinnati: City of Cincinnati.

Turner, Ralph H. and Lewis M. Killian. 1987. Collective Behavior. Third edition. Englewood Cliffs, NJ: Prentice Hall.

ARTICLE 11

The Dialectics of Resistance: An Analysis of the GI Movement

JAMES R. HAYES

The signing of the Indochina peace agreements in early 1973 officially ended American participation in the Vietnam conflict. Military officials would probably be the first to admit that they, more than any other group in society, experienced the first sigh of relief. Throughout most of the war, the military was subjected to invectives emanating from a war-weary civilian sector, as well as disgruntled, antiwar, antimilitary GIs. While civil-military relations have a well-documented tradition of animosity, organized protest within the ranks is without parallel in American military history. For military traditionalists, the presence of a small but vocal minority of soldiers raising the old ideal of a "democratic military" produced some acute anxiety. Contrary to its functionalist image of human nature and dissent, the military has been forced to come to grips with the reality that internal discontent runs deeper than the mere disaffections of a few disruptive, "bad" individuals (House Committee on Internal Security, 1972; Olson, Note 1; Special Subcommittee on Disciplinary Problems in the Navy, 1973). What were once considered to be private troubles came to be recognized as a public issue.

This article will briefly describe and analyze the effort by a minority of GIs to create an antiwar, antimilitary movement with the Vietnam-era military. I will present an attenuated chronology of the movement, along with an analysis of what appear to be major causal variables in its genesis and development.

THE MILITARY FIGHTS ITSELF

Beginning in the latter part of the 1960s a movement of soldier dissent unprecedented in military history began to gather momentum. Originating primarily as an antiwar movement, it escalated to a point where it was a force waging a battle against military authority and legitimacy. While desertion, AWOLs, drug use, and even fraggings (Linden, 1972) have long plagued the United States military, organized resistance appears to be a uniquely Vietnam-era phenomenon. The social movement characteristics exhibited by the movement, e.g., a sense of group identity and solidarity, consciously articulated ideologies, movement organizations, distinguish it from other more spontaneous and transitory uprisings such as the "Back Home Movement" in the aftermath of World War II. Adjustment responses such as drug use and various types of withdrawal reactions such as desertion and AWOL will not be discussed in the context of this article; the degree to which these various forms of dissent are politically motivated is open to debate (Berens, 1969; Gardner, 1972; Helmer, Note 2; House Committee, 1972; Musil, 1973; Williams, 1971).

Hayes, James R. (1975). The dialectics of resistance: An analysis of the GI movement. *Journal of Social Issues, 31* (4), 125–139.

Although there has been one well publicized instance of an officers' organization, The Concerned Officers Movement (COM), an antiwar group that dissociated itself from the more radical GI groups (Staff, 1970; Zwerdling, 1970), and a lesser-known and smaller group, The Concerned Graduates of the Military, Naval, and Air Force Academies, headquartered in San Francisco and largely limited to ex-officers in that area (Staff, 1970), the GI movement has for the most part been comprised of lower-ranking enlisted personnel ("enlisted" referring to status and not to mode of entry into the service), predominantly army but cutting across all branches of the armed services. Short of revolutionary in outlook and ideology, the movement has aimed primarily at institutional structural reform. There has been no accurate measure of the numerical strength of the movement, and the estimates vary according to source—the military appears to underestimate while movement sympathizers tend to exaggerate (House Committee, 1972; Sherrill, 1971; Staff, 1970; Stapp, 1970; Waterhouse & Wizard, 1971). It is safe to say, however, that the movement represents only a small fraction of GIs.

The Early Years

Like other movements of the period, the GI movement emerged in a rather piecemeal and disorderly fashion (Waterhouse & Wizard, 1971). Blumer (1951) argued that movements tend to emerge as rather amorphous, poorly organized, and formless entities, develop in periods of cultural drift, and the early action tends to be individualistic in nature and lacking group consciousness. The GI movement witnessed its beginning in a series of individual acts of resistance against the war. These initial exemplar acts occurred during a period (1965–1967) in which the Vietnam conflict and American military involvement in it were becoming increasingly important concerns for both the civilian and military sectors. (For evidence of the rapid rise in interest in the problem from 1964–1968 see Schuman and Converse, 1970.)

One of the first publicized incidents of resistance occurred in November of 1965 when Lt. Henry H. Howe, Jr. participated in an antiwar demonstration in El Paso, Texas (Waters, 1967). Howe was courtmartialed and charged with disrespectful utterances toward public officials for carrying a sign which read: "End Johnson's Fascist Aggression in Vietnam" and "Let's Have More Than a Choice Between Petty Ignorant Fascists in 1968." In December of 1965, Howe was convicted and sentenced to two years hard labor (later reduced to one) and dishonorably discharged (*CAMP News,* 1972). Howe's conviction raised the ire of some because, as Sherman (1968) states, the military presented no clear evidence that Howe's conduct threatened military discipline and order, particularly in light of the fact that he was off-duty as well as out of uniform.

The most celebrated case of GI antiwar resistance during 1966 took place on June 30, when three enlisted men at Ft. Hood refused shipment to Vietnam on the grounds that it was an immoral war. The refusal by Pvt. Dennis Mora, Pfc. James Johnson, and Pvt. David Samas was the first case of overt resistance against shipment to the war zone (*CAMP News,* 1972). All were given dishonorable discharges and forfeiture of all pay; Samas and Johnson were sentenced to five years at hard labor, Mora to three. The case of the "Ft. Hood Three" gained broader significance when a number of civilian antiwar activists became involved in it in an effort to make it a cause celebre. Although most civilian activists still viewed the GI with some disdain, a few were beginning to realize that the GI could be a potential ally in the antiwar struggle.

Perhaps the most significant and important individual act of antiwar resistance in the entire 1965–1967 period was the case of Capt. Howard Levy. Levy, a dermatologist, refused to train Green Beret medics for duty in Vietnam, citing the commission of war crimes by the special forces as one reason. Levy was accused not only of disobeying an order, but also of attempting to "crush the spirit" of enlisted men with his continued criticism of the war (Dimona, 1972). On June 3, 1967, Levy was sentenced to three years hard labor and dismissed from the service. The Levy case received nation-wide attention and the military had created a martyr. Less than two months after Levy's conviction, on July 27, two black marines, Pfc. George Daniels and Cpl. William Harvey, were arrested for taking part in a barracks discussion where they argued that blacks should not take part in the Vietnam War. They were convicted; Daniels was sentenced to ten years hard labor and Harvey to six (The *Ally*, July 1968). Their conviction and subsequent sentencing not only raised more questions about extreme military oppression but was also attacked as racist. Another case of officer resistance to the war also took place in 1967 when Air Force Capt. Dale Noyd was convicted and imprisoned for refusing to train pilots for Vietnam.

The above examples constitute only a select number of antiwar acts that occurred in 1965–1967. The formative years of the movement were typified by a number of different individuals engaging in similar behaviors, i.e., protesting the war, but acting largely independently of each other with no real communication existing among them. The early resisters played a key role by drawing attention to the possibility of political dissent in the military, and, perhaps more importantly, by using the war issue as a vehicle, they brought to the surface the larger issue of constitutional rights for military personnel, particularly enlisted persons. They did, however, suffer a heavy toll for their actions as prison sentences and dishonorable discharges constituted the backbone of the military defense.

The Big Year: 1968

The individual acts of confrontation which characterized the 1965–1967 years continued throughout the duration of the war. Beginning in 1968, the frequency of individual acts of resistance declined, and dissent of a collective nature took precedence (Blake, Note 3). It was also in 1968 that some of the defining traits of a social movement were first discernible. What had been uncoordinated and disconnected acts of resistance began to coalesce around an organizational framework. The organizational network was decentralized, in that no central decision-making headquarters existed, and segmented, in the sense that a number of groups arose and operated essentially independent of each other, linked only by a common mission and communications network. Consciousness of membership and joint interaction were created by the establishment of the GI underground press—the *Bond, FTA, Vietnam GI,* The *Ally*—and coffeehouses—Mad Anthony's, the UFO, and the Olso Strut. Movement cells, such as the American Serviceman's Union (ASU) and the FTA, developed programs and ideologies. The ASU and FTA were followed in 1969 by the GIs United Against the War in Vietnam (GIs-United), and the Movement for a Democratic Military (MDM). In May of 1969, the GI Alliance was constituted in Washington to serve as an umbrella organization with the intention of coordinating the actions of the various movement cell organizations (Staff, 1970). While the specific ideological positions of the GI groups varied some, their goals overlapped considerably and called for such things as an end to racism in the military, collective bargaining, federal minimum wage standards, and, most importantly, full constitutional rights for all enlisted people (Halstead, 1970; Stapp, 1970; Waterhouse & Wizard, 1971).

1968 proved to be a banner year for the GI movement in a variety of ways. Collective resistance against the war came to the forefront and manifested itself in a variety of styles. In addition to the war-related protest, stockade rebellions added a new dimension to GI resistance.

A new variety of antiwar resistance originated in 1968 as a number of military personnel across the country took sanctuary in various churches and universities. In July, nine GIs representing all four services chained themselves together inside a San Francisco church and held a 48-hour vigil in protest of the war (The *Ally*, August 1968). Army Pfc. Michael Locianto was arrested in August after he had taken sanctuary in a Greenwich Village church following his refusal to go to Vietnam. Also protesting the war, Marine Cpl. Paul Olimpieri took sanctuary in the Harvard Divinity School in the fall of 1968. In November, Army Pvt. John Michael O'Connor was arrested by military police after he had taken refuge in the Student Union at the Massachusetts Institute of Technology (The *Ally*, December 1968); approximately 1000 MIT students tried to shield O'Connor from the police in that instance. On November 8th, Army Pvt. William Brakefield and Airman David Copp were arrested after they had sought sanctuary on the campus of New York City College (The *Ally*, December 1968) The use of sanctuaries, particularly churches by antiwar GIs was increasingly facilitated as more and more clergy adopted an antiwar stance.

1968 also saw a dramatic growth in the number of GIs participating in antiwar demonstrations and teach-ins. The most significant participation occurred on October 12th when GI and civilian antiwar marches were held in Los Angeles, Atlanta, Washington, New York, and Chicago. The *Veterans Stars and Stripes for Peace* (1968) reported that an estimated 200 GIs led the march in Chicago. The *Ally* (November 1968) stated that approximately 700 GIs took part in the October 12th march in San Francisco.

At Ft. Campbell, Kentucky, 35 GIs held an October 12th antiwar rally in sympathy with the nation-wide protests (*Flag In Action*, 1968); the stockade was turned back over to authorities only after the military police were ordered to shoot to kill. An estimated 40–50 prisoners from the navy, marines, and army held the stockade in Danang, Vietnam for three days in August, protesting poor conditions and military authoritarianism (The *Ally*, September 1968); one cell-block was burned to the ground in this eruption. Also in Vietnam during August, GIs revolted at the Long Binh stockade, and a GI was killed by the military police and another 59 were wounded before the riot was under control (*Where It's At*, 1968). The most publicized case of collective resistance within stockades occurred in October when 27 inmates of the Presidio stockade (San Francisco) mutinied in protest over the slaying of a fellow prisoner (Gardner, 1970). The trial of the "Presidio 27" brought massive criticism upon the military due to the severe nature of the punishment meted out to the resisters. As a result of extreme pressure, the military reduced many of the sentences.

Stockade rebellions increased after 1968 and brought with them increased publicity over the less than adequate conditions under which inmates were forced to live. More importantly, stockade rebellions served to emphasize what a growing number of GIs were beginning to realize: the military's basic denial of any kind of rights and freedoms for enlisted individuals.

Although the above account of resistance in 1968 deals only with a small number of cases, it does illustrate that resistance was not only taking on a collective nature but it also was no longer solely confined to the war issue. More and more enlisted people were defining the military per se as oppressive, and deciding to confront it rather than withdraw. As the self-generated protest increased, dissident GIs saw large numbers of civilian radicals and antiwar groups taking an interest in them and willing to aid them in their struggle.

The Final Period

In 1969 and the following years, the issue of constitutional rights came to the forefront of the GI movement. The war, however, remained as the most appropriate vehicle through which to confront this issue. This larger concern had been precipitated by the military's reaction to and handling of antiwar dissenters. The military inadvertently pricked the consciousness of some hitherto uninvolved GIs and civilians by its heavy-handed repression in dealing with the initial dissent. The dilemma confronting the movement at that time was one of transforming what appeared to be a growing body of partisan support into active support. In general, enlisted personnel were well aware that any gains made by the movement would be in the form of "public goods," i.e., benefits which would accrue to all GIs regardless of whether or not they took an active role in the movement (Olson, 1968). Although initially direct confrontation of military authority, such as refusals of orders and distributing "subversive" literature on base, functioned as the main tactic, less risky behavior, such as rap sessions and political meetings in the barracks, were also employed with the hope that these relatively safe actions would increasingly involve larger numbers of GIs (Gardner, 1972). Despite these efforts, the majority of GIs preferred to remain sympathetic bystanders.

In 1970, GI participation in antiwar demonstrations was considerable. Although the possibility of punitive sanctions loomed large, the 1969 directive on dissent issued by the Department of Defense made such participation legal if the demonstration was off the base in the United States, and if GIs participating were off-duty and out of uniform. Various GI papers stressed the legality of participation and many advertised names and addresses of lawyers willing to defend any GI punished for participating. The largest nation-wide participation of GIs was in May in what the GIs termed "Armed Farces Day." This demonstration was held in conjunction with the traditional "Armed Forces Day" celebrations. GIs at Ft. Hood, Ft. Bliss, Ft. Bragg, Ft. Lewis, Ft. Devens, and others turned out to protest the war and the military. Estimates of the numbers involved ranged from 1500 at Ft. Bragg and 500 at Ft. Hood down to 20–30 at Ft. Devens (Blake, Note 3). Black soldiers continued to step up their fight against racism. In July, 250 black GIs revolted at Ft. Hood, burning two "Re-Up" offices and a BEQ building (Chicago Area Military Project, Note 4). At Ft. Carson, also during July, 200 black soldiers seized a section of the base while fighting off the military police. In Heidelberg, West Germany, 1000 black and white GIs held a July rally against racism in the army. While these demonstrations by black military personnel were not the first signs of a growing antiracism, the expanding scope and intensity of this resistance in conjunction with the antiwar, antimilitary position of many white enlisted people did present a formidable threat to the brass, at least the military defined it as such.

By 1971, there were approximately 26 antimilitary and antiwar coffeehouses, along with an estimated 144 underground GI papers and a nationwide network of GI counseling services (Heinl, 1972; Stanton, 1973). The estimate of 144 newspapers appears a staggering figure; however, it must be remembered that a significant number of these papers were very short-lived due to financial problems, military harassment, and staff turnovers. The papers themselves fell into two general categories: (a) "basc papers" which dealt primarily with the activities on a particular base and were generally confined to that specific military installation, and (b) "national papers" representing more of a news service publication, which detailed resistance and courtmartial cases at bases all across the country and overseas. The national papers were distributed nation-wide to GIs and interested civilians, largely through subscriptions. Through the GI press, activist GIs were aware that their colleagues at other bases were engaged in similar acts of resistance, and they were constantly in touch with the types of responses on the part of military authorities. The papers continually published self-help items for GIs, informing them of various groups and lawyers willing to defend them, as well as information pertaining to such things as conscientious objection and rights under the Uniform Code of Military Justice. The establishment and proliferation of the GI press served to bridge some of the structural limitations GIs faced in regard to communication and mobility, and helped to foster a feeling of consciousness of membership and interaction between activist GIs and movement cell organization (Finn, 1971; Glessing, 1970; Nelson, 1972; Rivkin, 1970).

In 1971 and 1972 resistance directed against the military and the war continued. GIs joined civilians in demonstrations around the country, as well as conducting their own protests on the post. In addition to statewide resistance, there were numerous reports out of Vietnam detailing refusals to engage the enemy on the part of some combat troops (Boyle, 1973; *Camp News*, 1972; Waterhouse & Wizard, 1971). While GI and antiwar civilian groups were quick to exploit the different protests as indicative of the strength of the GI movement, there remains some question as to whether these incidents were indeed related to the GI movement or more a result of the immediate situational contingencies of combat. Boyle (1973) argues that a number of troop revolts in Vietnam were private affairs by GIs who were either on drugs, scared, or angry over the fact of having to risk their lives to capture a piece of land. He goes on to say, though, that as the war continued, an increasing number of GIs began to question the war itself and turned to organized resistance to protest their being in Vietnam (Boyle, 1973). While the GI movement may have been, in part, a motivating factor behind the sporadic instances of combat refusal in Vietnam, it is equally true that the movement was basically ineffectual in creating any type of massive resistance among combat troops. Similar examples of troop demoralization occurred in Korea as that war was winding down. . . .

SUMMARY AND CONCLUSION

This account of the genesis and development of the GI movement is far from complete and total. It does serve to illustrate, however, that although the United States military has always been faced with some internal dissension, especially during periods of mass mobilization, only during the Vietnam War has there emerged a full-scale protest movement among enlisted personnel.

The GI movement in its initial phases was self-generated. It arose in a period of conduciveness created by increasing civilian disenchantment with the war and the emergence of numerous other protest movements in the 1960s. As the military witnessed a large influx of civilians into the ranks, antiwar resistance continued receiving new impetus from the increasing publicity given it by the mass media, from a policy of severe repression by the military, and from the growing coalition between activist GIs and their civilian counterparts. The civilian movement provided legal aid, financial resources, ideologies, and organizers. Military reaction not only served as a most important shot-in-the-arm for the movement, but also served to move dissent away from a sole concern with the war (military policy) to the larger issue of constitutional rights (military authority) for enlisted personnel. While all of the above factors were necessary for the rise of the GI movement, none of them taken alone was sufficient. It was the admixture of all of them which gave rise to a movement among some enlisted persons in opposition to the war and to the military in general.

Perhaps the internal conflict that confronted the military during the last decade represents the most cogent argument against an all-volunteer armed force. To the extent that the military can control who enters the service and for how long, the "civilian" influence brought in by temporary employees, i.e., draftees, would be greatly reduced. . . .

REFERENCES

The *Ally*. July 1968.

The *Ally*. August 1968.

The *Ally*. September 1968.

The *Ally*. November 1968.

The *Ally*. December 1968.

Armed forces: Dissent in uniform. *Time*, April 25, 1969. pp. 20–21.

Berens, R. J. AWOL in Sweden. *Army Digest*, June 24, 1969, pp. 6–7.

Blumer, H. Collective behavior. In A. M. Lee (Ed.), *Principles of sociology*. New York: Barnes & Noble, 1951.

Boyle, R. *GI revolts: The breakdown of the U.S. Army in Vietnam*. San Francisco: United Front Press, 1973.

CAMP News. December 1972.

CAMP News. May 1973.

Dimona, J. *Great court-martial cases*. New York: Grosset & Dunlap, 1972.

Finn, J. *Conscience and command: Justice and discipline in the military*. New York: Vintage Books, 1971.

Flag in Action. December 1968.

Gardner, F. *The unlawful concert*. New York: Viking Press, 1970.

Gardner, F. The future of desertion. In A. Kopkind & J. Ridgeway (Eds.), *Decade of crisis*. New York: World, 1972.

Glessing, R. J. *The underground press in America*. Bloomington: University of Indiana Press, 1970.

Halstead, F. *GIs speak out against the war*. New York: Pathfinder Press, 1970.

Heinl, R. D. The collapse of the armed forces. In House Committee on Internal Security. *Investigations of Attempts to Subvert the United States Armed Forces*. Washington, D.C.: U.S. Government Printing Office, 1972.

House Committee on Internal Security, *Investigations of Attempts to Subvert the United States Armed Forces* (3 Vols.). Washington, D.C.: U.S. Government Printing Office, 1972.

Kopkind, A., & Gardner, F. Crackdown on GIs. In A. Kopkind & J. Ridgeway (Eds.), *Decade of crisis*. New York: World, 1972.

Linden, E. The demoralization of an army: Fragging and other withdrawal symptoms. *Saturday Review*, January 8, 1972, pp. 12–17; 55.

Lipsky, M. Protest as a political resource. *The American Political Science Review*, 1968, 62 (December), 1144–1158.

Musil, R. K. The truth about deserters. *The Nation*, April 16, 1973, pp. 495–499.

Nelson, J. The underground press. In M. C. Emery & T. C. Smythe (Eds), *Readings in mass communication*. Iowa: W. C. Brown, 1972.

Olson, M., Jr. *The logic of collective action*. New York: Schocken, 1968.

Radine, L. B. *The taming of the troops: Modern techniques of social control in the U.S. Army*. Unpublished doctoral dissertation, Washington University, St. Louis, 1973.

Rivkin, R. *GI rights and army justice: The draftees guide to military life and law*. New York: Grove Press, 1970.

Schuman, H., & Converse, P. E. Silent majorities and the Vietnam war. *Scientific American*, 1970, (Offprint No. 656).

Sherman, E. F. Dissenters and deserters. *The New Republic*, January 6, 1968, pp. 23–36.

Sherrill, R. *Military justice is to justice as military music is to music*. New York: Perennial Library, 1971.

Special Subcommittee on Disciplinary Problems in the Navy, *Report No. 92–81*. Washington, D.C.: U.S. Government Printing Office, 1973.

Staff. The GI antiwar movement: Little action and money and few GIs. *Armed Forces Journal*, September 7, 1970, pp. 32–33; 39.

Stanton, M.D. The soldier. In D. Spiegel & P. Keith-Spiegel (Eds.), *Outsiders USA*. San Francisco: Rinehart Press, 1973.

Stapp, A. *Up against the brass*. New York: Simon & Schuster, 1970.

Veterans Stars and Stripes for Peace. October 1968.

Walton, G. *The tarnished shield*. New York: Dodd, Mead, 1973.

Waterhouse, L. G., & Wizard, M.C. *Turning the guns around: Notes on the GI movement*. New York: Praeger, 1971.

Waters, M. A. *GIs and the fight against the war*. New York: Pathfinder Press, 1967.

Where It's At, 1968, 1(3).

Williams, R. N. *The new exiles: American war resisters in Canada*. New York: Liveright, 1971.

Zwerdling, D. Concerned brass. *The New Republic*, September 19, 1970, pp. 10–11.

ARTICLE 12

On Participation in Political Protest Movements

ANTHONY M. ORUM

To those of us interested in American politics, one of the most impressive facts in recent years is the number and variety of political protest movements. Since the late 1950s, more or less organized efforts for political change have been developed by young blacks and young whites, on college campuses and in urban ghettos, among conservatives and liberals. Many of those efforts have left enduring marks on American history and on the American polity. In one case, the Presidential campaign of the American Independent Party candidate altered the balance of power between the major political parties; in another instance, the anti-Vietnamese war effort brought about the premature political retirement of an incumbent President; and after the civil rights protests of the 1960s, new laws extended or implemented access to electoral participation.

To the chagrin of some scholars, myself included, our understanding of the dynamics of these movements for political change, especially the motivations which prompt people to participate in them, has lagged behind the rise and spread of the movements themselves. Many social scientists and laymen persist in believing that political protest movements, for example, the student Left, consist primarily of frustrated people who have nothing better to do with their time and no better device to relieve their discontent. That notion has been elaborated and formalized in five currently popular theories designed to explain why people participate in protest movements: status inconsistency, cumulative deprivation, relative deprivation, rising expectations, and social isolation. The first four of these theories are essentially very similar to one another relying on a causal sequence that leads from conflicting norms or expectations to psychological tension and, finally, to active involvement in political protest movements. The last theory—social isolation— assumes a different perspective on the social conditions which originate the causal sequence, but concurs with the other theories on the psychological circumstances that produce political protest.

This paper argues that those theories are at best only partly correct. In addition, it proposes a new way of examining participation in political protest movements, in the hope of deepening our understanding of the complex social-psychological elements involved in their formation . . .

ANALYZING NEGATIVE ANTECEDENTS

I shall begin by reviewing recent theories and empirical studies of participation in political protest movements. Extensive definitions of such movements and of participation will be left until the last section of this paper, where I propose my own perspective. Nevertheless, in order to avoid confusion I offer the following preliminary definitions: a political protest movement is an organization, or cluster of organizations, whose purpose is to change the established political system; participation in such movements can refer to any number of activities, but in most empirical research, it refers to some form of endorsement of, or belief in, a political movement.

Status Inconsistency

The status inconsistency thesis, introduced by Lenski (1954), assumes that—

> *Social status is multidimensional and hierarchical. Individuals are located in social space in terms of their positions on a variety of dimensions of status—occupation, education, income, ethnicity, etc. Each person occupies a particular status configuration, determined by his location on each of the component dimensions. Thus, some status sets will be "crystallized" in the sense that all of the component statuses give rise to similar values and expectations while others will not. The theory argues that those individuals whose positions on the different dimensions are not crystallized—those whose status memberships give rise to conflicting values and expectations—are likely to experience more strain and tensions than people whose status sets are crystallized (Treiman, 1966, pp. 651–652).*

Certain patterns of inconsistency, it is further claimed, are particularly apt to produce psychological tensions, for instance those which involve an ascribed status, like ethnicity, and an achieved status, like educational attainment. The theory argues that those tensions are likely to lead to unusual forms of behavior or attitudes, such as uncommonly high levels of antipathy toward minority groups.

Geschwender (1967), one of the first scholars to recognize the potential usefulness of status inconsistency theory in explaining the popular appeal of protest movements, argues that people who suffer from the internal conflicts created by status inconsistency may seek relief from their discomfort by committing themselves to radical movements. The participation of middle class black Americans in the civil rights movement of the 1960s and the involvement of middle class Jews in European Socialist parties, he points out, provide *prima facie* evidence for this view. Along parallel lines, Rush (1967) concludes that the "status politics" notion of Hofstadter (1963), Lipset (1963), and others, which was proposed in the 1950s to explain the origins of McCarthyism and similar right-wing political sentiments in America, evolved out of the same intellectual traditions as Lenski's idea of status inconsistency and bears a close resemblance to it.

Although most often tested for its capacity to predict conventional political beliefs (Kelly & Chambliss, 1966; Kenkel, 1956; and Lenski, 1954), the theory of status inconsistency has also been examined for its adequacy in explaining the support of political protest movements. Using education, income, and occupation as measures of status, Rush (1967), for example, finds a relationship between status inconsistency and right-wing extremist beliefs, status inconsistents being the more apt to endorse such ideas. Like several other investigators, including Lenski himself, Rush unfortunately assumes that the inconsistency, or strain, effect is a linear function of his measures of status; consequently, his method of analysis does not permit him to determine whether his data represent a simple additive effect of the status measures or an additive effect *plus* a component due to inconsistency, or strain (see Blalock, 1966, pp. 55–58). Researchers who apply an additive statistical model to data where status inconsistency effects are thought to hold consistently find that such a model provides a reasonably accurate prediction of results (see, for example, Portes, 1972; Treiman, 1966). Thus, suspicion is cast on any study that purports to have uncovered the existence of status inconsistency but fails to consider results based on a simple additive model.

Involvement in the recent black civil rights movement in the United States has been the subject of several different attempts to test status inconsistency or related theses. Gary Marx (1967) found an interaction or inconsistency effect of occupation and education on support for civil rights militancy; but, again, it is difficult to unravel the separate input of each variable from the interaction component. An investigation by Pinard, Von Eschen, and Kirk (1969) of Maryland civil rights activities in 1961 allegedly revealed inconsistency effects as well, but these data are subject to the same difficulty in interpretation as Marx's. And one other investigation of the correlates of civil rights activism (Surace & Seeman, 1967) found that status concern accounts for only minor variation in the civil rights activity of both blacks and whites. Finally, Portes' study (1971, 1972) of support for left-wing radicalism in Chile in the late 1960s also uncovered no relationship between status inconsistency and left-wing politics.

On balance, several observations can be made regarding studies of status inconsistency and engagement in political protest movements. First, existing evidence provides very limited support for a line between the two. Second, in view of the fact that an additive statistical model provides a reasonable explanation of the distribution of some political attitudes, more accurate and parsimonious predictions might be made if one assumes that such attitudes are a result of social learning rather than the outcome of psychological tensions. For instance, after discovering that an additive model fit data on social mobility and participation in voluntary associations, Vorwaller (1970) suggests that a socialization process may be at work.

> *when the mobile person is located socially and economically in his destination status but has not yet acquired all of the behavioral and attitudinal accoutrements typical of that status. He may be in an intermediate state of the process of adjusting his behavior so that it is consistent with the normative influences of his destination status (p. 483).*

So, too, one might account for the involvement of many, if not most, people in protest movements by relying on principles of learning and socialization rather than invoking complex psychological mechanisms as the status inconsistency argument does. Third, it is too early to make definitive statements about the usefulness of status inconsistency theory in explaining movement involvement: it has still undergone comparatively few empirical tests. No one has yet shown that there are real interconnections among status inconsistency, psychological strain, and belief or participation in movements. Until such links are demonstrated faith in the theory must rest on grounds other than scientific ones.

Cumulative Deprivation

Although now the least popular of the five theories, cumulative deprivation still received some attention in the literature (Geschwender, 1964; Pinard, 1967). Its central claim is that fundamental and cumulative economic impoverishment eventually creates the dissatisfaction necessary to make people participate in a political protest movement. It seems to make most sense in instances in which members of the working or lower classes are the heaviest supporters of a political movement as, for example, the types of extremist movements which Lipset (1960) claims received widespread support among the working classes, or the support for George Wallace in the 1968 U.S. Presidential election campaign (Converse, Miller, Rusk, & Wolfe, 1969; Lipset & Raab, 1969; Orum, 1970).

Recent studies of protest movements—or their equivalents—find virtually no evidence for the cumulative deprivation theory. The exceptions are, however, noteworthy. Among them are Zeitlin's study of Cuban workers (1966), which reveals that workers who experienced the greatest economic insecurity prior to the Cuban Revolution were its strongest supporters. And, in Detroit, Leggett (1964) found that workers subject to the most severe economic insecurity tended to be the most class conscious—a necessary condition for involvement in political movements according to Marxian theory.

But the number of investigations which show no link between cumulative deprivation and political involvement far outweigh the exceptions. Pinard (1967) reports: "The data presented support the hypothesis that the Social Credit Party in Quebec failed, as did other political movements of both the left and right, to enlist the support of the poor at least as long as the parties remained relative weak" (p. 262). Pinard's references to other movements include the Poujadist movement in France in the 1950s, the Cooperative Commonwealth Federation in Canada studied by Lipset (1950), and support for Barry Goldwater in the 1964 U.S. Presidential election campaign. Portes' investigation in Chile (1971) also provides no evidence for the cumulative deprivation model, inasmuch as he discovers that neither socioeconomic status per se nor the intensity of subjective frustration among the lower classes led to a disproportionate degree of endorsement for radical politics. Segal's study (1969) of Chilean hospital personnel confirms Portes' results, as do the findings of Petras and Zeitlin (1968); each shows that groups other than the deprived are most likely to engage in movements for social and political change.

Turning to protest movements in the United States, one finds little evidence in favor of the cumulative deprivation thesis. Observers of the participation of black Americans in the recent civil rights movement found that it was principally middle class persons who favored or joined those activities (Marx, 1967; Matthews & Prothro, 1966; Orbell, 1967; Orum, 1972; Searles & Williams, 1962) Studies of white student protest activity in the 1960s revealed that the most prosperous and privileged of students participated in unusually large numbers (Block, Haan, & Smith, 1968; Braungart, 1966; Flacks, 1967; Lyonns, 1965; Peterson, 1968; Watts & Whittaker, 1966). Westby and Braungart (1966) demonstrated that members of the left-wing organization, Students for a Democratic Society, were more likely to come from middle class backgrounds whereas those who belong to right-wing groups like the Young Americans for Freedom were more apt to come from working class homes. (Nevertheless, since most members of YAF are found on college campuses, we cannot conclude that cumulative deprivation plays a central role in prompting them to participate.) Possibly the only contemporary case which supports the claims of the cumulative deprivation hypothesis is the electoral support mobilized for George Wallace in the 1964 primary and the 1968 general elections in the United States. But even a large share of that vote, especially in the South, seems to have resulted from a variety of factors; and the principal ones had little to do with miseries engendered by cumulative deprivation (Orum, 1970; Rohter, 1970). Finally, as I noted earlier, favorable sentiments for Senator Joseph McCarthy did not originate from the most deprived quarters of the American population (Hofstadter, 1963; Lipset, 1963).

Relative Deprivation

The lack of evidence to uphold the cumulative deprivation theory has led, among other things, to a belief that social and political protest movements gain most of their participants from the ranks of those who experience relative deprivation. This view point argues that "discontent, and subsequently, social rebellion, may arise among people who evaluate their achievements by reference to the standards and accomplishments of some similarly situated persons who differ only in terms of having different or more numerous advantages" (Orum & Orum, 1968, p. 523). Karl Marx laid down the essence of this notion, stating that—

> *A house may be large or small; as long as the surrounding houses are small it satisfies all social demands for a dwelling. But let a palace arise beside the little house, and it shrinks from a little house to a hut (Quoted in Ladd, 1966, p. 24).*

Although the relative deprivation thesis is essentially similar to the status inconsistency argument, as Geschwender (1964) notes, it is useful to distinguish between the two, if only because they are often treated as separate and independent explanations.

The most frequent recent attention to the relation between relative deprivation and movement participation has been in regard to explaining the origins of black civil rights activities in the United States (Ladd, 1966; Pettigrew, 1964; Searles & Williams, 1962; Thompson, 1965). In their examination of the correlates of civil rights activism among Southern black college students, Searles and Williams (1962) were among the first to recognize the possible importance of relative deprivation. Finding that middle class students represented the majority of participants, they speculated that the impetus to participation came from the deprivation middle class black students experienced when comparing themselves to middle class white students. Since then, other observations reinforce the conclusion that middle class black Americans were disproportionately represented in the civil rights movement (Marx, 1967; Matthews & Prothro, 1966; Orbell, 1967). Nevertheless, Orum and Orum (1968) found that black students from relatively deprived backgrounds, i.e., ones whose father's education was high but whose family income was low, were no more likely to participate than other black students. Their inspection of differential participation among the lower and middle class black students in settings of varying socioeconomic composition likewise revealed negative results.

The one overriding fact that emerges from recent studies is that middle class persons are the more apt to endorse, or actively participate in, political protest movements. Yet not a single study shows that such persons actually experience a sense of deprivation relative to others in their social world. No results prevent us from inferring that other factors, perhaps the level of education or degree of political awareness, play an equally, if not more, prominent role in people's support of protest movements.

Rising Expectations

Although the thesis of rising expectations resembles the status inconsistency and relative deprivation arguments, it too has been treated as a special source of protest movements and merits separate consideration here.

The rising expectations argument suggests that if, because of a partial fulfillment of their ambitions, people are subject to heightened aspirations, they may then become disenchanted by the too gradual improvement of their lot, and channel their discontent in a political protest movement. In depicting the origins of the English, American, French, and Russian Revolutions, Brinton (1958) relies heavily on this idea. He observes that the "economic grievances of certain groups—not so much economic distress, as a feeling that their opportunities for getting on in this world are unduly limited by political arrangements—seem to be one of the symptoms of revolution" (p. 36). Davies' attempt (1962) to develop a theory of revolution also embodies the central elements of the rising expectations model insofar as it connects the conditions of heightened aspirations with blocked opportunities. Among other proponents of this theory is Meier (1967), who regards it as the impetus for the recent black protest in the United States.

No matter how plausible the theory appears, one must evaluate the evidence on which it rests. In their sample of 386 participants in a civil rights demonstration in Maryland in 1961, Von Eschen, Kirk, and Pinard (1969) test and confirm the following proposition: "The greater the gap between a demonstrator's occupational aspirations and his expectations, the more intense was his participation in the movement" (p. 312). This held true for white and black demonstrators alike. In contrast, in a study of 3,500 black college students, Orum and Orum (1968) uncovered no support at all for the thesis of rising expectations. For example, they tested the hypothesis that students who feel that their employment opportunities are limited are the most likely to engage in the civil rights movement. The evidence for this hypothesis as well as two others provided no support for the theory. And Portes' study (1971) of Chilean supporters of left-wing radicalism also provided no support for a similar hypothesis.

Despite its popularity, this viewpoint has not received systematic and intense attention in empirical studies. Nonetheless, since the previous results concerning studies of status inconsistency and relative deprivation are also relevant here in view of the similarity of their basic notions, it is reasonable to suppose that the rising expectations argument is not especially helpful in explaining participation in protest movements.

Isolation

The fifth, and final, model to be discussed here is substantially different from the others, inasmuch as it does not deal with movement participation in terms of economic or status-related strains. This is the motion of isolation, depicted systematically in Kornhauser's work on mass society (1959), as well as in other investigations (Cohn, 1957; Talmon, 1962). According to Kornhauser, social isolation produces an availability for participation in political protest movements, and a susceptibility to political demagogues; for example, the Poujadist movement in France and the Nazi movement in Germany. Isolation may appear in a variety of forms, but is most commonly seen in the social isolation of recent migrants . . . as well as the isolation of those who do not belong to voluntary associations.

Of the five notions, the isolation thesis has received the least support in empirical studies. The several investigations of black protest activity in the United States all found that the least isolated individuals, in a broad sense, were also the most active or the most committed to civil rights militancy. Searles and Williams (1962) discovered that the most active black student civil rights participants were also extremely active in other campus groups. Orum (1972) found that black students who were most active on their college campuses—indeed those who were members of the campus political elite—were also much more likely to join and be active in the black student protest. Gary Marx (1967) found that organizational memberships—voting in 1960 and an overall index of social participation—are each positively and strongly related to civil rights militancy. Using an attitudinal dimension of parallel meaning, Surace and Seeman (1967) showed that a generalized sense of powerlessness has but a trivial impact on civil rights activism. And in his study of left-wing radicalism in Chile, Portes (1971) is unable to confirm the migration interpretation of the isolation thesis. Thus, this view, like all the others discussed here, receives little empirical verification . . . .

THE PATHS TO PARTICIPATION: A SYNTHESIS

My effort to provide some new directions will begin with a basic observation: in the life cycle of any protest movement, deprivation and isolation models, as well as socialization or organizational approaches, are all likely to explain why some groups of people will participate. But each will not work equally well on all occasions or for all varieties and degrees of participation in a movement. My intention here will be to demonstrate how a single theoretical scheme can embrace that complexity.

Four separate mechanisms lead to participation in political protest movements, each corresponding to a major strand of research.

The first strand is *socialization*. Unfortunately it has been the most overlooked by contemporary inquiries; nevertheless, it is a vital source for one segment of movement participants. This segment, which I shall refer to as the *social affinity* segment, are people who enter a movement for one of two reasons: because their own values have an affinity with the espoused purposes of a political movement, or because their friends or other associates are themselves drawn into the political movement. In general, this segment represents the earliest joiners of a movement, and certainly seems to be among the more vocal.

I shall refer to the second strand of inquiry into participation as the *deprivation* strand, which encompasses absolute and relative deprivation models together with the rising expectations view discussed earlier in this paper—all more or less derived from the Marxian mode of analysis, with its emphasis on the connections between deprivation, class consciousness, and political formations. The group of people brought into a movement through this mechanism, the *relatively deprived,* are generally those who have experienced some setbacks in their lives and believe that their situation does not, or even will not, meet their goals or expectations. Many have had fewer hardships, in absolute numbers or even in intensity, than others; but what is critical is that they *perceive* themselves to have been deprived with respect to goals which they may have set or wished to achieve. Recent interpretations of this approach, particularly in the industrialized countries of the world, suggest that many of these people are middle class. I believe that they represent the largest single potential source for most protest movements—and it is they, and their dissatisfactions, whom movements most attempt to exploit.

The third strand of insight into participation in movements derives from the *psychopolitical* school of research in political behavior, among whom I include researchers like Angus Campbell and his colleagues at Michigan, who have studied the antecedents of voting behavior. Such scholars find that the people who tend to turn out regularly to vote are those who feel they can affect the political system in some way; conversely, those who do not turn out to vote are generally those who feel they cannot affect the political system. It is the former one most often finds in political movement activities, those to whom I shall refer as *political effectuals:* people who feel they can affect the political system, largely because they have affected it in the past through a variety of channels, particularly through their involvement in political and quasi-political organizations. They are the people with political expertise, the types likely to "hire on" at an early stage, because of their administrative and organizational experience; and, without question they are the group most necessary for the ultimate victory of any political movement.

The fourth and final strand of inquiry into protest movement participation, the *mass society* perspective originated by Kornhauser (1959), helps us identify the fourth critical segment in protest movements, the periodically *unengaged.* In my opinion, this segment is also of vital importance to the success of a movement and predominates in movements, or stages of movements, devoted chiefly to physical action. Without people who have time on their hands, as it were, great revolutions would probably never get off the ground. Among these people are many singled out by Kornhauser: for instance, the unemployed, students, the old, and the young. All have in common a single characteristic, viz., they can use substantial amounts of their time more or less as they please; hence, they are more able to involve themselves in a movement's activities than people whose work is more structured and routinized.

By integrating these four approaches and major strands of research a model of participation in political protest movements can be developed. My representation of this model, in the form of a path diagram, is shown in Figure 1. The variables in that diagram, identified and elaborated below, are conceptual ones, and require some clarification before their precise relationship to participation, and the exact routes to participation which they affect, are discussed.

Participation (X_1). This variable refers to the amount of time, activity, or money contributed to a protest movement. We often know only whether or not a person participated (or claimed to participate). That is only one way of operationalizing the concept; however, its use alone will dramatically affect the predictions we make.

Political Trust (X_2). This variable refers to a person's belief that the political system is performing its tasks satisfactorily. As Gamson (1968) puts it, this dimension refers to a person's feelings about the outputs of the system, e.g., its policies or symbolic gestures; and

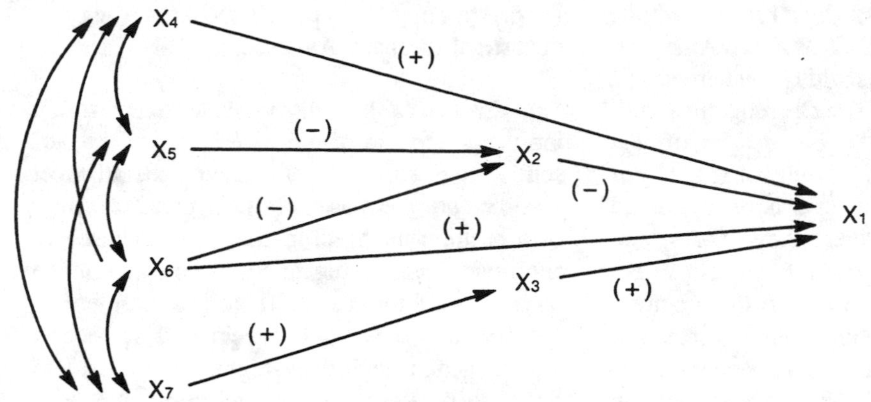

X_1 = Participation
X_2 = Political trust
X_3 = Political efficacy
X_4 = Unstructured work routine
X_5 = Subjective dissatisfaction
X_6 – Subgroup identification
X_7 = Self-esteem

FIGURE 1 A Causal Model of the Antecedents of Participation

it can operate with respect to any facet or type of system, e.g., authorities or local political systems, respectively.

Political Efficacy (X_3). This variable refers to the belief that one can affect what happens in the political system at some level of the system, and through some means, e.g., voluntary associations or writing to one's congressional representatives.

Unstructured Work Routine (X_4). This variable designates the amount of flexibility one has in determining when one will work. Groups typically high in such flexibility are students, the unemployed or periodically employed workers, college professors, and housewives; those typically low in this dimension are factory workers and white-collar employees in 9-to-5 jobs. Essentially what the former groups possess and the latter do not is more freedom to choose exactly how they will spend their time.

Subjective Dissatisfaction (X_5). This variable refers to an individual's belief that he is in some respects deprived. Most often this refers to a discrepancy between one's current situation and one's expectations; sometimes it refers to the belief that one's future will not measure up to one's hopes for it. The situation itself frequently refers to personal achievement in terms of life goals; sometimes, however, it may be more specific, referring to expectations for family life, work life, and so on. People who perceive (or are perceived by significant others to have) a fairly substantial discrepancy between their actual and expected situations are commonly referred to as the "relatively deprived"; they perceive that they are deprived relative to their own as well as to others' expectations for them.

Subgroup Identification (X_6). This variable refers to a more or less conscious identification with the subgroup in whose name a political movement, in effect, acts. It must be precisely and carefully identified for each protest movement. For example, the subgroup of the civil rights movement in the 1960s, taken as a whole, was blacks; for the pre-1968 Wallace American Independent Party, it was white Southerners. (It is essential to note that such subgroups will change over time, often by design of the movement's leaders, becoming narrower or broader. Obviously movements hope to expand the subgroup whose interest they express but many movements have gone into an eclipse because their leaders failed to identify the subgroup boundaries appropriately. Some successful movements, like the civil rights movement in the late 1960s, suffered a demise because, among other reasons, they tried to expand their boundaries too far: civil rights leaders expanded the movement's representation from blacks to the "poor," a subgroup at once too broad and too distasteful for many Americans.)

Self-Esteem ***(X_7).*** This variable refers to an individual's sense of regard for himself or herself. People with high self-esteem generally feel that they are the masters of their own fate, their own destiny; they feel in control of themselves and their situation, regardless of how an outside observer might access it. There is a close correspondence between self-esteem and subjective dissatisfaction, with those higher on self-esteem likely to be lower on dissatisfaction, and conversely. It is important, nonetheless, to distinguish between the two because each is likely to vary somewhat independently of the other . . . .

REFERENCES

Aberbach, J. A., & Walker, J. C. Political trust and racial ideology. *American Political Science Review,* December 1970, 64, 1199–1219.

Bandura, A., & Walters, R. H. *Social learning and personality development*. New York: Holt, Rinehart and Winston, 1963.

Berkowitz, L. *Aggression: A social psychological analysis*. New York: McGraw-Hill, 1962.

Blalock, H. M. The identification problem and theory building: The case of status inconsistency. *American Sociological Review,* February 1966, 31, 52–61.

Block, J., Haan, N., & Smith, M. B. Activism and apathy in contemporary adolescents. In James F. Adams (Ed.), *Understanding adolescence: Current developments in adolescent psychology*. Boston: Allyn and Bacon, 1968. Pp. 198–231.

Braungart, R. G. SDS and YAF: Backgrounds of student political activists. Department of Sociology, Pennsylvania State University, 1966. Mimeo.

Brinton, C. *The anatomy of revolution*. New York: Vintage Books, 1958.

Cohn, N. *The pursuit of the millennium*. New York: Harper and Brothers, 1957.

Converse, P. E., Miller, W. E., Rusk, J. G., & Wolfe, A. G. Continuity and change in American politics: Parties and issues in the 1968 election. *American Political Science review,* December 1969, 63, 1083–1105.

Davies, J. C. Toward a theory of revolution. *American Sociological Review,* February 1962, 27, 5–19.

Davies, J. C. (Ed.) *When men revolt and why*. New York: Free Press, 1971.

Dollard, J., Doob, L. W., Miller, N. E., Mowrer, O. H., & Sears, R. R. *Frustration and aggression*. New Haven: Yale University Press, 1939.

Flacks, R. The liberated generation: An exploration of the roots of student protest. *Journal of Social Issues,* Winter 1967, 23, 52–75.

Forward, J. R., & Williams, Jay R. Internal-external control and black military. *Journal of Social Issues,* Winter 1970, 26, 75–92.

Fraser, J. The mistrustful-efficacious hypothesis and political participation. *Journal of Politics,* May 1970, 32, 444–449.

Gamson, W. A. *Power and discontent*. Homewood, Ill.: Dorsey Press, 1968.

Geschwender, J. A. Social structure and the Negro revolt: An examination of some hypotheses. *Social Forces*. December 1964, 43, 248–256.

Geschwender, J. A. Continuities in the theories of status consistency and cognitive dissonance. *Social Forces,* December 1967, 46, 160–171.

Gurin, P., Gurin, G., Lao, R. C., & Beattie M. Internal-external control in the motivational dynamics of Negro youth. *Journal of Social Issues,* Summer 1969, 25, 29–53.

Hagedorn, R., & Labovitz, S. Participation in community associations by occupation: A test of three theories. *American Sociological Review*, April 1968, 33, 272–283.

Hofstadter, R. The pseudo-conservative revolt. In Daniel Bell (Ed.), *The radical right*. Garden City, L.I., N.Y.: Doubleday & Co., 1963. Pp. 63–80.

Hyman, H. A. Dimensions of social-psychological change in the Negro population. In Angus Campbell and Philip E. Converse (Eds), *The human meaning of social change*. New York: Russell Sage Foundation, 1972. Pp. 339–390.

Kelly, K. Dl, & Chambliss, W. J. Status inconsistency and political attitudes. *American Sociological Review*, June 1966, 31, 375–382.

Kenkel, W. F. The relationship between status consistency and political-economic attitudes. *American Sociological Review*, June 1956, 21, 365–368.

Kornhauser, W. *The politics of mass society*. New York: Free Press, 1959.

Ladd, E. C., Jr. *Negro political leadership in the South*. Ithaca: Cornell University Press, 1966.

Lane, R. E. *Political life*. Glencoe, Ill.: Free Press, 1959.

Leggett, J. Economic insecurity and working class consciousness. *American Sociological Review*, April 1964, 29, 226–234.

Lenski, G. Status crystallization: A non-vertical dimension of social status. *American Sociological Review*, August 1954, 19, 405–413.

Lenski, G. Social participation and status crystallization. *American Sociological Review*, August 1956, 21, 458–464.

Orum, A. M. *Black students in protest: A study of the origins of the black student movement*. Arnold and Caroline Rose Monograph Series. Washington, D.C.: American Sociological Association, 1972.

Orum, A. M. & Orum, Amy W. The class and status bases of Negro student protest. *Social Science Quarterly*, December 1968, 49, 521–533.

Paige, J. M. Political orientation and riot participation. *American Sociological Review*, October 1971, 36, 810–820.

Peterson, R. E. The student Left in American higher education. *Daedalus*, Winter 1968, 97, 293–317.

Petras, J. & Zeitlin, M. Miners and agrarian radicalism. In James Petras and Maurice Zeitlin (Eds.), *Latin American revolution or reform?* Greenwich, Conn.: Fawcett, 1968. Pp. 235–248.

Pettigrew, T. *A profile of the Negro American*. Princeton, N. J.: D. Van Nostrand Co., 1964.

Pinard, M. Poverty and political movements. *Social Problems*, Fall 1967, 15, 250–263.

Pinard, M. Mass society and political movements: A new formulation. *American Journal of Sociology*, May 1968, 37, 682–690.

Pinard, M., Von Eschen, D., & Kirk, J. Processes of recruitment in the sit-in movement. *Public Opinion Quarterly*, Fall 1968, 33, 355–369.

Portes, A. On the logic of post-factum explanations: The hypothesis of lower-class frustration as the cause of leftist radicalism. *Social Forces*, September 1971, 50, 26–44.

Portes, A. A status inconsistency and lower-class leftist radicalism. *Sociological Quarterly*, Summer 1972, 13, 361–382.

Portes, A. A model for the prediction of lower-class radicalism. Paper presented at the Annual Meeting of the American Sociological Association, New York City, August 1973.

Rohter, I. S. The genesis of political radicalism: The case of the radical right. In Roberta Sigel (Ed.), *Learning about politics: A reader in political socialization*. New York: Random House, 1970. Pp. 626–651.

Rush, G. B. Status consistency and right wing extremism. *American Sociological Review*, February 1967, 32, 86–92. Searles, R., & Williams, J. A., Jr. Negro college students' participation in sit-ins. *Social Forces*, March 1962, 40, 215–219.

Segal, B. E. Dissatisfaction and desire for change among Chilean hospital workers. *American Journal of Sociology*, November 1969, 75, 375–388.

Smith, D. H. A psychological model of individual participation in formal voluntary organizations: Application to some Chilean data. *American Journal of Sociology*, November 1969, 72, 249–266.

Surace, S. J. & Seeman, M. Some correlates of civil rights activism. *Social Forces*, December 1967, 46, 197–207.

Talmon, Y. Pursuit of the millennium: The relation between religious and social change. *European Journal of Sociology*, March 1962, 3, 125–148.

Thompson, D. The rise of the Negro protest. *Annals of the American Academy of Political and Social Science*, January 1965, 357, 18–29.

Treiman, D. J. Status discrepancy and prejudice. *American journal of Sociology,* May 1966, 71, 651–664.

Von Eschen, D., Kirk, J., & Pinard, M. The conditions of direct action in a democratic society. *Western Political Quarterly,* June 1969, 22, 309–325.

Vorwaller, D. J. Social mobility and membership in voluntary associations. *American Journal of Sociology,* January 1970, 75, 481–495.

Watts, W., & Whittaker, D. Free speech advocates at Berkeley. *Journal of Applied Behavioral Science,* 1966, 2, 41–62.

Westby, David L., & Braungart, R. Class and politics in the family backgrounds of student political activists. *American Sociological Review,* October 1966, 31, 690–692.

Zeitlin, M. Economic insecurity and the political attitudes of Cuban workers. *American Sociological Review,* February 1966, 31, 31–51.

ARTICLE 13

Relative Deprivation and Social Movements: A Critical Look at Twenty Years of Theory and Research

JOAN NEFF GURNEY
KATHLEEN J. TIERNEY

. . . *The Concept of Relative Deprivation.* The SM literature contains several implicit and explicit definitions of RD. Gurr (1970) and Morrison (1973), for example, both employ a relatively broad definition of RD as the perception that individual achievements have failed to keep pace with individual expectations. James Geschwender defines RD somewhat more narrowly, using the motion of reference groups. He argues RD is the perception that one's membership group is in a disadvantageous position, relative to some other group. However, he asserts status inconsistency and rising expectations can also be subsumed under the RD concept (Geschwender, 1964). A common thread in the literature is that RD is a *perceived* discrepancy between expectations and reality. Wilson (1973) and Runciman (1966) even argue there need not be an objective referent corresponding to the perception.

One difficulty in virtually all conceptualizations of RD is that the nature of the relationship between objective conditions and perceptions is never delineated. This may be due in part to the fact that theorists typically make distinctions among types and patterns of RD, without clarifying what these distinctions mean, or what they imply for measurement. Gurr (1970), for example, discusses three main "patterns" of RD: detrimental, aspirational, and progressive. Additionally, he identifies four "sources" of value expectations: past conditions, abstract ideals, standards of a leader, and reference groups. Morrison (1971) distinguishes two "types" of RD—detrimental and aspirational—which he defines in a manner similar to Gurr. Feierabend et al. (1969) present graphs of five "patterns" of rapid social change they claim are highly conducive to the development of systemic frustration a concept which they define in RD terms.

These distinctions confuse, rather than clarify, the concept. Should types, patterns, or sources be thought of as objective circumstances or as perceptions? Does aspirational, detrimental, or progressive deprivation refer to structural circumstances from which the perception of RD arises or to qualitatively different types of perceptions? Questions like these are important because they imply the way RD should be measured. For example, if detrimental, aspirational, and other variants are viewed as sources of RD, then logically RD becomes an intervening perceptual variable which explains the relation-

Gurney, Joan Neff, & Tierney, Kathleen J. (1982, Winter). Relative deprivation and social movements: A critical look at twenty years of theory and research. *Sociological Quarterly, 23,* 33–47.

ship between structural conditions and resultant social movement activity. This view necessitates measuring the perceptions of a population under a set of conditions A, B, and C in order to determine which condition or combination of conditions leads to the development of RD. While some authors (e.g., Davies) advocate this approach, it is not used. Instead, discussions blur the distinction between structural conditions which may give rise to RD and the perception of RD itself. The confusion of structural and psychological levels has led to misguided attempts to infer individual attitudes from macroeconomic indices, such as the GNP.

Even resource mobilization theorists acknowledge that deprivations of various kinds may play a role as background factors in emerging social movements (cf. Oberschall, 1973; McCarthy and Zald, 1973). Before the RD concept can have general utility, however, certain issues must be resolved. As indicated, there needs to be a greater degree of consensus on the definition of RD. First, the question of whether it should be used solely in reference group terms, or used more broadly to refer to any negative discrepancy between aspirations and achievements, needs to be addressed. In addition, greater consideration should be given to how to define RD—in objective or subjective terms. Writers may wish to employ the concept in both senses. On the other hand, they may wish to define RD solely in perceptual terms; if so, they should do so consistently. Finally, they should measure the concept at the individual level and attempt to clarify the linkages between RD and its objective antecedents and consequents.

Theoretical Bases of the RD Perspective. The link between RD and SM's is grounded in longstanding principles of social psychology, specifically either frustration-aggression theory or cognitive balance approaches. Several writers employ the frustration-aggression model to explain linkages between RD and the occurrence of civil strife (Gurr, 1969, 1970); revolution (Davies, 1962, 1969); or political violence (Feierabend et al., 1969). The cognitive balance approach is similar to the frustration-aggression model in that it posits an underlying state of individual psychological tension that is relieved by SM participation. Although this perspective is not as well developed in the literature as the frustration-aggression approach, at least two proponents (Morrison, 1973; Geschwender, 1964, 1968) make a cognitive balance approach central to their formulations. Morrison sees RD as a type of cognitive dissonance (between a legitimate expectation and the belief it will not be fulfilled) which produces psychic tension, leading to tension-reduction activities such as "organized group action to change the structural source of the blockage" (1973:109–10). Drawing on Lenski's status inconsistency formulations (1954, 1956), Geschwender (1964) explains black social movement participation by arguing the blacks in the 1960s were increasingly status inconsistent both in an absolute sense and in relation to whites. Later he argues RD is a result of cognitive dissonance having its origins in status inconsistency (Geschwender, 1968).

The adequacy of both these theoretical models can be challenged on several grounds. Each problem area is discussed briefly below.

1. *Strength of the association between underlying psychological processes and specific tension-reducing activities.* Social-psychological research suggest that regardless of which of the two perspectives is adopted, the strength of the association between psychological tensions and SM activities will be extremely weak, at best. The original version of the frustration-aggression hypothesis posited a necessary and sufficient relationship between the two variables (Dollard et al., 1939). This stance was modified by Miller (1941), who argued aggression is but one possible consequence of frustration. In the decades following these initial statements, there have been numerous suggestions for refinement of the original hypothesis. A long list of contingent fac-

tors has been suggested: individual differences in tolerance for frustration; effects of aggression-eliciting stimuli; anticipations or expectations of goal achievement; the role of modeling in shaping aggressive behavior (Berkowitz, 1969); strength and arbitrariness of frustration; and the instrumental value of aggression for the individual (Buss, 1961). In short, a body of scholarly work suggest the nature of strength of the link between frustration and aggression is an open question. Unfortunately, the frustration-aggression hypothesis has too often been treated as an assumption in the RD literature. Little consideration is given to the notion there may be responses to deprivation-included frustration other than a collective aggressive response. It is instead assumed that there is a critical point beyond which accumulated frustrations explode into revolt or revolution. What the nature of this point is and how long it takes to reach it are relatively untouched topics in the RD literature. Similarly, a major problem with cognitive imbalance is that SM participation is only one among several ways an individual might deal with a general feeling of dissatisfaction. As Festinger (1957) notes, dissonance reduction may be affected by changing one's attitudes or cognitions as well as by changing one's behavior. Lenski (1954) likewise states alternative responses to status inconsistency include blaming self, blaming others, and withdrawal, as well as supporting efforts to change the social structure. It is not enough to assert that cognitive dissonance and/or status inconsistency create tensions which lead to the development of SM's. At the very least, there appears to be a need for greater specification of the conditions under which one outcome, rather than others, will occur.

2. *Strength of the association between attitudes and behavior.* As Deutscher (1966) notes, a number of scholars, e.g., LaPiere, Mills, Merton, and Blumer, caution against accepting an individual's attitude as an indicator of possible future action. The existence of an attitude-behavior discrepancy has also been borne out time after time in empirical research. For example, in his classic review of studies concerning attitudes and behavior, Wicker concluded there is "little evidence to support the postulated existence of stable, underlying attitudes within the individual which influence both his verbal expressions and his actions" (1969:75). By the mid-1970s, negative results of research attempting to show attitude-behavior congruence, together with work on the influence of contingent factors on the attitude-behavior link (cf. DeFleur and Westie, 1958; Acock and DeFleur, 1972) led to the conclusion by at least one writer that "the bivariate relationship between attitude and behavior is no longer a research issue" (Liska, 1974:270). More recent research tends to support this conclusion. (See Schuman and Johnson, 1976; Andrews and Kandel, 1979, for discussions of work on attitude-behavior linkages.) The notion that behavior is explained only tenuously, if at all, by underlying individual dispositions is potentially devastating to the RD formulation, which rests partially on an assumption of correspondence between individual frustration or cognitive discomfort and participation in collective action.

3. *Nominalistic assumptions and convergence theories of collective behavior.* By extending to the group level a perspective formulated for and tested at the level of the individual behavior, RD theorists not only engage in reductionism but also adopt a position of nominalism and additivity, assuming collective action results from the coming together of frustrated individuals. Oberschall criticizes Gurr's theory on this account, calling it "basically psychological and individualist" (1978:301). Taking a nominalist position on SM phenomena also entails an assumption of homogeneity or uniformity of action and thoughts among participants—an assumption many writers in the area of collective behavior and social movements are no longer willing to make (cf. Turner and Killian, 1972; Orum, 1974; Marx and Wood, 1975). Because they portray movements

as aggregates of persons who share common tendencies or predispositions, cognitive balance and frustration-aggression versions of RD are both convergence theories (Turner, 1964). As such, they are more characterizations than explanations, positing a sociopsychological similarity among participants that may be more illusory than real (Turner and Killian, 1972). Recent work on social movement participation avoids this assumption, emphasizing instead the heterogeneity of participants' backgrounds, beliefs, motivations (Marx and Wood, 1975) and stressing differential paths to movement activism (Orum, 1974) and the importance of interpersonal ties and organization factors (Wilson and Orum, 1974) in mobilizing people into SM's.

4. *Nature of the purported causal linkages.* The bulk of the literature has treated RD as an independent, rather than dependent variable, reviewed RD as a necessary, but not sufficient, cause of SM's, and posited a unidirectional relationship between RD and SM's rather than a feedback or cyclical relationship. One consequence of the focus on RD as a variable which causes, promotes, or facilitates the development of SM's is that RD theorists (except perhaps Gurr, 1970; Sears and McConahay, 1970) generally give little attention to the emergence of RD itself, i.e., to how a sizeable proportion of a population comes to share a perception of illegitimate status or privilege discrepancies. To state that RD arises when people perceive that their expectations are not being met and that those expectations may be based upon past experiences, future hopes, or the experiences of another group is merely description, not explanation. The more interesting and yet relatively untouched questions center on the collectivization of RD; i.e., how the perception of RD comes to serve as a motivating force for a substantial portion of a population; how individuals who feel RD come to see their situation as requiring a collective solution; and what proportion of a population, or how many people must experience RD before the emergence a SM becomes likely. In a "grass roots" perspective such as RD, these questions, rather than being ignored, should be given considerable importance. However, among the macrolevel researchers, Sears and McConahay (1970) are virtually the only writers to address the idea of collectivization of grievances.

Writers also make little distinction between RD and frustration or psychological tension. Although they generally agree the perception of RD leads to feelings of frustration or dissonance-induced tension, which in turn find relief in SM activity, they blur the distinction between RD and the resulting feelings of tension, treating the connection as obvious and automatic. Feelings of frustration are seen as equivalent to RD. Little consideration is given to the possibility that a person whose expectations have been violated may respond by scaling down future aspirations rather than by enduring frustration or acting to reduce it.

Blurring the distinctions between RD an feelings of frustration also exacerbates the problem of moving from the structural to the psychological level without considering the steps in between. Researchers who use economic indices as measures of RD tend to relate these indices to SM activity directly, without employing any intervening measure of the level of frustration present in the population. The untested assumption is that "structural" RD is directly related to feelings of frustration or tension. The intervening variable is rarely measured, in part because it is confounded with the independent variable, "structural" RD, and in part because direct measures of frustration are not as readily available as national socioeconomic indices.

Theorists in the RD tradition generally propose RD as a necessary, but not sufficient, cause of SM activity (Davies, 1962; Geschwender et al., 1969; Gurr, 1969; Morrison, 1973). While there is common-sense appeal in this notion, it requires empirical support. Moreover, even if it *were* borne out empirically, the link could also prove relatively trivial: nonparticipants, as well as movement participants, might be experiencing feelings of RD, and to a similar extent; RD might be present in varying degrees among participants; and, in fact, there might conceivably be greater variation in RD levels among participants than between participants and nonparticipants (Marx and Holzner, 1977). Even if established empirically, the fact that SM joiners may be experienced RD might still tell us very little about the processes operating in movement emergence. This is essentially the point made by McPhail (1971), who reanalyzed data from several riot participation studies and found that even in that minority of studies where RD was found to be related to participation, the links were extremely weak.

RD theorists typically posit a unidirectional, rather than a cyclical or feedback model, in describing the RD/SM linkage. Scholars also discount the possibility that SM's themselves may be instrumental in producing perceptions of RD. It is possible structural inequality may exist prior to SM formation, but the perception of it—which RD theorists maintain is the most important factor explaining movement participation—may arise only after the movement has begun to do its work (Portes, 1971). Because RD research is typically *post hoc*, it cannot show whether perceptions of RD were a cause or a consequence of collective action.

EMPIRICAL ADEQUACY OF RD FORMULATIONS

This section begins with an assessment of how consistently and coherently the RD approach has been used in SM research and moves to a discussion of RD indicators. At the end of the section, we ask whether researchers have employed appropriate procedures for testing RD theory.

Consistency and Coherence of RD Research. How much agreement is there on the uses of the concept in empirical research? A look at the literature over the past twenty years suggest empirical work is characterized by considerable variety and eclecticism. Studies differ widely not only in their underlying theoretical rationales but also on the types of indicators used; the level at which variables are measured; the degree to which individual perceptions are emphasized, and the phenomena explained. There is little consensus on nominal and operational definitions, a great disparity in data-gathering strategies, and a marked tendency to specify a wide array of additional variables in different analyses. Measurement strategies are not always consistent with conceptualization. For example, while most researchers locate the sources of movement activity in intrapsychic processes, the studies are divided between those which obtain aggregate data on RD (Aberle, 1966; Davies, 1962, 1969; Feierabend et al., 1969; Geschwender, 1964; Gurr, 1969, 1970) and those which use self-report data on individuals (Bowen et al., 1968; Crawford and Naditch, 1970; Geschwender and Singer, 1970; Grofman and Muller, 1973; Pinard, Kirk, and von Eschen, 1969; Searles and Williams, 1962; Sears and McConahay, 1970). Writers using the frustration-aggression framework might be expected to relate individual psychological tension to movement activity; yet researchers such as Gurr do not do so but instead infer RD from economic and political indicators. Placing theoretical emphasis on perceptions does not necessarily lead to empirical investigation of perceptions. Geschwender and Singer (1970), for example, stress the importance of perception in their theoretical discussion; however, even though they gather data by means of interviews with individuals, rather than asking about perceptions, they employ indirect measures (income, education, occupation) and infer RD from these.

The literature also varies on what is being explained: movement emergence or individual participation. Some researchers (Searles and Williams, 1962; Bowen et al., 1968; Pinard, Kirk, and von Eschen, 1969) clearly are concerned with the latter. Others (Gurr, 1969, 1970; Feierabend et al., 1969) seem more interested in the origins of movement activity. Still others are concerned with both (Aberle, 1966) or seem not to be aware of the distinction (Crawford and Naditch, 1970).

Indicators of RD in Empirical Research. As used in the literature, RD is a very abstract concept, which could have many dimensions and any number of attitudinal and behavioral referents, including cognitions, beliefs, and attitudes with past, present, and future time orientations. In contrast with theoretical treatments, operationalizations of the concept in research tend to be narrow and unidimensional, with researchers adhering to a "one concept-one indicator" strategy.

Further, the RD concept has as its basis some rather complex reasoning about the ways people react to change in the area of valued goods, relative to others in society; RD research tends to oversimplify the relationship between deprivation and subsequent behavior. Since RD formulations are based loosely on the notion of reference groups, and since societies differ in the extent to which comparisons with other groups are meaningful to members, it seems logical to assume variations might occur in the extent to which structural conditions give rise to comparisons and the perception of RD among members of different societies. (For example, lower-caste Indians and ghetto-dwelling American blacks probably perceive differently the rich people they observe, due to differences in societal beliefs about mobility.) Yet cross-cultural research using the RD concept appears to assume that contextual factors operative similarly in all cultures, resulting in comparable levels of frustration or dissonance as well as in relatively equivalent amounts of movement activity.

Another problem with RD indicators was mentioned earlier; i.e., the reluctance on the part of many researchers to measure RD at the individual level, where theory states important processes are occurring. Feierabend et al. are aware of the difficulties with inferring psychological states from other data: "The most certain way to ascertain systemic frustration is through field work in the many countries, administering questionnaires . . . for the purpose of this study, an inexpensive and very indirect method was adopted" (1969: 257–58).

The use of indirect methods can be justified, provided researchers obtain independent evidence—from their own or other studies— linking structural strain of the kind discussed in theories of RD with individual perceptions of inadequate rewards or with feelings of frustration. However, this is not done in studies liking RD and SM's. We agree with Orum, who sees this omission as a major weakness in RD research: "As Hyman (1972) notes, theories which speak of the importance of discontent and dissatisfaction in prompting participation in political movements *must* develop indicators of those dimensions and cannot simply rely on the indicators of objective social statuses and status discrepancies" (1974: 192).

In short, researchers take as given the very link which must be empirically established to render RD theory plausible. Their failure to link convincingly psychological states with antecedent societal conditions on the one hand and with subsequent movement participation on the other is the Achilles heel of RD research.

Design of the Research and Adequacy of Findings. We now briefly discuss the empirical literature in terms of the extent to which studies show that RD and SM's are associated with one another; whether it has been demonstrated that changes in RD levels are accompanied by changes in SM phenomena; whether RD has been shown to precede SM activity in time; and whether alternative explanations which might account for social movement emergence or individual participation are considered.

1. *Association between RD and SM's.* Empirical work on the topic fails convincingly to demonstrate that Rd and SM's are associated. The typical strategy for such research is to find situations where SM activity is present and to look there for evidence of RD. This approach is seen in the work of Davies (1962, 1969) whose J-

curve hypothesis is illustrated via brief historical accounts of such events as the French Revolution and Dorr's Rebellion. Each example he presents supports the J-curve idea; there are no negative cases mentioned—no attempt to determine whether any revolution occurred without a J-curve, and no cases in which rising expectations were not followed by a revolution. Much of the quantitative research also fails to provide evidence of the existence of RD independent of the existence of SM activity. Findings which demonstrate that all B (movement participants) are A (relatively deprived) cannot be used to support statements about the extent to which members of A are members of B. A more valid approach would measure RD within heterogeneous populations and then seek data on movement activity among individuals or in societies manifesting different levels of RD.

A second caution against accepting findings showing an association between RD and SM's is that "we cannot in general infer from synchronic to diachronic correlation" (Galtung, 1967: 472). Empirical associations between two variables found by means of data gathered at a single point in time cannot be used as evidence for a broader, continuing association between the variables unless much more is either known or assumed about the strength and the direction of causal connections and the stability of contextual factors over time.

Finally, the argument for an association between RD and SM's is countered by other research (Lauer, 1972; Nelson, 1970; Orum, 1972) which fails to give support for RD hypotheses.

2. *Covariation.* It is commonly argued RD contributes to SM's because changes in RD levels are linked with changes in movement activity. While arguments are made to show that there is concomitant variation of the two phenomena, two weaknesses call these arguments into question: the lack of time reference in the research and the lack of attention to the question of what constitutes a critical level of RD.

Assertions about causal relationships which do not contain time specification are unfalsifiable because, in a given unit, changes in any X will be followed by changes in some Y, if sufficient time is permitted to lapse (Gibbs, 1972). Most RD studies refer to time only sketchily, if at all. Davies (1969) in his essay on the relationship between need satisfaction and revolution, seems to believe there is a relatively short time lapse—about two years— between frustrating social changes and societal dislocation, but this is never stated explicitly. Gurr confuses the issue further by suggesting that a comparatively short "critical period" may occur soon after the satisfaction of a salient value starts to decrease and that over time, "levels of value expectation or the salience of values, or both, are likely to decline; the victim is likely to become resigned to this condition" (1970—80). Thus, researchers' claims that covariation of RD and SM phenomena had been demonstrated should be viewed with skepticism.

Similarly, the question "How much is enough?" is dodged by most researchers. While Gurr, in his major theoretical statement (1970) distinguishes the dimensions of intensity and scope of RD and suggests ways to measure them, writers in general are mute on the question of the carrying capacity of societal tolerance for RD.

3. *Time order.* Despite the frequent assertions that a causal relationship between RD and SM's has been demonstrated, the majority of studies do not show RD existed prior to the onset of movement activity. On the whole, studies begin by positing, rather than testing, the assumption that RD precedes SM's. Crawford and Naditch state, for example: "We assume . . . that the causal sequence typically begins with the social system or background factors, which then lead to the psychological states of relative deprivation/gratification . . . and that these psychological states in turn cause the indicator behavior patterns" (1970: 216).

As noted, RD studies tend to be synchronic and *post hoc.* Data are gathered after a riot, or after a movement is under way, thus making it impossible to determine whether RD actually preceded the activity. The argument that the causal connection is the other way—that movement participation leads to a heightened sense of awareness of RD in members (Portes, 1971; Useem, 1980)—is equally plausible.

4. RD *research and competing explanations of movement phenomena.* In order to argue that one variable is influenced by another, other factors which might be confounded with the independent variable must be controlled for. Has RD research produced convincing evidence that social movements are traceable to deprivational states and not to other factors? This question can be approached first by considering methodology and second by considering theoretical/substantive issues.

a. Methodological aspects: Broadly speaking, empirical research on RD and SM's employs historical/descriptive case studies or multivariate analyses of individual or societal level data. Authors of historical and case studies (Aberle, 1966; Davies, 1969) attempt to provide evidence of causal connection by showing that RD and SM's are associated over time, by marshaling a preponderance of evidence for their arguments and by making comparisons and contrasts. These studies do not attempt to test hypotheses systematically; rather, they try to demonstrate that data are consistent with the framework of RD theory.

Matching and sampling are used in hypothesis-testing studies in the RD literature, but, unfortunately, they are used so haphazardly as to render the bulk of the research highly suspect. Examples of less-than-adequate designs include that of Bowen et al. (1968) which uses random samples, but no controls; that of Crawford and Naditch (1970) which reports high RD levels among samples of individuals living in riot-stricken sections of communities, but which does not contain data on RD in nonriot areas; and that of Geschwender and Singer (1970) which employs matching techniques, but on a nonrepresentative sample. (They find high RD levels among a random sample of Detroit "rioters," compared with a control group, but their "rioters" are a sample of persons arrested and incarcerated during the riots.) Finally, recall that those studies which use more elaborate methodology (Feierabend et al., 1969; Gurr, 1969, 1970) do not focus on the perception of deprivation itself but, rather infer individual psychological stress from aggregate-level data.

b. Substantive aspects: Recent research suggests other theoretical orientations may fit well with observed patterns of movement development and individual participation. The social control/resource mobilization approach is one such orientation (cf. Snyder and Tilly, 1972; Leites and Wolfe, 1970; Oberschall, 1973; McCarthy and Zald, 1973). These rationalist macrolevel perspectives have a parallel on the microlevel in approaches which view social movement activity as emerging in part from individual assessments of the costs and benefits of participating in collective action (cf. Fireman and Gamson, 1979; Oliver, 1980).

The social participation view of SM's (Marx, 1967; Orum, 1972) is another prominent microlevel perspective. According to this view, the most significant common characteristic of movement participants is not RD but prior organizational membership and involvement in other political activities.

Despite unresolved theoretical and conceptual problems, the RD perspective has grown—largely due to the efforts of energetic and creative researchers. However, viewed critically, research on RD and SM's fares no better than theory: it assumes too much, demonstrates too little. Although studies have helped dispel older myths about SM's, empirical research has failed to score decisive points for the RD approach and currently appears to be losing ground against theories offering alternative explanations for SM phenomena. In conclusion, we discuss possible reasons for the persistence of the approach and try to speculate about what the future may hold for SM research. . . .

REFERENCES

Aberle, David. 1966. The Peyote Religion Among the Navaho. New York: Wenner-Gren Foundation for Anthropological Research.

Acock, Alan, and Melvin De Fleur. 1972. "A configurational approach to contingent consistency in the attitude and behavior relationships." American Sociological Review 37 (December): 714–26.

Andrews, K. and D. Kandel. 1979. "Attitudes and behavior: a specification of the contingent consistency hypothesis." American Sociological Review 44 (April): 298–310.

Berk, Richard. 1974. Collective Behavior. Dubuque, Iowa: William C. Brown.

Berkowitz, Leonard. 1969. "The frustration-aggression hypothesis revisited." Pp. 1–28 in Leonard Berkowitz (ed.), Roots of Aggression. New York: Atherton Press.

Blumer, Herbert. 1951. "Collective behavior." Pp. 208–10 in A. M. Lee (ed.), Principles of Sociology. New York: Barnes and Noble.

Bottomore, T. B. 1963. Karl Marx: Early Writings. New York: McGraw-Hill.

Bowen, Don, Elinor Bowen, Sheldon Galoiser, and Louis H. Masotti. 1968. "Deprivation, mobility and orientation toward protest of the urban poor." American Behavioral Scientist (March–April): 20–24.

Buss, Arnold. 1961. The Psychology of Aggression. New York: John Wiley.

Crawford, Thomas, and Murray Naditch. 1970. "Relative deprivation, powerlessness, and militancy: the psychology of social protest." Psychiatry 33 (May): 208–23.

Davies, James. 1962. "Toward a theory of revolution." American Sociological Review 27 (February): 5–19.

———. 1969. "The J-curve of rising and declining satisfactions as a cause of some great revolutions and a contained rebellion." Pp. 547–76 in H. D. Graham and T. R. Gurr (eds.), Violence in America: Historical and Comparative Perspectives. Washington, D.C.: U.s. Government Printing Office.

———. 1971. When Men Revolt and Why: A Reader in Political Violence and Revolution. New York: Free Press.

DeFleur, M., and F. Westie. 1958. "Verbal attitudes and overt acts: an experiment on the salience of attitudes." American Sociological Review 23 (October): 667–73.

Deutscher, Irwin. 1966. "Words and deeds: social science and social policy." Social Problems 13 (Winter): 235–54.

Dollard, John, Leonard Doob, Neal Miller, O. Mowrer, and Robert Sears. 1939. Frustration and Aggression. New Haven: Yale University Press.

Feierabend, Ivo, Rosalind Feierabend, and Betty Nesvold. 1969. "Social change and political violence: cross national patterns." Pp. 497–545 in H. D. Graham and T. R. Gurr (eds.), Violence in America: Historical and Comparative Perspectives. Washington, D.C.: U.S. Government Printing Office.

Festinger, Leon. 1957. A Theory of Cognitive Dissonance. Stanford, Calif.: Stanford University Press.

Fireman, B., and W. Gamson. 1979. "Utilitarian logic in the resource mobilization perspective." In Mayer Zald and John McCarthy (eds.), The Dynamics of Social Movements: Resource Mobilization, Social Control and Tactics. Cambridge: Winthrop Publisher.

Freud, Sigmund. 1921. Group Psychology and the Analysis of the Ego. London: Hogarth.

Galtung, Johan. 1967. Theory and Methods of Social Research. New York: Columbia University Press.

Gamson, William. 1975. The Strategy of Social Protest. Homewood, Ill.: Dorsey.

Geschwender, James. 1964. "Social structure and the Negro revolt: an examination of some hypotheses." Social Forces 43 (December): 248–56.

———. 1968. "Explorations in the theory of social movements and revolutions." Social Forces 47 (December): 127–35.

Geschwender, James A., Benjamin D. Singer, and Richard W. Osborn. 1969. "Social Isolation and Riot Participation." Paper presented at annual meetings of American Sociological Association.

———, and Benjamin Singer. 1970. "Deprivation and the Detroit riot." Social Problems 17 (Spring): 457–63.

Gibbs, Jack. 1972. Sociological Theory Construction. Hinsdale, Ill.: Dryden Press.

Grofman, B., and E. Muller. 1973. "The strange case of relative gratification and potential for political violence: the V-curve hypothesis." American Political Science Review 67:514–39.

Gurr, Ted. 1969. "A comparative study of civil strife." Pp. 443–91 in H. D. Graham and T. R. Gurr (eds.), Violence in America: Historical and Comparative Perspectives. Washington, D.C.: U.S. Government Printing Office.

———. 1970. Why Men Rebel. Princeton: Princeton University Press.

Hinkle, Roscoe, and Gisela Hinkle. 1954. The Development of Modern Sociology. New York: Random House.

Hoffer, Eric. The True Believer, New York: Harper and Row.

Isaac, L., E. Mutran, and S. Stryker. 1980. "Political protest orientations among black and white adults." American Sociological Review 45 (April): 191–2133.

Jenkins, C., and C. Perrow. 1977. "Insurgency of the powerless: farm workers' movements (1946–72)." American Sociological Review 42 (April): 249–68.

Korpi, Walter. 1974. "Conflict, power, and relative deprivation." American Political Science Review 38 (December): 1569–78.

Lauer, Robert. 1972. "Social movements: an interactionist analysis." The Sociological Quarterly 13 (Summer): 315–28.

Leites, Nathan, and Charles Wolf, Jr. 1970. Rebellion and Authority. Chicago: Markham.

Lenski, Gerhard. 1954. "Status crystallization: a non-vertical dimension of social status." American Sociological Review 19 (August): 405–13.

———. 1956. "Social participation and status crystallization." American Sociological Review 21 (August): 458–64.

Liska, Allen. 1974. "Emergent issues in the attitude-behavior consistency controversy." American Sociological Review 39 (April): 261–72.

McCarthy, John, and Mayer Zald. 1973. The Trend of Social Movements in America: Professionalization and Resource Mobilization. Morristown, N.J.: General Learning Press.

———. 1977. "Resource mobilization and social movements: a partial theory." American Journal of Sociology 82 (May): 1212–41.

McPhail, Clark. 1971. "Civil disorder participation: a critical examination of recent research." American Sociological Review 36 (December): 1058–73.

Marx, G. 1967. Protest and Prejudice: A Study of Belief in the Black Community. New York: Harper and Row.

———, and J. Wood. 1975. "Strands of theory and research in collective behavior." Annual Review of Sociology 1:363–428.

Marx, J., and B. Holzner, 1977. "The social construction of strain and ideological models of grievance in contemporary movements." Pacific Sociological Review (August): 411–33.

Merton, Robert, and A. Kitt. 1950. "Contributions to the theory of reference group behavior." In R. Merton and P. Lazarsfeld (eds.), Studies in the Scope and Method of *The American Soldier*. Glencoe, Ill.: Free Press.

Miller, Neal. 1941. "The frustration-aggression hypothesis." Psychological Review 48 (July): 337–42.

Morrison, Denton. 1973. "Some notes toward theory on relative deprivation, social movements, and social change." Pp. 103–16 in R. R. Evans (ed.), Social Movements: A Reader and Source Book. Chicago: Rand McNally.

———, and Allan Steeves. 1967. "Deprivation, discontent, and social movement participation: evidence on a contemporary farmers' movement, the NFO." Rural Sociology 32 (December: 414–34.

Nelson, Joan. 1970. "The urban poor: disruption or political integration in third world cities?" World Politics 22 (April): 393–414.

Oberschall, Anthony. 1973. Social Conflict and Social Movements. Englewood Cliffs, N.J.: Prentice-Hall.

———. 1978. "Theories of social conflict." Annual Review of Sociology 4:291–315.

Oliver, P. 1980. "Rewards and punishments as selective incentives for collective action: theoretical investigations." American Journal of Sociology 85:1356–75.

Orum, Anthony. 1972. Black Students in Protest: A Study of the Origins of the Black Student Movement. Arnold and Caroline Rose Monograph Series. Washington, D.C.: American Sociological Association.

———. 1974. "On participation in political protest movements." Journal of Applied Behavioral Science 10:181–207.

Pinard, Maurice, Jerome Kirk, and Donald von Eschen. 1969. "processes of recruitment in the sit-in movement." Public Opinion Quarterly 33 (Fall): 355–69.

Portes, Alejandro. 1971. "On the logic of post-factum explanations: they hypothesis of lower-class frustration as the cause of leftist radicalism." Social forces 50 (September): 26–44.

Runciman, W. 1966. Relative Deprivation and Social Justice. Berkeley: University of California Press.

Sayles, Marnie. 1981. "Relative deprivation and collective protest: an impoverished theory?" Paper presented at the Annual Meetings of the American Sociological Association, Toronto.

Schuman, H., and M. Johnson. 1976. "Attitudes and behavior." Pp. 161–207 in A. Inkeles, J. Coleman, and N. Smelser (eds.), Annual Review of Sociology 2. Palo Alto: Annual Reviews.

Searles, Ruth, and J. Allen Williams, Jr. 1962. "Negro college students' participation in sit-ins." Social Forces 40 (March): 215–20.

Sears, D., and J. McConahay. 1970. "Racial socialization, comparison levels, and the Watts riot." Journal of Social Issues 26:121–40.

Skolnick, James. 1969. The Politics of Protest. New York: Simon and Schuster.

Snyder, David, and Charles Tilly. 1972. "Hardship and collective violence in France, 1830 to 1960." American Sociological Review 37 (October): 520–32.

Stouffer, S., E. Suchman, L. DeVinney, S. Star, and R. Williams. 1949. The American Soldier. Vols. 1–4. Princeton: Princeton University Press.

Tilly, Charles. 1978. From Mobilization to Revolution. Reading, Mass.: Addison-Wesley.

Tocqueville, Alexis de. 1966. The Old Regime and the French Revolution. Stuart Gilbert (trans,). Garden City, N.Y.: Doubleday and Company.

Traugott, M. 1978. "Reconceiving and social movements." Social Problems 26:38–49.

Turner, Ralph. 1964. "Collective behavior." Pp. 382–425 in R. E. L. Faris (ed.), Handbook of Modern Sociology. Chicago: Rand McNally.

———, and Lewis Killian. 1972. Collective Behavior, 2d ed. Englewood Cliffs, N.J.: Prentice-Hall.

Useem, B. 1980. "Solidarity model, breakdown model, and the Boston anti-busing movement." American Sociological Review 45 (June): 357–69.

Wicker, Allan. 1969. "Attitudes vs. action: the relationship of verbal and overt behavioral responses to attitude objects." Journal of Social Issues 25 (Autumn): 41–78.

Wilson, John. 1973. Introduction to Social Movements. New York: Basic Books.

Wilson, K., and A. Orum. 1976. "Mobilizing people for collective action." Journal of Political and Military Sociology 4:187–202.

PART THREE

Early Mobilization

Early mobilization is the stage when issues and goals become formulated and begin to shape collective action. Concurrently, leadership roles undergo elaboration and articulation from their initial stages of self and other appointment. It is at the mobilization stage that memberships are enlarged and deployed, and collective actions assume patterns of elaborated and formalized organizational strategies.

These early organizational activities differ between types of collectivities, and are commonly observed to differ, for example, among groups protesting esoteric issues, self-help groups, collectivities that appear to achieve immediately large-scale organization because of the popularity of their claims, social movements that rapidly achieve efficient organizational structure, and highly controversial or "deviant" groups that may remain underground for survival.

A specific example is the highly esoteric and member-oriented religious cult known as the Serpent Handlers, which operates throughout West Virginia and Kentucky and other parts of Appalachia. Members live in isolated hill areas, are typically poor, have low formal education, and are well known to one another prior to membership and participation. Recruitment, addressed more systematically later in this book, is highly selective and follows tight-knit networking contacts. Protection from potentially hostile critics and a curious press focusing on the psychological needs of the "deprived" membership, and insistence on membership compliance with a "pure" ideological perspective (e.g., no "backsliders") are necessary for the forward thrust of these groups.

By contrast, those protest groups, which are high on public acceptance and, relatedly, articulate mainstream values such as Mothers Against Drunk Drivers (MADD), have early advantages during the initial mobilization stage. It is possible for them to attend less to public opinion and to devote more attention and resources to the expansions of their membership base and the enlargement of resources for action.

The early mobilization stage, like the later formal organizational stage, *which may or may not be achieved* (see below), will vary in actions and structures according to variations on two major dimensions. These are (1) whether the collectivity pursues change in the existing social order (political, social, moral, etc.) or focuses primarily on services to the membership (which includes most voluntary, self-help organizations such as Alcoholics Anonymous) and (2) whether the climate of public opinion toward the collectivity is favorable or unfavorable. Although these are variable dimensions (i.e., no protest or member-focused group is concentrated *entirely* on social or member issues or is *universally* well received or rejected), most incidents of collective action and/or movement organizations can be ordered by these dimensions and their implications for early mobilization can be directly inferred.

For those collectivities with an external target (*societal* rather than member oriented) that enjoy widespread public support, early mobilization can be in pursuit of additional public support, greater resources, and larger memberships. Increased organizational resources represent success and more power for enlarged actions. Groups such as MADD fit this pattern of mobilization; within a few months of its initial formulation, the organization was receiving national exposure on network television. Most environmental groups also fit these conditions.

Groups pursuing social change not widely supported by the public, especially those focusing on changes in the normative structure of society, such as the women's movement and the civil rights movement, will typically be mobilized around a small coterie of significant members. An oligarchy or small, tight leadership core is a typical feature of these organizations. This was true for the early formulation of Marcus Garvey's "Back to Africa" movement earlier in this century. It has also been the case for the ebb and flow of the women's movement. In this section, Naomi Rosenthal, Meryl Fingrutd, Michele Ethier, Roberta Karant, and David McDonald (Article 14) note the importance of networks for the continuation and expansion of the women's movement. In a later section (Article 35), Verta Taylor elaborates on how the women's movement maintained a small, tight but retreatist structure during "abeyance" periods, in contrast to overt, direct protests during periods of greater public acceptance and increasing membership.

Groups focusing on member services are typically disapproved of by larger society if they are perceived as maintaining some type of cult or as subversive in the pursuit of their goals. The so-called Moonies came to be perceived in this manner. In their case, the reaction centered on "deprogramming" their members through their actual physical removal, largely at parental or friends' requests. Some persons became known as professional deprogrammers. Americans historically have feared cults and the word has come to be associated with evil, extremist actions. Cult members are variously referred as either perpetrators or as victims; the case of Patty Hearst became extraordinary because of the shift of public perception from victim to perpetrator to victim.

Early mobilization for member-serving groups (also called *expressive* as opposed to *instrumental* for those with social change goals) in disfavor with their societies typically incorporate strategies of secrecy, physical isolation, and strict boundaries. This is the case because when groups attempt to combine an intrusive and socialization control of members with an outreach effort that opens them to scrutiny, they invite intrusion and critical monitoring. In the case of the Mormons, success was achieved in the face of a suspicious environment through rigid and ingenious physical isolation in Utah.

Early mobilization of people serving groups with favorable environmental support appears to follow simpler organizational strategies. Whether religious self-improvement or lifestyle changes, members and their host organizations are applauded for attempting to better themselves. Still, an evolution of such organizations can be observed—a shift from some environmental suspicion to acceptance. Alcoholics Anonymous, founded in 1935 (see Article 23), followed such a course. Early AA groups were perceived as cult-like; acceptance later came with larger memberships and favorable media treatments.

In the following articles, Naomi Rosenthall and her colleagues (Article 14) set forth an excellent research strategy of network as well as cluster and analytical techniques to shed light on the nineteenth-century women reform movement in New York state. This covers an early mobilization stage. Interpersonal contacts and highly cohesive friendship cliques were highly instrumental in the maintenance and growth of the suffrage and women's rights organizations and the period of their collective activity between 1840 and 1914. A similar period of informal coteries of the women's movement is also documented by Verta Taylor (Article 35) for the women's movement during the twentieth century.

Precipitating environmental conditions are also documented by B. E. Aguirre, E. L. Quarentelli, and Jorge L. Mendoza (Article 15). They review the literature on the effects of participation in fads and on the identification and career of fads, and then test hypotheses from data on incidents of streaking on college campuses in the spring of 1974. A model of innovation diffusion, consisting of relative school prestige, sanctions, mass media effects, and the complexity and heterogeneity of schools, is also tested. Streaking incidents were heterogeneous, suggesting that the oddness, impulsivity, inconsequentiality, novelty, and ahistoric development of fads have been exaggerated. The authors also note the importance of environmental settings for the emergence of streaking, which again underscores the importance of setting conditions for the mobilization of collective action.

Stages of collective behavior, as outlined by Smelser's theory (Article 2), are tested by E. L. Quarantelli and James R. Hundley, Jr. (Article 16). The authors use information from their observations of a student demonstration to test Smelser's predictions regarding the six determinants of an outburst. Results do not support a key prediction of the theory, which is that the nature and influence of generalized hostile beliefs are sufficient and/or necessary for early mobilization.

Even crowds that may never reach a stage of formalized protest in the way of a social movement organization can be observed to follow a mobilization sequence. This occurs in a series of micro-organizational stages beginning with a concentration of members (e.g., a traffic jam), milling (persons get out of their cars to observe the obstruction), ephemeral leadership (one person begins to command attention and define symbols as well as normative expectations on what the standard drivers should do), and a series of supportive statuses and roles (some observing, others circulating rumors, etc.). A dramaturgical approach to this process is outlined by David Snow, the late Louis A. Zurcher, and Robert Peters (Article 17) for the University of Texas football victory celebrations. An important contribution of this research is its demonstration of the importance of the ecological context of collective action for understanding the events. It also documents how the patterns of interaction among actors, spectators, and the public-shaped collective behavior. Results confirm the dance-like nature of the relationships between agents of social control, members of the gatherings, and the institutionally situated nature of acts.

Lewis M. Killian (Article 18) used archival and participant information to analyze the mobilization of bus boycotts and sit-ins that occurred in Tallahassee, Florida, between 1955 and 1965. His findings challenge the assertion that spontaneity and sociocultural emergence are *not* important factors in understanding social movements. A significant contribution of this research and its theoretical implications are its *contextual* meanings for the phenemona of spontaneity and emergence.

ARTICLE 14

Social Movements and Network Analysis: A Case Study of Nineteenth-Century Women's Reform in New York State

NAOMI ROSENTHAL
MERYL FINGRUTD
MICHELE ETHIER
ROBERTA KARANT
DAVID MCDONALD

Social movements provide weapons for the powerless. They create milieus for people or groups with few formal institutional ties and for ideas that are not part of the institutional consensus. Social movements tend to question both accepted relations of power and the ideological underpinnings of those relations. Therefore, it is not surprising that innovative ideas often take shape with social movement organizations as they develop programs, agendas, and justifications for the world they want to create. But because the ultimate success of an insurgent program is dependent on its mobilization of broad support, such organizations must find avenues to introduce their agendas into wider discourse. Because institutional routes are usually blocked, social movement groups find allies among other insurgent groups. In this article, we examine the activities of 19th-century women reform leaders in New York State and their affiliations as a case study of relations among social movements.

Social movement theorists traditionally have searched for explanations of the rise, growth, and decline of movements by using variables that do not relate directly to the efforts of movement participants: propensities of mobs and crowds, psychological pathologies, processes inevitable to marginal groups, and cost-benefit effects. More recently, however, social scientists have begun to appreciate the relations between social movement development and the context of everyday life (McCarthy and Zald 1979). In this view, social movements adopt the same survival strategies used by more socially integrated and accepted organizations and institutions; they need to find, develop, and acquire such resources as money, publicity, expertise (Oberschall 1973), membership (Barkan 1979; Useem 1975; Schwartz, Rosenthal, and Schwartz 1981), strategic repertoires (Tilly 1978; Schwartz 1976), sympathetic publics (Turner 1969; McCarthy and Zald 1973; Freeman 1979), and communication networks (Turner 1969; Freeman 1975; Molotch 1979).

Curtis and Zurcher (1973) contend that social movements are really multiorganizational fields, that is, networks of organizations. These networks are important because they reduce

Rosenthal, Naomi, Fingrutd, Meryl, Ethier, Michele, Karant, Roberta, & McDonald, David. (1985, March). Social movements and network analysis: A case study of nineteenth-century women's reform in New York state. *American Journal of Sociology, 90,* 1022–1054. Reprinted with permission of The University of Chicago Press.

sources of environmental uncertainty (Allen 1974), increase the chances for effectiveness (Zald 1967; Kunz 1969), aid in accumulating and establishing the legitimacy of movement programs (Esman and Blaise 1966; Levine and White 1961), and create an esprit de corps among participants (Aveni 1978; Granovetter 1973). Because its posture of reform usually isolates a social movement from established social, political, or economic institutions, the development of support networks has the potential to create an audience for ideas that previously had little or no voice in public dialogue. We argue here that social movements usually appear within the context of, and depend on the existence of, other social movements.

Like other developing organizations, social movements tend to form alliances with groups that can offer them aid and support. This is not to say that social movements do not have problems specific to their own development and success. They often have few, if any, institutional bases, and their ideologies tend to challenge the status quo. Programs that are innovative or "risky" (Granovetter 1973) will not easily acquire the resources they need. They cannot rely on links that formal organizations have by virtue of an existing network of social relations and obligations. We expect that links with other social movement groups and the creation of networks are crucial aspects of the development and growth of a social movement group.

Social scientists who have been concerned with linkages (though not necessarily in social movement organizations) have highlighted two kinds of affiliations. Granovetter (1973) discussed the importance of weak ties for microsociological analysis. He argued that although strong ties create the tight bonds that characterize close affinity of ideas and close coordination of action—the sustenance of energy, comradery, spirit, and morale—weak ties allow for wider transmission of ideas.

> *Whatever is to be diffused can reach a larger number of people and traverse greater social distance (i.e. path length) when passed through weak ties rather than strong. If one tells a rumor to all his close friends, and they do likewise, many will hear the rumor a second and third time, since those linked by strong ties tend to share friends. If the motivation to spread the rumor is dampened a bit on each wave of retelling, then the rumor moving through strong ties is much more likely to be limited to a few cliques than that going via weak ones; bridges will not be crossed. [1973, p. 1366]*

In a later article (1982), Granovetter demonstrated the relevance of this concept for groups. Similarly, Aveni (1978) writes about the importance of linkage strength and linkage breadth for social movement groups. Linkage strength describes the possibility for real transference of influence and resources among or between social movement organizations. Linkage breadth provides for incorporation of a diverse number of sources that increase the "likelihood that the movement organization will be able to sustain itself and carry out its programs" (p. 190).

If social movements exist within a climate of other social movements and the resultant ties function to sustain the work of the movement, we should be able to see both integration and interchange in a study of social movements in any particular historical period. We have chosen the activities of 19th-century women reform leaders in New York State as a case study of relations among social movements. Focusing on the links among the organizations they created, we map and analyze the network of relations and the directionality of ties among the many reform movement organizations and groups that engaged the energies of these women.

HISTORY AND BIOGRAPHY

At the beginning of the 19th century, women constituted one of the most institutionally isolated groups in American society. They nevertheless became workers in abolitionism, temperance, trade unions, charity reform groups, progressivism, socialism in all its myriad forms, peace organizations, and a variety of new religious and professional groups—all in addition to their constant involvement in the struggle for women's rights. During this period, the strength, popularity, and relevance of their movement fluctuated considerably, as the shape of social movement activity allied with changing issues and agendas. But from about 1840 until World War I, women increasingly participated in the entire range of political, social, religious, and economic reform efforts. Women from all walks of life, but particularly from the middle class, emerged from splendid, culturally prescribed, but socially isolated, places and burst into public prominence in speaking, writing, marching, organizing, and educating—traveling across the nation to do so. There were, in fact, few social movements of the period in which women did not eventually participate in significant numbers (Flexner 1975). One might even argue that the social movement agenda of the period was largely set by women.

Because women's activities during this period were so diverse, an examination of the activities of prominent 19th- and early 20th-century New York women reformers should provide information on the breadth of women's activity during the period, as well as the extend and shape of interorganizational linkages. Most of the historical work on women of this epoch concentrates on women's rights organizing and feminism. Although feminism existed as an organized movement for approximately 75 years before World War I, it never existed alone. Feminism was not only embedded in a general movement for reform in American society; it was also at the center of ideological crosscurrents that encompassed liberal, radical, conservative, and elitist thought (Kraditor 1971; Gordon 1976).

Eleanor Flexner (1975) emphasized the significance of social networks forged in educational institutions, abolitionist activity, and other organizations to the development of the women's rights movement. She also tied feminism to other currents of social reform in a much more explicit fashion than had prior historians. Nevertheless, Flexner restricted her analysis and evidence to an impressionistic survey of the careers of a handful of leaders. This trailblazing work was followed by a variety of social histories linking movements in a similar fashion (see esp. Trattner 1974; Walters 1978; Leach 1980; Berg 1980; Bordin 1981). It is our contention that the network phenomenon glimpsed by Flexner and others can be documented by a systematic study of the overlaps among the whole spectrum of 19th-century movements in which women were involved.

Historians have usually relied on the biographies of one or two central figures to show connections between one movement and another. Ruth Bordin (1981), for example, claims an intense connection between the Women's Christian Temperance Union (WCTU) and the woman's rights movement on the basis of the activities and ideology of an early leader of the WCTU, Frances Willard. Flexner (1975) links feminism and antislavery agitation through the persons of the Grimké sisters, Lucretia Mott, and Lucy Stone. Beyond the dangers of basing conclusions on small, unrepresentative samples of unique leaders, this unsystematic and impressionistic approach cannot produce a portrait of the network of interaction among the large number of movement organizations that functioned during the era.

Because most of the work on the rise and diffusion of the feminist movement has been done by social historians interested in placing feminism in an ideological and social context, it has concentrated on the growth and development of feminist ideology, leadership, and programs within the framework of a changing United States (O'Neill 1969; Kraditor 1971; Flexner 1975; Gordon 1976; DuBois 1978). We agree with the logical presuppositions of the historical focus. Relations between organizations are created by people. Network chains are formed by people interacting in different organizations or groupings at the same time (and over time). As Aveni (1978) points out: "In the final analysis, linkages are between people and without the appropriate personnel to cultivate and sustain extra-organizational relationships, no resource mobilization will occur."

These networks show the potential for group interaction. Dual affiliation, therefore, creates mechanisms for cross-fertilization and communication and may reflect congruence of purpose. If a leader in one organization is also a leader in another, that is significant to both organizations. Yet the activities of one or two figures may reflect idiosyncratic behavior rather than the propensities of other movement leaders and participants. For example, the fact that Margaret Sanger moved from the Industrial Workers of the World (IWW, an anarcho-syndicalist organization) to a central role in the creation of the birth control movement does not tell us much about relations between the larger anarchist movement and the movement for birth control. What is required to bridge the gap between individual and social movement biography is a way to investigate systematically the links among social movement groups as they are created by a multiplicity of leaders.

Our work attempts to give an overview of a variety of reform organizations in which these women participated and the networks created by their efforts. If movements are multiorganizational fields, we should be able, using network analysis, to map the field for a sense of its weak and strong ties and to look at the direction of links. We will not, however, describe the actual content of the ties. For example, we will not be able to say exactly how much resource sharing or what kind of ideological affinity existed between two organizations that were linked to each other. We will look at potential channels for interaction created by the multiple affiliations of women in the sam;e rather than delineate which channels were activated. This overview allows us to put the smaller pieces of historical description of the contact between and among organizations into a broader perspective that illuminates the shapes not only of the early feminist movement but of social movement relations in general. Moreover, this study allows us to test the efficacy of applying network analysis to the sequential activities of individuals (McPherson 1982) by comparing the picture of social movement activity derived from the analysis with historical descriptions.

THE DATA

The data for this study consist of the organizational careers of nationally noted women reformers who resided in New York State. Women were selected by the following procedure:

1. We compiled a list of all women who ever resided in New York State mentioned in three biographical dictionaries covering the period 1820–1914 (*Notable American Women, 1607–1950: A Woman of the Century;* and *Who's Who, 1914–15);* all New York women mentioned in books and articles about specific social movements, organizations, and events of the period (such as *The History of the Woman's Club Movement in America* [1898] and Ira Kipnes's *The American Socialist Movement, 1897–1912* [1952]); and women, such as Florence Kelley, who were the subjects of special biographies.

2. We excluded those who resided in New York State for less than 10 years of their careers as reform activists. This avoided inclusion of women whose reform careers took place essentially out of state and women who moved out of state before their activity began. Belva Lockwood, for example, a lawyer, women's rights activist, and peace worker, was excluded from the study because she moved to Washington, D.C., in 1866 after six years of activism in New York State.

3. We eliminated those who were not active reformers for at least 10 years during the period under study (1820–1914). Agnes Smedley, an author, foreign correspondent, champion of revolutionary China, and activist in leftist politics, was not included in the study because she did not come to New York until 1916.

4. We included only women who were notable as reformers rather than women prominent in other spheres. Although Georgiana Barrymore, a famous actress of the period, was an advocate of women's rights, she was excluded because she was not a leader in reform. On the other hand, Maria Mitchell, a noted scientist, was included because she was also a founder and officer of Sorosis (an early club for literary women), the Association for the Advancement of Women (AAW), and the American Social Science Association. Mary Harriman, a wealthy philanthropist, was excluded because she was not active in reform organizations, although she supported a wide variety of charities.

5. We excluded women whose career biographies could not be assembled from printed sources. We could not, for example, locate any information on Lavinia Waight, founder of the United Tailoresses Society of New York. We eventually eliminated 25 individuals (11% of the total 227) from the study because of either insufficient information or inability to determine whether, as in the case of Mary Ann (Marianne) Johnson of Brooklyn, we had located one or two women.

We thus compiled a sample of 202 prominent women reformers whose biographical profiles include extensive information about their organizational affiliations, institutional as well as movement oriented, both in and out of state. These women were born between 1770 and 1890 and, according to the printed sources available, constituted the major leadership in state-centered reform activity between 1840 and 1914. The organizational affiliations of these 202 women provide the basic data set for our analysis.

THE METHOD

This study employs network analysis, which has largely been used in analyzing cross-sectional data. It has been employed in studies of adolescent communities (Coleman 1971), friendship configurations (Bott 1971), occupations (Granovetter 1973), corporate structures (Mintz and Schwartz 1981), and church hierarchies (White 1971). It allows us to use the individual affiliations of prominent women reformers to create relational matrices for group-to-group interaction, because of the properties of dual networks (Breiger 1974; McPherson 1982). These matrices can then help map the interconnections between organizations, measure the intensity of these interconnections, discover clusters of proximate organizations, and identify the groups central to clusters. This method, therefore, has enormous potential as a strategy for understanding intermovement relationships, illuminating the texture and shape of social movement clusters, creating new historical syntheses, and defining social movement boundaries.

The matrices for network analysis were formed in a three-step process. We first made a list of all the groups with which members of the sample were affiliated. In constructing this data set, we made no a priori judgements about which social movement contained a given organization, campaign, or event. For example, the Anti-Slavery Society was listed separately from Anti-Slavery Advocacy, the Bible and Tract Mission and the Bible and Tract Society were entered as two organizations, and each suffrage organization was listed as unique. We ignored only branch differences. Thus, the New York City YWCA and the National YWCA were both listed as YWCA. In addition, we included every organization to which members of the group belonged, even if the organization did not appear, at first glance, to be part of a social movement.

This procedure resulted in a list of 1,015 organizations. Then, by sorting the first list, we compiled a second list of every person in the sample and every organization with which that individual was affiliated. These two lists were used to generate a third list, which included all pairs of organizations that had at least one member in common. The National Labor Union and the International Council of Women, for example, constitute a dyad because Susan B. Anthony belonged to both. This third list, which contained 10,393 dyads (or 2% of the 514,60 dyads possible between 1,015 organizations), was used for the development of a matrix that showed the number of links (ties) created between each pair of organizations. All organizations had at least one tie to one other organization, because every member of the sample was active in at least two organizations. But many potential pairs of organizations—such as the WCTU and the NAACP—were not tied to each other at all.

The matrix, then, consists of a tally of links between dyads. Looking, for example, at the dyad created by the NAACP and the Socialist party, we see three links (a tie of three) because three women belonged to both organizations. The matrix of all dyads provides the basis for our analysis of relations among organizations. For each group, we compiled a list of all other organizations to which it was linked. By analyzing these individual and collective profiles, we outlined the general configurations of organizational relations.

The analysis that follows uses centrality analysis, which assesses the importance of each organization in the network in the light of the number of other groups to which it is linked, the numbers of shared members with each of these groups, and the centrality of the groups to which the organization is linked (Bonacich 1972; Mariolis 1983; Bearden et al. 1975; Mizruchi 1982; Mintz and Schwartz 1981). Centrality analysis identifies the most central nodes in the network. Two related methods, clique detection and peak analysis, locate and describe any separate clusters of organizations.

THE FINDINGS

The Network

Of the 1,015 organizations to which these women belonged, 1,004 constitute a single continuous network. The total number of ties in the matrix is 22,676, an average of 22 ties for each organization, because each tie is counted twice. We can appreciate the relative density of this network by comparing it with the network of corporate interlocks discussed by Mintz and Schwartz (1984). Their replication of previous studies found an average of 10 links for each of 1,131 corporations (of which 999 were tied into one network).

To describe the general shape and texture of the network, we look at summary figures. Table 1 shows the intensity of the ties connecting the 10,393 dyads in this network. The most striking feature of this table is that 94.3% of all dyads have only one member in common. We arbitrarily labeled ties of one and two as weak, three as moderate, and four or more as strong. In this way, we limited strong ties to the most infrequent cases. Because the sample is limited to leaders, we reasoned that a tie of four or more would represent a significant overlap between two organizations.

Because of both the large number of ties and the predominance of weak ties in the network, no graphic representation is possible. We cannot even draw a map of relations among the 50 most central organizations. Consider the case of the AAW, the seventh most central organization in the network. It was tied to relatively few organizations (90, which is below the average of 94 for the top 50), but it was linked to 30 of the other 49 most central organizations. A map of the links among the top 50 organizations would require approximately 750 lines, an unmanageable number.

Given the relative density of ties, we can see a network of many weakly tied organizations,

TABLE 1 Distribution of Ties (N = 10,393)

NUMBER OF COMMON MEMBERS	% OF DYADS
1	94.3
2	4.2
3	1.0
4 or more*	.7
Total	100.2

Note. —Percentages do not total 100 due to rounding error.

* The strong ties were distributed as follows, with number of common members followed in parentheses by number of dyads: 4 (31), 5 (17), 6 (13), 7 (4), 8 (5), 9 (1), 14 (1). Total number of dyads is 72.

with a small percentage that are more heavily linked. This result is amplified further by centrality analysis.

Centrality

The pure number of ties that one organization has with others is not enough to indicate its influence or the degree to which that organization might or might not be central in the network or be in a position to exert leverage in it. For example, 24 women out of the total 202 were active in the WCTU. Only Woman's Rights Conventions and Sorosis involved more members of our sample. Both the National Woman Suffrage Association (NWSA) and the National American Woman Suffrage Association (NAWSA) had exactly the same number of members from our sample of prominent women as the WCTU. Yet the WCTU, which comes twenty-fifth in our centrality analysis, has 142 weak ties, only three moderate ties, and no strong ties at all. The NWSA has 16 strong ties in addition to three moderate ties and 95 weak ties. Therefore, although the WCTU is an important organization by virtue of the large number of organizations to which it is tied, it cannot be considered as central as the suffrage groups, because its relationship to other groups is not as intense.

The degree to which an organization is or is not tied to highly central organizations also determines its centrality. The National Woman's Loyal League (organized in 1863 by Elizabeth Cady Stanton and Susan B. Anthony to fight for passage of the Thirteenth Amendment) is ninth in centrality, although it has only 93 ties to 58 organizations and only eight members of the sample belonged to it. But it is tied to the five most central organizations in the network and has strong ties to four of them. The Daughters of the American Revolution (DAR), on the other hand, is forty-sixth in centrality although it has 118 ties to 106 organizations. Nine members of the sample belonged to the DAR and it has ties to 14 of 45 more central organizations, but it has only one strong tie (and that is to an organization ranked thirteenth in centrality) and two moderate ties (one to the NAWSA and the other to the Republican party).

. . . Centrality, breadth, and strength of ties are related to number of affiliates. The number of links created, the average number of women in the links, and the number of affiliated women all have high correlations with centrality $r = .60, .72.$ and .51, respectively). The centrality scores for the top three organizations are relatively high. The fourth highest score drops to .67. This indicates to us that the three most central organizations play significant roles in the network. In fact, much of the density of the network is a result of the influence of the three most central organizations and their ties. These are the Woman's Rights Conventions (with 253 links to 154 organizations), the NWSA (209 links to 114 organizations), and the NAWSA (329 links to 232 organizations). Among them the three organizations participate in 5% of all the dyads in the network. They have large numbers of both weak and strong ties (linkage strength and linkage breadth) and are therefore the avenues for both coordination and diversification within the network. These groups were central focuses for woman's rights organizing and suffrage campaigns, and they are the core of cohesion in the network.

The first Woman's Rights Convention was held in 1848, organized by Elizabeth Cady Stanton. Conventions were then held several times a year in various regions of the country and under various auspices. For this sample, however, the conventions were not important after 1870. The NWSA, founded in 1869 by Stanton and Susan B. Anthony, centered its activity on the fight for a national suffrage amendment but was also at the forefront of a variety of other women's rights issues. The strength of the NWSA lay largely in the Middle Atlantic states. It functioned during a period when women's rights organizing was most marginal, after the break between abolitionist and women's suffrage forces and before the development of other strong alliances (Flexner 1975; DuBois 1978). Its major rival was the

American Woman Suffrage Association (AWSA), an organization centered in Boston, which advocated state-oriented suffrage campaigns. Only two women in this New York-centered sample were affiliated with the AWSA: Antoinette Blackwell and Phebe Hanaford. In 1890, the NWSA and the AWSA merged into the NAWSA.

The centrality of these three groups in the network confirms historical contentions that, at least nationally, suffrage and women's rights organizing dominated the 100 years of reform activity in which women were involved.

Of the top 50 organizations, 35 are tied directly to the most central organization (Woman's Rights Conventions). The remaining 15 are tied indirectly to it through one intermediary organization. In fact, no organization in the main network is more than three links away from the most central organization. For example, Birth Control Advocacy is connected to Woman's Rights Conventions through Free Love Advocacy, which is directly linked to Woman's Rights Conventions.

The tendencies within the network indicate that the Woman's Rights Conventions, the NWSA, and the NAWSA were umbrella groups for all other organizations in the network. They served as links between diverse organizations and provided a means for unifying groups, despite the fact that, numerically, their national membership was smaller than that of such groups as the WCTU and the General Federation of Women's Clubs. Their influence, created by large numbers of both weak and strong ties, provided channels for interaction, sharing of resources, communication, and coordination. . . .

CONCLUSIONS

Summary of Findings

We have shown that network analysis can be successfully applied to historical data, that it can both amplify and correct historical propositions about structural links, and that empirical work of this kind leads to a better theoretical understanding of social movements. More specifically, our findings indicate the following: (1) The reform movements in which women participated between 1840 and 1914 were highly interlocked, (2) network density was a result of both the influence of women's rights organizing and a large number of weak ties, (3) distinct clusters within the network emerged when the influence of the three most central organizations and ties of less than three were eliminated, (4) there were three distinct periods of women's organizing in which directionality indicates differing relations among organizations, (5) nationally prominent women were more ideologically focused than local women, and (6) leadership clustering delineates bounded movements.

Discussion

On the basis of our findings we would expect social movement networks to be dense. Further comparative research is required, however, to test this claim. Our sample might be anomalous, because the study is limited to the 19th century and to women's reform. Either of these factors could produce a degree of density that would not exist in other social movement networks. In our view, however, the institutional isolation of groups that engage in social movement activity will inevitably produce extremely thick networks.

In the course of our analysis we became increasingly aware of the applicability of Granovetter's theories about weak and strong ties in networks. Weak ties create density within social movement networks. In fact, they tend to mask boundaries. Furthermore, clusters are generally bridged by weak ties (although most weak ties are not bridges). Strong ties, on the other hand, characterize bonds between organizations within a movement. Strong ties cross clusters only when (as in the case of women's rights organizations) a common focus already exists or is created (Feld 1981). We argue, then, that two kinds of interactions emerge from weak and strong ties. Both provide avenues for the creation of large audiences and the possibility of unifying around single issues in cross-movement campaigns. Weak ties are channels for communication with diverse publics. Strong ties, however, show more enduring bonds. They demonstrate the existence of alliances. It is through these channels that resources (both material and ideological) flow from one organization to another, exchange of leadership may occur, and influence and control can be exercised. The balance of weak and strong ties for any given organization in a network is illustrative of its place in that network, whereas the pattern of strong and weak ties within a network illuminates the character of relations between groups.

We would expect social movements that are at the peak of activity and that have become respectable to have large numbers of weak ties. Groups that are institutionally isolated and whose ideas are socially marginal would have a relatively small proportion of weak ties. Finally, we would expect groups that play highly unifying roles within a network of social movements to have large numbers of both weak and strong ties. We would not expect ratios of weak to strong ties to be constant over time, because some movements become part of the mainstream and see their programs adopted, either wholly or partially. At other times, movements that have enjoyed some institutional support eventually become marginal.

The first tendency is illustrated by the case of the WCTU. This respectable, extremely large, turn-of-the-century organization was characterized by a large number of weak ties. Moreover, the cluster in our network that was most institutionally linked (as witnessed by its connection to the Republican party after 1910), the Woman's Club Movement, had relatively few strong ties internally and was weakly linked to large numbers of organizations outside the cluster. The reverse is true of the other two clusters, which were much less institutionally connected, although the cluster around the WTUL had connections to women's colleges as well as to investigative committees. Finally, the third tendency is illustrated by the most important feminist groups—Woman's Rights Conventions, the NWSA, and the NAWSA. Both nationally and in Wellsville, women's rights groups had a large number of strong ties, which reached to the central hubs of rather diverse clusters and organizations and drew them together. But they also had a large number of weak ties, which reached to all parts of the network.

In order to survive, social movements must form ties with other movements and groups. Insofar as they aim, in both their formal and informal aspects, to change the social structure but do not have access to resources, members, and audiences enjoyed by institutionally based actors, they must create an alternative system of resources. This alternative system must be composed of other social movements as long as few institutional avenues exist.

REFERENCES

Allen, Michael P. 1974. "The Structure of Interorganizational Elite Corporate Directorates." *American Sociological Review* 39:393–403.

Aveni, Adrian F. 1978. "Organizational Linkages and Resource Mobilization: The Significance of Linkage Strength and Breadth." *Sociological Quarterly* 19:185–202.

Banks, Olive. 1981. *Faces of Feminism.* Oxford: Robertson.

Barkan, Steven E. 1979. "Strategic, Tactical and Organizational Dilemmas of the Protest Movement against Nuclear Power." *Social Problems* 27:19–42.

Bearden, James, et al. 1975. "The Nature and Extent of Banking Centrality in Corporate Networks." Paper presented at the annual meeting of the American Sociological Association, San Francisco.

Berg, Barbara J. 1980. *The Remembered Gate: Origins of American Feminism, the Woman and the City, 1800–1860.* Oxford: Oxford University Press.

Blair, Karen J. 1980. *The Clubwoman as Feminist: True Womanhood Redefined, 1868–1914*. New York: Holmes & Meier.

Bonacich, Phillip. 1972. "Techniques for Analyzing Overlapping Memberships." Pp. 186–95 in *Sociological Methodology 1972*, edited by H. L. Costner. San Francisco: Jossey-Bass.

Bordin, Ruth. 1981. *Woman and Temperance: The Quest for Power and Liberty, 1873–1900*. Philadelphia: Temple University Press.

Bott, Elizabeth. 1971. *Family and Social Network: Roles, Norms and External Relations in Ordinary Urban Families*. 2d ed. New York: Free Press.

Breiger, Ronald L. 1974. "The Duality of Persons and Groups." *Social Forces* 53:181–89.

Coleman, James R. 1971. *The Adolescent Society*. New York: Free Press.

Cott, Nancy F. 1977. *The Bonds of Womanhood*. New Haven, Conn.: Yale University Press.

Croly, Jane C. 1898. *The History of the Woman's Club Movement in America*. New York: H. G. Allen.

Curtis, Russell, and Louis A. Zurcher. 1973. "Stable Resources of Protest Movements: The Multi-organization Field." *Social Forces* 52:53–61.

DuBois, Ellen C. 1978. *Feminism and Suffrage: The Emergence of an Independent Women's Movement in America, 1848–1869*. Ithaca, N.Y.: Cornell University Press.

Esman, Milton J., and Hans C. Blaise. 1966. "Institution Building Research: The Guiding Concepts." Photocopied. Pittsburgh: University of Pittsburgh.

Feld, Scott. 1981. "The Focused Organization of Social Ties." *American Journal of Sociology* 86:1015–35.

Flexner, Eleanor. 1975. *Century of Struggle: The Woman's Rights Movement in the U.S.* New York: Atheneum.

Freeman, Jo. 1975. *The Politics of Women's Liberation*. New York: McKay.

——. 1979. "Resource Mobilization and Strategy: A Model for Analyzing Social Movement Organization Actions." Pp. 167–89 in McCarthy and Zald, eds.

Gordon, Linda. 1976. *Woman's Body, Woman's Rights*. New York: Grossman.

Granovetter, Mark S. 1973. "The Strength of Weak Ties." *American Journal of Sociology* 78:1360–80.

——. 1982. "The Strength of Weak Ties: A Network Theory Revisited." Pp. 105–30 in *Social Structure and Network Analysis*, edited by P. V. Marsden and N. Lin. Beverly Hills, Calif.: Sage.

Hersh, Barbara G. 1978. *The Slavery of Sex: Feminist Abolitionists in America*. Urbana: University of Illinois Press.

James, Edward T., et al., eds. 1971. *Notable American Women, 1607–1950: A Biographical Dictionary*. Cambridge, Mass.: Harvard University Press, Belknap.

Kipnes, Ira. 1952. *The American Socialist Movement, 1897–1912*. New York: Monthly Review Press.

Kraditor, Aileen S. 1971. *The Ideas of the Woman's Suffrage Movement, 1890–1920*. Garden City, N.Y.: Doubleday.

Kunz, Phillip R. 1969. "Sponsorship and Organizational Stability: Boy Scout Troops." *American Journal of Sociology* 74:666–75.

Leach, William. 1980. *True Love and Perfect Union: The Feminist Reform of Sex and Society*. New York: Basic.

Levine, Sol, and Paul E. White. 1961. "Exchange as a Conceptual Framework for the Study of Interorganizational Relationships." *Administrative Science Quarterly* 5:555–601.

McCarthy, John D., and Mayer N. Zald. 1973. *The Trend of Social Movements in America: Professionalization and Resource Mobilization*. Morristown, N.J.: General Learning.

———. eds. 1979. *The Dynamics of Social Movements*. Cambridge, Mass.: Winthrop.

McPherson, J. Miller, 1982. "Hypernetwork Sampling: Duality and Differentiation among Voluntary Organizations." *Social Networks* 3:225–49.

Mariolis, Peter. 1983. "Interlocking Directorates and Financial Groups: A Peak Analysis." *Sociological Spectrum* 16:243–56.

Mariolis, Peter, Beth Mintz, and Michael Schwartz. 1975. "Centrality Analysis: A Methodology for Network Analysis." Paper presented at the annual meeting of the American Sociological Association, Boston.

Mintz, Beth, and Michael Schwartz. 1981. "Interlocking Directorates and Interest Group Formation." *American Sociological Review* 46:851–69.

———. 1984. *Bank Hegemony: Corporate Networks and Intercorporate Power*. Chicago: University of Chicago Press.

Mizruchi, Mark S. 1982. *The Structure of the American Intercorporate Network, 1904–1974*. New York: Sage.

Molotch, Harvey. 1979. "Media and Movements." Pp. 71–93 in McCarthy and Zald, eds.

Moore, Robert L. 1977. *In Search of White Crows: Spiritualism, Parapsychology and American Culture*. New York: Oxford University Press.

Oberschall, Anthony. 1973. *Social Conflicts and Social Movements*. Englewood Cliffs, N.J.: Prentice-Hall.

O'Neill, William. 1969. *Everyone Was Brave*. Chicago: Quadrangle.

Paulson, Ross E. 1973. *Women's Suffrage and Prohibition: A Comparative Study of Equality and Social Control*. Glenview, Ill.: Scott, Foresman.

Rosenberg, Rosalind. 1982. *Beyond Separate Spheres: Intellectual Roots of Modern Feminism*. New Haven, Conn.: Yale University Press.

Roy, William G. 1983. "The Unfolding of the Interlocking Directorate Structure of the United States." *American Sociological Review* 48:248–54.

Schwartz, Michael. 1976. *Radical Protest and Social Structure: The Southern Farmers' Alliance and the Cotton Tenancy System*. New York: Academic Press.

Schwartz, Michael, Naomi B. Rosenthal, and Laura Schwartz. 1981. "Leader-Member Conflict in Protest Organizations: The Case of the Southern Farmers' Alliance." *Social Problems* 29:22–36.

Tilly, Charles. 1978. *From Mobilization to Revolution*. Reading, Mass.: Addison-Wesley.

Trattner, Walter. 1974. *From Poor Law to Welfare State*. New York: Free Press.

Turner, Ralph H. 1969. "The Public Perception of Protest." *American Sociological Review* 34:815–31.

Useem, Michael. 1975. *Protest Movements in America*. Indianapolis: Bobbs-Merrill.

Walters, Ronald G. 1978. *American Reformers, 1815–1860*. New York: Hill & Wang.

Wertheimer, Barbara M. 1977. *We Were There: The Story of Working Women in America*. New York: Pantheon.

White, Harrison. 1971. *Chains of Opportunity*. Cambridge, Mass.: Harvard University Press.

Who's Who, 1914–15. 1915. Chicago: Marquis.

Willard, Frances E., and Mary A. Livermore, eds. (1893) 1967. *A Woman of the Century: Fourteen-hundred-seventy Biographical Sketches Accompanied by Portraits of Leading American Women in All Walks of Life*. Detroit: Gale.

Zald, Mayer N. 1967. "Urban Differentiation, Characteristics of Boards of Directors and Organization Effectiveness." *American Journal of Sociology* 73:216–72.

ARTICLE 15

The Collective Behavior of Fads: The Characteristics, Effects, and Career of Streaking

B. E. AGUIRRE
E. L. QUARANTELLI
JORGE L. MENDOZA

REVIEW OF THE LITERATURE

. . . Fads—a nontraditional preoccupation by diffuse collectivities on a circumscribed object or process are often considered as a form of collective behavior. Beginning with Park and Burgess (1924), fads have been listed as a substantive topic of interest for the field of collective behavior (e.g., Dawson and Gettys 1929; Turner and Killian 1957; Lang and Lang 1968; Lofland 1981). Yet, fads are seriously understudied. Although specific discussions of them abound, no one has presented a systematic conceptual and theoretical statement about them. We organized the major ideas on fads according to how they are identified, the effects of participation in fads, and their careers. Three themes focus on how to identify fads, one centers on the effect of participation, and five on their careers. We then test these themes with information on the fad of streaking.

In the last two decades, a number of ideas on collective behavior have been discarded and new ones have taken their place. These ideas concern panic flight, rioting crowds, participation in crowds, emergent behavior in natural disasters, and social-movement mobilization. This paper further revises our understanding of collective behavior by examining a prominent fad and questioning dominant social science definitions of it as homogeneous, odd, novel, nonutilitarian collective behavior, spread by imitation or the activation of the latent tendencies of people. For heuristic purposes, we use the emergent norm conceptual framework in collective-behavior theory, which emphasizes similarities and continuities between collective behavior and institutionalized social life and documents the emergence of new norms, values, social relations and communication patterns in the social organization of fads (Turner and Killian 1987). This theoretical framework models the spread of fads, not as contagion or convergence behavior, but as instances of innovation diffusion. It also supports our hypothesis that fads are heterogeneous expressions of social life and, like all other forms of social life, have histories, multiple effects, and meaningful normative constraints.

Descriptive Characteristics of Fads

(1) *Homogeneity.* Frequently cited as a major feature of fads is the idea that fad behavior is homogeneous in different times and places (e.g., Turner and Killian 1957, p. 207; Sebald 1968, p. 219; Lofland 1981, p. 445). (2) *Novelty.* Fads are

Aguirre, B. E., Quarantelli, E. L., & Mendoza, Jorge L. (1988, August). The collective behavior of fads: The characteristics, effects, and career of streaking. *American Sociological Review, 53,* 569–584. Reprinted by permission of the American Sociological Association.

presumed to involve novelty (e.g., Davis 1949, p. 79; Lang and Lang 1961, p. 526; Fairchild 1965, p. 113) and new behavior that differs from existing routines. This idea first introduced by Ross (1915, p. 80) persists in the notion that fads have no histories (e.g., Blumer 1968, p. 344; but see Klapp 1972, p. 308). (3) *Oddness*. Fads seem to be odd by existing cultural norms. They evoke social disapproval because those not involved in them perceive fads as ridiculous, dangerous, immoral, bizarre, if not deviant behavior (e.g., Davis 1949, p. 79; Jolly 1967, p. 14; Blumer 1968, p. 276; Lofland 1981, p. 445). Earlier writers saw fads as irresponsible or irrational (e.g., Bernard 1926, p. 546; Sapir 1931, p. 139; Davis 1949, p. 79).

Effects of Participation

(4) *Nonutilitarian Behavior*. Irrespective of the reasons people participate in fads the literature portrays fad behavior as nonutilitarian and lacking in consequentiality for their participants (e.g., LaPiere 1938, p. 177; Smelser 1962: Brown 1965, p. 719; Klapp 1972. p. 314; Lofland 1981, p. 445). This is often attributed to the content areas in which fads occur. The words *frivolous* and *superficial* are frequently used by earlier and later writers to refer to fads, while few writers argue that fad behavior occurs in all areas of social life and deserves serious consideration (e.g., Bernard 1926, p. 545; Turner and Killian 1972, p. 130).

Career of Fads

(5) *Suddenness*. Fads appear suddenly and are unexpected. They are said to be the result of impulse and are perceived as not involving calculated acts or deliberate adoption, but as spontaneous caprice (e.g., Gold 1964, p. 256; Blumer 1969, p. 276; Lofland 1981, p. 445). (6) *Rapid Spread*. Fads spread rapidly and, unlike fashions that diffuse downward, originate in any social stratum (e.g., Doob 1952, p. 386; Lang and Lang 1961, p. 486; Fairchild 1965, p. 113). Fads are limited to a small proportion of the population than are fashions (Davis 1949, p. 179). Some writers believe adolescents are particularly vulnerable to becoming involved in fads (e.g., Sebald 1968), although most emphasize that fads will spread only in certain segments of the population. (7) *Quick Acceptance and Short-Lived*. Fads obtain rapid acceptance and popularity. They peak quickly, with a rapid acceleration in the rate of adoption (e.g., Blumer 1968, p. 344). The most frequent generalization about fads is that they are short-lived (e.g., LaPiere 1938, p. 187; Klapp 1972, p. 312; Lofland 1981, p. 445; Brown 1965, p. 717; Turner and Killian 1972, p. 129). Once they pass they are gone forever.

Convergence and Contagion

Analytically, the spread of fads is interpreted as a form of imitation or manifestation of latent tendencies (for criticisms of these approaches, see Turner 1960; Milgram and Toch 1969). The latent or *convergence* explanation of the spread of fads has taken different forms. Doob (1952, p. 396) states that "innovations become fads only when they are perceived by people and when they satisfy some predispositions." Other writers (Blumer 1968, p. 342) suggest that fads, like fashions, "may be ways of rediscovering the self through novel yet socially sanctioned departures from prevailing social forms." LaPiere's (1938, pp. 463–64) emphasis on tension that is felt by collectivities of people and released during the *spree* continues to have resonance, as in Rose's (1982, pp. 193–94) *revels*. Better known is Smelser's (1962) idea of the function that positive wish fulfillment has in the *craze*, in which large numbers of people share predispositions in the form of anxieties, ambiguities, and strains that are resolved through the development and resolution of a collective fantasy.

The imitation or *contagion* explanation is one of the oldest in the literature (e.g., Dawson and Gettys 1929). The contagious spread of faddish behavior is caused by suggestion, imitation, identification and circular interaction, and rumor (e.g., Young 1944, p. 327; Gold 1964, pp. 256–57), which amplified by the mass media (Miller and Borhek 1978), creates impulsive and highly emotional crowd behavior.

The Model of Adoption

The emergent norm framework endorses a *social-interaction* view of the spread of fads. From this newer perspective, fads, like other forms of collective behavior, occur in novel, unexpected, or "out of the ordinary" circumstances in which people are forced to create meanings to orient their behavior. They do this while interacting with others in the absence of preestablished procedures for coordinating actions and identifying members, leaders,and shared objectives. This emergent "definition of the situation" limits and justifies the behavior of the collectivity and is changed by it (Turner and Killian 1987, p. 3).

The emergence of shared rules, meanings, and emotions in collective behavior depends on communication and cues in the situation rather than on physiological arousal. The diffusion of fads follows preexisting networks of relations and involves learning behavior from others (Perry and Pugh 1978, pp. 58–75). As Sullivan (1977, p. 50) has pointed out, research indicates that, as predicted by the emergent-norm framework, participants have diverse motives, goals, and patterns of involvement. This suggests that participation in fads does not call for special sociopsychological explanations.

This emergent-norm perspective informs our effort to develop a macrolevel innovation adoption model of streaking. Here, the probability of adopting the innovation is affected by changes in the context in which individuals learn and accept an emerging collective definition of the situation.

We hypothesize that five contextual components affect the emergent definitions of the situation and the probability of the occurrence of faddish behavior in the schools at risk of adoption. These include the institutional prestige of the neighboring schools that previously experienced streaking; the severity of social control used by those schools; the accuracy of the mass media reports of the streaking events; the heterogeneity and complexity of previous streaking events; and the sociocultural heterogeneity of the schools at risk of adoption.

This adoption model assumes temporal dependence among fad episodes, so that earlier events affect the occurrence and characteristics of later events. This assumption is also made in the analysis of social movements (Oliver 1985, p. 17) and diffusion of innovations (e.g., Rogers and Shoemaker 1971). In both fads and social movements, individuals, not groups, typically decide whether to participate. However a macro-level explanation of fad adoption is possible because individuals decide in interaction with others in a social context in which the emerging collective definition of the situation importantly determines the person's course of action.

We derive five predictions from the model of adoption:

School Prestige. The higher the social prestige of the *relevant* significant schools that previously experienced the fad, the greater the probability that other schools will also adopt the innovation. We assume that schools belong to larger systems of social stratification that affect what goes on in them. This systemic nature of the units in which collective behavior may occur has been noted more extreme versions of this view, the universality of fads is said to result from the fact that "they have a natural root in human nature" (Blumer 1968, pp. 344–45).

We endorse the alternative view that fads are rooted in specific social organizations. This view is voiced only occasionally and is in the diffusion of social-movement activities (Oberschall 1980, p. 52). In the present context, the nearer and higher the prestige of the schools that experienced the fad, the greater the probability that other schools will follow suit.

Sanctions. The greater the sanctions and controls that innovating schools practiced toward fad participants, the *lower* the probability that other schools will follow suit. This is because, as in social movements, "diffusion occurs partly as a result of a reassessment by potential activists and participants and by authorities of the chances of success and the costs of collective action after the outcomes of similar collective action elsewhere become known to them" (Oberschall 1980, p. 52).

Mass Media. The more accurately mass media covered significant schools that experienced the fad, the greater the probability of subsequent adoption. The dissemination of information about streaking events occurred through various means such as visits of students to other campuses, personal and telephone conversations, and letters, putting students from one university or college in touch with those at other schools. The accuracy of the mass media coverage of previous streaking episodes also affected the sort of information about the fad that prospective adopters received (Hirsch 1972).

Complexity and Heterogeneity. The greater the complexity and heterogeneity of previous streaking events, the greater the probability that schools will adopt the fad. The innovation is more likely to be adopted when the complexity of the previous incidents of the fad in neighboring schools is greater. The complexity of streaking incidents is a stimulus for potential adopters. For example, if many males and females, students and nonstudents, streaked repeatedly day and night, on and off campus, then many categories of persons in other nearby schools could identify with the faddish behavior. As a result, the events are no longer performed by only the rowdy but become acceptable to many potential adopters. Similarly, heterogeneity *among* streaking events in different schools increases the accessibility of the cultural innovation to potential adopters.

The importance of the degree of complexity of previous events for modeling the diffusion of collective-behavior forms is recognized by a number of scholars. For instance, Oberschall (1980, p. 48) argues that the success of collective action is measured by its impact on public opinion, which is a function of the number of participants in the episode. The greater the number of participants, the greater the impact on public opinion, the greater the success of collective action, and the higher the probability of subsequent collective action. Similarly, McPhail (1984), focusing on more elementary forms of collective behavior, states that extraordinary behavioral configurations have to be audible and visible to be recognized and considered before they can be adopted or rejected. Extraordinary behavior that is recurrent, widespread, very audible, and visible is more likely to be noted and considered.

The degree of heterogeneity *among* previous streaking events also affects the probability that schools will adopt the fad. Adoption is more likely when previous streaking events differ widely in their complexity, since they would offer a wider range of available adoptive-action patterns. The risk of adoption increases when previous incidents of streaking occur in a variety of ways and settings, individually and collectively, so that potential adopters have many different "scripts" for participating in the fad. Alternatively, the adoption of an innovation ends not only because fewer people are practicing it, with the consequent decline in its value to prospective adopters, but also partly because the faddish idea is exhausted and cannot generate new behavioral scripts; homogeneity sets in (Oberschall 1980, p. 51; Turner and Killian 1957, p. 211).

School Heterogeneity. We test the effect of social setting on the adoption of fads by hypothesizing that the greater the sociocultural heterogeneity of the schools at risk of adoption, the greater the probability of adoption. Social structure is generally down-played in the sociological literature as an important influence on the occurrence and complexity of faddish events. Fads, unlike fashion, for example, are believed to occur in any type of society, traditional or modern (Gold 1964, p. 257: Blumer 1968, p. 344). In applied primarily to modern societies with complex mass-communication systems (e.g., Meyersohn and Katz 1957; Jolly 1967). According to this view, a fad is more likely to occur and elicit more complex and heterogeneous behavior, the greater the level of social and cultural heterogeneity of social organizations (Smelser 1962, p. 175): Two facilitating factors are increasing level of heterogeneity of the norms and values governing social interaction in social organizations and increasing levels of social mobility and social differentiation of social organizations.

The sociocultural context of collective behavior supplies resources for organizing it and helps define the situation as one that may or may not be rewarding for participation in fads. The greater the heterogeneity of the social organization, the greater the freedom the individual has from overarching hegemonic value systems, the greater the opportunity and desire of people to experiment and try the new, the more likely that some people will have interests that correspond to the innovation developing elsewhere, and the greater are the mobilizable resources available for the adoption of the innovation (Mohr 1978). Blau and Slaughter (1971) have shown that student demonstrations are most likely to occur in large academic institutions than in small ones.

We have identified nine major themes in the relevant literature concerning the characteristics, effects, and career of fads. From our model of adoption, we derived five predictions. Do these themes and predictions stand up in our study of streaking?

DATA AND METHODS

The data are derived from a national study of the streaking fad that appeared in the spring of 1974 (Taylor and Quarantelli 1974), which concentrated on institutions of higher education, since they were the major settings where streaking events occurred (e.g., Evans and Miller 1975; Anderson 1977). Some of the data were obtained from a mail survey of all (1,543) colleges and universities in the continental United States with more than 1,000 students. A 24-item, mostly forced-choice questionnaire was mailed to the deans of student affairs or equivalent officials. . . .

RESULTS

Characteristics

Homogeneity of Streaking Events. The established view predicts that one category or cluster accounts for most streaking events because their characteristics would be similar. We reexamine this assumption of homogeneous behavior. While at one level of analysis, streakers do the same thing everywhere (i.e., take off their clothes in public), the emphasis on homogeneity ignores variation in fad behaviors and in the social relationships among participants. The range of this variation is captured by the two polar unitary concepts of mass and compact crowd (Blumer 1964; 1969), which highlight the continuum of sociocultural complexity of streaking behaviors and relationships. Following conventional usage, we distinguish mass from compact crowd. In the crowd, the participants interact with one another, define and orient their joint action by communicating, and develop a division of labor and a common goal to guide their behavior.

We assume that faddish behavior varies in its degree of homogeneity (Lange and Lang 1961, p. 179; Landecker 1981). A fad is composed of many spatially an temporally separate incidents that generate and reflect to a greater or lesser extent the new emergent norms and values that guide and justify the enactment of the new social relations and use of material culture characterizing the fad. We should be able to order incidents in a fad in terms of their degree of sociocultural complexity.

This alternative formulation implies that different subtypes of streaking events appear, which order themselves on a continuum from the most fleeting, inchoate, and masslike manifestations to its most complex, developed, compact crowdlike state. This predicted ordering of the clusters was called a complexity continuum (cf. Lang and Lang 1961, p. 197; Anderson 1977, p. 224).

The attributes used to construct the clusters are an important set of conceptual dimensions of the social organization of fads. As an ideal type, the most complex or highly crystallized social structure would involve hundreds of men and women, both students and nonstudents, streaking together over extended periods of time by themselves and in groups of various sizes, motivated to establish or to break a school record, and engaging in mooning. The event would occur during both day and night, on and off campus, and in many different locales on campus. The least complex social structure would have the reverse set of characteristics. None of the clusters duplicated these two ideal extremes. Nevertheless, the results of the cluster analysis support the prediction that there are several types of streaking events that can be ordered according to level of complexity.

Cluster 1 is the least complex form of social organization. It represents very fleeting, masslike instances of streaking. Sixty-nine percent of the events in this cluster involved only one or two persons. In fact, in 84 percent of the cases, only one person engaged in streaking at any given time. In almost all (98 percent) of these instances, males and females streaked separately and nonstudents did not participate (91 percent). Almost three-quarters (72 percent) lasted only one day, and most (95 percent) did not involve establishing a record for mooning (99 percent). The great majority of events (80 percent) occurred only during the day, on campus (95 percent), and in fewer than two different places on campus (97 percent).

Cluster 12 differs most from cluster 1. It is the most complex form of social organization found in this research; 73 percent of its streaking events involved 100 or more males and females (88 percent), with students and nonstudents streaking together (68 percent). Of these events, 97 percent were lengthy (about a week or more) and characterized by mixture of acting units (91 percent). Sixty-four percent involved breaking or establishing a school record, as well as mooning (73 percent). Almost all occurred both at day and night (94 percent), on and off campus (76 percent), and in three or four places on campus (82 percent). The remaining 10 clusters fall between these two extremes.

The distribution of the complexity variable has a boundary region, composed of clusters 6 and 7, and two opposite areas. One of these areas is made up of clusters 8 through 12 and accounts for 25 percent of the streaking events. Very complex streaking events are quite rare; cluster 12 accounts for 5 percent of all streaking events. The other area of decreasing complexity is formed by clusters 5 through 1 and accounts for 62 percent of all the streaking events. Highly uncrystallized streaking events are quite common; one-fifth of all streaking events are in cluster 1, the least complex cluster we observed. These streaking episodes most commonly resembled the mass behavior that previously has been assumed to characterize fads.

Equally important, however, many streaking events were highly heterogeneous. At first glance, streaking behavior appears to be homogeneous, acted out by members of a mass. Some of the events labeled streaking do fit this definition, but a majority do not. Despite limitations inherent in the simple act of appearing and running round in the nude, there was substantial variation in how the act itself was organized. Contrary to traditional views, which tend to emphasize the similarity and homogeneity of fad activity, streaking showed considerable variation and a wide range of innovations. There were important differences in the way the behavior was organized and enacted on different campuses (see below).

Novelty. The characterization of fad behavior as novel and odd is also suspect. The duration of the streaking fad considerably predated and postdated public mass media attention. The behavior had been institutionalized on some campuses for decades prior to 1974, and streaking incidents were still emerging in some schools months and even years after they had stopped elsewhere. Newspaper articles document that running in the nude, while perhaps not commonly known as streaking, was widely practiced before and after the 1974 incidents (Anderson 1977, p. 227; Evans and Miller 1975, p. 402). The long-term existence of the behavior makes the origin of the fad difficult to determine. Multiple claimants to creatorship of streaking exist (e.g., on Long Island during the American Revolutionary War, by American students vacationing in Mexico in the spring of 1965, at the University of Maryland, Whitworth College, University of Colorado at Boulder, Southern Methodist University, Air Force Academy, in the San Fernando Valley, in Lakewood, California, in Westchester, New Jersey). It is probable that streaking, like other fads, has multiple origins. Streaking was not novel to some segments of the population. There is always a pool of potentially faddish behaviors practiced by individuals or small groups in society (cf. Aronson 1952; Miller 1985, p. 154), and, like social problems (Blumer 1971), social movements (Lofland 1977), and fashion (Meyersohn and Katz 1957), only a few fads are legitimized, becoming part of universal culture.

Oddness. In most instances, streaking was defined in the student subculture and by school social-control agencies as harmless fun (e.g., Grimes, Pinhey, and Zurcher 1977, p. 1226; Anderson 1977, p. 225; Evans and Miller 1975, p. 408), acceptable in certain locations on campus and not in others (e.g., it was generally taboo to streak in classes where tests were being given). Moreover, the nudity involved was considered nonsexual by students and social-control agents. A new set of norms emerged, creating the context of the activity. This symbolic redefinition of fads is an important precondition to ensure their legitimacy; they must be perceived as odd, but not too od. Otherwise, public disorder, rather than faddish behavior, occurs. Modern-day fads do not exhibit the complete social transgression of the festivals of antiquity; they are not "full and blasphemous experience" (Duvignaud 1980, p. 15).

Streaking was interpreted as deviant behavior on some campuses, usually by school officials. In some of these instances, stiff sanctions led to conflicts, which in a dozen cases produced major riots (Evans and Miller 1975, p. 407). While we do not have sufficient information to study this issue, we conjecture that there is an element of play in activity fads such as streaking (Heckel 1978, p. 147), where reactions occur within the limits imposed by the emergent consensus. The game ends when the lines are breached. This interpretation supports Brown and Goldin's (1973, p. 131) emphasis on the transactional character of social control in instances of faddish behavior. Social-control agents adjust their actions to often-conflicting expectations of powerful constituencies (Anderson 1977, p. 232).

Effects of Participation

Nonutilitarian behavior. Streaking often had noticeable and important consequences. Like cults (Quarantelli and Wenger 1973) and fashions (Simmel 1957), participation generated new feelings of cohesion and separateness. Streaking was consequential at different levels of analysis. Apart from the obvious fun, streaking was used by small groups and residents of dormitories on campus to compete for status (e.g., Heckel 1978, p. 147). Interschool competition was also quite common (Anderson 1977, p. 223), increasing solidarity among the students. It forced television networks, school administrations, and police departments to develop new policies toward streakers. City councils and state legislatures throughout the country reacted by passing new laws on indecent public exposure and lewd and offensive behavior. Streaking was seen as a threat by dedicated nudists who worried about its impact on public opinion about nudism. Streaking was widely acknowledged in the press as an act of intergenerational symbolic protest, influenced by the then-new Woodstock sexual morality of the 60s and 70s. Deaths occurred in streaking-related accidents. Tass publicized streaking as yet another indication of the rebelliousness and unhappiness of young people in "crisis-plagued" capitalist societies. Finally, streaking had economic consequences: J.C. Penney and Sears Roebuck canceled the marketing of new lines of tennis shoes with "streaks" labels and apparel manufacturers began selling streaking medallions, uniforms, and for fashion-minded women, costly belts made of golden elk skin and pheasant feathers. It is clear that even an activity fad like streaking has noticeable effects on society. Product fads such as the citizen's band radio fad of 1976 and 1977 have even greater impact (Miller 1985, p. 141; see also Skolnik 1978). More broadly, the consequentiality of fads is documented in the history of technology; significant technological innovations (e.g., the bicycle) often appear as fads before they become permanent elements of the culture.

Career of Fads

Descriptive Model of Diffusion. The results support the prevailing descriptive model of the career of fads, which assumes a sudden, rapid, widespread, short-lived diffusion (e.g., Miller 1985, pp. 144–48). As shown in Figure 1, the streaking fad can be represented by a positively skewed, rapidly accelerating slope, a brief but unstable asymptote, and a precipitous decline.

Figure 1 illustrates the overall frequency of occurrence of streaking events between February and April 1974. The average daily number of newspaper articles and television reports on streaking events in institutions of higher education in the United States is also plotted. Ten streaking events had occurred by the end of February. This increased to 55 events during the first three days of March. The highest average daily frequencies occurred during the next five days (March 4–8). This peak was caused in part by the March 5 report on streaking by the three major television networks. Daily frequencies of streaking events then dropped considerably, averaging four by the middle of April. It must be stressed, however, that the fad behavior did not disappear

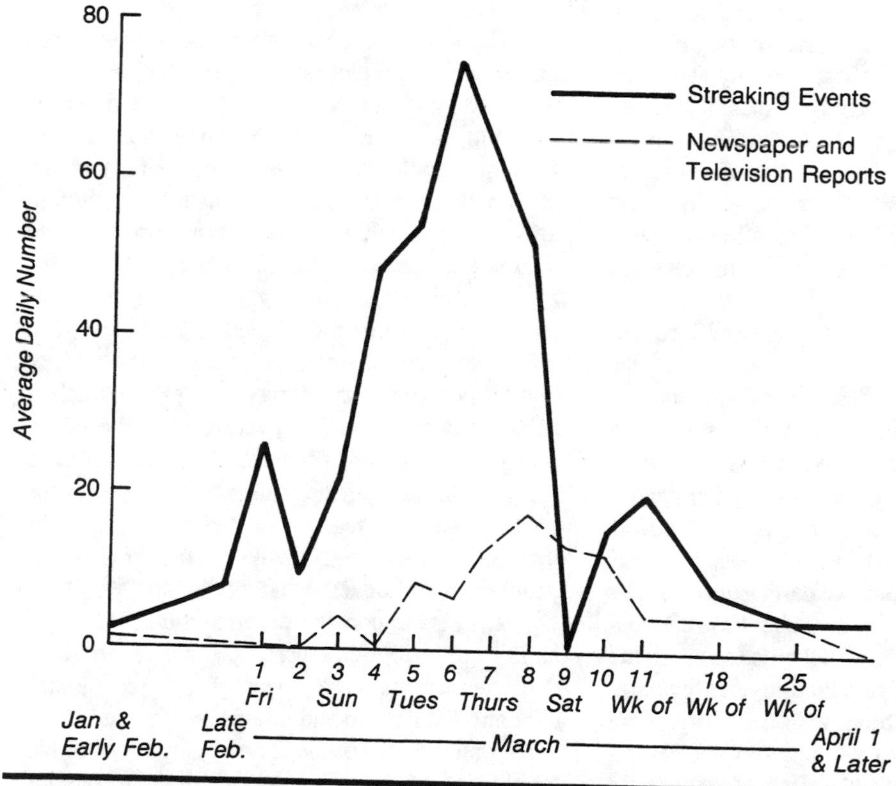

FIGURE 1 Incidents and Newspaper and Television Reports of Streaking

altogether. Schools experienced streaking incidents both before and after the streaking fad.

Our initial speculation was that, as with fictitious riots and imaginary panics, a discrepancy would exist between the events and the reporting of the events. This was not the case; the line for the mass media reports resembles the line for the events, although it trails them.

The sudden increase in the frequency of streaking events shown in Figure 1 was not solely a result of individuals experiencing an impulse to streak. Rather, a great deal of planning and organization went into the streaking events that we observed or for which documentary evidence could be obtained. Some division of labor was nearly always present; streaking without an audience has no meaning (McFadden 1974). Most cases involved organizers, actors, spectators, reporters and TV camera crews, and social-control personnel (e.g., school administrators, police) in the compact collectivities. The act of streaking was only the surface manifestation of pre- and post-group interactions that took many forms.

Streaking often involved calculated, planned actions by small groups like fraternities, sororities, or residents of floors or wings of particular dormitories (Anderson 1977, p. 227). The most active core often consisted of members of such preexisting social networks. Conscious selection governed time and place of the event. Usually, during the large-scale, highly crystallized instances we observed a quasi-scheduling of the behavior occurred as the result of informal understandings among social control agents and the organizers of the collective behavior. Some events were preplanned, to the extent that explicit negotiations about the organization and limits of allowable behavior took place between social control agents and groups of potential participants.

Actual manifestors of the behavior were chosen ahead of time. Personal skills, such as the ability to run fast, ski, ride motorcycles, or parachute, were needed. There was also a "streaking uniform," consisting of white tennis shoes, and ski caps, stocking caps, or Halloween masks. In many instances, streakers had a supporting cast, ranging from "transportation corps" and "musical bands" to "public relations agents" spreading the word about the forthcoming attractions. An anthem, "The Stripper," became quite popular.

The Model of Adoption

Single-Variable Models. Results of proportional-hazard linear modeling of the adoption of the fad of streaking are presented in two sections: the bivariate relationships, showing the effect of each predictor on the risk of streaking, and the overall stepwise reduced multivariate model, to assess the relative importance of the predictors. (See endnote.)

As predicted by our model, greater prestige of schools previously experiencing streaking increased the probability of adoption ($R = -.13, p < .0001$) (cf. Evans and Miller 1975, p. 406).

The variables in the second component contradicted our predictions; the greater the social reactions and sanctions evoked by previous streaking episodes, the higher the probability of subsequent adoption. Results show that the risk of streaking increased as police took action against the streakers, as administrators received complaints, took positions, or made statements against streakers, and as greater administrative punishments were meted out to streakers. The effect of sanctions was to increase the probability of adoption of the streaking fad in schools still at risk; the deterrent effect postulated in the adoption model was not observed. The exception to this generalization is the finding that the greater the extent of negative reaction of students in campuses that had experienced streaking, the greater the people's unwillingness to adopt the fad.

Results support the prediction that the probability of adoption increased when previous streaking events were correctly reported by student and local radio and television stations. Likewise, predictions for the fourth component of the model are supported. The risk of adoption increases with greater levels of complexity of previous streaking events ($R = .20, p < .0001$) and with greater degrees of heterogeneity among these events ($R = .09, p < .0001$).

Table 1 also supports the hypothesis that the greater the sociocultural heterogeneity of the schools at risk of adoption, the greater the probability of adoption. The probability of schools experiencing streaking incidents increased directly with size of student bodies ($R = .09, p < .0001$) and whether the schools at risk were universities and colleges rather than technical institutes or professional schools ($R = -.08, p < .0001$). Moreover, the greater the number of fraternities and sororities on campuses, the greater the probability of adoption of the streaking fad ($R = .10, p < .0001$).

Increasing levels of contextual heterogeneity lead to increased levels of complexity. Type of school, size of enrollment, number of fraternities, prestige of school, and social control of the schools were used as indicators of campuses' social and cultural heterogeneity (schools in the sample with predominantly black student bodies, with consequent high level of cultural homogeneity, did not experience streaking events.) Complexity, the dependent variable, is the numeric ordering of the clusters. It varies from 1 (most uncrystallized) to 12 (most crystallized). The mean of complexity for the entire sample of schools is 4.91 (see Table 2).

Seventy-eight percent of the 1,016 schools for which there was information experienced

TABLE 1 Predicting the Risk of Adoption of Streaking Behavior: Single-Variable Models

PREDICTORS	BETA	CHI-SQUARE	*R*
Components 1. Characteristics of sending schools			
Prestige of schools streaking previously	–.15	50	–.13
Component 2. Societal reactions			
Reaction of city police	–.37	5	–.03
Reaction of campus police	–.18	2	.00
Reaction of students	–.64	14	–.06
Reaction of faculty	–.01	00	.00
Public position by administration	1.51	75	.15
Administration-received complaints	2.05	103	.18
Number of punishments	1.10	45	.12
Official statement	1.17	36	.11
Component 3. Mass media coverage			
Coverage by student newspapers	–.53	18	–.07
Coverage by local city newspapers	–.57	36	–.11
Coverage by local radio and T.V. stations	–.37	20	–.08
Component 4. Characteristics of previous streaking events			
Degree of complexity	.26	122	.20
Standard deviation of complexity	.14	22	.09
Component 5. Social heterogeneity of schools at risk of adoption			
Size of student enrollment	.08	26	.09
Type of school	–.18	20	–.08
Number of fraternities	.01	30	.10

TABLE 2 Multiple Classification Analysis of Level of Complexity of Streaking Events with Characteristics of Schools as Factors

FACTORS	*N*	UNADJUSTED DEVIATION FROM GRAND MEAN[a]	ADJUSTED DEVIATION FROM GRAND MEAN[b]
Number of fraternities			
1. 0–5	429	−1.18	−.41
2. 6–12	78	.06	−.16
3. 13–23	93	.64	.23
4. 24–40	91	1.61	.53
5. 41–142	92	3.22	1.31
Size of school enrollment		(.44)	(.17)
1. <4000	452	−.89	−.35
2. 4,000–8,000	141	.43	.37
3. 8,000–16,000	123	1.27	.38
4. 16,000>	67	2.74	.85
		(.34)	(.12)
Prestige of school			
1. High	111	2.82	.80
2.	295	.66	.47
3.	105	−.11	.39
4.	263	−1.84	−1.00
5. Low	9	−1.25	−.45
		(.45)	(.21)
Type of school			
1. University	156	2.50	.58
2. College	398	.04	.18
3. Technical institute, other	23	−.74	.15
4. Professional schools	6	−.91	−1.24
5. Two-year community college	167	−2.19	−.83
6. Branch of university	33	−.55	−.56
		(.44)	(.15)
Social control of school			
1. Private—secular	131	.36	.08
2. Private—Catholic	49	−.16	−.51
3. Private—other religions	90	−.27	−.58
4. Public	513	−.03	.13
		(.05)	(.08)[c]
Grand Mean	4.91		
Multiple R^2	.26		

[a] Numbers in parentheses are eta coefficients.
[b] Numbers in parentheses are betas (standardized regression coefficients).
[c] Significance of $F = .22$.

streaking events. The analysis in Table 2 is limited to these schools and does not predict the probability that streaking would occur. Rather, the hypothesis is that if streaking occurs, the level of complexity of streaking events increases directly with the heterogeneity of the social organization of the schools.

The results support the prediction that greater sociocultural heterogeneity is associated with greater degree of complexity. Schools with larger student bodies experienced more complex streaking episodes than smaller schools; schools with higher levels of prestige experienced more complex streaking events than their less prestigious counterparts; universities and colleges had more complex streaking events than other types of schools; and, finally, schools with more fraternities and sororities experienced more complex episodes. Schools with the most fraternities (41 or more) had the highest unadjusted mean complexity score observed (8.13). This finding corroborates Anderson's (1977) observations of the importance of fraternities in streaking. Contextual resources, such as those mobilized by fraternities, are important facilitators of faddish activities. This finding also supports the prediction of emergent-norm theory (Turner and Killian 1987, p. 9) about the importance of preexisting social groupings in collective behavior and is similar to the findings of studies of social-movement dynamics that have shown the importance of mobilizable social and cultural resources, such as those available to preexisting organizations and to friendship and kin networks in the creation of social-movement actions.

TABLE 3 Predicting the Risk of Adoption of Streaking Behavior: Multiple-Variables Reduced Model

	BETA	CHI-SQUARE	PARTIAL *R*
Prestige of schools streaking previously	–.09	7	–.04
Reaction of campus police	2.42	64	.14
Reaction of students	–1.30	16	–.07
Reaction of faculty	1.35	40	.11
Public Position by administration	1.25	19	.07
Coverage by local city newspapers	–.82	35	–.11
Degree of complexity	.41	85	.17
Size of student enrollment	.05	8	.05
Overall model		414	.38

Multiple-Variable Reduced Model. Relative statistical importance of the predictors in the adoption model is shown in Table 3; variables that were statistically insignificant at the .01 level are excluded. The overall *R* is .38.

All five components of the adoption model are represented by the predictors in this reduced multivariate solution (see Table 3). The sign of all but one of the predictors (reaction of campus police) remain unchanged from the bivariate analyses. Reaction of faculty, insignificant in a bivariate context, is significant now; the risk of adoption increases as the reaction of the faculty to the fad becomes more negative. The most powerful predictor of adoption of the fad was the degree of complexity (R = .17) of previous streaking episodes, representing the strength of the stimulus that previous streaking events provided to potential adopters. This was followed in importance by reaction of campus police (R = .14), reaction of faculty (R = .11), and coverage by local city newspapers (R = –.11). These results show that the relative prestige of schools and degree of sociocultural heterogeneity of potential adopter schools are less important components in explaining adoption.

The relative stability of the signs and sizes of the coefficients in the bivariate and multivariate contexts argue against spuriousness. For instance, while it is true that greater sanctions attract more mass media attention, which in turn increases the risk of adoption, both sanctions and mass media have separate, significant effects on adoption. . . .

ENDNOTE

Lagged variables: The variables in components 1, 2, 3, and 4 of the proportional-hazard linear model of the adoption of streaking are one time period-lagged variables. These variables represent mean averages computed separately from the schools experiencing streaking for each combination of the states in the country and the 16 time periods under observation. Schools that did not experience streaking constituted the censored cases in the analysis (Allison 1984, pp. 27–29). The test of the adoption model is restricted to states with 38 or more schools in the sample to insure that there would be mean average scores for each time period for each of the states and that there would be sufficient number of cases to make these mean average scores stable. There are 364 schools in this test. The first component in the model of the diffusion of streaking is the institutional prestige of the schools. The second component is represented by eight lagged variables. Two questions ask whether or not campus and city police departments took action against the streakers; two questions ask if the reactions of students and faculty members were mostly positive, mixed or negative; and four questions ask about the reaction of schools administrators. The third component in the model is represented by three lagged variables that ask if the streaking event was correctly, partly correctly, or incorrectly reported by student newspapers, local newspapers, and local radio and television stations. The fourth component is operationalized by two variables, measuring the level of complexity of streaking events and the standard deviation of this variable. The fifth component in the model is represented by three *nonlagged* variables. The first variable presents information on the size of the student enrollment. It ranges from 1 for schools with enrollments of about 1,000 students, to 17 for schools with more than 30,000 students. The second variable is the type of school, ordered from high to low heterogeneity as follows: universities, colleges, branches of universities, two-year community colleges, technical schools, and professional schools (Carnegie Foundation 1976). The third variable is the number of college fraternities and sororities.

REFERENCES

Allison, Paul D. 1984, *Event History Analysis*. Beverly Hills, CA: Sage.

Anderson, William. 1977. "The Social Organization and Social Control of a Fad." *Urban Life* 6:221–40.

Aronson, Sidney. 1952. "The Sociology of the Bicycle." *Social Forces* 30:305–12.

Bernard. L. L. 1926. *An Introduction to Social Psychology*. New York: Holt.

Blau, Peter M. and Ellen L. Slaughter, 1971. "Institutional Condition and Student Demonstrations." *Social Problems* 18:474–87.

Blumer, Herber. 1964. "Collective Behavior." Pp. 165–200 in *An Outline of the Principles of Sociology,* edited by Alfred Lee. New York: Barnes and Noble.

———. 1968. "Fashion." Pp. 341–45 in *International Encyclopedia of the Social Sciences*. New York: Macmillan.

———. 1969. "Fashion: From Class Differentiation to Collective Section." *Sociological Quarterly* 10:275–91.

———. 1971. "Social Problems as Collective Behavior." *Social Problems* 18:298–306.

Brown, Michael and Amy Goldin. 1973. *Collective Behavior: A Review and Reinterpretation of the Literature*. Pacific Palisades. CA: Goodyear.

Brown, Roger. 1965. *Social Psychology*. New York: Free Press.

Carnegie Foundation. 1976. *A Classification of Institutions of Higher Education*. Berkeley, CA: The Carnegie Foundations for the Advancement of Teaching.

Cox, D. R. 1972. "Regression Models and Life Tables." *Journal of the Royal Statistical Society,* series B 34:187–202.

Davis, Kingsley. 1949. *Human Society*. New York: Macmillan.

Dawson, Carl and Warren Gettys. 1929. *An Introduction to Sociology*. New York: Ronald.

Doob, Leonard. 1952. *Social Psychology*. New York: Holt.

Duvignaud, Jean. 1980. "Festivals: A Sociological Approach." *Cultures* 3:13–25.

Evans, Robert and Jerry Miller, 1975. "Barely an End in Sight." Pp. 401–17 in *Readings in Collective Behavior,* edited by Robert Evans. Chicago: Rand McNally.

Fairchild, Henry. 1965. *Dictionary of Sociology and Related Sciences*. New York: Littlefield Adams.

Grimes. Michael D., Thomas K. Pinhey, and Louis A. Zurcher, 1977. "Note on Student's Reaction to 'Streakers' and 'Streaking'" *Perceptual and Motor Skills* 45:1226.

Gold, Ray. 1964. "Fad." Pp. 256–57 in *A Dictionary of Social Science,* edited by Julius Gould and William Kolb. New York: Free Press.

Harrell, Frank E., Jr. 1983. "The PHGLM Procedure." Pp. 267–94 in *SUGI Supplemental Library User's Guide,* edited by Stephanie R. Joyner, Gary. IN:SAS Institute Inc.

Heckel, Robert V. 1978. "Grin and Bare it. Focus of Control in Streakers." *Journal of Community Psychology* 4:145–48.

Hirsch, Paul. 1972. "Processing Fads and Fashions: An Organizational-set Analyses of cultural Industry Systems." *American Journal of Sociology* 77:639–59.

Jolly, Howard. 1967. *Popular Music: A Study in Collective Behavior*. Ph.D. diss., Stanford University.

Klapp, Orrin. 1972. *Currents of Unrest: An Introduction to Collective Behavior*. New York: Holt, Rinehart, and Winston.

Landecker, Werner S. 1981. *Class Crystallization.* New Brunswick, NJ: Rutgers University Press.

Lang, Kurt and Gladys Lang. 1961. *Collective Behavior*. New York:Crowell.

———. 1968. "Collective Behavior." Pp. 556–65 in *International Encyclopedia of the Social Science V*. New York: Macmillan.

LaPiere, Richard. 1938. *Collective Behavior*. New York: McGraw Hill.

Lofland, John. 1977. "The Boom and Bust Patterns of social Movements: Toward Analysis of Life History Scenarios," Unpublished ms.

———. 1981. "Collective Behavior: Elementary Forms." Pp. 413–46 in *Social Psychology Today: Sociological Perspectives,* edited by M. Rosenberg and Ralph Turner. New York: Basic Books.

McFadden, Robert D. 1974. "Streaking: A Mad Dash to Where?" *New York Times*. March 8. p[. 35, 41.

McPhail, Clark. 1984. "The Complexity of Collective Behavior and of Gatherings: From a Definition and Some Elementary Forms to a Taxonomy and a Scale." Unpublished ms.

Meyersohn. Rolf and Elihu Katz. 1957. "Notes on a Natural History of Fads." *American Journal of Sociology* 62:594–601.

Milgram, S. and H. Toch. 1969. "Collective Behavior: Crowds and Social Movements." Pp. 507–610 in *Handbook of Social Psychology, vol. 4,* edited by Garner Lindzey and Elliott Aronson, Reading, MA: Addison-Wesley.

Miller, David L. 1985. *Introduction to Collective Behavior*. Belmont, CA: Wadsworth Publishing Company.

Miller, J.L.L. and J.T. Borhek. 1978. "Contagion Reconsidered." *Sociological Symposium* 24:63–80.

Mohr, Lawrence B. 1978. "Determinants of Innovation in Organization," Pp. 312–17 in *Collective Behavior and Social Movements,* edited by Louis E. Genevie. Itasca, IL: F.E. Peacock.

Oberschall, Anthony. 1980. "Loosely Structured Collective Conflict: A Theory and An Application." Pp. 45–68 in *Research in Social Movements, Conflicts and Change 3,* edited by L. Kreberg, JAI Press.

Oliver, Pamela. 1985, "Bringing the Crowd Back In: The Nonorganizational Elements of Social Movements," Unpublished ms.

Park, Robert and Ernest Burgess. 1924. *Introduction to the Science of Sociology*. Chicago, IL: University of Chicago Press.

Perry, Joseph and M.D. Pugh. 1978. *Collective*

Ross, E.A. 1915. *Social Sciences*. New York: Macmillan.

Sapir, Edward. 1931. "Fashion." Pp. 139–44 in *Encyclopedia of the Social Sciences.* New York: Macmillan.

Sebald, Hans. 1968. *Adolescence: A Sociological Analysis*. Englewood Cliffs, NY: Prentice-Hall.

Simmel, Georg. 1957. "Fashion." *The American Journal of Sociology* 62:541–58.

Skolnik, Peter L. 1978. *Fads, America's Crazes, Fevers and Fancies*. New York: Crowell.

Smelser, Neil. 1962. *Theory of Collective Behavior*. New York: Free Press.

Sullivan, Thomas J. 1977. "The Critical Mass" in Crowd Behavior: Crowd Size, Contagion and the Evolution of Riots." *Humboldt Journal of Social Relations* 4:46–59.

Turner, Ralph. 1960. "Collective Behavior," Pp. 384–92 in *Handbook of Modern Sociology,* edited by E. Faris. New York: Rand McNally.

Turner, Ralph and Lewis Killian, 1957. *Collective Behavior*. Englewood Cliffs, NJ: Prentice-Hall.

———. 1972. *Collective Behavior*. Englewood Cliffs, NJ: Prentice-Hall.

———. 1987. *Collective Behavior*. Englewood Cliffs, NJ: Prentice-Hall.

Young, Kimball. 1944. *Social Psychology*. New York: Appleton Century Crofts. *Behavior. Response to Social Stress*. St. Paul, MN:West.

Taylor, Verta and E. L. Quarantelli. 1974. Spring 1974 Streaking Survey [MRDF]. Columbus, OH: Verta Taylor and E.L. Quarantelli (producer). College Station, TX: B.E. Aguirre, Department of Sociology, Texas A&M University (distributor).

Quarantelli, E. L. and Dennis Wenger. 1973. "A Voice from the Thirteenth Century: The Characteristics and Conditions for the Emergence of a Quija Board Cult." *Urban Life and Culture:* 379–400.

Ray, Alice Allen. 1982. *SAS User's Guide: Statistics*. Gary, NC: SAS Institute Inc.

Robson, John, 1977. *Baird's Manual of American College Fraternities*. Menasha, WI: Baird's Manual Foundation, Inc.

Rogers, Everett M. And F. Floyd Shoemaker. 1971. *Communication and Innovations. A Cross-cultural Approach*. New York: Free Press.

Romesburg, H. Charles. 1984. *Cluster Analysis for Researchers*. Belmont, CA: Lifetime learning Corporation.

Rose, Jerry. 1982. *Outbreaks. The Sociology of Collective Behavior*. New York: Free Press.

ARTICLE 16

A Test of Some Propositions about Crowd Formation and Behavior

E. L. QUARANTELLI
JAMES R. HUNDLEY, JR.

. . . What does Smelser say about crowd activity? Little, in one sense, because he usually talks of a hostile outburst rather than a crowd. Still, almost all of the sources cited as documentation and most of the examples drawn from the literature indicate that the new term substantially encompasses what is covered by the more traditional sociological label of "crowd."

A hostile outburst is formally defined as "mobilization for action under hostile belief." The behavior is identified by its objectives as revealed in the beliefs of group members. Or as Smelser more specifically states, "to fit our definition the participants in an outburst must be bent on attacking someone considered responsible for a disturbing state of affairs." As we shall discuss later, there is a problem with this formulation for it lends itself to an equating of the features by which a hostile outburst is to be identified, with the social factors which lead to the appearance of the phenomenon.

It is said that there are six necessary conditions or determinants of an outburst. These are: structural conduciveness, structural strain, a generalized hostile belief, precipitating factors, a mobilization-for-action, and particular reactions of social control agencies. These conditions do not necessarily develop in the order stated, but all have to be present for the appearance of a hostile outburst.

We have examined the propositions involved in the six conditions by looking at data gathered in connection with the following incident.

> Early in February, 1964, *The Candle*, a daily campus newspaper of a state university located in a major metropolitan area, appeared one morning with a large black headline proclaiming the arrest of a coed for not paying a five dollar jaywalking ticket. The headline read: "COED IN JAIL 1½ HOURS: CRIME? JAYWALKING," The front page, on which there was a photograph of the city jail, was exclusively devoted to stories about the arrest. Also displayed on the front page was a boxed-in story with the caption—"WE'D GO INTO CLASSROOM FOR HER IF NECESSARY." This statement was attributed to a sergeant at police headquarters.
>
> To outward appearances, nothing unusual happened on the university campus during the day. However, just before 5 P.M. students deliberately began to jaywalk into the evening rush hour traffic on the city's main thoroughfare just outside the front entrance to the campus area. Within minutes, scores of automobiles and buses were totally blocked from movement in any direction by the

Excerpted from Quarantelli, E.L., & Hundley, James R. Jr. (1975). In Robert R. Evans (Ed.), *Readings in collective behavior* (pp. 370–385). Chicago: Rand McNally, with permission of Robert R. Evans.

students milling in the street. At first, the crowd, although getting ever larger and more disorderly, remained at that location with participants climbing and standing on top of buses and battering cars that attempted to force their ways through. After about an hour, one segment of the crowd, perhaps 1,000 in number, marched about three miles to the downtown area. As police cars retreated in front of it, this crowd eventually worked its way to police headquarters in the heart of the central business district. Milling around in front of the station with some vocal elements demanding an apology from the police for arresting the coed, the crowd was confronted by the chief of police. After a rather noisy but inconclusive exchange, the participants marched back to rejoin the other part of the crowd that had remained at the original point of the massive jaywalk. A large bonfire was built in the middle of the street around which the participants milled in a somewhat desultory fashion, the only somewhat sustained action being an effort for about an hour to destroy a traffic light. Around 11:15 P.M., a little more than six hours after the first students spilled into the street, the crowd dissolved of its own accord without any intervention on the part of the large number of policemen that had assembled around the university area. Seven students were arrested during the course of the evening, but only two had been participants in the active core of the crowd.

The behavior of the crowd disrupted city traffic substantially at the height of the rush hour, and blocked, for six hours, the busiest thoroughfare in the metropolitan area. In addition, around a half dozen cars were severely battered, one being partly dismantled. Later estimates indicated that three to four thousand dollars' worth of damage had been done to store fronts and other property. The bonfire badly buckled the street and eventually one thousand dollars had to be spent to repair the pavement. Finally, the keeping of the afternoon police shift on overtime duty cost the city over five thousand dollars.

The authors of this article, partly because of having been given a half hour forewarning that a "demonstration" was likely, were able to obtain a variety of primary data on the incident. Taking the data obtained, what did we find when we used them to test Smelser's notions about the necessary conditions for the appearance of a hostile outburst? As we shall show below, we found that, while our data were consistent with four of the conditions advanced, that is, with respect to structural conduciveness, structural strain, precipitating factors, and the reactions of social control agencies, the data do not equally support the two most crucial conditions posited: a generalized hostile belief and mobilization-for-action.

STRUCTURAL CONDUCIVENESS

By structural conduciveness is meant "a setting which is either permissive of hostility or prohibitive of other responses, or both." Smelser states that there are three aspects: a figure, class or agency to which responsibility can be assigned for the disturbing state of affairs; the absence or failure of channels for expressing grievances; and ecological and other situational variables that facilitate the possibility of communication among the aggrieved.

These three factors were all present in our particular example. The police department was clearly perceived as responsible not only for the disturbing event (i.e., the arrest), but for a whole prior series of such events revolving around not only jaywalking tickets, but traffic fines and civil liberty violations On-campus channels for expressing grievances to off-campus sources were visualized as in effectual and often nonexistent. Finally, conditions were very conducive for communications among the students. The story of the arrest carried in the student newspaper (read by 88 percent of the 884 students in our sample) had been extensively discussed during the day as students moved from one class to another. Second, the local radio station most listened to by students had announced at 3:55 P.M. that a "demonstration" was going to occur an hour later (the 12 percent of our sample that heard this announcement were primarily dormitory residents so the news diffused rapidly). Third, several telephone calls asking support for a "demonstration" had been made early in the afternoon by a clique of students to friends elsewhere on campus. While direct support was not evoked, it did alert some students to a possible protest effort. Fourth, the initial group of agitators initiated the "demonstration" very near the most heavily student-traversed intersection around the campus.

Thus, aspects of structural conduciveness postulated by Smelser were present in the pre-crowd setting examined.

STRUCTURAL STRAIN

Smelser gives a very complex explanation of structural strain. However, the basic point is that impaired social relations are present in the pre-crowd situation. This impairment is along traditional if not institutionalized lines of social cleavages and tends to be focused on a particular issue.

Structural strain of long duration was definitely present in the case we are considering. Strong mutual dislike characterized police-student relationships in general. Students believed that the police were very biased in their statement of the college population. An indication of the strength of the feeling is given by the fact that 32 percent of our respondents volunteered negative comments about the police, although no questionnaire item directly or indirectly made any allusion to that organization or its personnel. (From the way remarks were couched, an unfavorable attitude towards police definitely had existed prior to the arrest of the girl.)

Again, the condition posited by Smelser was clearly present in the pre-crowd stage of our example.

GENERALIZED HOSTILE BELIEF

Smelser suggests five elements or stages in the creation of a generalized hostile belief. These include ambiguity, anxiety, assignment of responsibility for threats to identified agents, a focused desire to punish or restrict the particular responsible agent, and an omnipotent belief in the ability of the attackers to remove or harm the agent of "evil."

It is said that one of four factors can control ambiguity and stop the creation of the belief. If information is supplied, leadership is authoritative, norms are created, or faith in a set of values is maintained, ambiguity is controlled. In the situation we studied, no information was issued by the police or city government about possible future arrests. Neither the university administration nor official student groups provided any leadership in response to the jailing. No new rules were offered to handle further police-student relationships. And the faith of students in police adherence to principles of justice and fairness had long ago eroded. These observations therefore support Smelser's contention about ambiguity.

However, anxiety is visualized as rooted in ambiguous situations and as a generalized response not tied to precisely definable objects. Smelser states "it is a vague and incomprehensible uneasiness about unknown threats. Because these threats are undefined, *they contain potentially enormous power of destruction.*"

Our data do not support the notion that many, if any at all, of the pre-crowd participants perceived either an undefined danger or that the consequences of the threat were "boundless" or "unlimited." To understand this it is necessary to consider what is postulated as the third element or stage in the creation of a generalized hostile belief. Basically, a short-circuiting process is supposed to occur. As we understand it, the distinctive character of a generalized belief is a definition of the situation which jumps from an extremely high level of generality to specific "person, places, situations" or "events." The diffuse, almost free-floating anxiety becomes focused on specific agents which are seen as responsible for the anxiety-producing state of affairs.

However, our data indicate that the police have traditionally been visualized as a source of trouble to the students. Such anxiety as existed was not vague and diffuse and attributed to an unknown source. Students knew who gave out tickets; who made arrests. The police were held responsible for such activity long before the arrest of the coed. In short, there was no short-circuiting process in this particular incident. It follows that if anxiety existed it could not be boundless. This is partly illustrated by the fact that some respondents specifically indicated that they had ignored previous parking and traffic tickets. It is part of the student subculture on this particular campus to delay or to avoid paying tickets at all. Whatever negative feeling students had about the police, it was not anxiety in the way Smelser uses the term.

The point might be raised that the key event in this situation was the unexpected arrest rather than the giving out of jaywalking tickets and that the arrest itself generated anxiety. However, here again the specific agent involved in the action was clear cut–it was the police. More important, our questionnaire data do not indicate that the arrest generated much anxiety. Certainly there was nothing created that even remotely approached being seen as an unlimited threat that contained "potentially enormous power of destruction."

The fourth element or stage in the creation of a hostile belief supposedly, is ". . . a desire to punish, remove, damage, or restrict the responsible agent." We found two problems with this formulation.

First, it is difficult to understand exactly and specifically what should be taken as a manifestation of the indicated desire. Is the milling of a generally cheering and happily singing group in front of a police station while a few participants shout for apologies from a police chief an indication of a "desire to punish, remove, damage, or restrict the responsible agent"? Our visual observations and an analysis of the response to the question of why the students were participating would not fully support such a contention. For example, seldom did conversation in the crowd segment that marched downtown deal with matters that overtly could be interpreted as attacks against the police. Cries of "come on and join the fun" were far more frequent than "we'll show those cops." Only seven percent of our respondents indicated that they participated because they felt that they were protesting something. In short, relatively few students (although in total numbers they could have amounted to nearly two hundred participants) even saw it as a "demonstration."

Neither was there any short-circuiting or overt focusing of the generalized aggression on a specific agent. The crowd we studied had not specifically gone to police headquarters to confront the chief. It was fortuitous he was present and on his own initiative faced the crowd. In fact, it was not until the marchers were deep into the downtown area that they even turned in the direction of police headquarters (for reasons to be discussed later). Furthermore, our questionnaire data do not have more than two or three references to the arresting officer or other policemen involved in the original arrest incident. Crowd attention never turned to them. There was no short-circuiting or channeling of generalized aggression towards them as particular responsible agents either.

The second problem alluded to above with respect to the fourth element or stage in the creation of a hostile belief, has to do with the matter of numbers, or even more basically with the issue of homogeneity. How many persons have to have the desire *"to move against"* the responsible agent? Would this condition be met if only the more active participants in the crowd had the desire? Although perhaps unintended, the formulation advanced by Smelser along this line implicitly assumes substantial initial homogeneity or orientation among the crowd participants. To be sure, he makes a distinction between real and derived phases of recruitment into a crowd, but the earliest joiners or at least the core of the hostile outburst would initially appear to have to be composed of persons with the same orientation or generalized belief.

When we examine the crowd we had under study, what do we find with respect to its homogeneity? Put very simply, the crowd we studied was very heterogeneous. From the initial to the later stages it was marked by considerable diversity of orientation and belief. It is difficult to see anything resembling a widely shared intent to move against responsible agents. As discussed later, even the initial agitators were primarily interested in seeing if they could repeat an earlier success of theirs in getting a crowd per se to form. Participants joined the developing crowd, in their words, "to have fun, to see a real riot, because everyone in the hall went, to compare with other crowds I've been in, out of curiosity, my friends asked me to," and even "to make some observations for my collective behavior course."

Without doubt, many students on this campus were hostile towards the police. But this feeling was not directly related to anxiety. More important, the hostile attitude was but one of a variety of orientations prevailing among participants, including agitators, during all phases of the crowd development. As far as we can judge from our data, a generalized hostile belief was never a major— much less dominant—orientation, a desire to move against a particular responsible agent never prevailed.

The fifth step or element of the generalized hostile belief is said to involve an exaggerated perception of the "ability of the attackers to punish or harm the agent of evil." It is also stated that there develops an overestimation of the results that are to be achieved once the responsible agent is punished. This stage is seen as involving a generalized sense of omnipotence, which is short-circuited to specific results.

Our data do not support the notion of omnipotence in any major way. A few students thought their actions might lead the police to reconsider their ticketing and arrest policies. However, there is little evidence that many thought this activity would lead to major changes in the generally negative relationship between students and the police. More frequently voiced in the crowd were remarks to the effect that "nothing is going to come out of this but possible trouble for ourselves." There was not any exaggerated belief that by their actions, the crowd participants would "set the world right" or any illusion that the police would henceforth ignore the students.

Regarding a generalized hostile belief we can therefore say we found clear-cut support in our data only for the first stage or element postulated, i.e., ambiguity. The other four stages suggested could only be harmonized with our observations by adding qualifications and making reformulations of such a nature as to change the meanings of the basic elements posited by Smelser. Our crowd never underwent the short-circuiting process hypothesized in the last three stages. It was and remained a heterogeneous group held together neither by a common hostile belief, nor by a shared, single definition of the situation (i.e., a common mass perception).

PRECIPITATING FACTORS

Certain factors are said to confirm, sharpen, or exaggerate the effects of the conditions of conduciveness, strain, or generalized hostile belief. Apparently precipitants may, but do not necessarily, stir generalized aggression and focus it on definite situations. Smelser lists six ways in which the factors, not important in themselves, may support the other conditions.

In the particular crowd we studied, the news of the jailing of the coed can be taken as the major precipitating factor. The news of this event certainly confirmed and sharpened some of the already discussed conditions of conduciveness and strain, although it seems to have added little at all to the spread of a generalized belief. It was of course about eight hours after the news of the arrest before the crowd started to form. The actual formation was precipitated by the sporadic but deliberate cases of jaywalking at the intersection. However, as Smelser notes, there may be more than one precipitating factor, and what is a condition in one time context may be a precipitating factor in a shorter time span. At any rate, our data generally support Smelser's notion of precipitating factors, if they are not seen as necessarily contributing only to the spread of a generalized hostile belief.

MOBILIZATION-FOR-ACTION

The occurrence of mobilization action which supposedly marks the outbreak of hostility, is primarily discussed in terms of leadership, the organization of the crowd, and what is called the "shape" of the hostility curve.

Smelser states that leadership in a hostile outburst takes one of three forms—a model who unwittingly triggers action, a deliberate instigator, or a formal group that is part of an existing organization. Leaders supposedly spur the outward expression of the hostile attitude. Actually, the formulation is vague and not too systematic. More important, there seems to be an ignoring of the interactional aspects which lead to the development of diversity and changes of direction in the behavior of crowd participants.

The incident we examined was initially led by a clique of students who purposefully attempted to get other students to assemble near the intersection off the university campus. This group of from six to eight upperclassmen lived in one of the campus resident halls. Around noon on the day of the incident they started to discuss the *Candle* article about the jailing of the coed. In the course of the conversation the matter of violation of civil liberties and their own personal experiences with jaywalking tickets were discussed. But in the words of one of them, "the guys were more interested in seeing if they could get a crowd out there." This group had twice previously been successful in generating a large turnout at the airport to greet the returning basketball team. Following the pattern of their prior successes, they first telephoned a radio station (after getting a busy signal at another) to say that a "demonstration" was going to occur. They then called friends and acquaintances, mostly in fraternities, urging them to get other students to the intersection at five o'clock that afternoon. Callers "tried to appeal to Greek loyalties." However, these calls did not generate much enthusiastic response and our data show that those called seldom informed others of the possible event. (The call to the radio station did evoke an announcement on the 3:55 P.M. newscast that a "demonstration" was going to occur in an hour right off the university campus.) Less than one percent of our sample had heard, prior to the newscast, of a possible "demonstration." In this sense, the initial deliberate instigation through personal channels had failed. Even within the same resident hall, another small group which was to play an important keynoting part in the early stages of the crowd formation, learned of the supposed demonstration through the newscast rather than through personal contact.

The original agitators, motivated by the desire to have "fun" and to see if their activity would bear results, themselves went near the intersection about 4:30 P.M. They found more than the usual mass egress of persons from the campus. Some students, having heard the radio announcements or learned the news from others, had come to the scene primarily to see what would happen. Such spectators, our data show, were far more motivated by curiosity than hostility. Consequently, while the bulk of the students present were those who normally left the university grounds at that time of the day, more than 20 percent of our respondents said they unexpectedly came upon a larger than usual mass of students at the campus entrance.

The agitators, posting themselves on the far side of the main thoroughfare, three different times made major attempts to talk passing students into collective jaywalking. When this failed, four of them started a chant of "we'll win, we can't be beat, where we want, we'll cross the street," and another of "red rover, red rover, you can't come over." This attracted attention and drew even more students to the location but provoked no untoward action suggesting the vocal utterances were equivalent to belief. It was not until four members of the clique locked arms and jaywalked at 4:49 P.M., that other students also started to jaywalk. Even this activity ceased after a minute or two. Jaywalking was not recommenced until a non-clique student suddenly dashed into the middle of the street, and pretended to direct traffic. Even at this point only about fifty students actively participated in jaywalking and they did not block vehicular traffic since they waited to run across the street when cars were not moving. Persons first started to mill in the street itself when a TV mobile unit car arrived on the scene and provided a major focus of attention (at around 5 P.M.). Furthermore, the crowd actually crystallized only when members of the second aforementioned resident hall group arrived on the scene with an American flag and a sign (lettered Jaywalking 401). Their appearance led to conscious and successful efforts to block vehicular traffic.

The leader-follower relationship even in the first stages of this crowd involved a far more complex pattern than seems to be implied in Smelser's remarks on leadership. Even in the early period there were four different sequential foci of leadership. Likewise, there was no automatic or direct response by spectators to the ongoing behavior. In fact, at different points in time "leaders" failed to provoke the outward expression of the supposed underlying hostile attitude. This was also true at later stages of the crowd. Thus, even an hour after jaywalking activities had started, there were thousands more students watching from the side-walk and carefully avoiding stepping into the street than there were students milling in the middle of the avenue. (A measurement of the spatial area after the event revealed that no more than 1,000 persons could have been standing in the street even if the intersection had been devoid of blocked cars and buses, which of course it was not.)

According to Smelser, the organization of the attack in the hostile outburst varies considerably and is influenced by three factors: The degree of preexisting structure, ecological factors, and the operation of the agencies of social control. He states that "unless this prior organization itself is disrupted . . . the organization of the hostile outburst will correspond to the degree of preexisting organization." If by "prior organization" is meant the structure brought to the scene of the outburst, our data do not fully support this hypothesis. Not only were the first few agitators replaced by far numerous others but the behavior became more varies. What originally had some gross organization in the sense of the focus on a relative small core of initial participants engaged primarily in jaywalking, in the course of the early intensive milling became multiple small groups undertaking different actions. Some students pulled electric wires from blocked buses and pounded car and bus sides. Others talked with drivers and passengers in the stalled vehicles. Alongside them still other students reacted forcefully to cars attempting to force their way through. A few participants climbed atop bus tops, to the cheers of other students simply standing in the street. At a later stage not only did the crowd split into two parts with one marching downtown, but many participants left and returned. Thus, at least 25 percent of our respondents went away from the scene at least once only to return later in the evening. (A number even went to eat supper in dormitories before coming back.) Behavior ranged from coordinated and organized to uncoordinated and individualistic.

In this discussion of ecological factors Smelser states that the organization of a hostile outburst is also very dependent ". . . on the location and accessibility of objects of attack." The intersection at which the students gathered is widely known in the university community as a traditional convergence point for campus "demonstrators." Despite this as well as the fact it is one of the busiest points in the city insofar as traffic is concerned, it is equally known that police are seldom present in its vicinity at rush hours or at any other time. The march downtown might appear dictated by the fact that the major thoroughfare in the city went past the campus right into the heart of the central business district. However, as described earlier, the crowd did not originally head for police headquarters. In the course of interacting with one another, some members of the crowd at the intersection just off the campus suggested marching downtown. (Overheard discussion among participants indicated they remembered that another student crowd two years earlier had marched that way.) Also, once downtown, the crowd had to make a sharp right hand turn off the main street and double back two blocks to get to police headquarters. The decision to march to the police station emerged in the course of the interaction when the marchers were already past the building insofar as the direction of their movement was concerned. Ecological factors were not crucial in either the initial or later direction of crowd movement; far more important were interactional processes.

According to Smelser, the third factor affecting the organization of an outburst is the operation of agencies of social control. The rapidity and effectiveness of response of these agencies can counter an outburst and affect its organization and development. However, the exact ways the response is so affected are not really discussed. One is puzzled how such an analysis would handle in our instance the nature of the interaction that allowed the police chief to walk openly all around the crowd in its last three hours of existence without evoking any manifest hostility whatsoever.

Smelser locates "factors" which supposedly determine the nature of the response, but he poorly indicates which dimensions of organization are affected by the preexisting structure, the ecological variables, and the operation of social control agencies. A more basic problem, as we have tried to indicate in our discussions of these points, is that an understanding of what evolves in crowds requires the paying of close attention to the interaction patterns. Too strict a structural deterministic kind of approach hinders such a kind of analysis.

According to Smelser, a third aspect of the mobilization-for-action determinant is the spread of the hostile outburst. He states, "Hostility . . . can be divided for analytic purposes into a real and a derived phase. . . ." There is the supposition that an initial building up of hostility and subsequent expressive outburst is due to the structural determinants already discussed. However, the situation is conducive to the expression of *further hostility* unrelated to the conditions giving rise to the initial outburst. In fact, as soon as the real phase of hostility subsides, the derived phase builds up and maintains the hostile outburst if certain other circumstances are present such as structural conduciveness. As an outburst continues through time, participants with varying motivations *for hostility* will become involved. They may move from one object of attack to another, and different parts of the crowd may attack different objects simultaneously.

Our data do not lend much support to these notions. The crowd did not move from one object of attack to another. This is partly illustrated by the fact that after the first hour or so, all blocked cars and buses were allowed to go free and such automobiles as managed o avoid police roadblocks set up some distance away were unmolested in going through the intersection. A later effort to generate attention on an effigy hung from a nearby flagpole failed to move the participants around the bonfire. In fact, except for a relatively half-hearted attempt to destroy the traffic light, the crowd members did not do much of anything the last three and a half hours, except to walk around the bonfire in the middle of the street. Police and college officials in and around the crowd were generally ignored. Participants openly expressed a variety of reasons for their involvement, with the desire to express hostility being a minor theme. As already indicated, that part of the crowd that marched downtown was hardly goal-focused. (Actually there were two abortive efforts to start a movement away from the intersection before a segment of the crowd finally broke away.)

We did find that when time of involvement was checked against motivation, the later participants were less likely to give protest motives. But while our data do support the idea of something akin to a real and derived phase, the process is far more complex than a simple "drawing in" of persons with hostile orientations. Most later joiners of the crowd were moved far more by activation of personal ties with others than by a perception of an opportunity to give vent to their hostile attitudes. In fact, persons with hostile feelings who were not associating with friends and acquaintances on the scene tended to leave the crowd completely rather early in the course of events.

Smelser does not state that the action of social control agencies is a separate and necessary condition for a hostile outburst to emerge. Actions of such groups only add to the mobilization determinant. However, with respect to the behavior and completion of a hostile outburst, Smelser offers the hypotheses that outbursts will cease if: (1) communication is prevented; (2) interaction between leaders and followers is prevented; (3) officials do not vacillate in the use of force; and (4) officials refrain from entering the issues and remain unyielding on the principle of maintaining law and order.

The crowd we studied lasted for a little more than six hours. Communication among the participants was not prevented, the police abandoned the university area to the students and retreated when the marchers moved downtown, and the police were a party to the issue itself and at least partially involved in the crowd behavior. These factors partly help explain the excessive length of the disturbance, and generally support Smelser's statements about the effect of the behavior of the social control agencies on the development and continuation of crowd activity.

DISCUSSION

It might appear if four out of six conditions hypothesized by Smelser are supported by our data that this would lend strong support to the particular theoretical formulation involved. However, the four conditions are not the crucial ones; few other students of crowd formation and behavior would generally disagree with them. The two other conditions posited for a hostile outburst are a much more crucial test. It was noted earlier that a hostile outburst is defined as mobilization for action under hostile belief. Yet it is exactly these two features—the postulation of a generalized hostile belief and the mobilization-for-action condition—that are least supported by our data.

Three possibilities suggest themselves. (1) Our data are invalid and thus the propositions are not denied. This we do not accept. While our data are largely qualitative and not as fully systematic as might be desired, they are far better than the selective examples understandably used by Smelser to illustrate his proposition. Certainly our data provide an empirical test of sorts and thus are more convincing evidence than simple illustrations. (2) Our data are valid and thus the propositions are challenged. This of course is the opposite position of the one just discussed. However, if the two points on which we have focused are central to Smelser's formulation, we have to conclude that the overall model as to hostile outbursts is partly questionable along some lines. At least the approach seems to be rather weak in dealing with collective phenomena in which there is not considerable homogeneity of participants, and in assuming a structural determinism of behavior which substantially underplays the function of social interaction in the formation and development of emergent groups. This is a possible conclusion that can be drawn from our study.

There is, however, another possibility. It is that (3) what we studied was not what Smelser conceptualizes as a hostile outburst. If that is so, no test has been made of any of the propositions involved. When an idea type is compared to an empirical instance, it must be asked if the case material is appropriate to test the type (and the larger theory from which it is derived).

However, we not only believe our case was a valid test; more important, we feel our examination of a specific empirical instance revealed some possible weakness in the basic conceptualization itself. That is, the very concept of hostile outburst itself presents some theoretical as well as empirical difficulties. This obviously is more a matter of interpretation than of data or evidence as such, but let us try to indicate what we have in mind.

Smelser's formulation supposedly embraces all instances of collective behavior. It would seem beyond dispute that the empirical phenomenon we described and discussed was such an instance. It clearly was not institutionalized behavior. While there were some traditional aspects to it peculiar to the college campus on which it developed, the overall phenomenon was collective behavior as the term is generally understood. If so, the example must be classifiable as one of the five seemingly all inclusive collective behavior types postulated by Smelser. If our "crowd" is not an example of a hostile outburst, it is even less identifiable as any of the other four types discussed. It lacked, for example, the four general structural conditions said to be conducive to the appearance of a wish-fulfilling craze; it also did not have a precipitating factor giving evidence for tremendous rewards that Smelser states is equally necessary for a craze. In other words, granting our example is generic collective behavior, it certainly comes closer to being classed as a hostile outburst than any of the other four types postulated.

Smelser does exclude from his definition of a hostile outburst "mere disturbances of the peace, revelous displays of crowd, etc." But the case we examined went beyond such activity (e.g., a car was partly dismantled); many of the participants although not anxious had a hostile attitude toward the police and at times *some* of them overtly expressed it (e.g., in front of police headquarters). The negative collective acts earlier described, although they were never continuous or a dominant pattern, seem beyond mere revelry of frivolous celebrants or simple disorderly behavior by a collection of individuals. Furthermore, the police, community and college officials, entrapped and delayed motorists and bus riders, the mass media outlets, store owners, and other vocal elements in the city, campus student leaders, etc., in their initial as well as later reactions all defined it as something more than just an inconsequential and very localized disturbing incident.

Smelser does state that "the participants in an outburst must be bent on attacking someone considered responsible for a disturbing state of affairs. This brings us to the center of the problem. As already noted, how many participants must hold the hostile attitude, and in what way must the hostility be expressed before the phenomenon can be classed as a hostile outburst? Perhaps most important of all, what is to be done in a case such as we have described, where there were both hostile beliefs and behavior (although far more of the former than the latter), but where these were intermingled with and generally subordinate to other kinds of quite different actions and attitudes?

It could be argued that we are trying to force a case with heterogeneous dimensions into a pure or ideal type in a theoretical scheme. On the other hand, the position can be taken that Smelser's basic conceptualization involves an inherent difficulty. One common element is used both to identify and to account in great part for certain phenomena. That is, a hostile outburst is defined in terms of actions on the basis of hostile beliefs, and hostile beliefs in turn are seen as a major determinant of the emergence of the behavior. In essence, the formulation falls back on a single key attitudinal or belief state as both a major component of the definition and the explanation of hostile outbursts.

In many respects, Smelser's formulation is a variant of what Turner has recently called the "convergence theory" of crowd behavior. In this kind of explanation the crowd is thought of as resulting from the convergence of a number of people who share the same predispositions which "are activated by the event or object toward which their common attention is directed." As Turner notes, such a view has difficulty in accounting for shifts in crowd behavior, the organization of the crowd, and the different group definitions developed in the interaction among the participants. These, of course, are among the very points which do not seem to be adequately dealt with by Smelser's formulation when applied to our particular case study.

Our analysis has been somewhat negative rather than positive and probably has obscured one of the uncontestable and substantial merits of the formulation by Smelser. Far beyond any previous scholar he has advanced a set of propositions that are at least partly testable. This he has provided and quite well. Without his original formulation, our own effort at an empirical test could not have been attempted. It is only through the setting forth of theoretical statements such as those advanced by Smelser that empirical researchers will increasingly be able to go beyond mere descriptions of specific crowds to more abstract analyses of crowds in general. . . .

ARTICLE 17

Victory Celebrations as Theater: A Dramaturgical Approach to Crowd Behavior

DAVID A. SNOW
LOUIS A. ZURCHER
ROBERT PETERS

... The purpose of this paper is twofold: (1) to contribute empirical data on crowd behavior by describing and analyzing a series of college football victory celebrations; and (2) to apply a dramaturgical analysis to crowd behavior, focusing on interaction rather than on the cognitive or demographic characteristics of the participants. The intent is not to displace existing approaches to the study of the crowd. Rather, it is to complement them, particularly the emergent norm thesis and the gaming or rational calculus perspective.

DATA AND PROCEDURES

On five consecutive Saturday evenings from October 8, 1977 to November 5, 1977, students from The University of Texas and other Austin residents converged on the main street bordering the University and transformed it into an arena for celebrating the victories of the University football team. Data about the celebrations were derived from three sources. Following a team approach to fieldwork, we first observed the celebration *in situ*. One of the authors, who lived within earshot of the celebrations, assumed the role of a participant observer for each of the episodes. Another author, although attending some of the celebrations, functioned mainly as a detached observer. The participant observer roamed through the different spatial sectors of the celebrations, occasionally hitching a ride on a parading vehicle, and talked with representatives of the different segments of the crowd. He was able to record hundreds of behaviors and gestures and the interview informally several of the participants. The detached observer, functioning primarily as a cross-examiner, critically appraised the fieldnotes and interviewed the participant observer. Each Monday following a celebration the participant observer and the detached observer would meet in a debriefing session and establish a research agenda in the event of another celebration.

As a check on our own observations and fieldnotes, 15 university students, each of whom had participated in the victory crowds, were interviewed in the weeks following the celebrations. We were less interested in the representativeness of the student respondents than we were in how well their recollections corresponded with our own observations.

The third data source consisted of press accounts in the campus and city newspaper. These accounts, including letters to the editors regarding the celebrations, were examined for informa-

Snow, David A., Zurcher, Louis A., & Peters, Robert. (1981). Victory celebrations as theater: A dramaturgical approach to crowd behavior. *Symbolic Interaction, 4* (1), 21–41.

tion about community reaction and for evidence confirming or disconfirming our observations. Although the three data sources yielded no major inconsistencies, it might appear that the data base was thin. We would argue, however, that the data we collected are far better than none, especially in a substantive area rife with theoretical speculation about phenomena that have too infrequently been directly studied.

THE VICTORY CELEBRATIONS

On October 8, 1977, The University of Texas football team unexpectedly defeated its archrival, the University of Oklahoma, for the first time in seven years. Immediately following the game's conclusion (4:30 p.m.), many students and other local fans began driving along "the Drag," the section of Guadalupe Street bounding the western edge of the University campus.... Even though the game had not been played at "home," by 8:00 p.m. approximately 3,000 people had gathered on the Drag. There was bumper-to-bumper traffic between Nineteenth and Twenty-Sixth Streets (which constitute the northern and southern boundaries of the University campus). The street resounded with the din of honking horns and shouts of "we're No. 1!" The celebration, which was likened to "a big New Year's party" by one participant, lasted until early Sunday morning.

Throughout the evening six types of participants and corresponding behaviors were clearly discernible.... The first type consisted of the vehicular paraders or occupants of the motor vehicles who, as the focus of attention, constituted the main performers. A few of the cars had roof-mounted loudspeakers blaring "we're No. 1." All of the vehicles were filled with celebrants who, hanging out the car windows or sitting on the car roofs, guzzled beer, yelled, flashed the "Hook-em-Horns" sign, and slapped hands with other paraders and spectators who lined the street.

The second group of participants consisted of relatively passive spectators who sat on the cement wall that separates the University campus from the public sidewalk. Periodically a few of these spectators would yell and flash the "Hook-em" sign, but their main activity was viewing.

The third type were the more animated spectators. Congregated mainly on the west side of the Drag immediately north of Twenty-Second Street, these participants actively supported the vehicular paraders by shaking their hands and cheering them on. Immediately behind these spectators was the fourth set of participants. This group consisted of a small number of people who were dancing to the rock music blaring out of a record store.

The fifth type was represented by males who stood across from the Student Union just south of Twenty-Third Street. Whenever a car or pickup approached, they would slap the side and top of the vehicle and attempt to "grope" the female occupants.

The sixth group of participants was comprised of the police scattered along the Drag. Decidedly friendly, the police appeared to function more as supportive viewers than as control agents. Except for keeping the autos within their appropriate lanes and occasionally asking some of the more animated spectators to move back, the police maintained a low and cordial profile. This was reflected in part by the fact that none of the participants at this first celebration were arrested, even though many of them were in fact breaking the law.

The following Saturday (October 15), Texas' football team came from behind in the final quarter to defeat the University of Arkansas. Moments after the game, fans again converged on the Drag. They began celebrating in a manner similar to the previous week, but with three discernible differences. First, there was a greater number of vehicular paraders. Not only was the traffic backed-up further than the previous week, but there were more celebrants sitting in and on the cars and pickups. Second, females were not being molested by male spectators. Third, not only had the number of spectators increased, but they had become more animated. As before, the police did little to dampen the jovial mood or to stop the celebration, which could still be heard from a mile away at 4:30 Sunday morning.

While Texas was defeating Southern Methodist University on Saturday, October 22, No. 1 ranked University of Michigan was losing to the University of Minnesota. This upset, coupled with Texas' win, meant that Texas would probably become the No. 1 ranked team in the nation. Partly because of this unanticipated turn of events, the ensuing celebration was the largest and most vociferous to date. Honking horns rhythmically pounded out "we're No. 1" while riders waved Texas state flags, shook hands with spectators and tossed cans of beer to those weaving in and out of the bumper-to-bumper traffic which extended 15 blocks in either direction. But most of this activity was not evident until the vehicular paraders entered the area of Guadalupe that had been transformed into an arena for celebration. As paraders entered the "stage," their level of animation increased and the noise became almost deafening. The crowd activity reached its peak in the vicinity of Twenty-Third Street and the student Union . . . , where the number of spectators was most dense. Again, the police were unobtrusive. Most of the time they stood watching the celebrants, occasionally shaking hands with some of them and flashing the "Hook-em" sign.

Following Texas' defeat of Texas Tech University on Saturday, October 29, fans again converged on the Drag. With bumper-to-bumper traffic extending for 34 blocks by early evening, it appeared as if the celebration would be the wildest to date. The fact that this was the first celebration to follow a home game also suggested a likely increase in intensity. However, the celebration was subdued and constrained in comparison to those previous. There was less physical contact between paraders and spectators. There were fewer celebrants per vehicle. There was less hand-slapping and little rhythmical horn-blowing. The overall volume of noise had decreased.

These changes in the behavior of the celebrants seemed largely due to a shift in police strategy and demeanor. The number of officers had increased from the previous week's level of approximately 5 per block to a new level of 8 to 10 per block. In addition, the majority of the policemen were now suited in high leather boots and riot helmets. Now, rather than shaking hands and flashing the "Hook-em" sign, the police were concentrating on directing traffic, keeping celebrants off the tops and hoods of cars, and keeping spectators out of the street. In contrast to the earlier celebrations, the police were occasionally arresting lawbreaking celebrants.

Since these changes in police behavior interfered with the celebrating, some of the celebrants later in the evening (11 p.m.) shifted their activity further down the Drag where there were fewer police. Whereas the segment of the Drag directly across from the Student Union had functioned as "center stage," a substitute area was appropriated and redefined for celebration by some of the spectators. Until police reinforcements arrived at the new site, celebrants were once again sitting on car hoods and hanging out the windows, honking the car horns, walking back and forth between cars, shaking hands, and screaming "we're No. 1."

Texas' defeat of the University of Houston on Saturday, November 5, provided the impetus for another celebration. However, this post-game celebration was even more muted than the previous one. The major categories of actors returned, but their behavior had changed dramatically, as if the script had been rewritten. Though there were at least 1,000 celebrators on the Drag, there was little yelling. There were only scattered horn blowing and few overfilled cars and pickups. The mood was one of caution; the watchword was "Ssshhh." The apparent reason for the change was a significant increase in the number of police assigned to the Drag. Officers were standing every 30 to 40 feet on the center dividing line and on each side of the street. Police were stationed north of Twenty-Sixth Street for the first time since the celebrations had begun. The officers had been instructed (for reasons that will be discussed later) to reduce the overall level of noise.

Whenever a horn was blown, the officer who spotted the violator would stop the vehicle or shine his flashlight on the side of the auto and the next policeman would stop the car. As a result of this tactic, the noise was greatly reduced.

Nonetheless, some vehicular paraders, coaxed by the spectators, continued to drive up and down the Drag. Whenever a car horn sounded, spectators in the immediate area would applaud and cheer. If a parader received a citation, the police were booed. Though the encouragement did not lead to an increase in the actual amount of horn blowing, it did help produce an atmosphere conducive to taunting the police. Many paraders would shout "honk, honk" as they passed police; others mockingly would put a finger to their lips in the "Ssshhh" position. In response, one officer commented, "I'd almost rather they did honk. At least there would be something to do." As the evening progressed, it became evident that the interaction between the police and the vehicular paraders had now become the focus of attention.

The following Saturday, November 12, when Texas defeated Texas Christian University, the only actors to appear on the Drag in full force were the police. There was little celebration; traffic was near normal. There were several reasons for the apparent disinterest in celebration. First, although Texas won, the victory was anticipated. Second, the Saturday morning edition of the city newspaper indicated that the police would attempt "to put a damper on any celebration." As on the previous Saturday, there were approximately 10 police per block. Moreover, they were giving a traffic citation to anyone who blew a car horn. This show of force and "crack-down" strategy seemed to intimidate potential celebrants. Only three "honks" were heard and recorded within a 15 minute period between 8 p.m. and 9 p.m. A third countervailing factor was the rumor that "a sniper would be on the Drag" on Saturday evening. Both Friday's edition of the campus newspaper and the Saturday morning edition of the city newspaper reported that the Austin police had received an anonymous letter warning that the writer would "shoot up the Drag Saturday night" in the event of another celebration. Although the police were "pretty satisfied it (was) just a crank," such a threat could not be fully discounted, especially since it stimulated memories of a sniper who in 1967 had terrorized the University of Texas campus. A fourth countervailing factor was the annual sausage festival (Wurstfest) south of Austin. The festival provided an entertainment alternative to the Drag, thereby siphoning many potential celebrants. Finally, it is reasonable to assume that for many of the participants the celebrations were becoming routine and predictable; the novelty had worn off.

After five weeks, the series of victory celebrations had run its course. In the weeks that followed, Texas won its final two regularly scheduled games. Neither were followed by a victory celebration of the kind that had occurred earlier.

ANALYSIS AND DISCUSSION

Students of collective behavior have long debated its proper conceptualization (Brissett, 1968; Couch, 1968, 1970; Currie and Skolnick, 1970; Marx, 1970; Smelser, 1970; Turner, 1964a, 1964b; Weller and Quarantelli, 1973). However, most scholars would agree that the victory celebrations on the Drag constituted a series of crowd episodes. On each occasion there was a large number of people in close physical contact within a limited spatial area. There was a common focus of attention. Though some "assembling instruction" (McPhail and Miller, 1973) such as shouts of "to the Drag" were heard after the first celebration, the assemblage and ensuing behaviors were relatively spontaneous and unplanned. The celebrations were neither on the community or university calendars nor were they the product of prior formal organization. This is not to suggest that the celebrations were devoid of organization or patterned behavior. To the contrary, it appeared as if the actions of the different segments of the crowd fit together, as if they were aligned in a complementary fashion. How can that coordination be best explained? How did the lines of action exhibited by the different categories of participants fit together and contribute to the development of the celebrations? Additionally, what accounts for the shift in the behavior of some of the participants and for the change in the character of the celebrations?

The dominant theories of collective behavior do not fully enough address these questions. In fact, they are contradicted by much of what we observed and heard.

Convergence Theory

Convergence theory views the action of crowd participants as parallel or homogeneous, and attributes this presumed uniformity of action to hypothetically shared backgrounds or dispositions among the participants (Allport, 1924; Feuer, 1969; Gurr, 1970; Klapp, 1969; Miller and Dollard, 1941; Toch, 1965). The key to understanding crowd behavior is seen as residing within the characteristics of the participants rather than within what transpires once they become part of the collectivity. This view was of little use for understanding the victory celebrations. The crowds were characterized by differential participation, and the crowd members were not of one mind or background. The majority of participants appeared to be U. T. students, but "students" hardly constitute a homogeneous lot in background, orientation and allegiance to the university football team. This is especially true at a large state university. Moreover, we observed considerable variation in the age, sex, ethnicity and style of dress of the participants. The convergence assumption that crowd participants are similarly motivated is also inconsistent with our data. Some participants indicated they were in the crowd because of "curiosity," some because they were diehard Longhorn fans, some because they thought it would be "fun," some because they had "nothing better to do," some because they were coaxed by friends, and some, such as the police, because it was their duty.

Contagion Theory

Contagion theory seems equally unhelpful when applied to the celebrations. It also views the crowd as a monolithic entity characterized by uniformity of behavior. Rather than explaining the presumed homogeneity of action in terms of shared characteristics that precede the formation of the crowd, contagion theorists (Blumer, 1951; Freud, 1922; LeBon, 1903) attribute it to a breakdown of participants' cognitive abilities. The reduction in rational faculty, coupled with the anonymity supposedly provided by the crowd, renders the participant susceptible to the uncritical acceptance and mechanical production of whatever suggestion is encountered. Hence, everyone behaves alike.

Our observations do not support that view. As already emphasized, the victory crowds did not involve uniformity of action. Instead, the celebrations were the work of several categories of participants engaging in rather disparate behaviors. Additionally, most of the participants could not be classified as social isolates or anonymous individuals lost in the crowd. Friends and acquaintances rode together in parading vehicles. Many of the spectators were in the company of familiar others. The police officers were at least acquainted with each other.

The hypothetical link between crowd behavior and crippled cognition (LeBon, 1903) or noninterpretive interaction (Blumer, 1951) is also at odds with much of what transpired. When the police first began to make a concerted effort to halt the horn-blowing, for example, most people who blew their car horns almost simultaneously waved to the spectators. Since this action increased the possibility of being stopped by the police, it might appear to have been mindless or nonreflective behavior. But the police at that time were only warning violators rather than giving them citations. Hence, the violators had little, if anything, to lose. Moreover, the risk of being admonished by a police officer is likely to have been offset by the receipt of recognition from the cheering spectators. What may have seemed to have been indicative of "irrational" behavior appears to have been the obverse. That is, the behavior of some of the participants appears to have been based at least in part on consideration of potential rewards and costs. This interpretation is also suggested by the response of the vehicular paraders when the police increased their ranks and became more intent on reducing the overall level of noise. Rather than continuing to celebrate as before, the vehicular paraders as well as many of the spectators became more cautious, modifying their activities so as to decrease the prospect of being arrested. They still celebrated, but in a more subdued way.

Rational Calculus or Gaming Theory

Since the adjustment of one's actions in response to changes in the behavior of another is indicative of interpretive interaction rather than circular reaction, our observations are consistent with the rational calculus or gaming approach to crowd behavior (Berk, 1974a, 1974b; Brown, 1965). This perspective argues that crowd participants "exercise a substantial degree of rational decision-making and" are therefore no "less rational than in other contexts" (Berk, 1974a: 356). Crowd behavior is thus thought to be contingent on "enough crowd members" reaching "parallel assessments which make action for all a good bet" (Berk, 1974a: 368). In other words, collective action in a particular direction is attributed to an aggregation of individual decisions defining actions as more rewarding or less costly than inaction. By emphasizing the rational element in crowd behavior, we think that the gaming perspective provides a necessary and empirically sound corrective to the one-sided image of crowd participants suggested by the convergence and contagion approaches. But the individual remains the primary unit of analysis and cognitive processes, albeit rational in character, the focus of attention. Consequently, the gaming model is not directly helpful to understanding how the actions of different segments of the crowd fit together and contribute to its flow and direction.

Risky-Shift Theory

The risky-shift variant of the rational calculus approach suggests that the direction of collective action is determined by a natural selection process (Johnson, 1974; Johnson, et al., 1977; Johnson and Feinberg, 1977). It hypothesizes that the course of action taken—from a number of possibilities suggested by leaders or keynoters—is the one which is congruent with the dominant mood or opinion within the crowd. A shift in the direction of high risk, for instance, is regarded as most likely when the dispositions of crowd members are skewed in the direction of risk-taking. Those people who are not disposed to shift are likely to withdraw from the crowd, thereby moving the crowd towards greater consensus and uniformity of action. Accordingly, whether a particular keynoter's or leader's exhortations function to move the crowd in one direction or another is dependent on the distribution of dispositions throughout the crowd.

This line of explanation may be especially pertinent in those situations where there are identifiable leaders calling for different lines of action. However, it is often unclear in many crowd situations whether there are in fact any leaders. Throughout the victory celebrations there were innovators who might be construed as keynoters, but certainly not as leaders in the traditional sense. Moreover, the innovators tended to be groups of people acting in concert rather than single individuals. The argument that the direction of collective action is primarily a function of the congruence between leaders' exhortations and dispositions within the crowd thus seems to pertain to crowds with clearly defined leaders and followers rather than to crowds comprised of several categories of actors. As a consequence, interaction between various segments of the crowd is ignored by risky-shift theory.

Emergent Norm Theory

The approach that appears best to explain the victory celebrations is the emergent norm thesis developed by Turner and Killian (1957, 1972; Turner, 1964a, 1964b). Crowd behavior is taken to be regulated by a definition of the situation. The definition emerges from a process of crowd-specific interaction and hypothetically functions in a normative manner by encouraging behavior in accordance with the definition. While one could reasonably argue that the actions of the various groups of victory celebrants were normatively regulated, it is questionable whether there was a single dominant norm which all the participants supported. To the contrary, it appeared that whatever the emergent normative constraints, they were *specific to the various categories of actors* rather than to the collectivity as a whole. Additionally, the alteration in the patterns of activity we observed do not seem to be fully explained by the emergent norm thesis. Each week there were changes in behavioral patterns, with some being modified, some being added, and some deleted. During the initial celebration, for example, there was no distinctive pattern of horn-blowing. In the following week the honking of horns to the rhythm of "we're No. 1" emerged as a dominant pattern, and then faded during the final celebrations. It might be argued that the shifts were due to the emergence of new norms; but such an answer strikes us as tautological. Moreover, it leaves unanswered the question of what accounts for the emergence of one particular pattern of behavior rather than another, and the question of how norms specific to different components of the crowd fit together in an interactive pattern.

Summary of the Dominant Theories

The existing approaches to crowd behavior do not adequately account for the victory celebrations that developed on the Drag. Those approaches either ignore or gloss over the existence of various categories of actors, the ongoing interaction between them, and the role the interaction plays in determining the direction and character of crowd behavior. There are three reasons for the oversights. First, the approaches fall prey to the perceptual trap of taking the behavior of the most conspicuous element of the crowd as typifying the whole crowd, thereby giving rise to the "illusion of unanimity" (Turner and Killian, 1972: 22). Attention is directed away from the less dramatic segment of the crowd and their contributions to the collective episode. As a consequence, the range of interactions that occur within collective encounters are ignored. Turner and Killian (1972), who originally criticized the convergence and contagion approaches on these grounds, fall prey to this perceptual trap by emphasizing the emergence of a dominant norm that applies to all participants. Second, for all but emergent norm theory, individual participants and their states-of-mind (i.e., frustration, hostility, rationality) are the focus of research and analysis. Attention is thereby deflected away from crowd-specific interaction. Third, the bulk of the data on which much theoretical speculation is based has been derived from either laboratory experiments or post-facto interviews with participants. The importance of interaction between various segments of participants in relation to the development and direction of crowd behavior has been given insufficient attention.

A DRAMATURGICAL APPROACH

Dramaturgy, as a mode of analysis, articulates the patterns of behavior occurring whenever two or more persons come into each other's presence. Attention is focused on social interaction rather than on the individual and his or her background characteristics and cognitive states. Drawing on the imagery of the theater, interactants are viewed as conducting themselves *as if* they were theoretical performers, spectators, or alternating between the two. Whenever one's behaviors or gestures are the object of another's attention, he or she is seen, metaphorically speaking, as being "on stage" (performing). When one is engaged in the business of monitoring others, he or she is defined as audience or spectator. The nature of the audience's behavior is a consequence of members' "impressions" about the performance. The performer's subsequent behavior is in turn influenced by his or her reading of the audience. The character of much social action is regarded as a consequence of the adjustments interactants make to "the impressions" they formulate about each other.

We suggest that the character and direction of the victory crowds we observed can be best understood in terms of the interaction among the participants who either functioned as performers and spectators, or alternated between the two categories. We will first consider the performers, and then examine the "proximal spectators" and their relative influence. Since the police functioned as both spectators and performers, their behavior and influence are considered in relation to another audience, the bystanders or "distal spectators."

Task Performers

During the course of the celebrations a variety of activities were readily observable. Wright (1978), who similarly reported considerable behavioral heterogeneity during his first-hand examination of collective encounters, has suggested that these behaviors may be differentiated according to whether they are "task" or "crowd" activities. Crowd activities refer to redundant behaviors seemingly universal to all collective encounters, such as assemblage and milling. Task activities include those behaviors that are particular to and necessary for the attainment of a specific goal or resolution of a specific problem. From a dramaturgical standpoint, we would add that task activities constitute the primary objects of attention, and that those crowd participants engaging in such activities constitute the task performers.

Throughout the celebrations several task performers were clearly observable, such as the vehicular paraders, the "gropers," the dancers, and the police. There was even a group of religious fundamentalists that appeared one evening in an effort to promote their cause and recruit members. What distinguished the various task performers from the spectators is that rather than visually attending to the business of others, they engaged in activities specific to the tasks of celebrating, dancing, molesting women, or promoting Jesus. It was these performances that provided the spectators with something to view.

However, not all of the task performances were equally attended to be the spectators. Indeed it appeared as if all but the vehicular paraders, and later the police, were ignored. Consequently, it is useful to classify task activities according to the amount of attention they receive, and according to their salience to the character of the collective encounter. Those behaviors which are the major focus of attention and which give meaning to the occasion can be regarded as the *main task activity*. Those task performances subordinate to the main task activity constitute side or *subordinate task activities*. Put metaphorically, the major task activity is the main performance. It is on center stage. In contrast, the remaining task activities are side shows, subordinate and often parasitic to the main event. In the victory crowds the vehicular paraders functioned as the main task performers, at least until the fifth celebration when the police and their interaction with the paraders became the focus of attention.

Since the activities of the vehicular paraders were more in keeping with the spirit of the occasion, it is understandable why they, rather than the other task performances, were the focus of attention. But why did the paraders keep performing? Why was the performance confined to a specific spatial area? What defined "the stage?" What accounted not only for alteration in the behavior of the vehicular paraders, but also for the shift in orientation of the police? To answer these questions we must consider the spectators in detail.

Proximal Spectators

By proximal spectators we mean those physically co-present participants who function primarily as viewers. Whether voluntary of involuntary, animated or passive, their major activity consisted of watching the paraders celebrate.

Turner and Killian (1972: 93–94) have noted that spectators constitute an important element of the crowd because they swell its ranks and thereby create the impression of solidarity. Our observations suggest that spectators function not only in this supportive manner, but they also define the character of the activity they observe. In some instances, spectators offered verbal or gestural support for a new line of activity exhibited by innovative paraders. In other instances spectators called for specific lines of action. Those "calls" included thrusting out an open palm in order "to get five" from the passing paraders, yelling for the performers to ignore the police, and urging the performers to get on with "the show." When the police began to curtail the noise, for example, groups of spectators would call for the paraders to honk their horns. Rather than only responding to the main task performance and accepting the activity as given, the more animated spectators attempted to influence the character of the celebration.

The presence of spectators also functioned to determine the level of animation and noise produced by the vehicular paraders. Whenever spectators were absent, the paraders were relatively quiet and motionless. The only apparent activity occurred when a car approached from the opposite direction and blew its horn. However, as the vehicles approached an area where spectators were present, the paraders would "go into play"; that is, they would begin to yell, blow their horns, hang out the window, and flash the "Hook-em-Horns" sign. This interactional pattern was so dominant that paraders would cease to celebrate once out of view of the spectators. Then, after turning their cars around and getting back on the Drag, the paraders would "turn on" or "come into play" once again.

The influence of the presence of spectators was demonstrated even more dramatically during the fourth celebration when many of the spectators moved north of the Drag, redefining the portion of Guadalupe between Twenty-Ninth and Thirty-First Street as the "new stage." The vehicular paraders driving into that area went into "play," performing as they had earlier when the Drag was defined as the arena for celebration.

These observations indicate that the audience more than the main task performers defined the stage or area in which the celebrations were conducted. It is thus reasonable to suggest that in this particular series of crowd episodes the audience, rather than being merely supportive or facilitative, was structurally essential. Simply put: no audience, no victory celebrations.

Social Control Agents and Distal Spectators

Another group of actors which comprised part of the crowd and influenced the course and character of the celebrations were the police. We emphasized earlier that the character of the fourth celebration was strikingly different from those previous. Not only was there a discernible change in the behavior of the vehicular paraders, who had become more constrained, but there was a corresponding shift in the orientation of the police. Our observations suggest that the alteration in the activity of the main task performers was largely due to the change in the demeanor of the police.

Initially the police viewed the celebrations as good clean fun. They maintained a low profile, alternating between being supportive spectators and subordinate task performers. As one of the commanding officers commented after the first celebration:

> *This crowd was in a partying mood . . . not a trouble-making mood. They were not intent on tearing up anything. Far be it from us to interfere with a good party.*

In the midst of the third celebration another officer, who stood on the sidewalk watching the "party," similarly commented that "there's not much else we can do. They're just having fun." There were other lines of action that might have been pursued, but the police had adopted a policy of nonintervention. In the middle of the week prior to the fourth celebration a public information officer confessed that the police had been "rather lenient the last three weeks," adding that "we have not put some people in jail that we could have." However, shortly after the fourth celebration began it was clear that the police had redefined the crowd activity as something other than "fun." Twice as many officers were assigned to the Drag, and they were wearing riot helmets and high boots. They were also less congenial and more task oriented. Instead of standing on the sidelines and flashing the "Hook-em-Horns" sign, they were now stopping the paraders. They directed people to remain in their cars and to refrain from blowing their car horns. They issued warnings and citations. Finally, and most significantly, by the end of the evening the police had arrested several celebrants.

In attempting to control the proceedings, the police had become a focus of attention for both the vehicular paraders and the proximal spectators. They were competing with the vehicular paraders for control of "center stage," while simultaneously neutralizing the influence of the animated spectators. What was previously an occasion condoned or tolerated by the police had been redefined as an occasion that needed to be controlled and diffused. What transpired between the third and fourth celebrations to account for the change?

The answer to this question requires consideration of another audience that Turner and Killian (1972: 238–240) have termed a "bystander public." The concept denotes a diffuse collectivity that emerges when prolonged crowd behavior is perceived as a threat to personal routines and public order. According to Turner and Killian (1972: 238), bystanders have no particular stake in the demonstration, celebration, or conflict that constitutes an object of attention. Rather, they are concerned with the "restoration of order and the elimination of danger and inconvenience," whether real or anticipated. Since our observations indicate that each celebration prompted the emergence of bystander spectators, and that their responses were not all unfavorable, we find it necessary to broaden the conceptualization. Accordingly, we define a bystander public or audience as a diffuse collectivity of distal spectators who indirectly monitor an instance of crowd behavior and respond to it, either favorably or unfavorably, by registering their respective views with the media, the press, and/or with community officials. Although not directly involved in the crowd attended to, distal spectators can effect its career and outcome by indirectly influencing one or more groups of participants.

Our research indicates that the emergence of distal spectators did indeed influence the behavior of the police in particular and the character of the celebrations in general. This observation is suggested by the data derived from a content analysis of all celebration-related articles, editorials, and letters-to-the-editors appearing in the *Austin American Statesman* and the University *Daily Texan* from the day after the first celebration to seven days following the last regularly scheduled game. As indicated in Figure 2, which summarizes the findings, it was not until the week following the third celebration that distal spectators began to clamor for the control and dissolution of the celebrations. Since the change in police demeanor and strategy occurred during the following (fourth) celebration, we argue that the shift was largely attributable to the emergence of distal spectators who viewed the celebrations negatively, publicly calling for the restoration of order.

Prior to the third celebration, distal spectators, including the press, responded favorably to the victory crowds. Following the first celebration, for example, the city newspaper referred to the celebration as "Happy Days;" and a letter to the editor encouraged celebrants to "Keep (their) Horns High." The following week such terms as

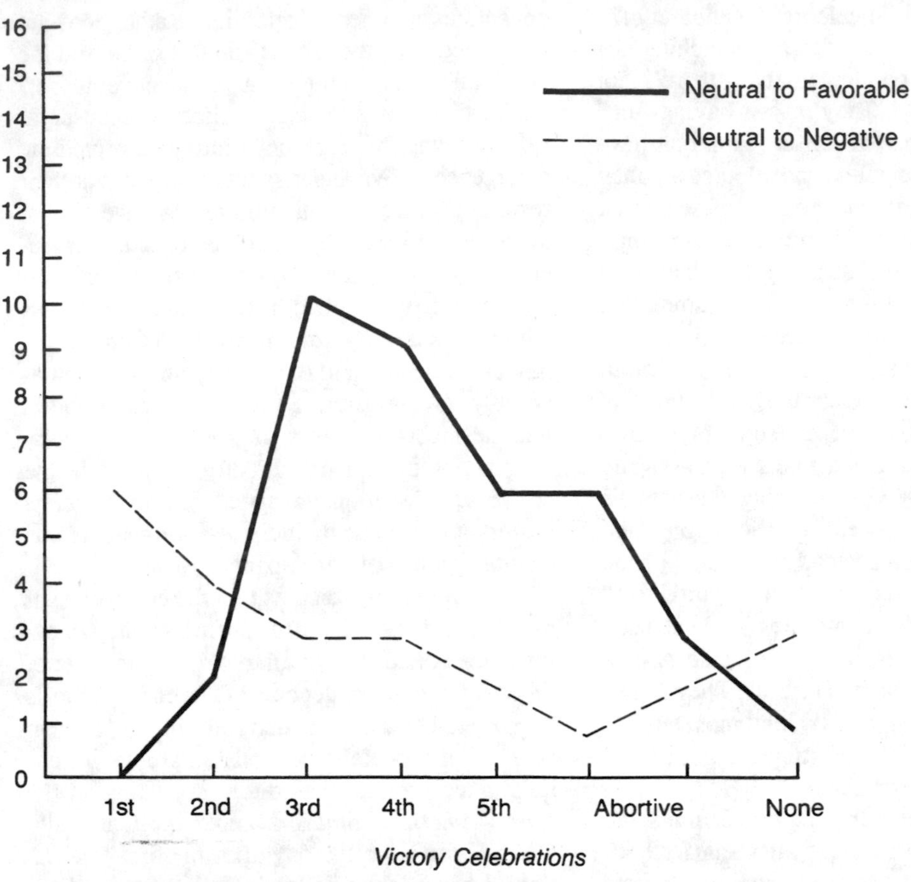

FIGURE 2 Number of Articles and Editorials Responding Favorably or Negatively to the Celebrations

"ecstasy" and "joy" were still being used to describe the celebrations. However, by the end of the week following the third celebration it was clear that either there had been a change in attitude among distal spectators or that a less congenial group of distal spectators had emerged. Whatever the case, not only had the celebrations become more of a community issue, as evidenced by the increase in the number of newspaper accounts devoted to them (see Figure 2), but the celebrations were now being described as "unruly," "childish," "drunken sprees," "expensive," and "public disturbances." In response to the negative public reaction, local officials urged the celebrants to "cool it." On the Thursday following the third celebration, the city mayor issued a press release in which she called on the police to "clamp down" on the celebrants whose actions "would harm any citizen, damage property or abuse any individual's rights." In a letter appearing in the campus newspaper on the same day, a university official called on "students to exercise . . . maturity and good judgment," and warned that continued celebration would make "large numbers of students subject to traffic citations, arrests, and prosecution."

In light of the distal spectators redefinition of the celebrations as "disturbances," and their demand for celebrant restraint and police vigilance, the change in police behavior is understandable.

Although this change altered the character of the fourth celebration, distal spectators continued to pressure public officials to control the "fanatics" and put an end to the "curse." The police thus maintained their "show-of-force" and "crack-down" strategy. As a result, the fifth celebration was the most subdued to date. In the weeks that followed, the police were the only group of actors to appear in significant presence. By the time the last regularly scheduled game was completed, it was clear that the police had become the main task performers. The Drag was once again a street rather than an arena for celebration. As one supportive distal spectator commented, "the spectacle wasn't loyal Texas fans waving their horns, but the 80 or so cops who lined the Drag."

In summary, our observations suggest that just as the activity of the vehicular paraders was influenced by the proximal spectators, including the police, so the police activity, and ultimately the character of the celebrations, was influenced by the emergence of distal spectators calling for the restoration of order.

CONCLUSIONS AND IMPLICATIONS

This paper has described and analyzed a series of victory celebrations that were observed as they evolved. Post hoc analysis revealed that existing theories of crowd behavior were either contradicted by our observations or did not adequately account for the heterogeneity of activity observed. Nor did they account for the interaction among the various categories of participants, or for the shifts in behavior of the participants and the resultant change in the character of the celebrations. Subsequent analysis indicated that the celebrations could best be understood from a dramaturgical standpoint. Dramaturgy views social action as the consequence of the adjustments interactants make to the impressions they formulate about each other in specific situations. Behavior is seen as situationally-constructed action. As such it cannot be accounted for by reference to predispositions, whether they be demographic or cognitive. When applied to crowd behavior, dramaturgy shifts emphasis from concern with the backgrounds and dispositions of the participants to the emergent and ephemeral roles (Zurcher, 1979) they construct. Such an approach provides little insight into socio-historical conditions that give rise to crowd behavior. Nor does dramaturgy account for why some individuals rather than others participate in specific crowd episodes. But dramaturgy does focus attention on what has generally been regarded as a key defining characteristic of crowd behavior but which has seldom been the object of empirical investigation— crowd-specific interaction. Therein lies the analytic strength and utility of a dramaturgical approach to crowd behavior.

Several theoretical, conceptual, and research implications for understanding crowd behavior emerge from our observations and from our application of dramaturgy.

First, a dramaturgical approach to crowd behavior neither contradicts nor displaces the gaming or emergent norm perspectives. Instead, it complements them and provides a perspective into which both can be integrated. Since interaction, from a dramaturgical standpoint, is contingent upon the role-taking and role-making processes (Brissett and Edgley, 1975), a dramaturgical approach to crowds assumes what the gaming or rational calculus perspective emphasizes—rationality on behalf of crowd participants.

A dramaturgical approach to crowd behavior also acknowledges the salience of emergent norms, but with two qualifications. First, there is seldom, if ever, one overarching norm that influences the behavior of all participants. Rather, there are different norms that are specific to different categories of actors. Second, a dramaturgical view suggests that emergent normative understandings are largely the function of verbal and non-verbal interactions and negotiation between main task performers and spectators.

Second, the observation that the character and direction of the celebrations were largely the result of interaction among several categories of performers and spectators suggests that spectators are structurally essential for the emergence of some, and perhaps all, forms of crowd behavior. Although several scholars have suggested that spectators contribute to the overall context of collective encounters, they are generally regarded as being a relatively passive and nonessential element in the crowd process (Turner and Killian, 1972; Wright, 1978). Certainly collective task performers could carry out their tasks independently of spectators (Wright, 1978: 71). But would they? Our findings suggest that both proximal and distal spectators not only help to define the arena in which crowd behavior occurs, but that they also influence the pattern of activity they observe. We thus argue, from a dramaturgical standpoint, that the relationship between spectators and task performers is reciprocal and frequently interdependent. The extent to which this interdependence obtains is an empirical question. But until the relationship between performers and spectators is better understood for different types of crowd behavior, analyses which fail to examine the influence of spectators are likely to be one-sided and incomplete.

Third, our findings raise additional questions about "sequenced" approaches to crowd behavior. For example, it would have been impossible to describe the pattern and evolution of the victory celebrations according to Smelser's (1962) stages of collective behavior. The *ad hoc* nature of the interactions among different types of participants, and the shifting of those situational interactions, defies categorizing by a fixed and limited set of stages. Heirich's (1971) work on the "spiraling" nature of crowd behavior, though not specific enough about interactive phenomenon, seems more useful and consistent with our observation and analysis.

A fourth implication pertains to the relation between crowd behavior and everyday behavior. Crowds have generally been viewed as explicable only in terms of concepts specific to collective behavior itself. With the exception of a few scholars (Berk, 1974a; Brissett, 1968; Brown and Goldin, 1973; Couch, 1968, 1970; Johnson, 1974, 1977; McPhail and Miller, 1973; Turner and Killian, 1972; Weller and Quarantelli, 1973), discussions of crowd behavior have eschewed concepts relevant to everyday, institutional life. This tradition has emphasized the difference between collective and everyday behavior. Moreover, it has undermined integration of theories of social behavior.

In contrast, the dramaturgical approach applies to both crowd and everyday behavior. The interactive mechanisms that characterize social interaction in everyday life are assumed to be operative in crowd behavior. The differences are largely spatial and temporal in character. Everyday behavior is usually scheduled and acted in spatial areas or structures designed and traditionally used for such behaviors. Crowd behavior, on the other hand, is more likely to be unscheduled and staged in spatial areas and structures that were designed and are currently used for purposes other than crowds—that is, for so-called institutional or everyday behavior.

Implicit within the foregoing distinction between everyday and crowd behavior is an expanded conception of crowd behavior. It is behavior that is not only guided by emergent norms (Turner, 1964a 1964b; Turner and Killian, 1972) or characterized by emergent social relationships (Weller and Quarantelli, 1973). It is also characterized by the appropriation and use of a spatial area (street, park, mall) or physical structure (building) for purposes other than those for which it was intended at a particular time. It may well be that the collective appropriation of space for purposes other than intended constitutes, from a phenomenological standpoint, a key factor in defining crowd behavior as something special. It is the unanticipated appropriation that alerts us that something out-of-the-ordinary is occurring. Football fans charging onto the playing field with 30 seconds remaining in the game is thus viewed as an instance of crowd behavior; fans charging onto the field 30 seconds after the game is completed is seen as ordinary fan behavior. Viewed from a dramaturgical standpoint, crowd behavior may thus be regarded as a social production constructed during the course of interaction in a spatial area or structure that has been appropriated and redefined for purposes other than designed or intended at a particular point time. Crowd behavior, therefore, along with everyday behavior, is not only an interactional phenomenon, but has a spatial and temporal dimension as well. The relative weight of each of these components in the generation of crowds, and the manner in which the components interact in the processes of crowd behavior, are fertile areas for further research.

REFERENCES

Allport, Floyd H. 1924. Social Psychology. Boston: Houghton.

Aveni, Adrian F. 1977. "The not-so-lonely crowd: friendship groups in collective behavior." Sociometry 40: 96–99.

Berk, Richard A. 1974a. "A gaming approach to crowd behavior." American Sociological Review 39: 355–73.

Berk, Richard A. 1974b. "Collective behavior." Dubuque, Iowa: Wm. C. Brown.

Blumer, Herbert. 1951. "Collective behavior." Pp. 167–222 in A. M. Lee (ed.), Principles of Sociology. New York: Barnes and Noble.

Blumer, Herbert. 1957. "Collective behavior." Pp. 127–58 on J. B. Gittler (ed.), Review of Sociology Analysis of a Decade. New York: Wiley.

Brissett, Dennis. 1968. "Collective behavior: the sense of a rubric." American Journal of Sociology 74: 70–78.

Brissett, Dennis and Charles Edgley (eds.). 1975. Life as Theater: A Dramaturgical Sourcebook. Chicago: Aldine Publishing Company.

Brown, Michael and Amy Goldin. 1973. Collective Behavior. Pacific Palisades, CA.: Goodyear.

Brown, Roger. 1965. Social Psychology. New York: Free Press.

Burke, Kenneth. 1962. A Grammar of Motives and A Rhetoric of Motives. New York: The World Publishing Co.

Burke, Kenneth. 1965. Permanence and Change. Chicago: Bobbs-Merrill.

Couch, Carl J. 1968. "Collective behavior: an examination of some stereotypes." Social Problems 15: 310–22.

Couch, Carl J. 1970. "Dimensions of association in collective behavior episodes." Sociometry 33: 475–71.

Currie, Elliot and Jerome Skolnick. 1970. "A critical note on conceptions of collective behavior." Annals of the American Academy of Political and Social Sciences 391: 34–45.

Feuer, Lewis L. 1969. The Conflict of Generations. New York: Basic Books.

Fisher, Charles S. 1972. "Observing a crowd." Pp. 187–221 in J. D. Douglas (ed.), Research on Deviance. New York: Random House.

Freud, Sigmund. 1922. Group Psychology and the Analysis of the Ego. London: The Hogarth Press.

Goffman, Erving. 1959. The Presentation of Self in Everyday Life. Garden City, New York: Doubleday.

Gurr, Ted R. 1970. Why Men Rebel. Princeton, N.J.: Princeton University Press.

Heirich, Max. 1971. The Spiral of Conflict: Berkeley, 1964. New York: Columbia University Press.

Johnson, Norris R. 1974. "Collective behavior as group induced shift." Sociological Inquiry 44: 105–10.

Johnson, Norris R. and William E. Feinberg. 1977. "A computer simulation of the emergence of consensus in crowds." American Sociological Review 42: 505–21.

Johnson, Norris R., James G. Stemler and Deborah Hunter. 1977. "Crowd behavior as risky-shift: a laboratory experiment." Sociometry 40: 183–87.

Klapp, Orrin E. 1969. Collective Search for Identity. New York: Holt, Rinehart and Winston.

Klapp, Orrin E. 1972. Currents of Unrest: An Introduction to Collective Behavior. New York: Holt, Rinehart and Winston.

Lang, Kurt and Gladys Lang. 1968. "Collective behavior." Pp. 556–65 in D. L. Sills (ed.), International Encyclopedia of the Social Sciences. New York: MacMillan and Free Press.

LeBon, Gustave. 1903. The Crowd. London: Unwin.

Marx, Gary T. 1970. "Issueless riots." Annals of the American Academy of Political and Social Sciences 391: 21–33.

Marx, Gary T. and James L. Wood. 1975. "Strands of theory and research in collective behavior." Pp. 363–428 in A. Inkeles, J. Coleman and N. Smelser (eds.), Annual Review of Sociology. Vol. 1. Palo Alto, CA.: Annual Reviews, Inc.

McPhail, Clark. 1969. "Student walkout: a fortuitous examination of elementary collective behavior." Social Problems 16: 441–455.

McPhail, Clark and David Miller. 1973. "The assembling process: a theoretical and empirical examination." American Sociological Review 38: 721–35.

Messinger, Sheldon E., Harold Sampson and Robert D. Towne. 1975. "Life as theater: some notes on the dramaturgic approach to social reality." Pp. 32–42 in D. Brissett and C. Edgley (eds.), Life as Theater, Chicago: Aldine.

Milgram, Stanley and Hans Toch. 1969. "Collective behavior: crowds and social movements." Pp. 507–610 in G. Lindzey and E. Aronson (eds.), The Handbook of Social Psychology, Vol. 4. Reading, Mass.: Addison-Wesley.

Miller, Neal E. and John Dollard. 1941. Social Learning and Imitation. New Haven: Yale University Press.

Oberschall, Anthony. 1973. Social Conflict and Social Movements, Englewood Cliffs, N.J.: Prentice-Hall.

Perry, Joseph B. and M. D. Pugh. 1978. Collective Behavior: Response to Social Stress. New York: West Publishing Co.

Quarantelli, Enrico L. and James R. Hundley, Jr. 1960. "A test of some propositions about crowd formation and behavior." Pp. 538–54 in R. R. Evans (ed.), Readings in Collective Behavior. Chicago: Rand McNally.

Seidler, John, Katharine Meyer and Lois MacGillivray. 1976. "Collecting data on crowds and rallies: a new methods of stationary sampling." Social Forces 55: 507–519.

Smelser, Neil J. 1962. Theory of Collective Behavior. New York: Free Press.

Smelser, Neil J. 1970. "Two critics in search of a bias: a response to Currie and Skolnick." Annals of the American Academy of Political and Social Sciences 391: 46–55.

Toch, Hans. 1965. The Social Psychology of Social Movements. Indianapolis: Bobbs-Merrill.

Turner, Ralph H. 1964a. "Collective behavior." Pp. 382–455 in R. E. L. Faris (ed.), Handbook of Modern Sociology. Chicago: Rand McNally.

Turner, Ralph H. 1964b. "New theoretical frameworks." Sociological Quarterly 5: 122–32.

Turner, Ralph H. and Lewis M. Killian. 1957. Collective Behavior. Englewood Cliffs, N.J.: Prentice-Hall.

Turner, Ralph H. and Lewis M. Killian. 1972. Collective Behavior, 2nd Ed. Englewood Cliffs, N.J.: Prentice-Hall.

Turner, Ralph H. and Samuel J. Surace. 1956. "Zootsuiters and mexican symbols in crowd behavior." American Journal of Sociology 62: 14–20.

Weller, Jack M. and Enrico L. Quarantelli. 1973. "Neglected characteristics of collective behavior." American Journal of Sociology 79: 665–85.

Wright, Sam. 1978. Crowds and Riots: A Study in Social Organization. Beverly Hills, CA.: Sage Publications.

Zurcher, Louis. 1979. "Role selection: the influence of internalized vocabularies of motive." Symbolic Interaction 2: 16–30.

ARTICLE 18

Organization, Rationality and Spontaneity in the Civil Rights Movement

LEWIS M. KILLIAN

Continuity and emergence, planning and impulse, organizational strategy and individual spontaneity are polar tendencies which have been observed in the careers of social movements. "Classical collective-behavior" theorists have been charged with placing too much emphasis on the emergence of new norms and structures and thus reflecting and reinforcing the stereotyped conceptions of irrationality and spontaneity identified by Couch (1968). A concise characterization of "classical collective-behavior theory" is advanced by Aldon Morris (1981:745) when he writes:

> *Social movements are theorized to be relatively spontaneous and unstructured. Movement participants are often portrayed as nonrational actors functioning outside of normative constraints and propelled by high levels of strain.*

Morris (1981:745) adds that collective-behavior theorists "do not deny that organizations and institutional processes play a role in collective behavior," but he feels that they misinterpret them by holding that they "emerge in the course of movements and become important in their later stages." While he does not completely dismiss spontaneity as a factor, he feels that collective-behavior theorists have emphasized it too much, with a consequent neglect of internal structure (Morris, 1981:746).

Morris and other theorists identifying themselves with one or another variety of Resource Mobilization Theory have sought to discredit the older model which they believe to have dominated the theory of social movements. The alternative they offer, characterized by James Wood and Maurice Jackson (1982) as a "rational calculation approach," views social movements "as deriving from actors rationally estimating their chances of success by using social movements to attain their goals." These actors are seen to calculate their chances of victory and defeat and act accordingly" (Wood and Jackson, 1982:36). Morris (1981:746) declares that a central proposition of Resource Mobilization Theory is that "collective action is rooted in organizational structure and carried out by rational actors attempting to realize their ends." Thus individual rationality and organizational direction are placed in opposition to spontaneity and emergent structures. "Organizations, institutions, pre-existing communication networks, and rational actors are all seen as important resources playing crucial roles in the emergence and outcome of collective action," says Morris (1981:745).

Killian, Lewis M. (1984, December). Organization, rationality and spontaneity in the civil rights movement. *American Sociological Review, 49,* 770–783. Reprinted by permission of the American Sociological Association.

Taking a broader, more political perspective, Doug McAdam (1982) emphasizes the importance of "indigenous organizational strength," but only within a favorable structure of political opportunities. Pre-existing organizations are held to be crucial, for "in the absence of this supportive organizational context, the aggrieved population is likely to be deprived of the capacity for collective action even when confronted with a favorable structure of political opportunities" (McAdam, 1982:48). The rationality of individual action within such an organizational context is still emphasized.

Both Morris and McAdam frequently use the term "network" along with "structure" and "organization" as if they were interchangeable. The concept of pre-existing networks and the emphasis on their importance to the emergence of social movements are often associated with the work of Jo Freeman (1973, 1979) on the women's liberation movement, although the idea was advanced in 1960 by students of Ralph Turner, a "classic collective-behavior" theorist (Jackson et al., 1960). While Freeman clearly differentiates pre-existing communication networks from masses of unrelated individuals, she suggests that these networks can range from highly structured, formal organizations to rudimentary, informal associations of like-minded people at the grass roots. She makes it clear that the various types cannot be treated as interchangeable when she states, "What is needed is a model within which strategic considerations, both planned and spontaneous, leader-directed and grassroots, can be analyzed" (Freeman, 1979:170). While Freeman is critical of individualistic, grassroots theories of social movements, she clearly sees spontaneous action as being important and networks as sometimes evolving, sometimes fully formed at the outset.

STUDIES OF THE CIVIL RIGHTS MOVEMENT

Empirical support for challenges to classical collective-behavior theories comes from revisionist studies of the Civil Rights Movement (Morris, 1981; McAdam, 1982). Concentrating on the Sit-In Movement of 1960, Morris (1981:764) concluded that "pre-existing social structures provided the sit-ins with the resources and communication networks needed for their emergence and development." This, he argued, refuted the standard account that the Southern Christian Leadership Conference, the Congress of Racial Equality, the National Association for the Advancement of Colored People, and adult community leaders had rushed into a dynamic campus movement after it was well under way. Secondly, he concluded that it was the existence of a well-developed and widespread internal organization that led to the rapid spread of the sit-ins. The notion that spontaneity was an important aspect of the movement was an illusion—"the rapidity with which the sit-ins were organized gave the appearance that they were spontaneous"—but it was accepted, he charges, by such diverse students as Howard Zinn (1964), Meier and Rudwick (1973), and Piven and Cloward (1977). Morris (1981:754) saw the pre-existing internal organizations as centering around the black church as the coordinating unit in the typical movement center which perfected strategy and directed action between 1955 and 1960. Morris (1981:764) presented all three of his conclusions as refutations of what he criticized as a persistent portrayal of internal organization "as an after-the-fact accretion on student spontaneity."

McAdam (1982) traces the roots of indigenous organizational strength farther back, to 1876, and shows the importance of not only southern black churches but also black colleges and NAACP chapters as constituent parts of the organizational base. Whereas Morris takes up his analysis in 1960, McAdam begins with the Montgomery Bus Boycott of 1955. His "political process model" differs from a resource mobilization model in the addition of a factor which he calls "cognitive liberation"—the development by people of a collective definition of their situation "as unjust and subject to change through collective action" (McAdam, 1982:51). Finally, both researchers concur in their images of movement participants. They are seen as political beings "distinguished from nonparticipants on the basis of their greater integration into the established organizations of the minority community" (McAdam, 1982:63). They are rational actors working intentionally to achieve their ends, and their collective action is rooted in the pre-existing organizational structure of the minority community. Although neither spontaneous, impromptu action nor new movement organizations are explicitly ruled out in these analyses, they are ignored or treated as incidental to social movement development.

A part of the Civil Rights Movement mentioned only briefly by these authors is that which took place in Tallahassee, Florida, beginning in 1956. Interpretations of this submovement by Killian and Smith and others who studied it seem to fit collective-behavior theory better than the theories espoused by Morris and McAdam. Although not given notice in both contemporary and historical accounts equal to that accorded events in Montgomery, Greensboro, Little Rock and Selma, the Tallahassee Bus Boycott of 1956 and the lunchcounter sit-ins of 1960 were thoroughly studied by sociologist on the scene. As a result of continued interest by faculty members at both Florida A and M University and Florida State University additional data became available in later years. In 1978 Professor Jackson Ice of Florida State University taped 21 lengthy interviews with former participants in the events of the fifties and sixties. In May, 1981, Florida A and M University sponsored a symposium on the 25th anniversary of the Tallahassee Bus Boycott. One of the highlights was a speech by Wilhemina Jakes, one of the two women whose arrest had precipitated the protest.

The availability of these resources, some embodying the research of social scientists done a decade or more ago, some being contemporary reconstructions by participants, made possible a reexamination of that part of the "standard account" of the Civil Rights Movement which involved Tallahassee. Specific events and sequences of events were reexamined in the light of revisionist critiques of the earlier research. The data, including published studies, an unpublished doctoral dissertation, and transcripts of interviews and speeches made between 1978 and 1981, were reviewed with the following questions in mind:

1. Which critical events could be characterized as spontaneous and which were clearly the result of strategic planning?
2. What was the role of pre-existing, local, minority organizations as compared with that of organizations which emerged during the course of the movement?
3. What was the relationship between pre-existing and emergent organizations?
4. What was the relationship of local movement organizations with external sources of support and other movement centers?

In his unpublished doctoral dissertation, "The Tallahassee Sit-Ins and CORE," Robert M. White (1964) characterized the Civil Rights Movement in Tallahassee as a "sub-movement" within the larger, region-wide Civil Rights Movement. Its course ran so nearly parallel to that of the larger movement that the casual observer might easily conclude that it was being directed from a central command post, unless simple contagion could explain the parallels. The Montgomery Bus Boycott began in December, 1955; the Tallahassee Boycott in May, 1956. The demands in each were worded almost identically. The Greensboro sit-ins occurred on February 1, 1960, while several students from Florida A and M University were arrested during a sit-in on February 20.

THE BUS BOYCOTTS: MONTGOMERY AND TALLAHASSEE

The widely held belief that Rosa Parks was a woman who had no conception of herself as a social activist but instead impulsively defied a white bus driver because her feet hurt has been discredited. She had a long history of active participation in the local and state NAACP organizations, and had been put off Montgomery buses several times previously for refusing to move to the rear. Apparently, however, she had not planned this particular act of defiance as the beginning of a campaign against bus segregation. Even though her act was spontaneous, her old friend E. D. Nixon, president of the Montgomery NAACP, saw it as a strategic opportunity. After signing the bond for her release, he called nineteen black ministers, including Martin Luther King, Jr., and asked them to join in sponsoring a boycott. Nixon revealed in an interview with journalist Milton Viorst (1979:27–28) that the idea of a boycott was not something that just sprang into his head:

> *We talked about the bus boycott all year. I kept saying that the only way we're going to do any good is to hit those people right where it hurts, and that's in the pocketbook.*

While the Montgomery NAACP was clearly involved in the initiation of the bus protest and continued its legal fight against segregated seating, the emergence of the Montgomery Improvement Association made the boycott what McAdam (1982:138) terms a "church-based operation headed by a minister." He accepts Pat Watters's (1971) assertion that all the other southern boycotts and the organizations conducting them were imitations of this model.

McAdam (1982:138) mentions the Tallahassee Bus Boycott as one of these imitations and accepts the version of its origins advanced by Thomas R. Brooks: "The Reverend Charles K. Steele visited his friend, Martin Luther King, in the winter of 1956, and returned home to Tallahassee, Florida, to organize a bus boycott." What happened in Tallahassee does not sustain this version of Steele's role, however, and upon close examination the sequence of events proves to be quite different from that in Montgomery.

The precipitating incident was the consequence of what was clearly a spontaneous action by two students with no record of activism and no organizational connections outside Florida A and M University. Moreover, they never became activists in the movement they "started," going almost immediately into final examinations and then returning to their homes for the summer, much relieved to get out of Tallahassee and the glare of publicity. The incident was described 25 years later by Wilhemina Jakes (1981), one of the two women.

> *The bus boycott came into focus when Carrie and I boarded a city bus here in Tallahassee on Saturday afternoon. We dropped our dimes into the meter and sat next to a white lady on the seat behind the driver. It was the only seat available. When we sat down, the driver said, "You girls can't sit there." I said, "Why?" He said, "You just can't sit there." I got up, went to him and said, "Give me back my dime and I will get off." He said, "I can't give you your dime." I returned to my seat and I sat. He drove the bus to the nearest service station; he went into the station and made a call. He returned to the bus and parked and said, "Everyone remain seated." Within five minutes three cars loaded with policemen came. Two of the officers came on the bus. They talked with the driver and then came over to Carrie and I. One of the officers said, "Are you girls having a problem?" I explained to him what had happened and told him that I would get off if the driver would give me my dime. He then said, "You girls want to ride—then I'll give you a ride; come with me." So Carrie and I, we followed the officer to his car and got in. He took us to the police station. When we got there it appeared as if the entire police force was there to greet us. It was somewhat frightening. He charged us for inciting a riot. We were really surprised and shocked. The dean of city students sent a bondsman to bail us out. The next morning when we read the paper, "Carrie Patterson and Wilhemina Jakes arrested for Inciting a Riot," we tried to call our parents and let them know what had happened, and that we were alright. Then about 9 a.m. Sunday Reverend Steele and a representative of the NAACP came to see us. They told us that when they read the paper they thought that we were still in jail and they had been there to bond us out. We told them the story: they offered us their support.*

Perhaps Steele eventually would have, like E. D. Nixon, seized upon this incident as the occasion for organizing a bus boycott, mobilizing the resources of internal organizations such as the NAACP and the black churches to support the effort. He never had the opportunity to initiate the boycott, for events transpired very quickly after his inconsequential visit to the two women. Late Sunday afternoon a cross was burned in front of their off-campus residence. They fled to a dormitory, and the word of the cross-burning spread rapidly over the campus. By the next morning the officers of the Student Government Association had posted notices calling for a mass meeting of students. In the words of Jakes (1981), "The student body met the next morning. Carrie and I were asked not to attend the meeting. We did not attend. Immediately following this meeting, the Tallahassee Bus Boycott began." The Chaplain of Florida A and M University confirmed this account:

> *Students were there in full number, it was a full auditorium, as many faculty as could get in—many of us were there. Well, the students decided that they would protest the action of the bus company and the police officers, and that they would withdraw student patronage of the bus company and that they would ask the community to join them in withdrawing patronage or boycott the bus company. (Ice—Hudson Interview, 1978)*

On questioning, Chaplain Hudson could not remember whether any of the leaders of the black community were there. This was a meeting called by the student leaders and conducted by them. Indeed, the Dean of Students, who had posted bond for the two co-eds, thought that no one but students were at the meeting (Ice—Miles Interviews, 1978).

Hudson, while a university official, was also president of the Tallahassee Interdenominational Ministerial Alliance, an association of black ministers. He says he called a special meeting of the Alliance on Tuesday, the day after the boycott had started. Steele, a member of the Alliance but also president of the local NAACP, claims that he and Hudson got together and called a joint meeting (Ice—Steele Interview, 1978). Hudson's version is that he and the pastor of the church in which the meeting was to be held "contacted community leaders and all other interested persons who would like to meet and talk over the situation" (Ice—Hudson, 1978).

The black ministers assembled at this meeting and set up a committee to talk to the bus company officials. It was headed not by Steele but by J. Metz Rollins, one of the newest ministers. What proved to be a more significant action was the calling of a mass meeting for that night. Steele was the one who proposed this, but the student-inspired bus boycott had already been under way and spreading for 24 hours.

The mass meeting was attended by a large portion of those black leaders, both lay and clerical, who had been engaged in any sort of civic activity in previous years. At this point it is evident that what Morris has identified as essential pre-existing social structures were becoming involved in the emerging movement—but only after the protest had been initiated by the students. What was the nature of these organizations and what resources could they provide?

There were the black churches which did, as in other southern communities, come to constitute important resources. Up until the beginning of the bus boycott, however, none of them included social protest on their agenda. The largest black social structure in Tallahassee was the Florida A and M student body, but despite the existence of a student government it did not constitute so much a formal organization as a communication network—all students belonged but few were active participants. Again, this structure had no history of social activism.

There did exist a local chapter of the NAACP as well as a student chapter at the university. Steele had been president of the Tallahassee chapter for about two years—he had moved to the city only three years before the boycott. There also existed an organization called the Tallahassee Civic League, something like a black Rotary Club, and there was the Ministerial Alliance. Smith and Killian (1958:6) characterized the organizational activity—or the lack of it—in the two years between the 1954 school desegregation decision and the boycott in these words:

> *Perhaps because of the peaceful accommodation in race relations, Tallahassee was virtually devoid of organizations active in intergroup relations at the time of the Supreme Court ruling. The local chapter of the NAACP was small and weak. . . .*
>
> *It was not until the formation of the Negro Inter-Civic Council that any organization embarked on a program of action either for or against any form of segregation in Tallahassee.*

The Inter-Civic Council (ICC) was born at the mass meeting. It constituted a merger of the NAACP, the Ministerial Alliance and the Civic League. The NAACP was the only one of the three with an action orientation, but it had been relatively inactive. Steele made it plain why the black community, goaded into action by the students, did not unite under the banner of the NAACP:

> *It was the decision of the people and the fear of some people that if the NAACP sponsored it [the boycott] it would be jeopardized by authorities, so they decided to form a new organization that they were not acquainted with. (Ice—Steele, 1978).*

Although Steele was elected president of the new body, it was not just the NAACP under a new name. As Steele himself said to Ice, it was named the Inter-Civic Council because "it would include representatives from all of the civic organizations in town interested in racial progress."

From the officers of the ICC came the "new leaders" identified by Killian and Smith (1960) in their study of Negro protest leaders. The change in the style of leadership from accommodating to militant was accompanied by a change of personnel. Not all of the new leaders were ministers, although most were. One of the most important was Dan Speed, a businessman who later became a minister but continued to operate his grocery and market near the university campus. He was elected to chair the transportation committee, charged with the task of organizing a car pool in support of the boycott. A model for such a system already existed in Montgomery, and it is likely that the Tallahassee leaders knew about it.

Although white opponents of the ICC did attempt to represent it as merely the NAACP in disguise, manipulated by "outside agitators," it was an autonomous organization. It was identified by the black community as being the primary organization supporting the boycott. Its leaders were not the same people who had been known as "Negro leaders" before the boycott. Under their leadership it engaged in a broad range of activities, as described by Killian and Smith (1960:257):

> *Finally these "new" leaders have sought to keep the Negro community of Tallahassee militant and dynamic by continuing weekly meetings of the ICC, the organization formed to promote the bus protests, conducting institutes on non-violence, taking preliminary steps toward school integration, working to get more Negroes registered and voting, and making many local and nonlocal public appearances in connection with the uplift of Negroes.*

The pre-existing organizations provided a communication network and a cadre of potential activists when the students precipitated a crisis. They did not become movement organizations in the sense that the emergent ICC did. The Civic League continued to exist but lost its prominence, and the NAACP, as a separate organization, was in evidence primarily as a channel through which outside aid could be obtained.

There is no evidence, however, that either outside aid or influence were of any significance in the initiation of the Tallahassee submovement, despite the suggestion that Steele conferred with King and then went back to organize the boycott. Although he had known King since the latter was a boy—"Martin was born the same year that I started preaching"—he did not credit him with originating the idea of a bus boycott. Like many other black ministers in the South, he knew that the Reverend Theodore Jemison had led the first bus boycott of modern times in Baton Rouge in 1953. In fact, Steele seemed to consider the Tallahassee movement as a rival of the Montgomery movement rather than an offshoot. When asked, "Did he [King] give you some words of encouragement or advice?" he answered:

> *No. He gave us encouragement. Fact is they gave us $3,000 during our struggle. From Montgomery. But as far as our sitting down and he say you do this, we didn't have that because in the first place I considered Tallahassee beyond Montgomery. I still think that. Our demands were greater than Montgomery, our results were greater than Montgomery. We had 98 percent, we put the bus company off the road, we put black drivers on before they did, and so on. And another thing, I have pictured the Montgomery effort as being the handwriting on the wall for the South, and I've considered Tallahassee as a little Daniel came along and interpreted that handwriting. (Ice—Steele, 1978)*

Not until the boycott was well under way and the car pool in full operation did the external resources of the NAACP come into play in Tallahassee. No lawsuit challenging the segregation ordinance was ever filed, but when drivers in the car pool were arrested for operating "For Hire" vehicles without a license the state NAACP office sent a lawyer from Tampa to defend them.

The resources available to the ICC were meager and there is no evidence that the activists in Tallahassee, from the two co-eds to the leaders, anticipated the possible costs of the movement. Smith and Killian (1958:19) observed in 1958, "There is no evidence that this movement was planned in advance of the events of May 27, 1956. In fact, the confusion of the first few days of the movement strongly indicates a lack of planning." Human resources, people who would boycott the buses, attend mass meetings, drive in the car pool and contribute money when collections were taken, quickly rallied to the emergent movement. Large sums of money to pay for the car pool were harder to come by. They were badly needed to provide bail and to pay legal costs for arrested drivers and the 21 members of the ICC Executive Committee arrested and charged with operating a transportation system without a franchise. Neither the pre-existing organizations nor the new movement organization had large "war chests." According to Steele, most of the money was raised through his personal efforts, with no external organizational support. He stated:

> *I was running hither and thither all over the country trying to raise $11,000. See, Martin Luther King could go to New York—I remember he went to New York one year and spoke six times in various areas in the New York area and raised $6,000. I could go to New York and speak the same number of times, maybe I would raise $1,500. Usually someone interested in Tallahassee would arrange an itinerary for me and I would speak in Newark, Brooklyn, New York. Then I'd preach on Sunday for my expense money. (Ice—Steele, 1978)*

Another important source of funds was not an organization but an individual—Dan Speed, Chair of the Transportation Committee. He was selected for this role because he was a very successful businessman who owned a store which was something of a community center. He described his role as the "banker" of the movement in the following exchange:

Q: How many cars did you need in this transportation system?

A: Oh, we had about 60, an average of 60 cars. I can answer that because when we first got started we didn't have any money.

Q: It must have cost a lot of money for those volunteers.

A: I financed it.

Q: How much did that cost you?

A: It cost me a whole lot. I gave them credit, they paid my money back. I was reimbursed on monies they raised, collections. (Ice— Speed. 1978)

Speed was not, of course, the only individual who contributed or lent funds. Chaplain Hudson, also an officer of the ICC, remembers that there was a Ways and Means Committee which "included such faithful women as 'Mother' Cora

Stokes and 'Mother' Robbins and others." Its task was fundraising. These women were distinguished and had earned the honorific "Mother" by long and faithful service in the various churches to which they belonged.

The Tallahassee Bus Boycott did not terminate in any clear-cut resolution of the issues. The demand for the employment of black drivers was met during the third month. After the Supreme Court declared segregation on city buses in Montgomery unconstitutional, the City Commission resorted to the device of a seat-assignment ordinance in attempting to prevent integrated seating. Three university students were arrested for refusing to sit in seats assigned by a bus driver. During ensuing months, while these and other cases wended their way through the courts, blacks gradually returned to the buses but not in the numbers prevailing before the boycott. At the same time, enforcement of the seating ordinance became increasingly lax; the bus company had no desire to lose its black customers again.

THE SIT-INS

It might seem that the ICC, which continued to exist as an organization, would have become the core of one of the movement centers which, in Morris's analysis, provided the organizational foundation for the subsequent student sit-in movement. Steele had become vice-president of the Southern Christian Leadership Conference and continued as Chair of the ICC, although there was no formal relationship between the two organizations until the mid-1960s. He continued as president of the Tallahassee NAACP until 1960, when he was forced to resign because of what amounted to a jurisdictional dispute with ICC. Most of the black churches continued to be connected to the ICC through their ministers. Yet, according to White (1964:70), following the bus boycott:

> *As the movement tempo subsided . . . the new leaders and their movement organization stabilized at a position of inactivity. The NAACP-ICC combine, the new leaders, and the condition of no communication between Negro and white power structures were institutionalized as conventional patterns in the community.*

The Florida A and M student body was mobilized into action once again, however, but not as part of the Civil Rights Movement. A black co-ed was raped by four white men. In Smith's (1961:225) words:

> *Again, the student body took action. They closed the University by refusing to attend classes, held mass meetings, and soon they were on national TV demanding justice.*

On February 1, 1960, the lunch-counter sit-in in Greensboro, North Carolina, occurred, and became known as the beginning of the "sit-in movement." Louis Lomax (1962:121), a black journalist, called it "the second major battle of the Negro revolt" and a "revolt against both segregation and the entrenched Negro leadership." He also dramatized it as an entirely spontaneous action, taken without planning or organizational influence.

> *Greensboro happened by itself; nobody planned it, nobody pulled any strings. Negro students simply got tired and sat down. Once they made their move, however, three national civil rights organizations came into town to help them. This was the beginning of a pattern that would spread over the Deep South. (Lomax, 1962:122)*

It is this image of spontaneity and lack of structure which Morris challenges by showing that the four Greensboro youths had been active members of an NAACP youth council at one time or another, had participated in action-oriented churches in Durham, and knew about the less well-publicized sit-ins which had occurred in the preceding three years. He counters with the declaration, "Thus, the myth that four college students got up one day and sat-in at Woolworth's—and sparked the movement—dries up like a 'raisin in the sun' when confronted with the evidence" (Morris, 1981:755).

According to McAdam (1982:139), the student sit-in movement spread in the following weeks, first within North Carolina, then to neighboring states, and then to "such traditional centers of southern black life as Tallahassee, Atlanta and Montgomery." He suggests, "The uniform nature of these demonstrations again suggests the presence of a well-developed communication network linking the southern black college campuses into a loosely integrated institutional network" (McAdam, 1982:138).

The event in Tallahassee to which he refers was a lunch-counter sit-in on February 13 conducted by eight Florida A and M Students and two black high school students. It was organized by CORE—the newest civil rights organization in the city. No demonstrators were arrested; they simply sat at the counter for two and a half hours without being served.

How did thc Tallahassee submovement become part of the spreading sit-in movement? Was it planned on the model of the sit-ins which had occurred in North Carolina the previous week? What was the involvement of the indigenous organizations which had developed during the bus boycott? When did outside resources from the national leadership organizations come into the community? Why was the sit-in sponsored by CORE, a new campus-based organization, rather than by the NAACP combine led by Steele?

White's detailed account of the career of Tallahassee CORE offers many answers to these questions. By the summer of 1959 both the Tallahassee NAACP and ICC had become relatively inactive. The two local organizations had overlapping leadership, particularly through Steele, Speed and Daisy Young, who served as secretary for both. Speed provided free rent [and] an office for the joint headquarters in the building in which his store was located. In an interview in 1983 he asserted, however, that the organizations maintained their separate identities. Daisy Young confirmed this, describing how Steele was forced to give up the presidency of the NAACP when he sought to bring King into a march on Tallahassee planned by the state NAACP.

The person who brought CORE to Tallahassee was a co-ed at Florida A and M University who had not been involved in the previous boycott. During the summer of 1959 she attended a CORE-sponsored Interracial Action Institute in Miami. Upon returning to Tallahassee in the fall, she set about organizing a chapter of CORE, seeking support from a small circle of fellow students and white students from Florida State University who, during the previous two years, had been attempting to organize an inter-university organization. ICC had been a black organization, although it did receive some surreptitious support from a few whites. By its constitution, CORE had to be interracial. Patricia Stephens succeeded in her efforts, helped by a CORE field secretary who came to Tallahassee for an organizational meeting.

While needing the support of the pre-existing organizations, CORE was a new and independent organization. The chief conncting links between it and the earlier ones were Daisy Young, who became a member of the executive committee of CORE, and Dan Speed's building, where CORE was also given space. On one occasion CORE even used ICC stationery (White, 1964:112). According to White, however, the key figure in CORE during the sit-ins was the faculty adviser, a young man who had lived in the community for only five years and had not been a leader in the bus boycott, if he was involved at all.

Organized early in the fall, Tallahassee CORE's first action was a test of the success of the bus boycott. Members conducted test rides on city buses and found that drivers were no longer attempting to make black passengers sit in the rear. Next, on November 11, 1959, 3 members actually sat down at a white lunch counter in Tallahassee and requested service—nearly 3 months before the Greensboro incident. This, too, was merely a test, and the black students left when they were refused. On December 1, two more CORE members requested service at a lunch counter and were refused. This early, unpublicized series of tests was not intended as demonstrations nor were they CORE's only activities. The main effort had been in another direction, testing the compliance of bus companies serving Tallahassee with the Morgan decision forbidding segregation in interstate travel.

The first sit-in *demonstration* by Tallahassee CORE was not spontaneous but neither was it planned as part of a well-thoughtout, ongoing strategy. This was the sit-in on February 13, two weeks after Greensboro. White (1964:112) describes how it came about:

> *Early in the month of February national CORE contacted Tallahassee CORE by telephone to inform them of a forthcoming region-wide sympathy sit-in. It was to begin at eleven o'clock on the thirteenth of February and to end at two o'clock on the same day. A meeting was quickly called, at which time the members of Tallahassee CORE decided to participate in the regional sit-in. . . . Eight Florida A and M students and two Negro high school students [Steele's sons] volunteered to participate in the project. The project group, according to [the faculty adviser], was "hastily organized . . . and with too little preparation."*

It was not until a week later, February 20, that the first sit-in demonstrators were arrested in Tallahassee. This demonstration had been planned by local CORE. After the arrests the NAACP-ICC did become involved for, according to White (1964:117), the faculty adviser "contacted three NAACP leaders" and "bond was furnished by a local NAACP-ICC leader." During the following week a more extended organizational network became involved.

> *Legal aid was secured from the NAACP office in Miami, a Tallahassee CORE Defense Fund was established, and an appeal was made to national CORE for financial aid. (White, 1964:117)*

At the same time, it appears that CORE was operating quite independently of the other indigenous organizations until such time as financial or legal aid was required. It also appears that they had no assurances of the availability of such aid before their costly ventures.

Events which followed arrests during a major sit-in demonstration on March 12 illustrate the mixture of planning and spontaneity. These sit-ins were carefully planned, following the manual, *CORE Rules for Action*. After the arrests, which took place about 11:30 a.m., the president of CORE returned to the Florida A and M campus, entered the cafeteria, and said to the lunch-time crowd, "The police have arrested FAMU and FSU students at Woolworth's. Let's march on Woolworth's and McCrory's—to fill the jails if necessary" (White, 1964:123). This impromptu action, taken without the consent of other members of the executive committee or other organizations, was in direct violation of CORE rules. It resulted in a march of about 100 students to the downtown area, the arrest of 17 more, and a confrontation with a group of club-wielding whites. No violence occurred and the students returned to the campus. Later in the afternoon, however, a march of from 800 to 1,000 students was stopped by police, who attacked the marchers with tear gas and then "began indiscriminately arresting students who remained in the general area" (White, 1964:127).

Again Tallahassee CORE had to seek outside aid:

> *Late Saturday night, the CORE Executive Council contacted national CORE to seek advice about getting legal aid for the arrested demonstrators. They were advised to contact the Miami branch of the NAACP, which they did and out of which they were offered legal aid as requested. (White, 1964:128)*

As in the early days of the bus boycott, Tallahassee was once more in crisis. Yet the "New Leadership" which emerged during the boycott was not leading this phase of the movement. SCLC, of which Steele was vice-president, was never involved; a representative who went from Nashville to Florida to offer SCLC's collaboration was rebuffed. Furthermore, although White indicates that the individual NAACP-ICC leaders helped to arrange bond after the first arrest, they were not acting as officers of the two organizations. White (1964:129) says of the officers of CORE, "They held joint meetings with some of the more active NAACP-ICC leaders, who, after the second arrests, had indicated to CORE that they were interested in assuming some leadership in local interracial activities." On March 23 there was a joint NAACP-ICC-CORE mass meeting in a Negro church; the main speaker was the new national field secretary of CORE.

Although CORE continued with its social action through a drive to raise funds to help the arrested students and a selective buying campaign aimed at downtown merchants, there were no more sit-in demonstrations. There was, however, extensive debate over whether to have more. During one meeting, this time to discuss a possible "kneel-in" on the steps of the capitol, the lack of integration within the movement center was revealed. White (1964:151) reports:

> *It was at this meeting that an NAACP-ICC leader [Steele] openly objected to CORE conducting demonstrations without the approval of the "adult leaders," since it is they (adult leaders) who "must answer for the consequences anyway." [The faculty adviser] answered his assertion with a rather mild challenge, but did not debate the issue. However, after the committee meeting, CORE members voiced strong dissatisfaction with the NAACP-ICC leaders' comments.*

Movement activities continued in Tallahassee until after the passage of the 1964 Civil Rights Act. They involved attacks on segregation in restaurants and theaters and resulted in even more arrests. At one time, over 500 students were in jail. All of these activities were led by CORE and involved Florida A and M students and some high school students.

In 1961, after both the bus boycott and the sit-ins, Charles U. Smith assessed the roles of students, of various movement organizations and of the black community. First he wrote:

> *Through mass meetings and other demonstrations the FAMU student body was able to influence the majority of the Negro community of Tallahassee to boycott the city bus service for several months. They found that the adult members of the Negro community would listen to their ideas and cooperate with their efforts. (Smith, 1961:225)*

Of the emergence of the sit-ins he stated:

> *By the time the sit-in demonstrations began in Greensboro in 1959, the FAMU student body were emotionally and spiritually prepared to enter into any legitimate fray on behalf of the rights of Negroes, and it was only incidental to this preparedness that CORE organized a chapter in Tallahassee in the Fall of 1959. This writer is firmly convinced that even without the support of CORE, it would only have been a matter of time until members of the FAMU student body started their own demonstrations. (Smith, 1961:226–27).*

Finally, of the adult community Smith said:

> *Adult, non-student participation in Tallahassee has been largely confined to arranging bail bonds and assisting with the procurement of legal counsel for the students. (Smith, 1961:229)*

There was another, less tangible, type of support provided by the adult community—the moral support for the activists expressed from the pulpits of the black churches. There were many black ministers who, from the time of the emergence of the ICC, constituted a significant portion of the new, protest leadership. The best known of these adult leaders was the charismatic and energetic C. K. Steele. His activities not only made him one of the best known and most feared blacks in Tallahassee but also extended beyond the city because of his dynamism as a speaker, his unquestionable courage and his position in the SCLC. Yet there is no evidence that he was a grand strategist of the civil rights movement in Tallahassee, as was widely believed in the white community.

During the period when CORE was the dominant movement organization, after the sit-ins began, Patricia Stephens was a strong leader showing a marked degree of autonomy. Asked how much influence Steele had on CORE's decisions, Daisy Young replied, "You could have a meeting and think a decision had been made but

Pat felt that since she had brought CORE here the decisions were hers. She believed in drastic action. So you'd find out she'd decided to do something drastic that hadn't been decided on at the meeting!" (Killian—Young Interview, 1984).

Furthermore, Steele did not underestimate the crucial contribution of the students. In 1978 he declared:

> *Without the students, there would have been no protest, there would have been no movement. They are the militants. They are the soldiers. You don't have a great number of people in a community or a city who have either the time or the energy really to get in a march. (Ice—Steele, 1978)*

While the students could be aptly characterized as "soldiers," they were not troops who merely followed. They were themselves leaders who, by their actions, created crises and galvanized the whole black community into action. Some of their actions were spontaneous; the most significant organizations were emergent ones.

THE MEANING OF SPONTANEITY AND EMERGENCE

The concepts "spontaneity" and "emergence," "spontaneous" and "emergent," are of critical importance in the analysis of social movements, yet just what they mean to scholars who use them is far from clear. Like many sociological concepts they are borrowed from lay language but used as if they had the precision desired in scientific discourse. Some attempt at clarification is demanded before the preceding case history is analyzed.

"Spontaneity" hardly qualifies as a sociological concept—it seems more like an ordinary adjective used occasionally by sociologists as if the meaning were self-evident. Perhaps the association alleged to exist between it and classical collective-behavior theory is related to Herbert Blumer's usage in his oft-cited essay on collective behavior, originally published in 1939 but reprinted in later editions of *Principles of Sociology* ([1946] 1951). There he defined collective behavior as that which arises "spontaneously" and "is not due to pre-established understandings or traditions" (Blumer, [1946] 1951:168). A little farther on he wrote, "Milling, collective excitement and social contagion are present, in varying degrees, in all instances of spontaneous group behavior" (Blumer, [1946] 1951:176). Here there is an implication that spontaneous behavior is emotional, impulsive, even irrational—the ideas ascribed by some critics to both Gustave LeBon and classical collective-behavior theorists. Yet by dictionary definition and in much of popular usage the term is more strongly related to such synonyms as "unpremeditated" and "unplanned" than to "impulsive." *Webster's Collegiate Thesaurus* lists as the antonym "premeditated." Other contrasting terms given are "deliberate, predetermined, preplanned, studied, and thought-out" (1976:772).

It is this meaning which is evident in Jo Freeman's (1979:170) call for a model in which decisions, both planned and spontaneous, can be analyzed. It is in this sense that "spontaneous" will be used in this analysis. Human actors can and do make on-the-spot decisions which are not part of a plan for continuous action and whose consequences are unanticipated. Such decisions and the resulting actions may or may not be accompanied by excitement or strong emotions. Whether they are rational must be determined by application of the same criteria by which the rationality of planned actions is judged (see Turner and Killian, 1972:9).

"Emergence" occurs more frequently in sociological and psychological writings. George H. Mead (1982:108) said of the act, one of his central concerns, "The act is novelty, an emergent." But he also made explicit what he meant by "novelty," relating it to emergence when he said, "the novel is constantly happening and the recognition of this gets its expression in more general terms in the concept of emergence. Emergence involves a reorganization but the reorganization brings in something that was not there before" (Mead, 1934:198). Irving Zeitlin contends that the concept of emergence is central to what he describes as "the dialectical philosophy" of Mead. Thus, says Zeitlin (1973:233), "There is then a dialectical relation between the individual and his world resulting in the reconstitution of both."

Blumer not only elaborated on the emergent nature of the individual act but also extended his analysis to what he called "joint" or "collective" action. He took for granted the relationship of such action to earlier structures and norms, saying, "One is on treacherous and empirically invalid grounds if he thinks that any given form of joint action can be sliced off from its historical linkage, as if its makeup and character arose out of the air through spontaneous generation instead of growing out of what went before" (Blumer, 1969:17). He balanced this emphasis on the influence of pre-existing structures and traditions with stress on the formation, or emergence, of every instance of joint action through the interaction of individual participants. Thus he asserted:

> *In dealing with collectivities and with joint action one can easily be trapped in and erroneous position by failing to recognize that the joint action of the collectivity is an interlinkage of the separate acts of the participants. This failure leads one to overlook the fact that a joint action always has to undergo a process of formation; even though it may be a well-established and repetitive form of social action, each instance of it has to be formed anew. (Blumer, 1969:17)*

It is this notion of the construction of new, in the sense of reorganized, modified or transformed, norms and structure which is embodied in the emergent-norm approach advanced by Turner and Killian (1972). This approach was derived not only from the Mead-Blumer symbolic interactionist tradition but also from the social-psychological theories and experiments of Muzafer Sherif. The latter saw the principle of "levels" and the corollary processes of emergence and continuity as essential to understanding not only the relationship between individual and group behavior but also that between the past and the present, declaring:

> *It is becoming a recognized fact that the emergence of different and new qualities—structural transformations—occurs not only on the level of human group interaction, but also on all levels of physical, biological and historical events. In particular the work of Gestalt psychologists on perception and in other fields has helped to establish the fact of structural properties of wholes, interdependence of parts, qualitative transformations with the coming of new factors into the situation. (Sherif, 1948:157)*

"Emergence" does not imply discontinuity with the past. It is complementary to continuity, but sensitizes the observer to that which is new without denying its roots in that which has gone before. To speak of the emergence of new structures and norms in a social movement, such as the one described here, is not to deny the influence of pre-existing organizations.

ANALYSIS OF THE CASE HISTORY

While reflecting the importance of pre-existing organizations and strategically planned action, the civil rights movement in Tallahassee also highlights the significance of spontaneous action and the emergence of new structures. This may be an idiosyncratic case which can shed no light on social movement theory or it may represent a variation, a less frequently occurring subtype, of the pattern presented by Morris and McAdam in their much more comprehensive studies. It may be that if the events in more of the other submovements or movement centers were examined on the microsociological level similar modifications of the revisionist models would appear warranted. What are the theoretical implications if we take the Tallahassee case as significant?

First, if we take the term "spontaneity" to denote the unplanned nature of an event or action rather than its irrationality or novelty, it is clear from the Tallahassee case that this element cannot be ignored. Spontaneity is especially likely to be important in the early stages of a social movement and during periods of transition from one type of action to another. Thus the precipitating act of the two co-eds clearly meets this criterion for spontaneity. The reactions of the bus driver and the police were not anticipated, nor was the burning of a cross in front of their residence. There is simply no evidence that they expected to precipitate a boycott. The other point at which spontaneity is evident is in the transition from the period of quiescence after the boycott had run its course to the new phase of demonstrations, beginning with the activities of CORE in late 1959. The early activities of this campus-based organization, which was even newer to the community that the ICC, had a groping, impromptu character. This changed when conducting lunch-counter sit-ins became the primary activity. There was greater coordination with national CORE, but the very significant marches on Tallahassee by Florida A and M students on March 12, precipitated by Pat Stephens's impromptu action and ending with a mass confrontation with the police, showed the continuing importance of spontaneous action even during a period of careful planning. Furthermore, from the outset Florida A and M students undertook costly actions with little or no assurance that the resources to "cover their bets" would be forthcoming.

At the same time, the importance of pre-existing structures—both organizations and networks—is inescapably evident. The student body, the black churches and the local NAACP constituted the "supportive organizational context" which McAdam (1982:48) emphasizes and the cooptable communication network stressed by Freeman (1983:9). Yet there is no indication that either the student leaders who called the first mass meeting or the leaders of the black community who mobilized the community in support of the impromptu boycott had any more than a vague idea of what resources they could rally. Neither the black churches nor the black secular organizations had any record of participation in the kind of social action being proposed, action which would require both personal and financial sacrifice. The movement was launched more on faith than on the basis of an inventory of resources in reserve, internal or external.

The pre-existing organizations, of crucial importance during the first few days, were soon displaced by an emergent structure, the Inter-Civic Council, and were transformed in the process of merging into it. Smith, who was present at the organizational meeting, said in an interview in 1983:

> *I know the NAACP had been sporadically active in the state . . . but in Tallahassee the NAACP was present but was not attacking racial segregation at all. I think the reason that the ICC was formed on the second day of the bus boycott was because there was no organization situated strategically enough and viable enough to carry out this activity. . . . It was thought that this would be a special organization that would cut across religious lines, lay lines, involve the lay community, the religious community, the student community, and that's how this organization came into existence. (Killian—Smith Interview, 1983)*

The ICC endured even after the boycott, along with the older organizations. While it, in combination with the NAACP, became involved in and supported the sit-in movement, it did not plan, lead or control it. White (1964:231) says of the relationship. "From the very first CORE meeting three leaders of the NAACP-ICC combine, acting in individual capacities, kept in touch with the submovement. . . . As an organization, the NAACP group remained indifferent and aloof from the submovement. Even the three friendly NAACP-ICC leaders remained outside of the submovement structure, and communicated their interest in its activities to the two established leaders." Once again a new, student-based organization acted independently to precipitate a crisis and revitalize the movement.

Next, in considering pre-existing structures it is important to distinguish between organizations and networks, as Freeman implies. Social structures lying toward the network or grass-roots pole of the continuum, such as the student body and the members of the several churches, are well suited to provide resources and serve as communication networks but not to function as coordinating staffs which devise strategy and direct action. They are very different from protest organizations devoted single-mindedly to promoting change, such as ICC, CORE, SCLC, SNCC and even the NAACP. It may be hypothesized that it was because the latter were, as movement organizations, both protest oriented and emergent (NAACP excepted) that many of them had careers which were spectacular but brief.

Recognizing that pre-existing structures have a critical influence on the development and course of social movement does not justify neglecting the emergent properties which make a social movement novel. Even as older organizations continue to exist they are transformed as they become parts of a new gestalt in which protest constitutes a common goal. Both continuity and emergence were evident in the Tallahassee Civil Rights Movement, as in all social movements.

Finally, the absence of clearly available resources at the time when precipitating actions were taken suggests the greater relative importance of social-psychological factors as against tangible resources. It is obvious that both the bus boycott and the sit-ins in Tallahassee emerged in a nationwide atmosphere in which black protest not only appeared more feasible than ever before but was even becoming normative, especially for black students. Smith (1961:228) even suggested in 1961 that for black college students "a spirit of competition has found its way into the civil rights arena, and no college or university wants to be left behind or be found wanting in this kind of courage and conviction." Events in Montgomery, Little Rock and Greensboro, as well as the rallying of the students and the black community in Tallahassee during the bus boycott and the rape case, justified the hope and faith of students and then of adult activists that resources to back up their bold actions existed and could be mobilized.

This sort of feeling is more akin to Ralph Turner's concept "the sense of injustice" (Turner and Killian, 1972:259) and McAdam's (1982:34) later "cognitive liberation" than to the utilitarian assessment of resources suggested by some versions of Resource Mobilization Theory. Freeman (1979:172) suggests a bridge between different *types* of resources when she defines the potential time and commitment which people may provide as an *intangible* resource, saying, "People are the primary intangible resource of a movement, and movements rely very heavily upon them." Martha Prescod Norman (1983), a former SNCC field worker, portrayed this intangible factor graphically when she reminisced:

> *One of the things I learned from organizing was how many resources even powerless people have. We didn't have resources of wealth, prestige, political power. Our main resources was faith in ourselves—faith that if we had our souls and bodies we could change the world!*

CONCLUSION

New developments in theory have reminded us that organization, resources and planning are essential to the success of a social movement and should not be neglected in practice or in research. V.I. Lenin's famous work, "What Is to Be Done?" was a call for systematic and methodical preparation for the work which a revolutionary movement would have to do. Yet he emphasized the complex relation between planning and spontaneity when he wrote:

> *We have spoken all the time about systematic and methodical preparation, but we have no desire in the least to suggest that the autocracy may fall only as a result of a properly prepared siege or organized attack. Such a view would be stupid and doctrinaire. On the contrary, it is quite possible, and historically far more probable, that the autocracy will fall under the pressure of one of those spontaneous outbursts or unforeseen political complications which constantly threaten if from all sides. But no political party, if it desires to avoid adventurist tactics, can base its activities on expectations of such outbursts and complications. We must proceed along our road, and*

> *steadily carry out our systematic work, and the less we count on the unexpected, the less likely are we to be taken by surprise by any "historical turn." (Lenin, 1929:116)*

Again, it is being suggested that while spontaneous, unplanned and unforeseen events have a high probability of precipitating social movements they are never sufficient to generate viable structures capable of sustained activities. While never relying on it, planners must be prepared for the unexpected, Lenin seems to be saying.

Hence we conclude that while organization and rational planning are key variable, social movement theory must take into account spontaneity and emergence and the forces which generate them. It must treat as important, not as irrational, the feeling states and the cognitions which sometimes cause individuals to throw caution to the winds and act in the face of great or unknown odds. It must include as an essential part of its analysis how social movement organizations and their leaders deal with the changes in the course of a movement which unpredictable, spontaneous actions introduce, and how they themselves are transformed or even superseded in the process.

POSTSCRIPT: THE POLITICAL CONTEXT OF RESEARCH

Writing some twenty years after the events occurred, Morris concluded from his data that theorists of the period placed too much emphasis on spontaneity and lack of structure in the Civil Rights Movement. Having reviewed some of the data, the present author concludes that in the Tallahassee case there were indeed spontaneous acts which were of central significance and that emergent organizations were more important that pre-existing ones. From the beginning of the current research it has been evident, however, that there was another reason why many contemporary observers emphasized any evidence they discovered indicating spontaneity and lack of planning. This was essentially a political reason, stemming not from a conservative bias but from sympathy for the values of the Civil Rights Movement. One of the charges most frequently used as a weapon to discredit the Movement was the accusation. "Our local blacks were satisfied until outside agitators like the NAACP came in and stirred them up." In Tallahassee, despite clear evidence to the contrary, the white press and the authorities persisted in the belief that somebody must have "put these two women up to sitting on the front of that bus." Glenda Rabby (1984:324), the latest scholar to study the events of this period, writes that a serious white accusation was that Tallahassee racial disturbance were engineered by outside agitators, out-of-town troublemakers, the national NAACP, or, even worse, the international communist party." There was an enduring belief in the white community that both the bus boycott and the sit-ins were the result of a conspiracy led by Steele and other "newcomers."Evidence of spontaneity, of impulsive protest against tired feet as well as against white supremacy, and of lack of organization and planning was welcome as ammunition against such charges to those researchers who wrote as the conflict was going on.

REFERENCES

Blumer, Herbert. [1946] 1951. "Collective behavior." Pp. 167–222 in A. M. Lee (ed.), Principles of Sociology. New York: Barnes & Noble.

Blumer, Herbert, 1969. Symbolic Interactionism: Perspective and Method. Englewood Cliffs, NJ: Prentice-Hall.

Couch, Carl. 1968. "Collective behavior: an examination of some stereotypes." Social Problems 15:310–22.

Freeman, Jo. 1973. "The origins of the Women's Liberation Movement." American Journal of Sociology 78:792–811.

Freeman, Jo. 1979. "Resource mobilization and strategy: a model for analyzing social movement organization actions." Pp. 167–89 in Mayer N. Zald and John D. McCarthy (eds.), The Dynamics of Social Movements. Cambridge, MA: Winthrop.

———. 1983. "On the origins of social movements." Pp. 8–30 in Jo Freeman (ed.), Social Movements in the Sixties and Seventies. New York: Longman.

Jakes, Wilhemina. 1981. Address given at Twenty-Fifth Anniversary Observance of the Tallahassee Bus Boycott, Tallahassee, FL. (Taped)

Jackson, Maurice, Eleanora Peterson, James Bull, Sverre Monsen and Patricia Richmond. 1960. "The failure of an incipient social movement." Pacific Sociological Review 3:35–40.

Killian, Lewis M. and Charles U. Smith. 1960. "Negro protest leaders in a southern community." Social Forces 38:253–57.

Lenin, V. I. 1929. "What Is To Be Done?" from V. I. Lenin, Collected Works, Volume 4:116. New York: International Publishers.

Lomax, Louis. 1962. The Negro Revolt, New York: New American Library.

McAdam, Doug. 1982. Political Process and the Development of Black Insurgency, 1930–1970. Chicago: University of Chicago Press.

Mead, George H. 1934. Mind, Self and Society, Charles W. Morris, ed. Chicago, University of Chicago Press.

———. 1982. The Individual and the Social Self. David L. Miller, ed. Chicago: University of Chicago Press.

Meier, August and Elliot Rudwick. 1973. CORE: A Study in the Civil Rights Movement, 1942–1968. New York: Oxford University Press.

Morris, Aldon. 1981. "Black southern sit-in movement: an analysis of internal organization." American Sociological Review 46:744–67.

Norman, Martha Prescod. 1983. Address given at Conference. "The Sixties Speak to the Eighties." University of Massachusetts, Amherst.

Piven, Frances Fox and Richard A. Cloward. 1977. Poor People's Movements. New York: Vintage.

Rabby, Glenda A. 1984. "Out of the past: the Civil Rights Movement in Tallahassee, Florida." Unpublished dissertation. Department of Sociology, Florida State University.

Sherif, Muzafer. 1948. An Outline of Social Psychology. New York: Harper & Row.

Smith, Charles U. 1961. "The sit-ins and the new Negro student." Journal of Intergroup Relations 2:223–29.

Smith, Charles U. and Lewis M. Killian. 1958. The Tallahassee Bus Protest. Field Reports on Desegregation in the South. New York: Anti-Defamation League of B'nai B'Rith.

Turner, Ralph H. and Lewis M, Killian. 1972. Collective Behavior, Englewood Cliffs, NJ: Prentice-Hall.

Viorst, Milton, 1979. Fire in the Streets. New York: Simon & Schuster.

Watters, Pat. 1971. Down to Now: Reflections on the Southern Civil Rights Movement. New York: Pantheon.

Webster's Collegiate Thesaurus. 1976. Springfield, MA: G. and C. Merriam Company.

White, Robert M. 1964. "The Tallahassee sit-ins and CORE." Unpublished dissertation. Department of Sociology, Florida State University.

Wood, James L. and Maurice Jackson. 1982. Social Movements. Belmont, CA: Wadsworth.

Zeitlin, Irving M. 1973. Rethinking Sociology: A Critique of Contemporary Theory. Englewood Cliffs, NJ: Prentice Hall.

Zinn, Howard. 1964. SNCC: The New Abolitionists. Boston: Beacon Press.

PART FOUR

Organizational Arrangements of Collective Behavior and Social Movements

Little in the way of collective behavior ever enjoys the acceptance, resources, and stability of a formal organizational structure. Furthermore, even social movements, with the advantages of sharply defined protest goals and people committed to the pursuit of these aims, may not achieve a formal organizational base. The consideration of "organizational elements" of social movement organizations (hereafter designated as SMOs) include those arrangements by which complex social actions accompanying the goals of the SMOs can be coordinated to achieve social (i.e., goals *external* to the group) or membership changes (i.e., goals *internal* to the group). These organizational and/or bureaucratic elements include hierarchies of authority, divisions of labor, leader and follower compliance structures, reward distributions (e.g., promotions, group honors) and punishments (e.g., demotions, member degradations, member-expelling actions), written records, and organizational procedures (e.g., manifestos, orders for meetings and committee appointments, etc.).

Protest or deviant groups achieving formalized organizational structures typically engage in issues favorably received by large segments of the society and do not represent an *extreme* threat to the public order. Again, as noted earlier, Mothers Against Drunk Drivers (MADD) received early public support and quickly achieved effective organizational operations, including sophisticated legal lobbying and highly technical public relations activities. Both anti-abortion and pro-choice forces are well supported. The advantages of their committed memberships, including fund-raising ability and previous organizational experience, contributed to the effective transformation of the tactics of these groups from informal and episodic actions to organizationally guided strategies engaging in formal and sustained activities.

A more controversial example than any of the above, but still meeting with favorable environmental support early in their efforts, was the National Organization for the Reform of Marijuana Laws (NORMAL). Led by highly informed persons familiar with both the statistics of usage and the ineffectiveness of sanctions, and with the ability to convert this information into news for public consumption, this collectivity quickly moved from an informal network to an extensive organizational operation. Some controversial groups subject to widespread prejudice and, at times, political and legal repression can achieve effective organizational advantages through ecological and environmental supports. Further, these types are aided by the appearance of highly skilled and committed leaders and members. The union movements of the early part of this century and the collective resistance of coal miners to federal government pressures during World War II are cases fitting the above environmental and member conditions. The former succeeded by the large numbers of concentrated workers who achieved an ecology of power, especially work stoppage in focused work settings. The latter was able to succeed because of the isolation of the miners throughout Appalachia from the external, national centers of opinion pressures.

In addition, some seemingly hopeless beginnings, such as the early Mormons and the initial actions of Martin Luther and, later, John Wesley, appear to have overcome an initial overt resistance and to reach the large bureaucratic and institutionalized forms they possess today. This is due to the atypical strengths of their leaders and because there was a "covert receptivity" to the issues raised by these early leaders that were misperceived by the existing institutional elites.

For current protest groups, the movement from informal networks of interested members to formal organizational operations enjoys a new and unique component: the existence and potential mainpulations of the mass media. No one who observed the televised depictions of the white citizenry and National Guard in Little Rock, or the uses of water hoses and guard dogs on protesting blacks in Birmingham, Alabama, can fail to note the importance of a mass media for generating favorable public opinion and, subsequently, large organizational operations from which new and different protests emerged.

Several organizational issues exist in the treatment of the social movement organization, including, as noted above, their evolution and their continued operations and subsequent effects. For one, SMOs have been found to be linked with one another. The "Child Savers" of the late nineteenth century, resulting in the first juvenile court in Cook County (Chicago), Illinois, were found to contain large numbers of members who had participated in other movements such as emancipation and suffrage.

An anti-pornography group was noted by Curtis and Zurcher (Article 19) to emanate from a Knights of Columbus chapter and, from there, to gain power and an influential base from linkages with 29 other church, civic, and youth-serving organizations. The new organization gained immediate organizational and leadership resources from these other existing organizations.

Such organizational links are often maintained and even extended through the existence of a large number of persons who have participated in many different organizations. Terminology currently in the literature in reference to these persons include *moral entrepreneurs* and *true believers* depending on the issues and the positions of persons making these designations. In the next section, for example, it is noted by James Max Fendrich and Kenneth L. Lovoy (Article 34) that persons participating in "Mississippi Summer" during the early 1950s were since found to have belonged to many different movement "causes," including environmental issues, minority interests, housing, public policy, and other public controversies.

SMOs typically differ from more institutionalized forms, such as public bureaucracies (e.g., schools) or business organizations, especially in their *initial or formative* stages, by their more amorphous structure, flexibility of purposes, and permeability of boundaries. Related to these organizational properties, Gary T. Marx (Article 20) notes how some controversial civil rights and anti-war organizations of the 1960s were infiltrated by government agents and how these agents provoked the protest groups to engage in illegal and controversial actions that damaged their public, moral reputations. Overall, it has been concluded that the more successful SMOs are those that, in effect, are most like institutionalized types.

A final structural proposition we would offer here is that protest groups that contain highly centralized and bureaucratic operations have been found to be more successful than those not achieving the advantages of this formality of operation. Still, a question remains that has not been sufficiently answered by the current research: Did success lead to greater bureaucratization and centralization or did the latter organizational characteristics lead to the success of the movements?

The beginning article of this section by Russell L. Curtis, Jr. and the late Louis A. Zurcher, Jr. (Article 19) centers on the forms of social movement organizations that are contingent on whether the goals are *expressive* (i.e., member change focused) or *instrumental* (i.e., focused outside of the immediate organizational realm). The nature of recruitment, whether highly selective or open, provides the other important dimension. They combine highly selective (exclusive) or open (inclusive) memberships with the nature of goals to define leadership styles and member compliance patterns. These conclusions were also anticipated in the discussions above.

Gary T. Marx, as noted above, focuses on social control agents and notes that they are not sufficiently represented in most social science studies of collective behavior and social movements (Article 20). His research on agent provocateurs and informants fills an important knowledge gap. Particularly noteworthy is Marx's analysis of role conflict and exposure of FBI and local police agents.

Carol Mueller and Thomas Dimieri (Article 21) address one of the least studied areas in the collective behavior and social movement literature: the existing preference structure or belief systems of populations pertaining to social change. There are very few studies of the structure of belief systems within social movement and countermovement organizations. This article compares the structure of beliefs of activists favoring and opposing the equal rights for women (ERA) referendum in Massachusetts in 1976. The results challenge the assumption that "belief polarization is the psychological counterpart of social (organized) polarization" by showing that the beliefs of activists opposed to ERA are more fragmented than the beliefs of activists favoring the ERA.

In Article 22, Michael Schwartz, Naomi Rosenthal, and Laura Schwartz detail the factors leading to conflict in an important social movement organization—the Southern Farmer's Alliance. Changing fortunes of political economy, personality factors, and shifting ecological and technological arrangements are all noted in detailing the importance of conflict in this SMO.

Leonard Blumberg (Article 23) details the fortunes of a modern self-help organization that has grown from a small group—often designated in its early years as a "cult"—to a large (over two million members) membership now enjoying popular acceptance and amazing, expanded applications to over 50 other "problems." This is the fellowship of Alcoholics Anonymous. Blumberg's conclusions some 15 years ago in 1977 were prophetic. His view then was that this organization, though loosely formed and peer directed, constituted a social movement. AA's growth and influence since 1977 do nothing but underscore Blumberg's conclusions.

An important point of controversy in the literature, addressed by Pamela Oliver (Article 24), is the nature of the motivation of social movement activists. Are paid activists people with a long history of involvement in movements, the most dedicated and committed of movement members, or are they, as the resource mobilization approach suggests, incipient professionals, motivated less by ideology and more by material remuneration? The results of this research show that paid activists are as ideologically committed as volunteers, that their activism is facilitated by the material support they receive, and that they have longer histories of activism.

Related to the work of Oliver, Suzanne Staggenborg (Article 25) analyzes the consequences of leadership professionalization and organizational formalization in social movements. Her findings indicate that professional activists, although increasing the level of formalization of social movement organizations, do not begin new movements or create new tactics; formalization makes organizations mor resilient to adverse environmental conditions; and professionalization and formalization make it easier for organizations to work together.

An important contribution of the reading by David A. Snow, Louis A. Zurcher, Jr., and Sheldon Ekland-Olson (Article 26) is its fourfold typology in which the authors offer a conceptual map of the outreach and recruitment patterns of SMOs. The results demonstrate how methods of recruitment, whether through friends in one organization or through anonymous and public contacts in another, relate with the overall goals and public contacts of two religious groups. Suggested from this research, but not made explicit by the authors of this article, is that membership conformity and compliance, addressed by Curtis and Zurcher (Article 19), is integrally related with member recruitment strategies. Hare Krishna, recruiting publically, engages in intensive postjoining socialization that entails the movement of their members to different geographic locales. The Nicheren Shoshu, recruiting through interpersonal networks (friends and relatives), achieve consensus and compliance through homogeneous recruitment and the prejoining compliance that such outreach can achieve. As such, their members were found to remain in the local area after joining the group.

Next, Russell L. Curtis, Jr. and Louis A. Zurcher, Jr. (Article 27) present research on multiorganizational factors for social movements, here anti-pornography protest groups. The article shows how existing organizations affect the operations of a given SMO. It also shows that how these two anti-pornography organizations were linked with their communities shaped their subsequent goal specifications (i.e., tightly or loosely focused) and leadership styles (i.e., instrumental or expressive).

Related to many of the organizational propositions outlined above, the next selection by J. Craig Jenkins and Charles Perrow (Article 28) identified the environment of SMOs to be extremely important for protest success. As noted above, groups whose cause is intensely unpopular can overcome this opposition through attentions and/or support from outside groups. The findings of Jenkins and Perrow link the success of the United Farm Labor Union from 1965 to 1972 to outside support from the federal government, organized labor, and liberal organizations. Still unclear is the extent to which the findings are generalizable to other countries, time periods, or social movements.

ARTICLE 19

Social Movements: An Analytical Exploration of Organizational Forms

RUSSELL L. CURTIS, JR.
LOUIS A. ZURCHER, JR.

Social movements are consciously and purposively structured types of collective behavior which manifest norm or value-oriented strategies for action (Zald and Ash, 1966). They contrast generally with other collective behavior forms, such as crowds or crazes, which may either represent incipient stages of ongoing movements or truncated, sporadic forms which never achieve any formal level of organization (Smelser, 1962; Turner and Killian, 1957).

Most studies of social movements have been descriptive, and conceptually have concentrated upon such factors as ideological base, social-psychological characteristics of the members, or the general context of societal change. Relatively few analyses of social movements as complex organizations have been reported (Zald and Ash, 1966; Gordon and Babchuk, 1959; Messinger, 1955; Gusfield, 1957). Yet whatever else a social movement may be, it is a complex organization. McLaughlin (1969:4) noted that a social movement "includes among its salient characteristics a shared value system, a sense of community, norms for action, and an organizational structure." Similarly, Killian (1964:439–40) observed that social movements embody a structure of roles, positions and norms among the participants. He further argued that "it is as a structure develops, with leaders and their followers being identified as peculiarly and intensively concerned with the promotion of certain values, that the members of a society recognize that a social movement has arisen." This analysis will focus upon the *organizational* characteristics of social movements. Selected variables from the relevant literature will be integrated into a paradigm, and the potential of that paradigm illustrated with data and observations from studies of social movements.

THE PARADIGM

The review of the literature isolated what appeared to be two key variables among the characteristics of social movement organizations: the kinds of organizational goals and the conditions of membership.

Social movement organizations pursue ends—goals in fact are their *raison d'etre*. The goals can be classified according to whether they are *inward*, as in the case of member benefits or the cultivation of member satisfactions, or *outward*, as in the case of the existence of aims which are independent of the immediate organizational operations (Lang and Lang, 1961:488; Zald and Ash, 1966:331). This distinction is best shown by Gordon and Babchuk's (195) differentiation between organizations which are primarily "expressive" and those which are primarily "instrumental." The expressive organization manifests a goal-orientation towards satisfying the social and psychological needs of its members through acts of participation. The instrumental organization manifests a goal-orientation of accomplishing some specific task external to the organization.

The second key variable, the conditions of membership, refers to the accessibility of the organization to potential recruits and to the subsequent demands made upon them as members. Two types, previously elaborated by Zald and Ash (1966), are identified: "inclusive" organizations and "exclusive" organizations. The original use of the concepts tended to focus upon obligations of members after joining, with less attention to the specifics of recruitment procedures. We assume that the screening activities employed by an organization reflect the available reward sources which subsequently will be manifested in membership compliance procedure.

The "inclusive" type of social movement organization does not have rigorous screening mechanisms for membership selection; affiliation is largely determined by the volition of the potential members. For the new members there are "minimum levels of initial commitment—a pledge of general support without specific duties, a short indoctrination period or none at all" (Zald and Ash, 1966:331). On the other hand, the "exclusive" organization rigorously controls the affiliation process, defines affiliation as predominantly the prerogative of the organization rather than the potential member, and tends "to hold the new recruit to a long novitiate, to require the recruit to subject himself to the organization discipline and orders, and to draw from those having the heaviest initial commitment."

It is possible for a social movement organization to have a mixture of expressive and instrumental goal orientations, and/or a mixture of exclusive and inclusive membership requirements. The "mixed" organizational types do not denote medians or midpoints on the dimensions, but recognize the presence of both components within the same organization. The presence of a mixture of the components does not necessarily suggest internal conflict or schism, although it may reveal the potential for either. The component mixture probably reveals a sharing of diverse goals or satisfactions among the membership or, more likely (as suggested by Zald and Ash, 1966:332), indicates a difference in orientation between the leadership cadre and the followers.

As shown in Figure 1, a paradigm can be constructed from the three types of goals orientations (expressive, instrumental, and mixed expressive and instrumental) and the three types of membership requirements (exclusive, inclusive, and mixed exclusive and inclusive). The paradigm thus contains nine cells, each of which represents a further mix, in a given social movement organization, of goal orientations and membership requirements.

Within each of the nine cells four other related variables, drawn from the relevant literature, are distributed: the nature of membership incentives (solidary or purposive); the degree of environmental contact (highly specified, moderately specified, or broad); the leadership styles (persuading or directing); and the kinds of membership (homogeneous or heterogeneous).

The incentives for participation in social movement organizations can be divided, following Clark and Wilson (1961), into "solidary" and "purposive" types. Solidary incentives derive "in the main from the act of associating, and (include) such rewards as socializing, congeniality, the sense of group membership and identification, the status resulting from membership, fun and conviviality, the maintenance of social distinctions, and so on. Their common characteristic is that they intend to be independent of the precise ends of the association" (1961:134–135). Purposive incentives, on the other hand, "are intangible, but they derive in the main from the

		Goal Orientations		
		EXPRESSIVE (AND DIFFUSE)	**MIXED EXPRESSIVE AND INSTRUMENTAL**	**INSTRUMENTAL (AND SPECIFIC)**
Conditions of Membership	**EXCLUSIVE**	Solidary Incentives Highly Specified Contact with Environment Directing Leadership Style Homogeneous Membership	Solidary and Purposive Incentives Highly Specified Contact with Environment Directing Leadership Style Homogeneous Membership	Purposive Incentives Highly Specified Contact with Environment Directing Leadership Style Homogeneous Membership
	MIXED EXCLUSIVE AND INCLUSIVE	Solidary Incentives Moderately Specified Contact with Environment Directing and Persuading Leadership Style Moderately Homogeneous Membership	Solidary and Purposive Incentives Moderately Specified Contact with Environment Mixed Directing and Persuading Leadership Style Heterogeneous Membership	Purposive Incentives Moderately Specified Contact with Environment Mixed Leadership Style Heterogeneous Membership
	INCLUSIVE	Solidary Incentives Broad Contact with Environment Persuading Leadership Style Moderately Heterogeneous Membership	Solidary and Purposive Incentives Broad Contact with Environment Persuading Leadership Style Heterogeneous Membership	Purposive Incentives Broad Contact with Environment Persuading Leadership Style Heterogeneous Membership

FIGURE 1 Goals, Membership Requirements, and Related Structural Characteristics of Social Movement Organizations

stated ends of the association rather than from the simple act of associating. These inducements are to be found in the suprapersonal goals of the organization" (1961:142–146).

Social movements vary in the degree to which they interact with other components of their social environment. Some social movements by choice essentially are isolated within their communities of operation; others are broadly integrated with mutual overlapping memberships, and interlocking leadership structures.

The exclusive organization will achieve homogeneity of membership through the relative severity of its selection processes and membership obligations (cf., Zurcher and Curtis, 1973). The social movement characterized by expressive goals would manifest homogeneity in membership, since agreement in specific perspectives or orientations would be required under conditions of sharing solidary incentives.

The organizational conditions of exclusiveness and homogeneous membership can be seen to be associated with a direct leadership style. On the other hand, inclusiveness and a heterogeneous membership is less well served or influenced by arbitrariness in leaders, and can be seen to be associated with a persuading leadership style.

SOME THEORETICAL AND EMPIRICAL FEATURES OF THE PARADIGM

Any cross-classificatory model should contribute more to sociological analysis than the addition of an ordering scheme. Students of this mode of analysis have suggested that such paradigms should yield a synthesis of a wide array of components, a balance between observed and abstracted combinations, and a seminal construct for the derivation of hypotheses (cf., McKinney, 1969; and Lopreato and Alston, 1970).

One important characteristic of the paradigm presented in this analysis is that it recognizes the critical importance of goals in the development and implementation of social movement organizations. For the members of most social movements, the stated organizational ends must in themselves be invoked as a sufficient rationale for affiliation and participation.

The paradigm also identifies the important relationship which exists among the goals, environments, and internal structures of complex organizations in general (cf., Simpson and Gulley, 1962; and Blau, 1956). Gusfield (1955; 1957) reported changes in WCTU leadership styles following the repeal of the eighteenth amendment. Internal organizational changes have been associated with "succession crises" (Gouldner, 1954), the erosion of an ideological stance (Bittner, 1963), and the changing power of the organization within its community of response (Talmon, 1965). The paradigm orders a variety of structural permutations which emanate from either a change in the internal or the external components, followed by a realignment of other components. The instrumental-expressive dimension identifies salient aspects of the goal and environmental structure; the exclusive-inclusive dimension describes the critical differences in the internal organizational systems.

Membership compliance patterns are conceptually and operationally crucial in any organization. Etzioni (1965:654) observed that a "central finding of the comparative analysis of organizations is that organizations which differ in the kinds of power they apply, and in the alienation or commitment they generate, differ also, in many significant ways, in other aspects of the organizational structure." This would seem to be particularly true of social movement organizations. Such organizations are concerned with changes, or resistance to changes, in the social order. Consequently, their actions create potential conditions for counterreactions from the community of concern. Many intense stresses are placed upon the relational patterns within a social movement organization, both horizontally and vertically, and often membership incentives are difficult to maintain.

The paradigm accounts for the importance of compliance patterns in social movement organizations. The inclusive-exclusive dimension identified the intensity of membership compliance mechanisms; the expressive-instrumental distinction identifies the major operational forms of those mechanisms. In the case of expressive social movement organizations, the compliance mechanisms are solidary—they serve maintenance functions. In the case of instrumental organizations, the mechanisms are purposive—they direct goal achievement activity.

The functional interdependence of goals, environments, and internal structures in the paradigm affords the opportunity generally to divide social movement organizations into *congruent* and *non-congruent* types. The congruent combination of social movement organizations include: those with expressive goal orientations and exclusive membership conditions, and those with instrumental goal orientations and inclusive membership conditions. "Congruent" is used here as a hypothetical construct which identifies a structural correspondence among organizational components. The points of structural correspondence are inferred, in similar fashion to Etzioni's (1961) well-known application of the concept, from theoretically postulated interdependent characteristics as well as from empirically observed combinations of organizational types.

Consideration of the characteristics of congruent social movement organizations stimulates the derivation of postulates concerning the interaction among organizational components. For example, on the organizational level of analysis, one initially can postulate broadly that: conditions of membership and goal orientations influence and are influenced by variations in types of incentives, extent of contact with the environment, leadership style, and the degree of membership homogeneity.

The paradigm also can stimulate postulates more focused on the individual rather than the organizational level of abstraction. We offer two again quite general postulates, influenced by an exchange perspective (Thibaut and Kelley, 1959; Blau, 1964; Emerson, 1962). Weiss (1963) used a similar framework in his stimulus-response explanation of recruitment to and defection from social movement organizations. In the exclusive-expressive (congruent) type of social movement organization: the greater the demand which the organization stipulates and obtains from the membership, the more the organization must provide sources of rewards for such commitments, and the more the organization must compete favorably in the field of members' reward alternatives. Rewards which the organization can provide the individual include, among others: the pleasure of interaction with persons of similar orientation; status enhancement; support for life style; protection from the environment; and ameliorative mechanisms for stresses, tensions, and conditions of alienation (Bittner, 1963; Zald and Ash, 1966; Lofland and Stark, 1965; Simmons, 1964; Zurcher et al., 1971). The exclusive-expressive organization would demand intensive commitment from its members, and foster goals or purposes which identify the members (rather than extra-organizational targets) as the beneficiaries of organizational activity.

The second postulate on the individual level states that in the inclusive-instrumental (congruent) type of social movement organization: the more that members achieve rewards from their goal attainment activity, the less that organization will maintain conditions which contribute to the experiential rewards of the members from interpersonal relationships. In this case, the goals themselves establish a rationale for the members' presence and commitment. Most certainly there are some formal prescriptions for appropriate member behavior and interaction, but life style expectations are less structured than in the exclusive-expressive types of organizations. The goals of inclusive-instrumental organizations place them in direct contact and often direct conflict with other elements of their community of concern. The stresses of membership, as a result of interaction with "targets," may be high, and the exchange position of the organization consequently tenuous. The organization would be able to make fewer demands upon its membership beyond their commitment to activities which would achieve the organizational goal. Furthermore, the organization would not want to emphasize a "social" orientation among its members if that process were to interfere with the predominant task orientation.

The exchange rationale of the paradigm at the individual level can be elaborated by referring to the concept "reward alternatives." Because the memberships of exclusive-expressive organizations are the beneficiaries of the organization's purposes on the one hand and the objects of heavy organizational demands on the other, competitive options are seen as existing in the community of concern rather than in other organizations with parallel purposes. This obtains because the exclusive-expressive organization meets competition for reward alternatives by insulating its membership from the broader environments. Toch (1965:206–207) observed that organizations which provide the individual with a personal status, or with a unique ideological perspective, must necessarily impede the opportunities for achieving those benefits from other sources. The existence of social isolation or insulation mechanisms has also been observed for a small Southeastern sect (Simmons, 1964), Puritans (Rossel, 1970), a small California sect (Lofland and Stark, 1965), Jehovah's Witnesses (Zygmunt, 1970), Japanese "little utopias" (Plath, 1968), Amish (Wilson, 1970), and Doukeboor (Toch, 1965), among many others. In short, such social buffering mechanisms generally prevent participants from experiencing the accomplishments of other social movement organizations. Conventional society, or the systematic rejection of components of it, becomes the most viable source of rewards. The pre-organizational catalytic elements representing a large variety of personal dissatisfactions with the social order are, in turn, reinforced within the organizational setting. The original attraction to a peripheral position in the conventional order is extended by the social movement organization. Techniques which have been employed for these purposes include "the discreditation of other groups, the debunking of secular authority, the elevation of internal group roles to a position of dominance in the life organization of the members" (Zygmunt, 1970:942–943), and the monopolizing of member interests, the conventionalization of their lives, and the defining of all aspects of their roles within the movements (Bittner, 1963). Such control, resulting in commitment, serves to decrease the attractiveness which alternative social systems might hold for members.

The stand of the inclusive-instrumental organization, on the other hand, is one of changing components of the conventional social order. Thus only selected aspects of that order would be favored as sources of reward alternatives. If not, then other associations or movements with similar orientations would constitute viable options. The members' exchange position is enhanced if there are conditions of significant interorganizational competition. The changing orientations of the several civil rights organizations during the 1960's, for example, was in part due to the competition for members. During periods of intense activity or interorganizational competition, the number of recruits constitutes an index of the degree of activity, a symbol of success of movement operations, and a protective support in the face of a hostile environment. Under those conditions, the needs of the organization require the creation of an attractive recruitment position—a position which is nearly impossible if heavy demands and role restrictions are placed upon the members.

Some empirical evidence is available which supports the rationale both for the paradigm and for the identification of the two congruent social movement organization types (exclusive-expressive and inclusive-instrumental). In a study of Mexican-American voluntary associations which had resulted from social movements, Lane (1968) found that instrumental organizations were much more inclusive than were expressive organizations. That is, they were less likely to "screen" their member candidates, were larger in size, were less likely to charge dues, had less well attended meetings, and had members who were less dependent upon the organization as a source of rewards. Lane's sample of organizations is especially useful for our purposes, since their activities generally represented an indication of dissatisfaction with the members' ethnic status or of a desire to interact under relatively insulated conditions with other persons from the same ethnic group. Examples of some of the associations were The Federation for the Advancement of Mexican-Americans, The Political Association of Spanish-Speaking Organizations, The League of United Latin American Citizens, and Involvement of Mexican-Americans in Gainful Endeavor. Lane's results were consistent with the paradigm and with the theoretical identification of the two congruent types of social movement organizations.

SOME FURTHER DISCUSSION AND ILLUSTRATIONS OF THE PARADIGM

The Congruent Types

The inclusive-instrumental social movement organization faces the critical problems of maintaining purposive integration with a heterogeneous membership, and surviving in the face of either goal attainment or failure to reach goal attainment. The internal structure of the inclusive-instrumental organization is integrally related with the goal attainment process. Success, or the accomplishment of specific goals, can leave the organization without a purpose, and can influence its disbanding or goal transformation (Zald and Ash, 1966; Zurcher et al., 1971; Roche and Sachs, 1965; Zurcher and Curtis, 1973). Sustained failure to reach goal objectives yields similar strain, encouraging the organization to: modify its goals; expend more energy in organizational maintenance activity; intensify the original goal attainment process; withdraw from the environment (either organizationally or personally on the part of various members); or cease activities.

The Townsend Movement, for example, failed to achieve its program for the elderly, and subsequently increased its activities to maintain the organization *per se* (Messinger, 1955). The WCTU, confronted with the appeal of Prohibition, evolved from a predominantly upper middle class membership to a lower class membership, and shifted its orientation to greater expression of moral indignation (Gusfield, 1955; 1957). The National Infantile Paralysis Campaign (Sills, 1961) though not a social movement as such at the time of its shift in goals, sought new purposes after the introduction of the Salk Vaccine. Political parties, though crystalized forms of the original social movements, have been shown to modify their internal organization following changes in their community of concern (Heberle, 1951).

Critical problems for the exclusive-expressive social movement organization are the maintenance of doctrinal purity and member compliance mechanisms. Generally those problems are solved by organizational isolation from the larger society (Simmons, 1964). Bittner (1963), however, concluded that doctrinal purity would eventually erode in a social movement organization. Most of the evidence from such studies, at least when applied to the exclusive-expressive types as defined here, suggest that the integrity of the organizational boundaries, rather than internal changes *per se,* is the critical element for organizational survival. Puritans (Rossel, 1970), for example, as a result of organizational boundary challenges presented by the frontier, were unable to sustain both their strictures on members' behaviors and their doctrinal purity.

Some exclusive-expressive organizations have been able to maintain the integrity of their boundaries for a long period of time. Zygmunt commented on the organizational longevity of Jehovah's Witnesses:

> *The major key to the group's success in keeping its millennial hopes alive and in resisting secularization has been its development of an essentially self-confirming and socially isolating symbolic-interactional system which has sustained its basic convictions and reduced its stakes in the present*

> *world. . . . Empirical events were perceived as occurring within this broader nonempirical context and an understanding of their 'true' significance required viewing them within the frame of reference supplied by the group's symbolic system. (1970:941–942)*

The reactions of the community of concern toward congruent social movement organizations can have a significant impact upon internal organizational components. A hostile environment (criticisms, counter-movement organizational operations, etc.) can serve to increase the insulation of both the exclusive-expressive and inclusive-instrumental organizations. The hostility enhances the existing insulating and solidarity mechanisms of the exclusive-expressive type, and influences the inclusive-instrumental type to shift its instrumental orientation toward the expressive and exclusive dimensions. On the other hand, a reinforcing environment (favorable publicity, increased access to resources, overt citizen support, etc.) will increase the instrumental orientations of the inclusive-instrumental type and will influence the exclusive-expressive type to relax its insulating mechanisms. The tendency for both types of social movement organizations in conditions of reinforcing environment is toward the instrumental and inclusive dimensions.

Non-Congruent Types

The exclusive-instrumental organization is oriented towards specific tasks concerning changes in its community of concern, but nonetheless must maintain a relatively extensive set of prescriptions for member participatory behavior. Several civil rights organizations, especially during the 1950's and early 1960's, are examples of this type. Their goals were instrumental, but the strategy of nonviolence which they espoused demanded a disciplined membership (Vander Zanden, 1963). The combination of instrumental goal orientation with a highly disciplined membership tends to emerge in situations where goal achievements demand a highly strictured interaction with the environment. The stresses upon the members, however, are severe. Coles (1964) has reported the great personal costs of being a civil rights activist, including experiences of guilt feelings and states of depression. To a large extent, the personal demands must be equated with the movement purposes in order to justify or explain the stresses. Vander Zanden (1963) has described the justifications and rationalizations of such suffering by civil rights activists.

Because of the costs of participation in an inclusive-instrumental organization, it is suggested that goal failures would turn such movements inward (an increased expressive orientation), and that success would loosen organizational control over member behavior. That process is at least suggested by the trend of some civil rights organizations, in the 1960's, toward radicalism and/or violence.

The inclusive-expressive social movement organization appears on the surface to be a contradiction. On the one hand, there would be little member discipline; on the other hand, members are the beneficiaries of organizational activities. Historical examples of the inclusive-expressive type would be peyote cults, the cargo cult, and other varieties of millenary movements (Cohn, 1961; Lanternari, 1963; Talmon, 1962; and Wilson, 1970). Such movements are built upon the frustrations and anguish of groups with relatively little power and property, and such factors constitute the sources for inclusive-expressive organizations. The usual interpretations of the development of such movements are based upon psycho-personality factors, which contribute to individual anxieties (Lang and Lang, 1961; Toch, 1965; Catton, 1957). More current examples of this type of social movement organization might be the religious campaigns of Billy Graham, Oral Roberts, etc. While member expectations are continually espoused, there appear to be few efforts to effect a closely disciplined membership.

To maintain the inclusive-expressive organization, conditions which originally fostered the organization would have to persist. When situational definitions are equivocal, the identification of targets and conditions becomes a very important leadership function. Finally, the fact that many of these types of movement organizations are built upon dissatisfactions with the prevailing power order incorporates sources of divisiveness and friction, which ultimately can destroy the organizational forms (Zald and Ash, 1966; Talmon, 1962).

The Non-Congruent Types: Mixed Components

The appearance of inclusive and exclusive orientations and/or expressive and instrumental orientations in the same social movement organization suggests the possibility of schisms; central functions often appear to be fragile. It is possible, as pointed out earlier, that such differences reflect diversities in the orientations of the leadership cadre and the followers. It is also possible that congruent types of social movement organizations (inclusive-instrumental; exclusive-expressive) have secondary dimensions which align themselves along incongruent dimensions. The Black Muslims have combined an exclusive-expressive pattern with instrumental orientations (Lincoln, 1961; Beynon, 1938; Laue, 1964). Their instrumental tendencies, it can be argued, are of less significance than the exclusive-expressive nexus. To the extent that goals outside of the organization (creation of private schools, loan operations, housing, etc.) become ascendant, the organization would probably lose some of its expressive and, perhaps, exclusive components. In this instance, Malcolm X's toleration of other Black groups (SCLC, CORE, NAACP, etc.) can be seen as an example of a decrease in the insular, expressive posture of the Muslims (as suggested in comparisons of church and sect).

The combination of the instrumental-expressive pattern with an inclusive orientation obtains for movements which are more "respectable" than those with expressive and exclusive orientations. Their inclusiveness manifests an existing base of support of sentiments in the community, which draws recruits to the fold. An organization which provides a fair approximation of those characteristics would be the Salvation Army (Wilson, 1970). When such organizations experience minimal success, they tend to shift the balance of their orientations toward the expressive dimensions; clear success influences the crystalization of the organization, and a deemphasis of its expressive functions.

Those types of social movement organizations which contain mixed components can also be highly complex collectivities whose operations contain many diverse elements, nearly paralleling the patterns of established bureaucracy. The Sierra Club, for example, is a national complex organizational form which contains many independent chapters. Some of those chapters are primarily oriented toward and implement an aggressive, instrumental posture; others are primarily oriented toward expressiveness and member satisfaction through experiences in nature.

CONCLUSIONS AND IMPLICATIONS

Knowledge concerning the organizational characteristics is important both for theoretical and implied reasons. Social movement organizations and the behavioral and structural phenomena associated with them are at the vortex of social change. Studies of the structure, function, and dynamics of such organizations can contribute to the development of more productive theory explaining the pressures for, implementation of and resistances to social changes. Pertinent to the applications of such studies, Zald (1969) has noted that as society grows more complex and, relatedly, develops a highly educated and specialized citizenry, the development of ameliorative organizations in reaction to designated problems will rapidly increase. Many of those organizations will be at the center of social movements. Moore (1966) had suggested that utopian social forms, and an understanding of them, have utility for society.

REFERENCES

Beynon, Erdmann Doane. 1938. "The Voodoo cult among Negro migrants in Detroit." American Sociological Review 43(May): 894–907.

Bittner, Egon. 1963. "Radicalism and the organization of radical movement." American Sociological Review 28(December): 928–940.

Blau, Peter M. 1955. The Dynamics of Bureaucracy. Chicago: University of Chicago Press.

Blau, Peter M. 1964. Exchange and Power in Social Life. New York: John Wiley and Sons.

Blumer, Herbert. 1955. "Social movements." Pp. 99–220 in A. M. Lee (ed.), Principles of Sociology. New York: Barnes and Noble.

Cantril, Hadley. 1969. "The kingdom of Father Divine." Pp. 223–242 in Barry McLaughlin (ed.), Studies in Social Movements. New York: Free Press.

Catton, William R., Jr. 1957. "What kind of people does a religious cult attract?" American Sociological Review 22(October): 561–566.

Clark, Peter B., and James Q. Wilson. 1961. "Incentive systems: a theory of organizations." Administrative science Quarterly 6(September): 129–166.

Cohn, Norman. 1961. The Pursuit of the Millennium. New York: Harper and Row.

Coles, Robert. 1964. "social struggle and weariness." Psychiatry 27(November): 305–315.

Curtis, Russell L., Jr., and Louis A. Zurcher, Jr. 1971. "Voluntary associations and the social integration of the poor." Social Problems 18(winter): 339–357.

Davies, James. 1962. "Toward a theory of revolution." American Sociological Review 27(February): 5–19.

Emerson, R. E. 1962. "Power-dependence relations." American Sociological Review 27(February): 31–41.

Etzioni, Amatai. 1961. A Comparative Analysis of Complex Organizations. New York: Free Press.

Etzioni, Amatai. 1965. "Organizational control structure." Pp. 650–677 in James G. March (ed.), Handbook of Organizations. Chicago: Rand-McNally.

Festinger, Leon, H. W. Riecken, and Stanley Schachter. 1956. When Prophecy Fails. Minneapolis: University of Minnesota Press.

Friedland, William H. 1964. "For a sociological concept of charisma." Social Forces 43(October): 18–26.

Gerrard, Nathan L. 1968. "The Serpent-Handlers of West Virginia." Transaction 5(May): 22–28.

Gerth, Hans. 1940. "The Nazi party: its leadership and composition." American Journal of Sociology 45(January): 517–541.

Gordon, C. Wayne, and Nicholas Babchuk. 1959. "A typology of voluntary organizations." American Sociological Review 24(February): 22–29.

Gusfield, Joseph R. 1955. "Social structure and moral reform: a study of the Woman's Christian Temperance Union." American Journal of Sociology 61(November): 221–228.

Gusfield, Joseph R. 1957. "The problem of generations in an organizational structure." American Journal of Sociology 35(May): 323–330.

Heberle, Rudolf. 1951. Social Movements. New York: Appleton-Century-Crofts.

Jacoby, Arthur P. 1965. "Some correlates of instrumental and expressive orientations to associational membership." Sociological Inquiry 35(spring): 163–175.

Jacoby, Arthur P. 1966. "Personal influence and primary relationships: their effect on associational membership." Sociological Quarterly 7(winter): 76–84.

Killian, Lewis M. 1964. "Social movements." Pp. 426–455 in Robert E. L. Faris (ed.), Handbook of Modern Sociology. Chicago: Rand-McNally.

Lane, John. 1968. "Voluntary Associations Among Mexican Americans in San Antonio, Texas: Organizational and Leadership Characteristics." Austin, Texas: University of Texas. Unpublished Dissertation.

Lanternari, Vittorio. 1963. The Religions of the Oppressed. New York: Alfred E. Knopf.

Laue, James H. 1964. "A contemporary revitalization movement in American race relations: the 'Black Muslims.' " Social Forces 42(March): 315–323.

Lincoln, C. Eric. 1961. The Black Muslims in America. Boston: Beacon Press.

Lofland, John, and Rodney Stark. 1965. "Becoming a world-saver: a theory of conversion to a deviant perspective." American Sociological Review 30(December): 1965.

Lopreato, Joseph, and Letitia Alston. 1970. "Ideal types and the idealization strategy." American Sociological Review 35(February): 88–96.

McKinney, John C. 1969. "Typification, typologies and sociological theory." Social Forces 48(September): 1–12.

Messinger, Sheldon L. 1955. "Organizational transformation: a case study of a declining social movement." American Sociological Review 20(February): 3–10.

Moore, W. E. 1966. "The utility of utopias." American Sociological Review 31(December): 765–772.

Plath, David W. 1970. "Modernization and its discontents: Japan's little utopias." Pp. 90–107 in Joseph R. Gusfield (ed.), Protest, Reform and Revolt. New York: John Wiley and Sons, Inc.

Roche, John P., and Stephen Sachs. 1965. The bureaucrat and the enthusiast: an exploration of the leadership of social movements.;; Western Political Quarterly 8(June): 248–261.

Rossel, Robert D. 1970. "The great awakening: an historical analysis." American Journal of Sociology 75(May): 907–925.

Sills, David L. 1961. "The volunteers." Pp. 146–159 in Amatai Etzioni (ed.), Complex Organizations. New York: Holt, Rinehart and Company.

Simmons, J. L. 1964. "On maintaining deviant belief systems: a case study." Social Problems 11(winter) 250–256.

Simpson, Richard L., and William H. Gulley. 1962. "Goals, environmental pressures, and organizational characteristics." American Sociological Review 27(June): 344–351.

Smelser, N.J. 1962. Theory of Collective Behavior. New York: Free Press.

Talmon, Yonina. 1962. "Pursuit of the millennium: the relation between religious and social change." European Journal of Sociology 3(No. 1) 125–148.

Thibaut, John W., and Harold K. Kelley. 1959. The Social Psychology of Groups. New York: John Wiley and Sons.

Toch, Hans. 1965. The Social Psychology of Social Movements. Indianapolis: Bobbs-Merrill.

Turner, Ralph H. 1964. Collective behavior. Pp. 382–425 in R. E. L. Faris (ed.), Handbook of Modern Sociology, Chicago: Rand-McNally.

Vander Zanden, James W. 1959. "Resistance and social movements." Social Forces 37(May): 312–318.

Vander Zanden, James W. 1963. "The non-violent resistance movement against segregation." American Journal of Sociology 68(March): 544–550.

Wallace, Anthony F. C. 1956. "Revitalization movement." American Anthropologist 58(April): 264–281.

Weiss, Robert Frank. 1963. "Defection from social movements and subsequent recruitment to new movements." Sociometry 26(March): 1–20.

Wilson, Bryan. 1970. Religious Sects. Italy: Librex. (Commissioned by World University Library, London).

Zald, M. N., and Roberta Ash. 1966. "Social movement organizations: growth, decay and change." Social Forces 44(March): 327–341.

Zald, Mayer N. 1969. "The structure of society and social service integration." Social Science Quarterly 50(December): 557–567.

Zurcher, Louis A., and Russell Curtis, Jr. 1973. "A comparative analysis of propositions describing social movement organizations." Sociological Quarterly 14(spring): 175–188.

Zurcher, Louis A., R. George Kirkpatrick, Robert G. Cushing, and Charles K. Bowman. 1971. "The anti-pornography campaign: a symbolic crusade." Social Problems 19(fall): 217–238.

Zygmunt, Joseph F. 1970. "Prophetic failure and chiliastic identify: the case of Jehovah's Witnesses." American Journal of Sociology 75(May): 926–948.

ARTICLE 20

Thoughts on a Neglected Category of Social Movement Participant: The Agent Provocateur and the Informant

GARY T. MARX

This article considers the hitherto unexplored phenomenon of the informant as used by authorities in their response to social movements. The origins and motives of informants, their roles in radical groups, and factors conducive to their becoming agents provocateurs are explored. Suggestions for further research and conclusions about the effects of using informants are offered.

> *We shall provoke you to acts of terror and then crush you. [C. B. ZUBATOV, TSARIST POLICE DIRECTOR]*

> *There's a thousand guys in the field like me. [TOMMY THE TRAVELER]*

> *From the dawn of our history, internal law and order has had to depend in greater or less measure on the informer. [Police Manual] . . .*

SOME CATEGORIES FOR ANALYSIS

In theory, a distinction can be made between the informant who merely plays an information-gathering role and the agent provocateur who more assertively seeks to influence the actions taken by the group. Empirically applying this distinction is more difficult. There are pressures inherent in the role that push the informant toward provocation. The most passive informant, of course, has some influence on the setting by his mere presence. His presence can make a movement seem stronger than it actually is. If nothing else, he may provoke the kind of information he is looking for. He may pass on to authorities false, exaggerated, or misinterpreted information. This may move through several police agencies and bureaucratic levels, and can lead to police actions with self-fulfilling effects. Even an informer who does not concoct information may "provoke" violence if his identity becomes known to the infiltrated group. They may attack him, and this may lead to counterattacks from authorities. Some examples of this phenomenon are the Black Panthers in Baltimore, New Haven, and New Orleans and the Weathermen in Chicago.

The consequences of agent-provocateur actions are more obvious. The agent may go along with the illegal actions of the group, he may actually provoke such actions, or he may set up a situation in which the group appears to

Marx, Gary T. (1974, March). Thoughts on a neglected category of social movement participant: The agent provocateur and the informant. *American Journal of Sociology, 80,* 402–442. Reprinted with permission of The University of Chicago Press.

have taken or to be about to take illegal actions. This may be done to gain evidence for use in a trial, to encourage paranoia and internal dissension, and/or to damage the public image of a group.

An agent may work for the police, for an interest group, a foreign government, or for a rival social movement. Among important differentiating factors are whether the agent is a sworn police official or a civilian; whether the agent was planted in the group or was already a member when his or her activities stated; and whether motives stem primarily from ideology, police pressure, material gains, or personal ends. Before analyzing the phenomenon, let us review some recent examples.

- The FBI in Meridian, Mississippi, was reportedly involved in the payment of $36,500 to two members of the White Knights of the Ku Klux Klan (KKK) to arrange for two other Klansmen to mob a Jewish businessman's home. A trap was set in which one Klansman was killed and another arrested in the unsuccessful attempt (*Los Angeles Times*, February 13, 1970).
- A student, paid by a congressional investigating committee to provide information on student radicals, has revealed how he started a Students for Democratic Society (SDS) chapter at his local college in order to keep tabs on the left and "prevent" a student takeover of buildings (Meinhausen 1969).
- The University of Chicago chapter of the Dubois Club collapsed when its chairman, Gerald Kirk—an SDS activist, sociology major, and FBI informant—withdrew from it. Kirk told a congressional investigating committee that the group collapsed because he did not work hard enough on it (*Investigation of S.D.S.* 1969).
- In demonstrations at the University of Alabama, a police agent reportedly urged violence, set fire to at least one campus building, and threw fire bombs and other objects at police. His actions were used to declare unlawful assemblies in which approximately 150 people were arrested (*Los Angeles Times*, September 11, 1970).
- An SDS chairman described as "the best liked and most trusted person in the movement in South Carolina" was a state police agent who helped indict a number of his co-workers (Herbert 1971).
- A deputy sheriff, enrolled as a student at SUNY at Buffalo, posed as a campus radical for 8 months, and testified to a Senate subcommittee that he helped students build explosive devices and test them in deserted wooded areas (*Washington Post*, October 9, 1970).
- A "radical student" arrested by Kent police for illegal possession of a Chinese-made AK-47 rifle and rocket launcher turned out to be a Kent State University campus security guard (*Cleveland Plain Dealer* 1972).
- "Tommy the Traveler," posing as an SDS organizer, offered bombs, guns, and lessons in guerilla tactics to students on various New York campuses. Two students whom he had taught to make Molotov cocktails burned down the campus ROTC building and were immediately arrested (*New York Times*, June 7 and 19, 1970; Rosenbaum 1971).
- A police agent at Northeastern Illinois State College led an SDS sit-in and was expelled for two semesters for throwing the school's president off the stage. He was the only SDS Weatherman representative on his campus and actively recruited students to join his faction and to participate in the 1969 Chicago "Days of Rage." During the Chicago conspiracy trial, where he was a prosecution witness, he acknowledged proposing schemes for sabotaging public facilities and military vehicles (Donner 1971).
- A well-known Cambridge community activist and tenant organizer active in many leftist organizations, including the local SDS executive committee, who had been described as SDS's major link with "the area outside Harvard Yard," was a paid FBI informant for three years (*Boston Globe*, April 12, 1973).
- George Demerle, an ex-Birch Society member known in New York radical circles as "prince crazy," was an FBI informant. He admitted that he helped assemble bombs and was with Sam

Melville when they placed a duffle bag full of time bombs on an army truck. Demerle and three others were arrested on bomb conspiracy charges. Charges against Demerle were quietly dropped. He had also been active in the Progressive Labor party, the Revolutionary Contingent, the U.S. Committee to Aid the National Liberation Front of South Vietnam, the Yippies, the Crazies, and the New York Young Patriots (*New York Post*, May 23, 1970).

- An acting regional coordinator of the Vietnam Veterans against the War (VVAW) who advocated the need for "shooting and bombing"—and whose actions appear to have led to a bombing, a threat of bombing, an illegal demonstration at an air force base, and subsequent arrests—was an FBI informant for 9 months. His testimony resulted in indictment of VVAW leaders on conspiracy charges for plans to disrupt the Republican National Convention (Donner 1972).

- The informant who testified in the Father Berrigan case helped carry messages to those outside the prison. He claimed a knowledge of explosives and helped arrange meetings that led to an indictment charging the participants with conspiratorial activities (*New York Times*, February 7, 1971).

- Robert Hardy, an FBI informant, provided leadership, plans, diagrams, instructions, supplies, and transported people and equipment to the scene in the Camden draft board raid (*New York Times*, March 16, 1972).

- A Mexican-American leader helped organize the Brown Berets, while working as an informer for the Treasury Department in Texas and California. His actions permitted police to raid the Chicano Moratorium Committee and arrest some of its members (*Los Angeles Free Press*, February 4, 1972).

- After planting a bomb at a real estate office thought by many to be responsible for local housing segregation, Larry Ward, a young Seattle black described as "apolitical," was killed by waiting police. He reportedly had been paid $75 to place the bomb and was driven to the scene by an FBI informant. The latter, a convicted robber, had reportedly been released from prison after offering to help police solve a wave of bombings. He had at first tried to recruit an ex-Panther to place the bomb. He recalls "the police wanted a bomber and I got one for them. I didn't know Larry would be killed" (Waltz 1971).

- Three of the four members of a New York group called the Black Liberation Front were arrested for plotting to blow up the Statue of Liberty. The fourth, an undercover policeman, reportedly helped to draw up plans for carrying out the idea and provided police funds both to pay for the dynamite and to rent the car in which it was picked up. He had previously established credentials by having himself arrested, convicted, and fined for trying to make a citizen's arrest of Mayor Wagner (*New York Times*, February 16, 1965).

- In New York, 13 Black Panthers accused of conspiracy to bomb public places reportedly obtained 60 sticks of dynamite from an FBI informant (*New York Times*, May 8, 1970).

- A New York detective helped open the Harlem office and then headed the Bronx chapter of the Black Panthers. He joined the party before any of those he testified against in the Panther 13 trial. He acknowledged that his actions at times went beyond mere infiltration in order "to protect my cover" (*New York Times*, February 3 and 17, 1971).

- Another undercover policeman had charge of the distribution of the Panther newspaper in the metropolitan area and was acting lieutenant of finance (*New York Times*, March 5, 1971).

- Malcolm X's personal bodyguard, the man who delivered mouth-to-mouth resuscitation to him, was a New York detective who had been undercover for seven years. He started as a Muslim and later became active in the Panthers. He earned a black belt in karate and taught it to one black nationalist group he infiltrated (*New York Post*, December 2, 1970).

- In other cases involving the Black Panthers in Indiana and New York, police agents reportedly have induced black militants to burglarize and rob, offering them weapons, a map of the target, and even a getaway car (American Civil Liberties Union 1969; Chevigny 1972).

- Heavy police surveillance and the eventual shoot-out in Cleveland between a black nationalist group led by Ahmed Evans and police, which left several dead, came after a never-substantiated FBI informant's report that the group was gathering weapons in a plan to kill moderate black leaders (Masotti and Corsi 1969).
- The raid in Chicago where Fred Hampton and Mark Clark were killed was based on FBI informants' report of a weapons cache, though few weapons were found (*New York Times*, May 16, 1970). The chief of security for the Panthers at this time and Hampton's bodyguard was a paid FBI informer. In court testimony he revealed his duties to be "making sure that all members were properly armed and their weapons working, screening and investigating possible informers, and building security devices" (*New York Times*, February 13, 1974).

Numerous historical examples are also available from France, Russia, and England (Cookridge 1967; Venturi 1966). The English Cato Street conspiracy offers a classic case (Stanhope 1962). Benjamin Franklin seems to have had fluid allegiances between France and the United States. It has been argued that at one point Stalin was a police spy. (Hyde 1971); anti-Nazi resistance groups in occupied Europe were heavily infiltrated. From the Molly Maguires, through the Haymarket riots and the San Francisco Preparedness Parade bombing, and onward, there are many examples to be found in the American labor struggle (Lewis 1964; Huberman 1937). There are also parallel cases in international relations (Blackstock 1964).

At any given time period there are many American social movements, yet only a few are deemed worthy of infiltration. The placement of agents in movements is certainly selective. One area where police discretion could usefully be studied, it is probably a function of police perceptions of threat, the political pressures brought to bear upon police, and the means and ends of the movement. Among the 34 cases for which some information is available, 11 involved white campus groups; 11, predominantly white peace groups and/or economic groups; 10, black and Chicano groups; and only two, right-wing groups.

THE BACKGROUND OF AGENTS

Generalizations here must be both rather superficial and cautious. The agent is likely to share the characteristics of the group he works against. Most recently this has meant being young and/or belonging to a minority group. Certain observations can be made about the more than 34 cases that have become public and for which some information is available, though this is a small and not necessarily representative sample.

It is easy to conjure up superspy images of the highly experienced professional policeman who is everywhere conquering domestic dragons, and it appears that the FBI would like to give this appearance. In fact, a few agents might fit this image. Thus, Robert Pierson—who was assigned by the Illinois State's attorney's office and served as Jerry Rubin's bodyguard during the Democratic convention—graduated from the FBI training school, the Chicago Police Academy, the Counter-Intelligence Service at Fort Holabird, and was also a veteran of Army counterintelligence service.

Just as the United States has a special academy to train police from developing countries for political work, so various Americans experienced in foreign security work have returned to the home front. James Jarret, an ex-Green Beret working with the Los Angeles Police Department's intelligence squad, is said to have delivered a box of hand grenades to the house of two activists shortly before they were arrested for possessing hand grenades. He reportedly had past CIA experience in Indochina, Africa, and Latin America. Tommy the Traveler's father is said to have worked for the CIA. A civilian informer in

Seattle had a background in counterintelligence. The CIA has trained local police in intelligence matters (*New York Times,* February 6, 1973). There are also exchanges in the other direction. Thus, two former members of New York's Bureau of Special Services became active in the White House "plumbers' unit."

The elaborate preparations that characterize wartime spies generally seem absent. The stakes are not as great, a different type of information is sought, the "enemy" is less sophisticated at detection, infiltration takes place within the United States, and contact with supervising authorities is much simpler than in a foreign country. The myriad of cultural details noted by Goffman (1972) that might give an agent away were he in a different country (laundry marks, buttons on the wrong side, how he holds his fork, etc.) need not be as carefully attended to. Nevertheless, cover stories must often be created, and some of the same elements are present.

But given the local and decentralized nature of much American law enforcement, the relative openness of American society, and the lack of a tradition of political police, much infiltration of radical movements appears to be rather amateurish. In a majority of cases, civilians—rather than sworn police personnel—are used as informants. Civilians are much cheaper and give far greater coverage, but, more important, they easily share the attributes of the group to be infiltrated, which do not normally correspond closely to the police, who are more likely to be white, high school educated, over 30, Christian, male, American born, with a conventional life-style and world view. A police source observes that "undercover police agents are social or political chameleons selected precisely because of their ability to blend naturally into the background of the area to be studied" (Bouza 1967, p. 67). However, this is easier for some groups than for others. The social characteristics of the police may not have impeded access to the labor movement, to right-wing political groups, or to black groups—such as the Muslims and the Panthers—with a lower status base, but the New Left drew upon a different stratum of the population, namely, students and the intelligentsia.

When regular police are used as agents, it is often those who have recently joined the force, sometimes having purposely not undergone academy training. Their youthfulness not only makes their access easier, but it also makes them less recognizable as police officers and eliminates the need for elaborate cover stories. They may play "themselves," using their own names and biographies as much as is possible. In some cases (as at Columbia and SUNY at Buffalo), police who infiltrated student movements were regularly enrolled students. With increased emphasis on college-educated police and programs to facilitate going to school while serving on the force, this seems a natural arrangement. Another natural arrangement appeared in the case of New York City black policemen, some of whom had been Black Muslims for many years. However, in the fall of 1972, the New York City Muslims, apparently in fear of undercover agents, "expelled dozens of thier members who work as policemen" (*New York Times,* October 29, 1972).

Some civilian agents have had experiences conducive to deception. The agent in the Berrigan case had previously been arrested for impersonating an officer, fraud, and forgery. Several agents had led double lives as homosexuals and drug dealers.

Among civilian agents, a goodly percentage were previously or simultaneously informants for traditional criminal matters. This was particularly true in the black movement. This use of traditional criminal informants in political cases seems to come about because some groups such as the Panthers and Black Muslims sought to recruit from those with lower-class and criminal backgrounds. Legal protest and illegal drugs were part of the same youth culture. In the middle and late sixties, the line between protest and crime became blurred in the minds of the public and the police, as black violence and Weathermen activities occurred simultaneously with demonstrations, sit-ins, and other nonviolent actions.

Applying their previously held images of criminals and their rhetoric and procedures for handling criminal cases, the police engaged civilian informants and also sent their own officers into the ranks of those they viewed as criminals. Techniques for dealing with vice cases, when the state is a complainant, rather than a wronged individual, were easily transferred to political cases. The United States is unique in giving the same national police agency responsibility for the very different activities of counter-espionage and criminal investigations. Cold War rhetoric of the 1950s, which linked politics and crime—such as J. Edgar Hoover's references to the "Communist underworld"—undoubtedly strengthened the inclinations of the FBI and the police toward this kind of surveillance and detection. A pool of men trained in military intelligence was available.

The FBI procedure encourages what it calls "racial informants" among those who previously have been criminal informants. When local police used agents on the college campus, as with Tommy the Traveler and Charles Grim at the University of Alabama, the same agent often dealt in both drugs and politics. It is difficult to tell whether the agent was primarily concerned with politics, was using his radical political activities to help establish credibility in his undercover drug role, or was equally concerned with both. Some agents were paid simultaneously by local police to do narcotics and by the FBI to do politics. For both there is no complainant, and undercover work is necessary. In some cases where it was not possible to get a man for his politics, he could be gotten for his drugs. In addition, students involved in politics and drugs—and arrested for the latter—could sometimes be induced, to avoid prosecution, to work with the police in both areas.

In most cases, the agent simply appears on the scene without elaborate background preparations. He may loyally carry out routine tasks; recount tales of past activism or victimization by the system; propose daring schemes; offer to obtain resources such as weapons, supplies, and vehicles; and offer instruction in self-defense and the use of weapons and explosives.

THE MOTIVES OF AGENTS

Presumably we do not need to investigate the motives of the undercover agent who is a regular policeman or FBI agent. He is simply doing the job he is paid to do, although later in this paper we will discuss the fact that these agents sometimes go beyond what appears to be their mandate. Civilian agents, however, offer a variety of motives not so easy to detect. Some are patriotic Middle Americans and/or those insecure about their status. Others come from an urban criminal milieu where rewards of various kinds may be important, while others seem to be otherwise typical members of the group they inform on (whether the Klan or SDS) who have become disenchanted with their group or get hooked into the role by the police. There are also, no doubt, some described by a police manual as "demented, eccentric, nuisance types" (Harney and Cross 1960).

Patriotism

For those individuals who appear to be impelled by patriotism. motives appear largely ideological—to help the good guys and to hurt the bad guys. The police literature makes much of those who inform as a "civic duty" and implies that this is the most common motive in criminal cases. Young Americans for Freedom, a right-wing student group, infiltrates the left, as have various right-wing exiles from Communist countries. Organizations concerned with equal rights have infiltrated racist groups such as the Klan. Sectarian groups of both the left and the right sometimes infiltrate their closest competitors.

Insecurity about status, long thought to be a factor pushing individuals toward radical politics, may also push them toward superpatriotism and toward informing as a means of gaining acceptance from the dominant group. For example, while it is well-known that Jews were overrepresented in revolutionary groups in Russia, they also may have been overrepresented in the secret police. This appears to be a factor in several contemporary cases, such as with Tommy the Traveler, who is half-Thai, and with some new Americans from Communist countries.

Those with ideological or personal motives are more likely to initiate contact with police and volunteer their services. Some informants were offered draft deferments. Other informers are hooked into service by the police, who offer to trade their resources—immunity from prosecution or harassment, leniency with respect to charges, money, release from jail, help with naturalization, or problems with the government—in exchange for information.

Coercion

Among 15 civilian cases for which some information is available, nine volunteered and six appear to have been coerced into the role as a result of arrest or threatened arrest.

In the Meridian, Mississippi, Klan bombings, fear of police appears to have been the main motive; a detective states: "One of the informants believed we were going to kill him. We helped him believe it. We acted like we were going to do it" (*Los Angeles Times*, February 13, 1970). The informants were also given written assurance that they would be immune from prosecution in several cases of church bombing.

The British police have a saying that "today's arrest is tomorrow's snout." Arrest is an important means of recruitment. Charles Grim, who admitted throwing fire bombs and burning buildings at the University of Alabama, in recalling how initial troubles with police led to his recruitment as an agent, remembers being told by a detective: "'I'm going to throw you in jail if you don't cooperate with us,' and, being afraid of jail, as I am, I decided, well I'd better cooperate. These people had me by the throat and they knew it . . . it wasn't the money so much [his payment]; it was the fact that if I didn't do it with them they'd nail me" (Jacobs 1971).

The importance of police pressure can be seen in a bulletin to regular FBI agents that suggests that some activists "will be overcome by the overwhelming personalities of the contacting agent and volunteer to tell all—perhaps on a continuing basis" (*Win* 1972, p. 28).

Financial Reward

As with Gypo Nolan in Lian O'Flaherty's novel *The Informer* (1961), informing for some may be mainly a question of the need for money. The informer in the plot against Caesar Chavez was unemployed when he volunteered his services to the Kern County sheriff's office, who put him in touch with the state narcotic bureau (*New York Times*, January 2, 1972).

There is probably great variation in the amount of money paid informants, depending on the importance of the case, the agency involved, the credibility of the informant, and the like. Excluding narcotics cases, criminal informants at the local level may often receive nominal amounts. The informant in the Camden draft case received $60 a day from the FBI, the amount normally earned from his construction business. However, for some political cases the rewards may be considerable. According to some sources, the FBI was offering $2,000 for turning in Weathermen. One student activist at a large midwestern university went all the way through school on what amounted to an FBI scholarship. She received $300 a month and in return wrote what she believed were nondamaging, selective, general reports on the campus mood and student activism. She saw the job as a hustle, making it possible to get through school, and as a way to protect the student movement.

In 1971 when an FBI agent wished to give out a lump sum or monthly payment of more than $300 to an informant, he needed to receive authorization on a higher level (*Win* 1972, p. 28). Traditionally, federal agencies have had funds to pay informants, while local police have had very limited, if any, funds available.

Activist Disaffection

Formerly loyal members of a group may be motivated by a variety of reasons, political and personal: to avenge a loss, to try to change the course a group is taking, rivalries over leadership, personal vendettas, to put someone out of circulation, competition between groups, guilt over past activism, changes in political attitudes. Those who publicly break with a movement may be approached by authorities and encouraged to rejoin later as paid informants. Another motive is to prevent harm from befalling a group or individual the informant cares about. In the Camden, New Jersey, draft case, the informant, who has since renounced his past actions and claimed the FBI broke its word with him, described the group as "the finest group of Christian people I have ever been associated with" (Hardy 1972). He claims that he did not want those in the group, many of whom were his closest friends, to be hurt by committing illegal actions. Some individuals may feel guilt about their past activities and see cooperation with authorities as a way to atone or repay society. Or, sensing that a movement is on the losing end, they may cooperate with authorities in hopes of gaining favorable treatment after the fall.

Double Dealing: The Double Agent

There are also those activists who become agents with the hope that they can assist the movement by giving false information to authorities or by obtaining information about authorities. This "double agent" might betray to the authorities those within the movement who are out of favor or are seen as a threat by the agent. Some double agents seek to gain protection for their own radical activities. Other agents may be essentially apolitical and opportunistic, deceptively cooperating with both sides as this furthers their own interests.

One of the most interesting double agents was Aseff, a Russian police agent for 15 years, 5 of which were spent as head of what a historian writing in 1934 called "the largest and most important terrorist organization known to history" (Nikolajewsky 1934). While Aseff betrayed a large number of activists, he also arranged for a series of terrorist activities "the success of which focused on him the eyes of the world." These included the assassination of Plehve, the minister of the interior, and the Grand Duke Sergei, as well as an attempt against the tsar, the failure of which was not Aseff's fault.

The motivation of a double agent is, no doubt, exquisitely complex, varying both from one situation to another and from stage to stage in his career. He may enjoy a sense of power by deceiving everyone, experience cross-pressures, and be unclear as to which side he is really on. An unstable personality or changing pressure may mean a number of shifts in allegiance back and forth.

There may also be enjoyment of the intrigue and gamesmanship. Chess player and police agent Louis Tackwood, in a remark reminiscent of Georg Simmel's (1955) emphasis on the sense of power and possession surrounding the secret, states "they [the Los Angeles police he worked with] looked down on me, and all the time it was tickling me to even play counterplots on them and counterplots on the other side too. These are people who think they can conspire against me and they're playing with a master of conspiracy" (Citizens Research and Investigation Committee, 1973, p. 28).

Those Who Convert to the Movement

To be credible, the agent must share at least some of the class, age, ethnic, racial, religious, or sexual attributes of the group he or she is informing on. This is especially true when the movement is structured around issues related to these sources of identity. However, this very fact opens the agent to a susceptibility to sympathize with the anger, critique, and goals of the group. He may discover that the government's view of a group is wrong and became disenchanted with the questionable means used to deal with it. To be effective the agent must become a trusted member of the group. Yet the more he becomes a trusted member, the greater may be his concern about the betrayal and deception involved in his actions. Familiarity can breed liking as well as contempt, particularly to the extent that the agent is cut off from his familiar surroundings and friends and becomes immersed in a new life. He may experience severe cross-pressures and feelings of guilt, leading to his ineffectiveness as an agent or his becoming a convert to the movement he originally sets out to damage. This is the opposite of the person discussed earlier, who starts as an activist and later becomes an agent, though no doubt many of the same processes of conversion, withdrawal of allegiance, changes in self-conception, and reinterpretation of the past are involved.

Among well-known historic examples of this phenomenon are Father Gapon, a police agent and key figure in the 1905 uprising in Russia who became radicalized in the process, and Roman Malinovsky, an agent who apparently became converted to Bolshevism (Wolfe 1961, chap. 31). Conversion often seemed to be the case with those of working-class background who infiltrated the American labor movement during the 1930s. More recently it has been the case with several idealistic FBI agents and informants who concluded that the groups they infiltrated were not a serious threat and that by its actions the FBI helped create some of the problems it ostensibly wanted to control. One man in Seattle, who sought to help the FBI solve a series of bombings, quit and claimed that the FBI asked him to actually carry out bombings (*University Review* 1971). Another student, who worked for the House Un-American Activities Committee after infiltrating SDS, apparently came to enjoy the youth culture, which his rural fundamentalist background had kept from him, and became sympathetic to SDS (Meinhausen 1969). Four men who had gone as undercover agents for military intelligence to the UFO coffeehouse in Columbia, South Carolina, later came forward to testify for the defense. In the Camden draft and Chicano Mortorium Committee cases, the informants became angry and disillusioned when authorities were seen to break agreements. A black agent who voluntarily surfaced in Los Angeles with 10 years' experience as an informer in criminal and later political cases reports being inspired by Daniel Ellsberg. He states: "After the Angela [Davis] set-up by C.C.S. [the criminal conspiracy section of the Los Angeles Police Department], I couldn't take it any more. She was a good sister. So I decided to try and help you people after all the things I've done against the 'movement.' Kind of like paying you back" (Citizens Research and Investigation Committee 1973, p. 26). Other agents who are not converted may disagree with activists over specific means, yet come to agree that war, racism, and poverty are serious problems, and may subsequently view themselves as liberals.

The Agent Provocateur: Success through Excess

Perhaps more common than the tendency of the agent to become converted and lose his zeal is the opposite: overly zealous agents who exceed their mandate. This mandate, of course, varies and is not always clear. While agents are sometimes explicitly instructed to entrap, to give reports that would justify repression, and to foment discord in a movement, the constraints of a democratic society mean that the most commonly given instructions probably assign no more than a passive information-gathering role. Yet this role may be exceeded. It becomes important to ask why, in the words of the FBI, informants sometimes get "carried away" (*Win* 1972, p. 29).

Those attracted to play such roles may be somewhat unreliable to begin with. The willingness to take a job that involves the deception of activists while posing as their friend may also characterize people willing to deceive those who hire them, particularly if the agent believes his job is dependent on presenting information that indicates a threat to civil order. This economic incentive was very obvious during the 1930s, when labor spying and related activities were estimated to be an $80,000,000-a-year business. In testimony before the La Follette Commission, a United States senator reported his experiences as a prosecuting attorney to investigate such cases:

> *I found that what would happen would be that industrial spies would get into a union and then would go out and try to get decent union men to commit some crime, to blow up a transformer, to put dynamite under a building, or blow up something, drive nails into logs or set fire to mines . . . for the purpose of creating jobs for the spies' particular organization . . . they would frighten the lawyers and the officers of the company to such an extent that they would have to employ a great many more men to watch these "dangerous" men; and when the "dangerous" literature that was being passed out, or the suggestions that were being made by supposedly bad men, were traced down, they were almost invariably traced to the Pinkerton or the Burns or the Thiel detective who was lurking in the background. [Humberman 1937, pp. 96–97].*

It might seem logical that such activity would occur less often among sworn police personnel acting as undercover agents who have permanent jobs and are more directly accountable to their employers. However, in the cases considered here, police were at least as likely to move from passive information-gathering to provocation as were civilians. Perhaps the desire for citations and promotions serves as an incentive to enlarge the extent of the threat and aid in "a good pinch." Thus, the young new York policeman who infiltrated the group supposedly threatening to blow up the Statue of Liberty was promoted to detective and decorated after the successful conclusion of the case. Similar promotions have been given to other infiltrators.

The passing of faulty information is more likely to occur if the agent has his own ax to grind, whether ideological or personal. Exiles from Communist countries, for instance, without fresh evidence, may feel they know what a threat the group really is or would be if given the chance, even though it has not done anything yet. Such agents may thus feel free to encourage activists to take violent action or to report false information. They may feel that the group poses such a severe threat that any means (even lying to superiors) are necessary to destroy it.

The nature of the role may lead the informer beyond his assigned task. "Discovering" evidence that would serve to justify his role could help to alleviate his guilt or conflict over the role. Exaggerating the importance of the group may make him feel that what he does is significant. Further, wishful thinking, limited exposure, and selective perception may lead the agent to believe a group's own exaggerated estimates of its power and appeal and to confuse vague revolutionary rhetoric with specific plans. The functions of such rhetoric and the fantasy of violence that characterize some oppressed and powerless groups may not be fully appreciated. Further conducive to distortion of information may be factors noted by Wilensky (1967), such as the presence of competing specialized intelligence agencies (within and between police departments) and the hierarchical quasi-military organizational structure characteristic of police.

Deception is aided by the secrecy inherent in the role. It gives the agent an advantage over his employer, who in any given instance may find it hard to assess the accuracy of the information he gets (unless he has a number of such agents in the organization). While it may be true, as the leading police administration book suggests, that "certain police activities are best conducted in a milieu of privacy, removal from the mainstream of publicity and routine which often attends other facets of law enforcement." there are likely to be important problems of accountability, as with any activity carried out in secret (Eastman 1971, p. 159).

For the authorities, this secrecy can have dire consequences. Thus, Aseff, the Russian police spy who was born a Jew, arranged for the successful assassination of Plehve, the minister of interior who was initially responsible for hiring him as a police spy. The assassination was apparently a result of Plehve's responsibility for a wave of anti-Semitic pogroms (Nikolajewsky 1934). Aseff, of course, covered himself in the reports he regularly filed with police for 15 years.

His secret status offers the informant the opportunity to act in ways that would be avoided by more prudent activists who must content with arrest. He can swing with the movement and act out the emotions he may feel as a member of a disprivileged group or his general feelings of aggression, without fear of reprisal. For some it may be the best of two worlds. As Frank Donner (1971) observes: "The infiltrators's secret knowledge that he alone in the group is immune from accountability for his acts dissolves all restraints on his zeal."

The Role's Inherent Contradictions

The FBI may ask impossible things of its informants when it advises that they "should be privy to everything going on and should rise to the maximum level of their ability to the new left movement," but warns at the same time that they "should not become the person who carries the gun, throws the bomb, does the robbery or by some specific violative, overt act become a deeply involved participant" (*Win* 1972, p. 29). Even when the agent wishes to adhere to the FBI's directive about noninvolvement in such actions, he must face the dilemma that credibility and access come through activism. As Karmen (1974) notes, he must often choose between a passive peripheral role that gives him little information and influence and a more active role that will yield greater information and the ability to affect outcomes with the attendant difficulties of complicity and entrapment. In two-thirds of the 34 cases considered here, the specious activists appear to have gone beyond passive information gathering to active provocation.

The police literature gives rather little in the way of practical suggestions for the informant, aside from advising him not to become involved with women and to minimize emotional involvements generally. Most attention is given to the management of civilian informants.

Given the analysis above and the cases made public, it is not surprising to find an FBI memorandum stating "the key word in informants, according to bureau supervision is 'control'" (*Win* 1971, p. 29). The basic police handbook, Eastman's *Municipal Police Administration* (1971, p. 162), notes that "the non-police informant requires close supervision" and that his information is "often of dubious value." Another police observer advises constant investigation of the informant to determine his "varied and complex" motivating factors and adds that failure to do this invariably leads "to disaster or at least embarrassment" (McMann 1954, p. 44).

Because the informant may lie, exaggerate, misperceive, improperly evaluate, misunderstand his relationship with police, entrap, or be a double agent, police are warned to be careful. Devices for dealing with the problem include placing other agents, whose identity is kept secret, in the same operation; using electronic surveillance on the agent as well as the activists; careful checking; using police rather than civilians as infiltrators; and employing organization rather than individual responsibility for controlling the agent.

Unlike informants in ordinary criminal cases (excluding organized crime)—who are under the aegis of an individual officer and whose identity may not even be known by supervisors—informants in political cases are more likely to be centrally controlled. Presumably, this factor might introduce more reliability. Recent police literature makes much of the question of who should control the informant. Although noting that the investigator's sole control of the informant protects the latter's security and permits the organization to deny any official knowledge of the illegal transactions that may occur between the informant and policeman, it strongly argues for central control.

For those who must supervise, however, the problems are more complex than imagined by those who write instruction manuals. In their necessity to respond to bureaucratic pressures to come up with a certain number of arrests or information, they may not always question the quality of the information. The FBI agents must meet a quota of informants and devote a certain amount of time to generating political intelligence, regardless of whether or not any specific crime has occurred or seems imminent. According to one source, they needed at least 12 informants: six criminal, three national security, and three racial (*Newsweek* 1971). Finding the required number of informants may be difficult enough, without having to worry about reliability. When production rates are too high for the means at hand, innovation and reduced concern with quality are likely to emerge. One agent (Wall 1972) reports that to meet his quota he even picked names from a phone book and made up reports for them. But at other times, much bad or useless information may be seen as a reasonable trade-off for the occasional important piece of information it does provide. Also, the supervising policeman or FBI agent is probably less likely to question information about the supposed violent and subversive nature of a group consistent with his previous ideas about them. Finally, since entrapment rather than its avoidance may be an end desired by authorities, the quality of the information provided may be relatively unimportant.

EASE OF ENTRY INTO THE MOVEMENT

The agent's entry and rise to a position of leadership in an organization may be facilitated by the structure of that organization: those groups that are dedicated to unpopular or visionary causes are often small, experience high rates of turnover, and lack resources and people willing unselfishly to undertake the routine and time-consuming tasks required of activists, as well the dangerous and daring tasks that may be called for. The agent often brings badly needed special skills and resources. His ties to authorities may give him an added secret resource. As was the case with tsarist agents in the Communist party, he may be able to rise rapidly to a position of leadership in the organization through arranging for the arrest in its incumbent leaders or those who suspect him.

The particular ideology and organization of many of the black, student, and antiwar organizations of the 1960s undoubtedly facilitated the entry of informants, but probably made it unlikely that the agents could gather information that would be of much use to their employers. Generally speaking, the protest organizations of the 1960s consisted not of highly centralized, formally organized, tightly knit groups of experienced revolutionaries bent on carefully planned criminal conspiracies, but were instead decentralized, with fluid leadership and task assignments, shifting memberships, and an emphasis on participation. Members were generally not carefully screened, and requirements for activism were minimal. This was all the more true in the case of events— such as demonstrations, meetings, and marches—in which anyone could participate. The emergent noninstitutionalized, social movement character of the struggle meant constantly changing plans, shifting alliances, and spontaneous actions. Their ideology stressed peaceful nonviolent means, reform, democracy, openness, an antibureaucratic orientation, and optimistic faith in people, tolerance, community, and naivet about government surveillance. Most groups had nothing to hide. Furthermore, given the lack of a well-developed tradition of political police, most groups initially saw little reason to be suspicious. Unlike people in organized crime, they generally lacked the capacity to retaliate against informants, and kinship networks are not as important for recruitment. Furthermore, the impersonal character of urban life, with its many secondary and superficial relations, may create an atmosphere in which an agent can easily conceal personal information and deceive his fellows. In such a context, those whose allegiances were not to the espoused cause had easy access.

HOW AGENTS ARE EXPOSED

It appears that a majority of young civilian agents are active for only a short period of time, partly as a function of the rapidly changing nature of current social movements and the mobility associated with youth and schools. But it also results from having met their initial obligation (for those hooked into the role) from fear, guilt, or conversion, and from discovery.

Agents may be discovered when they surface as prosecution witnesses, when they take a public stand to warn of the dangers the movement poses, when they are neither charged nor arrested, or when they are released without bail during, or shortly after, raids. Such factors accounted for exposure in about 60% of the 34 cases. Conversion, or at least enough disenchantment with the role to publicize their former activities, accounted for another 20% of the cases. The final 20% were discovered in one of the following ways: they were recognized by someone who either knew them as a policeman or saw them with police; they revealed their identity in a faulty role performance; or they were denounced by a former ally.

The discovery of an agent may lead to an attack on him, to his expulsion—with great effort made to publicize his real identity—to efforts to make him a double agent or to feed him false information (a tactic favored by Lenin), and, last, to efforts to obtain a court injunction against his presence.

In some cases there may be efforts to convert, understand, and reach out to the agent. In other cases, he may simply be given drudging tasks and denied access to anything but public information.

Activists often react to the discovery of an agent, or to an accusation against someone, with great ambivalence. The member who attempts to reveal an agent, whether real or imagined, may face countercharges of being an agent or at least of damaging the movement through smear or slander and creating suspicion. Even where the evidence is incontrovertible, some activists will refuse to believe that a trusted colleague could voluntarily betray them. . . .

SOME DIVERSE CONSEQUENCES

The range of consequences which a theory of the agent provocateur must account for can be suggested, even if we are far from a theory able to do this.

The movement may sometimes benefit from the presence of an agent. Specious activists may help perpetrate a protest group by offering the kinds of resources and moral support that are often in short supply among those who take highly unpopular positions and engage in illegal actions. Because of their need to be accepted, agents often work very hard, are often very successful at gaining new recruits for the movement, and even at starting new branches of a movement. Even acts of violence provoked or committed by agents may have consequences quite different from those desired by authorities.

Given the dynamics of social movements, it is sometimes a risky business (from their perspective) for status quo elements to go around provoking protest. In an atmosphere of intense grievances, such as early 20th-century Russia, such actions may backfire. The strategic consequences envisioned by radicals may prove more correct than those envisioned by authorities. Organizations may profit from dramatic events that serve as example and inspiration to others. The subsequent repression of the group may create martyrs and sympathy for it and help to publicize its cause. The exposure of the role of the agent provocateur may further reduce the legitimacy of the government.

Yet the negative effects are more apparent and, on balance, more damaging. Discovery of an agent (and even perpetuation of the myth of the agent) may lead to feelings of demoralization, helplessness, cynicism, and immobilizing paranoia, and can serve to disintegrate a movement—

particularly if it is loosely structured, as was the case with many movements during the 1960s. When he is not discovered, the agent may encourage internal divisiveness and lines of action that are self-defeating or not in the best interests of the organization. A democratic organizational form may be made impossible. Agents who rise to positions of leadership within the movement may have an important effect in shaping policy.

The agent may directly or indirectly contribute to the violence and illegality associated with a group by the actions he takes to gain access and to maintain credibility, through his efforts to entrap others in illegal activity, through the often-violent response of activists to his presence when he is discovered and the subsequent counterresponse from authorities, and through the various self-fulfilling effects noted throughout this paper. This can serve to stigmatize the movement as violent, alienate it from its potential constituency, and focus attention away from the basic issues. Its leadership may be decimated through imprisonment and all the movements' resources and energy may have to be put into security, self-defense, and legal needs, even if activists are often not convicted.

The role of authorities in a democratic society in driving groups underground and making them revolutionary (or more revolutionary sooner than they might have been) by denying them the opportunity to retain the reformist stance they so often begin with has been noted before. The Panthers, for example, stated as a local reform-oriented self-defense group that became increasingly revolutionary and violent (in self-defense or retaliation). Their subsequent development was certainly a response in part to their internal ideology and the characteristics and wishes of members. But it is as certain that the killing of Panthers by police; raids of questioned legality on their offices; extensive surveillance and use of undercover agents; denial of basic civil liberties—such as the right to make political speeches and distribute their literature; excessive stops for traffic offenses; general harassment; and their stigmatization by national political leaders had an important effect on their subsequent ideology and behavior and hoped, to some extent, make true the original police assessments of them as a violent revolutionary group. The FBI, with agents on both sides, apparently played an important role in the split that occurred in the Black Panthers between the Huey Newton and Eldridge Cleaver factions. It is only through studying the interaction between the Panthers and social control agencies that their development can be understood.

There is also the issue of deflation. Social scientists, social movements, and history can be deprived of newsworthy events by the actions of police, as well as provided with them. Even where the informant plays a passive role, the nature of the group cannot help but be changed by the presence of specious activists. This is true of the participant-observer's role in general. . . .

CONCLUSION

This paper has not intended to grant causal primacy to the role of agents. Indeed, the demonology inherent in such a perspective is particularly unbecoming the careful social scientist. Leaders and organizers (whether specious or not) build social movements only when conditions are appropriate. With the exception of outright frame-ups, when illegal protest actions occur there is obviously an interaction between the agent and other activists involved in the illegal activity. This is what makes entrapment and encouragement such interesting and illusive concepts. Unless certain political themes and tensions are present in a society and/or certain personality predispositions present on the part of potential activists, the most skilled provocateur may be unable to provoke anyone, and his efforts may merely be viewed with amusement, if not suspiciousness.

What Blumer (1951) has called a general social movement is something that great men or great agents can neither create, nor, in a democratic context, stop, for that matter. Yet as we move to the origins and development of a given movement in a particular locale, and even more to particular protest events, agents are sometimes more than the epiphenomena they are generally considered. If agents are only one factor among a great many, they are of interest because their importance is all too often unrecognized and because in a ostensibly democratic society the government and its agents are morally and perhaps actually easier to hold accountable than are activists, who may deny all legitimacy to the government.

Understanding the role of agents provocateurs and informants can call attention to the importance of microlevel analysis for understanding social movements and of the need to study movements in relation to their political environments. It can sensitize us to ground our statements about social movements in careful empirical observations and can lead to an appreciation of the interactive and emergent character of much collective behavior beyond the causal impact of history, broad social structural variables, and the personality characteristics and attitudes of activists. On the individual level, one can, in the tradition of Erving Goffman, learn a considerable amount about the delicate problems of identity and self by looking at those who consciously project "false" selves. One can as well apply this perspective to the creation and presentation of "false" public images and events by social movements and their opponents. Such an approach can help further to link the study of politics and deviance implicit in the labeling perspective. The approach also offers an area in which to consider the always-uneasy balance between liberty and order; not the least important, it can call attention to, and perhaps help prevent, some of the violence and violations of civil liberties and due process to which irresponsible agents may contribute.

REFERENCES

Ahern, J. 1972. *Police in Trouble*. New York: Hawthorne.

American Civil Liberties Union. 1969. News Release. New York, December 24.

Barth, A. 1951. *The Loyalty of Free Men*. New York: Viking.

Becker, H. 1963. *Outsiders*. Glencoe, Ill.: Free Press.

Berger, P. 1966. *Invitation to Sociology*. New York: Doubleday.

Black, D. 1973. "The Mobilization of Law." *Journal of Legal Studies*, vol. 2 (January).

Blackstock, P. 1964. *The Strategy of Subversion*. Chicago: Quadrangle. [53] For example, Tommy the Traveler apparently tried to several years without success to encourage violent actions among the students he came in contact with on the small, isolated, rather nonpolitical colleges in up-state New York.

Blumer, H. 1951. "Collective Behavior." In *New Outline of the Principles of Sociology*, edited by H. Lee. New York: Barnes & Noble.

Boston Globe. December 16, 1972; April 12, 1973; December 7, 1973.

Bouza, A. 1967. "The Operations of a Police Intelligence Unit." M.A. thesis, City College of New York.

Burnham, D. 1972. "40,000 Police Agencies Can Be Wrong." *New York Times Book Review* (July 16).

Chakotin, S. 1939. *The Rape of the Masses*. London Book Service.

Chevigny, P. 1972. *Cops and Rebels*. New York: Random House.

Citizens Research and Investigation Committee and Louis E. Tackwood. 1973. *The Glass House Tapes*. New York: Avon.

Cleveland Plain Dealer. May 7, 1972.

Connor, W. 1972. "Manufacture of Deviance: The Case of the Soviet Purge, 1936–38." *American Sociological Review* 32 (August): 403–13.

Conrad, J. 1965. *Secret Agent*. New York: Doubleday.

Cookridge, E. H. 1967. *Set Europe Ablaze*. New York: Crowell.

Daly, R. 1973. *Target Blue*. New York: Dell.

Donner, F. 1971. "Theory and Practice of American Political Intelligence." *New York Review of Books*. (April 22).

___. 1972. "The Confessions of an FBI Informer." *Harpers* (December).

Draper, T. 1957. *The Roots of Communism.* New York: Viking.

Eastman, G. 1971. *Municipal Police Administration.* Washington, D.C.: International City Management Association.

Elliff, J. 1974. "The Scope and Basis of FBI Data Collection." In *Investigating the FBI,* edited by Pat Waters and Stephen Gillers. New York: Ballantine.

Emerson, T. 1974. "The FBI and the Bill of Rights." in *Investigating the FBI,* edited by Pat Waters and Stephen Gillers. New York: Ballantine.

Erickson, K. 1966. *The Wayward Puritans.* New York: Wiley.

FBI Law Enforcement Bulletin. 1962. Vol. 31 (October).

Festinger, L., et al. 1956. *When Prophecy Fails.* New York: Harper & Row.

Goffman, E. 1972. *Strategic Interaction.* New York: Ballantine.

Gollin, A. 1971. "Social Control in Non-violent Protest." Paper given at American Sociological Association meetings, Denver.

Hardy, R. 1972. Affidavit filed on behalf of Camden 28, Philadelphia.

Harney, M. L., and J. C. Cross. 1960. *The Informer in Law Enforcement.* Springfield, Ill.: Thomas.

Helmreich, W. 1973. *The Black Crusaders.* New York: Harper & Row.

Herbert, B. 1970–72. "With a Little Pork from Our Friends." *Rat* (December 12-January 6).

Huberman, L. 1937. *Labor Spy.* New York: Modern Age.

Hughes, E. 1962. "Good People and Dirty Work." *Social Problems* 10 (Summer): 3–11.

Hyde, H. M. 1971. "Was Stalin a Police Spy?" *London Times* (July 10).

Investigation of S.D.S. 1969. Committee on Internal Security. 91st Congress, 1st Session. Pt. 5, pp. 1654–1705 of hearings.

Jacobs, P. 1971. "Investigative Report." Unpublished transcript of Public Broadcasting Television show, October 6.

Karmen, A. In press. "Agents Provocateurs in the Contemporary U.S. New Left Movement." In *Criminology: A Radical Perspective.* Pacific Palisades, Calif.: Goodyear.

Levine, J. 1962. "Hoover and the Red Scare." *Nation,* vol. 195 (October).

Lewis, A. 1964. *Lament for the Molly Maguires.* New York: Harcourt, Brace & World.

Lindesmith, A. 1967. *The Addict and the Law.* New York: Random House.

Los Angeles Free Press. February 4, 1972.

Los Angeles Times. February 13 and September 11, 1970.

Lundy, J. 1969. "Police Undercover Agents." *George Washington Law Review 37* (March): 634–68.

McMann, M. 1954. "The Police and the Confidential Informant." M.A. thesis, University of Indiana.

Marx, G. 1974 "Cops as Robbers, Crime Facilitators, and Creators of False Records: Ironies of Social Control." Paper read at International Sociological Association meetings, Toronto.

Masotti, L., and J. Corsi. 1969 *Shootout in Cleveland.* Washington, D.C.: Government Printing Office.

Meinhausen, D. 1969. "The Changeling: The Story of a HUAC Spy in the Student Movement." *Hard Times,* no. 46 (October 6), pp. 1–4.

Merton, R. 1974. *Social Theory and Social Structure.* Glencoe, Ill.: Free Press.

Mills, J. 1973. *Report to the Commissioner.* New York: Simon & Schuster.

New York Post May 23, 1970; December 2, 1970.

New York Times. February 16, 1965; August 24, 1967; June 23, 1968; May 8 and 16, 1970; June 7 and 19, 1970; January 2, 1971; February 3, 4 and 17, 1971; March 5 and 11, 1971; June 13, 1971; January 2, 1972; March 16, 1972; October 29, 1972; February 6, 1973; November 1, 1973; and February 13, 1974.

Newsweek. 1971. "Hoover's FBI: Time for a Change?" (May 10).

Nikolajewsky, B. 1934. *Aseff the Spy: Russian Terrorist and Police Stool.* Garden City, N.J.: Doubleday.

O'Flaherty, L. 1961. *The Informer.* New York: Harcourt, Brace & World.

Pincus, W. 1974. "The Bureau's Budget: A Source of Power." In *Investigating the FBI,* edited by Pat Waters and Stephen Gillers. New York: Ballantine.

Preston, Jr., W. 1963. *Aliens and Dissenters.* Cambridge, Mass.: Harvard University Press.

Ramparts. 1970 "Where Are the Clark Kents of Yesteryear? They Are Infiltrating the Movement, and

Here Is How to Get Rid of Them." 19 (December): 39–42.

Rosenbaum, R. 1971. "Run, Tommy, Run!" *Esquire 76* (July): 51–58.

Sagarin, E., and D. MacNamara. 1970. "The Problem of Entrapment." *Crime and Delinquency*, 16 (October): 363–78.

Schur, E. 1972. *Labeling Deviant Behavior*. New York: Harper & Row.

Seale, B. 1970. *Seize the Time*. New York: Random House.

Shellow, R., and D. Roemer. 1966. "The Riot That Didn't Happen." *Social Problems* 14 (Fall): 221–33.

Simmel, G. 1955. *Conflict and the Web of Inter-Group Affiliations*. New York: Free Press.

Stanhope, J. 1962. *The Cato Street Conspiracy*. London: Cape.

Taft, P., and P. Ross. 1969. "American Labor Violence: Its Causes, Character, and Outcome." In *Violence in America: Historical and Comparative Perspectives*, edited by Fred Graham and Ted R. Gurr. Washington, D.C.: Government Printing Office.

Venturi, F. 1966. *The Roots of Revolution*. New York: Grosset & Dunlop.

University Review. 1971. "We Bombed in Seattle" (November).

Wall, R. 1972. "Special Agent for the FBI." *New York Review of Books* (January 27).

___. 1974. "Why I Got Out of It." In *Investigating the FBI*, edited by Pat Waters and Stephen Gillers. New York: Ballantine.

Waltz, J. 1971. "Staked out for Slaughter." *Nation* (July 5).

Wambaugh, J. 1972. *The Blue Knight*. New York: Dell.

Washington Post. October 9, 1970; October 17, 1971; March 15, 1974.

Wilensky, H. 1967. *Organizational Intelligence*. New York: Basic.

Win. 1972. "The Complete Collection of Political Documents Ripped Off from the FBI Office in Media, Pennsylvania, March 8, 1971" (March).

Wolfe, B. 1961. *Three Who Made a Revolution*. Boston: Beacon.

ARTICLE 21

The Structure of Belief Systems among Contending ERA Activists

CAROL MUELLER
THOMAS DIMIERI

. . . Are there systematic differences in the patterns of policy preferences held by social movement activists supporting and opposing change? For almost twenty years, Tilly has elaborated systematic differences at the structural level which distinguish proactive movements supporting change from reactive movements opposing. This paper extends that discussion by arguing that the organization of proactive and reactive belief systems differs systematically as well. Data to test this thesis are preferences on feminist policies held by activists working for and against an Equal Rights Amendment (ERA) to the state constitution of Massachusetts in 1976.

THE ORGANIZATION OF BELIEFS

Before addressing the central thesis of this paper, it is necessary to indicate what we mean by the organization or structuring of belief systems. Although beliefs can be highly complex systems of thought and meaning, we have followed the lead of political scientists in simplifying our subject by concentrating on the public policies that are proposed by a proactive movement and, in turn, opposed by a reactive movement. The belief systems approach which we employ is adapted for analysis of social movement ideologies from a rich tradition of research which has developed in response to Converse's classic paper, "The Nature of Belief Systems in Mass Publics."

The belief systems described by political scientists consist primarily of expressed preferences for candidates, issues, and parties (Campbell et al.). The consistency of preferences is evaluated over a policy domain such as domestic or foreign affairs. Consistent positions usually fall along a dimension ranging from liberal to conservative. Consistency of preferences may then be assessed for different groups in order to compare the coherence or integration of their belief systems and their correspondence with a liberal or conservative orientation. A previous paper (Mueller and Judd) discusses the appropriateness of this paradigm for the study of three important characteristics of social movement beliefs—constraint, consensus, and position extremity.

Constraint is a property of individuals describing the degree to which one belief or preference can be predicted from another. Consensus is a group property that describes the average variability on a set of specific beliefs within a group. Position extremity is the difference between average beliefs of two or more groups or populations where one average is taken as the standard. It is, thus, a property of the relationship between the two groups. Mueller and Judd found, for instance, that the sex role beliefs for members of a social movement organization (the Boston Chapter of the National Organization of Women) were more highly constrained for individual members and showed more consensus within the group than the same beliefs for women who belonged to a nonfeminist political organization (the Massachusetts Federation of Republican Women—MFRW). Not surprisingly, the average belief for NOW women was significantly more feminist on a 9-point scale than MFRW women. Thus, these three dimensions may be used to compare the structure and coherence of the policy preferences for activists supporting and opposing change.

Our thesis that proactive and reactive belief systems will differ systematically along these three dimensions is based on the ideas developed by Ferree and Miller for applying attribution theory to the study of social movement ideology. Following Tilly, they maintain that there are inherent differences in the degree and source of consensus in social movement belief systems depending on the type of demands or claims made by the movement. Reactive movements are those which seek to protect old rights; proactive movements demand new rights. Basic to the Ferree-Miller argument is the assumption that reactive demands are still legitimated by the prevailing culture while proactive demands are not. Because of this difference in legitimacy, the proactive movement asserts new rights which have not previously been accepted within the dominant culture as when unions sought the right to bargain collectively. Alternatively, the proactive movement may try to endow new groups with rights previously legitimated for others as when suffragists sought to obtain the vote for women after it had been extended to ever wider categories of men. In this challenge phase of its life cycle, the proactive movement must define and provide symbols for legitimating new, more desirable social arrangements. Consensus on the desirability of the new arrangements develops out of concrete social interaction within a homogeneous, intensively interacting group. In contrast, the demands of the reactive movement are legitimated by traditional definitions of right and obligations which provide a taken-for-granted basis of consensus. Legitimacy is gained by reference to time-honored slogans or symbols. When specific traditional rights are challenged, reactive demands are very specific also—stop busing or Stop ERA (see Mottl). Rather than develop a new ideology, a reactive movement seeks to attach an additional concern to an existing belief structure without denying its overall legitimacy.

If we examine the differences between reactive and proactive beliefs in terms of consensus, constraint, and position extremity, several propositions are suggested. On issues related to the grievances of social movement members, a proactive groups's beliefs should demonstrate greater consensus among group members, greater position extremity from the general public than the beliefs of the reactive group. These differences in the patterning of beliefs are primarily accounted for by two factors. Proactive groups have a greater dependence on social interaction to establish and to legitimate the new beliefs. In addition, the development of the proactive belief system arises as a challenge to older beliefs and the groups protected by them. These two conditions, high levels of interaction an a situation of group antagonism, are similar to conditions identified by political scientists as the basis for higher levels of belief constraint among different segments of the electorate (Aberbach and Walker; Nie et al.). Consensus seems to arise similarly on the group level (McClosky et al.). The average distance of proactive beliefs form those of the general public should be greater because of the innovative and initially illegitimate nature of proactive beliefs and the fact that these arise and are disseminated through concrete social interaction, a slow process similar to conversion (for a general discussion, see Gerlach and Hine; and, on the women's movement, Cassell).

The beliefs of reactive groups should show less constraint, less consensus, and less position extremity than the beliefs of the proactive group. This is due to the reactive group's essential adherence to the prevailing ideology. Because they only seek to reaffirm former rights, their beliefs should have a good deal of the looseness and contradictions associated with everyday definitions of the social world (see Bittner for this contrast). Grievances of the reactive group arise out of ad hoc situations created by changing conditions or a threat from a proactive movement. Thus, inadequate time is available to invest in the prolonged social interactions necessary for closely integrating the beliefs within either individuals or groups. The reactive group accepts most of the dominant ideology and seeks only minor restitution. As a result, it should be closer to the general public than a proactive group on most beliefs.

HYPOTHESES

These propositions are tested with interview data collected from opposing leaders of campaigns working for and against a Massachusetts referendum on a state Equal Rights Amendment (ERA) in 1976. This campaign is selected to represent Tilly's distinction between proactive and reactive social movements. He uses the proactive—reactive distinction to characterize the opposing political groups which are mobilized in response to major structural transformations in society (see Tilly et al.). Proactive groups mobilize to take advantage of structural changes; reactive groups mobilize to defend the old order. Such is the nature of the campaigns for the federal ERA.

A major transformation is occurring in the roles of women. These changes center around women's increasing entry into the paid labor force, the decline in fertility, and the increase in divorce and marital instability (see Klein for a comprehensive discussion of these trends). Some women are structurally positioned to experience these changes as the basis of new opportunities, rights, and privileges. Others occupy positions from which these changes are viewed as a threat to the traditional rights and privileges of wives and mothers. Women on both sides have organized politically. The ERA is the issue which has most dramatically represented these changes and what is being won and lost for many women. Since its material implications remain ambiguous, the focus on the ERA is probably due to its symbolic importance (Mueller). If proponents win, the amendment will lend the weight of Constitutional legitimacy to changes that are presently occurring in women's roles. If opponents defeat it, they will have won at least a temporary symbolic victory by denying Constitutional sanction to macrolevel sources of change which are less easily influenced by grassroots mobilization.

In stating the previous propositions more specifically as hypotheses, we are assuming that the ERA referendum of 1976 in Massachusetts occurred during the challenge phase of a social movement cycle. It seems likely to us that the ERA was one issue in a highly integrated set of feminist beliefs for proponents. This would be consistent with other reports that early ideological differences within the contemporary woman's movement had been resolved on most issues by the mid-seventies (Carden; Freeman). For opponents, however, the existence of a tightly constrained set of anti-feminist beliefs in 1976 was less likely. Reactive movements in defense of family and neighborhood that opposed busing (Mottl), abortion (Leahy), and the ERA (Arrington and Kyle; Brady and Tedin) had shown little evidence of coordination by 1976.

Thus the belief system framework applied to campaign activists working for and against the ERA suggests the following hypotheses:

1. Policy preferences on feminist issues will be significantly more constrained for individual members of the leadership supporting the ERA than for leaders opposing.

2. Consensus on policy preferences will be significantly greater within the leadership group supporting the ERA than within the opposing leadership group.

3. The average policy preference of leaders opposing the ERA will be less polarized from the views of women in the general population than that of leaders supporting the amendment.

Hypotheses 1 and 2 are tested with data from interviews with the leaders of groups working for and against the ERA in a 1976 Massachusetts referendum. For Hypothesis 3, a survey of Massachusetts adults conducted immediately after the 1976 election serves as baseline data for the measure of position extremity.

THE STUDY

Campaign Activists in Massachusetts

Frustrated with repeated failures to pass the federal ERA, NOW members submitted a bill in the 1971–72 legislative session to guarantee equal rights on the basis of race, creed, and national origin as well as sex. The state bill was allowed to die, however, after the 1972 passage of the federal amendment by Congress and 26 states, including Massachusetts. As momentum for the federal amendment slowed in 1973, the state bill was reintroduced. Lobbying for the bill was directed by a coalition including the Governor's Commission on the Status of Women, the (Boston) Mayor's Commission to Improve the Status of Women, the Massachusetts Women's Political Caucus, the Women's Equity Action League, and the Women's Lobby. It passed unanimously and without debate in August 1973.

In the two years before the bill was submitted to the legislature for a second and final vote, a national organization opposing the federal amendment, STOP ERA, had spread to 40 states. Arguments against the amendment were based on the general theme that the sex neutral guarantees of the ERA would destroy the family. In addition, the ERA would promote sexual promiscuity by bringing men and women together unnaturally in police cars, in prisons, on sports teams, and in combat units. It would also legalize abortion and homosexual marriages.

The impact of the national controversy generated by the arguments and organizing efforts of STOP ERA and its chief spokesperson, Phyllis Schlafly, became clear when hearings were called for the final vote on the Massachusetts ERA in February 1975. In a crowded hearing room, speakers from the conservative Women for Constitutional Government, who had affiliated with the national STOP ERA, surprised legislators as well as proponents. The hearings marked the beginning of a heated public controversy accompanied by intensive lobbying and letter writing. Only intensive lobbying and parliamentary maneuvering by the proponents achieved final approval in May by a vote of 217–55. The final step was a state referendum set for November 1976.

Immediately after the May 1975 vote, the ERA Coalition began to mobilize for a statewide campaign to reach voters. A highly centralized structure was developed with task forces for education, outreach, organization, fundraising, and media relations. The controversy of the previous spring and the defeats of state referenda in New York and New Jersey in the fall of 1975 led the Committee to expect a difficult campaign. In January of 1976, it launched its campaign with 23 committees located across the state. By summer, the Committee was able to hire a full-time campaign worker and open a downtown Boston headquarters. During the ten months of the campaign, the Committee was able to draw on a list of 5,000 identified volunteers throughout the state and recruited 75 speakers. Campaign funds of $66,000 were raised.

The opposition presented a very different picture. Despite their strong showing with the legislature in the spring of 1975, organized efforts against the ERA referendum did not begin until the summer of 1976. The campaign developed around two small and largely independent groups from the north and south of Boston—a STOP ERA affiliate in the north and an ad hoc group called ALERT on the South Shore. While the North Shore group recruited volunteers through the John Birch Society, position to abortion was the common link with the South Shore group. There was little role specialization or formal organization. Most of the half dozen core members of each group performed tasks encompassing the full range of campaign activities. The two groups not only failed to coordinate thier activities, but the chief public speaker against the ERA dissociated herself form the opposition leadership on several occasions. In their interviews, respondents noted continual difficulty in recruiting volunteers and raising money. The total campaign funds spent by the opposition were less than $5,000.

Samples

The study is based on interviews with ERA campaign leaders and statewide sample of Massachusetts residents. Leaders were initially defined as individuals who were influential in shaping policy for the two campaigns. In the process of identifying leaders, it was soon discovered that the Committee to Ratify was considerably larger and more formally organized than either STOP ERA or ALERT. Given the lack of comparability to the opposing campaign organizations, all members of STOP ERA and ALERT but only key decision-makers in the Committee to Ratify were identified and interviewed. In both cases, identification began with those who were publicly known. They, in turn, identified others and the process continued until no new persons were named. The total number interviewed was 17 proponents and 13 opponents. Of the 13 opposition leaders, 2 were men; all proponents were women. Only one leader, an opponent, refused to participate. Interviews of most proponents took place before the November election. All opposition leaders and key leaders of the Committee to Ratify were interviewed after the election because of their apprehensions that sensitive information might be released which would adversely affect their respective campaigns.

Interviews with Massachusetts residents were based on a stratified cluster sample of residents selected from telephone listings. Respondents were interviewed by students from Wellesley College over a two-week period immediately following the 1976 election. Based on U.S. Census data for Massachusetts minor adjustments by sex, age, and education were made in the sample. After weighting, the sample size was 407 of whom 306 had voted on the ERA. Because most discussion of the ERA has focused on the opposition of women, the comparison here between activists and voters is confined to the 167 women voters.

Feminist Policy Preferences

Data for describing campaign leaders' preferences on feminist policies consist of thirteen statements which were described to respondents as "specific demands that have been made in the name of changing women's status for the better." ... Respondents were asked to judge whether each demand would help improve women's place in society, neither help nor hurt, or hurt. Items considered "helpful" were scored as one, "hurt" as three, and "neither help nor hurt" as two. The items range from those which clearly require government action such as "government support for day care centers" to those which are almost entirely matters of private morality such as "giving women the same sexual freedom as men." Despite this range, most of the demands require government funding, tax incentives, executive action, judicial or legislative support. The items and question wording are from Ferree. Six of the items were also asked on the state survey of Massachusetts residents....

RESULTS

Like other studies of ERA activists (Arrington and Kyle; Brady and Tedin; Tedin et al.), proponents and opponents differed significantly on most social characteristics relevant to feminist beliefs ... Opponents were older and more likely to be married and housewives. Full-time employment, usually in a professional or technical job, was significantly more characteristic of proponents. Most striking, however, were differences in the importance of religion. . . . All of the opponents were currently members of a church or parish; all stated that religion was very important to them personally; and, two-thirds had received some part of their education in a religious school.

In contrast to opponents in southern states, however, the women who led the opposition to the ERA referendum in Massachusetts were predominantly Catholic. They also differed from ERA opponents studied elsewhere in their high level of education and involvement in electoral politics.

Despite unexpected similarities in levels of education and political participation, the general political orientations of the contending leaders differed in the expected direction. A conservatism score was based on level of concern for five issues (crime, morality in government, sexual morality, size of federal budget, and the military position of the U.S.) which had high loadings on the first factor in a single component factor analysis of eight concern items. Opponents scored almost twice as high as proponents on the conservatism score.

Organization affiliations reinforce differences in structural characteristics in political orientation. The inner core of decision-makers for the Committee to Ratify consisted largely of the women who had organized the Boston Chapter of NOW in the early seventies and were considered by more peripheral members of the Committee to be founders of the women's movement in Massachusetts. Eleven of the 17 proponent leaders belonged to NOW; 3 of the remaining 6 belonged to other feminist organizations. Affiliations with schools or professions predominated over social service and strictly civic concerns. Politically, affiliations with the Civil Liberties Union, Common Cause, the Congress of Racial Equality and Planned Parenthood reflected a consistent array of liberal concerns.

Over half of the opposition leaders from both the North Shore STOP ERA and the South Shore ALERT were recruited into ERA opposition through their affiliations with pro-life groups. Most of the others were members of conservative political organizations such as the John Birch Society, Eagle Forum, Women for Constitutional Government, and the Daughters of the American Revolution. Although a few belonged to professional organizations, they were more likely to be leaders of groups concerned with children—ranging from Scouts and the YMCA to the local school committee and auxiliary groups within their local churches.

Because the two campaigns were very different in both their duration and their degree of formal organization, it is also important in evaluating the hypotheses to consider whether the individual leaders in the two campaigns differed significantly in their campaign participation. Despite the earlier start of the Committee to Ratify, the proponent leaders we have interviewed did not differ significantly from opposition leaders in the number of years they had worked on the issue. Although one proponent had begun working for the state amendment before the federal ERA passed Congress in 1972, 85 percent of both proponents and opponents had been involved for no more than two years. In terms of the intensity of their participation, we also found no significant differences between the two groups of leaders in either the number of campaign activities attended weekly or the number of hours spent on the campaign per week.

Constraint on Feminist Policy Preferences

From Hypothesis 1, we expect to find that constraint on feminist policy preferences is higher among proponents than opponents. Traditionally, constraint has been assessed in political science by computing correlations between pairs of policy items across respondents within a group, averaging within groups and then comparing across groups (Campbell et al.; Converse). Previous research on belief systems has shown, however, that high levels of group consensus (and, thus, low variance) artificially reduce the degree of association among items (Barton and Parsons). A similar problem is found here among proponent activists on their policy preferences. . . . Instead of correlational techniques, we will follow the procedure outlined in Mueller and Judd of measuring constraint by calculating for each individual the variance of responses across the thirteen items. This measure of an individual's belief constraint is then averaged for each group.

Comparing the average within-individual variances on the thirteen policy items, we find an average variance of *.098* for proponents and *.710* for opponents. These two mean values are significantly different (*t* with *28 d.f. 8.63; p < .0001*) indicating the greater consistency (lower average variance) of policy preferences among proponents.

Consensus on Feminist Policy Preferences

While constraint provides a measure of homogeneity within the individual's belief system, consensus measures homogeneity of belief within each of the two groups of campaign leaders. Thus, from Hypothesis 2, we expect that within-group consensus will be greater among proponents than among opponents. Consensus is measured by comparing the variance across respondents on each of the thirteen items for the two groups separately. . . . No variance is found among supporters of ERA on eight of the thirteen policy items. On these items, all proponents gave the identical answer. Of the five remaining items, only two (six and twelve) have a lower variance for opponents than for proponents. Thus, it is not surprising that the average variance over the thirteen items for opponents (*.366*) is more than three times that of proponents. (*.110*). Using a *t*-test for matched samples, these average group variances are found to differ significantly (*t* with *12 d.f. 2.9655*, *p* < .01). We find, then, that not only are ERA proponents more consistent than opponents in their policy preferences as individuals, but they also show a much higher level of consensus within the group.

Polarization on Feminist Policy Preferences

For Hypothesis 3, we expect to find that the average policy position (support or opposition) of ERA opposition leaders is closer to that of women in the electorate than to the average position of the proponent leaders. To make this comparison, women in the electorate are divided into those who reported a favorable vote on the ERA (*N* =124) and those who reported a negative vote (*N* =43). We then calculate an individual's average score over all preference items and compare the average individual differences between the four groups—proponent and opponent activists and voters. For these tests on positive extremity, the six policy questions are used for which we have comparable data from both leaders and voters.

. . . Average individual preferences on feminist policies range from ERA proponents at the most favorable end (lowest value) to ERA opponents at the opposite end (highest value). Mean values for the two groups of voters fall in order between the two extremes. The same ranking on support for feminist policies holds among the four groups on the six individual items as well. In terms of individual averages over the six policy questions, the positions of proponents and opponents are significantly different for both leaders and voters. . . . A woman's vote on the ERA predicts her position on only half of the individual policy questions. This is because most women voters, regardless of their vote on the ERA, accept the demand of equal pay for equal work as well as the value of electing more women to public office. On the abortion issue, both groups of voters are very near the neutral position of *2.0*, although the variances indicate considerable difference of opinion in both groups of voters. For the other three issues, the ERA vote predicts the policy position.

If Hypothesis 3 is correct, the difference between the policy preference position of women voters and proponent leaders will be significant while that between voters and opponents will not. The *t* values indicate that this is not the case. The position of opponent as well as proponent leaders is significantly different from that of women voters as a whole (row three). In addition, we find that both groups of leaders not only hold policy positions significantly different from women who voted against them on the ERA, but also from those who voted with them. Thus, women voters on both sides of the ERA issue hold moderate positions on other feminist policies in comparison with the campaign leaders. Contrary to our expectations, they are no closer to opponents than to proponents. . . .

Before discussing the implications of these results, an obvious caveat is in order. This extensive discussion is based primarily on interviews with a small number of campaign leaders. Such a careful examination of the patterning of their policy preferences seemed justified for several reasons. Most importantly, there are seldom more than a handful of people directing a political campaign despite, as in the case of the proponents, a volunteer army of 5,000. Also, by comparing the patterning of preferences between opposing leadership groups with those of women in the general population, we have also provided a context for evaluating the unique type of structures which distinguish activists from nonactivists. Finally, our approach has the added advantage of collecting data during and immediately following a campaign.

CONCLUSIONS

Previous theories of social movement interaction have drawn on the conflict theories of social psychologists to argue that beliefs polarize symmetrically in a situation of conflict. Oberschall, for instance, has argued that belief polarization is the psychological counterpart of social polarization between opposing social movements. The two are considered mutually supporting processes in which conciliatory individuals are driven out of leadership positions in opposing movements and moderate or inconsistent attitudes are eliminated from the beliefs of participants on both sides of the conflict. Drawing on the work in social psychology of Sherif and Deutsch, Oberschall implies that conflict produces two sets of consistent but opposing beliefs within each of the contending movements.

The finding here that policy preferences on feminist issues are more fragmented among reactive opponents then proactive supporters of the ERA does not appear to support this assumption. We have found that the beliefs of a reactive counter-movement are not the mirror image of proactive beliefs. Anti-ERA activists are not as consistently anti-feminist as pro-ERA activists are consistently pro-feminist. As a group, the ERA opponents support feminist policies which would encourage young women to enter the professions as well as policies guaranteeing women's right to equal pay for equal work. The fragmentation of their beliefs is even more strongly demonstrated in the greater variation of their individual responses compared to the activists supporting the ERA. Thus, they disagree more among themselves than proponents on eleven of the thirteen issues. Even on the issue of abortion, they are more divided than proponents.

There are several ways of accounting for the discrepancy between our findings and Oberschall's theory of attitudinal polarization, but we have found two most promising for further exploration. The first approach would give Oberschall the benefit of the doubt by suggesting that the conflict between opposing movements observed here has not been sustained long enough for symmetrical belief polarization to occur. There is recent evidence to support this alternative. In the four years following collection of our data in the 1976 Massachusetts ERA campaign, a national, right wing political movement has coalesced at the organizational level around "pro-family" issues. Along with many issues concerning the public schools, the pro-family program includes opposition to the feminist policies of abortion, homosexual rights, and the ERA (Crawford). This coalition of economic conservatives, evangelicals, and single-issue groups dominated the Republican Platform Committee in the summer of 1980 just as it had demonstrated increasing political effectiveness in the electoral campaigns of the late seventies. Despite their increased importance in electoral politics, however, it is not known whether this coalition has developed among its activists a level of consensus in defense of traditional norms and values comparable to the belief consensus of the proactive feminist movement which preceded it. Comparable levels of consensus and constraint in the pro-family movement would support Oberschall's use of a belief polarization model adapted from research on conflict in small groups and require a different level of explanation.

An alternative interpretation raises the question whether the social psychological model of polarization used by Oberschall is appropriate for the structural level to which it is applied. It seems plausible that the polarization which occurs between social movements may be quite different from that in small groups. For instance, the greater scale of social movements makes it much more likely that communication will be indirect rather than face-to-face. The mediation of the media as the means of communication also introduces a third party to the conflict and the possibility of coalition (see Lipsky). The importance of media support is accentuated by the fact that social movements struggle for control of the historic symbols conveying legitimacy to rights and privileges as well as for tangible rewards.

Most importantly, however, the emphasis of Ferree and Miller's work on the divergent processes by which consensus and legitimacy are achieved in proactive and reactive movements suggest that asymmetry rather than symmetry of belief structure is more likely at any given time. The presumption in favor of asymmetry is based on the premise that the belief system of a reactive movement always enjoys more cultural legitimacy than that of a proactive movement. From this assumption follows the challenge posture of the proactivists; the guarantee of opposition; a mobilization strategy of conversion through the intense interaction of homogeneous groups; and the great constraint, consensus, and extremity of beliefs described here.

Equally important to the presumption of asymmetry, however, is the sequencing of life cycles of proactive and reactive movements. There is the strong likelihood that proactive movements will achieve initial successes before reactive movements mobilize (Mottl). In the past two decades, for instance, reactive movements have not mobilized until a proactive movement had won the support of one or more major institutions. The ERA had passed Congress with overwhelming approval before Phyllis Schlafly began nationwide mobilization for STOP ERA in late 1972. Supreme Court decisions favorable to proactive claims for busing and abortion were also handed down before the anti-busing and "right-to-life" movements became widespread. Thus, recent U.S. history suggests that reactive groups may not even appear until their claims have already lost the support of some major institutions. Because of this precedence of the proactive movement, asymmetry in belief structure seems more likely than symmetry at any given point in the rise of the proactive movement.

Life cycle phasing may also reverse the direction of asymmetry found here. There is obviously a stage in the development of a successful proactive movement when the legitimacy of some portion of its program is established and these claims become part of the taken-for-granted assumptions of its beneficiaries as well as powerful institutions in society. Under these circumstances, reactive belief systems may retain their legitimacy at the local or regional level but take on a defensive stance at the level of national culture as the temperance movement did in the period after World War I (Gusfield). To the extent that a reactive movement withdraws from the national culture and formulates its own world view, the structural characteristics of its beliefs may come to approximate those of the proactivists described here with high levels of consensus, constraint, and position extremity. To discover whether such structure exists, however, will require that investigators frame their questions within the context of the reactivists' world view.

One last comment is in order. Tilly's distinction between reactive and proactive movements has been an essential ingredient in this study of social movement beliefs. This may at first appear incongruous because Tilly is best known for his contributions to the resource mobilization perspective which has generally ignored the part played by beliefs. Tilly's theoretical work, however, has generally accorded more influence to beliefs than that of others in the resource mobilization tradition. While Oberschall and McCarthy and Zald (a, b) have emphasized rational decision-making and the allocation of tangible resources to the pursuit of collective goals, Tilly has insisted that the analysis of collective action take into account "... a group's conception of its aims and rights" (c, 42–3). Although Tilly's empirical work emphasizes the origins of competing claims in macro-structural changes, the proactive-reactive distinction is, in fact, made at the cultural level in terms of a collectively shared sense of the legitimacy of claims both propounded and defended. We find Tilly's proactive-reactive distinction a critical juncture for joining structural and ideological analyses of social movements. . . .

REFERENCES

Aberbach, J. D., and J. L. Walker. 1979. "The Meaning of Black Power: A Comparison of White and Black Interpretations of a Political Slogan." American Political Science Review 64(June): 367–88.

Arrington, T. S., and P.A. Kyle. 1978. "Equal Rights Amendment Activists in North Carolina." *Signs* 3(Spring):666–80.

Barton, A. H., and R. W. Parsons. 1977. "Measuring Belief System Structure." *Public Opinion Quarterly* 41:159–80.

Bem, Daryl. 1970. *Beliefs, Attitudes, and Human Affairs*. Belmont: Brooks/Cole.

Bittner, E. 1963. "Radicalism and the Organization of Radical Movements." *American Sociological Review* 28(December):928–40.

Brady, D., and K. L. Tedin. 1976. "Ladies in Pink: Religion and Political Ideology in the Anti-ERA Movement." *Social Science Quarterly* 36(March):564–75.

Campbell, Angus, Philip E. Converse, Warren E. Miller, and Donald E. Stokes. 1960. *The American Voter*. New York: Wiley.

Cassell, Joan. 1977. *A Group Called Women*. New York: McKay.

Carden, M. L. 1977. "The Proliferation of a Social Movement: Ideology and Individual Incentive in the Contemporary Feminist Movement." In Louis Kreisberg (ed.), *Research on Social Movements: Conflict and Change*. Greenwich: JAI Press.

Converse, P. E. 1964. "The Nature of Belief Systems in Mass Publics." In David E. Apter (ed.), *Ideology and Discontent*. New York: Free Press.

Crawford, Alan. 1980. *Thunder on the Right*. New York: Pantheon Books.

Deutsch, M. 1969. "Conflicts: Productive and Destructive." *Journal of Social Issues* 25(1): 7–41.

Ferree, Myra. 1975. The Emerging Constituency: Feminism, Employment and the Working Class. Unpublished Ph.D. dissertation, Harvard University.

Ferree, Myra, and F. Miller. 1979. "Social Movement Ideologies." Unpublished manuscript.

Freeman, J. 1979. "The Women's Liberation Movement: Its Origins, Organizations, Activities, and Ideas." In Jo Freeman, (ed.), *Women: A Feminist Perspective*. Palo Alto: Mayfield.

Gerlach, Luther P., and Virginia H. Hine. 1970. *People, Power and Change: Movements of Social Transformation*. Indianapolis: Bobbs-Merrill.

Gusfield, Joseph R. 1972. *Symbolic Crusade*. Urbana: University of Illinois Press.

Klein, Ethel. 1979. A Social Learning Perspective on Political Mobilization. Unpublished Ph.D. dissertation. University of Michigan.

Leahy, Peter J. 1976. "Mobilization and Recruitment of Leadership to Anti-Abortion Movement: A Test of Some Hypotheses." Paper presented at the annual meeting of the Southwestern Sociological Society.

Lipsky, M. 1968. "Protest as a Political Resource." *American Political Science Review* 62(December):1144–58.

McCarthy, John D., and Mayer N. Zald. a:1973. *The Trends of Social Movements in America: Professionalization and Resource Mobilization.* Morristown: General Learning Press.

———. b:1976. "Resource Mobilization and Social Movements: A Partial Theory." *American Journal of Sociology* 82(May):1212–38.

McClosky, H., P.J. Hoffman, and R. O'Hara. 1960. "Issue Conflict and Consensus Among Party Leaders and Followers." *American Political Science Review* 58(June):361–82.

Mottl, T. L. 1980. "The Analysis of Counter Movements." *Social Problems* 27(June):620–35.

Mueller, Carol. 1976. "Rancorous Conflict and Opposition to the ERA." Working Paper No. 37, Center for Research on Women. Wellesley College.

Mueller, C., and C. Judd. 1981. "Belief Consensus and Belief Constraint." *Social Forces* 60(September):182–87.

Nie, Norman H., and Sidney Verba, and John R. Petrocik. 1976. *The Changing American Voter.* Cambridge: Harvard University Press.

Oberschall, Anthony. 1973. *Social Conflict and Social Movements.* Englewood Cliffs: Prentice-Hall.

Sherif, Muzafer. 1966. *In Common Predicament: The Social Psychology of Intergroup Conflict and Cooperation.* Boston: Houghton Mifflin.

Tedin, K. L., D. W. Brady, M. E. Buxton, B. M. Gorman, and J. L. Thompson. 1977. "Social Background and Political Differences Between Pro- and Anti-ERA Activists." *American Politics Quarterly* 5(July):395–408.

Tilly, Charles. a:1964. *The Vendee.* Cambridge: Harvard University Press.

———. b:1969. "Collective Violence in European Perspective." In Hugh Graham and Ted Gurr, *Violence in America.* New York: Bantam.

———. c:1978. *From Mobilization to Revolution.* Reading: Addison-Wesley.

Tilly, Charles, Louis Tilly, and Richard Tilly. 1975. *The Rebellious Century, 1830–1930.* Cambridge: Harvard University Press.

ARTICLE 22

Leader-Member Conflict in Protest Organizations: The Case of the Southern Farmers' Alliance

MICHAEL SCHWARTZ
NAOMI ROSENTHAL
LAURA SCHWARTZ

For nearly sixty years, Robert Michels' "iron law of oligarchy" has been invoked to explain both the dominance of leadership elites in modern protest movement organizations and the frequent displacement of movement goals within the organizational framework. Michels saw protest movements as the only political weapon available to common people, but he was extremely pessimistic about the ability of the masses to maintain control over their own creations.

Michels' (1962) reasoning was based on two presumptions, one structural and the other psychological. First, the size of mass organizations and the need for functional specialization inevitably create a structural impetus for the transformation to oligarchy. Second, apathy and hero worship, always ingredients in membership involvement, inevitably provide a conducive psychological atmosphere for its development (Cassinelli, 1953:781). These underlying factors produce a dynamic which results in dictatorial control by a leadership clique:

> *The technical specialization that inevitably results from all extensive organization renders necessary what is called expert leadership. Consequently, the power of determination comes to be considered one of the specific attributes of leadership, and is gradually withdrawn from the masses, to be concentrated in the hands of the leaders alone . . . (Michels, 1962:70).*

Once in control, the leaders consolidate their privilege and transform the original goals:

> *At the outset leaders arise SPONTANEOUSLY: their functions are ACCESSORY and GRATUITOUS. Soon, however, they become PROFESSIONAL leaders, and in this second stage of development they are STABLE and IRREMOVABLE (Michels, 1962:364, author's emphasis).*

This compelling vision has become the foundation for many of the most enduring precepts used by theorists of social movement behavior, especially those who analyze social movements as psycho-social phenomenon. Michels' keen logic meshes nicely into Weber's (1947) notion of charismatic leadership and bureaucratic rationalization. It provides a foundation for such diverse concepts as role specialization (Lang and Lang, 1961) and functional requirements of leadership (Smelser, 1962), and has become central to the presumption that a wholly internal set of dynamics condition the fate of protest movement organizations. . . .

THE CASE OF THE SOUTHERN FARMERS' ALLIANCE

The Southern Farmers' Alliance (SFA) was the largest and most active of the protest groups which formed the basis of the Populist Party in the 1890s. The SFA was founded in the late 1870s as the successor to the Grange (Goodwin, 1976; Schwartz, 1976; Woodward, 1938) and grew into the largest unified farmers' organization in U.S. history. Between 1885 and 1890, the SFA initiated a remarkably broad and comprehensive set of programs designed to reform and revolutionize the one-crop cotton tenancy system. Strikes, cooperatives, boycotts, counter-institutions, political lobbying, and physical force were all tried without lasting results. In 1892, the SFA collapsed and was superseded by the Populist Party which, in its turn, died after its large-scale, third-party electoral efforts were frustrated. Many historians have concluded that these failures prove the impossibility of meaningful agrarian reform in the late nineteenth century (Hicks, 1925, 1931; Woodward, 1938). However, these interpretations have rested on the uninvestigated assumption that the farmers' protest organizations (the most important of which was the SFA) could not be effective in resisting the consolidation of the tenant farming system and the further impoverishment of the southern farmer. This assumption is unwarranted: a study of the internal dynamics of the SFA reveals the existence of potentially successful reform policies. Had these strategies prevailed, the misery of cotton sharecropping might have been alleviated (Schwartz, 1976). However, these tendencies failed to win over the organization, and the consequent failure of agrarian reform was an organizational problem, instead of an inevitable consequence of the structure of southern society. This reinterpretation of SFA failure relies on an understanding of leader-member conflict, since this conflict was central to the development and crystallization of the losing strategies which the group pursued.

Leadership

Once the SFA became a force in the cotton-growing South, it attracted individuals from all rural strata who were discontented with their economic circumstances. In those southern states with considerable commercial, industrial or non-cotton agricultural areas, plantation owners found themselves with many grievances. A substantial number joined the SFA and rapidly rose to leadership positions (Schwartz, 1976:95). This was facilitated by the SFA's growth, which involved the merger of two different kinds of organizations. One type—the sort we ordinarily associate with populist movements—recruited large numbers of poor farmers into clubs and depended upon mass action for its power. The other type of constituent group depended upon the individual power of prestigious cotton planters and did not emphasize mass organization. Its members were usually large cotton landlords with grievances quite different from their poorer brethren. The dissolution of these groups, and the subsequent appearance of their members in prominent positions in the SFA, became the major recruiting device for SFA leadership in many states.

In North Carolina, the Farmers' Clubs, a looseknit protest group made up almost exclusively of plantation owners, dissolved in 1888 and urged its members to enter the SFA, which had proven itself the more viable organization. Within a year, large planters, previously members of the Farmers' Clubs, had risen to the state presidency, the state lectureship (the only full-time office), and other major offices. The Farmers' Club newspaper, *The Progressive Farmer*, had become the statewide organ of the SFA and the editor, L. L. Polk (a nephew of U.S. President Polk), was soon afterward elected National Farmers' Alliance president (Schwartz, 1976).

The Virginia Farmers' Assembly had only 200 members, largely planters, but it "included many of the most distinguished names in the state." By 1889, 170 of these individuals had joined the SFA where they held most of the leadership positions (Sheldon, 1935:24).

The recruitment of planters to state-wide and local leadership positions can also be documented in Alabama (Bratten, 1938; Hackney, 1966; Rogers, 1962) and Georgia (Woodward, 1938). The phenomenon was less significant in South Carolina and Mississippi, where discontented plantation owners successfully captured the state government without joining the SFA (Simkins, 1944). In Texas, Arkansas, Louisiana, Tennessee, and Florida the evidence is fragmentary, but it seems to point to a substantial, if not dominant, landlord presence (Knauss, 1926; Lucia, 1943; Martin, 1924; Morgan, 1889; Saloutos, 1969; Schwartz, 1976).

At the national level, a more systematic study is possible. The SFA, like many other organizations, proudly printed brief biographies of its leaders. Fifty-one biographies, representing every important national leader of the two major organizations which merged to form the SFA in 1888, illustrate the social origins of leadership. We obtained information about occupation, education, wealth, and the holding of political office. Comparing leaders with members we found the following differences between the two groups: Eighteen percent of leaders (compared with less than 5 percent of members) were wealthy; 38 percent of leaders (less than 3 percent of members) were college educated; 26 percent of leaders (less than 3 percent of members) held previous political office. In a combined index, 65 percent of the leaders possessed at least one of these characteristics, while the membership figure is under 11 percent. There can be little dispute that the social origins of the leaders were dramatically different from those of the members. Furthermore, 93 percent of SFA members were farmers. In contrast, only 53 percent of leaders farmed and one-third of the farming leaders had other occupations as well.

The figures support a functionalist analysis that leaders were recruited because of the special skills they possessed. The non-farmers all had useful training: editorial skills, public-speaking experience and administrative backgrounds. Twelve of the 17 farmers who had other occupations also had special leadership skills. Moreover, the holding of public office implied organizing skills: education included a whole array of useful attributes and wealth implied material resources and local prominence. These are crucial for any protest group, and individuals with these attributes would be pushed or recruited into leadership roles.

This interpretation should not be stretched too far with the data at hand. If recruitment followed a purely functionalist pattern, people with elite attributes would be given roles which reflected their elite skills. This did not occur with any regularity. most newspaper editors in the SFA had previous experience in journalism, but beyond that, elite skills did not match SFA positions. Wealthy members did not concentrate in business management positions. Political office holders did not concentrate in proselytizing positions. In short, special occupational background did not imply a special role in the organization. This lack of consistency may reflect the possibility for individuals to move into leadership roles different from those of their original expertise. Therefore, we conclude that the evidence suggests, but does not prove, that functional recruitment occurred.

Our discussion thus far points to two conclusions which support the hypothesis that SFA leaders were recruited from different strata than members:

1. Leaders were drawn from a different pool than members.
2. Leaders on the state level were landlords. On the national level they had political experi-

ence, were highly educated, and had greater wealth than their followers.

Membership

Before proceeding to a discussion of the consequences of these leadership characteristics, we offer a portrait of the membership. In doing so, we outline the economic and social interest of the rank-and-file, and therefore bring into focus the significance of differential recruitment in the SFA.

Most accounts of populism characterize the SFA as an organization of small farm owners (yeomen) looking for a way to make small farming profitable and, therefore, avoid descending into debt peonage and sharecropping (Hicks, 1931; Saloutos, 1969; Woodward, 1951). Little systematic work, however, has been done to validate this assertion. Data are scanty and membership figures are always unreliable. It is, therefore, difficult to actually test this critical proposition.

This study relies upon the organizational records of the state alliances. The SFA held annual state conventions and the published proceedings always contained the names of the counties represented, but in the SFA's early years the organization was nurtured in small sectors of each state. We identified counties which were the site of early SFA strength by searching convention minutes and accounts. To determine the socio-economic character of early SFA members, we collated this information with data from the U.S. Bureau of the Census (1890; 1915). Since the analysis involved cohorts and not individuals, we inferred characteristics of SFA members from the demographic composition of the areas in which they resided.

Table 1 shows the proportion small owners and the proportion white, as well as the amount of cotton planted, for counties organized by the SFA before 1889. The major strength came from counties where there were few blacks, a large number of owner-operated farms, and a large amount of cotton acreage. (It is generally accepted that over 10,000 acres of cotton planted was the hallmark of a "cotton-county.") In Texas, the 18 early SFA counties averaged 60 percent yeoman and 95 percent white, compared with 40 percent yeoman and 79 percent white for the major cotton counties in the state. In Mississippi, a state with only 42 percent white population and 57 percent yeoman, the five early SFA counties were 82 percent white and 60 percent yeoman. In the same year (1886), five SFA counties in Tennessee showed many fewer blacks and a great many more yeoman than the surrounding area.

This pattern is broken by the data on Alabama, Florida and North Carolina, where the 42 counties organized by 1887 included 33 with less than 70 percent yeoman population, 17 with less than 60 percent and six with less than 50 percent.

TABLE 1 Acreage in Cotton, Average Percent Yeoman, and Average Percent Black in Counties Organized by the Southern Farmers' Alliance

STATE	MEAN ACREAGE IN COTTON	MEAN PERCENT YEOMAN, 1890	MEAN PERCENT WHITE, 1890	YEAR	NUMBER OF COUNTIES
Texas	33,700	60%	95%	1886	18
Tennessee	21,000	60%	78%	1885	5
Mississippi	16,400	66%	82%	1886	5
Alabama	33,000	58%	66%	1887	18
Florida	8,400	79%	62%	1887	17
North Carolina	29,400	63%	62%	1887	7
North Carolina	17,300	62%	62%	1888	46

Sources: U.S. Bureau of the Census, 1890, 1915.

The key to understanding this lies in analyzing the figures for year of organization. Alabama, Florida, and North Carolina were organized in 1887, while the Texas, Tennessee and Mississippi figures related to SFA organization in 1886 or earlier. The difference is one of SFA program and of organizing orientation. Before 1887, the SFA was oriented towards local actions, mounted by yeomen who had cash on hand with which to support selective buying campaigns. No real effort was made to send organizers or proselytizers to areas with few yeomen. In heavily black or tenant counties, even where there were many white yeomen, local merchants could outlast SFA actions by serving blacks and/or tenants. Thus the possibility of successful action, based on white yeomanry alone, was greatly inhibited. Even though there were ample white yeomen to be organized, the presence of blacks or tenants greatly inhibited SFA organization during the early years.

Later, SFA activity shifted to state-wide economic programs or political pressure. With the focus on these programs, it made more sense to organize white in heavily black areas. Since those counties tended to be more depressed than areas with white yeomen exclusively, they were often among the first counties organized. Furthermore, using travelling organizers greatly increased the likelihood of reaching these counties.

The tenancy figures in Table 1 would seem to undermine this explanation, since the figure for Alabama, Florida, and North Carolina show that yeomanry was high in the counties organized. However, in Florida there were only five counties with less than 60 percent yeomen; three of them were organized in the first few months of proselytizing. (The other two were over 80 percent black and hardly had enough whites to sustain any white organization.) Similarly, in North Carolina all 11 counties with less than 50 percent yeomanry, and 16 of 20 with less than 60 percent white, were organized by 1888.

The evidence suggests, therefore, that early SFA membership was largely restricted to white yeomanry with cash on hand. Later, when the organizing thrust switched from local boycotts to statewide coordinated action, the SFA spread to heavily black and tenantized areas. Hence, by the late 1880's, the SFA was composed of a cross section of white yeomen and tenant farmers.

Although this evidence is by no means complete, it helps form a picture of SFA membership in the early years. This picture is confirmed by the one extant survey of SFA membership, conducted from the South Carolina State Alliance in early 1889 (*National Economist*, May 27, 1889). Haphazardly gathered and poorly reported, the evidence alone would be a poor indicator of the backgrounds of SFA members. Nevertheless, the survey confirms the data offered here. Of 12,500 SFA members who responded to the survey, 8,665 listed their occupations: 93 percent were farmers, with 64 percent of the farmers yeomen and 36 percent tenants. Since over 50 percent of South Carolina farmers were tenants, these figures suggest that the SFA made its early and most extensive appeal to yeomen. Since the number of tenant members is probably underestimated in this survey, and since even without accounting for this factor, over one-third of the membership were tenants, we can see that the SFA was by no means restricted to yeomen.

Before discussing tensions within the organization, let us briefly summarize our findings. The SFA made headway in heavily yeoman cotton regions. It experienced early difficulty in reaching into sections based on tenant farming, but later overcame this resistance and spread to these areas, even in counties which were predominantly black. The consistency of results indicates that the possibility of mistaking the characteristics of the group because of selectivity within the region is remote. The SFA recruited small cotton farmers who either owned or rented their farms. These members brought to the organization an extensive set of grievances, problems, and demands concerning low cotton prices, high supply costs, and chronic indebtedness (Brooks, 1914; Hicks, 1931; Schwartz, 1976; Woodward, 1938).

Leader-Member Tension

Two sets of interests coexisted within the SFA. The leaders represented landlords and included a considerable contingent of people who had previously held political office and entertained further political ambitions. The rank-and-file was almost exclusively small owners and tenants, searching for solutions to their economic problems. Thus, the leaders and members had different interests as well as their common commitment to the defense of the agrarian system. This commitment allowed different constituencies with different goals to coexist within the organization–but it did not prevent clashes between the two groups.

As the leaders consolidated their power and concentrated on their own political and economic interests, they threatened to alter the stance and thrust of the organization. Simultaneously, rank-and-file members began to challenge the leadership. The class interests of the two groups (leaders and followers) were actually incompatible. The members were, however, unable to permanently regain control of the movement; the leaders took actions which would eventually destroy the organization.

There is evidence that SFA members often understood these tendencies. One indication of these concerns can be found in the complaints of members against politician-leaders. Consider the following letters to SFA newspapers:

> *One of our greatest faults is that we elect or promote men to prominent offices in our order who either hold or have held prominent political offices. I consider that a weak point in our organic law. Can you point out a single one at the present time elected to any political office who is not under the thumb and influence of either of the old political bosses? (Florida Dispatch, July 4, 1889).*

> *I wish there was an article in our constitution prohibiting politicians from membership in the Alliance, and where a member turns politician to dismiss him from the order at once. Because they were welded to their idol, they will never be any more than a firebrand in our ranks (Florida Dispatch, July 4, 1889).*

> *One of the great dangers to [Alliance] success and usefulness lies in the fact that unworthy men in no way directly connected with tilling the soil as a means of sustenance . . . seek membership in its ranks that their own ends may be accomplished, regardless of the welfare of the order (Raleigh Progressive Farmer, September 19, 1889).*

The leaders responded by advocating programs to centralize the control of the organization. For example, before 1887, recruitment had been handled by local groups. But state leadership soon gave themselves the job—appointing state lecturers to attract members (instead of giving support to local efforts), and having these lecturers collect dues directly, pocketing half the cash as wages while sending the remainder to the state organization (*Florida Dispatch*, October 10, 1887). Rather than finance conventions through fund-raising among membership, the leadership accepted inducements from merchants and cities to hold the conventions in their towns—making the choice of site more dependent upon ease of financing than upon membership convenience (Blood, 1893:39; Knauss, 1926:310; *National Economist*, December 20, 1890; Proctor, 1950:162). State-wide SFA newspapers shifted their priorities from internal education and local emphasis to circulation and membership drives (Schwartz, 1976:118). When major programs were begun, the state leaders developed new, centralized structures to direct them, instead of using already existent clubs and locally controlled mechanisms (Schwartz, 1976:239; Smith, 1945).

While these developments were part of a process of internal centralization, they did not necessarily hinder the organization's development. Nor did they reflect the "external" interests of the leadership, either as a group of landlords seeking to impose their own policies on poorer farmers, or as ambitious individuals. Instead, they seem to suggest an internally developing oligarchy consolidating and perpetuating its control while preserving the organization.

However, three further examples illustrate the broader forces at work and demonstrate that leadership policies could and did threaten the viability of the SFA as a protest group. By mid-1886, the SFA, with around 100,000 members, had become a major force in Texas. Nevertheless, it was facing considerable difficulty. Local boycotts, the main activity until then, had failed and it had become clear that without a new program the organization would atrophy and die. At the August convention in Clebourne, Texas, the leaders proposed to refocus the organization's energy on lobbying the Texas state legislature, participating in political conventions, and endorsing candidates. Though this program passed, it triggered a minority revolt at the convention, and this revolt spread so quickly afterward that it threatened to destroy the organization. The rank-and-file rapidly mobilized against the new policy, throwing its support to the dissidents who favored the already established economic orientation. Ultimately, after losing many members and the threat of an actual division, the leaders resigned and a new convention was called. The second convention adopted a new economic program and a national organizing drive (Drew, 1891:283; Dunning, 1891:40; Hicks and Burkhart, 1929:264; Hunt, 1935:31; *National Economist*, December 14, 1889; Smith, 1945:355).

This conflict over policy did not reflect a conservative orientation of the leaders. They sought to shift the group away from economic action into the political arena. If successful, the transfer to politics would have brought SFA leaders into friendly contact with major political leaders, made them well known throughout the state, and given them a large constituency for their political careers.

A political elite tried to use the SFA as a vehicle for political advancement. But political lobbying did not offer any promise of direct or immediate alleviation of debt, improvement in cotton prices, or reduction of rental costs—the issues that concerned members. And, since the success of this strategy depended upon the future votes of SFA members, the members' antagonism was effective, even though the convention had endorsed the proposals. The leaders were defeated; this led to the development of statewide and national economic actions which became the hallmark of the SFA. Members' resistance was the key element in the SFA's expansion from a 100,000-member group in Texas to a massive southern organization with national visibility.

Various interpretations of this incident within Michels' framework are possible. It can be seen as an example of resource mobilization, using the logic of McCarthy and Exalt (1977): leaders tapped the broadest potential vein of resources to advance the organizations' interest. If, in so doing, they ignored the wishes (and perhaps even the interests) of the members, this illustrates that a crucial factor in organizational behavior is material support from outsiders who have only a tangential interest in the welfare of the membership.

The incident can also be viewed from the perspective of Froelich et al. (1971), who argue that leadership is independent of membership and view leaders as entrepreneurs searching for the optimum combination of resources with which to advance their careers. Seen in this light, the shift into politics was simply a judgment by the disembodied leaders that such a move would further their own political careers.

These interpretations assume that the leaders desired to enhance their own standing *within the organization*. McCarthy and Exalt (1977) and Froelich et al. (1971) sharpen our understanding of the formation of oligarchy and offer a more detailed analysis of the type of leadership behavior which is consistent with such an argument. Nevertheless, lurking beneath this apparent consistency with Michels' theory is a nagging inconsistency. The attempted transfer of SFA activity from the economic to the electoral realm represented a dramatic and forceful change in direction. This was resisted at the convention and was ultimately overthrown by a massive rebellion from local groups. The leadership had tampered with a stable set of ongoing relationships within the organization, risking organizational suicide in order to pursue a policy which was risky to the organization. It was not a safe move. These events contradict Michels' formulation which provided the foundation of later analyses of intra-organizational conflict. Thus, the leaders jeopardized the organization for a policy which was, at best, uncertain. A conservative, self-serving leadership would not do this. Internal oligarchies can only maintain themselves if the organization as a whole is secure. The switch to electoral politics guaranteed major disruption and threatened the very existence of the organization. The leaders' political background suggests that the underlying motive was electoral ambition and that the death of the SFA was acceptable if it resulted in promising electoral careers.

This sense of misfit in Michels' logic is made more explicit by a consideration of SFA policies towards black members. While the SFA was the least racist of any white group in southern history (it adopted many overtly anti-racist positions and was sometimes successful in mobilizing whites behind policies of cross-racial unity), most historians agree that racism was a major factor in its demise. The easily mobilized prejudice of white southerners made it difficult for black and white farmers to achieve the unity that might have proven capable of resisting the growth, extension and impoverishment of the tenant farming system (Allen, 1974; Goodwin, 1976; Schwartz, 1976; Woodward, 1938:195). A major factor in this weakness was the exclusion of blacks from the SFA and the establishment of a separate, fraternal Colored Farmers' Alliance (Abramowitz, 1947, 1950, 1953). The two groups were meant to coordinate their programs and structures at local, state and national levels, but such coordination was difficult to achieve.

Although the history of southern racism suggests that this exclusion would be endorsed by white SFA members, this was not entirely the case. In 1888–1889, the two major SFA organizations amalgamated into one unified group of about 600,000 members. One group, the Agricultural Wheel, had been racially integrated. The leaders who negotiated the merger agreed that blacks would be expelled from the Wheel and sent into the Colored Farmers' Alliance. This decision was challenged by members of the rank-and-file, led by the Mississippi delegation which had passed a motion at its state convention denouncing exclusion:

> *Resolved: That we do not think it advisable, prudent or just to go into a union with the Farmers' Alliance or with any organization that requires us to exclude a part of our members. We having taken into our organization the colored people, and having full assurance that the order has been of mutual benefit to us, we are opposed to excluding them from membership in the proposed organization, unless they prefer a separate organization with the same objects and aims (Morgan, 1889:104).*

These protests were defeated, apparently through the intervention of wealthy farmers who were strongly represented among the leadership. These landlords did not want their black tenants organized around SFA demands, even though such organizing would have given white tenants and yeomen more leverage on the system (Dunning, 1891:74; Morgan, 1889:104; Saloutos, 1969:79; Schwartz, 1976:95).

A different balance of power within the SFA could have produced a different SFA posture in subsequent events. Racial exclusion was organized by the leaders and opposed by some of the members. The consequences of recruitment of landlords to leadership positions, therefore, extended far beyond the confines of intra-organizational life; it helped to determine the entire posture and future of SFA policy.

The exclusion of blacks from direct membership in the SFA was not the end of racial tension within the organization; and whenever this tension became visible, the same lines of division emerged. For example, during a state-wide boycott movement in 1889, North Carolina Alliance county organizations began to recruit members and chapters of the Colored Farmers' Alliance.

The state president at the time was Elias Carr, a large planter whose plantations were manned almost exclusively by black tenants. Carr opposed the recruitment of black members and even opposed coordination between the colored and white alliances on this issue. Moreover, when members raised the issue of the relationship between the white and colored alliances, Carr, in the columns of the state-wide *Progressive Farmer*, denied any fraternal relationship. This duplicity was maintained throughout the period of Carr's regime and until the demise of the SFA itself. Moreover, in 1889, while the national convention was passing a reunification measure between the white and colored alliances (as well as a strong statement of support of the demands of black farmers), the North Carolina leadership combined resistance to these policies with a continuing denial of any fraternity between the organizations (Schwartz, 1976).

Though these incidents are only a sample from a wide range of similar occurrences, as many authors have noted, the SFA worked diligently for interracial unity (Goodwin, 1976; Hackney, 1966; Woodward, 1938, 1951). The leaders in this instance, however, pursued racist policies even when members were receptive to racial inclusion. This illustrates an important process which is usually ignored by theorists of intra-organizational dynamics: the leadership imposed upon its membership a policy calculated to substantially reduce the overall size—and therefore the overall power—of the organization. As leaders, these individuals would certainly benefit from an expanding base and increasing membership. Indeed, many of Michels' conclusions rest upon precisely such an argument. For example, Michels himself argues that the deradicalization of social democratic programs in Germany were explicit attempts to expand the support base of the political party. The leadership sacrificed the interests of the current membership in order to appeal to other groups and thus enhance its own security (Michels, 1962:163).

In thc racial exclusion in the SFA, however, we see that planter leadership reduced membership (and therefore undermined its own internal authority) to create an organization which would be more receptive to the needs of plantation owners. This policy served the outside interests of the leadership rather than their interests as an internal oligarchy. In this case, an analysis of the class allegiances of movement leaders is essential for an understanding of their behavior in the organization. Michels' argument will not do.

From 1889 to 1890, the SFA, responding to a 100 percent price increase, carried out a national boycott of jute bagging—a commodity used to wrap bales of cotton. At the critical juncture in 1890, there were at least two plausible courses of action; the most appealing was a deescalation of the boycott with a partial victory. Instead of adopting one of the two available means of salvaging the aims of the boycott, leadership puts its own resources and energy into setting the stage for SFA entry into political lobbying and electoral efforts. It set up legislative committees to represent the SFA in state capitals and to influence the choice of political candidates (Martin, 1924:31). It made shaky coalitions with other farmers' groups which could only be useful in coordinating political endorsements (Proctor, 1950). And it arranged an expensive convention in out-of-the-way Ocala, Florida. This convention signalled the beginning of SFA participation in electoral politics and projected SFA leaders into the political center stage, culminating in the election of many to state and local offices (Hicks, 1931:170; Martin, 1924; Proctor, 1950; Woodward, 1938).

In the meantime, the boycott was allowed to die in the most devastating manner: the farmers were forced to rewrap their cotton at great expense. This demoralized the membership and began a process of disintegration which culminated in the death of the organization (*Florida Dispatch*, October 10, 1889; *National Economist*, May-December, 1889; Schwartz, 1976:225; Smith, 1945:346). Instead of adopting compromises and conservative actions which might have preserved or strengthened the organization, leaders propelled it into self-destructive political action.

CONCLUSION

An oligarchy formed within the leadership of the Southern Farmers' Alliance in much the manner that Michels would predict. The leadership group was, however, more than an internally generated clique. It was largely dominated by the planter class of the southern tenant farming system, and by individuals with a history of political ambition and office holding. The leaders had different outside loyalties than most of the members. The attempted entry into Texas politics was a reckless and difficult enterprise which threatened the existence of the organization. The exclusion of blacks substantially weakened the membership base, limiting both the SFA's size and its potential political effectiveness. The abandonment of economic activity in favor of electoral politics was self-conscious attempt to abandon the organization as a whole, and it ultimately succeeded. All three policies were at variance with Michels' prediction: the first risked the existence of the organization; the second guaranteed a limited appeal; and the third led to the demise of the very structure that conferred leadership. These policies are readily understandable in the context of an analysis of the outside interests and loyalties of the leadership group. In each case leaders sought to pursue programs which would aggrandize the planter class, advance the political careers of SFA officeholders, or both; they thus came into conflict with a sometimes-militant, sometime-passive, constituency.

REFERENCES

Abramowitz, Carl. 1974. "Agrarian reformers and the negro question." Negro History Bulletin 11 (March):128–139.

Abramowitz, Carl. 1950. "The Negro in the agrarian revolt." Agricultural History 24 (April):88–95.

Abramowitz, Carl. 1953. "The Negro in the populist movement." Journal of Negro History 38 (July):257–289.

Allen, Robert. 1974. Reluctant Reformers. Washington, D.C.: Howard University Press.

Ash, Roberta. 1972. Social Movements in America. Chicago: Markham Publishing Company.

Barkan, Steven E. 1979. "Strategic, tactical and organizational dilemmas of the protest movement against nuclear power." Social Problems 27 (October):19–42.

Blood, F. G. 1893. Handbook and History of the National Farmers' Alliance and Individual Union. Washington, D.C.: Farmers' Alliance.

Bratten, O. M. 1938. "Elmore County politics, 1890–1900." Unpublished Masters dissertation, University of Alabama.

Breines, W. 1979. "Community and organization: The new left as a social movement 1962–1968." Unpublished Ph.D. dissertation, Brandeis University, Boston, Mass.

Brooks, Robert P. 1914. The Agrarian Revolution in Georgia. Madison, Wisconsin: Bulletin of the University of Wisconsin, History Series (Vol. 3).

Carden, Maren Lockwood. 1974. The New Feminist Movement. New York: Russell Sage.

Cassinelli, C. W. 1953. "The iron law of oligarchy." American Political Science Review 47 (September):773–784.

Cloward, Richard A. and Frances Fox Piven. 1977. Poor People's Movements: Why They Succeed, How They Fail. New York: Pantheon.

Drew, Frank M. 1891. "The present farmers' movement." Political Science Quarterly 14 (June):282–310.

Dunning, Nelson A. 1891. The Farmer's Alliance History and Agricultural Digest. Washington, D.C.: Farmers' Alliance.

Florida Dispatch 1887–1890. Official newspaper of the Florida Farmers' Alliance. Jacksonville, Florida.

Freeman, Jo. 1975. The Politics of Women's Liberation. New York: D. McKay.

Froelich, Norman, Joe A. Oppenheimer and Oran R. Young. 1971. Political Leadership and Collective Goods. Princeton: Princeton University Press.

Gamson, William A. 1975. The Strategy of Social Protest. Homewood, Illinois: The Dorsey Press.

Goodwin, Lawrence. 1976. Democratic Promise. New York: Oxford University Press.

Gordon, Hans. 1971. "Robert Michels and the study of political parties." British Journal of Political Science 1 (April):155–172.

Hackney, Francis. 1966. "From populism to progressivism in Alabama, 1890–9110." Unpublished Ph.D. dissertation, Yale University, New Haven, Connecticut.

Hicks, John D. 1925. "The Farmers' Alliance in North Carolina." North Carolina Historical Review 2(April): 162–187.

Hicks, John D. 1931. The Populist Revolt. Minneapolis: University of Minnesota Press.

Hicks, John D. and John D. Burkhart. 1929. "The Farmers' Alliance." North Carolina Historical Review 6 (July):254–280.

Hunt, Robert Lee. 1935. A History of Farmers' Movements in the Southwest, 1873–1925. College Station, Texas: University of Texas.

Jenkins, J. Craig and Charles Perrow. 1977. "Insurgency of the powerless: Farm worker movements 1946–1972," American Sociological Review 42(April):249–268.

Kelso, William Alton. 1978. American Democratic Theory. Westport, Connecticut: Greenwood Press.

Knauss, James O. 1926. "The Farmers' Alliance in Florida." South Atlantic Quarterly 25 (July):300–315.

Lang, Kurt and Gladys Lang. 1961. Collective Dynamics. New York: Crowell.

Lipset, Semour M., Martin A. Trow and James S. Coleman. 1956. Union Democracy. Glencoe: Free Press.

Lucia, Daniel. 1943. "The Louisiana people's party." Louisiana Historical Quarterly 26 (October):1055–1149.

McCarthy, John D. and Mayer N. Exalt. 1977. "Resource mobilization and social movements: A partial theory." American Journal of Sociology 82(May):1212–1241.

Martin, Roscoe. 1924. The People's Party in Texas. Austin, Texas: University of Texas Press.

Michels, Robert. 1962. [1911] Political Parties: A Sociological Study of the Oligarchical Tendencies of Modern Democracy. New York: Free Press.

Morgan, W. Scott. 1889. History of the Wheel and Alliance and the Impending Revolution. Fort Scott, Kansas: Farmers' Alliance.

National Economist 1889–1893. Official newspaper of the Farmers' Alliance, Agricultural Wheel and Farmers' Union. Washington, D.C.

Oberschall, Anthony. 1973. Social Conflict and Social Movements. Englewood Cliffs, New Jersey: Prentice-Hall.

Proctor, Samuel. 1950. "The National Farmers' Alliance convention of 1890 and its 'Ocala Demands'." Florida Historical Quarterly 28(January):161–181.

Raleigh Progressive Farmer. 1889. Official newspaper of the north Carolina Farmers' Alliance. Raleigh, North Carolina.

Redstockings. 1978. Feminist Revolution. New York: Random House.

Rogers, William W. 1962. "The Farmers' Alliance in Alabama," The Alabama Review 15(January):5–18.

Rothschild-Whitt, Joyce. 1976. "Conditions favoring participatory democratic organizations." Sociological Inquiry 46(2):75–86.

Saloutos, Theodore. 1969. Farmer Movements in the South, 1860– 1933. Berkeley: University of California.

Schwartz, Michael. 1976. Radical Protest and Social Structure. New York: Academic Press.

Sheldon, William D. 1935. Populism in the Old Dominion: Virginia Farm Politics, 1885–1900. Princeton, New Jersey: Princeton University Press.

Simkins, Francis Butler, 1944. Pitchfork Ben Tillman of South Carolina. Baton Rouge, Louisiana: University of Louisiana.

Smelser, Neil J. 1962. Collective Behavior. New York: Free Press.

Smith, Ralph. 1945. "The Farmers' Alliance in Texas, 1875–1900." Southwestern Historical Quarterly 48 (January): 346–369.

U.S. Bureau of the Census. 1890. Agriculture. Vol. 5 of Eleventh Census of the United States, Washington, D.C.: Government Printing Office.

U.S. Bureau of the Census. 1915. Farms, Farm Characteristics, Livestock and Products, Crops, Fruits, Values. Vol. 2 of the United States Census of Agriculture, Washington, D.C.: Government Printing Office.

U.S. Bureau of the Census. 1965. The Statistical History of the United States from Colonial Times to the Present. Stanford, Connecticut: Fairfield Publishers.

U.S. Bureau of the Census. 1968. Negro Population in the United States, 1790–1915. New York: Arno Press.

Useem, Michael. 1979. Protest Movements in America. Indianapolis, Indiana: Bobbs-Merrill.

Weber, Max. 1947. Theory of Social and Economic Organization. New York: Free Press.

Woodward, C. Vann. 1938. Tom Watson, Agrarian Rebel. New York: Free Press.

Woodward, C. Vann. 1951. Origins of the New South, 1877–1913. Baton Rouge: University of Louisiana.

Zald, Meyer N. and Roberta Ash. 1966. "Social movement organizations: Growth, decay and change." Social Forces 44(March):327–340.

ARTICLE 23

The Ideology of a Therapeutic Social Movement: Alcoholics Anonymous

LEONARD BLUMBERG

. . . Every social movement has a story of origin promulgated by its leaders and accepted by its followers. Usually the promulgators claim to have discovered the principles of the movement (which they say are but re-enunciations of sacred principles from the past), or they claim that the principles of the movement were gifts from a divine source. Usually the actual origins of the movement, being unrecorded, are difficult if not impossible to reconstruct. Fortunately, this is not the case for A.A. Rarely does the leadership of a social movement take the pains that Bill W.—William Wilson—took to explain the immediate sources of A.A. If inventions are unique syntheses of previously exiting elements, and if one accepts the concept of social inventions, then Bill W. and his associates clearly invented the ideology and practices of A.A. (By "ideology" is meant the central governing set of beliefs or assertions which explain the predicament in which people find themselves, which provide a focus for the behavior of those who subscribe to this set of beliefs, which justify one set of practices rather than another, and which form the basis for the program advocated to others.)

The present discussion is an exposition of the elements of this ideology. It explores several "sources behind the sources" of A.A. The hope is to gain a better understanding of the origins of one of the most persuasive and widely accepted therapeutic social movements of our day.

For purposes of discussion, the "roots" of A.A. may be arbitrarily divided into medical, psychological and religious sources. Within each major source, there are a number of possible influences which vary in their significance. These are considered in turn. Attitudes and information that have a reasonable likelihood of having been influential during the formative period of A.A., rather than all possible influences on Bill W. and his associates, are examined.

In *Alcoholics Anonymous Comes of Age*, Bill W. acknowledged the importance to A.A. of William D. Silkworth, M.D., "the benign little doctor who loved drunks. . . . [H]e supplied us with the tools with which to puncture the toughest alcoholic ego, those shattering phrases by which he described our illness: *the obsession of the mind* that compels us to drink and the *allergy of the body* that condemns us to go mad or die" (1, p. 13). When Bill W. was discouraged because in the first six months he had not converted anyone, it was Silkworth who quoted William James's statement that "transforming spiritual experiences are nearly always founded on calamity and collapse" (1, pp. 13, 64). Dr. Silkworth also advised Bill W. to stop preaching and to start with a medical discussion. If "drunks" realize the

Reprinted with permission from *Journal of Studies on Alcohol,* vol. 38, pp. 2122–43, 1977.

medical consequences of alcohol, Silkworth argued, they may become desperate enough to accept Bill W.'s spiritual approach (1, p. 13). That Bill W. was deeply grateful was evident in the appeal that he and his associates made in 1951 to raise funds so that Dr. Silkworth could retire to New Hampshire. Dr. Silkworth died in 1951, not very long after that solicitation was made. Bill W.'s sense of affection and personal loss is expressed in a notation on a copy of their appeal for funds (found in the archives of the General Service Conference of A.A.): "Thank Heaven we started this before Silkie went!"

Dr. Silkworth graduates from Princeton University, took his M.D. degree at New York University and interned at Bellevue Hospital in New York City. A specialist in neuropsychiatry, he was a member of the psychiatric staff of the U.S. Army Hospital at Plattsburgh, New York, during World War I. From 1919 to 1929, he was an associate physician at the Neurological Institute of Presbyterian Hospital in New York City. From 1932 until his death, he was physician-in-charge and then medical superintendent of the Charles B. Towns Hospital in New York City, and from 1945 he served also as director of the alcoholism treatment center of Knickerbocker Hospital.

Dr. Silkworth, alone or with others, wrote and had published eight articles, including the anonymous introduction to *Alcoholics Anonymous* (1, p. 168; 2), the first book-length statement by Bill W. and his associates. The earliest of Dr. Silkworth's writings was published in 1937 and the latest in 1950. Five were about A.A. and the other three approached drunkenness and alcoholism as organic problems. "Alcoholism as manifestation of allergy" (3) stated his position: "The physical treatment of these patients has heretofore been unsatisfactory. But if we recognize the condition as a species of anaphylaxis occurring in persons constitutionally susceptible to sensitization by alcohol, the problem resolves itself into two factors. First, the revitalizing and normalizing of cells, and second, the energizing of the normalized cells into producing their own defensive mechanism. . . . [O]n the mental side, from our point of view, the situation is a practical one and must be met through the medium of intelligence and not emotion. Nothing is to be gained by substituting one emotion for another. The patient cannot use alcohol at all for physiological reasons. He must understand and accept the situation as a law of nature operating inexorably. Once he has fully and intelligently grasped the facts of the matter he will shape his policy accordingly." Thus, Dr. Silkworth was thoroughly imbued with a medical approach while committed to total abstinence as a part of therapy. . . .

For many years the dominant medical influence at Towns Hospital was Dr. Alexander Lambert. Towns often cited him in his writings. Lambert was an attending physician at Bellevue Hospital from 1894 to 1933, and also served for a long time as head of the alcohol and drug addiction ward at Bellevue; he was president of the American Medical Association in 1919–20, a member of the Committee on Narcotic Addiction of the Mayor of the City of New York in 1927, and was a member of a similar State commission. During the course of an extremely active professional career he wrote at least 75 articles or chapters in books, of which a handful dealt with alcoholism and the treatment of alcoholics. Lambert accepted a disease concept of alcoholism, not as unusual point of view for the period.

It is highly probable that, as a professional in the field of alcoholism, Dr. Lambert was familiar with the *Quarterly Journal of Inebriety* published by the American Association for the Study and Cure of Inebriety and its successor organization, the American Medical Society for the Study of Alcohol and Other Narcotics. The American Association for the Study and Cure of Inebriety was formed in 1870 to advocate the disease theory of alcoholism. In its earliest declaration of principles its membership, largely physicians, asserted that alcoholism is a disease and that alcoholism is curable "in the same sense that other diseases are." A number of meanings were given to the term "disease" as it was discussed in the *Journal,* which was published from 1876 to 1914. As far as the Association's leadership was concerned, the disease theory may more nearly be referred to as a disease ideology (as the term ideology is used in the present report). There can be little doubt that by Lambert's time the disease concept of alcoholism had penetrated into the medical care of alcoholics. Although the disease concept was still obscure generally and rejected by the Prohibitionist Movement, a nascent treatment specialty had developed and was practiced in designation residential institutions managed largely by physicians and in specialized hospital wards such as Bellevue's.

For reasons that are obscure, Lambert made no mention of the Association and its *Journal* when he discussed the disease concept of alcoholism. Instead, he referred to Anstie's study, which was published in 1868, as the turning point in medical classification (11, p. 121). Anstie defined alcoholism as "a disease of the general nervous system, induced by continued excesses in the use of alcoholic liquor" (12, p. 63). This organic condition spread through the entire body but had its origin in the nervous system and the degenerative effects of prolonged and heavy use of alcohol. Anstie argued that alcoholism, "the form of the disease, which we have so far considered, is decidedly curable, tending in fact to right itself of the simple adoption of a plan of complete abstinence from the exciting cause of the mischief, combined with a nourishing and supporting diet" (12, p. 74).

Anstie regarded alcoholism as a kind of "narcotic," or chemical, poisoning, and the treatment, therefore, was to remove the poison and build up the depleted organism with a high protein diet. His position was not much different from those of the American Association for the Study and Cure of Inebriety and Towns and Lambert. The problem with abstinence, said Anstie, is not physical but moral. "The danger of pursuing this course is not a physical one, but a moral one: All kinds of pledges which, as it were, *bind* the individual, have a tendency to lessen the force of such motion of personal responsibility as he may retain; he is apt to rest his confidence on the oath or formal resolution which he has taken, instead of teaching himself the virtue of self-restraint, as he would have to do if he were to accustom himself to the moderate use of alcoholic liquors" (12, p. 86). Anstie, in the terminology of our own day, viewed the means of preventing a relapse as psychological, while he viewed its clinical treatment as medical.

It seems evident that Dr. Lambert subscribed to a disease concept and that his orientation was distinctly medical; Dr. Silkworth aligned himself with his medical background when he took the position that alcoholism was a disease. It is this medical categorization that found its way into the ideology and practice of A.A. Although it does not necessarily follow that Dr. Silkworth's thinking was influenced by Dr. Lambert's, the fact that he studied at Bellevue while Dr. Lambert was in charge of the alcohol and drug addiction ward is highly suggestive.

PSYCHOLOGICAL AND RELIGIOUS SOURCES

Bill W. was in and out of the Charles B. Towns Hospital. One day an old drinking buddy, Ebby, told Bill W. how he had "gotten religion" with the Oxford Group Movement, the evangelist campaign started by Frank Buchman in the 1920s. Ebby had been influenced by a fellow Oxford Grouper, Roland H. (Mr. R.), a businessman who had had conversations with Dr. Carl Jung. Jung had told Roland H. that he could not help him because Roland H. was in the grip of an uncontrollable disease; the only likely route to cure was a radical religious experience. Since Dr. Silkworth had recently told Bill W. that his case was hopeless, Ebby's message hit a responsive chord. Bill W., drunk again, went to Towns Hospital, was sedated and detoxicated. As he lay in bed during the recovery period he prayed for a demonstration of the Divine Presence: "If there be a God, will He show Himself! The result was instant, electric, beyond description. The place seemed to light up, blinding white. I knew only ecstasy and seemed on a mountain. A great wind blew, enveloping and penetrating me. To me, it was not of air, but of Spirit. Blazing, there came the tremendous thought. 'You are a free man.' Then the ecstasy subsided. I now found myself in a new world of consciousness which was suffused by a Presence. One with the universe, a great peace stole over me" (13, p. 10).

When he had a little time to reflect on this experience, Bill W. began to test it. Was he hallucinating and on the verge of madness or was this a genuine religious experience? Dr. Silkworth assured him that he was not mad, that conversion experiences sometimes were reported by "hopeless alcoholics" who had then been "turned around" and recovered from their alcoholism. He referred Bill W. to William James' *Varieties of Religious Experience* (14), and Ebby gave him a copy of the book to read.

That Bill W. and his early associates carefully studied James's *Varieties of Religious Experience*, there can be no doubt. Special attention was probably given to Lectures IX and X, which deal with conversion and were the ones to which Dr. Silkworth had referred Bill W. on several occasions. Lecture VIII, "The Divided Self," may also have been influential because it describes the condition before conversion: "To be converted, to be regenerated, to receive grace, to experience religion, to gain an assurance, are so many phrases which denote the process, gradual or sudden, by which a self hitherto divided, and consciously wrong, inferior and unhappy, becomes unified and consciously right, superior and happy, in consequence of its firmer hold upon religious realities" (14, p. 189). In this opening sentence of Lecture IX, William James aptly described Bill W.'s conversion experience in Towns Hospital.

Lectures IX and X are replete with examples of conversions, but only two clearly involved alcoholics. The story of one of the converts, an Oxford University graduate, might have given reassurance that educated middle-class people could not only have alcohol problems but could subsequently be converted, finding not only a solution to their alcohol problems but also a general orientation of their lives. The second case was probably more relevant to the experience of Bill W. and his associates, for it dealt with the conversion of Samuel H. Hadley, "who, after his conversion [and as superintendent of the Jerry McAuley Water Street Helping Hand Mission], became an active and useful rescuer of drunkards in New York" (14, p. 201). In footnotes, James referred to a publication of the McAuley Water Street Mission that discussed other examples of the conversion of alcoholics. Lectures IX and X also alluded to John B. Gough, an alcoholic who was converted during the Washingtonian Movement and became a prominent Prohibitionist lecturer (15).

The significance of the *Varieties of Religious Experience* is that it generalized discussion of the conversion experience, which had been limited to adolescent conversion, and in that more generalized form attracted wide interest and attention. The influence of Carl Jung on Bill W. is well-documented (1, pp. 6–7; 4, pp. 231–232, 362–364) but more indirect. Jung's interests were far broader than alcoholics and their treatment. One can only speculate on the source of his observation that conversion might be a cure of last resort for alcoholics. It may be that he had read *Varieties of Religious Experience*, which was published in German in 1907 (16).

Substantively, James's lectures on conversion drew heavily on the work of James H. Leuba (17) and Edwin D. Starbuck (18). That part of Starbuck's book that is most relevant for the present discussion appeared in an article in 1897 (19). It is a reasonable possibility that Bill W. consulted Leuba's and Starbuck's works, which were cited frequently by James.

Leuba referred to John B. Gough as "the famous temperance orator, who is moved to renovation by his misery, by nothing else" (17, p. 325); Leuba quoted sections of Gough's *Autobiography* describing the depressed condition of the alcoholic. As Dr. Silkworth pointed out to Bill W., William James made it clear that "transforming spiritual experiences are nearly always founded on calamity and collapse" (1, pp. 13,

64). Leuba emphasized this reversal, and also pointed out that a second precondition to conversion is self-surrender. (The Third Step of A.A. is, "We made a decision to turn our will and our lives over to the care of God as we understood Him.") Leuba also quoted S. H. Hadley and commented: "In this record the approach towards complete surrender can be followed step by step. He has laid aside pride enough to respond to the invitation and thereby confess publicly his inability to cease drinking. Old crimes, and that which the settlement of them will require of him, pass before his mind; for a moment he hesitates to accept the attitude towards them which submission to God would demand. His humble prayer for succor, and its effect, indicate that all the resistance of which he was conscious had given away, and that, as he called upon Christ, he threw himself unreservedly at his feet" (17, p. 332).

At the end of his article, Leuba summarized the conversion experiences of 17 people, including the Oxford graduate to whom James had referred; of these, 7 were clearly alcoholics who stopped drinking after their conversion. Leuba said of 2 of these cases: "G. and O. had repeatedly signed abstinence pledges, and had made desperate, but vain efforts to keep them. It was only when all hope of succeeding by their own strength had gone that redemption came" (17, p. 367).

Starbuck graphically described the phenomenon that A.A. people refer to as "hitting bottom" and the subsequent conversion experience. The crisis comes when "the divine urging has become imperative and irresistible. Here is the critical point, the tragic moment. The subject resorts to evasion of good influences, pointing out the perfection of the present self, the imperfection of others, and anything to preserve the old self intact. It is more often a distress, a deep undefinable feeling of reluctance, which is perhaps a complex of all surface considerations which a thorough break in habits and associations would involve. He continues until complete exhaustion takes away the power of striving; he becomes nothing; his will is broken; he surrenders himself to the higher forces that are trying to claim him; he accepts the higher life as his own" (19, p. 305). Insofar as Starbuck influenced James's discussion of "The Divided Self" (Lecture VIII) and its subsequent unification through conversion (14, pp. 166–188), Starbuck influenced the development of A.A. . . .

Bill W. acknowledged the religious influence of Rev. Samuel Moor Shoemaker and the Oxford Group Movement in the formation of A.A.'s ideas of self-examination, acknowledgment of character defects, restitution for harm done, and working with others (1, p. 39).

Shoemaker, an active member of the Student Christian Movement and a Christian pacifist when he graduated from Princeton University in 1916, volunteered to work for the Young Men's Christian Association in Texas and later in England. He had been strongly impressed by the preaching of Sherwood Eddy, an evangelical leader in the YMCA, and when Eddy suggested that he go to China with him as a part of the Princeton-in-China program, Shoemaker agreed. As Mrs. Shoemaker tells it, he arrived on 29 October 1917, and rapidly got down to a mixed job of teaching insurance to Chinese students and teaching Christianity to a group of interested persons—mostly Chinese government officials (22, pp. 25–27). In the next several months his small group of "inquirers" about Christianity dropped from 20 to 7. Sam was upset and discouraged. Then on 19 January 1918, he met Frank Buchman, a rising star with an evangelistic style of teaching religion, who "rang the changes" on the Four Absolutes: Honesty, Purity, Unselfishness and Love (22, p. 24). Shoemaker had a conversion experience: "I felt only a sense of release as I went to bed that cold, crisp January night. But— to change the figure— it was as if something that had been out of joint had slipped back again where it belonged. I felt forgiven and free. The ways seemed open to God through Christ" (22, p. 25). The next morning he felt that he needed to talk to someone, and traveled from Peking's West City, where he was living, to the East City to visit a young Chinese businessman who was in his class on Christianity. He confessed to his student that he felt that fault was with himself, not with those who had come to learn from him. He then told his student about the experience of the previous night and assured him that he too could have a conversion experience if he would "let God in completely." The student had a conversion that very day.

Frank Buchman encouraged Shoemaker to appear before groups and to give public witness to his experiences: he introduced him to other converts, and in the following weeks and months maintained a direct personal tie with Shoemaker through a heavy correspondence (22, p. 26). With the help of Frank Buchman and others, Shoemaker developed a style of personal evangelism that he used throughout his career. Much later in life, for example, with the help of Admiral Ben Moreel, former head of the Jones and Laughlin Steel Corporation, he began a series of religious meetings to steel plants, country clubs, and other settings so that God might be "the same to Pittsburgh as steel is to Pittsburgh.

Sam Shoemaker came to New York's Calvary Protestant Episcopal Church, at 4th Avenue and 21st Street, in 1925. Organized in 1835, it had always had a missionary orientation—the Protestant Episcopal City Mission Society had four of Calvary's founders on its board (22, p. 46). Its sixth rector, Rev. Francis Lister Hawks, who served from 1850 to 1862, founded the Missionary Association of Calvary Church and erected a chapel and lodging house for vagrants on East 23rd Street (22, p. 47). It is clear, therefore, that a home missionary orientation to housing for Skid Row people was a pre-Civil War phenomenon in New York City. Rev. Hawks had been rector of St. Thomas's Protestant Episcopal Church in New York City from 1831 to 1843, but during that period he was busy with this church and various scholarly, literary and educational ventures. He may have been aware of the Washingtonians, but he took no significant part in the movement.

In the post-Civil War period, Rev. Henry Yates Satterless reorganized the 23rd Street facility as the Galilee Mission "to save needy men" (22, p. 47). By the time Sam Shoemaker came to New York in 1925, the mission facilities had been boarded up and the program discontinued. The Olive Tree Inn, founded in the 1880s by Satterless, was still operating next door to the closed Galilee Mission, charging 25 cents a night for lodging (22, p. 84). Shoemaker decided that he would reopen the 23rd Street mission building as the Calvary Mission, using the approach of personal evangelism that had been shaped and influenced by Frank Buchman, and put Henry Hadley II in charge of it. Henry Hadley II was the son of the S. H. Hadley who had been director of Jerry McAuley's Helping Hand Mission and who was mentioned by William James; Henry had been converted three days after his father's death in 1906 and had since been traveling the country (22, p. 188).

It was in the Calvary Mission, whose work came to be interpreted as a mission to alcoholics, that Roland H. and Ebby first encountered the Oxford Group Movement. Shoemaker saw the Calvary Mission as an effort to extend the principles and procedures of the Buchmanite approach to the down-and-out in contrast to the well-to-do Princeton undergraduates with whom he had worked after his return from China. By 1932 Shoemaker felt the urgency of providing some leadership to the Oxford Group Movement (which had not attempted to expand in the United States), and was granted a six-month leave of absence from Calvary Church. Shoemaker was, in effect, the American head of the group during this period, when he led an Oxford Group from coast to coast in the United States and Canada.

Shoemaker continued to be extremely active with the Oxford Group Movement until 1941, when he broke with Buchman, charging that Buchman had become "dictatorial" and that Buchman's activities had become too divisive for the Christian Church. It is probable that Shoemaker had been uncomfortable with Buchman's style for some time. As to why he broke with him at this time rather than earlier or later, it is plausible, as Eister (23) suggests, that Shoemaker felt

Buchman's public statements about Hitler and the Nazis were intolerable; Shoemaker may have found it necessary to dissociate himself so that he (Shoemaker) would not be discredited and could continue to perceive himself as religiously effective (23, pp. 61–62). (We have the example of the discrediting of Lindbergh during the same period, and we know that he worked had to achieve political rehabilitation.) In a larger context, however, Shoemaker's break with Buchman reflected Shoemaker's desire to continue to work within traditional Christianity while Buchman, who had been "divisive" from almost the beginning of his ministerial career, progressively moved away from the traditional Christianity.

Over the years, Shoemaker moved from the Christian socialism that tended to permeate the pre-World War I YMCA-Student Christian Movement ot a more conservative sociopolitical position. His early pacifism disappeared during the course of World War II. In the postwar years, he took a vigorous anti-Communist position, but called on Christians to be pro-Christian rather than anti-Russian. By the time Shoemaker broke with the Oxford Group–Moral Re-Armament Movement, A.A. had already passed through its formative period.

Insofar as A.A. is concerned, the critical influence on Shoemaker seems to have been Frank Buchman and his brand of Christian evangelism. There seems to be no evidence that the Washingtonian-like beliefs and practices of Shoemaker came from another source.

Frank N. D. Buchman, the progenitor of Oxford Group–Moral Re-Armament religious evangelism, was born and raised in the Pennsylvania Dutch country that is a major part of the regional ethnic heritage. From a Lutheran family, he was educated partly in public schools and partly in the Perkiomen School, an academy operated by the Schwenkfelder sect of German pietists, before he went to the Lutheran-sponsored Muhlenberg College in Allentown, Pennsylvania. He studied at Mt. Airy [Lutheran] Theological School in Philadelphia and was ordained a Lutheran minister.

In 1902, Buchman accepted a call to the Lutheran Church in Overbrook, then an outlying and well-to-do section of Philadelphia. The experience in the parish ministry was not very satisfying for him, but during that period he offered shelter and hospitality to a number of young men who desperately needed help, and he found his calling in a ministry to young persons in need. The ministerium apparently recognized his service, because in 1905 it announced that he would direct a new hospice to be opened some blocks west of the Philadelphia Skid Row.

Buchman gradually developed his skill in "personal evangelism" at that hospice, but quit in despair in 1907 because of his persistent conflicts with representatives of the ministerium; they could not tolerate his slipshod management of the hospice's finances, and he could not tolerate their insistence that he be up-and-about early in the day (even though he had been up half the night counseling one of the young men in his care) (24, pp. 27–29, 34–35).

Buchman was angry and depressed by the conflict with the ministerium, and after some months of nursing his feelings he decided to go to England. In July 1908, Buchman wandered into a chapel at Keswick, Cumberland, and chanced to hear a sermon by a woman evangelist. During that sermon he had a conversion experience. He was a changed man, of course, and returned to the United States to take a job as secretary of the YMCA-Student Christian Movement at Penn State College in 1909. He knew that he wanted to engage in personal evangelism, and at Penn State he was successful in organizing large numbers of young men into Bible study groups and in counseling them about the most intimate kind of behavior. To individual counseling he added a group approach. He also found it effective to attract the "big men on campus" as models for other students.

Buchman then moved to Hartford Theological Seminary, where his evangelistic approach raised a storm because it was perceived as divisive. By the spring of 1918, Frank Buchman had moved to China. It was there that he held the first "house party" in the home of a wealthy Chinese lawyer-diplomat (25, p. 54). The house party involved a weekend of good food, plenty of talk, witnessing, soul-searching, personal counseling and conversion; originally held in homes of the well-to-do, house parties were later held in hotels and resorts frequented by the well-to-do. Buchman made valuable British contacts in China, and in 1921 he went to Oxford and Cambridge to conduct a campaign of personal evangelism. He made a sufficient number of converts there to give him justification for labeling his activities "The Oxford Group Movement," again using the Oxbridge status to make his own religious approach respectable. Some years later, the name was changed to "Moral Re-Armament." . . .

The Washingtonian Total Abstinence Movement, begun in Baltimore in 1840, was primarily therapeutic in the same sense that A.A. is therapeutic. It swept the settled part of the United States over the next several years and then rapidly declined; the 1845 annual report of the Executive Committee of the American Temperance Union observed that "if the Washingtonian Movement has in a considerable measure spent its force, still its results are mighty; and many reformed men snatched from the burning, and standing upon their feet with true hearts and a right spirit, have become valuable aids in carrying forward the work of universal redemption." The movement and its successors were discussed in some detail by Maxwell (28, 29) who outlined the following similarities and differences between the Washingtonians and A.A.: *Similarities*—alcoholics helping each other; the needs and interests of alcoholics being central, despite mixed membership, because of the predominance of their numbers, control or enthusiasm; weekly meetings; sharing of experiences; fellowship of the group or constant availability of its members; reliance upon the power of Good; and total abstinence from alcohol. *Differences*—A.A.'s exclusively alcoholic membership; singleness of purpose, i.e., to stay abstinent; clear-cut program of recovery; anonymity; traditional practices to minimize hazard to the group.

The ideology of A.A. is clearly not traceable to the Washingtonians. It seems reasonable to conclude that the similarities of the two movements are based in part on the fact that they both faced alcohol as a problem and on their descent from the common ancestor of Protestant religious practice. Otherwise, the historical relationship between the two movements is remote.

But what of the differences? Bill W. and his associates came from diverse backgrounds and their discussions in the early days were fraught with controversy. One way to resolve controversy and to head off divisiveness was to limit the focus of the group to alcoholism; thus participants could differ on theology and politics and the group itself would not be threatened. Bill W. and his associates thereby incorporated the pluralist approach to social and moral reform that was common to the United States of their day—to attract a diversity of members and interested followers on the basis of a single purpose.

Beyond that pragmatic approach to their movement, the context in which Bill W. and his associates worked was sharply different from that of the Washingtonians. Thus, the Washingtonians and A.A. stand in almost opposite positions with respect to the Temperance and Prohibition Movements. The Temperance Movement was relatively unimportant in the late 1830s, and its members were sharply divided into advocates of moderate drinking and "ultras," who demanded total abstinence. The Washingtonians were ultraists in their pledge, and in the conflict within the Temperance Movement of that period they helped the ultras win out over the moderates. "Temperance" came to mean total abstinence. Subsequently, the advocates of political action, the prohibitionists, drove out the Washingtonians, who were advocates of moral suasion; "temperance" then came to mean Prohibition. The growing political effectiveness of 19th-century moral reformers was evident when Prohibition became law in the United States. During the course of the agitation for Prohibition, the Washingtonian position of moral suasion was thoroughly discredited as a social policy with respect to drunkenness. Between the Civil War and World War I the disease concept of alcoholism became accepted among the physicians who had developed a nascent medical specialty based on that disease theory. The concept was ultimately transmitted through Dr. Silkworth to A.A.

By contrast, A.A. developed after the defeat of Prohibition. While organizationally the Prohibitionist Movement still exists, it is socially and politically impotent in the Unites States today. A.A. is closer to the mental health movement than to the Prohibitionist Movement. While A.A. is ultraist, it is not Prohibitionist; it advocates moral suasion, and it avoids political controversy in order to avoid the drinking population's residual fear of and hostility toward Prohibition. Given the fact that Prohibition became discredited as a social policy in the United States but that drunkenness has persisted, moral suasion, the rejected alternative of the Washingtonians, was rediscovered and reapplied in a new sociopolitical context.

What may occur is challenge to the total abstinence (ultraist) component of A.A. ideology by those who argue that it is possible to resume social drinking. It is too soon to tell, but A.A.'s remarkable growth rate may slow down as the resistance to total abstinence builds up. Social movements often do not die; rather, they fade away through a process of ideological and organizational transformation. Can A.A. encompass the moderate as well as the ultraist positions? Again, it is too soon to tell, but it seems likely that if this transformation of A.A. takes place at all it will probably come through a more careful specification of the disease concept of alcoholism. If this takes place, then we can look forward to a period of vigorous debate of the findings of biomedical and psychological research. The question is whether A.A. can update Dr. Silkworth's theories of the early 1930s without setting loose too many schismatic tendencies.

REFERENCES

1. [W., Bill.] Alcoholics Anonymous comes of age. New York: Harper; 1957.
2. Silkworth, W. D. The doctor's opinion. Pp. 1–9. In: [W., Bill.] Alcoholics Anonymous: the story of how many thousands of men and women have recovered from alcoholism. New York; Works Publishing; 1946.
3. Silkworth, W. D. Alcoholism as manifestation of allergy. Med. Rec., NY 145: 249–251, 1937.
4. Thomsen, R. Bill W. New York; Harper Row; 1975.
5. Lambert, A. Care and control of the alcoholic. Boston med. surg. J. 166: 615–621, 1912.
6. Towns, C. B. The alcoholic problem considered in its institutional, medical, and sociological aspects. New York; 1917. [Published by the author.]
7. Turner, J. E. The history of the first inebriate asylum in the world, by its founder: an account of his indictment, also a sketch of the Woman's National Hospital, by its projector. New York; 1888. [Published by the author.]
8. Towns, C. B. Habits that handicap; the remedy for narcotic, alcohol, tobacco and other drug addictions. New York; Funk & Wagnalls; 1920.
9. Towns, C. B. The present and future of narcotive pathology. Med. Rev. of Rev., N.Y. 23: 35–37; 113–119; 195–201; 1917.
10. Towns, C. B. Drug and alcohol sickness. New York; Barbour; 1932.
11. Lambert, A. Some statistics and studies from the alcoholic wards of Bellevue Hospital. Med. surg. Rep. Bellevue Hosp. 1: 113– 154, 1904.
12. Anstie, F. E. Alcoholism. In: Reynolds, J. R., ed. A system of medicine. Vol. 2. London: Macmillan; 1868.
13. [W., Bill.] Three talks to medical societies by Bill W., co-founder of Alcoholics Anonymous. New York; Alcoholics Anonymous World Services; 1973.
14. James, W. The varieties of religious experience. New York; Longman's, Green: 1928. [Orig. 1902.]

15. Gough, J. B. Autobiography, and personal recollections of John B. Gough with twenty-six years' experience as a public speaker. Springfield, MA; Bill. Nichols; 1869.
16. James, W. Die religise Erfahrung in ihrer Mannigfaltigkeit; Materialien and Studien zu einer Psychologie and Pathologie des religisen Lebens. Leipzig; Hinrichs; 1907.
17. Leuba, J. H. A study in the psychology of religious phenomena. Amer. J. Psychol. 7: 309–385, 1896.
18. Starbuck, E. D. The psychology of religion. New York; Scribner's; 1899.
19. Starbuck, E. D. A study of conversion. Amer J. Psychol. 8: 268—308, 1897.
20. Bonner, A. Jerry McAuley and his mission. Neptune, NJ; Loizeaux; 1967.
21. Rosenberg, C. S. Religion and the rise of the American city; the New York City mission movement. Ithaca, NY; Cornell University; 1971.
22. Shoemaker, H. S. I stand by the door. New York; Harper & Row; 1967.
23. Eister, A. W. Drawing room conversion. Durham, NC; Duke University; 1950.
24. Driberg, T. The mystery of moral re-armament. London; Secker & Warburg; 1964.
25. Clark, W. H. The Oxford group, its history and significance. New York; Bookman; 1951.
26. Pollack, J. C. Moody; a biographical portrait of the pacesetter in modern mass evangelism. New York; Macmillan; 1963.
27. Findlay, J. F., Jr. Dwight L. Moody, American evangelist, 1837—1899. Chicago; University of Chicago Press; 1969.
28. Maxwell, M. A. Social factors in the Alcoholics Anonymous program. Ph.D. dissertation, University of Texas–Austin; 1949.
29. Maxwell, M. A. The Washingtonian movement. Quart. J. Stud. Alc. 11: 410–451, 1950.

ARTICLE 24

The Mobilization of Paid and Volunteer Activists in the Neighborhood Movement

PAMELA OLIVER

. . . There have been paid activists in social movements for at least two hundred years and probably longer. At the turn of the century, there was extensive debate in socialist circles about whether working-class movements should pay their leaders (Lenin, 1973:137–176; Michels, 1962:129–152). Nevertheless, collective behavior theorists writing about social movements generally devote a great deal of attention to the traits and activities of movement leaders without discussing whether they are provided livelihoods for the activism (Turner and Killian, 1972:388–405; Smelser, 1962:296–298, Lang and Lang, 1961:517–524; Killian, 1964:440–443). A few writers mention paid activists in passing, suggesting for example that they are more strongly committed to a movement because their livelihood depends upon it (Lang and Lang, 1961:526). Collective behavior theorists are doubtless well aware that some activists are paid, but have not considered the matter to be worthy of specific analytic attention, possibly because they assume that paid activists are supported by contributions from movement participants.

McCarthy and Zald (1973) changed the thinking of social movement theorists when they challenged this collective wisdom. They argued that the trend of the 1960s (which seemed to be continuing into the 1970s) was for more and more activists to be paid for their activism and for the source of that support to come from institutions or conscience contributors outside any membership base of potential beneficiaries; they argued that this trend has important consequences for social movements. McCarthy and Zald went on to argue that a new kind of social movement has emerged, a "professional social movement," characterized by a paid leadership cadre and the absence of any genuine participating membership. Interestingly, three other works published that same year commented on this phenomenon (Oberschall, 1973:161; John Wilson, 1973:182; James Q. Wilson, 1972:203); clearly an important historical trend was being noticed by many of the major theorists in the field.

In this paper I propose to address systematically one of the questions raised by McCarthy and Zald's work, but not pursued by them or subsequent writers: the mobilization of paid activists as compared to the mobilization of volunteer activists. I shall do this by laying out the two alternative theories of mobilization common in the social movement literature and showing the relation of these models to McCarthy and Zald's work as well as to other works which have addressed the problem. These models suggest em-

Oliver, Pamela. (1983). The mobilization of paid and volunteer activists in the neighborhood movement. *Research in Social Movements, 5*, 133–170.

pirical predictions about the differences or similarities between paid and volunteer activists; these predictions are developed in some detail, drawing on the relevant literature.

A partial test of these propositions is provided by data collected from a sample of paid and volunteer activists who attended the 1979 convention of the National Association of Neighborhoods. Despite some serious limitations in the sample (which are described in detail below), these data are important—perhaps unique—because there are sufficient numbers of similarly-situated paid and volunteer activists to permit statistical comparisons. Even though the data permit only cautious empirical generalizations, they provide strong support for a theoretical model that integrates resources and commitment in the process of mobilization. . . .

TWO THEORETICAL APPROACHES

This paper focuses on the mobilization of activists. By "activists" I mean those persons who commit a relatively large amount of time and effort to movement activities; they are generally part of the leadership cadre of movement organizations. The distinction between inner hard-working circles and outer circles of less involved participants is common in the literature (Lenin, 1973:137–176; John Wilson, 1973:306; Killian, 1964:443).

Activists may be paid or volunteer. McCarthy and Zald's concept of a "professional social movement" combines the presence of paid activists with the absence of a genuine membership base. These characteristics are, in fact, separable: Some movement organizations have both paid activists and genuine participating memberships, and some have neither (that is, may have only an all-volunteer cadre). Distinctions among kinds of paid activists are developed in the appendix.

By "mobilization of activists" I refer to the processes whereby people come to devote significant amounts of time and energy to a movement, that is, to the processes whereby they become activists rather than passive supporters or occasional participants.

Although the distinction between mobilizing activists and mobilizing less involved supporters has often been blurred, two traditions may be identified in explaining the mobilization of activists. These may be labeled commitment models and collective action models. These two traditions are not necessarily incompatible, although they have developed somewhat distinctly. Some theorists from each tradition have incorporated elements of the other into their theories. To foreshadow the conclusions of this paper, I believe the evidence indicates that a correct understanding of the mobilization of paid activists requires an integration of these two traditions.

Although not necessarily older in the history of ideas (see Oberschall, 1973:1–29), the commitment tradition is older in the sociological study of social movements. There are two key ideas in this tradition. The first is that people become involved in social movements because of changes in beliefs, values, and norms and that these involve emotional responses to events. The second is that commitment is a progressive process, with earlier experiences drawing the person into greater and greater involvement in and identification with the movement. Comprehensive treatments of commitment processes identify rituals and customs that tend to increase the recruit's dependence on the movement and to decrease his or her involvement outside of the movement (Turner and Killian, 1972:335–360; John Wilson, 1973:300–328; Gerlach and Hine, 1970:99–158; Kornhauser, 1962; Becker, 1960).

If they are mentioned by commitment theorists, paid activists are viewed as the most committed members of all, for they have cast their lot with the movement and they depend upon it for their very survival (John Wilson, 1973:306; Lang and Lang, 1961:526). It is nearly always either explicitly stated or implicitly assumed that paid activists rise through progressive commitment from the ranks of volunteers. Lenin explicitly argued that the professional revolutionary cadre should be chosen from the talented members of the mass base (1973:137–176), and most commitment theorists retain this image (e.g., John Wilson, 1973:306).

In contrast with the commitment tradition, the collection action tradition is based on the idea that people decide whether to participate in a social movement according to their expectations of benefits and costs. Most theoretical work is informed by Olson's *The Logic of Collective Action* (1965), which argues that pursuit of a group interest invokes the public goods problem from economics in which every actor prefers to share in the collective benefit without having to incur the costs of cooperating in the collective action; this implies that collective action requires private or selective incentives to reward those who cooperate with collective action or to punish those who do not. A subsequent critical literature has shown that Olson overstates the generality of his claims (Oliver, 1980; Frohlich and Oppenheimer, 1970; Frohlich et al., 1975; Chamberlin, 1974; Schofield, 1975; Bonacich et al., 1976; Smith, 1976), but the work remains important for calling attention to the problematic nature of mobilization. The resource mobilization perspective on social movements is based on collective action models of mobilization.

Paid activists are central to collective action theory, for a salary is an important private incentive for collective action. People who are paid for their actions in pursuit of a collective good do not experience the dilemma of the free rider problem. Completion of the logic of paid activism requires specifying who will pay the activist and under what conditions (Oliver, 1980). Entrepreneurial theorists argue that the activist absorbs the cost of creating a payment system in the expectation of making a profit by doing so (Frohlich et al., 1971; Frohlich and Oppenheimer, 1978:66–89). Alternately, persons or institutions who attach high value to the collective good and who have more money than time may prefer to hire an activist rather than be one themselves.

In its pure form, the collective action theory borrowed from economists assumes that activists are motivated by material gain, either from the collective good or their salaries as paid activists, or both. The assumption that people are motivated only by their own personal material gain is obviously incorrect, and a number of theorists within the collective action tradition modify the concepts of benefit and cost to take account of other motivations. James Q. Wilson argues that there are three basic kinds of incentives: *material incentives,* which are intangible rewards arising from the association with others; and *purposive incentives,* which are intangible rewards deriving from the sense of satisfaction of having contributed to the attainment of a worthwhile cause (1973:30–34). Fireman and Gamson (1979) construct an argument in a different way that arrives essentially at the same conclusion. Collective action models should include not only material self-interest but group solidarity that leads an actor to value group benefits and consciousness that leads an actor to want to contribute to a collective good. Much of Fireman and Gamson's article discusses the ways in which organizers and entrepreneurs (that is, paid activists) can induce other (that is, volunteers) to participate in collective action.

Both of these modifications to collective action models contain terms that interface with the commitment models, although the dynamic elements of commitment processes are only partially captured in Fireman and Gamson's work and hardly mentioned in James Q. Wilson's. Conversely, the classic discussions of commitment cited above interface with collective action models. They discuss such topics as turning resources over to the movement, bridge-burning rituals cutting off alternate actions, and shifts from extra-movement to intra-movement social ties, all of which can be recast as costs and benefits in collective action models.

A. Mobilizing Paid Activists

The issue can now be posed simply. Are paid and volunteer activists mobilized through the same basic process, or are they mobilized in different ways? Are paid activists just activists who happened to be paid, or are they fundamentally different from volunteers? Do the factors which distinguish paid from volunteer activists arise in the larger society or within the internal processes of the movement?

The commitment tradition strongly suggests that paid and volunteer activists mobilize through the same processes, the paid only more so. Conversely, the collective action tradition implies that paid activists are mobilized, in ways different from volunteers, by the possibility of drawing a salary.

Even though the issue is not exactly isomorphic with the two theoretical traditions on mobilization, they are strongly related. Commitment theorists (if they mention paid activists explicitly at all) state that paid activists are the most committed activists and rise from the ranks of volunteers, implying that paid and volunteer activists are mobilized in the same general process.

On the other hand, collective action theory implies that paid and volunteer activists are often mobilized differently. Since paid activists are compensated by salaries, they require less interest in the public good and/or less concern with purposive incentives than do volunteers. McCarthy and Zald's articles imply that paid activists respond to different constraints in mobilizing than do volunteers (1973:18–25). James Q. Wilson speaks of an organization hiring staff in a way that implies that they would not necessarily come from the ranks of volunteers (1973:225–228). Oberschall analyzes the risks and rewards of mobilizing and argues that paid activists incur lower risks than other activists (1973:161), again implying that the two groups are affected by different factors in mobilizing.

Although commitment theories suggest similarities and collective action theories differences in the mobilization of paid and volunteer activists, there are ambiguities and contradictions in each stream of work. Commitment theories are strangely silent about the mobilization of leaders, particularly the kind that collective action theorists call entrepreneurs. A great deal of attention has been devoted to the motivations of the followers of charismatic and other leaders, and to the attributes of leaders that make people follow them (Turner and Killian, 1972:388–405; Lang and Lang, 1961:517–524; Killian, 1964:440–443, John Wilson, 1973:194–225; Heberle, 1951:286–290), but I know of none devoted to the question of what makes a leader want to be a leader. Such leaders are often supported by their followings—making them paid activists in the terms of the paper—and some treatments hint at financial exploitation of the following, but the suggestion of material gain as motivation has not been pursued in this tradition.

For their part, collective action theorists are contradictory in their treatment of the obvious empirical phenomenon of intense ideological commitment among paid activists. Salaries are material incentives, and the main thrust of collective action theorists is to emphasize the importance of salaries in attracting activists. But James Q. Wilson (1973:227) and others suggest a salary might be a sacrifice if it is less than a person could earn in a non-movement job. McCarthy and Zald, especially in their 1973 article, talk about the dedication of young activists, the tone implying that committed activists look for ways to be paid for their activism rather than being attracted by the prospect of a paying job. A willingness to make a sacrifice or an active seeking support for activism sounds more like a result of a commitment process than a materially-oriented response to resource levels, but none of these authors sorts out these contradictions into a coherent model of the mobilization of paid activists.

PREDICTIONS FROM THE THEORIES

The data I have available do not contain direct information about activist careers or mobilization processes, but it is possible to derive a number of competing cross-sectional hypotheses from the theoretical traditions summarized above.

A. Social Characteristics

A number of theorists provide predictions for the economic positions or backgrounds that are most likely to produce movement activists. Obviously, if paid and volunteer activists are mobilized by the same factors and processes, then they should appear to come from the same general population; if they are mobilized in different ways, they should come from different populations.

Pure commitment models make no particular predictions about the social characteristics of activists. Different ideologies will have appeal for different people depending upon their situation and experience, but no particular occupational group is treated as logically more predisposed to activism than any other.

By contrast, resource mobilization theorists make specific predictions about the occupations of volunteer activists. McCarthy and Zald put greatest emphasis on the convenience of action and predict that volunteer activists come from occupations with discretionary time (such as students and professionals), particularly when tactics require transitory teams (1973:9–11; 1977:1236).

Oberschall emphasizes the ratio of possible rewards to the risk of retaliation and argues that volunteer activists are persons for whom the risk of retaliation from the opposition is relatively low, either because they are in relatively secure occupations (such as free professionals or small business owners whose clientele are of the aggrieved population) or because their upward mobility is blocked and they have nothing to gain from refraining from movement activity (1973:159–171). Thus, Oberschall predicts that activists will be from the higher, secure strata, from groups whose income is independent of the opposition, and from the very lowest strata who have nothing to lose.

No theorist makes specific predictions about comparing paid and volunteer activists. McCarthy and Zald's notion of discretionary time as an explanation for the occupations of activists simply explains why paid activists are important, since they can devote all their time to the movement. But Oberschall's discussion of risks and rewards implies that the persons attracted to paid activism will be those for whom it is a relatively lucrative or secure position, that is, those whose occupational opportunities in the society in general are lower. These would be people who have blocked channels of access due to discriminatory social barriers, or those whose education or skills fit them poorly for high-paying jobs.

B. Networks

There is strong evidence that persons mobilized for a social movement tend to be well integrated into social and organizational networks. Oberschall (1973:103–113) cites a great deal of evidence to support this position and to refute Kornhauser's mass society hypothesis; he also argues that those mobilized first are especially likely to be well-integrated (:135). Gerlach and Hine (1979:79–98) stress the importance of personal networks in recruiting and mobilizing converts to the Pentecostal and Black Power movements as does John Wilson's review of the literature (1973:131–133). Snow and his colleagues (1980) review a number of different studies of movement recruitment and conclude that people are mobilized through personal influence networks.

This evidence about networks applies to the mobilization of volunteer activists. Now if, as the commitment modes predict, paid activists work their way up through the ranks of the volunteers, they should be just as integrated—if not more integrated—into the social and organizational networks of their communities as the volunteers. By the same logic, paid activists would exhibit the same density of social connections to the movements' constituencies as volunteers would.

On the other hand, if paid activists are mobilized for the movement by the material incentive of a salary, they would not necessarily exhibit the same patterns of social integration as volunteers. Although I have found no author who makes an explicit prediction about social ties to the larger community, McCarthy and Zald argue that paid activists are more likely than volunteers to be divorced from their constituencies (1973:17–18), and that the true membership base of social movement organizations with paid leadership is smaller than the true membership base of organizations with volunteer leadership (1973:20–23). This difference between paid and volunteer would be predicted to hold true especially for those activists whose salaries are paid from sources external to the movement's membership base (which is true of virtually all paid neighborhood activists).

C. Ideological Commitment and Involvement

Commitment models of paid activism imply the clear predictions that paid activists will, on the average, exhibit greater ideological connection to the movement and will have had longer histories of activism in that movement than volunteers. This follows necessarily from the assumption that paid activists work their way through the ranks of volunteers. As indicated above, commitment theorists generally assume that paid activists are leaders supported from sources internal to the movement; it is not clear if they would change these predictions for activists supported from external sources.

Pure collective action models ignore ideology and simply examine the balance of collective benefits and individual incentives versus costs; these pure models would predict no particular ideological differences between activists and nonactivists, or between paid and volunteer activists. However, the modified collective action models that admit intangibles such as purposive incentives do yield specific predictions about ideology and paid activists. Since tangible and intangible incentives are proposed to be additive, paid activists should be *less* ideologically motivated than volunteers at comparable levels of involvement. This is because volunteers would presumably be motivated solely by purposive incentives, while paid activists would have both. McCarthy and Zald's suggestion that paid activists are more responsive to ebbs and flows in resources than are volunteers is consistent with this analysis: They view all social movement organizations as responsive to resource levels (1977:1224–5), but imply that sensitivity to resource flows is especially characteristic of movements controlled by professional activists (1973:18–25; 1977:12–4–5). Oberschall explicitly argues that being paid reduces the cost of activism (1973:161), which would seem to suggest that lower ideological motivation would be necessary. James Q. Wilson's discussion of organizations hiring staff implies that staff do not necessarily have the attachment to the movement of the volunteers who hire them (1973:225–230). His discussion of movement entrepreneurs argues that they are generally motivated by purposive incentives and willing to forego material gain (:196–197). Entrepreneurs foregoing material gain would show up as volunteers in a cross-sectional analysis, although persons who had foregone gain in the past and who were now being supported by the movement they created could be expected to show high ideological commitment as paid activists.

The suggestion proposed by Wilson (1973:226) that movement staff may view their paid activism as a sacrifice would make the generation of testable propositions difficult. However, if paid activism is a sacrifice, it should be greater the better the activist's alternative occupations. Thus, paid activists with higher education or skill levels should be more ideologically motivated than those with lower education or skill levels. For similar reasons, better paid professional activists should be less ideologically motivated (on the average) than less paid movement activists.

Commitment theories imply that paid activists will have longer average histories of movement activism than volunteers. Collective action theories do not yield clear predictions about the relative lengths of activist histories. The mobilization of paid activists may precede or follow the mobilization of volunteers, depending in part on whether their source of support is internal or external to the movement.

D. History and Generations

McCarthy and Zald offer historical evidence that external support for social movements increased during the 1960s (1973:12–16). If this historical argument is correct (and I have seen nothing to dispute it), it must affect any empirical study of paid and volunteer activists in the recent period. For McCarthy and Zald, working in the collective action tradition, the important thing about the 1960s is the amount of resources available to support movement activists. But the commitment tradition calls our attention to the 1960s as a period in which many people, especially those who were of college age, became extremely involved in and committed to the civil rights and anti-war movements. Both theories require that attention be paid to the impact of the 1960s trends on people who came of age during the decade.

Building on the writings of Mentre, Mannheim, and Hellpach, Heberle defines a *political generation* as "those individuals of approximately the same age who have shared, at the same age, certain politically relevant experiences" (1951:119–120). He suggests that people are most affected by decisive experiences as young adults, that different sub-groups within an age cohort might have different decisive experiences and form different political generations, that traditions based on decisive experiences may or may not be transmitted across generations, and that political generations have been important in movements such as Nazism, whose leaders were all young adults when the Versailles treaty was signed (:118–127).

It is widely believed that the turmoil of the civil rights and anti-war movements in the 1960s created a political generation. Numerous articles and books written during the period and immediately after it focused on the question of generations and adduced various kinds of data to support the claim that the youth of this period were qualitatively different from their elders, although there is debate about whether these differences were disjunctive. Comparisons of activist students with nonactivist students found that they were more likely to be politically radical; more likely to be liberal arts majors and especially social science majors; less likely to espouse "extrinsic reward values" such as money, prestige, and security; and more likely to plan to enter knowledge or social service careers (Braungart and Braungart, 1974; Demerath et al., 1971; Flacks, 1967, 1971; Kornberg and Brehm, 1971; Lipset, 1971; McFalls and Gallagher, 1975; Matthews and Prothro, 1966; Van Eschen et al., 1971).

The small accumulating literature on subsequent careers of movement activists suggests that they remain different from persons who were not student activists during their college days. The largest sample is Fendrich's, of male students who were in Tallahassee during the civil rights activities of 1960–1964; 95 white former Florida A & M students were surveyed in 1973. Men who had been arrested at civil rights demonstrations and student government leaders were disproportionately sampled. White civil rights activists were far more likely than nonactivists (including student government leaders) to have chosen academic professions or social service and creative occupations (a category that included paid activists), to claim to be politically radical, and to maintain a high level of political involvement as adults. Black activists were more likely to continue adult political activism but student activism was not correlated with political radicalism or occupational choice among blacks.

Other studies have found similar patterns for white 1960s activists: Isla Vista "Bank Burners"

(Whalen and Flacks, 1980), student protesters at Berkeley (Maidenberg and Meyer, 1970; Green, 1970) and Kent State (Adamek and Lewis, 1973), civil rights workers (Demerath et al., 1971), youth movement activists (Weiner and Stillman, 1979), radical leaders (Braungart and Braungart, 1980), and OEO Legal Service lawyers (Erlanger, 1977) tend to be more radical, less likely to pursue financially lucrative careers, and more likely to pursue social service occupations than nonactivists. I know of no comparable follow-up studies of black activists.

These historical effects are relevant to both commitment and decision models of the mobilization of paid activists. If 1960s activists remain politically active in the 1970s, this supports the idea that the process of being committed to a social movement leads to permanent changes in one's ideological beliefs and actions. It is clear that part of the ideology of the time led to a rejection of "establishment" (that is, business) jobs and a preference for employment in academic or social service occupations, which would serve ideologically acceptable goals. In this context, paid movement activism would be viewed as the most extreme instance of this ideological tendency, as a willingness to dedicate one's life to "the movement."

But the historical features of the 1960s are also relevant to collective action models of paid activism, for this decade witnessed not only intense ideologies and political conversion experiences, but a tremendous expansion in the money available to pay people to be social movement activists (McCarthy and Zald, 1973). Career decisions are typically made when people are in their late teens and early twenties. The 60s generation is the first that could (in large numbers) rationally choose a career in movement activism. Thus the ideological and economic impacts of the decade are intertwined and cannot be separated; we will only be able to assemble indirect suggestive evidence as to the relative weights of these two kinds of effects.

SOURCE OF DATA

Some of the observations I am able to make about the mobilization of paid and volunteer activists arise from my familiarity with published and verbal accounts of the neighborhood movement nationally and from my two and one-half years as a participant observer in the neighborhood movement in Louisville, Kentucky. Data uniquely relevant to the matter were obtained in a survey of the participants at the 1979 convention of the National Association of Neighborhoods (NAN). NAN was founded in 1976 by Milton Kotler, whose book *Neighborhood Government* (1970) articulates an ideology of extreme decentralization and local control. It is one of several national coalitions, including ACORN and National People's Action, each of which has a distinctive constituency and strategy, although they have significant overlaps and generally amicable interorganizational relations. NAN puts more priority on providing services and obtaining governmental funding, while ACORN emphasizes confrontations with powerful persons and institutions (Rathke et al., 1979; Kotler, 1979). NAN is generally controlled by its paid staff, although it has a participating membership of individuals and organizations.

RESULTS

A. Characteristics of the Activists

Occupations. Information about the neighborhood activists' occupations was obtained in a standard open-ended occupation item on a page titled "background information" . . . McCarthy and Zald's arguments about the importance of discretionary time receive strong support in this sample of activists: 43% are paid activists, and a total of 76% are in occupational situations with high discretionary time; only 12% are in occupations with little discretionary time. However, occupations with high discretionary time also tend to require high education, and education is known to be a strong correlate of all forms of political and organizational participation, so it is difficult to disentangle the two effects. Oberschall's claim that movement activists will come from independent occupations receives little support. Except for activists paid by movement organizations, the vast majority are employed by large, elite-controlled public or private organizations. There are only handfuls of independent professionals or small business owners among the activists.

Three-quarters of the paid movement activists are employed by independent neighborhood movement organizations. However, nearly all of these organizations are funded by some combination of government and foundation grants or contracts, so the boundary between movement-paid and government-paid activists is blurry. Many neighborhood organizations that are formally independent and private (such as neighborhood development corporations, community action agencies, and the more diversified groups of more recent origin) have achieved routinized, quasi-governmental status.

Nearly all of the paid activists have staff titles: only two are elected officers of associations. "Organizing" was mentioned as a part or all of their job description by 36%; another 16% described their job in terms related to the concept of organizing, terms such as advocacy or education. A large group, 37%, described their job as administrative or coordinative.

Age. The distribution of activists' ages in five-year ranges defined by the year the activist became 18. Activists span the entire range of adult ages, but most come from the years of peak adult responsibility, 23 to 47. Comparing the sample to the resident adult population of the United States using standard census categories indicates that the 35–44 age group is by far the most over-represented in the sample, and that representation in the sample has a bell-shaped distribution with those 18–21 and those over 65 most underrepresented (data not shown). Contrary to expectations established during the 1960s, this social movement is staffed not by the young, but by adults. Of course, many of these participants were young in the 1960s.

The percentage of paid activists within each age group because preliminary analysis revealed a significant deviation from linearity. Inspection of these percentages indicates that it is precisely those persons who reached maturity in the 1960s, and especially those who came of age in the latter half of the decade, who are most likely to become paid neighborhood activists. For this reason, subsequent analysis of the effect of age employs a dummy variable for membership in the 1960s cohort; those younger and those older are grouped together in the reference category.

Neighborhood Integration. The means, standard deviations, and coding conventions for the extent to which the activists have significant social ties to the neighborhoods in which they reside are shown.... It is difficult to interpret means of the neighborhood integration variables without a comparison group of nonactivists, but they seem to be at least as high as one would expect of comparable nonactivists.

Political Integration. Two indicators assess the activist's involvement with political activities besides the neighborhood movement.... The levels of activity reported on these variables appear higher than those obtained in general population samples (e.g., Verba and Nie, 1972), indicating that these activists are quite involved in community political affairs. This is consistent with Oberschall's predictions.

Movement Experience. Four indicators tap the activist's past involvement in social movements. ... Again, the means of these variables indicate rather higher levels of movement experience than would be obtained in the general population.

Movement Ideology. Three indicators assess the activists' adherence to movement-relevant ideologies.... The first assesses the person's general political orientation; the other two deal with issues directly relevant to the neighborhood movement. One question asked whether neighborhood organizations should concentrate on meeting local neighborhood needs even if they conflict with others, should concentrate on developing city-wide cooperation among neighborhood organizations, or should concentrate on linking up with a larger struggle for social justice. The first two choices were contrasted with the last. The other item derives from coding of open-ended responses to a question asking what issues the neighborhood movement should give first priority to. Those activists who listed any specific neighborhood-related problem were coded as having an issue orientation and contrasted with those who responded only in general abstract terms. These two items capture the extent to which the activist is concerned about the specific issues of the neighborhood movement as opposed to a diffuse interest in social change. The activists' general political orientations are significantly more liberal-to-radical than the general population. The other two items are not meaningful for nonactivists.

Demographic Variables. The last section . . . shows the means and standard deviations for sex, race, years of education, and whether the person is a college graduate. The sample has only slightly more women than men, is over a third minority, and is very highly educated. . . . Consistent with the assumptions of the collective action/resource mobilization tradition, the majority of the activists . . . seem to have an occupational interest in the goals of the neighborhood movement. Even considering only the volunteers, these activists are certainly not a representative sample of the kinds of people who live in urban neighborhoods. Contrary to Oberschall's discussions, there is little suggestion that these activists come from occupations independent of elite control; most are employed by elite-controlled or elite-funded organizations. However, Oberschall's logic would seem to apply only to a movement facing elite opposition (which he seems to assume faces all movements). His predictions would not seem to hold for a movement with elite sponsorship. (See Marx, 1979, for more about elite sponsorship of and opposition to movements.) Another proposition implied by Oberschall, that paid activists will come disproportionately from those with blocked channels of access due to discriminatory social barriers or from those whose education or skills fit them poorly for higher-paying jobs, also has not been confirmed: paid activists have higher average levels of education than volunteers and are not significantly more likely to be members of minority groups.

The second set of predictions involved social and organizational networks. Consistent with past research on social movement activists, the neighborhood activists in this sample appear to have rather high levels of social and political integration. However, there is no difference between paid and volunteer activists in this regard. This lack of a difference is consistent with the theory that paid activists come to their positions by way of volunteer activism, that is, they are mobilized into the movement by the same general processes and factors as volunteers are. Contrary to the implications of McCarthy and Zald's work, paid activists do not appear to be more likely than volunteers to be divorced from their constituencies, nor do they appear to have been recruited to paid activism by the lure of a job independent of ideological considerations.

The next set of predictions involved ideology and experience. Commitment models of paid activism imply that paid activists will exhibit greater ideological connection to the movement and have longer histories of movement activism than volunteers, predictions that follow necessarily from the assumption that paid activists work their ways up through the ranks of the volunteers. Even though the 1970s neighborhood movement violated the commitment theorists' assumption that paid activists are supported from internal movement sources, they nevertheless support such theorists' predictions about ideology and experience. Paid activists are more likely to have leftist political orientations and to report that they have spent greater proportions of their adult lives as "neighborhood activists" than volunteers. However, they are no different from volunteers on the indicators of specific neighborhood-movement ideology, when general political ideology is controlled. This, plus the strong correlation of leftist ideology with participation in the anti-war movement, strongly suggests that the motivation for paid neighborhood activism lies not in the neighborhood movement, but in previous social movements. The evidence is that a commitment process is involved, but not a commitment to the neighborhood movement itself. Rather, there appears to be a commitment to some larger movement or vision of a movement.

Contrary to the commitment models, the general logic of the collective action models implies that volunteers would be more motivated by purposive incentives or personal gain from the collective good than would paid activists. While many of the volunteers' occupations are consistent with the view that they are especially likely to experience personal gain from the goals of the neighborhood movement, there is little support for the view that volunteers are more ideologically or purposively motivated. It appears much more likely that it is the paid activists who are more ideologically motivated.

Concerning the possibility that paid activism is an economic sacrifice, it was argued that this would imply ideological differences among paid activists according to educational levels. . . . Persons with college degrees have more leftist political orientations than persons who do not, but this difference is statistically significant for paid activists and is not for volunteers. These data are consistent with the prediction from collective action theory, but not strongly confirming.

It is very clear that the 60's cohort, persons who came of age during the 1960's, are much more likely to be paid activists than others. This finding is quite consistent with what would be predicted from the values expressed by student activists in the 1960s, and with the literature on the subsequent political involvement and occupational careers of 1960s activists. Examination of the occupations of the volunteer activists will reveal that they are also likely to have chosen careers consistent with these predictions. These data strongly indicate that many of the 1970s neighborhood activists are heirs of the social movements and values of the 1960s. These patterns lend support to the view that activists in the 1960s experienced commitment processes that led to permanent changes in their political and occupational behavior.

However, money to pay social movement activists also became more readily available in the 1960s. The fact that, especially for whites, there is a cohort effect net of political experience from this decade suggests that the economic factor is also significant. In assessing the economic factor, however, it is important to remember that this is a sample of activists whose political experience is substantially more extensive and whose political attitudes are substantially more leftist than the general population. There is little evidence that the net cohort effect is due to political inexperience or ideological neutrality among paid activists; rather, persons not from this cohort who are just as politically experienced and politically leftist are far less likely to be paid activists. Since occupations are usually chosen in young adulthood, it is most likely that the cohort effect is due to the availability of such occupations at the time the person is making an occupational choice.

Since both cohort and political ideology and experience have effects on paid activism net of each other, it is clear that neither a pure commitment model nor a pure collective action model adequately explains the observed data. Both processes are obviously important in creating paid activists.

DISCUSSION

The evidence of these data is that paid neighborhood activists come from essentially the same pool as volunteers, except that they are more likely to have leftist political orientations as a result of their greater involvement in the social movements of the 1960s, have spent a somewhat greater proportion of their adult lives as neighborhood activists, and are more likely to have come of age in the 1960s. What does this mean for theories of the mobilization of activists, especially paid activists?

First, there is strong evidence that the decision to become a paid activist arises from social movement experience and commitment. The evidence strongly suggests that the values and activities of the social movements of the 1960s affected participants in ways that led them to continue lives of political activism, and led many of them to choose careers as paid activists. There is no evidence that paid activists are less socially or politically integrated than volunteer activists. The image of paid activists as being the especially committed, experienced, and ideologically motivated participants in a social movement seems justified. There is no evidence to support the idea that a salary may be an alternative or supplementary motivation for social movement activism.

Secondly, there is clear evidence that economic factors impose constraints on the limits of activist involvement. It seems fairly clear that ideological commitment alone is not sufficient to make a paid activist; there must also be the possibility of earning a livelihood in this way. In the 1960s, a generation just at the age of deciding their life's work not only encountered new values and experiences but perceived the possibility of making a career of activism in the rapidly increasing funding available for such work throughout the decade. Older generations of activists may have been just as committed (and many were also active in the 1960s social movements), but they had already chosen other careers. The 1970s generation came of age in a period of reduced activism and retrenchment in support for social movements; . . . they are somewhat more likely to have chosen non-movement occupations than the 1960s generation did.

The responses of these activists forces us to see resources as a constraint on activism, not as a motivation for it. Neighborhood activists—regardless of their backgrounds—speak for constituencies they are members of. But even for activists promoting causes of no immediate benefit to themselves, it seems unlikely that we will be able to say that they are activists *because* they can be paid to be activists. Rather, their desire to be social movement activists derives from fundamental beliefs and values acquired in the intense experiences of past social movements. Their beliefs and values lead them to seek ways of being able to devote full time to activism by being able to make a living doing it. They not only passively receive the benefits of increases in resources, they actively campaign for and promote resources for activism. (This is the implication of McCarthy and Zald's 1973 piece, an implication they contradicted in their 1977 work.)

To argue that paid activists are mobilized more by commitment experiences than by job opportunities is not to discount the significance of changes in job opportunities stressed by McCarthy and Zald. Job opportunities for paid activists allow activists to spend more time on activism, since they do not also have to earn a living. Job opportunities controlled by elite sponsors (as were the majority of those available in the 1960s and 1970s) raise important implications for social movements. Even though they have strong social and political ties to their communities, paid activists dependent on outsiders rather than their constituencies for their paychecks may well choose their specific actions and programs more in line with their sponsors' goals than their constituencies'. But in exploring these important issues, and other related ones, it is important to recognize that whatever the *consequences* of paid activists may be for social movement organizations in goal displacement or elite control, the *causes* of activist careers arise from commitment and ideology.

In sum, people became paid neighborhood activists through progressive social and ideological commitment constrained by the resources available to support their activism. A movement will have many paid activists when there is a conjunction of commitment experiences leading participants to dedicate themselves to the movement and resources to pay full-time activists arising at a point in activists' life cycles when they are making occupational choices.

Although this paper has compared in detail paid and volunteer activists in the neighborhood movement, its findings are significant for our more general understanding of social movement mobilization. It seems clear from the papers and discussions among participants at recent meetings that most theorists are abandoning polar contrasts between the collective behavior and resource mobilization traditions. The constructive task of building theory on the foundations of the best from both traditions seems well under way. In this context, the findings of this research call attention to several important issues.

First, the character of social movement participation is clearly affected by the presence or absence of resources. Different types of activism and activities require different amounts of resources. The occupations of the volunteers in this sample highlight the importance of discretionary time as a critical "resource." Paid activism clearly depends upon monetary resources. Material conditions clearly constrain collective action.

Secondly, mobilization for one social movement will generally be affected by past mobilizations. The history of social movements in America is replete with examples of activists from one movement becoming involved in another cause. Neither of the two main theoretical traditions in the sociological study of social movements has dealt well with continuity and historical context, or provided an adequate theoretical accounting of these phenomena. An older paper by Weiss (1963) using stimulus-response concepts may be a starting point for comparative studies of activists' shifts from movement to movement.

Thirdly, mobilization of people to activism clearly should be viewed as a process of progressive commitment, not as isolated decisions or sporadic outbursts. It is quite possible that the mobilization of activists is very different from the mobilization of occasional participants, although the implications of this possibility have rarely been explored. There is a good theoretical grounding for the study of activist mobilization since, as I discussed above, each of the two main theoretical traditions has links to the other; the combination seems likely to yield a good portrait of the process.

Finally, the work already underway to link theories of interests and decisions with theories of emotions and ideologies is clearly taking us in the proper direction toward our goal of understanding the mobilization of social movement participants. . . .

REFERENCES

Adamek, Raymond J., and Jerry M. Lewis. 1973. "Social control, violence and radicalization: The Kent State case." Social Forces 51: 342–347.

Alinsky, Saul. 1971. Rules for Radicals. New York: Random House.

Becker, Howard S. 1960. "Notes on the concept of commitment." American Journal of Sociology 61: 32–40.

Bengtson, Vern L., Michael J. Furlong, and Robert S. Laufer. 1974. "Time, aging, and the continuity of social structure: Themes and issues in generational analysis." Journal of Social Issues 30: 1–30.

Bonacich, Phillip, Gerald H. Shure, James P. Kahan, and Robert J. Meeker. 1976. "Cooperation and group size in the n-person prisoners' dilemma." Journal of Conflict Resolution 20: 687–706.

Braungart, Richard G., and Margaret M. Braungart. 1974. "Protest attitudes and behavior among college youth: A U.S. case study." Youth and Society 6: 219–248.

Braungart, Richard G., and Margaret M. Braungart. 1980. "Political career patterns of radical activists in the 1960s and 1970s: Some historical comparisons." Sociological Focus 13: 237–254.

Buss, Allan R. 1974. "Generational analysis: Description, explanation, and theory." Journal of Social Issues 30: 55–71.

Chamberlin, John. 1974. "Provision of collective goods as a function of group size." American Political Science Review 68: 707–716.

Demerath, N. J. III, Gerald Marwell, and Michael T. Aiken. 1971. Idealism: White Activists in a Black Movement. San Francisco: Jossey-Bass.

Dillick, Sidney. 1953. Community Organization for Neighborhood Development: Past and Present. New York: William Morrow and Company and Woman's Press.

Ecklein, Joan L., and Armand A. Lauffer. 1972. Community Organizers and Social Planners. New York: Wiley.

Erlanger, Howard S. 1977. "Social reform organizations and subsequent careers of participants: A follow-up study of early participants in the OEO Legal Services Program." American Sociological Review 42: 233–248.

Fendrich, James M. 1974. "Activists ten years later: A test of generational unit continuity." Journal of Social Issues 30: 95– 118.

Fendrich, James M. 1976. "Black and white activists ten years later: Political Socialization and adult left-wing politics." Youth and Society 8: 81–104.

Fendrich, James M. 1977. "Keeping the faith or pursuing the good life: A study of the consequences of participation in the civil rights movement." American Sociological Review 42: 144–157.

Fendrich, James M., and Ellis S. Krauss. 1978. "Student activism and adult left-wing politics: A causal model of political socialization for black, white and Japanese students of the 1960s generation." Research in Social Movements Conflicts and Change 1: 231–255.

Fendrich, James M., and Alison T. Tarleau. 1973. "Marching to a different drummer: Occupational and political correlates of former student activists." Social Forces 52: 245–253.

Fireman, Bruce, and William A. Gamson. 1979. "Utilitarian logic in the resource mobilization perspective." In Mayer N. Zald and John D. McCarthy, (eds.), The Dynamics of Social Movements: Resource Mobilization, Social Control and Tactics. Cambridge, MA: Winthrop.

Flacks, Richard. 1967. "The liberated generation: An exploration of the roots of student protest." Journal of Social Issues 23: 7– 14.

Flacks, Richard. 1971. Youth and Social Change. Chicago: Markham.

Frohlich, Norman, Thomas Hunt, Joe Oppenheimer, and R. Harrison Wagner. 1975. "Individual contributions for collective goods: Alternative models." Journal of Conflict Resolution 19: 310–329.

Frohlich, Norman and Joe A. Oppenheimer. 1970. "I get by with a little help from my friends." World Politics 23: 104–120.

Frohlich, Norman and Joe A. Oppenheimer. 1978. Modern Political Economy. Englewood Cliffs, NJ: Prentice-Hall.

Frohlich, Norman, Joe A. Oppenheimer, and Oran Young. 1971. Political Leadership and Collective Goods. Princeton: Princeton University Press.

Gamson, William A. 1975. The Strategy of Social Protest. Homewood, Ill.: The Dorsey Press.

Gerlach, Luther P., and Virginia H. Hine. 1970. People, Power, Change: Movements of Social Transformation. Indianapolis: Bobbs- Merrill.

Greene, W. 1970. "Where are the Savios of yesteryear?" New York Times Magazine 6: 6–10.

Grosser, Charles F. 1968. "Staff role in neighborhood organization." Pages 133, 145 in John B. Turner, Neighborhood Organization for Community Action. New York: National Association of Social Work.

Haan, Norma. 1975. "Hypothetical and actual moral reasoning in a situation of civil disobedience." Journal of Personality and Social Psychology 32: 255–270.

Heberle, Rudolf. 1951. Social Movements: An Introduction to Political Sociology. New York: Appleton Century-Crofts.

Kahn, Si. 1970. How People Get Power: Organizing Oppressed Communities for Action. New York: McGraw-Hill.

Kasschau, Patricia L, H. Edward Ransford, and Vern L. Bengtson. 1974. "Generational consciousness and youth movement participation. Contrasts in blue collar and white collar youth." Journal of Social Issues 30: 69–94.

Killian, Lewis M. 1964. "Social movements." In R. E. L. Faris (ed.), Handbook of Modern Sociology. Chicago: Rand McNally. 426– 455.

Kornberg, Alan, and Mary L. Brehm. 1971. "Ideology, institutional identification and campus activism." Social Forces 49: 445–459.

Kornhauser, William. 1962. "Social bases of political commitment: A study of liberals and radicals." Pages 321–339 in Arnold Rose (ed.), Human Behavior and Social Processes. Boston: Houghton Mifflin.

Kotler, Milton. 1969. Neighborhood Government: The Local Foundations of Political Life. Indianapolis: Bobbs-Merrill.

Kotler, Milton. 1979. "A public policy for neighborhood and community organizations." Social Policy 10. (2): 37, 43.

Kramer, Ralph M., and Harry Specht (eds.). 1974. Readings in Community Organization Practice. (Second Edition) Englewood Cliffs, NJ: Prentice-Hall.

Lang, Kurt, and Gladys Engel Lang. 1961. Collective Dynamics. New York: Thomas Y. Crowell Company.

Lenin, V. I. [1902] 1973. What Is To Be Done? Peking: Foreign Languages Press.

Lin, Nan. [1974–5]."The McIntire march: A study of recruitment and commitment." Public Opinion Quarterly 38: 562–573.

Lipset, Seymour M. 1971. "Youth and politics." Pages 743–792 in Robert K. Merton and Robert A. Nisbet (eds.), Contemporary Social Problems. New York: Harcourt, Brace and World.

Lofland, John. 1977. Doomsday Cult. (Enlarged Edition) New York: Irvington.

Lofland, John. 1979. "White-hot mobilization: Strategies of a millenarian movement." In Mayer Zald and John McCarthy (eds.), The Dynamics of Social Movements, 157–166. Cambridge, MA: Winthrop.

McCarthy, John D., and Mayer N. Zald. 1973. The Trend of Social Movements in America: Professionalization and Resource Mobilization. Morristown, NJ: General Learning Press.

McCarthy, John D., and Mayer N. Zald. 1977. "Resource mobilization and social movements: A partial theory." American Journal of Sociology 82: 1212–1241.

McFalls, Joseph A., and Bernard J. Gallagher, III. 1975. "Political orientations and occupational values." Paper presented at the American Sociological Association meetings, August, San Francisco.

McPhail, Clark, and David Miller. 1973. "The assembling process: A theoretical and empirical examination." American Sociological Review 38: 721–735.

Miadenberg, M, and P. Meyer. 1970. "The Berkeley rebels: Five years later." Paper presented at the annual meeting of the American Association for Public Opinion Research. Abstracted in Public Opinion Quarterly 24: 477–478.

Marx, Gary T. 1979. "External efforts to damage or facilitate social movements: Some patterns, explanations, outcomes, and complications." Pages 94–125 in Mayer Zald and John McCarthy (eds.), The Dynamics of Social Movements. Cambridge, MA: Winthrop.

Matthews, Donald, and James Prothro. 1966. Negroes and the New Southern Politics. New York: Harcourt, Brace and World.

Michels, Robert. [1915] 1962. Political Parties. New York: Collier.

Moe, Terry M. 1980. The Organization of Interests: Incentives and the Internal Dynamics of Political Interest Groups. Chicago: The University of Chicago Press.

Moymhan, Daniel P. 1965. "The professionalization of reform." The Public Interest 1: 6–16.

Moymhan, Daniel P. 1969. Maximum Feasible Misunderstanding: Community Action in the War on Poverty. New York: The Free Press.

Oberschall, Anthony. 1973. Social Conflict and Social Movements. Englewood Cliffs, NJ: Prentice-Hall.

O'Brien, David J. 1975. Neighborhood Organization and Interest-Group Processes. Princeton University Press.

Oliver, Pamela. 1980. "Rewards and punishments as selective incentives for collective action: Theoretical investigations." American Journal of Sociology 85: 1356–1375.

Olson, Mancur, Jr. 1965. The Logic of Collective Action. Cambridge, MA: Harvard University Press.

Perlman, Janice. 1979. "Grassroots empowerment and government response." Social Policy 10 (2): 16–21.

Rathke, Wade, Seth Borgos and Gary Delgado. 1979. "ACORN: Taking advantage of the fiscal crisis." Social Policy 10 (2): 35–36.

Schofield, Norman. 1975. "A game theoretic analysis of Olson's game of collective action." Journal of Conflict Resolution 19: 441–461.

Schwartz, Sanford M., and John D. McCarthy. 1978. "Marketing strategies for mass mobilization." Paper presented at the Annual Meeting of the Southern Sociological Society, New Orleans.

Smelser, Neil J. 1962. Theory of Collective Behavior. New York: Free Press.

Smith, Constance and Anne Freedman. 1972. Voluntary Associations: Perspectives on the Literature. Cambridge, MA: Harvard University Press.

Smith, David Horton. 1975. "Voluntary action and voluntary groups." Annual Review of Sociology 1: 247–270.

Smith, Jan. 1976. "Communities, associations, and the supply of collective goods." American Journal of Sociology 82: 291–308.

Snow, David A., Louis A. Zurcher, Jr., and Sheldon Ekland-Olson. 1980. "Social networks and social movements: A micro-structural approach to differential recruitment." American Sociological Review 45: 787–801.

Turner, Ralph II, and Lewis M. Killian. 1972. Collective Behavior. (Second Edition) Englewood Cliffs, NJ: Prentice-Hall.

Verba, Sidney, and Norman H. Nic. 1972. Participation in America. New York: Harper and Row.

Von Eschen, Donald, Jerome Kirk, and Maurice Pinard. 1971. "The organizational substructure of disorderly politics." Social Forces 49: 529–544.

Weiner R, and D. Stillman. 1979. Woodstock Census: The Nationwide Survey of the Sixties Generation. New York: Viking Press.

Weiss, Robert F. 1963. "Defection from social movements and subsequent recruitment to new movements." Sociometry 26: 1–20.

Whalen, Jack and Richard Flacks. 1980. "The Isla Vista "bank burners" ten years later: Notes on the fate of student activists." Sociological Focus 13: 215–236.

Wilson, James Q. 1973. Political Organizations. New York: Basic Books.

Wilson, John. 1973. Introduction to Social Movements. New York: Basic Books.

ARTICLE 25

The Consequences of Professionalization and Formalization in the Pro-Choice Movement

SUZANNE STAGGENBORG

. . . This paper explores the consequences of professionalization in social movements by analyzing the impact of leadership and organizational structure in the pro-choice movement. My analysis is based on documentary and interview data gathered on the pro-choice movement (Staggenborg 1985) and focuses on a sample of 13 pro-choice movement organizations, including 6 national organizations and 7 state and local organizations from Illinois and Chicago. . . . Documentary data cover the histories of the organizations from their beginnings to 1983. Fifty individuals were interviewed, including leaders and rank-and-file activists, who were active in the organizations during different periods. I analyze the changes in leadership and internal structures of the SMOs and the impact of these changes on the movement. In particular, I focus on changes in three major periods of the abortion conflict: the years prior to legalization of abortion in 1973; 1973 to 1976, when Congress first passed the Hyde Amendment cutoff of federal funding of abortion; and 1977–1983 following the anti-abortion victory on the Hyde Amendment. . . .

CONCEPTUAL DISTINCTIONS

Types of Leadership in SMOs

With the professionalization of social movements and the availability of funding for staff positions, several types of leaders are found in SMOs (cf. McCarthy and Zald 1977, p. 1227; Oliver 1983, pp. 163–64). *Professional managers* are paid staff who make careers out of movement work. Professional managers are likely to move from one SMO to another and from movement to movement over their careers (see McCarthy and Zald 1973, p. 15). Two types of *nonprofessional leaders* are *volunteer leaders nonprofessional staff leaders.* Volunteer leaders are not paid. Nonprofessional staff leaders are compensated for some or all of their time, but are not career activists. Rather, they serve as SMO staff for a short term and do not regard movement work as a career. As I argue below, there may be significant differences in orientation of leaders within this category based on whether the nonprofessional staff leader is temporarily dependent on the movement income for a living. Those who are dependent on the income may behave like professional managers in some respects, whereas those with other sources of income (or those willing to live at subsistence level) may behave more like volunteers. All three types of leaders are, by definition, involved in organizational decision making. All three are also included in the category of *activists,* as are other nonleader members who are actively involved in the SMO as opposed to being paper members.

Paid leaders, then, may or may not be "professionals" in the sense of making careers out of

Staggenborg, Suzanne. (1988, August). The consequences of professionalization and formalization in the pro-choice movment. *American Sociological Review, 53,* 585–606. Reprinted by permission of the American Sociological Association.

movement work and, as Oliver (1983, p. 158) shows, may come from the "same pool" as volunteers. Of course, leaders who do not begin as movement professionals may become career activists. Both professional and nonprofessional leaders learn skills (e.g., public relations skills) that they can easily transfer from one organization to another and from one cause to another. Both professionals and nonprofessionals can serve as *entrepreneurs*—leaders who initiate movements, organizations, and tactics (cf. Kleidman 1986, pp. 191–92). However, as I argue below, nonprofessional leaders are more likely to inititate movements (as opposed to SMOs) and tactics than are professionals.

Types of Movement Organizations

Changes in the structures of SMOs have occurred along with the professionalization of social movement leadership. In contrast to "classical" SMOs, which have mass memberships of beneficiary constituents. McCarthy and Zald (1973, 1977) argue that movement organizations with professional leadership have nonexistent or "paper" memberships and rely heavily on resources from constituents outside of the group(s) that benefit from movement achievements. Professional movement activists are thought to act as entrepreneurs who form such organizations by appealing to conscience constituents. The difficulty with this characterization of the structural changes in SMOs led by professionals is, as Oliver (1983) notes, that many such SMOs have both active and paper memberships. Similarly, organizations may rely on a mix of conscience and beneficiary constituents for resources.

An alternative characterization of structural differences in SMOs is based on difference in operating procedures. *Formalized* SMOs have established procedures or structures that enable them to perform certain tasks routinely and to continue to function with changes in leadership. Formalized SMOs have bureaucratic procedures for decision making, a developed division of labor with positions for various functions, explicit criteria for membership, and rules governing subunits (chapters or committees). For example, the formalized SMO may have a board of directors that meets a set number of times per year to make organizational policy: an executive committee of the board that meets more frequently to make administrative decisions; staff members who are responsible for contacts with the mass media, direct mail campaigns, and so forth; chapters that report to the national organization; and an individual rank-and-file membership. As I argue below, this type of SMO structure is associated with the professionalization of leadership. In contrast, *informal* SMOs have few established procedures, loose membership requirements, and minimal division of labor. Decisions in informal organizations tend to be made in an ad hoc rather than routine manner (cf. Rothschild-Whitt 1979, p. 513). The organizational structure of an informal SMO is frequently adjusted; assignments among personnel and procedures are developed to meet immediate needs. Because informal SMOs lack established procedures, individual leaders can exert an important influence on the organization; major changes in SMO structure and activities are likely to occur with changes in leadership. Any subunits of informal SMOs, such as work groups or chapters, tend to be autonomous and loosely connected to one another. Informal organizations are dominated by nonprofessional, largely volunteer, leaders.

THE IMPACT OF PROFESSIONAL LEADERSHIP

. . .

Professionalization and the Formalization of SMOs

Not only are movement entrepreneur and professional distinct roles, but movement entrepreneurs and other nonprofessionals are likely to differ from professional managers in their organizational structure preferences. While McCarthy and Zald (1977) suggest that movement entrepreneurs create "professional" SMOs, my data support the argument that movement entrepreneurs prefer informal structures and may resist creation of formalized SMOs run by professional leaders. The professionalization of social movements (i.e., the rise of career leadership) is associated with the formalization of SMOs for two reasons: (1) professional managers tend to formalize the organizations that they lead; and (2) the SMOs that have the resources to hire professional managers are those with formalized structures.

Movement entrepreneurs prefer informal structures that enable them to maintain personal control. As the analogy to business entrepreneurs suggests, movement entrepreneurs are risk-takers (cf. Oliver 1983) who initiate movement organizations without certainty of success, just as capitalist entrepreneurs risk investment in new products. Like capitalist entrepreneurs, movement entrepreneurs are likely to be personally involved in the enterprise, desiring personal control over decision making because they have taken the risks to establish an organization or movement. In contrast to the professional manager who brings skills to an organization and expects to operate within an established structure, movement entrepreneurs may try to prevent the creation of an organizational structure in which decision making is routinized and, therefore, less subject to personal control.

The history of leadership in NARAL, which was founded in 1969 as the National Association for the Repeal of Abortion Laws, reveals that conflict between entrepreneurial leadership and formalization occurs in some circumstances. NARAL founders were not professional movement organizers in the sense of being career movement activists; rather, they were persons who had become dedicated to the cause of legal abortion as a result of their prior experiences, primarily in the family planning and population movements that provided the most important organizational bases for the rise of the single-issue abortion movement (see Staggenborg 1985). Because the decision-making structure was informal . . . , a movement entrepreneur who became chairman of the executive committee exerted a large amount of control over the organization; as he commented in a 1984 interview about his own style of leadership:

> *Let's face it. . . . I don't believe in endless meetings, I like to make quick decisions. Maybe I acted unliaterally sometimes, although I was always careful to check with the executive committee. Some people objected to my calling [other members of the executive committee] and getting their approval on the phone. [But] we couldn't meet, we had to move fast, so I polled the exec committee around the country by phone. (Personal interview)*

Although there were some disagreements among NARAL executive committee members in the pre-1973 years, the informal decision-making structure seems to have worked fairly well at a time when the movement was very young, abortion was illegal in most states, and it was necessary to act quickly to take advantage of opportunities for action and to meet crises (e.g., the arrests of leaders involved in abortion referral activities).

After legalization, however, conflict over the decision-making structure occurred as NARAL attempted to establish itself as a lobbying force in Washington and to expand by organizing state affiliates. At this point, there was a power struggle within the organization between long-time leaders and entrepreneurs of NARAL and newer activists who objected to "power being concentrated in the hands of a few men in New York City" and who supported having persons "who are doing the work of the field—the State Coordinators" on the board (documents in NARAL of Illinois papers; University of Illinois at Chicago). The latter faction won a critical election in 1974 resulting in a turnover of leadership on the NARAL executive committee. Although the executive committee remained the decision-making body of the organization, practices such as the use of proxy votes and phone calls to make important decisions were discontinued (personal interview with 1974 NARAL executive director), resulting in more formalized decision-making procedures that involved more activists at different levels. Another major change that occurred at this point was that for the first time the executive director and other paid staff became more important than the nonprofessional entrepreneurs as NARAL leaders. It was only with the defeat of movement entrepreneurs as organizational leaders that NARAL began to formalize and eventually grew into a large organization capable of acting in institutionalized arenas.

If movement entrepreneurs interfere with the formalization of SMOs, as this case suggests, professional managers encourage formalization. While informal structures are associated with nonprofessional leadership, all of the organizations in my sample that have moved toward a more formal structure have done so under the leadership of professional managers. . . . Although further study of the leadership styles of professional managers compared to nonprofessional SMO leaders is necessary, my data suggest some reasons why professional managers tend to formalize the SMOs that they lead. Insofar as a bureaucratic or formalized structure is associated with organizational maintenance (Gamson 1975), professional leaders have a strong motivation to promote formalization: ongoing resources are needed to pay the salary of the professional manager. However, the motivation to promote financial stability is also shared by nonprofessional staff who are dependent on their income from the SMO position; moreover, it is possible to secure stable funding by means other than formalization. It is also important that professional managers are interested in using and developing organizing skills and expanding the SMOs they lead because this is what they do for a career. A formalized structure, with its developed division of labor enables the professional manager to achieve a degree of organizational development not possible in informal SMOs.

The case of the Abortion Rights Association of Illinois (formerly Illinois Citizens for the Medical Control of Abortion and later NARAL of Illinois) reveals the role of professional leadership in the creation of organizational stability and bureaucracy. From 1970 to 1976, ICMCA/ARA was led by a nonprofessional director who was paid a small salary, but who volunteered much of her time and was often not paid on time due to financial problems of the organization. She was extremely effective, but did not create a structure such that others could easily carry on her work. Rather, organizational activities were carried out by force of her personality. Moreover, volunteer efforts were channeled into instrumental tactics like lobbying, and little emphasis was placed on organizational maintenance activities such as fundraising. When she resigned in early 1976, ARA entered a period of severe decline due to inept leadership and neglect of organizational maintenance.

A new director hired in 1978 was the first to develop a stable source of financial resources for the SMO. Although not a professional manager, the new director was highly motivated to secure funding because, unlike the previous directors, she was a graduate student who did not have a husband who made enough money to support her while she volunteered her time. She needed the money from the job and did not intend to work as a volunteer when there was not enough money to pay her salary (about $11,000 a year for part-time work) as had previous directors. Consequently, she set about trying to figure out how to bring a stable income to the organization. She eventually was able to do so by personally convincing the owners of a number of abortion clinics in the city to make monthly financial contributions to NARAL (personal interview with 1978–80 NARAL of Illinois director). Thus, it was important that the leader of Illinois NARAL was someone who, while not a career activist, did need to be paid and was therefore motivated to provide the organization with financial stability. However, the financial stability was based on the personal appeal of the organization's director; the contributions from clinics were received as a result of personal relationships with clinic owners established by the NARAL director. After she left NARAL and a new director replaced her in the fall of 1980, the organization lost these contributions and went through a period of budget tightening.

It was not until the first career professional took over leadership of NARAL of Illinois that the organization became more formalized and less dependent on the personal characteristics of its leaders. The director hired in 1980, who stayed with NARAL until 1983, was a young woman who had previously done community organizing work and who, unlike her predecessor, wanted a career in "organizing." She did not have any experience working on the abortion issue prior to being hired as the director of Illinois NARAL, but saw the job as a good experience for her, a way to develop her own skills and enhance her career objectives. Like other leaders, the professional manager was highly committed to the goals of the movement, both because of pro-choice views formed prior to directing NARAL and because of her experiences in working with NARAL. But the professional director's orientation to her job led her to make important changes in the structure of the organization.

Until Illinois NARAL's first professional manager took over; the board of directors was selected from the same pool of long-time activists, many of whom were highly involved in other organizations like Planned Parenthood and not very active in ARA/NARAL. Consequently, there was little division of labor in the organization and it was heavily reliant on the abilities of its executive director. When she was hired in 1980, the new director insisted that the board selection procedures be revised so that active new volunteer recruits could serve on the board and so that the terms of service on the board were systematically rotated. This procedure was implemented in 1980, resulting in a board composed of active volunteers along with some old board members who continued to serve on a rotating basis to provide experience to NARAL. The result was that a formal procdure for bringing new and active members into the decision-making structure of the organization was established for the first time. This change was important in making the organization less exclusively dependent on its executive director for leadership. It also made volunteers more available to the executive director for use in organizational maintenance activities, such as the NARAL "house meeting" program, which provided an important source of funds to the SMO in the early 1980s. In Illinois NARAL and in other SMOs, . . . formalization occurred as professional managers took over leadership. Once a formalized structure is in place, SMOs are better able to mobilize resources and continue to hire professional staff (see below).

THE CONSEQUENCES OF FORMALIZATION

The Maintenance of Social Movement Organizations

While informal movement organizations may be necessary to initiate movements, formalized SMOs do not necessarily defuse protest as Piven and Cloward (1977) argue; rather, they often perform important functions (e.g., lobbying) following victories won by informal SMOs (Jenkins and Eckert 1986, p. 827). And, while informal SMOs may be necessary to create the pressure for elite patronage, formalized SMOs are the usual beneficiaries of foundation funding and other elite contributions (Haines 1984; Jenkins 1985b; Jenkins and Eckert 1986). Consequently, formalized SMOs are able to maintain themselves—and the movement—over a longer period of time than are informal SMOs. This is particularly important in periods such as the one following legalization of abortion, when movement issues are less pressing and mobilization of constituents is more difficult.

Jenkins (1985b, p. 10) argues that one of the reasons that formalized SMOs are able to sustain themselves is that foundations prefer dealing with organizations that have professional leaders and "the fiscal and management devices that foundations have often expected of their clients." In the case of the civil rights movement, foundations "selected the new organizations that became permanent features of the political landscape" through their funding choice (Jenkins 1985b, p. 15). It is important to recognize, however, that this selection process is a two-way street. Formalized SMOs do not just passively receive support from foundations and other elite constituents; they actively solicit these resources. They are able to do so because they have organizational structures and professional staff that facilitate the mobilization of elite resources. Most importantly, professional staff are likely to have the know-how necessary to secure funding (e.g., grant-writing skills and familiarity with procedures for securing tax-exempt status).

The ability of formalized SMOs to obtain foundation funding is part of a broader capacity for organizational maintenance superior to that of informal SMOs. Paid staff and leaders are critical to the maintenance of formalized SMOs because they can be relied on to be present to carry out tasks such as ongoing contact with the press and fundraising in a routine manner. A formalized structure ensures that there will be continuity in the performance of maintenance tasks and that the SMO will be prepared to take advantage of elite preferences and environmental opportunities (cf. Gamson 1975). Of course, volunteers might well have the skills to perform such tasks, and some informal SMOs do maintain themselves for a number of years, even in adverse environmental conditons (cf. Rupp and Taylor 1987). However, it is much more difficult to command the necessay time from volunteer activists on an ongoing basis. When informal SMOs do survive for many years, they are likely to remain small and exclusive, as was the case for the National Women's Party studied by Rupp and Taylor (1987) and Women Organized for Reproductive Choice in my sample.

The superior ability of formalized SMOs to maintain themselves is documented by the experiences of organizations in my sample.... On the national level, all of the surviving pro-choice organizations have at least moved in the direction of formalization.... The one organization that did not do so, the Reproductive Rights National Network, was formed in a period of intense constituent interest in the abortion issue created by events such as passage of the Hyde Amendment cutoff of Medicaid funding of abortion in late 1976 and the election of anti-abortion president Ronald Reagan in 1980, but was unable to maintain itself after this period. On the local level, the movement industry declined in the period after legalization due to the lack of formalized SMOs. ... The exception was Chicago NOW, which was moving toward formalization but which was concentrating its energies on the Equal Rights Amendment rather than on the abortion issue. In the period after the environmental stimulus of the Hyde Amendment, the local pro-choice SMOs that became stable were those that began to formalize. Among informal SMOs, only Women Organized for Reproductive Choice (WORC) has survived and it has remained a small organization. Thus, on both the national and local levels, formalized SMOs have been stable organizations that helped to sustain the movement during lulls in visible movement activity brought about by environmental developments.

Not only do formalized SMOs help keep a movement alive in periods when constituents become complacent, such as that following legalization of abortion, but they are prepared to take advantage of opportunities for mobilization when the environement changes. In the late 1970s, when the anti-abortion movement scored its first major victories, including the cutoff of Medicaid funding for abortions, adherents and constituents were alerted by visible threats to legal abortion, and the ability of the pro-choice movement to mobilize was greatly enhanced. However, it was important not only that the environment was conducive to mobilization but also that the pro-choice movement had formalized organizations that were stable and ready for combat (cf. Gamson 1975). In NARAL, professional leaders were available with the skills and know-how necessary to form a political action committee, launch a highly successful direct-mail drive, create an educational arm, obtain foundation grants, and organize state affiliates.

In contrast to the succes of NARAL and other formalized SMOs in mobilizing resources . . . informal movement organizations were not as prepared to take advantage of constituent concerns in the late 1970s. The Reproductive Rights National Network (known as R2N2), an informal SMO formed in the late 1970s, received a donation of money to undertake a direct-mail campaign during this period, but the attempt to raise money and recruit activists in this manner was unsuccessful because activists in the organization's national office did not have the experience to carry out the program properly (personal interviews with 1980–83 R2N2 coordinator and steering committee member). There might have been local activists in the organization with direct-mail skills who could have directed this campaign, but in this instance, and in others, the informal structure of the organization made access to such skills difficult to obtain. As one steering committee member commented in an interview, R2N2 suffered from "the classic leadership problem"— the difficulty of trying to get people "to do what they are supposed to do" and the problem of "no one being around" to coordinate work—that has long affected the "younger branch" of the women's movement (see Freeman 1975) of which R2N2 was a descendent. Ultimately, this structural problem led to the demise of R2N2 after the period of heightened constituent interest in abortion ended.

Formalized SMOs, then, are able to maintain themselves during periods when it is difficult to mobilize support and are consequently ready to expand when the environment becomes more conducive. An important reason for this is that they have paid leaders who create stability because they can be relied on to perform ongoing tasks necessary to organizational maintenance. However, stability is not simply a matter of having paid activists; it is also important that formalized SMOs have structures that ensure that taks are performed despite a turnover in personnel. It is the combination of formalized structure and professional leadership that facilitates organizational maintenance in SMOs.

Strategies and Tactics

While Piven and Cloward (1977) appear to be mistaken in their claim that formalized SMOs necessarily hasten the end of mass movements, their argument that formalization leads to a decline in militant direct-action tactics remains important. Formalization does affect the strategic and tactical choices of SMOs. First, formalized SMOs tend to engage in institutionalized tactics and typically do not initiate disruptive direct-action tactics. Second, formalized SMOs are more likely than informal SMOs to engage in activities that help to achieve organizational maintenance and expansion as well as influence on external targets.

Formalization and Institutionalized Tactics. The association between formalization and institutionalization of strategies and tactics occurs for two reasons: (1) As environmental developments push a movement into institutionalized arenas. SMOs often begin to formalize so they can engage in tactics such as legislative lobbying (cf. Cable 1984). Formalization allows SMOs to maintain the routines necessary for such tactics (e.g., ongoing contacts with legislators) through paid staff and an established division of labor. (2) Once SMOs are formalized, institutionalized tactics are preferred because they are more compatible with a formalized structure and with the schedules of professional activists. For example, institutionalized activities can be approved in advance; the amount and type of resources expended for such efforts can be controlled; and activities can be planned for the normal hours of the professional's working day.

The history of the pro-choice movement clearly reveals that formalization accelerated as environmental events forced the movement into institutionalized arenas. Prior to 1973, the movement to legalize abortion was an outsider to established politics. Although institutionalized tactics were employed in this period, no SMO confined its activities to institutionalized arenas; demonstrations and quasi-legal or illegal abortion-referral activities were common tactics. . . . After legalization in 1973, the arena for the abortion conflict switched to Congress and SMOs like NARAL began to formalize in order to act in that arena. After the Hyde amendment was passed in 1976, the political arena became the primary battlefield for the abortion conflict, and formalization of SMOs within the movement accelerated. Although informal SMOs in my sample did engage in some institutionalized tactics, the organizations that sustained a heavy use of tactics such as legislative lobbying and political campaign work were most commonly formalized SMOs.

It is possible for informal SMOs to engage in such tactics, but only as long as the leaders of the organization have the necessary know-how and other organizational resources. Formalized organizations are able to maintain such activities, despite changes in leadership, due to their structural division of labor.

Environmental forces and events, including countermovement activities, do place strong constraints on the tactics of SMOs. When environmental events call for nonroutine direct-action tactics, informal movement organizations typically play a critical role in initiating these tactics (Jenkins and Eckert 1986). In the case of the civil rights movement, for example, Morris (1984) shows that the formalized NAACP preferred to focus on legal and educational tactics, while informal SMOs were engaging in direct-action tactics. However, even the NAACP engaged in some direct-action tactics through its youth divisions at a time when it was clear that progress could only be made through tactics such as the sit-ins initiated by informal SMOs.

When formalized SMOs do engage in direct-action tactics, however, they are likely to be nondisruptive, planned versions of the tactics. NARAL's use of the "speak-out" tactic in the period following 1983 provides some evidence on this point. This was a period when the prochoice movement was beginning to take the offensive in the legislative and political arenas, particularly after anti-abortion forces failed in their attempt to pass a Human Life Bill through Congress in 1982 and the Supreme Court delivered a ruling in 1983 that struck down most of the restrictions on abortion that had been passed by state and local legislatures. The anti-abortion movement responded to these developments by forcing a switch away from the institutionalized arenas, in which pro-choice forces were beginning to gain the upper hand, to public relations tactics such as the film *The Silent Scream.* As a result of media coverage that began to focus on the issue of fetal rights (cf. Kalter 1985), prochoice organizations such as NARAL were forced to respond. NARAL chose to employ a version of the speak-out was a spontaneous type of public forum at which women spoke out about their experiences as women, relating their own stories about illegal abortions and so fourth. NARAL's version of this tactic was planned one; to focus media and public attention on women rather than on the fetus, NARAL asked women around the country to write letters about their experiences with abortion addressed to President Reagan and other elected officials and send the letters to NARAL and its affiliates. The letters were then read at public forums on a scheduled day. This case suggests that formalized organizations can switch from tactics in institutionalized arenas to other tactics when necessary, but the tactics they choose are likely to be orderly versions of direct-action tactics originated by informal SMOs.

Formalization and Organizational Maintenance Tactics. Not only are the tactics of formalized SMOs typically institutionalized, but they are also frequently geared toward organizational maintenance and expansion, in addition to more instrumental goals. This was certainly the case for NARAL and its affiliates, which embarked on a "grassroots organizing" strategy known as "Impact '80," intended to expand NARAL, and its political influence, in the late 1970s (see, for example, *NARAL News,* November 1978). It was also the case for NOW, which engaged in a number of high-profile tactics around abortion that were used in membership appeals in the 1980s (see, for example, *National NOW Times*, September/October 1979). In Chicago NOW, there was explicit discussion of the membership-expanding potential of the abortion issue in the late 1970s and early 1980s (personal interview with Chicago NOW executive director).

The experiences of organizations in my sample suggest that professional leaders play an important role in influencing organizations to adopt tactics that aid organizational maintenance. In several organizations, professional staff were responsible for undertaking direct-mail campaigns that helped to expand the organization. In NARAL, an experienced director who took over in 1974 began a direct-mail campaign that was later expanded by other professional leaders (person interviews with 1974–75 and 1975–81 NARAL executive directors). In the NWHN, an executive director succeeded in expanding organizational membership in the late 1970s through direct mail despite the concerns of nonprofessional leaders that direct mail would bring uncommitted members into the organization (personal interviews with NWHN board members). In ZPG, a professional manager was responsible for reversing the decline in individual membership in the organization through direct mail after he finally convined the nonprofessional leaders on the ZPG board to undertake the campaign (personal interview with 1976–80 ZPG executive director).

The case of Illinois NARAL is particularly valuable in revealing the role of professional leaders in advancing strategies that aid organizational expansion. In the early 1980s, the NARAL affiliate made important changes in its strategies and tactics, switching from an emphasis on legislative lobbying to heavy involvement in political campaign work. This switch was part of the national NARAL Impact '80 program, which began to be implemented by Illinois NARAL in 1979. However, it was not until the early 1980s, after a professional manager took over, that Illinois NARAL really became committed to the new tactics, which included political campaign work and workshops to train volunteers, house meetings to recruit new members, and an "I'm Pro-Choice and I Vote" postcard campaign.

One reason why the switch in mobilization tactics occurred after 1980 was that the national NARAL organization had by this time become much better organized in implementing the grassroots organizing program through training and grants to local affiliates. . . . As the national organization became more formalized, it was able to extend more aid through its bureaucratic structure to affiliates and to exert more influence over their tactics. In fact, NARAL affiliates signed formal contracts in exchange for national funds to carry out programs in the early 1980s. The other reason was that there were important differences in the state of the organization and in the orientations of the Illinois NARAL directors who served from 1978–1980 and from 1980–1983, which resulted in different strategies and tactics.

Because ARA was in a state of decline when she was hired in 1978, . . . the new director spent much of her time in administrative tasks; securing funding, renewing contacts with members, and organizing the office. Due to her organizational skills and attractive personal style, she was highly successful at reviving the organization. In doing so, she used the skills of constituents but did not create a formalized organization. NARAL's strategies and tactics were determined solely by the pragmatic and instrumental approach of the 1978–80 executive director. Rather than concentrating on bringing large numbers of activists into the organization, she recruited volunteers with particular skills, including her friends, for specific tasks. Tactics were aimed less at gaining exposure for NARAL than at accomplishing specific objectives. For example, when a Chicago alderman moved to introduce an ordinance in the city council restricting the availability of abortions, the NARAL director worked to have the measure killed through quiet, behind-the-scenes maneuvers. In this instance and in lobbying work in the state legislature, she made use of the skills and influence of seasoned activists.

Due to her success with such tactics and her lack of concern with organizational expansion, the 1978–80 director was not sold on the national NARAL "Impact '80" program, which was intended to expand NARAL and make the organization a visible political force. In accordance with the natioanl organization's wishes, she tried to implement the program, conducting a limited number of house meetings. Bus she remained unconvinced of their effectiveness, preferring more efficient methods of fundraising and recruitment. She had similar objections to other parts of the national NARAL grassroots organizing program. When I asked her about the political skills workshops, she replied:

> *I refused to do those political skills workshops. I didn't have time, I said [to national NARAL]. I'm doing the house meetings program—that's enough. I really just didn't think they were necessary—there are enough organizations like the League of Women Voters which do political skills training. From an organizational point of view, I guess it's good to do your own skills training to show that the organization is really involved. (Personal interview)*

Although she recognized the organizational value of such tactics, this director was not primarily concerned with organizational expansion, but with more specific goals, such as defeating particular pieces of anti-abortion legislation. She was accustomed to using individual skills for this work rather than mobilizing large numbers of activists. When asked about campaign work, she replied:

> *I do think the "I'm Pro-Choice and I Vote" [postcard campaign] was important in getting the message across to legislators and candidates in a public way. I put a lot of emphasis on [abortion] clinics for post cards because there was a ready-made setting for getting people to sign them. . . . As far as the campaign work, it was clear to me at the time that Reagan was going to be elected. It was too late in 1980 to make a difference. And, on the local level, there are already liberal groups . . . that almost always support pro-choice candidates anyway. . . . I'm just not that much on duplicating efforts which I think NARAL is doing with the campaign work. (Personal interview)*

As these comments indicate, the 1978–80 Illinois NARAL director preferred instrumental tactics rather than organizing tactics as a result of her background and experiences. She saw the house meetings as an inefficient way to raise money, and, while she recognized that political-skills workshops and campaign work were good for organizational visibility, she was not convinced of their effectiveness for achieving movement goals—her primary concern. She used the "I'm Pro-Choice and I Vote" postcards as a signal to legislators rather than as an organizing tool. Due to her influence, most of Illinois NARAL's activities during her tenure were instrumentally targeted at state legislators.

It was not until an executive director with experience in community organizing work and with ambitions for a movement career was hired in 1980 that the Illinois NARAL affilitate enthusiastically implemented the national NARAL grassroots organizing program. In contrast to her predecessor, who had no interest in organizing *per se*, the new director was anxious to engage in "organizing" work to expand the local affiliate and eagerly began to develop the house meeting program that was part of the national NARAL organizing strategy. One of the reasons that she was successful in dong so was that, as described above, she created a more formalized organization. Whereas her predecessor had been reluctant to delegate certain tasks, including speaking at house meetings, the new director made heavy use of a division of labor that had not existed in the previously informal SMO. Aided by her past experience with community organizing, she was highly successful at training volunteers to conduct house meetings and, with funds raised from the meetings and some financial aid from national NARAL, was able to hire an organizer to run the house meeting program, thereby increasing the division of labor in the SMO.

The new director's strategic approach was clearly influenced by her professional interest in organizing tactics. She used the NARAL house meeting program to raise money, but also as a means of bringing new activists into the NARAL organization. And just as the house meetings were used as an organizing tool, so were the NARAL postcards. As the NARAL director explained:

> *The best thing about the postcards was that they gave us new contacts. We would set up tables in different places and people would come up and sign and say things like "I'm really glad someone is doing something about this issue." And then we'd say, "Would you like to get more involved?" and we got a number of activists that way. We also got names for a mailing list. . . . So the postcards were good as a way of making contacts, a means of exposure for the organization. The actual effect of the postcards on legislators was, I think, minimal. I know some of the legislators never even opened the envelope; when we delivered an envelope-full to Springfield, they'd just throw them away. (Personal interview)*

Thus, Illinois NARAL employed tactics oriented toward organizational goals after moving toward formalization. This local case history suggests that professional leaders may be more likely than nonprofessional staff and volunteers to influence SMOs to engage in tactics that have organizational maintenance functions rather than strictly instrumental goals because they have organizational skills that they want to use and develop.

Coalition Work

The formalization of social movement organizations also has implications for coalition work within movements. In my sample, formalized SMOs have played the dominant roles in lasting coalitions. . . . Coalitions among formalized SMOs are easier to maintain than are coalitions among informal SMOs or between formalized and informal SMOs because formalized SMOs typically have staff persons who are available to act as organizational representatives to the coalition and routinely coordinate the coalition work. Just as paid staff can be relied on to carry out maintenance tasks for SMOs, they can also be relied on to maintain contact with the representatives of other SMOs in a coalition. When all of the SMO representatives are paid staff, coordination is easiest. While volunteers can represent SMOs in coalitions, it is more difficult to keep volunteers in contact with one another and to coordinate their work, particularly in the absence of a formalized coalition organization with paid staff of its own. Thus, paid staff help to maintain coalitions, thereby lessening the organizational problems of coalition work (see Staggenborg 1986, p. 387).

The experiences of the Illinois Pro-Choice Alliance (IPCA), a Chicago-based coalition organization, reveal the impact of organizational structure on coalition work. formalized movement organizations, including NARAL of Illinois and Chicago NOW, have played a major role in this coalition, while informal organizations, such as Women Organized for Reproductive Choice (WORC), have had a difficult time participating in the coalition. One past director of the Illinois Pro-Choice Alliance recognized this problem, commenting in an interview:

> *. . . there is a real difference between groups which have paid staff and the grassroots groups which are all volunteers. The groups with paid staff have a lot more opportunity to participate [in the coalition]—even trivial things like meeting times create problems. The groups with paid staff can meet in the Loop at lunch time—it makes it easier. Also . . . people from the grassroots groups tend to be intimidated by the paid staff, because as volunteers the grassroots people are less informed about the issue. Whereas for the staff, it's their job to be informed, and they have the resources behind them. . . . I think too that the grassroots people have higher expectations about*

what can be done. They're volunteers who may have worked all day, then they do this in the evenings; they're cause-oriented and they expect more out of people and projects. Paid staff are the opposite in that they work on the issue during the day and then want to go home to their families or whatever at night and leave it behind. They want to do projects with defined goals and time limits, projections as to the feasibility and all that. Not that paid staff are not committed people. I think it's good to have a balance between the grass-roots and staffed groups. Without the grassroots people, I think things would be overstructured; with just the grassroots people, well, there's too much burnout among them. The staffers tend to last a lot longer. (Personal interview)

These perceptions are borne out by the difficulties of Women Organized for Reproductive Choice in trying to participate in the IPCA. WORC members interviewed also spoke of the problems they had attending IPCA meetings at lunchtime in downtown Chicago, a time and place convenient for the staff of formalized SMO members of the coalition but difficult for WORC members, who tended to be women with full-time jobs in various parts of the city. Another reason for the difficulty is that the coalition has focused on institutionalized lobbying activities, tactics for which WORC members have neither the skills nor the ideological inclination. Efforts by WORC to get the coalition to engage in a broader range of tactics, including direct-action tactics, have been unsuccessful. On the national level, the Reproductive Rights National Network had nearly identical problems participating in the Abortion Information Exchange coalition (see Staggenborg 1986). Formalized SMOs play an important role in maintaining coalitions, but they also influence coalitions toward narrower, institutionalized strategies and tactics and make the participation of informal SMOs difficult.

CONCLUSION

While professionalization of leadership and formalization of SMOs are not inevitable outcomes of social movements, they are important trends in many movements (cf. McCarthy and Zald 1973, 1977; Gamson 1975, p. 91). There is little evidence, however, that professional leaders and formalized SMOs will replace informal SMOs and nonprofessionals as the initiators of social movements and collective action. While systmatic research on the influence of different types of movement leaders is needed, my data show that the roles of entrepreneur and professional manager are in some cases distinct. This is because environmental opportunities and preexisting organizational bases are critical determinants of movement mobilization; movement entrepreneurs do not manufacture grievances at will, but are influenced by the same environemental and organizational forces that mobilize other constituents. Contrary to the arguments of McCarthy and Zald (1973, 1977), nonprofessional leaders and informal SMOs remain important in initiating movements and tactics that are critical to the growth of insurgency (cf. McAdam 1983).

Professionalization of leadership has important implications for the maintenance and direction of social movement organizations. My data suggest that professional managers, as career activists, tend to formalize the organizations they lead in order to provide financial stability and the kind of division of labor that allows them to use and develop their organizational skills. Once formalized, SMOs continue to hire professional managers because they have the necessary resources. Contrary to the arguments of Piven and Cloward (1977), formalized SMOs do not diffuse protest but play an important role in maintaining themselves and the movement, particularly in unfavorable environmental conditions when it is difficult to mobilize constituents. Formalized SMOs are better able to maintain themselves than are informal ones, not only because they have paid staff who can be relied on to carry out organizational tasks, but also because a formalized structure ensures continuity despite changes in leadership and environmental conditions. Thus, a movement entrepreneur who prevents formalization by maintaining personal control over an

SMO may ultimately cause the organization's demise. A movement that consists solely of informal SMOs is likely to have a shorter lifetime than a movement that includes formalized SMOs. Similarly, a coalition of informal SMOs has less chance of survival than a coalition of formalized SMOs.

While formalization helps to maintain social movements, it is also associated with the institutionalization of collective action. Formalized SMOs engage in fewer disruptive tactics of the sort that pressure government authorities and other elites to make concessions or provide support than do informal SMOs. Formalized SMOs also tend to select strategies and tactics that enhance organizational maintenance. Given the prominent role of professional managers in formalized SMOs, these findings raise the Michels ([1915] 1962) question of whether formalized organizations with professional leaders inevitably become oligarchical and conservative, as Piven and Cloward (1977) argue. Based on my data, I dispute the conclusion that formalized SMOs necessarily become oligarchical. In fact, many seem more democratic than informal SMOs because they follow routinized procedures that make it more difficult for individual leaders to attain disproportionate power. As Freeman (1973) argues, "structureless" SMOs are most subject to domination by individuals.

The tendency of formalized SMOs to engage in more institutionalized strategies and tactics than informal SMOs might be interpreted as a conservative development, given findings that militant direct-action tactics force elite concessions (cf. Jenkins and Eckert 1986). Informal SMOs, with their more flexible structures, are more likely to innovate direct-action tactics. However, the institutionalization of movement tactics by formalized SMOs does not necessarily mean that movement goals become less radical; an alternative interpretation is that movement demands and representatives become incorporated into mainstream politics. For example, the National Organization for Women is now an important representative of women's interests in the political arena. While the long-term implications of this phenomenon for the social movement sector and the political system require further investigation, it is certainly possible for formalized SMOs to exert a progressive influence on the political system.

Finally, my research raises the question of whether movements inevitably become formalized or institutionalized, as suggested by classical theories of social movements, which argue that movements progress through stages toward institutionalization (see Lang and Lang 1961; Turner and Killian 1957 for discussions of such stage theories). In the case of the pro-choice movement, there has clearly been a trend toward formalization. As Gamson (1975, p. 91) notes, there does seem to be a kernel of truth to theories that posit an inevitable trend toward bureaucratization or formalization. However, as Gamson also notes, "the reality is considerably more complex" in that some SMOs begin with bureaucratic or formalized structures and others never develop formalized structures. Although neither Gamson nor I found cases of SMOs that developed informal structures after formalization, such a change is conceivable under certain circumstances (e.g., if nonprofessional staff are hired to replace professional managers, a development most likely at the local level). Classical theories of the "natural history" of a movement focus on the institutionalization of a movement as a whole and ignore variations in the experiences of different SMOs within the movement. My research shows that SMOs vary in the ways in which they deal with internal organizational problems and changes in the environment. Formalization is one important means of solving organizational problems, particularly as SMOs grow larger; however, SMOs can also develop alternative structures. Important variations exist within the two broad categories of SMO structure that I have identified; further empirical research on leadership roles and SMO structures and their impact on organizational goals and activities is necessary.

REFERENCES

Barr, Evan T. 1985. "Sour Grapes." *The New Republic* 193:20- -23.

Cable, Sherry. 1984. "Professionalization in Social Movement Organization: A Case Study of Pennsylvanians for Biblical Morality." *Sociological Focus* 17:287–304.

Carmen, Arlene and Howard Moody. 1973. *Abortion Counseling and Social Change*. Valley Forge, PA: Judson Press.

Delgado. Gary. 1986. *Organizing the Movement: The Roots and Growth of ACORN*. Philadelphia: Temple University Press.

D'Emilio, John. 1983. *Sexual Politics, Sexual Communities*. Chicago: University of Chicago Press.

Freeman, Jo. 1973. "The Tyranny of Structurelessness." *Ms*. 2:76–78, 86–89.

———. 1975. *The Politics of Women's Liberation*. New York: Longman.

———. 1979. "Resource Mobilization and Strategy: A Model for Analyzing Social Movement Organization actions." Pp. 167–89 in *The Dynamics of Social Movements,* edited by Mayer N. Zald and John D. McCarthy. Cambridge, MA: Winthrop.

Gamson, William A. 1975. *The Strategy of Social Protest*. Homewood, IL: Dorsey Press.

Haines, Herbert M. 1984. "Black Radicalization and the Funding of Civil Rights: 1957–1970." *Social Problems* 32:31–43.

Jenkins, J. Craig. 1983. "Resource Mobilization Theory and the Study of Social Movements." *Annual Review of Sociology* 9:527–53.

———. 1985a. *The Politics of Insurgency: The Farm Worker Movement in the 1960s*. New York: Columbia University Press.

———. 1985b. "Foundation Funding of Progressive Social Movements," Pp. 7–17 in *Grant Seekers Guide: Funding Sourcebook,* edited by Jill R. Shellow. Mt. Kisco, NY: Moyer Bell Ltd.

Jenkins, J. Craig and Craig M. Eckert. 1986. "Channeling Black Insurgency: Elite Patronage and Professional Social Movement Organizations in the Development of the Black Movement." *American Sociological Review* 51:812–829.

Kalter, Joanmarie. 1985. "Abortion Bias: How Network Coverage Has Tilted to the Pro-Lifers." *TV Guide* 33:7–17.

Kleidman, Robert. 1986. "Opposing 'The Good War': Mobilization and Professionalization in the Emergency Peace Campaign." *Research in Social Movements, Conflicts and Change* 9:177–200.

Lader, Lawrence. 1966. *Abortion*. Boston: Beacon Press.

———. 1973. *Abortion II: Making the Revolution*. Boston: Beacon Press.

Lang, Kurt and Gladys E. Lang. 1961. *Collective Dynamics*. New York: Thomas Y. Crowell.

McAdam, Doug. 1983. "Tactical Innovation and the Pace of Insurgency." *American Sociological Review* 48:735–54.

McCarthy, John D. and Mayer N. Zald. 1973. *The Trend of Social Movements in America: Professionalization and Resource Mobilization*. Moristown. NJ: General Learning Press.

———. 1977. "Resource Mobilization and Social Movements: A Partial Theory." *American Journal of Sociology* 82:1212–41.

McFarland, Andrew S. 1984. *Common Cause,* Chatham, NJ: Chatham House.

Michels, Robert [1915] 1962. *Political Parties*. New York: Collier.

Morris, Aldon D. 1984. *The Origins of the Civil Rights Movement: Black Communities Organizing for Change*. New York: Free Press.

NARAL of Illinois papers. Manuscripts Department, University of Illinois, Chicago, library.

Oberschall, Anthony. 1973. *Social Conflict and Social Movements*. Englewood Cliffs, NJ: Prentice-Hall.

Oliver, Pamela. 1983. "The Mobilization of Paid and Volunteer Activists in the Neighborhood Movement." *Research in Social Movements, Conflicts and Change* 5:133–70.

Piven, Frances Fox and Richard A. Cloward. 1977. *Poor People's Movements*. New York: Vintage Books.

Rauber, Paul. 1986. "With Friends Like These . . ." *Mother Jones* 11:35–37, 47–49.

Reinarman, Craig. 1985. "Social Movements and Social Problems: 'Mothers Against Drunk Drivers,' Restrictive Alcohol Laws and Social Control in the 1980s." Paper presented at the Annual Meeting of the Society for the Study of Social Problems, Washington, DC, Aug. 23–26.

Roche, John P. and Stephen Sachs. 1965. "The Bureaucrat and the Enthusiast: An Exploration of the Leadership of Social Movements." *Western Political Quarterly* 8:248–61.

Roeser, Thomas F. 1983. "The Pro-life Movement's Holy Terror." *Chicago Reader* 12(44):1. 14–24.

Rothschild-Whitt, Joyce. 1979. "The Collectivist Organization: An Alternative to Rational-Bureaucratic Models." *American Sociological Review* 44:509–27.

Rupp, Leila, J. and Verta Taylor, 1987. *Survival in the Doldrums*. New York: Oxford University Press.

Staggenborg, Suzanne. 1985. *Patterns of Collective Action in the Abortion Conflict: An Organizational Analysis of the Pro-Choice Movement*. Ph.D. diss., Northwestern University.

———. 1986. "Coalition Work in the Pro-Choice Movement: Organizational and Environmental Opportunities and Obstacles." *Social Problems* 33:374–90.

Turner, Ralph and Lewis Killian. 1957. *Collective Behavior*. Englewood Cliffs, NJ: Prentice-Hall.

Useem, Bert and Mayer N. Zald. 1982. "From Pressure Group to Social Movement: Organizational Dilemmas of the Effort to Promote Nuclear Power." *Social Problems* 30:144–56.

Walsh, Edward J. 1981. "Resource Mobilization and Citizen Protest in Communities Around Three Mile Island." *Social Problems* 29:1–21.

Zald, Mayer N. and Roberta Ash. 1966. "Social Movement Organizations: Growth, Decay and Change." *Social Forces* 44:327–41.

ARTICLE 26

Social Networks and Social Movements: A Microstructural Approach to Differential Recruitment

DAVID A. SNOW
LOUIS A. ZURCHER, JR.
SHELDON EKLAND-OLSON

. . . Four focal questions structure the inquiry: (1) What are the microstructural avenues of movement recruitment? (2) What accounts for the differential availability of people for movement participation? (3) What are the structural characteristics of social movements which predict different recruitment strategies and patterns? (4) What implications do different recruitment strategies and patterns have for the spread and growth of a movement?

DATA AND PROCEDURES

The article draws on three sets of data. The first is derived from an examination of social movement case studies through which we synthesize quantitative data pertaining to the recruitment process. References to the salience of such microstructural factors as social networks are not uncommon, but our review of the literature revealed that most of the references tend to be impressionistic. There is a dearth of hard data specifying the function of social networks in relation to differential recruitment to and the differential spread and growth of movements. However, we did find ten studies with quantitative data bearing directly on the recruitment process. The sample size of the ten studies varies from 31 to 310 participants, with the combined N totalling more than 1,200.

The second data set comes from an examination of recruitment to the Nichiren Shoshu Buddhist movement in America. These data were derived from the senior author's observations and experiences as a participant-observer for a year and a half, his informal interviews with recruits and members, and his examination of a random sample of members' testimonies appearing in the movement's newspaper, *The World Tribune.* Since most editions of the newspaper contain several members' testimonies, 504 were randomly selected from 1966 to 1974 (six per month), excluding a two-year period in which the newspaper was not readily available. Three hundred and thirty of the 504 testimonies provided information specifying mode of recruitment into the movement. These 330 cases, coupled with 15 other members from whom recruitment information was informally elicited, yielded a sample of 345. Informal interviews with 25 Hare Krishna

Snow, David A., Zurcher, Louis A. Jr., & Ekland-Olson, Sheldon. (1980, October). Social networks and social movements: A microstructural approach to differential recruitment. *American Sociological Review, 80,* 787–801. Reprinted by permission of the American Sociological Association.

devotees supplement the data pertaining to Nichiren Shoshu. Twenty of the interviews were with members of the Krishna commune in Los Angeles, and five were with members of the Dallas commune. The interviews were conducted during the course of six visits to the Los Angeles commune and two visits to the Dallas commune.

The third data set is derived from a nonrandom sample of University of Texas students. A questionnaire designed to gather information pertaining to movement recruitment and participation was administered to 550 students enrolled in ten different university courses in the Spring semester of 1979. The first part of the questionnaire contained a list of twenty-five social movement organizations within the Austin, Texas, area. The respondents were initially asked to indicate for each movement whether they were (a) unfamiliar with it; (b) familiar but not sympathetic or supportive; (c) sympathetic but not a participant; or (d) associated with it as a participant at one time or another. Three hundred of the 550 respondents indicated that they either were movement participants or were sympathetic with the objectives of one or more of the movements. Since we are concerned with differential recruitment, only the responses of the 135 participants and the 165 sympathizers are considered. The sympathetic nonparticipants constitute a kind of control group in that their responses shed light on the question of why it is that people who are in sympathy with and supportive of a movement's value orientation do not always participate in movement activities. A consideration of the responses of both participants and sympathizers should yield a better understanding of differential recruitment.

FINDINGS AND DISCUSSION

The Microstructural Avenues of Recruitment

Movement recruitment has generally been approached from a social-psychological/motivational level of analysis, with various states-of-mind or psychological attributes posited as the major causal variables (see Cantril, 1941; Feuer, 1969; Glock, 1964; Hoffer, 1951; Klapp, 1969; Toch, 1965). However reasonable the underlying assumption that some people are more susceptible than others to movement participation, that view deflects attention from the fact that recruitment cannot occur without prior contact with a recruitment agent. The potential participant has to be informed about and introduced into a particular movement. Thus, even if one accepts the popular contention that some individuals are predisposed social-psychologically to movement participation, the following question still remains: What determines which potential participants are most likely to come into contact with and be recruited into one movement rather than another, if into any movement at all?

It is a basic sociological tenet that social phenomena are not distributed randomly, but are structured according to aggregate or group membership, role incumbency, and the like. It thus seems reasonable to assume that movement recruitment, rather than being random or merely the function of social-psychological predispositions, will also be structured by certain sociospatial factors. Accordingly, we can begin to answer the above question by considering, first, the various sociospatial settings in which movements and potential participants can come into contact, and, second, the variety of generally available modes of communication through which information can be imparted.

Regarding the first concern, most spatial settings or domains of social life can be conceptualized in terms of a continuum ranging from public to private places. Examples of the former include shopping malls, community sidewalks, airports, bus stations, and city parks. Country clubs, an office, a sorority or fraternity house, and an apartment or home are illustrative of the latter.

The means of information dissemination can be conceptualized generally in terms of whether they are face-to-face or mediated. By face-to-face communication, we refer to all information, whether it be verbal or nonverbal, that is imparted when two or more individuals or groups are physically present. In contrast, mediated communication refers to information dissemination through institutionalized mass communication mechanisms, such as radio and television, or through institutionalized, but individualized and privatized, communication mechanisms such as the mail and telephone.

The cross-classification of these two dimensions suggests four general and fairly distinct microstructural avenues for movement information dissemination and recruitment. Figure 1 schematically summarizes these alternative avenues, each of which is distinguished by the spatial domain of social life in which contact can be established and the means through which information can be imparted.

Given the alternative microstructural avenues, the question arises as to the relative yield of each in terms of actual recruits. In other words, is recruitment among strangers in public places more productive than recruitment along the other avenues, or are movement recruits typically drawn from existing members' extra movement friends, acquaintances, and kin?

Examination of the movement literature strongly suggests that the network channel is the richest source of movement recruits. Numerous studies allude to the importance of social networks as a conduit for the spread of social movements. . . .

Our findings regarding recruitment to Nichiren Shoshu are consistent with those just presented. . . . Nichiren Shoshu members are typically recruited into the movement by one or more members with whom they have a preexisting, extra movement, interpersonal tie. Although Nichiren Shoshu members devote a considerable amount of time and energy to proselytizing in public places, these information dissemination and recruiting forays are not very productive. The senior author accompanied members on over forty such expeditions, and only twice were recruits attracted. In contrast, all but one of the twenty-five Krishna devotees we interviewed were recruited "off the street" by other members who were strangers at the time of contact. (Factors which account for the different recruitment patterns of Hare Krishna and the other movements will be discussed later.)

The important bridging function of social networks in relation to movement recruitment is further demonstrated by our findings regarding the sample of university students participating in

	FACE-TO-FACE	
	Face-to-face leafleting, petitioning, and proselytizing on sidewalks; participation in public events, such as parades; staging events for public consumption, such as sit-ins, protests, movement-sponsored conventions and festivals.	Door-to-door leafleting, petitioning, and proselytizing; information dissemination and recruitment among familiar others along the lines of promoter's extra-movement interpersonal networks.
PUBLIC CHANNELS		PRIVATE CHANNELS
	Promotion and recruitment via radio, television, and newspapers	Promotion and recruitment via mail and telephone.
	MEDIATED	

FIGURE 1 Classification of General Outreach and Engagement Possibilities for Movement Information Dissemination, Promotion, and Recruitment

various social movements. Additionally, these findings suggest that network linkages are not only important in accounting for differential recruitment into religious movements, but also for political movements. As indicated in Table 3, 63% of the students participating in political movements were drawn into their respective movement's orbit of influence by being linked to one or more members through a preexisting, extramovement interpersonal tie.

The findings associated with the three data sets not only corroborate each other, but they also clearly demonstrate the importance of preexisting social networks in structuring movement recruitment. It is thus reasonable to suggest the following summary proposition:

> *Proposition 1:* Those outsiders who are linked to one or more movement members through preexisting extramovement networks will have a greater probability of being contacted and recruited into that particular movement than will those individuals who are outside of members' extramovement networks.

The Importance of Social Networks in Accounting for Differential Availability

Proposition 1 and the data in which it is grounded suggest that recruitment among social networks is likely to be more productive than recruitment via the other microstructural avenues. However,

TABLE 3 Recruitment Avenues of a Sample of University Students Participating in Various Movements (Percentage)

	MOVEMENTS		
RECRUITMENT AVENUES	*Political (N:81) Percent*	*Religious (N:54) Percent*	*Totals (N:135) Percent*
Public Places	7	0	4
Social Networks	63	80	70
Mass Media	30	20	26
Mail/Telephone	0	0	0

the fact remains that not all relatives, friends or acquaintances of movement members participate in movement activities when invited. The findings reported in the preceding section indicate that, for all the movements studied, at least some members were recruited "off the street" or through the public media. The findings pertaining to Hare Krishna in particular suggest that some movements recruit most of their members through channels other than social networks. The question thus arises as to who out of the pool of individuals contacted either through existing ties or through other recruitment avenues is most likely to become a movement participant?

One plausible answer is suggested by the many works that posit a psychofunctional linkage between social-psychological attributes (conceptualized as susceptibilities) and the goals and ideologies of movements (construed as appeals). According to this view, participation in movement activities is largely a function of certain fertile dispositions, such as alienation (Bolton, 1972; Oppenheimer, 1968; Ransford, 1968), relative deprivation (Aberle, 1966; Davies, 1971; Glock, 1964; Gurr, 1970); and authoritarianism (Hoffer, 1951; Lipset, 1960; Lipset and Raab, 1973). Although of longstanding popularity, the social-psychological dispositional approach has in recent years been called into question on both theoretical and empirical grounds. Moreover, our research suggests that the reason why some rather than other individuals join a movement once they have been introduced to it can be explained in large part by their structural availability. Specifically, the findings pertaining to Nichiren Shoshu and the sample of movement sympathizers suggest that the reason for participating or not participating in movement activities once invited is largely contingent on the extent to which extramovement networks function as countervailing influences. Since sets of social relationships can be more or less demanding in regard to time, energy, and emotional attachment (Etzioni, 1975; Kanter, 1972), it follows that they can also vary in the extent to which they constitute countervailing influences or extraneous commitments (Becker, 1960) with respect to alternative networks and lines of action. Hence, some individuals will be more available for movement exploration and participation because of the possession of unscheduled or discretionary time and because of minimal countervailing risks or sanctions.

In the case of Nichiren Shoshu, these observations seem to hold for both those members recruited from the street and those recruited through social networks. Most were under 30, single, in a transitional role (such as that of student), employed in a line rather than in a managerial position, or in a state of occupational marginality. As a consequence, they tended to possess a greater amount of unscheduled time and generally lacked the kinds of extraneous commitments that are likely to inhibit movement participation. Aside from the absence of a social tie to one or more members prior to initial contact, those recruited from the street differed from those recruited through networks only in that they were structurally more available for participation. This observation is illustrated by the following account of how and why one street-recruit, a twenty-five-year-old male, came to join Nichiren Shoshu:

> *I found myself here in L.A. with nothing but the clothes I was wearing. I didn't know anybody. I didn't have a lot of money. It was a really strange situation.*
>
> *I had just flown into L.A. airport, and all my baggage came up missing. This was on a Saturday night. Since I didn't know anybody and didn't have any place to go, I went to the airport police station and was told to go to Travelers' Aid. But I learned that they wouldn't be open until Tuesday, since this was a Labor Day weekend. So I waited around the airport until Tuesday and then went down to Travelers' Aid. They sent me to the Welfare Department. After spending four days waiting and filling out forms, I was told that I couldn't qualify for welfare because I wasn't a California resident.*
>
> *At this point I didn't know what to do. So I spent a few nights at the Midnight Mission, and then decided to go to the Santa Monica Beach. That evening while I was walking around downtown Santa Monica, this guy came up to me and started talking about Nam-Myoho-Renge-Kyo (the Nichiren Shoshu chant), and asked if I would like to go to a meeting. Since I didn't have anything else to do, I went along.*
>
> *All of a sudden I find myself at this meeting where everybody was chanting. I didn't have the faintest idea about what was going on. I had never heard of the chant before, and didn't even know there was such a group as NSA. But since everybody was telling me to give chanting a try, I figured why not. I literally didn't have anything to lose. So I joined, and I've been chanting ever since—which is about four months.*

Although this account differs somewhat from the stories of other street-recruits in its particulars, it underscores what was common to the life-situation of the 85 street-recruits about whom we were able to gather information. They were either recent arrivals to or passing through the area in which they were recruited, or they were minimally involved in proximal and demanding social relationships. Although one might argue that these street-recruits were "susceptible" to the "appeals" of the movements they joined because they were "social isolates," "loners," or "outcasts," we do not subscribe to such an interpretation. Rather, we think it is sociologically more compelling to argue that individuals who join social movements share the kinds of demographic and social characteristics that allow them to follow their interests and/or engage in exploratory behavior to a greater extent than individuals who are bound to existing lines of action by such extraneous commitments as spouse, children, debts, job, and occupational reputation.

This microstructural interpretation is also suggested by our findings regarding the movement sympathizers in our sample of university students. By movement sympathizers, we refer to those individuals who indicate verbal support of or agreement with the goals of a movement, but who do not devote any time, energy, or other resources to advancing the movement's objectives.

. . . Most relevant to the present discussion is the finding that nearly two-thirds indicated that they did not have enough time to participate. Had their lines of action not been constrained by competing, extramovement commitments and demands, and had they been asked to participate by a member with whom they were acquainted, then presumably they would have become a participant or "constituent" rather than just a sympathizer or "adherent."

In light of these corroborating findings and observations, it seem reasonable to suggest that, given the existence of a social tie to one or more movement members, differential recruitment is largely a function of differential availability, which is best conceptualized as a microstructural phenomenon. That is, it is a function of how tightly individuals are tied to alternative networks and thus have commitments that hinder the recruitment efforts of social movement organizations. The following propositions summarize the argument. The first pertains to the relation between social networks and availability for movement participation. The second concerns the connection between structural availability and the probability of actual participation.

> *Proposition 2A:* The fewer and the weaker the social ties to alternative networks, the greater the structural availability for movement participation.
>
> *Proposition 2B:* The greater the structural availability for participation, the greater the probability of accepting the recruitment "invitation."

Here it might be argued that even though a social bond with one or more movement members and structural availability increase the probability of movement participation, they are not sufficient conditions. We would agree, especially since social action on behalf of noncoercive organizations is unlikely in the absence of instrumental, affective, or ideological alignment (Etzioni, 1975; Kanter, 1972; Parsons and Shils, 1962). However, it is important to emphasize that people seldom initially join movements per se. Rather they typically are asked to participate in movement activities. Furthermore, it is during the course of initial participation that they are provided with the "reasons" or "justifications" for what they have already done and for continuing participation. As C. Wright Mills emphasized some time ago (1940), vocabularies of motives are frequently supplied "after the act" to explain the "underlying causes of the act," even though they have little to say about how the act came about. We would thus argue that the "motives" for joining or continued participation are generally emergent and interactional rather than prestructured. That is, they arise out of a process of ongoing interaction with a movement organization and its recruitment agents. Although this alignment process has not received much empirical attention, its salience in relation to movement recruitment has been illustrated by Lofland's (1977a; 1977b) reexamination of the process by which one becomes a "Moonie" and by Snow's (1976) description of how Nichiren Shoshu strategically goes about the business of "luring" and "securing" recruits. In both cases the recruitment process is organized so as gradually to "sell" prospects on the "benefits" of participation and to provide them with "reasons" for remaining a member. This is not to suggest that prestructured cognitive states and tensions are irrelevant for understanding movement joining. Rather, it is to emphasize that they must be aligned with the movement's value orientation, given specific forms and means for expression and amelioration, and put into the service of the movement (Zygmunt, 1972). In light of these observations, we argue that initial and sustained participation is largely contingent on the countervailing influence of alternative networks and intensive interaction with movement members. Whereas the first factor determines whether one is structurally available for participation, the second factor gives rise to the rationale for participation.

Structural Influences on Movement Recruitment Strategies and Patterns

In analyzing the recruitment process from the point of view of the movement itself, the relationship between movement structure (as determined by its network attributes) and recruitment opportunities and patterns requires attention. As indicated earlier, there are four general outreach and engagement channels that movements can exploit for information dissemination and recruitment: (1) They can channel their promotion and recruitment efforts among strangers in public places by face-to-face means: (2) They can promote via the institutionalized, mass communication mechanisms; (3) They can recruit among strangers in private places by such means as door-to-door canvassing; (4) They can promote and recruit through members' extramovement social networks. The question thus arises as to what determines the patterning and channelling of a movement's recruitment efforts.

Depending on their resource base and strategy, all nonsecretive movement organizations interested in expanding their ranks can exploit the first three recruitment possibilities. However, not all such movements are structurally able to use the network channel to the same extent since they do not all constitute open networks. Some movements are more restrictive and exclusive than others in that membership eligibility is contingent on the possession of certain ascribed or achieved attributes. In other movements, such as Hare Krishna, core membership may even be contingent upon the severance of extramovement interpersonal ties. Since movement organizations can vary considerably. Accordingly, it seems reasonable to suggest the following propositions regarding the relation between a movement's network attributes and the channelling and patterning of its recruitment efforts:

Proposition 3A: Movements requiring exclusive participation by their members in movement activities will attract members primarily from public places rather than from among extramovement interpersonal associations and networks.

Proposition 3B: Movements which do not require exclusive participation by their members in movement activities will attract members primarily from among extramovement interpersonal associations and networks, rather than from public places.

These two propositions are suggested when we compare our findings regarding recruitment into Nichiren Shoshu with those pertaining to Hare Krishna. As mentioned earlier, more than three-quarters of our sample of NSA members reported that they were recruited into the movement by relatives, friends, or acquaintances. In contrast, only one of the twenty-five Krishna devotees we interviewed was recruited by a former acquaintance. Judah (1974:162) similarly found that only 3.32% of the Krishna devotees he interviewed "learned about it through a friend who was a devotee." The majority (66%) came into contact with the movement by encountering a public chanting session or a devotee in the street. Judah (1974:162–3) concludes that

> *. . . the results seem to indicate rather clearly the importance of the Movement's method of proselytizing. It has attracted the attention of many by its practice of chanting the Hare Krishna mantra in public. During these public ceremonies, other devotees sell the literature and engage the curious in conversation about Krishna.*

Anyone with firsthand knowledge of the Krishna movement will find little reason to quibble with Judah's (1974) observations. However, he fails to note that the movement in general and devotees in particular have little choice other than to turn to the streets in search of recruits. Since core membership in Hare Krishna requires an austere communal lifestyle and the severance of extramovement interpersonal ties, the movement is structurally compelled to concentrate its recruitment efforts in public places. Consequently, most of its members are recruited "off the streets."

In contrast, the Nichiren Shoshu movement does not involve communal life or require its members to sever their extramovement interpersonal ties. It is, therefore, structurally able to recruit both in public places and through members' extramovement networks. Consequently, it draws the bulk of its membership from those networks.

Implications of Recruitment Strategies for Movement Spread and Growth

The differential spread and growth of social movements has generally been analyzed in terms of the appeal of movement goals and value orientations to various target populations in the ambient society. That a movement's organizational structure, and particularly its network attributes, might function as an important determinant of its spread and growth has received only brief attention in the literature (Curtis and Zurcher, 1973; 1974; Messinger, 1955; Zald and Ash, 1966; Zurcher and Kirkpatrick, 1976). We now address this issue. Specifically, do differences in network attributes and recruitment opportunities have a significant impact on the success of a movement's recruitment efforts, as measured by the number of outsiders actually recruited? The answer hypothetically depends not only on a movement's value orientation, but also on whether recruitment among social networks typically yields a greater return than does recruitment "off the street" or through the media. If the latter is generally more productive, then a movement's network attributes would be of little relevance to its overall growth. However, if recruitment among strangers is not as effective as recruitment among movement members' acquaintances, friends, and relatives, then a movement's network attributes would constitute a significant and important variable in relation to its growth and spread.

Our findings indicate that for those movements which recruit both in public places and through networks, recruitment among acquaintances, friends, and kin is generally more successful than recruitment among strangers. We thus conclude that a movement's network attributes and corresponding recruitment patterns do indeed make a significant difference in a movement's recruitment efforts and growth. Hence, the following propositions:

Proposition 4A: The success of movement recruitment efforts, measured by the numbers of outsiders actually recruited, will vary with the extent to which movements are linked to other groups and networks via members' extramovement interpersonal ties, such that:

Proposition 4B: Movements which are linked to other groups and networks will normally grow at a more rapid rate and normally attain a larger membership than will movements which are structurally more isolated and closed.

Aside from a few exceptions (Craven and Wellman, 1974; Curtis and Zurcher, 1973; Turk, 1970), most social network analyses have focused on the individual and his or her interpersonal ties, with a paucity of social ties taken as evidence of objective or structural social isolation. That focus may be useful for understanding the structural determinants of individual behavioral patterns and propensities. However, it obscures the fact that social isolation can also occur at the group or movement level, as when a movement has few, if any, direct links with other groups and therefore constitutes a closed network or insulated system of social relations. When this occurs, Propositions 4A and 4B suggest that such movements will differ markedly from structurally less isolated movements in recruitment opportunities and patterns, and overall growth.

Empirical support is provided for the propositions by a comparison of the membership claims of the Nichiren Shoshu and Hare Krishna movement organizations in the United States. Since 1970 Nichiren Shoshu's membership claims have consistently hovered between 200,000 and 250,000. In contrast, members of the Los Angeles and Dallas Krishna communes have reported that the number of communal Krishna devotees throughout the country totals no more than 4,000. While efforts to reach an objective estimate of Nichiren Shoshu's membership suggest that it is about half of what the movement claims (see Snow, 1976:137–44), the point still remains that Nichiren Shoshu's membership far exceeds that of Hare Krishna. Given the fact that both are active, proselytizing movements, the question arises as to why the spread and growth of Nichiren Shoshu have far outdistanced those of Hare Krishna. Differences in the value orientation, promises, and membership demands of the two movements certainly constitute important variables in accounting for the difference in their spread and growth. However, Propositions 4A and 4B point to a perhaps more significant determinant of the differential spread and growth not only of these two movement organizations, but also of social movement organizations in general: the extent to which a movement organization is linked to or structurally isolated from other groups and networks within its environment of operation.

SUMMARY AND CONCLUSIONS

In recent years the study of differential recruitment to and the differential spread and growth of social movements has been characterized by concern with the process through which movement organizations strategically expand their ranks and mobilize support for their cause. Yet, as both Useem (1975:43) and Zald and McCarthy (1979:240) have noted, there has been relatively little systematic research conducted on the details of the influence process. In order to shed greater empirical and theoretical light on the recruitment process, we have presented data derived from three sources. Our findings indicate that the probability of being recruited into a particular movement is largely a function of two conditions: (1) links to one or more movement members through a preexisting or emergent interpersonal tie: and (2) the absence of countervailing networks. The first condition suggests who is most likely to be brought directly into a movement organization's orbit of influence and thereby subjected to its recruitment and reality-construction efforts. The second indicates who is structurally most available for participation and therefore most likely to accept the recruitment invitation. Our findings also indicate that a movement's recruitment strategies and its resultant growth will vary considerably in the degree to which it constitutes a closed or open network attributes of movement organizations and members function as important structural determinants of differential recruitment to and the differential growth of movement organizations.

Several theoretical and empirical implications are suggested by our findings and correspondent propositions. First, in contrast to the traditional assumption that movement recruitment efforts are largely a function of goals and ideology, our findings indicate that the mobilization process in general and the recruitment process in particular are likely to vary significantly with changes in organizational structure. Indeed, our findings indicate that movement goals and organizational structure may occasionally contradict each other. When this occurs, as in the case of Hare Krishna, the organizational structure will function as the more important determinant of recruitment patterns.

Second, since social networks constitute microstructures, the findings suggest that microstructural variables are of equal, and perhaps greater, importance than dispositional susceptibilities in the determination of differential recruitment. We do not urge that dispositions be wholly ignored in attempts to understand the recruitment process. The notion "disposition" perhaps usefully could be integrated with the network perspective by conceptualizing it in terms of the normative, instrumental and affective ties among current and potential participants. People can become encapsulated (Lofland, 1977a; 1977b) by a movement when they are "dispositionally" linked to the proselytizing network, and when that connection becomes expanded by exposure to increasingly broadened socialization messages.

Third, our analysis suggests that the question of "why" people join social movements cannot be adequately understood apart from an examination of the process of "how" individuals come to align themselves with a particular movement. Indeed, it is our contention that the "whys" or "reasons" for joining arise out of the recruitment process itself. We would thus argue that further examination of movement joining and participation should give more attention to how movements solicit, coax, and secure participants, and more attention to the factors that account for variations in recruitment strategies and their efficacy. An examination of such factors should move us beyond our current knowledge about the recruitment process, which has, according to Marx and Wood (1975:393), reached "a point of diminishing returns."

REFERENCES

Aberle, David. 1965. "A note on relative deprivation theory as applied to Millenarian and other cult movements." Pp. 537–41 in W. Lessa and E. Vogt (eds.), Reader in Comparative Religion: An Anthropological Approach. New York: Harper and Row.

Aberle, David. 1966. The Peyote Religion Among the Navaho. Chicago: Aldine.

Becker, Howard S. 1960. "Notes on the concept of commitment." American Journal of Sociology 66:32–40.

Bibby, Reginald W. and Merlin B. Brinkerhoff. 1974. "When proselytizing fails: an organizational analysis." Sociological Analysis 35:189–200.

Blumer, Herbert. 1951. "Collective behavior." Pp. 166–222 in A. M. Lee (ed.), New Outline of the Principles of Sociology. New York: Barnes and Noble.

Bolton, Charles D. 1972. "Alienation and action: a study of peace group members." American Journal of Sociology 78:537–61.

Bromley, David A. and Anson D. Shupe, Jr. 1979. "Moonies" in America. Beverly Hills: Sage.

Cantril, Hadley. 1941. The Psychology of Social Movements. New York: Wiley.

Craven, Paul and Barry Wellman. 1974. "The network city." Pp. 57—88 in M. Effrat (ed.), The Community: Approaches and Applications. New York: Free Press.

Curtis, Russell L., Jr., and Louis A. Zurcher, Jr. 1973. "Stable resources of protest movements: the multi-organizational field." Social Forces 52:53–61.

Curtis, Russell L., Jr., and Louis A. Zurcher, Jr. 1974. "Social movements: ana analytical exploration of organizational forms." Social Problems 21:356–70.

Daner, F. J. 1976. The American Children of Krishna: A Study of the Hare Krishna Movement. New York: Holt, Rinehart and Winston.

Darley, John M. and C. Daniel Batson. 1973. "From Jerusalem to Jericho: a study of situational and dispositional variables in helping behavior." Journal of Personality and Social Psychology 27:100–8.

Dator, James. 1969. Soka Gakkai: Builder of the Third Civilization. Seattle, Wash.: University of Washington Press.

Davies, James C. (ed.). 1971. When Men Revolt and Why. New York: Free Press.

Etzioni, Amatai. 1975. A Comparative Analysis of Complex Organizations. New York: Free Press.

Feuer, Lewis. 1969. The Conflict of Generations. New York: Basic Books.

Fireman, Bruce and William A. Gamson. 1979. "Utilitarian logic in the resource mobilization perspective." Pp. 8–44 in M. Zald and J. McCarthy (eds.), The Dynamics of Social Movements. Cambridge, Mass.: Winthrop Publishers.

Freeman, Jo. 1973. "The origins of the women's liberation movement." American Journal of Sociology 78:792–811.

Gerlach, Luther P. and Virginia H. Hine. 1970. People, Power, and Change: Movements of Social Transformation. Indianapolis: Bobbs- Merrill.

Glock, Charles Y. 1964. "The role of deprivation in the origin and evolution of religious groups." Pp. 24–36 in R. Lee and M. Marty (eds.), Religion and Social Conflict. New York: Oxford University Press.

Goffman, Erving. 1963. Behavior in Public Places. New York: Free Press.

Gurr, Ted R. 1970. Why Men Rebel. Princeton: Princeton University Press.

Harrison, Michael L. 1974. "Sources of recruitment to Catholic Pentecostalism." Journal for the Scientific Study of Religion 13:49–64.

Heirich, Max. 1977. "Change of heart: a test of some widely held theories about religious conversion." American Journal of Sociology 83:653–80.

Hoffer, Eric. 1951. The True Believer. New York: Harper and Row.

Jackson, Maurice, E. Peterson, J. Bull, S. Monsen and P. Richmond. 1960. "The failure of an incipient social movement." Pacific Sociological Review 3:35–40.

Judah, J. Stillson. 1974. Hare Krishna and the Counterculture. New York: Wiley.

Kanter, Rosabeth M. 1972. Commitment and Community: Communes and Utopias in Sociological Perspective. Cambridge, Mass.: Harvard University Press.

Klapp, Orrin. 1969. Collective Search for Identity. New York: Holt, Rinehart and Winston.

Lachman, Sheldon J. and Benjamin Singer. 1968. The Detroit Riot: 1967. Detroit: Behavior Research Institute.

Leahy, Peter J. 1975. "The anti-abortion movement: testing a theory of the rise and fall of social movements." Ph.D. dissertation. Department of Sociology, Syracuse University.

Lee, Robert. 1967. Stranger in the Land. London: Lutterworth.

Lewis, Steven H. and Robert E. Kraut. 1972. "Correlates of student political activism and ideology." Journal of Social Issues 28:131- -49.

Lipset, S. M. 1960. Political Man. New York: Doubleday and Company.

Lipset, S. M. and Earl Raab. 1973. The Politics of Unreason: Right-Wing Extremism in America, 1790–1970. New York: Harper and Row.

Lofland, John. 1966. Doomsday Cult. Englewood Cliffs, N.J.: Prentice-Hall.

Lofland, John. 1977a. Doomsday Cult. Enlarged Edition. New York: Irvington Publishers.

Lofland, John. 1977b. "Becoming a world-saver revisited." American Behavioral Scientist 20:805–19.

Lyman, Stanford M. and Marvin B. Scott. 1967. "Territoriality a neglected sociological dimension." Social Problems 15:236–48.

Marx, Gary T. 1969. Protest and Prejudice. New York: Harper and Row.

Marx, Gary T. and James Wood. 1975. "Strands of theory and research in collective behavior." Pp. 363–428 in A. Inkeles et al. (eds.), Annual Review of Sociology I. Palo Alto, Calif.: Annual Reviews.

McCarthy, John and Mayer Zald. 1973. The Trend of Social Movements in America: Professionalization and Resource Mobilization. Morristown, N.J.: General Learning Press.

McCarthy, John and Mayer Zald. 1977. "Resource mobilization and social movements: a partial theory." American Journal of Sociology 82:1212–41.

McPhail, Clark. 1971. "Civil disorder participation: a critical examination of recent research." American Sociological REview 36:1058–73.

McPhail, Clark and David Miller. 1973. "The assembling process: a theoretical and empirical examination." American Sociological Review 38:721–35.

Messinger, Sheldon L. 1955. "Organizational transformation: a case study of a declining social movement." American Sociological Review 20:3–10.

Mills, C. Wright. 1940. "Situated actions and vocabularies of motive." American Sociological Review 5:404–13.

Moinat, Sheryl, W. Raine, S. Burbeck and K. Davison. 1972. "Black ghetto residents as rioters." Journal of Social Issues 28:45–62.

Murata, Kiyoaki. 1969. Japan's New Buddhism: An Objective Account of Soka Gakkai. New York: John Weatherhill.

National Advisory Commission on Civil Disorders. 1968. Report of the National Advisory Commission on Civil Disorders. New York: Bantam Books.

Oberschall, Anthony. 1973. Social Conflict and Social Movements. Englewood Cliffs, N.J.: Prentice-hall.

Oppenheimer, Martin. 1968. "The student movement as a response to alienation." Journal of Human Relations 16:1–16.

Orum, Anthony. 1972.Black Students in Protest: A Study of the Origins of the Black Student Movement. Washington, D.C.: American Sociological Association, Arnold M. and Caroline Rose Monograph Series.

Parsons, T. and E. A. Shils. 1962. Toward a General Theory of Action. New York: Harper and Row.

Petras, James and Maurice Zeitlin. 1967. "Miners and agrarian radicalism." American Sociological Review 32:578–86.

Pinard, Maruice. 1971. The Rise of a Third Party: A Study in Crisis Politics. Englewood Cliffs, N.J.: Prentice-Hall.

Portes, Alejandro. 1971. "On the logic of post-factum explanations: the hypothesis of lower-class frustration as the cause of leftist radicalism." Social Forces 50:26–44.

Ransford, H. Edward. 1968. "Isolation, powerlessness and violence: a study of attitudes and participation in the Watts riot." American Journal of Sociology 73:581–91.

Sills, Davis L. 1957. The Volunteers. Glencoe, Ill.: Free Press.

Snow, David A. 1976. The Nichiren Shoshu Buddhist Movement in America: A Sociological Examination of Its Value Orientation, Recruitment Efforts and Spread. Ann Arbor, Mich.: University Microfilms.

Snow, David A. 1979. "A Dramaturgical Analysis of Movement Accommodation: Building Idiosyncrasy Credit as a Movement Mobilization Strategy." Symbolic Interaction 2:23–44.

Snow, David A. and Cynthia L. Phillips. 1980. "The Lofland-Stark conversion model: a critical reassessment." Social Problems 27:430–37.

Snyder, David and William R. Kelly. 1979. "Strategies for investigating violence and social change: illustrations from analyses of racial disorders and implications for mobilization research." Pp. 212–37 in M. Zald and J. McCarthy (eds.), The Dynamics of Social Movements. Cambridge, Mass.: Winthrop Publishers.

Snyder, David and Charles Tilly. 1972. "Hardship and collective violence in France, 1830–1960." American Sociological Review 37:520–32.

Tilly, Charles. 1978. From Mobilization to Revolution. Reading, Mass.: Addison-Wesley Publishing Co.

Toch, Hans. 1965. The Social Psychology of Social Movements. Indianapolis: Bobbs-Merrill.

Turk, Herman. 1970. "Interorganizational networks in urban society: initial perspectives and comparative research." American Sociological Review 35:1–20.

Turner, Ralph H. and Lewis M. Killian. 1972. Collective Behavior. Englewood Cliffs, N.J.: Prentice-Hall.

Tygart, Clarence E. and Norman Holt. 1972. "Examining the Weinberg and Walker typology of student activists." American Journal of Sociology 77_957–66.

Useem, Michael. 1975. Protest Movements in America. Indianapolis: Bobbs-Merrill.

Von Eschen, Donald, Jerome Kirk, and Maurice Pinard. 1971. "The organizational substructure of disorderly politics." Social Forces 49:529–44.

White, James W. 1970. The Sokagakkai and Mass Society. Stanford: Stanford University Press.

Wilson, John. 1973. Introduction to Social Movements. New York: Basic Books.

Wilson, Kenneth and Tony Orum. 1976. "Mobilizing people for collective political action." Journal of Political and Military Sociology 4:187–202.

Woelfel, Joseph, John Woelfel, James Gillham and Thomas McPhail. 1974. "Political radicalization as a communicational process." Communication Research 1:243–63.

Zald, Mayer N. and Roberta Ash. 1966. "Social movement organizations: growth, decay and change." Social Forces 44:327– 41.

Zald, Mayer N. and John D. McCarthy (eds.). 1979. The Dynamics of Social Movements: Resource Mobilization, Social Control, and Tactics. Cambridge, Mass.: Winthrop Publishers.

Zurcher, Louis A. and R. George Kirkpatrick. 1976. Citizens for Decency: Antipornography Crusades as .Status Defense. Austin, Texas: University of Texas Press.

Zurcher, Louis A. and David A. Snow. Forthcoming. "Collective behavior: social movements." In Morris Rosenberg and Ralph Turner (eds.), Sociological Contributions to Social Psychology. New York: Basic Books.

Zygmunt, Joseph. 1972. "Movements and motives: some unresolved issues in the psychology of social movements." Human Relations 25:449–67.

ARTICLE 27

Stable Resources of Protest Movements: The Multi-Organizational Field

RUSSELL L. CURTIS, JR.
LOUIS A. ZURCHER, JR.

Several authors have described the growth and transformation of protest organizations (Gusfield, 1963; Messinger, 1955; Zald and Ash, 1966) and the personality characteristics of participants (Davies, 1962; Lang and Lang, 1961; McCormack, 1950; Toch, 1969; Walzer, 1969; Weiss, 1963). But no previous research has specifically examined the operation of multi-organizational fields in the development and maintenance of protest organizations.

The concept "multi-organizational field" suggests that organizations in a community setting approximate an ordered, coordinated system. Interorganizational processes within the field can be identified on two levels, which conceptually overlap: the *organizational* level, where networks are established by joint activities, staff, boards of directors, target clientele, resources, etc.; the *individual* level, where networks are established by multiple affiliations of members. Research at the organizational level has reported: the commonality of community political and organizational textures (Greer and Orleans, 1962); the representation of the community as an ecology of games (Long, 1958); the interpenetration of organizational representation (Turk and Lefcowitz, 1962; Warren, 1967; Zald, 1969); and the interface between local urban structures and the larger society (Turk, 1970; Walton, 1967). Research at the individual level has reported: a pattern of multiple memberships in voluntary associations (Babchuk and Booth, 1969); the existence of "moral entrepreneurs" for whom moral issues become a central life interest to be pursued in varieties of organizational settings (Becker, 1963).

Multi-organizational fields should operate significantly (both on the organizational and the individual levels) in the emergence and maintenance of protest organizations. In this article, data and interpretations from a study of two anti-pornography organizations (hereafter, APOs) will reveal that: (1) APOs were enmeshed in a network of other community organizations (voluntary associations) in the larger multi-organizational field; (2) these interorganizational linkages were based on common interests, ideologies, audiences, or other shared characteristics; (3) participants in APOs shared memberships in other voluntary associations within the multi-organizational field; (4) differences between the two APOs in the kinds of alignments they had within the field were associated with differences in their goals, strategies, member recruitment patterns, member characteristics, goal achievements, and life span.

The material is presented in the sequence in which the two APOs developed. Few organiza-

Curtis, Russell L. Jr., & Zurcher, Louis A. Jr. (1973, September). Stable resources of protest movements: The multi-organizational field. *Social Forces, 52,* 53–61.

tional studies examine both the structure and dynamics of a single unit (see Brewer, 1971, for a commentary). This mode of presentation serves to emphasize the cumulative strength of the data and is convenient for an exploratory analysis. The discussion can be anticipated by referring to Diagram 1 which identifies the emergent relationships.

The first APO studied was located in a southwestern city (hereafter, Southtown) which is a governmental and educational center, has several tertiary industries, and a population of about *250,000*. The second APO was located in a primarily industrial city (hereafter, Midville) with a population of about *100,000*.

The investigators were able to maintain close observation of the Southtown APO from its beginning in February 1969. Six of the seven major APO meetings were attended by at least four investigators. Three of the meetings were tape recorded. The investigators also had access to small, informal meetings of the leadership, and to the organization's records, memos, newsletters, and other relevant documents. Over *150* unstructured interviews were conducted with Southtown participants: city officials, police officers, theatre managers, and other citizens knowledgeable about the APO. Extensive structured questionnaires were administered to a snowball sample of *49* active and central APO members (sampling was continued until respondents were being renominated and no new names were being added to the list).

Near the end of June 1969, the investigators were able to collect data on the Midville APO. For *17* days, six investigators visited Midville and gathered documents, newspaper accounts, and held more than *50* unstructured interviews with participants, city officials, bookstore employees, and other citizens knowledgeable about the APO. The task was more difficult than in Southtown not only because of the briefer period of study, but because the Midville operation had been active for over five years and, at the time of the study, was being sued for one million dollars by a retaliating bookstore. The structured questionnaire, following the same procedures described for Southtown, was administered to *36* active and central APO members. (The snowball procedure had yielded *42* potential respondents, *6* of whom had been named in the suit and had been advised by legal counsel not to be interviewed.)

FINDINGS AND INTERPRETATIONS

Brief Historical Overview of the APOs

The Midville APO was established and guided by the sporadic but enthusiastic efforts of *12* indi-

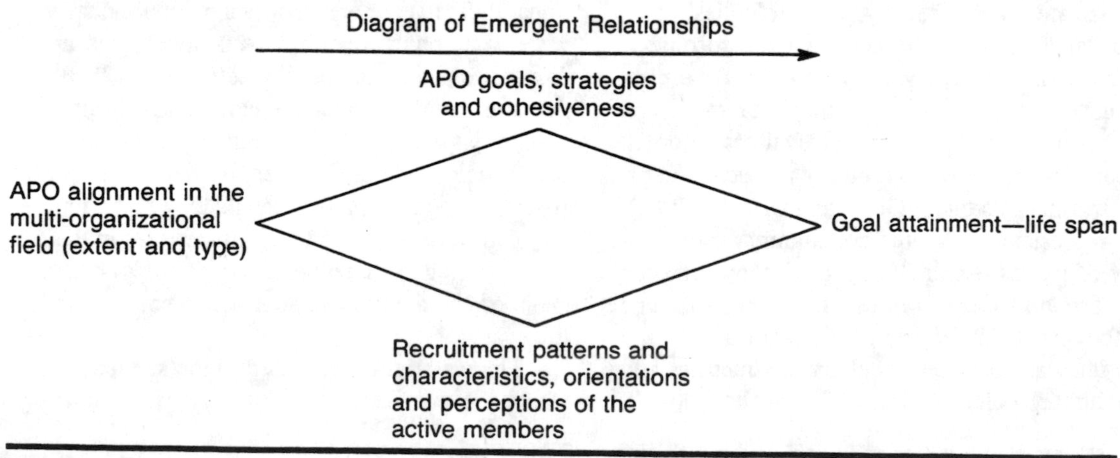

DIAGRAM 1

viduals, whose activities from 1961 to 1965 were confined mainly to getting in touch with various agencies, public officials, businessmen, and media representatives about the "problems" of "pornography." Several of the founding individuals were active in various religious organizations, but the APO was not formed as an adjunct or component of any of them. The APO was formally incorporated in 1965, and until 1969 conducted a number of activities, ranging from written complaints about "questionable" television programs to an "Action for Decency Day" formally approved by the city mayor.

In 1969, the Midville APO reached the zenith of its activity, catalyzed by the speech of an invited representative from a national anti-pornography organization, who stated that the city's local bookstore was one of the worst he had ever seen. The combination of this observation from an outside authority and thorough coverage in the local newspaper stimulated an intense crusade against the bookstore. Thirty-one community organizations, representing *16,000* persons, supported the APO. Crusade tactics included the purchase of materials supporting arrest-producing complaints, and the circulation of petitions (signed by *11,000* Midvillians) calling for removal of the bookstore. In reaction, a bookstore owner filed a $1,000,000 civil suit against the APO and other affiliates. The APO activities, at least those involving direct action against the bookstore, diminished sharply. At the completion of the data-gathering phase of this study the lawsuit was still pending. Since then, the lawsuit has been resolved without punitive judgment, the bookstore has opened two new branches and a theatre, and the APO continues to operate but with less vigor.

The Southtown APO emerged from one stable community voluntary association. Following a regularly scheduled meeting of a men's religious fraternal organization, a small group of members began to discuss the need for more "family film entertainment" in the city. As their reactions crystallized, the group designated itself an "action committee," and agreed that the chairman should meet with various city and state officials in the near future. When he later did so, the officials suggested the possibility of changes in the state anti-pornography statutes, and the need for the demonstration of community support for such changes. The chairman and other members of the APO steering group (who had decided to retain APO control within their own fraternal organization), actively solicited the support of church and civic organizations. With representatives from *11* such organizations, and other interested persons, a public meeting on pornography was held, and attended by over *200* citizens. About six weeks later, the APO sponsored a "decency rally," attended by nearly *2,500* persons and supported by *29* community organizations. At the rally and afterward, *2,800* citizens signed petitions calling for the passing of more restrictive anti-pornography legislation. Accordingly, legislation was passed and enacted about two months after the rally. With the enactment of the statutes, the Southtown APO ceased to exist. Later, the statutes were struck down in courts, and the availability of "pornography" has increased in Southtown.

The Multi-Organizational Field and APO Characteristics

Both APOs were enmeshed in multi-organizational fields. The Midville APO had ties with *31* other community organizations; the Southtown APO with *29*. Table 1 shows the types of organizations with which the APOs were linked—mostly youth-serving, church-related, or fraternal-service organizations. The pattern of alignments manifests the interests, goals and audiences shared by the APOs and the components of their multi-organizational fields. The APOs openly declared their intention to protect youth from the "evil" influences of pornography, to defend "decency" and "faith" against the onslaught of pornography and, by crusading against "smut," to serve the community and its citizens. Those declarations, and the ideologies and strategies they represented, appealed to the interests of youth-serving, church-related, and fraternal-service organizations.

. . . Ninety-four percent of Southtown and *89* percent of Midville members were affiliated with one or more community organizations. The multiple affiliations of members were concentrated primarily among fraternal-service, civic-political, and youth-serving organizations. The orientations of these organizational types again were compatible with APO orientations, this time on the individual level. . . . Compared with the Babchuk and Booth (1969) Nebraska random sample, APO active members were over-represented in affiliations with fraternal-service, civic-political, and youth-serving organizations, about equally represented in church- and job-related organizations, and underrepresented in recreational organizations—perhaps not an atypical pattern for the potential or actual moral crusader.

The differences between the organizational and individual patterns within APO fields invite interpretation. Fraternal-civic and youth-serving organizations tend to operate both on the organizational level (aligned with the APOs) and on the individual level (APO members were affiliated with them). Church-related organizations tended to operate primarily on the organizational level, and civic-political organizations on the individual level. The goals and strategies of APOs so appealed to some fraternal-service and youth-serving organizations that they became both alignment and recruitment sources. Church-related organizations were willing to align with APOs as entities, but were less a source of active members. Civic-political organizations were less willing to align as entities, but were good sources for recruitment. The data in this form are at best suggestive, and differences might completely be accounted for by some artifact of multiple membership. Further research might fruitfully draw on the distinction between individual and organizational levels in analyses of multi-organizational fields and their implications, especially as to motivations for and functions of alignment or affiliation.

Though both APOs were enmeshed in multi-organizational fields, the Southtown APO was the more closely integrated with its field. The list of *31* organizations reported to be aligned with the Midville APO when incorporated was almost entirely different from the list of alignees during the bookstore crusade. Of those alignees who took direct action against the bookstore, most did so relatively independently of the APO. For example, one of the anti-bookstore petition leaders commented that she was not representing the APO, but was just one of a "bunch of citizens" acting. Though several organizations lent their names to the Midville APO as a token of support, rarely did they send formal delegates to APO meetings.

The Southtown APO carefully developed alignments with its multi-organizational field, evolving from *11* alignees at its first public meeting to *29* at the decency rally, with a loss of only 2 in the interim. All the aligned organizations sent formal delegates to APO meetings, and they and the organizations they represented acted in concert under the direction of the APO leaders.

The greater organizational integrity of the Southtown APO and the tighter quality of its relations with the multi-organizational field were evident during the recruiting process. The Southtown APO tended to gain members through contact with potentially aligned organizations (who subsequently would send representatives). The Midville APO also followed that pattern, but more than the Southtown APO tended to approach individuals directly, rather than organizations or their formal representatives. Whereas the Southtown APO tended to recruit on the organizational level of the multi-organizational field, the Midville APO tended to recruit on the individual level. Among individuals, in Southtown most were recruited by APO leaders (75 percent) while such leaders were responsible for the affiliation of only *56* percent of Midville APO members. For the rest, *25* and *44* percent, respectively, affiliation was attributed to the influence of friends.

The quantity and quality of active member participation in other organizations indicated the greater integration of the Southtown APO with its multi-organizational field. As noted above, *94* percent of the Southtown APO members, as compared with *89* percent of Midville members, were affiliated with one or more community organizations. Furthermore, *62* percent of the Midville APO members indicated that they were *officers* in other organizations.

The degree of integration of such a protest organization with its multi-organizational field should be associated with the degree of goal clarity and specificity. Aligned organizations had to decide to align, and thus needed to know the risks and benefits of alignment. The Southtown APO was more integrated with its field, and it single-mindedly pursued the goal of "tougher" anti-pornography laws throughout its organizational life span. The Midville APO was less integrated with its field, and its goal continued throughout to be a vague and yet perpetual maintenance of community "decency."

Characteristics of the Active APO Members

The closer integration of the Southtown APO with its multi-organizational field, and its more focused recruitment procedure were reflected in the greater homogeneity of that organization's membership. The average age of Southtown APO members was *41.1* years, with a standard deviation of *9.85* years. The average age of Midville APO members was *48.0* years, with a standard deviation of *16.02* years. The marked difference in standard deviations suggests the greater homogeneity of age among Southtown members.

The Southtown median categories for both education and income contain larger percentages than the Midville categories. Midville's greater heterogeneity is not a matter of skewness, but the result of more cases at *both* extremes of the two distributions. Since levels of education and monthly family income were obtained for range options, standard deviations were not computed.

Previous studies indicate that membership in complex organizations tends to be firmer and more integrated for those who have orderly and successful occupational careers (Bruce, 1971; Vorwaller, 1970; Wilenski, 1961), who have an active interest in political activities (Erbe, 1964; Freedman and Axelrod, 1952; Hastings, 1954; Maccoby, 1958), and who have such personal attributes as high self-esteem, feelings of fate control, etc. (Bell, 1957; Hagedorn and Labovitz, 1968; Mizruchi, 1960; Rose, 1959). The members of the Southtown APO had been recruited in a more orderly and systematic fashion than the members of the Midville APO. They were more completely integrated into an APO which itself was more closely associated with other community organizations. Consequently, Southtown members should have reflected to a greater degree than Midville members some of the work, political and personal characteristics cited above. Ninety percent of Southtown members in contrast to *55* percent of Midville members liked their work. Fifty-nine percent of the Southtown members in contrast to *44* percent of the Midville members were "very interested" in politics. Eighty-one percent of Southtown members felt that election of a specific person to political office can influence daily life (a rough measure of political efficacy), in contrast to *69* percent of Midville members.

Thus, the closer integration of the Southtown APO with its multi-organizational field paralleled its greater membership homogeneity in age, education, and income, its higher indices of members' integration and satisfaction with work, and its greater degree of member political interest and sense of political efficacy.

Orientations and Perceptions of the Active Members

Consistent with the more ordered approach of its recruitment process, the organizational boundary of the Southtown APO was less diffuse than that of the Midville APO. Thirty-one percent of the Midville members indicated that they were not *official* members of that APO; only *6* percent of the Southtown members so indicated. Similarly, *42* percent of Midville members could not accurately name their APO; *27* percent of Southtown members could not accurately name theirs. In part, these differences could have been influenced by the hesitancy of Midville members to identify themselves publicly with an organization that was under civil suit. Yet, with the exception of those *6* who actually were named in the suit (none of whom are included in the sample), the members were not significantly threatened by the legal action. Some of them, in fact, viewed the suit as a victory, and as indication that they had made an impact on the "smut peddlers." The refusal rate for interviews was quite small—less than *3* percent in both Midville and Southtown.

Southtown more than Midville members also revealed their greater sense of identification with their APO by the level of their outreach activities. Ninety-one percent of Southtown members, as contrasted with *79* percent of Midville members, talked about APO activities with nonmembers outside of meetings and other scheduled events. Ninety-four percent of Southtown members, as contrasted with *61* percent of Midville members, were trying to recruit additional APO members.

More Southtown members (*96* percent) could articulate at least one specific APO goal than could Midville members (*78* percent). Similarly, more Southtown (*96* percent) than Midville members (*81* percent) could identify the APO strategy. Ninety-five percent of Southtown members were optimistic about the potential of the organization to accomplish its goal; *83* percent of Midville members were optimistic. The same pattern appears in optimism about the degree to which the community supported the APO (*79* percent of Southtown members perceived support; *69* percent of Midville members perceived support), and about the future of pornography in the United States (*64* percent of Midville respondents thought it would increase; *31* percent of Southtown respondents so thought). These perceptions and orientations indicate the greater organizational integrity of the Southtown APO, and reflect its higher degree of integration with its multi-organizational field.

The differential linkages of APOs with the multi-organizational field and the associated variations in membership and organization characteristics were also associated with both the success and the persistence of the organizations. The Southtown APO accomplished its specific goal of legislative change, and upon doing so summarily disbanded. The Midville APO has yet to accomplish its rather sweeping goal of maintaining "decency" and continues to operate, though at least temporarily with less vigor.

CONCLUSIONS

Both APOs depended on the recruited support of members and representatives from other community organizations, and were involved to a greater or lesser extent in a multi-organizational field. Compared with the Midville APO, the Southtown APO had closer and more ordered interaction and integration with its multi-organizational field. It had *greater* recruitment focus, use of organizational rather than extra-organizational contacts, and stability of aligned organizations. The Southtown APO was the more homogeneous (in age, education and income). Its members were more committed to and satisfied with their work. They had a greater interest in politics and a greater sense of political efficacy. Southtown members were more closely identified with their organization, and they knew more about it—its name, its goals and strategies. With this sense of identity went more sharply defined boundaries. Its members talked more with outsiders (outreach) and were more optimistic about achieving their goals, gaining community support, and reducing the distribution of pornography. Their aims were more specific and they were the prompter to disband once the goals had been attained.

The findings indicate that the characteristics of the multi-organizational field, and the degree to which a protest organization is integrated with it, are variables significantly associated with structural and membership characteristics of the organization itself. The findings support the contention that few organizations, unless their purposes include isolation or freedom from exogenous influence or contamination, can operate in an interorganizational void. Lastly, the findings disclose multiple affiliation career paths for voluntary association members.

The results of this study can be challenged as circumstantial, drawn from but two cases. But the pattern of parallel findings and predictive congruences is, if not convincing, at least strongly suggestive (See Gibbs, in press, for a discussion of the merits of predictive congruence for theory testing).

Each finding can be rewritten as an hypothesis, and should be tested with data from protest organizations of various sizes, intentions, approaches, durations and ideologies. (In this article we have dealt with protest organizations and multi-organizational fields generally conservative in orientation). Research which would isolate *independent* and *dependent* variables among the *associated* variables presented herein, and assessing the usefulness of dichotomizing the multi-organizational field into organizational and individual levels would be particularly valuable.

REFERENCES

Babchuk, N., and A. Booth. 1969. "Voluntary Association Membership: A Longitudinal Analysis." *American Sociological Review* 34(February):31–45.

Becker, Howard S. 1963. *Outsiders*. New York: Free Press.

Bell, W. 1957. "Anomie, Social Isolation and Class Structure." *Sociometry* 20(June):105–16.

Brewer, J. 1971. "Flow of Communications. Expert Qualifications and Organizational Authority Structures." *American Sociological Review* 36(June):475–84.

Bruce, J. M. 1971. "Intragenerational Occupational Mobility and Participation in Formal Associations." *Sociology Quarterly* 12(Winter):46–55.

Davies, J. C. 1962. "Toward a Theory of Revolution." *American Sociological Review* 27(February):5–19.

Erbe, W. 1964. "Social Involvement and Political Activity: A Replication and Elaboration." *American Sociological Review* 29(April):198–215.

Freedman, R., and M. Axelrod. 1952. "Who Belongs to What in a Great Metropolis." *Adult Leadership* 1(November):6–9.

Gibbs, Jack P. In press. *A Mode of Formal Theory Construction*. New York: Dryden.

Greer, S., and P. Orleans. 1962. "The Mass Society and Parapolitical Structure." *American Sociological Review* 27(October):634–46.

Gusfield, Joseph R. 1963. *Symbolic Crusade*. Urbana: University of Illinois Press.

Hagedorn, R., and S. Labovitz. 1968. "Occupational Characteristics and Participation in Voluntary Associations." *Social Forces* 47(September):16–27.

Hastings, P. K. 1954. "The Non-Voter in 1952: A Study of Pittsfield, Massachusetts." *Journal of Psychology* 38(Fall):301–12.

Lang, Kurt, and Gladys E. Lang. 1961. *Collective Dynamics*. New York: Crowell.

Long, N. E. 1958. "The Local Community as an Ecology of Games." *American Journal of Sociology* 64(November):251–61.

Maccoby, H. 1958. "The Differential Political Activity of Participants in a Voluntary Association." *American Sociological Review* 23(October):524–32.

McCormack, T. H. 1950. "The Motivation of Radicals." *American Journal of Sociology* 56(July):17–24.

Messinger, S. L. 1955. "Organizational Transformation: A Case Study of a Declining Social Movement." *American Sociological Review* 20(July):3–10.

Mizruchi, E. H. 1960. "Social Structure and Anomia in a Small City." *American Sociological Review* 25(October):645–54.

Rose, Arnold M. 1959. "Attitudinal Correlates of Social Participation." *Social Forces* 37(March):202–5.

———. 1967. *The Power Structure*. New York: Oxford University Press.

Toch, Hans. 1969. *The Social Psychology of Social Movements*. Indianapolis: Bobbs-Merrill.

Turk, H. 1970. "Interorganizational Networks in Urban Society: Initial Perspectives and Comparative Research." *American Sociological Review* 35(February):1–19.

Turk, H., and M. J. Lefcowitz. 1962. "Towards a Theory of Representation Between Groups." *Social Forces* 40(May):337– 41.

van den Berghe, P. L. 1966. "Checklists Versus Open-Ended Research: A Comment on a Brief Report on the Methodology of Stereotype Research." *Social Forces* 44(March):418–9.

Vorwaller, D. J. 1970. "Social Mobility and Membership in Voluntary Associations." *American Journal of Sociology* 75(January):481–95.

Walton, J. 1967. "The Vertical Axis of Community Organization and the Structure of Power." *Social Science Quarterly* 48(December):353–68.

Walzer, M. 1969. "Puritanism as a Revolutionary Ideology." In Barry McLaughlin (ed.), *Studies in Social Movements*. New York: Free Press.

Warren, R. L. 1967. "The Interorganizational Field as a Focus for Investigation." *Administrative Science Quarterly* 12(December):396–419.

Weiss, R. F. 1963. "Defection from Social Movements and Subsequent Recruitment to Social Movements." *Sociometry* 26(May):1–20.

Wilensky, H. L. 1961. "Orderly Careers and Social Participation: The Impact of Work History on Social Integration in the Middle Mass." *American Sociological Review* 26(August):521–39.

Zald, M. N. 1969. "The Structure of Society and Service Integration." *Social Science Quarterly* 50(December):557–67.

Zald, M. N. and R. Ash. 1966. "Social Movement Organizations: Growth, Decay and Change." *Social Forces* 44(March):327–41.

Zurcher, L. A., and C. K. Bowman. 1971. "The Natural History of an Ad Hoc Anti-Pornography Organization in Southtown, USA.11 In *Technical Reports of the Commission on Obscenity and Pornography*. Vol. 5. Washington: Government Printing Office.

Zurcher, L. A. and R. G. Cushing. 1971. "Some Individual Characteristics of Participants in Ad Hoc Anti-Pornography Organizations." In *Technical Reports of the Commission on Obscenity and Pornography*. Vol. 5. Washington: Government Printing Office.

Zurcher, L. A., and R. G. Kirkpatrick. 1971. "The Natural History of an Ad Hoc Anti-Pornography Organization in Midville, USA. In *Technical Reports of the Commission on Obscenity and Pornography*. Vol. 5. Washington: Government Printing Office.

Zurcher, L. A., R. G. Kirkpatrick, R. G. Cushing, and C. K. Bowman. 1971. "The Anti-Pornography Campaign: A Symbolic Crusade." *Social Problems* 19(Fall):217–38.

ARTICLE 28

Insurgency of the Powerless: Farm Worker Movements (1946–1972)

J. CRAIG JENKINS
CHARLES PERROW

... Our thesis is that the rise and dramatic success of farm worker insurgents in the late 1960s best can be explained by changes in the political environment the movement confronted, rather than by the internal characteristics of the movement organization and the social base upon which it drew. The salient environment consisted of the government, especially the federal government, and a coalition of liberal support organizations. We shall contrast the unsuccessful attempt to organize farm workes by the National Farm Labor Union from 1946 to 1952 with the strikingly successful one of the United Farm Workers from 1965 to 1972.

The immediate goals of both movements were the same—to secure union contracts. They both used the same tactics, namely, mass agricultural strikes, boycotts aided by organized labor, and political demands supported by the liberal community of the day. Both groups encountered identical and virtually insurmountable obstacles, namely, a weak bargaining position, farm worker poverty and a culture of resignation, high rates of migrancy and weak social cohesion, and a perpetual oversupply of farm labor, insuring that growers could break any strike.

The difference between the two challenges was the societal response that insurgent demands received. During the first challenge, government policies strongly favored agribusiness; support from liberal organizations and organized labor was weak and vacillating. By the time the second challenge was mounted, the political environment had changed dramatically. Government now was divided over policies pertaining to farm workes; liberals and organized labor had formed a reform coalition, attacking agribusiness privileges in public policy. The reform coalition then furnished the resources to launch the challenge. Once underway, the coalition continued to fend for the insurgents, providing additional resources and applying leverage to movement targets. The key changes, then, were in supprot organization and governmental actions. To demonstrate this, we will analyze macro-level changes in the activities of these groups as reported in the *New York Times Annual Index* between 1946 and 1972.

METHOD

To test this argument we need two bodies of information, one bearing on events leading to the initiation of insurgency and the other dealing with the political environment shaping challenge outcomes. For the first, we have drawn on published accounts of the movements, filled in and corroborated by extensive interviews conducted with movement participants and informed ob-

Jenkins, J. Craig, & Perrow, Charles. (1977, April). Insurgency of the powerless: Farm worker movements (1946–1972). *American Sociological Review, 42*, 249–268. Reprinted by permission of the American Sociological Association.

servers. For the second, we have turned to newspaper sources to provide a picture of the societal response to the two challengers. By content coding the abstracts of news stories that dealt with farm labor issues printed in the *New York Times* over a twenty-seven-year period (1946–1972), we can determine the types of groups concerned with the question of farm labor, whether their actions favored the structural changes advocated by insurgents, the types of activities in which they were engaged and, finally, the pattern of interaction prevailing between these various groups during the course of the respective challenges. This way we have a systematic data base against which to test hypotheses bearing on movement-environment interaction.

As with any data source, there are limits to the *Times* data. We cannot, for example, use it to test hypotheses on the internal dynamics of mobilization. For this, we have gone to interviews and published sources. Nor, as Danzger's (1975) work has recently indicated, can we view the *Times* reportage as a complete picture of *all* insurgent activity and environmental responses to insurgency. Since it is a national newspaper, the *New York Times* will not provide us with day-to-day coverage, for example, of police repression in Delano, California. Nor can we count on the *Times* to reveal the hidden bargains and machinations that might underlie public positions and alliances.

We do not ask it to do so. What we are using the *Times* for is to construct a systematic, reliable index of the publicly visible political activities that formed the environment of each challenge. By comparing statistics drawn from this data base and relating these measures to differences in challenge outcome, we can see if our environmental thesis holds up.

To see if the *New York Times* is a reliable source, we have compared the coverage given by the *Times* with that of two other newspapers, the *Chicago Tribune* for a more conservative picture and the *Los Angeles Times* for a more proximate source. After comparing the stories on farm labor carried by these three papers for one month (selected at the peak of activity for the three periods of analysis), we have concluded that the *New York Times* is basically a more complete version of the same "news." In the month selected from the first period (March, 1951), the *New York Times* covered seventeen events, only one of which was picked up by each of the other papers; no events in the "test" papers were missed by the *New York Times*. In the second period (April, 1958), the *New York Times* carried nine events, two of which the *Los Angeles Times* covered and none of which the *Tribune* covered; again the *New York Times* missed no events covered in the other papers. Only in the third period (October, 1968) did the *New York Times* miss an event, one involving a local organization that pressured the Los Angeles City Council to boycott grapes. This was reported in the *Los Angeles Times*. Of eight events covered by the *New York Times*, half appeared in the *Los Angeles Times* and none in the *Tribune*. In sum, if you want newspaper reportage on farm labor events, the *New York Times* is a more thorough source and reveals no clearly different bias than the other papers during one period of time, say, the NFLU challenge, than another, e.g., the UFW effort.

Finally, there is the question of whether news reportage, regardless of cross-validation with other news sources, is valid. Danzger (1975) has argued that news coverage is affected by editorial policy, and that systematic error creeps in because the geographic location of national wire service offices produces uneven reportage of relevant events. It is important to note that we code events, not news stories. The prominence given to stories by the editors of the *New York Times* is irrelevant, as are the evaluations of the events by news personnel. Additionally, our data set should be relatively immune to the main source of error identified by Danzger. Both insurgencies centered in the same locale. Assuming that the corrective mechanisms within the news agencies identified by Danzger were operative, time-series data should be less vulnerable to error than cross-sectional data. Also, we should note the limitations to Danzger's conclusions given his own data base. As Snyder and Kelly (1976) have demonstrated, news-based conflict data dealing with violence appear quite valid; more error exists in nonviolent protest data (employed in Danzger's test). Extending that distinction to our own data set, we can place more confidence in our measures of "concrete" activities than those for "symbolic" ones. . . .

PERIOD I: THE NFLU CONFLICT (1946–1955)

The first period illustrates in classical terms the obstacles to a sustained and successful farm worker challenge. In addition to the structural constraints restricting farm worker activity, the political environment confronting the insurgents was unfavorable. Government officials at all levels and branches came into the conflict predominantly on the side of the growers, despite the mandate of agencies such as the Department of Labor or the Education and Labor Committees in Congress to protect the interests of deprived groups like farm workers. Though external support was decisive in launching the challenge, it was weak and frequently ill-focused dealing with the consequences rather than the causes of farm worker grievances. When support was withdrawn, the challenge soon collapsed.

Chartered at the 1946 convention of the American Federation of Labor, the National Farm Labor Union set out to accomplish what predecessors had been unable to do—successfully organize the farm workers of California's "industrialized" agriculture. The leadership cadre was experienced and resourceful. H. L. Mitchell, President of the NFLU, was former head of the Southern Tenant Farmers Union; the Director of Organizations, Henry Hasiwar, had been an effective organizer in several industrial union drives during the 1930s; Ernesto Galarza, who assumed prime responsibility for publicity efforts, had served as political liaison for Latin American unions and had a Ph.D. in economics from Columbia University.

Initially, the strategy was quite conventional: enlist as many wrokers as possible from a single employer, call a strike, demand wage increases and union recognition, and picket to keep "scabs" out of the fields. American Federation of Labor affiliates would then provide strike relief and political support to keep the picket line going. An occasional church or student group would furnish money and boost morale.

But the government-sponsored alien labor or *bracero* program provided growers with an effective strike-bearing weapon. According to provisions of the law, *bracers* were not to be employed except in instances of domestic labor shortage and *never* to be employed in fields where domestic workers had walked out on strike. Yet in the two major tests of union power, the DiGiorgio strike of 1948 and the Imperial Valley strike of 1951, the flood of *braceros* undermined the strike effort of domestic workers (London and Anderson, 1970; Galarza, 1970; Jenkins, 1975: ch. 3). In the Imperial strike, the NFLU used citizen's arrests to enforce statutes prohibiting employment of *braceros* in labor disputed areas. However, local courts ruled against the tactic and the Immigration Service refused to remove alien "scabs" from the fields (Galarza, 1970: 78; Jenkins, 1975: ch.4). Nor were affairs changed when the *bracero* administration was transferred to the U.S. Department of Labor in 1951. Domestic workers were pushed out of crops by *braceros*, and *braceros* reappeared in the Los Baños strike of 1952 to break the challenge (Galarza, 1970: 79).

In response, the NFLU launched a two-pronged political challenge—a demand for termination of the *bracero* program and, to get around the problem of ineffective strikes, requests for organized labor's support of boycotts. Neither demand found a favorable audience. Lacking strong labor or liberal support, the demand for an end to the *bracero* traffic ended in minor reforms in the *bracero* administration (Galarza, 1970: ch.4). As for the boycott, despite initial success, it collapsed when a court injunction was issued (imporperly) on the grounds that the NFLU was covered by the "not cargo" provisions of the Taft-Hartley Act. The National Labor

Relations Board initially concurred and reversed its position over a year later. By then the Union's resources were exhausted and organized-labor support had long since collapsed (Galarza, 1970: 73–92).

. . . The curves delinearing government, liberal, and farm worker activities move roughly in concert. (Organized labor, though, played little public role in this or the next period.)

. . . Largely a reflection of the pressure campaign waged by the NFLU, the strongest correlation is between insurgents and favorable government activity (.63), concrete activities seemingly being more efficacious (.70 versus .49 for symbolic acts). *R* for insurgent/government activity drops only slightly when controls are introduced for liberal activity (.57), indicating that liberal activity was not necessary for this measure of official response.

The main issue for the period was labor supply. Looking at activities concerned with this issue, the correlation between insurgent and pro-farm worker government activities is high (.59); for the issue of living and working conditions, the relation disappears (–.80). The union attempted, through court actions, lobby efforts and public protest, to pressure government to end the *bracero* program since it was so central to the control of the labor supply. The official response, however, was largely symbolic. Though government tended to respond to concrete insurgency with favorable concrete actions, the majority of favorable governmental actions were actually symbolic (58%). Nor did many of these concrete moves decisively aid the farm worker cause. Key actions, such as pulling strikebreaking *bracers* out of the fields, did not occur.

What, then, are we to make of the fact that 50% of reported governmental actions were coded as favorable to the interest of farm workers? Was government responding to the conflict between insurgents and growers in some even-handed "pluralist" way? Here it is necessary to recall that we are using news media reportage on a social problem and efforts to redress that problem. The news media will be more sensitive to efforts attempting to define or solve that problem than to efforts to maintain the *status quo*. Consequently, unfavorable actions by government and growers are underrepresented in our data. If only 50% of news-reported government actions can be coded as favorable, then the full universe of governmental activities should, in the balance, be more favorable to growers.

The strength of this assertion is borne out by information on actions favorable to growers. . . . The correlation between pro-grower government activities and grower activities is quite high (.75), actually stronger than the respective *r* for insurgents. In quantitative tems, government was more responsive to agribusiness interests. Clearly, in critical instances, e.g., leaving *braceros* in struck fields, government policies favored growers over workers.

In addition to the predominantly unfavorable response of government, the NFLU failed to receive sustained, solid support from the liberal community. The major problem was the type of activities in which liberals engaged. When they acted, liberals consistently supported farm workers over growers but they rarely moved beyond symbolic proclamations. Only 24% of liberal actions during the period were concrete. By contrast, 38% during the UFW challenge were so. Even more indicative, though, is the modest level of the correlation between liberal and insurgent activity (.45). What concomitant activity did exist between these two groups involved only symbolic acts (.56 versus –.02 for concrete acts). Looking ahead, the respective *r*'s for the UFW challenge indicate a quite different liberal response, *r* was .83 and, for symbolic acts .06. Where the UFW experienced consistent and concrete support, the NFLU found itself relatively isolated.

Though liberals did not rush to the side of the NFLU, they did play a role in the pressure campaign. When controls are introduced for government activity on the relation between insurgents and liberals, the modestly positive relation turns negative (–.10). Insofar as liberals did act alongside insurgents, apparently it was in the presence of public officials. But there were problems even with this limited-scale liberal support. Liberals focused almost exclusively on the working and living conditions of farm workers. Following the lead of Progressive Party candicate Henry Wallace in 1948, several religious and "public interest" associations sponsored conferences and issued study reports publicizing deplorable camp conditions and child labor. In what might be considered a typical pattern of liberalism of the time, they were concerned with the plight of the workers rather than the fact of their powerlessness or the role of the *bracero* program in underwriting that powerlessness. It was a humanitarian, nonpolitical posture, easily dissipated by "red baiting" in Congressional investigations and "red scare" charges by growers and their political allies throughout the late 1940s and early 1950s. The two issues, poverty and the question of labor supply, were not to be linked by the liberal organizations until well into Period II.

PERIOD II: ELITE REFORM AND REALIGNMENT (1956–1964)

The late 1950s and the early 1960s, the second Eisenhower administration and the brief Kennedy period emerge from this and other studies in the larger project as a period of germination. Contrary to some interpretations, the remarkable insurgencies of the late 1960s did not originate with the Kennedy administration, but with developments that initially began to appear during Eisenhower's second term. Nor did the Kennedy years witness a dramatic escalation of insurgent activity. Indeed, in the case of farm workers, insurgency showed a decline.... For our purposes, the two presidential administrations can be treated as a single period, one that witnessed important realignments and shifts in political resources in the national polity, culminating in a supportive environment for insurgent activity.

Farm worker insurgency during the reform period was at a low ebb. Actions by farm worker insurgents dropped from 16% to 11% of all proworker activity. In 1956–1957 the NFLU, now renamed the National Agricultural Workes Union (NAWU), secured a small grant from the United Auto Workers, enabling it to hang on as a paper organization. Galarza, by then the only full-time cadre member, launched a publicity campaign to reveal maladministration and corruption within the *bracero* administration. Aside from a brief and ineffective organizing drive launched in 1959 by the Agricultural Workers Organizing Committee (AWOC), generating only one reported strike (in 1961), this was the sum of insurgent activity for the nine-year Period II.... Growers remained publicly inactive and seemingly secure in their positions, aroused only at renewal time for the *bracero* program to lobby bills through Congress. Until the insurgency of Period III began, growers retained a low profile in the *Times*.

With the direct adversaries largely retired from the public arena, affairs shifted into the hands of government and the liberals. Despite the absence of significant insurgency, the balance of forces in the naitonal polity had begun to shift. Actions favorable to the interests of farm workers increased from 50% to 73%, remaining on the same plane (75%) through the following UFW period. Beginning during the last years of the Eisenhower administration, three interrelated developments brought about this new supportive environment: (1) policy conflicts within the political elite that resulted in a more "balanced," neutral stance towards farm workers; (2) the formation of a reform coalition composed of liberal pressure groups and organized labor that, in the midst of elite divisions, was able to exercise greater political influence; (3) the erosion of the Congressional power-base of conservative rural interests, stemming immediately from reapportionment.

The concern of liberal pressure groups initially was focused on the need to improve housing and educational conditions of migrant workers. In 1956, the Democratic National Convention included a plank for increased welfare aid to migrants. The next year, the National Council of Churches, already involved in the early civil rights movement in the South, began a study of migrant camp conditions and child labor. In early 1958, several liberal pressure groups were joined by the AFL-CIO in attacking the *bracero* program, scoring administrative laxity, and arguing that federal labor policies were the origin of social problems. The two as yet unrelated issues—poverty and labor policies—were now firmly linked in the public debate.

The fusion of these two issues was significant. Of course, economic conditions already had been linked with social deprivations in public parlance, but the concern of liberal gorups in the past had been with inspection of housing, assurances of educational opportunity, and pubic health measures. To argue now that a public program of importing foreign labor perpetuated the list of conditions deplored by liberals was a substantial change. As later happened more generally with the New Left (cf. Perrow, 1972), the advocates of reform had begun to look at the source of problems in terms of a system.

About the same time, organized labor took a new interest in farm workers. In 1959, the AFL-CIO Executive Council abolished the NAWU and created the Agricultural Workers Organizing Committee (AWOC), headed by Norman Smith, a former UAW organizer. Despite strong financial backing, the AWOC produced little results. Concentrating on 4 A.M. "shake-ups" of day laborers, the AWOC managed to sponsor a number of "job actions" but only one major strike and little solid organization. Like the NFLU, the AWOC had to confront the problem of *bracero*. In the one reported strike, the Imperial Valley strike of February, 1961, the AWOC used violence to intimidate strikebreaking *braceros* and create an international incident over their presence. Officials quickly arrested the cadre, and the AWOC ceased to exist except on paper. Though the AWOC drive consumed over one million dollars of AFL-CIO funds, it produced neither contracts nor stable membership (London and Anderson, 1970: 47–50, 77). Yet, and this indicates the shift, this type of financial support had never before been offered by organized labor.

The final element in the formation of a supportive environment was a shift in governmental actions. Actions favorable to farm workers increased from the unfavorable 50% prevailing during Period I to a more "balanced" 68% of all governmental actions. Of these, the portion coded "concrete," and therefore more likely to have impact, increased from 40% in Period I to 65%. Indicative of the change taking place in official views, the focus of governmental attentions shifted from the labor supply issue (56% of favorable actions during Period I) to the question of farm workers' living and working conditions (73% during Period II).

The change in official actions stemmed, in part, from internal conflicts within the national political elite. Secretary of Labor James Mitchell was a surprise Eisenhower appointee from the Eastern wing of the Republican Party, a former labor consultant for New York department stores and a future protégé of Nelson Rockefeller. Mitchell took the Department of Labor in a more pro-union direction than was thought possible, at the time becoming a "strong man" in the cabinet because of his success in mollifying unions. In 1958, an open fight between the Taft and Eastern wings of the Republican Party developed, with the conservatives favoring a national "right-to-work" law. Mitchell, as an advocate of unionism and apparently jockying for position for the Republican Vice-Presidential nomination, became a figure of elite reform within Republican circles.

A second factor contributing to the shift in official actions was the pressure campaign launched by the reform coalition. The effects of the campaign can be captured, in part, from the *Times* data. Though the correlation between liberal activity and government activity favorable to farm workers is modest (.50), it is considerably higher than during the other perios (.33 for the first and .04 for the third) and it is independent of insurgent activity.

Tangible effects of the pressure campaign appeared almost immediately. In 1957, under pressure from the liberal reform coalition, the Department of Labor under Mitchell's guidance carried out an internal review of farm labor policies. The upshot was a series of executive orders to tighten up enforcement of regulations covering migrant camps (Craig, 1971: 151–5). When the economic recession of 1958–1959 arrived, sensitivity within the Administration to rising unemployment levels increased. In response, Mitchell vowed to enforce more fully the 1951 statutes requiring farm employment to be offered to domestic workers prior to importation of *braceros*. Growers, long accustomed to having their *bracero* requests met automatically, rebelled when asked to provide more justification (Jacobs, 1963: 183–4). In February, 1959, Mitchell took an even stronger step, joining the liberal reformers in support of legislation to extend minimum-wage laws to agriculture and to impose new restrictions on the use of *braceros*.

The following year, the division within the Eisenhower Administration opened up into a full-scale, cabinet-level battle over renewal of the *bracero* program. The Farm Bureau and the state grower associations engaged that other administration "strong man," Secretary of Agriculture Ezra Taft Benson, to defend the program. In testimony before the House Committee on Agriculture, the White House took a neutral stance; Benson defended the program, while Mitchell argued that the program exerted demonstrable adverse effects upon domestic workers and should be abolished (Craig, 1971: 156–61). Into this breach in the political elite stepped the liberal-labor support coalition. At the same time, the House Committee on Public Welfare opened hearings on health and camp conditions, giving the Cotton Council and the Meatcutters Union a chance to air opposing views.

Initially, the reform effort failed. In March, 1960, Secretary Mitchell withdrew his program, resolving the dispute on the cabinet level. The next month, agribusiness pushed a two-year renewal of the *bracero* program through Congress. But, for the first time, the issue had been debated seriously and a loose coalition of liberal pressure groups (e.g., National Council of Churches, National Advisory Committee of Farm Labor, NAACP) and organized labor had formed. Though the eventual termination of the *bracero* program did not undermine growers' ability to break strikes (there were other substitutes, e.g., "green card" commuters, illegal aliens), the fight against the program did refocus the concern of liberals and organized labor on the structural problem of farm worker powerlessness.

The reform coalition sustained the campaign over the next three years. In 1960, the Democratic platform condemned the *bracero* program. Once in office, the New Frontiersmen, though demanding no important statutory changes, did vow to enforce fully the laws restricting *bracero* use (Craig, 1971:174). By renewal time in 1963, the Kennedy Administration was in the pursuit of a public issue ("poverty") and courting minority-group votes. For the first time, the White House went formally on record against the program. Only at the last minute was a pressure campaign, mounted by Governor Pat Brown of California and the Department of State, responding to Mexican diplomatic pressure, able to save the program temporarily. Amid promises from Congressional farm bloc leaders that this was the last time the program would be renewed, a one-year extension was granted.

In addition to the efforts of the reform coalition, which played a critical role in other reforms of the same period, and the new elite-level neutrality, the fall of the *bracero* program stemmed from the narrowing power base of the Congressional farm bloc. Congressional reapportionment had visibly shaken the conservative farm bloc leaders. Searching for items in the farm program that could be scuttled without damaging the main planks, the farm bloc leaders fixed on the *bracero* program. The mechanization of the Texas cotton harvest had left California growers of specialty crops the main *bracero* users. When the test came, *bracero* users, as a narrow, special interest, could be sacrificed to keep the main planks of the farm program intact (Hawley, 1966).

Period II, then, emerges from this analysis as a period of reform and political realignment that dramatically altered the prospective fortunes of insurgents. Reforms, stemming from elite-level conflicts and a pressure campaign conducted by liberal public-interest organizations and organized labor, came about in the virtual absence of activity by farm worker insurgents. The activism of several key liberal organizations depended, in turn, upon broad economic trends, especially the growth of middle-class disposable income that might be invested in worthy causes (McCarthy and Zald, 1973). Insurgents did not stimulate these changes in the national polity. Rather, they were to prove the beneficiaries and, if anything, were stimulated by them.

PERIOD III: THE UFW SUCCESS (1965–1972)

During the NFLU period, the number of insurgent actions reported totalled 44. Most of these were symbolic in character, only 27% being concrete. Insurgency was brief, concentrated in a four-year period (1948–1951). However, in the third period, insurgency became sustained. Insurgent actions reached a new peak and remained at a high level throughout the period. A total of 143 actions conducted by farm worker insurgents were recorded. Significantly, 71% of these were concrete in character. By the end of the period, the success of the United Farm Workers was unmistakable. Over a hundred contracts had been signed; wages had been raised by almost a third; union hiring halls were in operation in every major agricultural area in California; farm workers, acting through ranch committees set up under each contract, were exercising a new set of powers.

The key to this dramatic success was the altered political environment within which the challenge operated. Though the potential for mobilizing a social base was slightly more favorable than before, the UFW never was able to launch effective strikes. Though the UFW cadre was experienced and talented, there is little reason to believe that they were markedly more so than the NFLU leadership; neither did the tactics of the challenge differ. the boycotts that secured success for the UFW also had been tried by the NFLU, but with quite different results. What had changed was the political environment—the liberal community now was willing to provide sustained, massive support for insurgency; the political elite had adopted a neutral stance toward farm workers.

As before, external support played a critical role in launching the challenge. The initial base for the United Farm Workers was Cesar Chavez's National Farm Workers Association (NFWA) and remnants of the AWOC still receiving some support form the AFL-CIO. During the 1950s, Chavez had been director of the Community Service Organization, an Alinsky-styled urban community-organization with strong ties to civil rights groups, liberal churches and foundations. Frustrated by the refusal of the CSO Board of Directors to move beyond issues salient to upwardly-mobile urban Mexican-Americans, Chavez resigned his post in the winter of 1961 and set out to organize a community organization among farm workers in the Central Valley of California. Drawing on his liberal contacts, Chavez was able to secure the backing of several liberal organizations which had developed a new concern with poverty and the problems of minority groups. The main sponsor was the California Migrant Ministry, a domestic mission of the National Council of Churches servicing migrant farm workers. During the late 1950s, the Migrant Ministry followed the prevailing policy change within the National Council, substituting community organization and social action programs for traditional evangelical ones (Pratt, 1972). By 1964, the Migrant Ministry had teamed up with Chavez, merging its own community organization (the FWO) with the NFWA and sponsoring the Chavez-directed effort.

By summer, 1965, the NFWA had over 500 active members and began shifting directions, expanding beyond economic benefit programs (e.g., a credit union, cooperative buying, etc.) to unionization. Several small "job actions" were sponsored. Operating nearby, the remaining active group of the AWOC, several Filipino work-crews, hoped to take advantage of grower uncertainty generated by termination of the *bracero* program. The AWOC launched a series of wage strikes, first in the Coachella Valley and then in the Delano-Arvin area of the San Joaquin Valley. With the AWOC out on strike, Chavez pressed the NFWA for a strike vote. On Mexican Independence Day, September 16th, the NFWA joined the picket lines (Chavez, 1966; Dunne, 1967; London and Anderson, 1970).

Though dramatic, the strike soon collapsed. Growers refused to meet with union representatives; a sufficient number of workers crossed the picket lines to prevent a major harvest loss. Over the next six years, the same pattern recurred—a dramatic strike holding for a week, grower intransigence, police intimidation, gradual replacement of the work force by playing upon ethnic rivalries and recruiting illegal aliens (cf. Dunne, 1967; London and Anderson, 1970; Matthiessen, 1969; Kushner, 1975; Taylor, 1975). What proved different from the NFLU experience was the ability of the insurgents, acting in the new political environment, to secure outside support.

Political protest was the mechanism through which much of this support was garnered. By dramatic actions designed to capture the attention of a sympathetic public and highlight the "justice" of their cause, insurgents were able to sustain the movement organization and exercise sufficient indirect leverage against growers to secure contracts. The UFW's use of protest tactics departed from that of rent strikers analyzed by Lipsky (1968; 1970). Though the basic mechanism was the same (namely, securing the sympathy of third parties to the conflict so that they would use their superior resources to intervene in support of the powerless), the commitments of supporting organizations and the uses to which outside support was put differed. Lipsky found that protest provided unreliable resources, that the news media and sympathetic public might ignore protestors' demands (cf. Goldenberg, 1975) and that, even when attentive, they often were easily satisfied with symbolic palliatives. Though the UFW experienced these problems, the presence of sustained sponsorship on the part of the Migrant Ministry and organized labor guaranteed a stable resource base.

Nor were the uses of protest-acquired resources the same. Lipsky's rent-strikers sought liberal pressure on public officials. For the UFW, protest actions were used to secure contributions and, in the form of a boycott, to exercise power against growers. Marches, symbolic arrests of clergy, and public speeches captured public attention; contributions from labor unions, theater showings and "radical chic" cocktail parties with proceeds to "*La Causa*" supplemented the budget provided by sponsors and membership dues.

Given the failure of strike actions, a successful outcome required indirect means of exercising power against growers. Sympathetic liberal organizations (e.g., churches, universities, etc.) refused to purchase "scab" grapes. More important, though, major grocery chains were pressured into refusing to handle "scab" products. To exercise that pressure, a combination of external resources had to be mobilized. Students had to contribute time to picketing grocery stores and shipping terminals; Catholic churches and labor unions had to donate office space for boycott houses; Railway Union members had to identify "scab" shipments for boycott pickets; Teamsters had to refuse to handle "hot cargo"; Butchers' union members had to call sympathy strikes when grocery managers continued to stock "scab" products; political candidates and elected officials had to endorse the boycott. The effectiveness of the boycott depended little upon the resources of mobilized farm workers; instead, they became a political symbol. It was the massive outpouring of support, especially from liberals and organized labor, that made the boycott effective and, thereby, forced growers to the bargaining table.

The strength of liberal-labor support for the UFW is indicated by the high level of concomitant activity between insurgents and their supporters. While the correlation of insurgent and liberal activities was modest in Period I (.45), it was strong during the third period (.62). More important, liberals were far more concrete in their support for insurgents. In the first period, concomitant activities were almost wholly symbolic (.56 versus .02 for concrete activities); during the UFW challenge, it was concrete activities (.81 versus .06 for symbolic activities). Nor do statistical controls for governmental actions favorable to farm workers reduce the correlation (r = .64). Given the fact that liberal activities rarely occurred jointly with pro-worker government activities (r = .04), it is clear that liberals directed their efforts toward supporting insurgents rather than pressuring government.

The more "balanced," neutral posture of government that was the product of the reform period continued. Sixty-nine percent of all official actions were favorable to farm workers (as against 50% and 68% in Periods I and II). Concretely, this meant that court rulings no longer routinely went against insurgents; federal poverty programs helped to "loosen" small town politics; hearings by the U.S. Civil Rights Commission and Congressional committees publicized "injustices" against farm workers; welfare legislation gave farm workers more economic security and afforded insurgents a legal basis to contest grower employment practices. National politicians, such as Senators Kennedy and McGovern, lent their resources to the cause.

The most striking changes in official actions took place on the federal level. Actions favorable to farm workers rose from 46% of federal level activity in the first period, to 63% in the second and 74% in the third. State and local government, more under the control of growers (cf. McConnell, 1953:177; Berger, 1971), followed a different pattern. In Period I, when growers had opposition only from insurgents, only 26% of official actions were judged favorable to workers. In Period II, when farm workers were acquiescent but the liberal-labor coalition was experiencing growing influence in national politics, 67% were favorable, slightly more than on the federal level. But when insurgency reappeared in Period III, the percent favorable dropped to 45%, far lower than the federal level. Government divided on the question, federal actions tending to be neutral, if not supportive, of insurgents while state actions, still under grower dominance, continued to oppose insurgents.

Significantly little of the pro-worker trend in governmental actions during the UFW period is associated with either insurgent or liberal activities. For insurgent and favorable government actions, r is low (.26 versus .63 during the NFLU period); the correlation between liberal organizations and favorable government actions drops to the lowest point in the study (.04 versus .33 and .50 for Periods I and II, respectively). Only organized labor appeared to be performing a pressure function. There is a modest correlation between symbolic activities by organized labor and government (.46), largely centering around the legitimacy of unionism in agriculture (r = .35). Official positions had already undergone important changes during the reform period. The termination of the *bracero* program had left government in a neutralized position. No longer a key player in the conflict, but still under the influence of the reform policies, government preserved its neutral stance despite less visible pressure from any of the partisans.

There was, of course, opposition on the part of growers and allied governmental actors. There were numerous instances of police harassment, large-scale purchases of boycotted products by the Department of Defense, and outspoken opposition from Governor Reagan and President Nixon.

However, growers had lost their entrenched political position. Public officials no longer acted so consistently to enhance grower interests and to contain the challenge. An indication of the sharpness of the displacement of growers is given by the levels of concomitance between grower actions and pro-grower governmental actions. In Period I, r for grower-government activity was .75; in Period II, .62. But, during the UFW challenge, the correlation dropped to a negligible .05. By the time the United Farm Workers struck in 1965, agricultural employers were no longer able to rely upon government, especially at the federal level, to be fully responsive to their interest in blocking unionization.

CONCLUSION

The critical factor separating the National Farm Labor Union failure from the United Farm Worker success was the societal response to insurgent demands. In most respects, the challenges were strikingly similar. In both instances, the leadership cadre came from outside the farm worker community; external sponsorship played a critical role in launching both insurgent organizations; both movements confronted similar obstacles to mobilizing a social base and mounting effective strikes; both resorted to political protest and boycotts. What produced the sharp difference in outcome was the difference in political environment encountered. The NFLU received token contributions, vacillating support for its boycott and confronted major acts of resistance by public authorities. In contrast, the UFW received massive contributions, sustained support for its boycotts and encountered a more "balanced," neutral official response.

The dramatic turnabout in the political environment originated in economic trends and political realignments that took place quite independent of any "push" from insurgents. During the reform period, conflicts erupted within the political elite over policies pertaining to farm workers. Elite divisions provided the opening for reform measures then being pressed by a newly active coalition of established liberal and labor organizations. Though the reforms did not directly effect success, the process entailed by reform did result in a new political environment, one which made a successful challenge possible.

If this analysis is correct, then several assumptions found in the classic literature are misleading. Rather than focusing on fluctuations in discontent to account for the emergence of insurgency, it seems more fruitful to assume that grievances are relatively constant and pervasive. Especially for deprived groups, lack of collective resources and controls exercised by superiors—not the absence of discontent—account for the relative infrequency of organized demands for change. For several of the movements of the 1960s, it was the interjection of resources from outside, not sharp increases in discontent, that led to insurgent efforts.

Nor does the political process centered around insurgency conform to the rules of a pluralist game. The American polity had not been uniformly permeable to all groups with significant grievances (cf. Gamson, 1975). Government does not act as a neutral agent, serving as umpire over the group contest. Public agencies and officials have interests of their own to protect, interests that often bring them into close alignment with well-organized private-interest groups. When insurgency arises threatening these private interests, public officials react by helping to contain insurgency and preserve the *status quo*. But if an opposing coalition of established organizations decides to sponsor an insurgent challenge, the normal bias in public policy can be checked. Sponsors then serve as protectors, insuring that the political elite remains neutral to the challenge.

The implications for other challenges are rather striking. If the support of the liberal community is necessary for the success of a challenge by a deprived group, then the liberal community is, in effect, able to determine the cutting edge for viable changes that conform to the interests of those groups still excluded from American politics. Moreover, there is the possibility of abandonment. Since liberal support can fade and political elites shift their stance, as has happened to the UFW since 1972, even the gains of the past may be endangered. The prospects for future insurgency, by this account, are dim. Until another major realignment takes place in American politics, we should not expect to see successful attempts to extend political citizenship to the excluded.

REFERENCES

Berger, Samuel. 1971. Dollar Harvest: The Story of the Farm Bureau. Lexington, Ma.: Heath.

Chavez, Cesar. 1966. "The organizer's tale." Pp. 138–47 in Staughton Lynd (ed.), American Labor Radicalism. New York: Wiley.

Chambers, Clarke. 1952. California Farm Organizations. Berkeley, Cal.: University of California Press.

Craig, Richard C. 1971. The *Bracero* Program. Austin, Tx.: University of Texas Press.

Dahl, Robert. 1967. Pluralist Democracy in the United States. Chicago: Rand McNally.

Danzger, M. Herbert. 1975. "Validating conflict data." American Sociological Review 40: 570–84.

Davies, James C. 1962. "Toward a theory of revolution." American Sociological Review 27:5–19.

Davies, James C. 1969. "The J-curve of rising and declining satisfactions as a cause of some great revolutions and a contained rebellion." Pp. 671–709 in Hugh Davis Graham and Fred Robert Gurr (eds.), Violence in America. New York: Bantam.

Dunne, John Gregory. 1967. Delano. New York: Farrar, Straus and Giroux.

Fisher, Lloyd. 1953. The Harvest Labor Market in California. Cambridge, Ma.: Harvard University Press.

Frisbee, Parker. 1975. "Illegal migration from Mexico to the United States; a longitudinal analysis." International Migration Review 9:3–14.

Fuller, Varden. 1967. "A new era for farm labor?" Industrial Relations 6:285–302.

Galarza, Ernesto. 1964. Merchants of Labor: The Mexican *Bracero* Story. San Jose, Ca.: Rosicrucian Press.

Galarza, Ernesto. 1970. Spiders in the House and Workers in the Field. London: University of Notre Dame Press.

Gamson, William. 1968. "Stable unrepresentation in American society." American Behavioral Scientist 12:15–21.

Gamson, William. 1975. The Strategy of Social Protest. Homewood, Il.: Dorsey.

Goldenberg, Edie. 1975. Making the News. Lexington, Ma.: Lexington Books.

Gurr, Ted. 1970. Why Men Rebel. Princeton, N.J.: Princeton University Press.

Gusfield, Joseph. 1968. "The study of social movements." Pp. 445–52 in David Sills (ed.), International Encyclopedia of the Social Sciences, Volume 14, New York: Macmillan.

Hawley, Ellis W. 1966. "The politics of the Mexican labor issue." Agricultural History 40, 3 (July): 157–76.

Hibbs, Douglas. 1973. Mass Political Violence. New York: Wiley.

Hilton, Bruce. 1969. The Delta Migrant Ministry. New York: Macmillan.

Jacobs, Paul. 1963. The State of the Unions. New York: Atheneum.

Jenkins, Craig. 1975. Farm Workers and the Powers: Farm Worker Insurgency (1946–1972). Unpublished Ph.D. dissertation. Department of Sociology, State University of New York, Stony Brook.

Kornhauser, Arthur. 1959. The Politics of Mass Society. Glencoe, Il.: Free Press.

Kushner, Sam. 1975. Long Road to Delano. New York: International Publishers.

Lang, Kurt and Gladys Lang. 1961. Collective Dynamics. New York: Crowell.

Lipsky, Michael. 1968. "Protest as political resource." American Political Science Review 62:1144–58.

Lipsky, Michael. 1970. Protest in City Politics. Chicago: Rand McNally.

London, Jaan and Henry Anderson. 1970. So Shall Ye Reap. New York: Crowell.

Matthiessen, Peter. 1969. *Sal Si Puedes:* Cesar Chavez and the New American Revolution. New York: Random House.

McCarthy, John and Mayer Zald. 1973. The Trend of Social Movements in America. Morristown, N.J.: General Learning Corporation.

McConnell, Grant. 1953. The Decline of American Democracy. New York: Atheneum.

McWilliams, Carey. 1939. Factories in the Fields. Boston: Little, Brown.

McWilliams, Carey. 1942. Ill Fares the Land. Boston: Little, Brown.

New York times. 1945–1974. New York Times Index. New York: New York Times.

Oberschall, Anthony. 1973. Social Conflict and Social Movements. Englewood Cliffs, N.J.: Prentice-Hall.

Perrow, Charles. 1972. The Radical Attack on Business. New York: McGraw-Hill.

Pratt, Henry J. 1972. The Liberalization of American Protestantism. Detroit, Mi.: Wayne State University Press.

Rose, Arnold. 1967. The Power Structure. New York: Oxford University Press.

Smelser, Neil J. 1962. The Theory of Collective Behavior. New York: Free Press.

Snyder, David and William Kelly. 1977. "Conflict intensity, media sensitivity and the validity of newspaper data." American Sociological Review 42:105–23.

Snyder, David and Charles Tilly. 1972. "Hardship and collective violence in France, 1830 to 1960." American Sociological Review 37:520–32.

Taylor, Ronald B. 1975. Chavez and the Farm Workers. Boston: Beacon.

Tilly, Charles. 1975. "Revolutions and collective violence." In F. I. Greenstein and N. Polsky (eds.), Handbook of Political Science. Reading, Ma.: Addison-Wesley.

Tilly, Charles, Louise Tilly and Richard Tilly. 1975. The Rebellious Century. Cambridge, Ma.: Harvard University Press.

Truman, David. 1951. The Governmental Process. New York: Knopf.

Turner, Ralph and Lewis Killian. 1957. Collective Behavior. Englewood Cliffs, N.J.: Prentice-Hall.

Turner, Ralph and Lewis Killian. 1972. Collective Behavior (2nd ed.). Englewood Cliffs, N.J.: Prentice-Hall.

Wilson, John. 1973. Introduction to Social Movements. New York: Basic Books.

PART FIVE

Movement Environments and Responses

Movement environments have received extensive attention during the past three decades in the collective behavior and social movement literature. Central to the issues, controversies, and ongoing syntheses is the question of whether movements are made by the environment or whether the movement shapes its environment. There is also the associated question of the interaction of movements and other forms of collective behavior with their environments. It is the latter question that appears to contain more subscription currently. However, it remains to be seen whether this synthesis strategy is an outcome of future research findings or is merely a convenient, current compromise.

Environments facilitating, shaping, and obstructing collective behavior and social movements contain several elements. Those we briefly address here are the availability of members, the moral and political receptivity of issues at stake, media and their impacts on the changing incidence and forms of noninstitutionalized collective actions, financial resources, and the existence of other movements—some of which are aligned and either convergent or competitive and some of which are hostile and obstructive.

The ecology of memberships was first elaborated by Karl Marx during the nineteenth century on the consequences of dense concentrations of workers within the productive organization and, more important, by his formulation of the "consciousness of kind" that would evolve outside the productive organization in what has been termed the *industrial community*. Awareness that one is not alone, that a shared perspective exists, and that the fellowship of shared issues among many people represents power and self-validation are important ingredients for organized protest. The brilliant formulations and insights by Marx were validated by the union movements of industrial nations throughout the early twentieth century. They were further supported by the *failure* of most farmworkers' and land reform movements unless, as indicated earlier, there was outside support for these movements. That Marx is often declared incorrect for the occurrence of successful communist movements in *agricultural* rather than industrial areas is greatly qualified by the fact that it was within the leading cities and intellectual centers (e.g., Moscow, Havana) of these societies that initial revolutionary support was generated.

Whether the environment is morally receptive refers to whether the issues raised by the protest or "deviant" group (in the perceptions of the larger society) are shared in some measures by outside members of the society. The National Organization for the Reform of Marijuana Laws is a case in point. In our view, the goals of this group would have met widespread opposition in the late 1950s and enjoyed support in the 1960s because of various medical findings suggesting the effects of the drug were not severe and the fact that usage and arrests for usage had permeated the upper middle classes of this country. Similarly, the goals of Mothers Against Drunk Drivers (MADD) would not have enjoyed much success just following the end of prohibition and may be on the decline today because of prison overcrowding and the forced early release of offenders who committed violent crimes against persons; drunk driving has suffered a lowered rank in the hierarchy of criminal offenses because of current prison conditions.

Media now can generate *instant* attention to the actions of a protest group. Leaders of protest marches, most recently those opposing armed attack on Iraqi forces, orchestrate crowd patrols to generate impressions of large numbers before television audiences. As noted in other introductory sections of this book, it is difficult to conceive of the success of the Civil Rights an Anti-War (i.e., Viet Nam) movements of the 1960s without recourse to the impact of television. Viet Nam, as several astute observers have noted, was our first televised war. War War II, by contrast, was well covered by photographs, especially essays appearing in *Life;* conflicts prior to that period were covered by print. As a case in point, protests over the assassination of Abraham Lincoln would be difficult to postulate, given that most citizens were unaware of the event until some two to three weeks after the occurrence.

Evidence on the overall impacts of mass media treatments of controversial protest actions is not conclusive. Without a doubt instant coverage brings us the protests on evening news. But a counterfactor also exists: Media enterprises are business organizations and are attentive to the attentions of more established, conservative subscribers and advertisers. Controversial coverages, regardless of their political directions or social implications, can offend supportive financial and political interests. They are often suppressed by them. Relatedly, financial resources vary between protest and/or "deviant" groups. Some social movement organizations (SMOs) hold a middle-class base and enjoy a solid financial base. Some environmental and animal rights groups are cases in point. Highly selective and esoteric groups may become objects of suspicion and, like the Moonies and Hare Krishna, place the burden of financial support on the members themselves. More conservative groups, such as the John Birch Society, had wealthy industrial and business contributors. Obviously, the more controversial the group, the more selective its financial resources. As a corollary, actions that give these groups "image problems," such as the bombings on college campuses of radical student organizations in the early 1970s and the confrontive actions of animal rights activists, create problems in financial solicitations. Although MADD currently continues to enjoy widespread public support, they have also been known to irritate and engender the covert opposition from certain segments of our criminal justice system.

Finally, in this brief account of environmental factors, SMOs may become opposed by other SMOs. In essence, movement organizations become part of the environment of other movement organizations. Clearly, pro-life and pro-choice forces are at organizational as well as ideological war. Following civil rights gains for blacks and other minorities, conservative protest groups such as the Ku Klux Klan and American Nazis grew in membership and media visibility. A former self-proclaimed member and leader of the Klan recently ran for a governership and pronounced his candidacy for the 1992 presidential election.

Not all successful movement organizations are actively opposed by other emerging SMOs, but during this century, there does seem to be a trend where one force will generate another of different or opposing ideological perspective. Feminists and the women's movement were met by countermovements during the 1970s. Even conservative Republican groups are being countered by more extreme conservative protest groups during the 1992 election. The Women's Temperance Christian Union succeeded but was continuously and effectively opposed by other groups during the prohibition period. Currently, as we write, there is a "Men's Movement," with accounts to the effect that this represents a a reaction to the women's movement, although some have suggested that secure men in the Men's Movement are true feminists! You be the judge.

In the selections that follow, Aldon Morris (Article 29) qualifies the conclusions of J. Craig Jenkins and Charles Perrow (Article 28) that internal resources are relatively less significant than outside resources in the emergence and success of social movements. Here, the student sit-in movement of the 1960s and the creation of movement centers (a very useful concept) were found to be supported and facilitated by key institutions in the black community (churches and colleges). An important finding is that the geographical spread of the sit-ins was a function of the network of relationships among the leaders and members of these institutions.

In the next selection, Barrie Thorne (Article 30) discusses two tactics (draft counseling and noncooperation) used by two organizations of the draft-resistance movement to establish credibility in public. The first tactic attempted to minimize differences between activists and the general public; the second maximized them in its stress on principle and risk taking. The strains of the two tactics are highlighted. The article is reminiscent of David A. Snow, Louis A. Zurcher, and Sheldon Ekland-Olson's (Article 26) concerns with the outreach and engagement patterns that are employed to disseminate information about social movements and to recruit members. We encourage you to peruse these two articles for their findings on the relationships of outreach and recruitment on the one hand and subsequent operations and SMO strategies on the other.

In Article 31, Ronald Lawson uses information on the rent-strike movement in New York City to discuss the general issue of social movement strategy and changes. It presents six innovations used by the movement and their effects on the nature of the rent strike. The reading also addresses the broader sociocultural changes that made the innovations appropriate and necessary. One of its important features is the discussion of the institutionalization of the rent strike, and its function in normal city politics.

Paul Luebke, in Article 32, shows the importance of both internal and external resources for the success of social movements. The article uses information from a movement opposed to an expressway. Initially, the two organizations active in the movement were a neighborhood association and a statewide political organization. The reading documents the tactics they used to create a citywide coalition against the expressway that eventually stopped its construction. The importance of enthusiasm in the collective mobilization of support for the cause is stressed.

ARTICLE 29

Black Southern Student Sit-In Movement: An Analysis of Internal Organization

ALDON MORRIS

Scholars of the Civil Rights movement (Zinn, 1964; Oppenheimer, 1964; Matthews and Prothro, 1966; Meier and Rudwick, 1973; Oberschall, 1973; McAdam, 1979) and Civil Rights activists agree that the black Southern student sit-in movement of 1960 was a crucial development. The sit-ins pumped new life into the Civil Rights movement and enabled it to win unprecedented victories. Moreover, the sit-ins exercised a profound tactical and strategic influence over the entire course of social and political upheavals of the 1960s.

Apart from having a jarring impact on race relations, the sit-ins signaled the possibility of militant action at both Northern and Southern white campuses (Haber, 1966; Obear, 1970; Sale, 1973). A critical mass of the early leaders of the white student movement acquired much of their training, organizing skills, and tactics from the black activists of the student sit-in movement (Sale, 1973; Westby, 1976). Thus, the beginning of the white student movement as well as the quickened pace of Civil Rights activity can be traced to the black student sit-in movement.

The sit-ins were important because their rapid spread across the South crystallized the conflict of the period and pulled many people directly into the movement. How is such a "burst" of collective action to be explained? A standard account of the sit-ins has emerged which maintains that the sit-ins were the product of an independent black student movement which represented a radical break from previous civil rights activities, organizations, and leadership of the Black community (e.g., Lomax, 1962; Zinn, 1964; Oppenheimer, 1964; Matthews and Prothro, 1966; Meier and Rudwick, 1973; Oberschall, 1973; Piven and Cloward, 1977).

In the standard account, various factors are argued to be the driving force behind the sit-ins, including impatience of the young, mass media coverage, outside resources made available by the liberal white community of the North, and support from the Federal Government. Although these writers differ over the proximate causes of the sit-ins, they nevertheless concur that the sit-ins broke from the organizational and institutional framework of the emerging Civil Rights movement. The data for the present study do not fit this standard account and suggest that a different account and interpretation of the sit-ins is warranted. The purpose of this paper is to present new data on the Southern student sit-in movement of 1960, and to provide a framework that will theoretically order the empirical findings.

DATA

This study of the sit-ins is part of a larger study on the origins of the Civil Rights movement

Morris, Aldon. (1981, December). Black southern student sit-in movement: An analysis of internal organization. *American Sociological Review, 46,* 744–767. Reprinted by permission of the American Sociological Association.

(Morris, forthcoming). A substantial part of the data were collected from primary sources—archives and interviews with Civil Rights participants. The archival research was conducted at various sites between May and September of 1978. Thousands of original documents (i.e., memoranda, letters, field reports, organizational histories and directives, interorganizational correspondences, etc.) generated by movement participants were examined. These data contained a wealth of information pertaining to key variables—organization, mobilization, finance, rationality, spontaneity—relevant to the study of movement.

Interviews with participants of the movement constituted the second source of data. Detailed interviews with over 50 Civil Rights leaders were conducted. Interviews made it possible to follow-up on many issues raised by the archival data: and, since these interviews were semi-open-ended, they revealed unexpected insights into the movement. Whenever statements were heard that seemed novel or promising, interviewees were given freedom to speak their piece. . . .

EARLY SIT-INS: FORERUNNERS

The first myth regarding the sit-in movement is that it started in Greensboro, North Carolina, on February 1, 1960. This research documents that Civil rights activists conducted sit-ins between 1957 and 1960 in at least fifteen cities: St. Louis, Missouri; Wichita and Kansas City, Kansas; Oklahoma City, Enid, Tulsa, and Stillwater, Oklahoma; Lexington and Louisville, Kentucky; Miami, Florida; Charleston, West Virginia; Sumter, South Carolina; East St. Louis, Illinois; Nashville, Tennessee; and Durham, North Carolina. The Greensboro sit-ins are important because they represent a unique link in a long chain of sit-ins. Although this paper concentrates on the uniqueness of the Greensboro link, there were important similarities in the entire chain. While other studies (Southern Regional Council, 1960; Oppenheimer, 1964; Matthews and Prothro, 1966; Meier and Rudwick, 1973) have not totally overlooked these earlier sit-ins, they fail to reveal their scope, connections, and extensive organizational base.

The early sit-ins were initiated by direct-action organizations. From interviews with participants in the early sit-ins (Moore, 1978; McCain, 1978; Lawson, 1978; Smith, 1978; McKissick, 1978, 1979; Luper, 1981; Randolph, 1981; Lewis, 1981) and published works (Southern Regional Council, 1960; Meier and Rudwick, 1973), I found that Civil Rights organizations initiated sit-ins in fourteen of the fifteen cities I have identified. The NAACP, primarily its Youth Councils either initiated or co-initiated sit-ins in nine of the fifteen cities. CORE, usually working with the NAACP, played an important initiating role in seven of the fifteen cities. The SCLC initiated one case and was involved in another. finally, the Durham Committee on Negro Affairs, working with the NAACP, initiated sit-ins in that city. From this data, we can conclude that these early sit-ins were a result of a multi-faceted organizational effort.

These sit-ins received substantial backing from their respective communities. The black church served as the major institutional force behind the sit-ins. Over two decades ago, E. Franklin Frazier argued that "for the Negro masses, in their social and moral isolation in American society, the Negro church community has been a nation within a nation" (Frazier, 1963:49). He argued that the church functioned as the central political arena in black society. Nearly all of the direct-action organizations that initiated these early sit-ins were closely associated with the church. The church supplied these organizations not only with an established communication network, but also leaders and organized masses, finances, and a safe environment in which to hold political meetings. Direct-action organizations clung to the church because their survival depended on it.

Not all black churches supported the sit-ins. The many that did often supported sit-ins in a critical but "invisible" manner. Thus, Mrs. Clara Luper, the organizer of the 1958 Oklahoma City sit-ins, wrote that the black church did not want to get involved, but church leaders told organizers, "we could meet in their churches. They would take up a collection for us and make announcements concerning our worthwhile activities" (Luper, 1979:3). This "covert" role was central. Interviewed activists revealed that clusters of churches were usually directly involved with the sit-ins. In addition to community support generated through the churches, these activists also received support from parents whose children were participating in demonstrations.

These sit-ins were organized by established leaders of the black community. The leaders did not spontaneously emerge in response to a crisis, but were organizational actors in the full sense of the word. Some sit-in leaders were also church leaders, taught school, and headed up the local direct-action organization; their extensive organizational linkages provided blocks of individuals to serve as demonstrators. Clara Luper wrote, "The fact that I was teaching American History at Dungee High School in Spencer, Oklahoma and was a member of the First Street Baptist Church furnished me with an ample number of young people who would become the nucleus of the Youth Council" (Luper, 1979:1). Mrs. Luper's case is not isolated; leaders of the early sit-ins were enmeshed in organizational networks and were integral members of the black community.

Rational planning was evident in this early wave of sit-ins. During the late fifties, the Revs. James Lawson and Kelly Miller Smith, both leaders of a direct-action organization—Nashville Christian Leadership Council—formed what they called a "nonviolent workshop." In these workshops, Lawson meticulously taught local college students the philosophy and tactics of nonviolent protest (D. Bevel, 1978; Lewis, 1978). In 1959, these students held "test" sit-ins in two department stores. Earlier, in 1957, members of the Oklahoma City NAACP Youth Council created what they called their "project," whose aim was to eliminate segregation in public accommodations (Luper, 1979:3). The project consisted of various committees and groups who planned sit-in strategies. After a year of planning, this group walked into the local Katz Drug Store and initiated their sit-in. In St. Louis in 1955, William clay organized an NAACP Youth Council. Through careful planning and twelve months of demonstrations, members of this organization were able to desegregate dining facilities at department stores (Meier and Rudwick, 1973:93). In Durham, North Carolina in 1958, black activists of the Durham committee on Negro Affairs conducted a survey of 5-and-10-cent stores in Durham (Southern Regional Council, 1960). The survey revealed that these stores were heavily dependent on black trade. Clearly, the sit-ins initiated by this group were based on rational planning. A similar picture emerges in Sumter, South Carolina and for all the early sit-ins.

Finally, these early sit-ins were sponsored by indigenous resources of the black community; the leadership was black, the bulk of the demonstrators were black, the strategies and tactics were formulated by blacks, and the finances came out of the pockets of blacks, while their serene spirituals echoed through the churches.

Most of the organizers of the early sit-ins knew each other and were well aware of each other's strategies of confrontation. Many of these activists were part of the militant wing of the NAACP. Following the Montgomery bus boycott, this group began to reorganize NAACP Youth Councils with the explicit purpose of initiating direct-action projects. This group of activists (e.g., Floyd McKissick, Daisy Bates, Ronald Walters, Hosea Williams, Barbara Posey, Clara Luper, etc.) viewed themselves as a distinct group, because the national NAACP usually did not approve of their direct-action approach or took a very ambivalent stance.

These militants of the NAACP built networks that detoured the conservative channels and organizational positions of their superiors. At NAACP meetings and conferences, they selected situations where they could present freely their plans and desires to engage in confrontational politics. At these gatherings, information regarding strategies was exchanged. Once acquainted, the activists remained in touch by phone and mail.

Thus, it is no accident that the early sit-ins occurred between 1957 and 1960. Other instances of 'direct action' also occurred during this period. For example, Mrs. Daisy Bates led black students affiliated with her NAACP Youth Council into the all-white Little Rock Central High School and forced President Eisenhower to send in National Guards. CORE, beginning to gain a foothold in the south, had the explicit goal of initiating direct-action projects. We have already noted that CORE activists were in close contact with other activists of the period. Though these early sit-ins and related activities were not part of a grandiose scheme, their joint occurrences, timing, and approaches were connected via organizational and personal networks.

SIT-IN CLUSTER

Organizational and personal networks produced the first cluster of sit-ins in Oklahoma in 1958. By tracing these networks, we can arrive at a basic understanding of this cluster and a clue to understanding the entire sit-in movement.

In August of 1958, the NAACP Youth Council of Wichita, Kansas, headed by Ronald Walters, initiated sit-ins at the lunch counters of a local drug store (Lewis, 1981). At the same time, Clara Luper and the young people in her NAACP Youth Council were training to conduct sit-ins in Oklahoma City. The adult leaders of these two groups knew each other; in addition to working for the same organization, several members of the two groups were personal friends. Following the initial sit-ins in Wichita, members of the two groups made numerous phone calls, exchanged information, and discussed mutual support. This direct contact was important because the local press refused to cover the sit-ins. In less than a week, Clara Luper's group in Oklahoma City initiated their planned sit-ins.

Shortly thereafter, sit-ins were conducted in Tulsa, Enid, and Stillwater, Oklahoma. Working through CORE and the local NAACP Youth Council, Clara Luper's personal friend, Mrs. Shirley Scaggins, organized the sit-ins in Tulsa (Luper, 1981). Mrs. Scaggins had recently lived in Oklahoma City and knew the details of Mrs. Luper's sit-in project. The two leaders worked in concert. At the same time, the NAACP Youth Council in Enid began to conduct sit-ins. A Mr. Mitchell who led that group (Luper, 1981) knew Mrs. Luper well. He had visited the Oklahoma Youth Council at the outset of their sit-in and discussed with them sit-in tactics and mutual support. The Stillwater sit-ins appear to have been conducted independently by black college students.

A process similar to that in Oklahoma occurred in East St. Louis, Illinois. Homer Randolph, who in late 1958 organized the East St. Louis sit-ins, had previously lived in Oklahoma City, knew Mrs. Luper well, and had young relatives who participated in the Oklahoma City sit-ins.

In short, the first sit-in cluster occurred in Oklahoma in 1958 and spread to cities within a hundred-mile radius via established organizational and personal networks. The majority of these early sit-ins were (1) connected rather than isolated, (2) initiated through organizations and personal ties, (3) rationally planned and led by established leaders, and (4) supported by indigenous resources. Thus, the Greensboro sit-ins did not mark the movement's beginning, but were links in the chain. But the Greensboro sit-ins were a unique link which triggered sit-ins across the South at an incredible pace. What happened in the black community between the late 1950s and early 1960s to produce such a movement?

EMERGENCE OF INTERNAL ORGANIZATION

During the mid-fifties the extensive internal organization of the Civil Rights movement began to crystalize in communities across the South.

During this period "direct action" organizations were being built by local activists. Community institutions—especially the black church—were becoming political. The "mass meeting" with political oratory and protest music became institutionalized. During the same period, CORE entered the South with intentions of initiating protest, and NAACP Youth Councils were reorganized by young militant adults who desired to engage in confrontational politics.

However, neither CORE nor the NAACP Youth Councils were capable of mobilizing wide-scale protest such as the sit-ins of 1960, because neither had a mass base in the black community. CORE was small, Northern-based, and white-led, largely unknown to Southern blacks. Historically, the NAACP had been unable to persuade more than 2% of the black population to become members. Furthermore, the national NAACP was oriented to legal strategies, not sit-ins. Following the 1954 school desegregation decision, the NAACP was further weakened by a severe attack by local white power structures. Members of the Southern white power structures attempted to drive local branches of NAACP out of existence by labeling them subversive and demanding they make their membership public. NAACP officials usually refused to comply with this demand because their members might suffer physical and economic reprisals if identified. NAACP's opponents argued in the local courts that this noncompliance confirmed their suspicion that NAACP was subversive, and the courts responded by issuing injunctions which prevented NAACP from operating in a number of southern states. For example the NAACP was outlawed in the state of Alabama from 1956 to 1965 (Morris, 1980). This repression forced the NAACP to become defensively-oriented and to commit its resources to court battles designed to save itself. Thus, neither CORE nor NAACP Youth Councils were able to provide the political base required to launch the massive sit-ins of 1960.

Nevertheless, between 1955 and 1960 new organizational and protest efforts were stirring in Southern black communities. The efforts attracted CORE southward and inspired the direct-action groups in the NAACP to reorganize its Youth Councils. The Montgomery bus boycott was the watershed. The importance of that boycott was that it revealed to the black community that mass protests could be successfully organized and initiated through indigenous resources and institutions.

The Montgomery bus boycott gave rise to both the Montgomery Improvement Association (MIA) and the Southern Christian Leadership Conference (SCLC). The MIA was organized in December 1955 to coordinate the activities of the mass bus boycott against segregated buses and to serve as the boycott's official decision-making body. The MIA was a local church-based Southern organization. Its leadership was dominated by local ministers of Montgomery, with the Rev. Martin Luther King serving as its first president. The dramatic Montgomery boycott triggered similar boycotts in a number of Southern cities. As in Montgomery, these boycotts were organized through the churches, with a local minister typically becoming the official leader. SCLC was organized in 1957 by activist clergymen from across the South to coordinate and consolidate the various local movements. SCLC's leadership was dominated by black ministers with King elected as its first president, and the major organizational posts were filled by ministers who led local movements. Thus, SCLC was organized to accomplish across the South what the MIA had in Montgomery. The emergence of MIA and SCLC reflected the dominant role that churches began to play in confrontational politics by the late 1950s.

The Montgomery bus boycott demonstrated the political potential of the black church and church-related direct-action organizations. By 1955 the massive migration of blacks from rural to urban areas was well underway, and many southern cities had substantial black populations. The black urban churches that emerged in these cities were quite different from their rural counterparts. The urban churches were larger, more numerous, and better financed, and were presided over by ministers who were better educated and whose sole occupation was the ministry (Mays and Nicholson, 1933; McAdam, 1979; Morris, 1980). Moreover, urban churches were owned, operated, and controlled by the black community.

These churches functioned as the institutional base of the Montgomery bus boycott. They supplied the movement with money, organized masses, leaders, highly developed communications, and relatively safe environments where mass meetings could be held to plan confrontations. This institutional base was in place prior to the boycott. Movement leaders transformed the churches into political resources and committed them to the ends of the movement. The new duty of the church finance committee was to collect money for the movement. The minister's new role was to use the pulpit to articulate the political responsibilities of the church community. The new role of the choir was to weave political messages into the serene spirituals. Regular church meetings were transformed into the "mass meeting" where blacks joined committees to guide protests, offered up collections to the movement, and acquired reliable information of the movement, which local radio and television stations refused to broadcast. The resources necessary to initiate a black movement were present in Montgomery and other communities. They were transformed into political resources and used to launch the first highly visible mass protest of the modern Civil Rights movement.

The important role of the MIA in the emergence of the modern Civil Rights movement is seldom grasped. As a nonbureaucratic, church-based organization, MIA's organizational affairs were conducted like church services rather than by rigid bureaucratic rules, as in the case of the NAACP. Ministers presided over the MIA the way they presided over their congregations. Ultimate authority inhered in the president, Dr. King. Decisions pertaining to local matters could be reached immediately. Diverse organizational tasks were delegated to the rank-and-file on the spot. Rules and procedures emerged by trial and error and could be altered when they inhibited direct action. Oratory, music, and charismatic personalities energized MIA's organizational affairs. The structure of the organization was designed to allow masses to participate directly in protest activities. The MIA proved to be appropriate for confrontational politics because it was mass-based, nonbureaucratic, Southern-led, and able to transform pre-existing church resources into political power.

Southern blacks took notice of the Montgomery movement. Activists from across the South visited Montgomery to observe the political roles of the church and the MIA. For example, when Hosea Williams (at the time, an activist associated with the NAACP in Savannah, Georgia) visited the Montgomery movement, he marvelled at its dynamics:

> *You had had NAACP lawsuits, you'd had NAACP chapters, who had much less than 5% participation anyplace. But here's a place [Montgomery] where they got masses of blacks—they couldn't get a church big enough where they could hold mass rallies. And then, none of them [masses] were riding the buses. I was interested in these strategies and their implementation and in learning how to mobilize the masses to move in concern. [Williams, 1978]*

Williams, like countless others, did more than marvel. In his words, "I went back to Savannah and organized the Youth Council and nonviolent movement." Thus, another direct-action organization emerged.

Black ministers were in the best position to organize church-related direct-action organizations in the South. Even while the Montgomery movement was in progress, ministers in other cities (e.g., Steele in Tallahassee, Shuttlesworth in Birmingham, and Davis in New Orleans) began to build mass-based movements patterned after the Montgomery movement. These ministers were not only in a position to organize and commit church resources to protest efforts, they were also linked to each other and the larger community via ministerial alliances. In short, between 1955 and 1960 a profound change in Southern black communities had begun. Confrontational politics were thrust to the foreground through new direct-action organizations closely allied with the church.

SCLC AND MOVEMENT CENTERS

The creation of the Southern Christian Leadership Conference (SCLC) in 1957 marked a critical organizational shift for the Civil Rights movement. The ministers who organized SCLC clearly understood the historic and central institutional importance of the church in black society. They knew that the church nurtured and produced most of the indigenous leaders, raised finances, and organized masses, as well as being a major force in other aspects of black culture. By 1957 these ministers, many of whom were leading movements in their local communities, consciously and explicitly concluded that the church was capable of functioning as the institutional vanguard of a mass-based black movement. Hence, they organized SCLC to be a Southern-wide, church-based protest organization.

Prior to SCLC, the major black protest organization—NAACP—had been closely linked with the church. Yet, before SCLC was created, the NAACP, and not the church, functioned as the organization through which protest was initiated. With the emergence of SCLC, the critical shift occurred whereby the church itself, rather than groups closely linked to it, began to function as the institutional center of protest.

In 1957 the organizers of SCLC sent out a call to fellow clergy men of the South to organize their congregations and communities for collective protest. The remarks of Rev. Smith of Nashville typified the action of protest-oriented ministers:

> *After the meeting [SCLC organizing meeting] and after the discussion that we had and all that, it became clear to me that we needed something in addition to NAACP. So I came back and I called some people together and formed what we named the Nashville Christian Leadership Council in order to address the same kind of issues that SCLC would be addressing. [Smith, 1978]*

Hundreds of ministers across the South took similar action.

From this collective effort resulted what can best be conceptualized as local movement centers of the Civil Rights movement, which usually had the following seven characteristics:

1. A cadre of social-change-oriented ministers and their congregations. Often one minister would become the local leader of a given center and his church would serve as the coordinating unit.
2. Direct action organizations of varied complexity. In many cities local churches served as quasi-direct-action organizations, while in others ministers built complex, church-related organizations (e.g., United Defense League of Baton Rouge, Montgomery Improvement Association, Alabama Christian Movement for Human Rights of Birmingham, Petersburg Improvement Association). NAACP Youth Councils and CORE affiliates also were components of the local centers.
3. Indigenous financing coordinated through the church.
4. Weekly mass meetings, which served as forums and where local residents were informed of relevant information and strategies regarding the movement. These meetings also built solidarity among the participants.
5. Dissemination of nonviolent tactics and strategies. The leaders articulated to the black community the message that social change would occur only through nonviolent direct action carried out by masses.
6. Adaptation of a rich church culture to political purposes. The black spirituals, sermons,

and prayers were used to deepen the participants' commitment to the struggle.

7. A mass-based orientation, rooted in the black community, through the church.

See Figure 1 for a schematic diagram of a typical local movement center.

Most scholars of the movement are silent about the period between the Montgomery bus boycott and the 1960 sit-ins. My analysis emphasizes that the organizational foundation of the Civil Rights movement was built during this period and active local movement centers were created in numerous Southern black communities. For instance, between 1957 and 1960 many local centers emerged in Virginia. Ministers such as Reverends Milton Reid, L. C. Johnson, Virgil Wood, Curtis Harris, and Wyatt Walker operated out of centers in Hopewell, Lynchburg, Portsmouth, and Petersburg. The direct action organizations of these cities were named Improvement Associations and were patterned after the original MIA. South Carolina also had its movement centers. For example, in 1955–1956, after whites began exerting economic pressure against blacks desiring school integration, the black community of Orangeburg initiated an economic boycott against twenty-three local firms. This extended boycott resulted in a vibrant movement center led by the Reverends Matthew McCollom, William Sample, and Alfred Issac and their congregations. Movement centers emerged in other South Carolina cities, such as Sumter, Columbia, and Florence, organized by James McCain of CORE and activist clergymen.

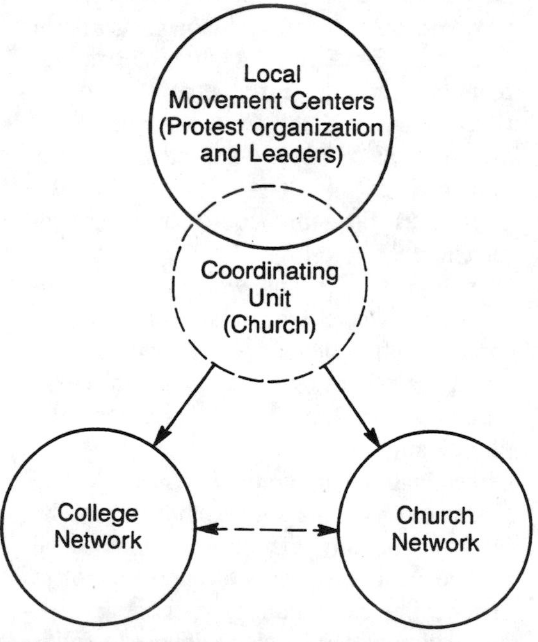

FIGURE 1. Structure of a Typical Local Movement Center

AMERICAN SOCIOLOGICAL REVIEW

In Durham, North Carolina, churches that made up the movement center were Union Baptist, pastored by Rev. Grady Davis; Ashbury Temple, pastored by Rev. Douglas Moore; Mount Zion, pastored by Rev. Fuller; St. Marks, pastored by Rev. Speaks; and St. Josephs, pastored by Rev. Swann. Movement centers were also to be found in cities of the deep South such as Montgomery and Birmingham, Alabama; Baton Rouge, Louisiana; and Tallahassee, Florida.

So prevalent were these centers throughout the South that when Gordon Carey, a CORE field investigator, surveyed the situation in 1959, he reported:

> *In some Southern cities such as Montgomery, Orangeburg, Tallahassee, and Birmingham nonviolent movements have been and are being carried on. But most of the South, with its near total segregation, has not been touched. Many places have felt the spirit of Martin Luther King, Jr. but too often this spirit has not been turned into positive action. [Carey, 1959, emphasis added]*

The "spirit" to which Carey referred was in fact the church-based movement centers he found throughout the South, most of which were affiliated with or patterned after SCLC.

Elsewhere (Morris, 1980), I have analyzed how, in the late 1950s, these centers were perfecting confrontation strategies, building organizations, leading marches, organizing voter drives, and radicalizing members of the community. Scholars (e.g., Oberschall, 1973:223) persistently dismiss these centers as weak, limited, and unwilling to confront the white power structure. Yet the evidence suggests a different interpretation. For example, Rev. Fred Shuttlesworth and his mass-based movement center continually confronted Bull Connor and the white power structure of Birmingham throughout the late fifties. As a consequence, Shuttlesworth's home and church were repeatedly bombed.

In short, between 1955 and 1960 many local movement centers were formed and hardened. These centers, which included NAACP Youth Councils and CORE chapters, constituted the new political reality of Southern black communities on the eve of the 1960 sit-ins. It was these structures that were able to generate and sustain a heavy volume of collective action.

THE GREENSBORO CONNECTION

On February 1, 1960 Ezell Blair Jr., Franklin McCain, Joe McNeil, and David Richmond, all students at North Carolina Agricultural and Technical College, sat-in at the Woolworth's lunch counter in Greensboro, North Carolina. Though most commentators mark this as the first sit-in, the four protesters knew that they were not the first to sit-in in the state of North Carolina. Sit-in activity in the state had begun in the late fifties, when a young black attorney, Floyd McKissick, and a young Board member of SCLC, Rev. Douglas Moore, and a small group of other young people (including a few whites from Duke University) began conducting sit-ins in Durham.

These early Durham sit-ins were part of the network of sit-ins which occurred between 1957 and 1960. The activists involved in the early sit-ins belonged to the NAACP Youth Division, which McKissick headed, and their own direct-action organization called the Durham Committee on Negro Affairs. During the late fifties, McKissick and Moore's group conducted sit-ins at local bus stations, waiting rooms, parks, hotels, and other places (McKissick, 1978). In 1957, Rev. Moore and others were arrested for sitting-in at a local ice-cream parlor. The subsequent legal case became known as the "Royal Ice Cream Case." McKissick, who also headed the local Boy Scout organization, periodically would take the young "all-American" scouts into segregated restaurants and order food. In short, this Durham group persistently confronted the white power structure in the late fifties.

The four students who sat-in at Greensboro and sparked the widespread sit-in movement had been members of the NAACP Youth Council, headed by McKissick. According to McKissick, he knew them all well and they knew all about the Durham activities. Martin Oppenheimer (1964:398), an early historian of the sit-ins, confirms this: "All of the boys were, or at some had been members of an NAACP Youth Council." Indeed, the four students had participated in numerous meetings in social-action oriented churches in Durham. Involvement with the NAACP Youth Council meant that they were not only informed about the Durham sit-ins, but also knew about many of the sit-ins conducted prior to 1960. Thus, the myth that four college students got up one day and sat-in at Woolworth's—and sparked the movement—dries up like a "raisin in the sun" when confronted with the evidence.

The National office of the NAACP and many conservative ministers refused to back the Greensboro sit-ins. The NAACP's renowned team of lawyers did not defend the "Greensboro Four." Nevertheless, on the same day they sat-in, the students contacted a lawyer whom they considered to be their friend, and Floyd McKissick became the lawyer for the "Greensboro Four." The network of college students and adult activists had begun to operate in earnest.

Well-forged networks existed between and among black churches and colleges in North Carolina, facilitated by the large number of colleges concentrated in the state. Indeed, ten black colleges existed within a ten-mile radius of Greensboro (Wolf, 1970:590). Interactions between colleges and churches were both frequent and intense; many colleges were originally founded by the churches. A number of North Carolina churches were referred to as "college churches" because they had large student memberships. These two sets of social organizations were also linked through college seminaries where black ministers received their theological training.

These church-student networks enabled activist-oriented students to become familiar with the emerging Civil Rights movement via local movement centers and made it possible for adult activists to tap the organizational resources of the colleges. Leaders of student governments and other campus groups facilitated student mobilization because they, like the ministers, had organizing skills and access to blocs of people. Moreover, the concentration of colleges in the state provided an extended network of contacts. Fraternity and sorority chapters linked students within and between campuses, as did dating patterns and joint cultural and athletic events. Finally, intercollegiate kinship and friendship networks were widespread, and student leaders were squarely tied to these networks. Similarly, black communities across North Carolina could be rapidly mobilized through the churches, since churches were linked through ministerial alliances and other networks. By 1960 these diverse and interlocking networks were capable of being politicized and coordinated through existing movement centers, making North Carolina an ideal state for the rapid diffusion of collective action.

Within a week of the Greensboro protest, sit-ins rapidly spread across the South. In an extensive study, the Southern Regional council (1960) reported that between February 1 and March 31 of 1960, major sit-in demonstrations and related activity had been conducted in at least sixty-nine Southern cities.

BEYOND GREENSBORO

As soon as the sit-ins started in Greensboro, the network of movement centers was activated. In the first week of February, 1960, students continued to sit-in daily at the local Woolworth's, and the protest population began to grow. The original four protesters were joined by hundreds of students from A & T College and several other local black colleges. Black high-school students and a few white college students also joined the protest. Influential local whites decided to close the Woolworth's in Greensboro, hoping to take the steam out of the developing mass-movement. It was too late.

Floyd McKissick, Rev. Douglas Moore, and others who had conducted previous sit-ins formulated plans to spread the movement across the state. They were joined by CORE's white field secretary, Gordon Carey, whose services had been requested by the local NAACP president. Carey arrived in Durham from New York on February the 7th and went directly to McKissick's home, where the sit-ins were being planned. Carey was a good choice because he had knowledge of nonviolent resistance and because of his earlier contact with movement centers in Southern black communities.

On February 8th—exactly one week after the Greensboro sit-ins— the demonstrations spread to nearby Durham and Winston-Salem. McKissick, Moore, Carey, and others helped organize these sit-ins, bringing students from the local colleges to churches where they were trained to conduct sit-ins. For example, the Durham students were trained at the same churches through which McKissick and Moore had planned direct action in the late 1950s. Following training and strategy sessions, the students went to the local lunch counters and sat-in.

The organizing effort was not limited to these two nearby cities. Within the first week of the Greensboro sit-in, McKissick, Carrey, and Rev. Moore made contact with activists in movement centers throughout North Carolina, South Carolina, and Virginia, urging them to train students for sit-ins. They not only phoned these activists, but traveled to various cities to provide assistance. Upon arrival they often found sit-in planning sessions already underway. According to Carey (1978), "when we reached these cities we went directly to the movement oriented churches." When asked why, Carey replied, "Well, that's where the protest activities were being planned and organized." Thus, these sit-ins were largely organized at the movement churches rather than on the campuses. To understand the sit-in movement, one must abandon the assumption that it was a collegiate phenomenon. For different reasons, Rev. Moore attempted to convey this same idea in the early days of the sit-ins: "If Woolworth and other stores think this is just another panty raid, they haven't had their sociologists in the field recently" (Moore, 1960). The sit-ins grew out of a context of organized movement centers.

As anticipated above, the Southern Christian Leadership Conference was central to the rise of the 1960 sit-in movement. It is critical to remember that when Rev. Moore and other organizers visited churches in North and South Carolina and Virginia, they discovered that church leaders were already training students for sit-ins. Speaking of the ministers who headed these movement churches, Carey (1978) reported, "All of these ministers were active in the Southern Christian Leadership Conference. At least 75% were getting inspiration from King." Additionally, these ministers had contacts with and often were leaders of both CORE and the activist wing of the NAACP.

Since the movement centers were already in place, they served as both receiving and transmitting "antennas" for the sit-ins. As receivers they gathered information of the sit-ins, and as transmitters they rebroadcast information throughout the networks. Because this internal network already existed, information was rapidly channeled to groups prepared to engage in nonviolent collective action.

During the second week of February 1960, plans were formulated to conduct sit-ins in a number of Southern cities. Communication and coordination between the cities was intensified. For example, early in the second week of February, the Rev. B. Elton Cox of High Point, North Carolina, and Rev. C. A. Ivory of Rock Hill, South Carolina, phoned McKissick and other leaders, informing them that their groups were "ready to go" (McKissick, 1978). Cox's group sat-in on February 11th and Ivory's on February 12th. Rev. Ivory organized and directed the Rock Hill sit-ins from his wheelchair. Within the week, sit-ins were being conducted in several cities in Virginia, most of them organized through the dense network of SCLC movement centers in that state (Southern Regional Council, 1960; Walker, 1978).

The movement hot lines reached far beyond the border states of North Carolina, South Carolina, and Virginia. Rev. Fred Shuttlesworth, an active leader of the Birmingham, Alabama, movement center, happened to be in North Carolina when the first wave of sit-ins occurred, fulfilling a speaking engagement for the leader of the High Point sit-ins—Rev. Cox. According to Shuttlesworth, "He [Rev. Cox] carried me by where these people were going to sit-in. . . . I called back to Atlanta, and told Ella [Baker] what was going on. I said, 'this is the thing. You must tell Martin [King] that we must get with this, and really this can shake up the world' " (Shuttlesworth, 1978). Baker, the Executive Director of SCLC, immediately began calling her contacts at various colleges, asking them, "What are you all going to do? It is time to move" (Baker, 1978).

Carey and Rev. Moore phoned the movement center in Nashville, Tennessee, and asked Rev. Lawson if they were ready to move. The student and church communities coordinated by the Nashville Christian Leadership Conference answered in the affirmative. According to Lawson,

> *Of course there was organizing because after the sit-in, the first one in February, people like Doug Moore, Ella Baker, myself, did call around to places that we knew, said, "Can you start? Are you ready? Can you go? And how can we help you?" So there was some of that too that went on. Even there the sit-in movement did not just spread spontaneously. I mean there was a readiness. And then there were, there were phone calls that went out to various communities where we knew peo-*

ple and where we knew student groups and where we knew minister groups, and said, you know, 'this is it, let's go,' [Lawson, 1978]

When asked, "Why did the student sit-in movement occur?" Lawson replied,

Because King and the Montgomery boycott and the whole development of that leadership that clustered around King had emerged and was ready and was preaching and teaching direct action, nonviolent action, and was clearly ready to act, ready to seed any movement that needed sustenance and growth. So there was ... in other words, the soil had been prepared. [Lawson, 1978]

These data provide insight into how a political movement can rapidly spread between geographically distant communities. The sit-ins spread across the South in a short period of time because activists, working through local movement centers, planned, coordinated, and sustained them. They spread despite the swinging billy clubs of policemen, despite Ku Klux Klansmen, white mobs, murderers, tear gas, and economic reprisals (Southern Regional Council, 1960; Matthews and Prothro, 1966; Oberschall, 1973). The pre-existing movement centers provided the resources and organization required to sustain the sit-ins in the face of opposition.

SIT-IN CLUSTERS OF 1960

The organizational and personal networks that produced the first cluster of sit-ins in Oklahoma in 1958 have already been described. The cluster concept can be applied to the entire set of sit-ins of February and March 1960. Many of the cities where sit-ins occurred can be grouped by geographic and temporal proximity. A cluster is defined as two or more cities within 75 miles of each other where sit-in activity took place within a span of 14 days. . . . Forty-one of the sixty-nine cities having sit-ins during this two-month period have been grouped because they meet these criteria. Within this period 59% of the cities that had sit-ins and related activity were part of clusters. The percentage of these cities forming sit-in clusters is even more striking in the first month: during February, 76% of cities having sit-ins were part of clusters, while during March the percentage dropped to 44%.

The clustering differentials between the two months can be explained by taking region into account. . . . In the first month (February) 85% of the cities having sit-ins were located in Southeastern and border states. This pattern had been established earlier, when most of the pre-1960 sit-ins occurred in border states. Most of the February sit-ins took place in cities of border states because repression against blacks was not as severe there as in the deep South. This made it possible for activists in border states to build dense networks of movement centers. We have already seen that North Carolina, South Carolina, and Virginia had numerous social-action churches and direct-action organizations. By the time the sit-ins occurred in Virginia, SCLC had affiliates throughout the state, and Rev. Wyatt Walker, who was the leader of Virginia's movement centers, was also the state Director of CORE and President of the local NAACP. Similar patterns existed in the other border states. Small wonder that in the month of February, 73% of cities having sit-ins were located in Virginia, North Carolina, and South Carolina. Similarly, these cities produced 88% of the February clusters. This clustering reflected both the great density of movement centers and a system of domination less stringent than that of the deep South.

. . . In March a major change took place: the majority of the sit-ins occurred in cities of the deep South. With a few exceptions, the sit-ins in the deep South did not occur in clusters. They occurred almost exclusively in Southern cities where movement centers were already established; Montgomery and Birmingham, Alabama; Baton Rouge and New Orleans, Louisiana; Tallahassee, Florida; Nashville and Memphis, Tennessee; and Atlanta and Savannah, Georgia. Repression would have been too great on student protesters operating outside of the protection of such centers in the deep South. Thus, the decrease in clustering in the deep South reflected both the high level of repression and the absence of dense networks of movement centers. Focusing on the internal movement centers enables us to explain both the clustering phenomenon and its absence.

Given the large proportion of sit-ins occurring in clusters, we can say that they did not spread randomly. The clusters represented the social and temporal space in which sit-ins were organized, coordinated, spread, and financed by the black community. Within these clusters, cars filled with organizers from SCLC, NAACP, and CORE raced between sit-in points relaying valuable information. Telephone lines and the community "grapevine" sent forth protest instructions and plans. These clusters were the sites of numerous midday and late night meetings where the black community assembled in the churches, filled the collection plates, and vowed to mortgage their homes to raise the necessary bail-bond money in case the protesting students were jailed. Black lawyers pledged their legal services to the movement and black physicians made their services available to injured demonstrators. Amidst these exciting scenes, black spirituals that had grown out of slavery calmed and deepened the participants' commitment. A detailed view of the Nashville sit-ins provides an example of these dynamics, because the Nashville movement epitomized the sit-ins whether they occurred singularly or in clusters.

THE NASHVILLE SIT-IN MOVEMENT

A well-developed, church-based movement center headed by Rev. Kelly Miller Smith was organized in Nashville during the late 1950s. The center, an affiliate of SCLC, was called the Nashville Christian Leadership Council (NCLC). Rev. James Lawson, an expert tactician of nonviolent protest, was in charge of NCLC's direct-action committee. Lawson received a call from Rev. Douglas Moore about two days after the Greensboro sit-ins began. The Nashville group was ready to act because a cadre of students had already received training in nonviolent direct action. They had conducted "test sit-ins" in two large department stores in downtown Nashville prior to the 1959 Christmas holidays. Moreover, the group had already made plans in late 1959 to begin continuous sit-ins in 1960 with the explicit intention of desegregating Nashville (Smith, 1978; D. Bevel, 1978). Thus, Greensboro provided the impetus for the Nashville group to carry out its pre-exiting strategy.

Rev. Smith's First Baptist Church became the coordinating unit of the Nashville sit-in movement. A decision to sit-in at local lunch counters on Saturday, February 13 1960, was arrived at after much debate. The adults (mostly ministers) of the NCLC met with the students at movement headquarters and tried to convince them to postpone the demonstrations for a couple of days until money could be raised. According to Rev. Smith (1978), "NCLC had $87.50 in the treasury. We had no lawyers, and we felt kind of a parental responsibility for those college kids. And we knew they were gonna be put in jail, and we didn't know what else would happen. And so some of us said, 'we need to wait until we get a lawyer, until we raise some funds.' "

NCLC leaders told the students that they could collect the money through the churches within a week. Then, according to Rev. Smith:

> *James Bevel, then a student at American Baptist Theological Seminary, said that, "I'm sick and tired of waiting,' which was a strange thing to come from a kid who was only about nineteen years old. You see, the rest of us were older.... [Bevel said] 'If you asked us to wait until next week, then next week something would come up and you'd say wait until the next week and maybe we never will get our freedom.' He said this, 'I believe that something will happen in the situation that will make for the solution to some of these problems we're talking about.' So we decided to go on. [Smith, 1978]*

The proximity of four black colleges in Nashville—Fisk University, Tennessee State College, American Baptist Theological Seminary, and Meharry Medical School—facilitated the mobilization of large numbers of students. In its extensive ties between students and churches, Nashville resembled the state of North Carolina. Indeed, John Lewis, James Bevel, and Bernard Lafayette, who became major sit-in leaders, were students at the American Baptist Theological Seminary and were taught there by Rev. Smith. Furthermore, they were student leaders:

> *John Lewis, Bernard and myself were the major participants in the seminary. All of us were like the top student leaders in our schools. I think John at the time was the president of the Student Council. I was a member of the Student Council. I was one of the editors of the yearbook. Bernard was an editor of the yearbook. So all of us were like the top leaders in our school. [J. Bevel, 1978]*

Thus the student leaders could rapidly mobilize other students because they already had access to organized groups. Other writers (Von Eschen et al., 1971; McAdam, 1979) have pointed out that these college networks played a key role in sit-in mobilization. However, the sit-in movement cannot be explained without also noting the crucial interaction between black college students and local movement centers. Speaking of Rev. Smith and his church, Bevel recalled, "the First Baptist basically had the Baptist people who went to Fisk and Meharry and Tennessee State, and the Seminary were basically members of his church" (J. Bevel, 1978). These students had been introduced to the Civil Rights movement while they attended church.

On the first day of the sit-ins in Nashville, students gathered in front of their respective campuses. NCLC sent cars to each college to transport the students to Rev. Smith's church. Again, the major organizational tasks were performed in the church which served as the coordinating unit of the local movement center, rather than on the campuses. Coordination of sit-in activity between the college community and the churches was made less difficult because many of the students (especially student leaders) were immersed in the local movement centers prior to the sit-ins. The pattern of close connection between student demonstrators and adult leaders had already existed in places such as Greensboro and even Oklahoma City in 1958; indeed, this pattern undergirded the entire movement. Rev. Jemison's (1978) remark that the Baton Rouge sit-in demonstrators "were schooled right over there at our church; they were sent out from here to go to the lunch counters" typifies the relationship between the students and the local movement centers. Jemison continued. "The student leaders attended church here. We had close ties because they were worshipping with us while we were working together."

Once the Nashville students arrived at movement headquarters, they participated in workshops where they learned the strategies of nonviolent confrontation from experts like Rev. Lawson, Rev. Metz Rollins, Rev. C. T. Vivian, and the core group of students that Lawson had already trained. This pool of trained leaders was a pre-existing resource housed by NCLC. After the workshops, the students were organized into groups with specific protest responsibilities, each having a spokesperson who had been trained by Lawson during the late 1950s. They then marched off to confront Nashville's segregated lunch counters and agents of social control.

The adult black community immediately mobilized to support the students. Shortly after the demonstration began, large numbers of students were arrested. According to Rev. Smith:

> *We just launched out on something that looked perfectly crazy and scores of people were being arrested, and paddy wagons were full and the people out in downtown couldn't understand what was going on, people just welcoming being arrested, that ran against everything they had ever seen. . . . I've forgotten how much we needed that day, and we got everything we needed. [That particular day?] Yes, sir. About $40,000. We needed something like $40,000 in fives. And we had all the money. Not in fives, but in bail. Every bit of it came up. You know—property and this kind of thing . . . and there were fourteen black*

> *lawyers in this town. Every black lawyer made himself available to us. [Smith, 1978]*

Thus, basic, pre-existing resources in the dominated community were used to accomplish political goals. It was suggested to Rev. Smith that a massive movement such as that in Nashville would need outside resources. He replied,

> *Now, let me quickly say to you that in early 1960, when we were really out there on the line, the community stood up. We stood together. This community had proven that this stereotyped notion of black folk can't work together is just false. We worked together a lot better than the white organizations. So those people fell in line. [Smith, 1978]*

Rev. Smith's comments are applicable beyond Nashville. For example, in Orangeburg, after hundreds of students were arrested and brutalized, the adult black community came solidly to their aid. Bond was set at $200 per student, and 388 students were arrested. Over $75,000 was needed, and adults came forth to put up their homes and property in order to get students out of jail. Rev. McCollom, the leader of the Orangeburg movement center, remarked that, "there was no schism between the student community and the adult community in Orangeburg" (McCollom, 1978). Jim McCain (1978) of CORE, who played a central role in organizing sit-ins across South Carolina and in Florida, reported that community support was widespread. According to Julian Bond (1980), a student leader of Atlanta's sit-ins, "black property owners put up bond which probably amounted to $100,000" to get sit-in demonstrators released from jail.

These patterns were repeated across the South. This community support should not be surprising, considering the number of ministers and congregations involved before and during the movement. Yet, Zinn, an eyewitness to many of these events, wrote, "Spontaneity and self-sufficiency were the hallmarks of the sit-ins; without adult advice or consent, the students planned and carried them through" (1964:29). This myopia illustrates the inadequacies of analyses that neglect or ignore the internal structure of oppressed communities and protest movements.

The continuing development of the Nashville sit-ins sheds further light on the interdependence of the movement and the black community. A formal structure called the Nashville Nonviolent Movement was developed to direct sit-in activities. Its two substructures, the Student Central Committee and the Nashville Christian Leadership Council, worked closely together and had overlapping membership (Reverends Lawson and Vivian were members of both groups). The Central Committee usually consisted of 25 to 30 students drawn from all the local colleges. NCLC represented adult ministers and the black community. The two groups established committees to accomplish specific tasks, including a finance committee, a telephone, publicity, and news committee, and a work committee. The work committee had subgroups responsible for painting protest signs and providing food and transportation. The city's black lawyers became the movement's defense team, students from Meharry Medical School were the medical team.

This intricate structure propelled and guided the sit-in movement of Nashville. A clear-cut division of labor developed between the Central Committee an the NCLC. The Central Committee's major responsibilities were to train, organize, and coordinate the demonstration. The NCLC developed the movement's financial structure and coordinated relations between the community and the student movement. Diane Nash Bevel, a major student leader of the Nashville sit-ins, was asked why the students did not take care of their own finances and build their own relationships with the larger community. She replied,

> *We didn't want to be bothered keeping track of money that was collected at the rallies and stuff. We were just pleased that NCLC would do that, and would handle the bookkeeping and all that trouble that went along with having money. . . .*

Besides, we were much too busy sitting-in and going to jail and that kind of thing. There wasn't really the stability of a bookkeeper, for instance. We didn't want to be bothered with developing that kind of stability. . . . We were very pleased to form this alliance with NCLC who would sponsor the rallies and coordinate the community support among the adult and keep track of the money, while we sat-in and . . . well, it took all our time, and we were really totally immersed in it. My day would sometimes start . . . well we'd have meetings in the morning at six o'clock, before classes, and work steady to extremely late at night, organizing the sit-ins, getting publicity out to the students that we were having a sit-in, and where and what time we would meet. Convincing people, and talking to people, calming people's fears, going to class, at the same time. It was a really busy, busy time for all of the people on the Central Committee. We were trying to teach nonviolence, maintain order among a large, large number of people. That was about all we could handle. [D. Bevel, 1978]

Students are ideal participants in protest activities. Usually they do not have families to support, employer's rules and dictates to follow, and crystallized ideas as to what is "impossible" and "unrealistic." Students have free time and boundless energy to pursue causes they consider worthwhile and imperative (Lipset and Wolin, 1965:3; McCarthy and Zald, 1973:10). McPhail's (1971:1069) finding that young, single, unemployed males were ideal participants in civil disorders and McPhail and Miller's (1973:726) discussion of availability for participation in the assembly process parallels this notion that students are ideal participants in protest activities. Nevertheless, although black students were able to engage in protest activities continuously because of their student status, a one-sided focus on them diverts attention from the larger community, which had undergone considerable radicalization. Speaking of the adults, James Bevel (1978), a student organizer of the Nashville sit-ins, remarked, "But when you talk to each individual, they talked just like we talked—the students. They had jobs and they were adults. But basically, their position would be just like ours. They played different roles because they were in different—they had to relate based on where they were in the community" (J. Bevel, 1978).

The adults of the NCLC organized the black community to support the militant student sit-in movement. Once the movement began, NCLC instituted weekly and sometimes daily mass meetings in the churches. Rev. Smith (1978) recalled,

Sometimes we had them more than once a week if we needed to. When things were really hot we called a meeting at eight o'clock in the morning. We'd call one for twelve that day, twelve noon, and the place would be full. We had what we called our wire service. People got on telephones, that was our wire service, and they would fill that building. They'd fill that building in just a matter of relatively short time."

At these mass meetings, ministers from across the city turned over the money that their respective churches had donated to the movement. Thousands of dollars were collected at the mass meetings while black adults, ministers, and students sang such lyrics as "Before I'd be a slave, I'd rather be buried in my grave." Then too, bundles of leaflets were given to adults at mass meetings who then distributed them throughout the black community. This shows how the movement built communication channels through which vital information, strategies, and plans were disseminated.

During the Nashville sit-ins, word went out to the black community not to shop downtown.

We didn't organize the boycott. We did not organize the boycott. The boycott came about. We don't know how it happened. I tell you there are a lot of little mystical elements in there, little spots that defy rational explanation. . . . Now, we promoted it. we adopted it. But we did not sit down one day and organize a boycott . . . ninety-nine percent of the black people in this community stayed away from downtown during the boycott. It was a fantastic thing—successful. It was fantastically successful. [Smith, 1978]

Yet the boycott was largely organized by NCLC. According to Bevel, Dr. Vivian Henderson, who was head of Fisk University's economic department and a member of NCLC, played a key role in the boycott, because

> *Vivian Henderson was basically responsible for calling the boycott. He got up at a mass meeting and said, 'at least what we could do to support students, if we've got any decency, we can stop paying bills and just don't shop until this thing is resolved.' A very indignant type of speech he made. It just caught on. All the bourgeois women would come to the meeting, and they just got on the phone and called up everybody, all the doctors' wives and things. They just got on the phone and called 300 or 400 people and told them don't shop downtown. Finally there was just a total boycott downtown. There would be no black people downtown at all. [J. Bevel 1978]*

Activists were stationed downtown to insure that blacks knew not to shop. According to Rev. Smith, shortly after the boycott was initiated, merchants began coming to his home wanting to talk. Diane Nash Bevel attributed the boycott's effectiveness to reduced profits during the Easter shopping season. It also changed the merchant's attitude toward the sit-ins.

> *It was interesting the difference that [the boycott] made in terms of how the managers were willing to talk with us, because see we had talked with the managers of the stores. We had a meeting at the very beginning and they had kind of listened to us politely, and said, 'well, we just can't do it. We can't desegregate the counters because we will lose money and that's the end of it.' So, after the economic withdrawal, they were eager to talk with us, and try to work up some solution. [D. Bevel, 1978]*

In early 1960 the white power structure of Nashville was forced to desegregate a number of private establishments and public transportation facilities. SNCC's *Student Voice* reported that in Nashville, "A long series of negotiations followed the demonstrations, and on May 10, 6 downtown stores integrated their lunch counters. Since this time others have followed suit, and some stores have hired Negroes in positions other than those of menial workers for the first time" (*Student Voice*, August, 1960). Daily demonstrations by hundred of students refusing to accept bond so that they could be released from jail, coupled with the boycott, gave blacks the upper hand in the conflict situation. Careful organization and planning was the hallmark of the Nashville sit-in movement.

The movement centers that emerged following the Montgomery bus boycott were developed around nonviolent approaches to social change. Indeed, the primary goal of these centers was to build nonviolent movement. Yet, nonviolent confrontations as a disciplined form of collective action was relatively new to the black masses of the South. The activists within the movement centers systematically introduced blacks to the nonviolent approach. They organized nonviolent workshops and conducted them on a routine basis in the churches and protest organizations. Literature from organizations (e.g., Fellowship of Reconciliation and CORE) that specialized in the nonviolent approach was made available through the centers. Skilled nonviolent strategists (e.g., Bayard Rustin, James Lawson, and Glenn Smiley) travelled between centers training leaders how to conduct nonviolent campaigns. The varied tactics—mass marches, negotiations, boycotts, sit-ins—associated with direct action became common knowledge to activists in the centers. Moreover, in the late fifties activists began experimenting with these tactics and urging the community to become involved with nonviolent confrontations. Meier and Rudwick (1976) have shown that sit-ins at segregated facilities were conducted by black activists in the nineteen forties and late fifties. But this tactic remained relatively isolated and sporadic and did not diffuse throughout the larger community. Meier and Rudwick (1976:384) conclude that diffusion did not occur before 1960 because the white mass-media failed to cover sit-ins. My analysis suggests another explanation: sit-ins prior to 1960 did not spread because the internal organization required for such a spread did not exist. In short, without viable internal social organization, innovations will remain sporadic and isolated. With organization, innovations can spread and be sustained. By 1960 the internal organization of the Civil Rights movement had amassed resources and organization specifically designed to execute nonviolent confrontations.

The sit-in tactic was well suited to the existing internal organization of the Civil Rights movement. It did not conflict with the procedures, ideology, or resources of the movement centers. Indeed, because the sit-in method was a legitimate tactic of the direct-action approach, it was quickly embraced by activists situated in the movement centers. Because these activists were already attempting to build nonviolent movements, they instantly realized that massive sit-ins could have a wide impact. Furthermore, they were well aware that they were in command of precisely the kinds of resources through which the sit-ins could be rapidly diffused. This is why they phoned activist groups and said, "This is it, let's go!" That is, the sit-ins became a tactical innovation within the movement because they fit into the framework of the existing internal organization.

In conclusion, this paper has attempted to demonstrate the important role that internal organization played in the sit-in movement. It is becoming commonplace for writers (e.g., Hubbard, 1968; Lipsky, 1968; Marx and Useem, 1971; McCarthy and Zald, 1973; Oberschall, 1973) to assert that the Civil Rights movement was dependent on outside resources: elites, courts, Northern white liberals, mass media, and the Federal Government. The present analysis suggests that this assertion may be premature, especially when the role of internal organization is ignored. Future research on collective action that treats internal organization as a topic in its own right will further increase our knowledge of the dynamics of social movements.

REFERENCES

Baker, Ella. 1978. Interview. New York, New York.

Bevel, Diane Nash. 1978. Interview. Chicago, Illinois. December 14.

Bevel, James. 1978. Interview. New York, New York. December 27.

Blumer, H. 1946. "Collective Behavior." Pp. 165–220 in A. M. Lee (ed.), New Outline of the Principles of Sociology. New York: Barnes & Noble.

Bond, Julian. 1980. Interview. Ann Arbor, Michigan. October 19.

Carey, Gordon. 1959. Report to CORE National Council. February 21– 22.

Carey, Gordon. 1978. Interview. Soul City, North Carolina. November 18 (Follow-up telephone interview November 1, 1979).

Coleman, James S., Eliher Katz, and Herbert Menzel. 1957. "The diffusion of an innovation among physicians." Sociometry 20:253– 70.

Frazier, E. Franklin. 1963. The Negro Church in America. New York: Schocken Books.

Gamson, William A. 1975. The Strategy of Social Protest. Homewood, Illinois: Dorsey Press.

Haber, Robert A. 1966. "From protest to radicalism: an appraisal of the student struggle 1960." Pp. 41–9 in Mitchell Cohen and Dennis Hale (eds.), The New Student Left. Boston: Dorsey.

Hubbard, Howard. 1968. "Five long hot summers and how they grew." Public Interest 12:3–24.

Jemison, Rev. T. J. 1978. Interview. Baton Rouge, Louisiana. October 16.

Jenkins, J. Craig and Charles Perrow. 1977. "Insurgency of the powerless: farm workers movements (1946–1972)." American Sociological Review 42:249–68.

Killian, Lewis M. 1968. The Impossible Revolution? New York: Random House.

Lang, Kurt and Gladys Lang. 1961. Collective Dynamics. New York: Crowell.

Lawson, James. 1978. Interview. Los Angeles, California, October 2 and 6.

Lewis, John. 1978. Interview. Washington, D.C. November 9.

Lewis, Chester. 1981. Interview. Wichita, Kansas. February 3.

Lionberger, H. F. 1960. Adoption of New Ideas and Practices. Ames : The Iowa State University Press.

Lipset, Seymour Martin and Sheldon S. Wolin. 1965. The Berkeley Student Revolt. Garden City, New York: Doubleday.

Lipsky, Michael. 1968. "Protest as a political resource." American Political Science Review 62:1114–58.

Lomax, Louis E. 1962. The Negro Revolt. New York: New American Library.

Luper, Clara. 1979. Behold the Walls. Jim Wire.

Luper, Clara. 1980. Interview. Oklahoma City, Oklahoma. (Follow-up interview, January 1981).

Marx, Gary T. and Michael Useem. 1971. "majority involvement in minority movements: civil rights, abolition, untouchability." Journal of Social Issues 27:81–104.

Mays, Benjamin and Joseph W. Nicholson. 1933. The Negro's Church. New York: Arno Press and the New York Times.

Matthews, Donald and James Prothro. 1966. Negroes and the New Southern Politics. New York: Harcourt, Brace,and World.

McAdam, Douglas. 1979. "Political process and the civil rights movement 1948–1962." Ph.D. dissertation. Department of Sociology, State University of New York at Stony Brook.

McCain, James. 1978. Interview. Sumter, South Carolina. November 18.

McCarthy, J. D. and M. N. Zald. 1973. The Social Trends of Social Movements in America: Professionalism and Resource Mobilization. Morristown, N.J.: General Learning Press.

McCollom, Rev. Matthew. 1979. Interview. Orangeburg, South Carolina. October 31.

McKissick, Floyd. 1978. Interview. Soul City, North Carolina. November 18 (Follow-up telephone interview November 2, 1979).

McPhail, Clark. 1971. "Civil disorder participation: a critical examination of recent research." American Sociological Review 36:1058–73.

McPhail, Clark. 1973. "The assembling process: a theoretical and empirical examination." American Sociological Review 38:721–35.

Meier, August and Elliot Rudwick. 1966. From Plantation to Ghetto. New York: Hill and Wang.

Meier, August and Elliot Rudwick. 1973. CORE A study in the Civil Rights Movement 1942–1968. Oxford University Press.

Meier, August and Elliot Rudwick. 1976. Along the Color Line. University of Illinois Press.

Moore, Douglas. 1960. Journal and Guide. Vol. LX, March 5, 1960.

Moore, Douglas. 1978. Interview. Washington, D.C. November 1.

Morris, Aldon. 1980. "The origins of the civil rights movement: an indigenous perspective." Ph.D. dissertation, Department of Sociology, State University of New York at Stony Brook.

Morris, Aldon. forthcoming. Origins of the Civil Rights Movement. New York: Free Press.

Obear, Frederick W. 1970. "Student activism in the sixties." Pp. 11–26 in Julian Foster and Durward Long (eds.), Protest: Student Activism in America 1970. New York: William Morrow.

Oberschall, Anthony. 1973. Social Conflict and Social Movements. Englewood Cliffs, N.J.: Prentice-Hall.

Oppenheimer, Martin. 1964. "The southern student movement: year 1." Journal of Negro Education 33:396–403.

Piven, Frances Fox, and Richard A. Cloward. 1977. Poor People's Movements. New York: Vintage.

Randolph, Homer. 1981. Interview. East St. Louis, Illinois.

Rogers, Everett M. 1962. Diffusion of Innovations. New York: The Free Press of Glencoe.

Sale, Kirkpatrick. 1973. SDS. New York: Vintage.

Shuttlesworth, Rev. Fred. 1978. Interview. Cincinnati, Ohio. September 12.

Smelser, Neil J. 1963. Theory of Collective Behavior. New York: Free Press.

Smith, Rev. Kelly Miller. 1978. Interview. Nashville, Tennessee. October 13.

Southern Regional Council. 1960. "The student protest movement, winter 1960." SRC-13, April 1.

Student Nonviolent Coordinating Committee. 1960. The Student Voice. August.

Tilly, Charles. 1978. From Mobilization to Revolution. Reading, Massachusetts: AddisonWesley.

Tilly, Charles, Louise Tilly, and Richard Tilly. 1975. The Rebellious Century 1830–1930. Cambridge, Massachusetts: Harvard University Press.

Turner, Ralph and Lewis Killian. 1957. Collective Behavior. Englewood Cliffs, N.J.: Prentice-Hall.

Von Eschen, Donald, Jerome Kirck, and Maurice Pinard. 1971. "The organizational substructure of disorderly politics." Social Forces 49:529–44.

Walker, Rev. Wyatt Tee. 1978. Interview. New York City, New York. September 29.

Westby, David L. 1976. The Clouded Vision: The Student Movement in the United States in the 1960s. London: Associated University Press.

Williams, Hosea. 1978. Interview. Atlanta, Georgia. September 22.

Wolff, Miles. 1970. Lunch at the Five and Ten. New York: Stien and Day.

Zinn, Howard. 1964. SNCC: The New Abolitionists. Boston: Beacon.

ARTICLE 30

Protest and the Problem of Credibility: Uses of Knowledge and Risk-Taking in the Draft Resistance Movement of the 1960's

BARRIE THORNE

. . . This is a comparison of different strategies of persuasion used by groups within the same movement. In Boston there were two organizations which were part of the Resistance, the nationwide movement which, from 1967–69, protested the draft and the Vietnam War (on the history of the Resistance, see Ferber and Lynd, 1971; Useem, 1973; Thorne, 1971). The groups shared a common origin and ideology, but differed in strategies and tactics. The Boston Draft Resistance Group used draft counseling (the offering of expert knowledge), and the New England Resistance used non-cooperation with the craft (encouraging risk-taking) to confront the federal government (the protest target), to mobilize participants, and the focus of this analysis to seek attention and credibility with outsiders.

This study is based on active participation, and observation, in the draft resistance movement in Boston between March, 1968, when the movement was building toward its peak, and July, 1969, when the Resistance was very much on the decline. I took an active role in both movement groups, and did not disguise the fact that I was doing research in addition to being a participant committed to the goals of the movement (for a discussion of the ethical and political problems involved, see Thorne, 1971).

DESCRIPTION OF THE TWO STRATEGIES

Draft Counseling: The Uses of Knowledge

The Boston Draft Resistance Group (B.D.R.G.) grew out of the New Left philosophy of community organizing, previously tried in Southern civil rights work and among the urban poor. B.D.R.G. organizers hoped to reach poor and working-class people, especially the draft eligible, and to use the draft issue to draw them into opposition to the Vietnam War, imperialism, and the structure of American society. To make contact with Selective Service registrants, B.D.R.G. workers canvassed from lists of 1=A's (a draft classification meaning "available for induction") and at pre-induction physicals, and—the central tactic—provided draft counseling.

Draft counseling involved compiling and disseminating extensive knowledge about Selective Service rules, regulations, and informal operating procedures information of great practical value to those "uptight with the draft," and hoping somehow to evade or resist conscription. B.D.R.G. expertise included knowledge of official regulations, and the accumulated wisdom of actual experience, gleaned from thousands of individual cases handled by the counseling group. For example, B.D.R.G. counselors knew if a given local draft board was easy or tough on conscientious objector applications, or what sort of evidence was most effective in getting a physical deferment. They offered practical tips which one could never learn from official sources, for example, "If you can get a peek at the form the last doctor fills out at the pre-induction physical, here's how you can tell if you flunked. . . ."

Offering this information through formal and informal draft counseling was a way of demystifying the Selective Service. It also provided the "bait" for bringing registrants to the B.D.R.G. office and into contact with the movement. In counseling sessions, B.D.R.G. workers combined technical information with political education, trying to "radicalize" those they talked with and to persuade them—however their individual draft situations turned out—actively to oppose the draft and the war. B.D.R.G. workers saw themselves primarily as political organizers, but technical expertise was essential in establishing their initial credibility with potential recruits and sympathizers.

Non-Cooperation: The Uses of Risk-Taking

The guiding vision of the early New England Resistance (N.E.R.) and other non-cooperation groups around the country was both simple and powerful: What if they gave a war and nobody came? If enough draft-age men refused to serve, the war and the draft would end. Even if they didn't get enough non-cooperators directly to stop the war, Resistance leaders hoped that by acting in a public and dramatic way, non-cooperators would embarrass the government and create a wave of national indignation. They provoked public confrontation with the government in order to spur more and more people into protest.

The taking of risks was essential to this strategy. The acts of non-cooperation—refusal to register, to carry a draft card, or to accept induction—carry a penalty of up to 5 years in prison and a $10,000 fine. The N.E.R. sought to increase the number and visibility of non-cooperators and to draw individual risk-takers into a community of support. This was partly done by staging public events built around these acts of risk: a series of draft card turn-ins, demonstrations for those refusing induction and coming to trial, and "symbolic sanctuaries" for indicted draft resisters and A.W.O.L. soldiers. The N.E.R. worked to mobilize large groups and to attract extensive media coverage for these events. Acts of risk were used to challenge the Selective Service System, to draw attention to the movement, and to claim legitimacy for organized opposition to the war and the draft.

THE PROCESS OF PERSUASION

One of the central goals of the Resistance was to reach outside audiences: to make new, active recruits to the movement (especially from among the draft-eligible); to gain political, financial, and other kinds of support from sympathetic third parties; to become widely publicized as a movement; and to persuade more and more people to oppose the war, the draft, and their underlying causes. The B.D.R.G. and the N.E.R. shared these goals, but their styles of proselytizing differed in ways closely tied to their different protest strategies.

Gaining Access to Outsiders

The first step of persuasion is to gain the attention of outsiders who might otherwise be apathetic, indifferent, or hostile to one's message. This is the process Lofland (1966) conceptualizes in terms of embodied and disembodied strategies of access.

Although members of both Resistance groups made personal, or embodied, contact with outsiders, this style of proselytizing was more strongly emphasized by the Boston Draft Resistance Group. The central B.D.R.G. activities—draft counseling, canvassing from lists of 1-A's and talking with registrants at pre-induction physicals—all facilitated personal contact with outsiders. The New England Resistance emphasis on staging large, well-publicized events (demonstrations, draft card turn-ins, sanctuaries), replete with extensive leafletting and media coverage, entailed a more indirect, or disembodied form of contact with the public. Around Resistance circles it was often said that the N.E.R. was "media-oriented" and geared to creating "spectacles." In contrast, the B.D.R.G. was more low-key, routine, and workaday.

The Use of Knowledge to Gain Access

To make personal contact with outsiders, B.D.R.G. organizers devised ways to accost strangers and solicit encounters which could be turned to proselytizing purposes. B.D.R.G. workers regularly showed up at local draft boards on days when pre-induction physicals were scheduled, to talk with registrants waiting for the bus which would take them to the army base, where physicals were held (this project was known as the "Early Morning Show"). The organizers capitalized on the fact that most registrants were anxious, curious, and uncertain about what to expect; they were in an exposed position, relatively open to being approached by strangers (Goffman, 1963:125–128). Posing as pre-inductees, male B.D.R.G. workers would accost waiting registrants and engage them in what initially sounded like idle talk ("Goin' for your physical today? Think you can get out?"), but which could be turned into a proselytizing chat. Mutual accessibility was facilitated by the appearance of being in the same boat, of both being in a cohort going through a pre-induction physical. Female B.D.R.G. workers were more visibly outsiders, since women (except for draft board clerks) are rarely present at any stage of the pre-induction physical. Women organizers usually began encounters with pre-inductees by explaining their presence and implicitly offering help ("I'm from a group that does draft counseling."), but, not infrequently, the registrants they accosted implied that the encounter had the sexual overtones which seem to go with women soliciting in public places. Female activists often found themselves in a marginal and ambiguous position (Throne, 1975).

Goffman (1963:127) points to the special accessibility of an individual who is in "patent need of help." Registrants obviously vulnerable to the draft had anxieties which the B.D.R.G. equipped itself to meet, and by eliciting problems and offering services, organizers found a way to establish contact with strangers. The typical Early Morning Show pitch involved bringing out a problem ("Are you 1-A?" "Do you have any physical conditions that might get you out?") and then suggesting that the movement could provide solutions ("if you come to our office, we can tell you how to appeal a 1-A . . ."). By being knowledgeable about the Selective Service and the special dilemmas of draft-age men, Resistance organizers found a way to accost outsiders and to engage their interests.

These proselytizing expeditions met with mixed success. Some registrants ignored or rejected the overtures of B.D.R.G. organizers; conversations sometimes developed into heated arguments about the Vietnam War or the anti-war movement. Even if a friendly conversation ensued, it was never clear if one's efforts had made an impact.

The Use of Risk-Taking to Gain Access

In contrast with the person-to-person approach of the B.D.R.G., the New England Resistance used strategies of access which were more colorful, spectacular, and theatric. Demonstrations, marches, and sanctuaries drew attention to the Resistance movement and helped publicize its issues. These events, in contrast with the more muted and less newsworthy style of draft counseling, often drew media coverage, which brought anti-draft protest to the attention of mass audiences, as well as physical onlookers.

Risk-taking enhanced the dramatic appeal of N.E.R. events, and helped draw the attention of outsiders. Acts of non-cooperation were unexpected, fateful, and to many, inexplicable. When the risk was assumed voluntarily, and by people whom it was difficult to discredit on other grounds, the acts assumed even greater significance. During a meeting to plan support for indicted men, a resister spoke of the "shock value" of non-cooperation:

> *Here us straight, middle-class guys from the suburbs are getting ready to go to prison, to become felons, to wear uniforms and be known by a number, it surprises people. . . . When we talk to student audiences, it gives them pause to realize that several years ago we were also neatly secured with 2-S [student] deferments, and here we are.*

Acts of risk-taking raise the implicit question: "Why would a person do a thing like that?" This curiosity became a foot in the door, a point of initial contact between the N.E.R. and outsiders. Risk helped create a platform for resisters to explain their motives, describe their intentions, and to present the Resistance message. In the same meeting, a resister spoke of the access to outsiders which his jeopardy provided:

> *You can really use your situation to rap to people. Like back in my hometown I'll go into a grocery store and be rapping with Mrs. Jones. She'll say 'What are you doing these days?' And I'll say 'Getting ready to go to trial on May 3rd.' It really blows their minds, and we have great discussions.*

Establishing Credibility

Gaining access to outside parties is only the first step in the process of persuasion; access and attention are not equivalent to agreement, sympathy, or even to being taken seriously. The next step of persuasion involves establishing credibility and gaining a respectful hearing, rather than being rejected, ridiculed, or quickly ignored.

Other parties—Selective Service and court officials, political antagonists, and hostile outsiders—were quick to impute discrediting motives to opponents of the war and the draft. Outsiders referred to non-cooperators as "cowards," "draft dodgers," "draft evaders," "criminals," "communists," and "fools." The Resistance continually sought to counter these discrediting labels, to persuade outsiders that opposition to the war and the draft was a just, a rightful position, and that those who protested and resisted conscription were heroes rather than cowards or criminals.

Knowledge and Credibility

The Boston Draft Resistance Group used expertise to claim credibility in the eyes of the public. B.D.R.G. organizers "knew what they were talking about"; they often excelled even Selective Service officials in their detailed, technical knowledge about the draft; they were also well-informed about the history of American involvement in the Vietnam War.

Draft counselors sought to establish legitimacy and to gain a clientele, which was also a potential constituency, through devices which many professions have used in gaining a special niche in society (see Hughes, 1971; Freidson, 1970). They claimed a special body of expert knowledge and skill, gained through a period of formal training (the B.D.R.G. ran regular training sessions and informal apprenticeships for new draft counselors). Of course, draft counselors lacked formal certification or license, and their training period was brief; they did not call themselves "professionals" ("professionalism" was a pejorative term around the movement); their services were free; and being a draft counselor was rarely a central or prolonged source of personal identity. But draft counselors did develop a strong sense of being experts, of developing and offering skilled knowledge, and of taking responsibility for individual cases much as professionals take on clients.

B.D.R.G. expertise was widely acknowledged in the Boston area. On busy days as many as 30 draft registrants would come in person to the B.D.R.G. office for information, and numerous others telephoned for advice. A major Boston newspaper ran a column of draft information and advice written by two B.D.R.G. counselors; it was seen as a coup for the Resistance that the newspaper asked the anti-draft movement, rather than Selective Service officials, to write the column.

Risk-Taking and Credibility

While the B.D.R.G. used knowledge to establish legitimacy with outsiders, the N.E.R. relied more on risk-taking. Many draft resisters assumed risk voluntarily, by giving up or refusing to seek deferments. This voluntary assumption of risk expressed strong individual commitment to opposing the war and the draft (the rhetoric of non-cooperation included phrases like "show the sincerity of our beliefs" and "this movement is worth my life"). Non-cooperators were intent on explaining and justifying their acts, on showing the public that they protested the war and the draft on moral and political grounds, and not out of private or selfish motives.

Resisters used every occasion to put forward their statements of motive, their reasons for refusing to cooperate with the draft. Draft card turn-ins, induction refusal demonstrations, and trials gave resisters public forums for explaining and justifying their acts, and elaborating the Resistance perspective.

The fact of risk became a way of claiming legitimacy, of giving weight to "raps" against the war and the draft, since "communications media and potential allies will consider more soberly the complaints of people who are understood to be placing themselves in jeopardy" (Lipsky, 1968:1150). One of the founders of the N.E.R. expressed a belief held by many resisters:

> *Turning in my card put me in a position to organize other guys, to talk to people from my own situation of jeopardy.*

Another resister talked about the persuasive impact of his position of risk:

> *I do a lot of public speaking for the Resistance, and sometimes there are hecklers there. But it's the hecklers who often stay around the longest afterwards, and we've had some incredibly good talks. My having turned in my card gives credibility to what I say. They see that I'm willing to jeopardize myself. I could have a deferment, probably two deferments: I'm legally deaf in one ear, which is an automatic 4-F, and as a Quaker and a pacifist, I could probably get a C.O.*

It was often claimed that being in jeopardy was of special value in reaching those groups (such as soldiers, and working-class registrants with limited access to deferments) who themselves ran unusual risks because of the war and the draft.

CONTRASTING STYLES OF PERSUASION

To be most effective in persuading outsiders to join or become sympathetic with a movement, should the proselytizers minimize differences between themselves and those they hope to reach? Or should they set themselves apart, establishing a visible alternative and evoking a partisan response? This debate dominated many tactical discussions within the anti-war movement, and was a point of tension within the Resistance. The protest strategies of the B.D.R.G. and the N.E.R. involved contrasting styles of persuasion. Draft counseling, or the offering of expert service on a person-to-person basis, involved minimizing differences and bridging the gap between B.D.R.G. organizers and those they sought to reach. In contrast, the acts of risk which were central to the large, media-oriented events of the N.E.R., tended to set non-cooperators apart and to encourage a more polarizing style of persuasion.

Implicit in the B.D.R.G. strategy was an assumption that persuasion is most effective when there is a common ground, a basis for identification, between proselytizers and their audience. The B.D.R.G. sought especially to reach draft registrants from working-class communities, who, ineligible for many special deferments and lacking middle-class know-how to evade the draft, carried a disproportionate burden on the draft and the war. Realizing that these groups were often alienated by long hair and other symbols of the counter-culture, B.D.R.G. workers avoided flamboyant styles of appearance and manner. They talked about the importance of "learning to speak the idiom of those we are trying to reach." With relatively short hair and a generally "straight" appearance, B.D.R.G. workers could pose as pre-inductees, and more easily make contact with registrants at draft boards and at the army base.

In proselytizing expeditions. B.D.R.G. organizers often used what Lofland (1966) calls "covert presentations." The message was muted, and various phrases (such as "draft resistance") were withheld to avoid alienating the listener before contact had been established. Those who went on Early Morning Show expeditions or canvassed registrants often presented themselves as draft counselors, as technical specialists in the problems of draft-age men. Expertise provided entree. The political pitch, the Resistance message, came later.

In contrast, New England Resistance presentations were typically more overt, involving sharp differentiation from outsiders. Some referred to the "shock tactics" of the N.E.R. whose members were set apart from other draft registrants by the fact of being non-cooperators, of having violated the law. They also tended to dress and live in the ways of the counter-culture; being "hip" was a subtle but important criterion for acceptance in the central core of the N.E.R. The N.E.R. mode of dress tended to long hair and scruffy clothes, with touches of flair and self-expression, and ever-present political buttons. Buttons (the omega, the national symbol of draft resistance, and special buttons issued for demonstrations) became a form of mobile political advertising, raising questions ("What does the omega mean?" "Why does that say April 3rd?"), and provoking response ("You're a resister are you? Well, I'm with you!"; "Why don't you go back to Russia where you belong!").

N.E.R. events tended to force partisanship. Demonstrations, draft card turn-ins, marches, and sanctuaries were public events which set participants (who in a sense became performers) apart from on-lookers or media audiences. These events were not intended to be passively watched or consumed; they were partly staged for persuasive effect, to force people to take sides and thereby enlist them in the protest cause.

While B.D.R.G. members muted differences between themselves and those they hoped to reach, N.E.R. activists "testified in and out of season," provoking a partisan response. Two events, where people from both Resistance groups were present, illustrate these contrasting ways of approaching third parties and potential recruits. One was a fancy cocktail party given in a suburban home to raise money for the legal defense of draft resisters. People from both the B.D.R.G. and N.E.R. were invited, free, although the other guests paid for admission and drinks as part of the fund-raising. These guests ("rich liberals from the suburbs," they were typed in Resistance circles) were important allies for the movement, although they were sometimes regarded with cynicism. The B.D.R.G. contingent arrived on time and in apparel presentable in the straight world: the women wore dresses, and the men wore suits, or at least a spruced-up demeanor. N.E.R. people came late, wearing their usual scruffy clothes, and looking haggard and preoccupied. The Arlington Street Church sanctuary was in process, and they made it clear that the cocktail party was a brief interlude, a Movement duty before returning to the scene of the action. While the B.D.R.G. group mingled, making polite conversation with the guests, N.E.R. people brought Resistance literature, leaflets, and political buttons to sell and hand around.

The other incident took place at the army base, in an early joint effort to infiltrate and to reach registrants going through pre-induction physicals. A report of this event in the October, 1967 N.E.R. newsletter acknowledged the contrasting styles of the two groups:

> *Unblessed, as an organization, with respectable and/or officious looking guys, we [the N.E.R.] did not manage to get anybody inside the Army Base. They asked for our papers when the bus stopped at the gates. We showed them our drivers' licenses, high school honor society cards, etc., but*

this is not what they had in mind. We got thrown off the bus. The B.D.R.G. got lots of people on, being blessed with a number of respectable, officious, etc. guys. Like Roger King, who dressed up in a khaki shirt and made it past 12 guards by explaining to each in a loud military voice that he was going in to inquire about his 'reserve points.' We were jealous. But we got good publicity. Of the 173 pictures taken of the demonstration outside the gates, most showed the 'October 16' button worn by people from the [N.E.R. The button advertised the first draft card turn-in]. . . . One of these appeared in the Boston Globe on September 13th, page 24. The rest were taken by Army Base security officers, and will not immediately be made available to the general public.

In short, in contacts with outsiders B.D.R.G. workers sought to blend in, to proselytize in an unobtrusive, person-to-person manner. N.E.R. workers were more visible. They sought to polarize, rather than to build identification through compromise, and they were more oriented to the media. The demands of the media for events that were unusual, dramatic, and visually interesting helped shape the differentiating style of the N.E.R.

HOW THE STRATEGIES WORKED OUT OVER TIME

How successful were these various tactics for gaining attention, establishing credibility, and making converts? Part of the frustration of the movement was that it was difficult to determine success. Through Early Morning Shows, draft counseling, and other projects, the B.D.R.G. made contact with thousands of registrants. But few became active B.D.R.G. members, an it was difficult to know how many others were politicized or drawn into even partial sympathy with the movement point of view. During its peak of activity, the N.E.R. achieved media coverage and became widely known. But publicity must be distinguished from persuasion, and it was impossible to gauge the impact of the Resistance on mass audiences. Each strategy had built-in strains which became apparent over time; the strategies inevitably fell short of the original visions behind them. All of this contributed to the eventual demise of the movement.

Problems with the Strategy of Draft Counseling

Draft counseling, the core activity of the B.D.R.G., was supposed to combine technical information with a political message. The service aspect of counseling involved drawing on expert knowledge to help registrants with their individual draft problems. The counseling also had a political purpose: to persuade counselees to protest the war and the draft.

B.D.R.G. counselors sought ways to give a political thrust to their conversations with registrants, by relating specific anxieties to their institutional causes and by turning the conversation to topics like the Vietnam War and American imperialism. But B.D.R.G. counselors often found that this kind of talk came across as forced, artificial and manipulative, and that counselees were unresponsive. Counseling sessions vacillated between technical and political content, and less politically committed counselors often avoided the political side. It was difficult to be a technical expert and a missionary at the same time, especially when one's clients wanted technical advice but not a radical testimony.

It was the political side of B.D.R.G. draft counseling which justified the activity in the eyes of the radical movement. It was the service, the technical expertise, which most counselees valued and sought, and which was the basis of much of the legitimacy of the B.D.R.G. in the eyes of outsiders. Some counselors complained (usually outside the B.D.R.G. office) that they got a "heavy political rap" and not enough technical help. Movement critics were prone to voice the opposite complaint: that the B.D.R.G. was merely providing "service counseling" and "had no politics." One leader of the New England Resistance sarcastically referred to the organization as "B.D.R. and G., Counselors."

Draft counselors themselves vacillated between the dual, not always harmonious goals of providing service and proselytizing for a political movement. Some counselors kept score on how many registrants they had helped avoid induction; "I've kept 80 percent of my counselees out!" was a typical proud announcement, which reflected one way of measuring success. But the more seasoned political activists emphasized the goal of radicalizing counselees and noted that getting someone a deferment is not equivalent to making a radical. In those terms, success meant that a counselee was moved towards active opposition to the war and had come to identify with the radical movement—whether or not he received a desired deferment. Although it was difficult to measure political impact, over time more and more people in the B.D.R.G. and other New Left groups began to believe that the B.D.R.G. was primarily a service organization and did not live up to its radical claims.

This opinion was strengthened by the fact that although the group set out to teach working-class and poor communities, in fact most of the B.D.R.G. constituency was middle-class. Estimates varied, but anyone familiar with the B.D.R.G. would admit that at least two-thirds and perhaps as many as 90 percent of all counselees were white, middle-class college students. This fact undercut an early B.D.R.G. rationale: that the organization would spread knowledge about the Selective Service and an anti-war perspective into communities which lacked the tools to avoid being drafted. In the eyes of many radicals, the B.D.R.G. ended up an adjunct to an already privileged social class. This disillusionment—the sense that the B.D.R.G. reached the wrong audience and for the wrong reasons—contributed to the eventual decline of the movement organization.

Problems with Non-Cooperation

The non-cooperation strategy also fell short of the original vision. It did not have the direct and immediate impact on the draft which the N.E.R. founders had envisaged. The estimated 4,000 non-cooperators nationwide (the N.E.R. claimed around 700 non-cooperators in the Boston area) had no apparent effect on the government; the war and the draft continued, with no hint of a manpower shortage. In many ways, the non-cooperation branch of the Resistance resembled a millenarian movement, looking ahead to a movement of great transformation, investing present actions in a hoped-for future hour. But the hour didn't come, and when even the most optimistic had to admit that the draft was in no danger of crumbling, morale collapsed.

Furthermore, for many, perhaps the majority, of those who turned in draft cards, the act did not make a significant personal difference. Many were not heard from again after their initial acts of risk-taking, and there was strong indication that the majority of resisters did not stick with non-cooperation (by asking for a new draft card, accepting a deferment, fleeing to Canada, or submitting to induction). Although the N.E.R. called itself a "club of resisters," most resisters did not opt for full-time moment activity; some seemed to feel that by turning in their draft cards, they had "done their thing to end the war" and were absolved from any further political activity. Gradually N.E.R. leaders began to reconsider the strategy of voluntarily sending large numbers of men to prison, and to wonder if they wouldn't have more political effect by staying out.

The N.E.R. was not always satisfied with its approach to outside audiences. From the beginning, there were those who disagreed with the claim that being a non-cooperator was in itself a persuasive stance. Those concerned with recruiting in non-middle-class communities argued that non-cooperation had limited appeal; they claimed that, more often than not, working-class and black registrants thought resisters foolish to volunteer for jail. Critics of non-cooperation argued that the strategy was moralistic and elitist, and that it thwarted, rather than facilitated reaching outsiders with a political message.

Around Boston movement circles, people often described the N.E.R. as "fixed on staging spectacles," "apocalyptic," and "crisis-oriented."

This group seemed always to be "where it's at," in the center of crisis, risk, and the 6 o'clock news. In its efforts to stay newsworthy, the N.E.R. adopted a theatric style of protest, and shifted rapidly from one type of event to another. After a few draft card turn-ins, the event lost its novelty; the N.E.R. then began to stage sanctuaries, which, in turn ceased to get media coverage after a few months. The N.E.R. sought publicity, exposure, and confrontation; it moved from crisis to crisis with little follow-through or routinization. As a result, it had an unstable relationship to its constituency.

Taken as a whole, the draft resistance movement had difficulty mobilizing individual registrants into a lasting collectivity and building cohesive and growing protest organizations with committed membership. The separate histories of the Boston Draft Resistance Group and the New England Resistance can be analyzed in terms of their central strategies, the problems and strains involved, and gradual moves to disenchantment.

CONCLUSION

This comparison of two groups within the same protest movement— one based on a strategy of risk-taking and the other on disseminating expert knowledge—has shown different methods of approaching outside audiences and trying to persuade them to support the movement. In its bid for credibility, the Boston Draft Resistance Group used person-to-person persuasion, relying on expertise to gain attention and legitimacy. This strategy involved a strain between the offering of technical advice (which was seen as a means to reach outsiders, but which often became the only connection with them) and the protest goal of spreading radical opposition to the war and the draft. In the end, many activists concluded that political purposes had been unduly compromised by efforts to gain credibility.

In contrast, the New England Resistance developed around a strategy which visibly set it apart from outsiders. Non-cooperation with the draft entailed serious personal risks, and the demeanor of resisters, and the large dramatic events which were their forte, conveyed a strongly partisan stance. The non-cooperation strategy succeeded in making the movement visible and in attracting media attention; as an approach to persuasion, it involved forcing choices rather than making compromises. However, some began to conclude that the choice was too often against the Resistance, that non-cooperation set the group too far apart and was not sufficiently persuasive to potential recruits and allies.

Comparison of these two strategies and their implicit strains highlights a dilemma many protest movements have experienced: to gain legitimacy involves the risk of compromising the movement's beliefs and political goals—but to stay apart, to be true to the group's differences with the existing culture, may limit the movement's effectiveness. Wilson (1973:167–8) alludes to the same dilemma:

> *Organizing collective effort to change the world demands acceptance of part of that world as a constraint upon one's own behavior, especially if one belongs to a minority. Social movements are forced to adapt themselves to present social norms and institutions in the ambient society, and yet they must maintain their own sense of apartness and purity, their own distinct identity, to retain membership commitment and avoid the dilution of co-optation.*

This analysis may be extended to other movements with strategies based on the use of expert knowledge, or on risk-taking. Draft counseling is one example of what appears to be a trend: a number of recent social movements have developed forms of counseling, turning a quasi-professional activity towards political objectives. For example, women's liberation groups have established abortion counseling and rape counseling as service activities with a proselytizing dimension, and the National Welfare Rights Organization has counseled those on welfare about ways to work the system (Piven and Cloward, 1971:320–338). This trend seems worthy of further analysis.

Organized protest has often involved risk, especially when movement activities have run counter to the law, or become a focus of social control (Wilson, 1974). There are parallels between the strategic use of risk-taking in the draft resistance movement, the early rights movement (the jeopardy of early Freedom Riders in the south, for example), and the United Farmworkers Movement (the risks undertaken by striking members of the U.F.W.). This deliberate use of risk as part of protest strategies could be compared with the impact of risks unanticipated by movement groups, e.g., the killings at Kent State.

Whatever the chosen strategy, protest movements are up against great odds. They typically confront powerful institutions (in the case of the Resistance, nothing less than the federal government, the military, and the law). The success of protest often depends on gaining recruits and sympathizers from an indifferent or even antagonistic outside world. Yet protest movements do have effects which reach beyond themselves, and in tracing the history of particular protest strategies, one can better understand both social change, and resistance of change.

REFERENCES

Bowers, John Waite and Donovan J. Ochs. 1971. The Rhetoric of Agitation and Control. Reading, Massachusetts: Addison-Wesley.

Burke, Kenneth. 1950. A Rhetoric of Motives. Englewood Cliffs: Prentice-hall.

Ferber, Michael and Staughton Lynd. 1971. The Resistance. Boston: Beacon Press.

Freeman, Jo. 1975. The Politics of Women's Liberation. New York: David McKay.

Freidson, Eliot. 1970. Profession of Medicine. New York: Dodd, Mead & Co.

Gerlach, Luther P. and Virginia H. Hine. 1970. People, Power, Change: Movements of Social Transformation. Indianapolis: Bobbs- Merrill.

Goffman, Erving. 1963. Behavior in Public Places. New York: Free Press.

Hughes, Everett C. 1971. The Sociological Eye: Selected Papers. Chicago: Aldine-Atherton.

Keniston, Kenneth. 1973. Radicals and Militants: An Annotated Bibliography of Empirical Research on Campus Unrest. Lexington, Massachusetts: Lexington Books.

Klumpp, James F. 1973. "Challenge of radical rhetoric: radicalization at Columbia." Western Speech 37 (Summer): 146–156.

Lipsky, Michael. 1968. "Protest as a political resource." American Political Science Review 62 (December): 1144–1158.

Lofland, John. 1966. Doomsday Cult. Englewood Cliffs: Prentice- Hall.

Oberschall, Anthony. 1973. Social Conflict and Social Movements. Englewood Cliffs: Prentice-hall.

Piven, Frances Fox and Richard A. Cloward. 1971. Regulating the Poor: The Functions of Public Welfare. New York: Pantheon.

Scott, Robert L. and Donald K. Smith. 1969. "The rhetoric of confrontation." The Quarterly Journal of Speech 55 (February): 1– 8.

Simons, Herbert W. 1972. "Persuasion in social conflicts: a critique of prevailing conceptions and a framework for future research." Speech Monographs 39 (November): 227–247.

Smelser, Neil J. 1962. Theory of Collective Behavior. New York: The Free Press.

Thorne, Barrie. 1971. Resisting the Draft: An Ethnography of the Draft Resistance Movement. Unpublished Ph.D. dissertation, Brandeis University.

Thorne, Barrie, 1975. "Women in the draft resistance movement: a case study of sex roles and social movements." Sex Roles 1 (June):179–195.

Turner, Ralph H. and Lewis M. Killian. 1972. Collective Behavior (Second Edition). Englewood Cliffs: Prentice-Hall.

Useem, Michael. 1973. Conscription, Protest, and Social Conflict: The Life and Death of a Draft Resistance Movement. New York: Wiley-Interscience.

Wilson, John. 1973. Introduction to Social Movements. New York: Basic Books.

Wilson, John. 1974. "The effects of social control on social movements." Paper presented at 69th annual meeting of American Sociological Association. Montreal, Canada.

ARTICLE 31

Origins and Evolution of a Social Movement Strategy

The Rent Strike in New York City, 1904–1980

RONALD LAWSON

. . . The purpose of this article is to test and expand Tilly's hypotheses concerning the origins and evolution of social movement strategies. Its vehicle is the rent strike as used within the tenant movement in New York City. The rent strike—the concerted withholding of rents by tenants—which was first introduced in 1904, became the dominant strategy of the tenant movement, and to a large extent set its identity. The origins of the strategy and the emergence and diffusion of six key innovations over a 76 year period are described, and then the patterns found are analyzed.

RESEARCH METHODS

Data concerning the tenant movement in New York City were collected during a large study between 1973 and 1980 funded primarily by NIMH. The study had two foci: historical and current. Citywide, local, and ethnic newspapers; and legislative, housing agency, and, where available, tenant organization files were consulted and oral history interviews carried out concerning the historical period. Participant observation, two surveys—one of citywide federation and neighborhood organization leaders, the other of leaders, members and nonmembers in organized buildings—and the tenant press and organization files were the main sources of data concerning the 1970s. Because of its significance to the movement, one of the chief concerns of the research was the rent strike strategy, including its origins, variations, evolution, and effectiveness. Because of this concern, and because the research methods used allowed familiarity with a wide range of tenant organizations over time, the data concerning the evolution of the rent strike are excellent.

DATA

The First Rent Strikes

For half a century before 1904, legislators had fashioned regulations to remedy the reported evils of New York City's overcrowded slums. But the tenants, those immediately affected by these conditions and the high prevailing rent levels, had not protested. Early in the new century, as the flow of immigrants reached toward an all-time peak, thus exacerbating the critical housing shortage and fueling a speculative housing mar-

Lawson, Ronald. (1983, March). Origins and evolution of a social movement strategy: The rent strike in New York City, 1904–1980. *Urban Affairs Quarterly, 18,* 371–395. Reprinted by permission of Sage Publications, Inc.

ket, rent increases became especially frequent. Finally, when in 1904 yet another general increase of 20% to 30% was mooted, the *Daily Forward,* a Yiddish-language socialist newspaper, urged action against the rapacious landlords. The tenants of the Lower East Side Jewish quarter responded by forming "tenant unions" in their buildings, and collectively withholding their rents. Reports during the next month indicated that 800 tenement houses had struck, and that 2000 tenants were threatened with eviction (Joselit, forthcoming).

Although the law recognized no defense for nonpayment of rent, the rent strikers nevertheless exerted considerable leverage against their landlords. Court fees and movers' charges made evictions costly, while the specter of rent losses was raised by the attempts by the lawyer of the new umbrella neighborhood tenant organization to tie up cases in court on technical grounds and by the picketing of buildings to discourage applications from prospective tenants. Consequently, many of the landlords chose to negotiate with their strikers, agreeing to reductions in the proposed increases. Cases were settled rapidly, with the whole strike lasting barely a month.

Similar, much larger and more bitter rent strikes were again triggered by steep rent increases in the winter of 1907–1908, and from 1917 through 1920 (Joselit, forthcoming; Spencer, forthcoming). Because of the size of these actions and the increasing involvement of the Socialist Party, both were interpreted as posing political threats, as well as pressuring landlords individually. So great was the fear generated during the latter period of turmoil, which coincided with the postwar and post-Bolshevik revolution "red scare," that the state legislature introduced rent controls in 1920 in order to defuse the issue.

The Evolving Strategy: Six Innovations

The original form of the rent strike evolved through a series of six innovations.

Innovation I. The first innovation, introduced in the mid-1930s, sharply altered the scope of the typical rent strike. Whereas the initial strikes had been mass actions involving many buildings simultaneously, these strikes were confined typically to a single building seeking to settle its individual problem.

Innovation II. In 1963, strikers began to invoke a law that had in fact been available since 1929, but had only rarely been used (Lipsky, 1970: 137). Recodified routinely as Section 755 of the Real Property Actions and Proceedings Law in 1961, it provided for the placing of rent monies in escrow in court until all violations against a property had been removed.

Innovation III. In 1970, the Metropolitan Council on Housing, the dominant tenant federation in New York City (Lawson, 1982), began to promote the "rolling rent strike," the main purpose of which was to allow tenants to regain control of their withheld rent monies from the courts. Since judges now regularly insisted that rents be deposited in court even when tenants did not evoke a 755 defense, strikers strove to postpone court appearances and to negotiate directly with their landlords. They never pleaded a 755 defense, and if nevertheless ordered to place rents in escrow, they chose instead to pay them directly to the landlord in order to avoid losing control of future rents. They then withheld the next month's rent. The object was to use lengthy court fights and fear of tenants' skipping with owed rents in their possession to persuade landlords to negotiate.

Innovation IV. In the early 1970s, the tenant movement expanded to encompass a broader range of SES groups. However, in spite of real fears of blight and decay encroaching on their neighborhoods, many middle-income tenants regarded the rent strike as too radical a strategy. Consequently, the "rent slowdown" was invented by an organizer working among such tenants.

This was not really a strike, but a strategy whereby tenants held back their rents until the middle of the month, when the tenant leader handed them all to the landlord. For a landlord, it was an eloquent demonstration of tenant togetherness, and therefore also a warning. For tenants, it was in fact an organizational and emotional preparation for a strike should the landlord ignore the warning.

Innovation V. The rolling rent strike as preempted after 1973, when a firm legal basis for rent withholding under conditions of decay or the absence of services gradually emerged, and judges encouraged tenants and landlords to negotiate settlements under the auspices of the court. Landlord-tenant relations had previously been dominated by a traditional understanding of the lease, which was not seen as a contract in common law where a failure by one party to meet his or her obligations would have voided the obligations of the other party. Instead, most leases required tenants to keep paying rents regardless of how the landlord maintained the property. However, by the early 1970s, Warranty of Habitability legislation, incorporating contractlike elements into the law and allowing for rent abatements when the landlords failed to live up to their obligations, had been enacted by several states. The introduction of negotiations into court in New York City was a practical move toward acceptance of a similar position, and case law also began to recognize an "implied warranty of habitability." Finally, the state legislature confirmed the new understanding of the lease as contract in an act introduced in 1975 at the behest of a new politically active federation, the New York State Tenants' Coalition.

Innovation VI. With the spread of housing abandonment and the destruction of their neighborhoods, poor tenants began, in the early 1970s, to form tenant organizations to a larger extent than ever before. Since their chief problems were decay and lack of services, they naturally conducted rent strikes. However, the strategy often failed to gain them meaningful repairs. Instead, after several months they found themselves still cold and their buildings in disrepair, but holding large joint bank accounts. Frequently, too, they were facing final abandonment by landlords who had given up any pretense of providing services or keeping promises, and had also ceased trying to collect rents or to con them into allowing raids on their rent kitties. As frustration mounted, a significant strategic innovation took form: the spending of accumulated rent monies on needed services and repairs. Tenants were taking control of their buildings.

The success of this innovation has resulted in the incorporation of tenant control and even plans for tenant ownership in several programs. Funds, too, have been provided to rehabilitate many of the tenant-controlled buildings.

A Transformed Strategy

In total, these innovations amounted to a transformation of the rent strike strategy:

1. The size and length of the average strike changed drastically. The first strikes were large (with hundreds of buildings involved concurrently), short (sudden-death strikes culminating in a few days), and infrequent (three waves of activity totaling less than 4 years spread over 16 years, with almost no action between). On the other hand, recent strikes have been localized (normally limited to conflict over a single building), much longer (typically lasting at least several months), and frequent (many actions overlapping one another, but not in a concerted manner).

2. The key issues provoking rent strikes have changed and broadened. Initially, rent increases were the focus. But after rent issues were politicized to the point where they were dealt with mainly in the legislative sphere, the foci of strikes shifted to decay in building condition, absence of services, and the refusal of a landlord to recognize the tenant organization in his building.

3. The way in which rent monies are used as leverage has passed thorough several distinct phases. Initially, strikes culminated quickly in court or through direct negotiations. Later, monies were placed in court pending the making of repairs. Then the rolling rent strike had tenants begin the withholding process again and again in order to retain control of their money; the slowdown was not a strike, but a joint delay of payment; and the Warranty of Habitability finally legitimated the use of rent withholding as a bargaining tool, while those for whom no bargain was possible jointly used their rents to purchase needed services and repairs. Today, tenants in many buildings spend their rent or use it in court to bargain for repairs. Some more timid tenants continue to invoke the rent slowdown.

4. The typical locus of leverage has varied from a decision imposed at a court hearing; to negotiations in court corridors, or arbitrated by a judge, or entirely separate from the courts; to direct assumption of control of buildings.

5. Ancillary tactics increasing the leverage of the rent strike strategy have developed over time. Initially, they were limited to rallies and picketing, which fell into what Lofland and Fink (1982:4) define as "symbolic protests," the lowest of their four subdivisions of protest politics. Later, harassment of landlord targets was added—directly through picketing their homes and distributing leaflets to their neighbors, and indirectly by pressuring the banks holding mortgages on their properties to act on the clause that threatens foreclosure if a building is not properly maintained. This strategy falls within Lofland and Fink's "interventions," the third of their categories. Finally, tenant control of their buildings establishes alternate institutions, defined as the highest level of system challenge. This is only true, however, if official sanction is not received.

6. Over time, the rent strike was transformed from what was perceived as a revolutionary threat to a mechanism for redress of grievances recognized in law and official programs. Its practice was routinized through the adoption of standard formats (such as those detailed in organizing manuals), and as it acquired its own jurisprudence (both laws and bureaucracies). Moreover, its participants eventually included representatives of the entire SES spectrum of the tenant population. During this period, the rent strike "lost much of its expressive function, its festive air, its revolutionary potential"; but it also became "a much more widely accessible, less risky way of making demands" (Tilly, 1978:147). As such, its progress parallels that of the earlier French labor strike. Its symbolic meaning had been transformed.

ANALYSIS

Classifying the Rent Strike Strategy

In his detailed system, Sharp (1973:226) classifies rent withholding under the general heading of "methods of economic noncooperation," subheading "economic boycotts," subsection "action by consumers." Here it is listed with various forms of consumer boycott. However, while the typical boycott involves a decision not to purchase, rent strikers withhold payment for housing they are already inhabiting. Subjectively, New York rent strikers have not thought of themselves as akin to consumer boycotters—their analogy is much more likely to be the labor strike. Lofland and Fink's (1982) more general system places them in such company within "noncooperation," the second of their four categories. But again there is a key difference between the two strategies: While typical striking workers withdraw their labor from the workplace and lose their wages, rent strikers continue to live in their dwellings while withholding payment for them. They accumulate bargaining leverage with the landlord in the rent owed, while at the same time there is an implied threat that they could skip without paying, and so escape housing costs for the period of the strike.

Thus the rent strike overlaps Turner's (1970) elemental categories both sequentially and concurrently. A sequence may begin with attempts at persuasion, as tenants perhaps send letters to their landlord asking attention to their grievances. When there is no effective response, they may add coercion in the form of the threat of a rent strike. An actual strike contains both the bargaining and coercive elements outlined above.

Why Was This Strategy Selected?

There is no evidence that New York tenants, as such, joined together in protest prior to 1904 (Joselit, forthcoming; Heskin, 1981). consequently, they had no strategic repertoire of their own, although many strategies were in use around them and were no doubt being used by the tenants themselves in other roles. When they finally acted, why did tenants create a new strategy rather than select one of those in use around them? What are the roots of the rent strike?

Piven and Cloward's (1977:14) explanation of how strategies are chosen from the array available—that choices are "determined by the institutional context in which people lie and work"—fits this situation excellently. (The fit of the theory may not be as good when intervention strategies such as sit-ins are employed, but it has high explanatory power for strategies of noncooperation.) Tenants were experiencing exploitation, in the form of sharp rent increases, in their homes, and this focused discontent on the rapacious landlords, whom they saw as profiteering from their distress. As tenants, they were aggregated in buildings where they had opportunities to get to know one another, to discuss their antipathies toward their common landlord, and to develop common identities as the tenants of their building (Lawson and Barton, 1980:238–239). And since the main duty expected of them in their role of tenant was to pay rent, this became the obvious focal point for defiance.

Although there had been bitter rent strikes by farmers in the Hudson River Valley a half century earlier (Heskin, 1981:186), there is no sign that these urban tenants were aware of this precedent. But they were very familiar with labor unions, and had often, as members of the United Hebrew Trades, engaged in labor strikes. This was the strategy that they borrowed. Their self-consciousness in this is illustrated by the name they gave the organizations they formed in their buildings: "tenant unions." These organizations naturally became the basic unit of their movement (Lawson, 1982).

The rent strike spread rapidly from building to building within the Jewish quarter because many tenants were confronted with large rent increases concurrently, and because of the preexisting social structures within that community (Morris, 1981:746). These included synagogues and other Jewish institutions, the Socialist Party and its Yiddish press, and labor unions such as the United Hebrew Trades.

Explaining the Evolution of the Strategy

Why did the rent strike evolve in the manner recounted above? . . .

Changing Issues. The evolution of the strategy was linked to changes in the issues to which the strikes were responding. This was because the various forms of strike did not match different goals equally. The first strikes responded to across-the-board rent increases, which invited mass action. But after 1920 the main direct tenant-landlord confrontations shifted to service and maintenance crises, which were normally building-specific. Still later, tenants had to cope with advanced decay and abandonment. These concerns were matched, respectively, by the mass strike, the various forms of single building strikes, and the taking control of rent money expenditure.

Changes in the Economic and Political Context. When the Great Depression caused a rapid rise in the vacancy rate, it gave rent strikes greater leverage because landlords realized that it could be difficult to replace evicted tenants. The Depression also made the locally elected judges more sympathetic to the complaints of tenants. This period was therefore an opportune time to introduce the single building strike, which clearly lacked the political impact of the earlier mass strikes. Similarly, the background of the burgeoning civil rights movement in 1963 not only allowed Jesse Gray to find response to his organizing among Harlem's tenants (he had been working with them with little success for 10 years prior to that), but it also prepared third parties to enter as "conscience constituents" (Monti, 1979; Lipsky, 1970: 172). However, the most significant change in the economic and political context was the growing crisis over housing abandonment after 1965, which in 15 years destroyed over 200,000 apartments in New York City (Lowry, 1970:3; Salins, 1980:1). This crisis created shared concern between the tenant movement and the city government, which was eager to preserve the housing stock from further decay. These shared interests prepared the way for the acceptance of innovations that allowed strikers to win repairs, such as the various forms of putting rent monies into court pending repair, the acceptance of the legitimacy of rent withholding as a bargaining mechanism when seeking repairs, the spending of rent monies directly on repairs, and the espousal of tenant control and ownership in management and rehabilitation programs with large budgets.

Changes in the Legal/Judicial Context. When the first strike broke out in 1904, New York law already required landlords to go to court in order to evict tenants. Since the strikers also saw themselves as emulating the labor movement, it is not surprising that as the rent strike evolved, it became closely related to legal machinery, litigation, and legislation. The legal environment included being able to quash a warrant of eviction for nonpayment of rent at any time preceding its execution, an important protection for strikers, especially those in single building actions; the rules for proper service of an eviction notice; the protection of tenant activists from retaliatory eviction after 1943 under the provisions of New York's various rent regulations; and the various defenses for nonpayment, beginning with jurisdictional questions and evolving over a 50-year period from the transformation of constructive eviction in 1929 to the Warranty of Habitability decisions and legislation in the 1970s. Changes in the attitudes of judges also impinged on the effectiveness of various strike forms. For example, after the reorganization of the courts abolished local court districts in 1962, judges became much more concerned with enforcing the letter of the law, and focused hearings on the question of whether or not rents had been paid. This left the tenant lawyers in 1963–1964 with few legal alternatives to the defense of Section 755, which placed rents in escrow pending repairs. In the 1930s, however, the locally elected judges often used their influence to persuade landlords to compromise with strikers; and judges in the new Housing Court after 1973, rather than finding for one party, often sent both sides into the corridors to negotiate and then recorded the settlements arrived at.

Previous Forms No Longer Adequate. Innovations were often introduced after previous strike forms ceased to be effective. One example was just mentioned: Strikers invoked Section 755 when judges no longer worked for compromise in court. But 755 also proved to have disadvantages: It reduced the leverage of the strikers, since there was no longer danger that they would skip with the withheld rents; oftentimes only token repairs were made; and landlords received all the money of tenants who moved or paid late, even when no repairs had been done. Eventually the Metropolitan Council, the federation that had originally helped to promote Section 755, declared such provisions "strikebreakers to avoid," and devised the rolling rent strike in its place (Shiliom, 1971:39). But landlords then proved unwilling to recognize tenant organizations and negotiate with them out of court (which was the object of the new strategic form), and the courts became clogged at a time when action was desperately needed to stem housing deterioration. Consequently, tenant lawyers and judges cooperated to facilitate negotiations in court by recognizing an implied Warranty of Habitability, which had the effects of securing recognition for building organizations and legalizing the rent strike. This innovation in turn, quickly proved inadequate for tenants facing abandonment. The tenants then innovated once more, directing the expenditure of their rents toward mitigating their problems.

The rent strike strategy, though originally borrowed by analogy from the labor movement, evolved thereafter within the tenant movement, independent of its source. Its evolution occurred in response to changes in the issues facing the tenant movement and as forms of the strategy in use proved inadequate. Shifts in the economic, political, judicial, and legal environment also helped shape the strategy, partly by undermining the forms in use. And some of the latter changes, such as the decisions that contributed toward the legalization of the strategy and so undermined the rolling strike, were in part a feedback mechanism, themselves responding to the implementation of the strategy.

Mechanisms of Innovation. The first mechanism of innovations was improvisation. This sometimes grew out of the experience of some building on the periphery of the movement (as with the introduction of the single-building strike and of the spending of rent money); and was sometimes thought out by strategists (often "movement lawyers") in one part of the movement, such as a federation (the rolling rent strike, the push for Warranty of Habitability legislation) or a neighborhood organization (the rent slowdown, decisions to utilize procedures that placed rent monies in court escrow). The multilevel pyramidal organization of the movement, with at least several organizations at each of three levels, was important in providing opportunities for experimentation without the danger of committing the whole movement to a mistaken strategy (Lawson, 1982).

The Diffusion of Innovations. The communications networks radiating from each of the federations were vital to the spread of successful innovations, which was via imitation. . . . Some strategic innovations (the rolling rent strike, for example) were consciously promoted by federations in their newspapers, handbooks, and workshops. Others (notably, rent spending) were spread primarily by word of mouth among organizers plugged into federation networks. Lawyers, too, publicized the legal forms by using them (implied Warranty of Habitability, Section 755). On the other hand, although the slowdown continued to be used by organizations where it had evolved, it was not publicized because of the isolation of these organizations and because the main federation did not promote it.

Initially, the rise and fall of strategic forms (the mass strike, then the options for individual buildings in the 1930s) were tied to the waxing and waning of the particular issues to which they were addressed. Later, however, as the strategic options available multiplied, conscious promotion helped certain forms become established (the rolling rent strike, for example), or helped others phase out (755). On the other hand, some forms that at first were not deliberately promoted (rent spending, in-court negotiations), took hold as word of their results and favor among participating tenants became known. Again, although the slowdown failed to spread owing to lack of either planned or word-of-mouth publicity, its success maintained it as a viable strategy among those who knew of it. That is, for a strategic innovation to diffuse throughout the movement, it was important that it receive publicity. However, its effectiveness and the response to it by tenants involved with it were more important than whether it was consciously promoted—so long as its users were tied strongly into movement networks.

Variations in the Use of Strategic Forms. To what extent did the use of strategic forms by the many SMOs within the tenant movement vary? There was considerable uniformity among those using the strike before World War II because of the time gaps between the fading of one form and the emergence of another, and the hegemony of a single federation or of the Socialist Party, an equivalent during the early years. Even in the 1960s, when several possible forms were available, considerable uniformity remained: 755 was generally accepted because of the publicity given the Harlem strike. The only standouts were the lawyers experimenting with other legal forms as they became available, or pressing for direct negotiations. Later, when 755 was replaced by the rolling strike, the Metropolitan Council's influence was such that the only initial nonconformists were lawyers continuing to promote the legal forms.

However, the situation changed with the growing diversity of the movement in the 1970s, when multiple federations emerged, representing tenants from different parts of the SES spectrum and often addressing different issues (Lawson, 1982). For the first time, different forms of the rent strike coexisted: middle income, conservative tenants conducted slowdowns, those who were more aggressive organized strikes that were designed to culminate in negotiations with their landlords in court, while those tenants with missing or unresponsive landlords provided themselves with services and repairs by taking control either unofficially or officially.

Contrary to the expectations of Tilly (1978:155), competition or maneuvering among tenant organizations has not been central to innovations in the rent strike strategy. The structure of the movement is such that this competition is minimized: Building organizations have their own discrete territories (their particular buildings), as do most neighborhood organizations, and when the latter do overlap they tend to deal with different constituencies, such as tenants with or without landlords, because of issue specialization. It is only when there are multiple federations or when segments of the movement are tied closely to opposed political parties that there is likely to be strong competition for the symbolic leadership of the movement. Thus, organizations identified with the mainstream parties rejected rent strikes between 1917 and 1920 because they were being organized by socialists (Spencer, forthcoming). A certain amount of competition did surface in the 1960s, but between rival tenant lawyers rather than tenant organizations. It was with the emergence of multiple major federations after 1973 that competition increased. While the rolling strike was widely adopted in 1970 because of the hegemony of the Metropolitan Council, strategic diversification developed in the mid-1970s because this hegemony collapsed.

Nevertheless, in spite of this pattern, the variation in strategies tended to break down as certain approaches became visibly successful and were adopted by other groups because their usefulness had become apparent. Thus, the Metropolitan Council, which worked mainly with buildings with landlords, reluctantly dropped the rolling strike and became identified with negotiations in court because its constituency wanted settlements. But as decay and abandonment spread, the council eventually began to allow its tenants to buy fuel with their rent monies when they were cold—a strategy that had been developed among neighborhood organizations belonging to two other federations whose constituencies had originally been drawn from more decayed areas of the city. . . .

CONCLUSION

Piven and Cloward (1977:14, 21) have argued that "the forms of political protest are . . . determined by the institutional context in which people live and work," and that "it is typically by rebelling against the rules and authorities associated with their everyday activities that people protest." Charles Tilly (1978) has suggested that collective actors choose their strategies from a repertoire with which they are familiar. This study shows that the rent strike was the logical form of rebellion by tenants within their institution, and that it was borrowed from the labor strike, with which the tenants concerned were very familiar.

This study also confirms Tilly's finding that gradual change can, over time, transform a strategy. It also confirms his hunches that the mechanisms through which strategies evolve are improvisation and imitation, and that changes are often in response to the repression and/or facilitation of authorities and other actors making up the movement's external environment (especially the changing legal environment which is in part a response to the implementation of the rent strike). The chief reasons for the evolution of the rent strike were the changing interests of the strikers and the realization of the disadvantages of previously favored forms.

The article also considered how innovations were diffused through the movement, and found that publicity via word of mouth was as significant as conscious promotion in publicizing successful innovations as long as the innovators and users were well plugged into movement networks.

An examination of variations in the use of strategic forms by the organizations within the tenant movement found that there was considerable uniformity in practice until the 1970s, when multiple strategic forms coexisted. Since multiple federations emerged at the time, the competition among them began to include the strike strategies employed. However, the patterned variations began to break down once certain strategic innovations became visibly more successful, for organizations switched to the forms most suitable to their needs.

Finally, it was argued that the prime impact of the strike was direct rather than via third parties. Political effectiveness depended on mass strikes, which virtually disappeared after 1920. The impact at the building level was strengthened, however, as the strategy developed and was eventually legalized. It was concluded that the rent strike has become so accepted and involved with government programs that it is now institutionalized.

REFERENCES

Boyer, P. (1978) Urban Masses and the Moral Order in America. Cambridge, MA: Harvard Univ. Press.

Freeman, J. (1979) "Resource mobilization and strategy: a model for analyzing social movement actions," 167–189 in M. Zald and J. McCarthy (eds.) The Dynamics of Social Movements. Cambridge, MA: Winthrop.

Gamson, W. (1975) The Strategy of Social Protest. Homewood, IL: Irwin.

Gamson, W. (1968) Power and Discontent. Homewood, IL: Irwin.

Hiskin, A. (1981) "The history of tenants in the United States, struggle and ideology." Int. J. of Urban and Regional Research 5 (June):178–204.

Joselit, J. (forthcoming) "1850–1915: the birth of tenant action," in R. Lawson (ed.) From "Tenant Rebellion" to Tenant Management: the Evolution of the Tenant Movement in New York, 1904–1981.

Lawson, R. (1982) "A decentralized but moving pyramid: the evolution and consequences of the structure of the tenant movement," in J. Freeman (ed.) The Politics of Social Movements. New York: Longman.

——— and S. Barton (1980) "Sex roles in social movements: a case study of the tenant movement in New York City," Signs: J. of Women in Culture and Society 6 (Winter): 230–247.

Lipsky, M. (1970) Protest and City Politics. Chicago: Rand McNally.

Lofland, J. and M. Fink (1982) Symbolic Sit-ins: Protest Occupations of the California Capitol. Washington, DC: Univ. Press of America.

Lowry, I. (1970) Rental Housing in New York City, Vol. 1, Confronting the Crisis. Santa Monica, CA: Rand.

Monti, D. (1980) "The relation between terrorism and domestic civil disorders." Terrorism 4: 123–141.

———. (1979) "Patterns of conflict preceding the 1964 riots: Harlem and Bedford-Stuyvesant." J. of Conflict Resolution 23 (March): 41–69.

Morris, A. (1981) "Black southern sit-in movement: an analysis of internal organization." Amer. Soc. Rev. 46 (December): 744–767.

Piven, F. and R. Cloward (1977) Poor Peoples' Movements: Why They Succeed: How They Fail. New York: Pantheon.

Salins, P. (1980) The Ecology of Housing Destruction. New York: New York Univ. Press.

Schwartz, J. and B. Schwartz (forthcoming) "1943–1971: tenants, landlords, and planners in the rent control era," in R. Lawson (ed.) From "Tenant Rebellion" to Tenant Management: the Evolution of the Tenant Movement in New York 1904–1981.

Sharp, G. (1973) The Politics of Nonviolent Action. Boston: Sargent.

Shiliom, D. (1971) Your Home is Your Hassle. New York: Metropolitan Council of Housing.

Spencer, J. (forthcoming) "Sustained mass mobilization as political leverage: the post-world war I crisis and the passage of the emergency rent laws of 1920," in R. Lawson (ed.) From "Tenant Rebellion" to Tenant Management: the Evolution of the Tenant Movement in New York, 1904–1981.

Tilly, C. (1980a) "How (and to some extent why) to study British contention." Center for Research on Social Organization, Working Paper 212, University of Michigan.

———. (1980b) "Charivaris, repertoires and politics." Center or Research on Social Organization, Working Paper 214, University of Michigan.

———. (1979) "Repertoires of contention in American and Britain, 1750–1830," pp. 126–155 in M. Zald and J. McCarthy (eds.) The Dynamics of Social Movements. Cambridge, MA: Winthrop.

———. (1978) From Mobilization to Revolution. Reading, MA: Addison-Wesley.

Turner, R. (1970) "Determinants of social movement strategies," pp. 145–164, in T. Shibutani (ed.) Human Nature and Collective Behavior. Englewood Cliffs, NJ: Prentice-Hall.

ARTICLE 32

Activists and Asphalt: A Successful Anti-Expressway Movement in a "New South City"

PAUL LUEBKE

In recent years, the study of social movements by American social scientists has followed a new approach, usually termed the resource mobilization perspective (McCarthy and Zald 1977). The traditional approach, rooted in the collective behavior research of the Chicago sociologists (see Blumer 1939), emphasizes the importance of frustration leading to "mushrooming discontent" (Turner and Killian 1972:247). Growing discontent leads to "popular excitement" (Blumer 1939:259), which takes on organizational form because of movement leaders. As Wilson (1973:90) has noted, the focus of the traditional approach is on social movements as products of antecedent conditions.

By contrast, the resource mobilization approach emphasizes the incentives, costs, and benefits that movement participants consider *before* a movement is launched (McCarthy and Zald 1977:1216). Further, this approach assumes that potential beneficiaries of movements cannot "sustain challenges, especially effective ones, on their own" (Jenkins and Perrow 1977:251). Movement supporters must be divided into "beneficiary constituents" and "conscience constituents," i.e., organizations and persons who do not receive a direct benefit for supporting the movement (McCarthy and Zald 1977:1222). The focus of the resource mobilization approach is on social movements as a consequence of skilled resource utilization, with little regard to the level of discontent (Jenkins and Perrow 1977:250).

This paper demonstrates the greater utility of the resource mobilization approach in analyzing the growth of Durham's successful anti-expressway movement, but not without revision of that model. Defining resource mobilization as the bringing together of previously unapplied human energy and skills (Tilly 1978:69), this paper suggests that the ability of a movement organization to inspire others to action is an important psychological resource. Such resources have been ignored by the resource mobilization model in favor of an economistic emphasis on costs and benefits (see McCarthy and Zald 1977; Oberschall 1973; Leites and Wolf 1970:150). Further, low-income groups' organizational contributions have been minimized in the resource mobilization model's focus on the skills of the better-educated (see Jenkins and Perrow 1977; McCarthy and Zald 1973). This paper also suggests the importance of continuing young White political movements, especially in the southern United States, during the 1980s.

A successful social movement was organized by low-income Black neighborhood resi-

Reproduced by permission of the Society for Applied Anthropology from *Human Organization, 40* (Fall), 256–263.

dents and postcollege young Whites in Durham, North Carolina in 1978 and 1979. Together, they blocked an expressway plan that would have destroyed the Black neighborhood. The young Whites who were instrumental in the formation of the movement supported the anti-highway perspective of the Black neighborhood residents, but also had their own reasons for opposing the road: as residents of Durham, they opposed the proposed expressway because it would come near their homes and promote easy access to the suburbs. Thus, the young Whites were not only sympathetic (conscience) participants, they were self-interested (beneficiary) activists in the anti-expressway movement. . . .

The Black neighborhood, known as Crest Street, was threatened by an expressway proposal which city government, state officials, Durham businessmen, and Duke University administrators contended was absolutely essential to relieve traffic congestion near Duke Medical Center in West Durham. Expressway proponents argued that the neighborhood would have to be relocated in order to promote "progress" in Durham as a whole (Luebke 1980). The young White community activists belonged to People's Alliance (PA), a decentralized statewide political organization (with chapters in three North Carolina cities), which had been formed in 1975 by persons whose most common bond was their politicization by the many reform social movements on and off the campuses during the 1960s and early 1970s (see Howard 1974). PA allied with the Crest Street Community Organization (CSC) and forged a citywide Black-White coalition which persuaded the Durham City Council in February 1979 to reverse its earlier votes and to oppose the expressway plan. . . .

REACTING TO THE EXPRESSWAY PROPOSAL

Like their counterparts in many urban areas in the 1950s, Durham's leaders had believed that its growth required an expressway to bring employees and shoppers downtown. Few foresaw that the shopping center and mall phenomenon would contribute to the decline of the downtown shopping district (see Kasarda 1978). This belief in "progress" had been shared by Black as well as White business people, so much so that Black business and political leaders had agreed to the destruction of the Black commercial district and the adjoining neighborhoods to allow for construction of the first leg of the expressway in the late 1960s.

Only later did Blacks confront many broken promises—a business district never rebuilt and working people relocated without sufficient government support. They saw that the poor were placed in housing projects that were far worse—not far better as had been promised—than the single-family dwellings that most had lived in before the expressway. This once-substantial community, a cluster of businesses, homes, and churches, had been irreparably destroyed by the first expressway project (*Durham Morning Herald*, Sept. 22, 1966).

By 1977, the expressway had been extended westward to within a half a mile of the Crest Street neighborhood. City and state officials, eager to proceed with the highway, offered relocation assistance. But Crest Street residents believed that they should not be required to move, that their community cohesiveness could not be reestablished in a housing project (see Friedman 1978; Kasarda and Janowitz 1974), and that their community had been selected for the expressway right-of-way because they were Black and poor.

Because of the low median income of Crest Street's 200 families, neighborhood leaders were able to request and receive legal assistance from the Durham-based North Central Legal Assistance Program. Beginning in late 1977, neighborhood residents became the clients of two Legal Assistance attorneys, who worked cooperatively and continuously with CSC, the neighborhood's political organization.

CSC had the option of opposing the expressway solely on legal grounds by filing a racial discrimination suit against the North Carolina Department of Transportation (NCDOT), or of opposing the road politically as well, by lobbying the Durham City Council. Unlike many Southern cities, Durham had had a Black representative on the city council since 1948, and a second Black was elected in 1953 (Burgess 1962:118). By the mid-1970s about one-third of the 13-member council could be viewed as moderate-to-liberal. In November 1977, three progressives, a Black and two Whites, were elected replacing three White conservatives.

Although CSC considered a city council majority vote against the expressway to be a long-shot possibility, none of the three established progressive citizens' groups agreed. The city-wide Durham Committee on the Affairs of Black People (DCABP), generally viewed as one of the strongest Black political organizations in the South, agreed with CSC's contention that race was a chief reason for the highway's routing through Crest Street, but the committee's major interest seemed to be having CSC lobby for a better relocation plan than other Durham Blacks had received a decade earlier. The Duke University-based White liberal Durham Voters Alliance agreed that Crest Street should be saved, but doubted that a highway project with so much long-standing support from the "power structure" could be halted. Carolina Action, a statewide working class organization based on the ACORN model (Kopkind 1975) with whom CSC was then affiliated, joined the pessimistic chorus after a Black city council member recommended publicly in December 1977 that CSC should be less hostile to the state highway engineers who were planning the expressway project.

For CSC, the eagerness of PA members to adopt a political rather than a legal strategy was a welcome contrast. The 25 core members ("constituents") of Durham PA in early 1978 were typically White college graduates, in their mid-20s to mid-30s, working in lower-status, White-collar jobs (special education teacher rather than college professor; paralegal rather than lawyer). The activists possessed "organizational skills" (Taylor and Potter 1978); they could assess a political problem, divide up research or action tasks at a meeting, and expect that the tasks be completed. All constituents who were old enough had actively opposed the Vietnam War and had also been sympathetic to or active in the civil rights, women's, and ecology movements.

Several differences between PA and its organizational allies in Durham city politics appear to explain the greater optimism of PA and its willingness to undertake the long-shot political strategy at the city council level. First, as former participants in campus-based reform movements of the 1960s and early 1970s, PA members were psychically prepared for "long hauls"; none of these movements had produced immediate or easy victories. Second, in contrast to leaders of the other progressive groups, most PA members had not been active in Durham city politics before 1977 and thus had not seen Durham's conservative business-political elite flex its political muscle during the early 1970s. That strength was intimidating to the more established progressive groups.

Third, PA *had* observed three progressive council candidates defeat three conservatives in the fall 1977 elections, and those three newcomers had committed themselves publicly against the expressway. PA saw three of the necessary seven votes at hand, believed that political tides were flowing against the conservatives, and hoped that education of the public and council members could produce the additional four votes. Finally, PA recognized an unusual opportunity to fight simultaneously for a number of its political values (Fireman and Gamson 1979): racial justice, interracial cooperation, anti-suburbanization, energy conservation, and environmental protection.

In reviewing the growth of the movement, PA summarized its organizational tasks as falling into three categories: establishing a well-reasoned case against the highway, broadening the coalition to include a wide spectrum of Black and White political groups, and producing large numbers of supporters.

The willingness of PA constituents to build the movement with volunteers meant that money, a frequent concern in social movement activity (McCarthy and Zald 1977), was not of major importance. Rather, donations of large amounts of "discretionary time" (McCarthy and Zald 1977:1236) from members was crucial. A PA-sponsored public meeting on the expressway issue in February 1978 led to the formation of a 15-member education committee, which outlined a research paper opposing the highway on racial, economic, and environmental grounds. Arguments about racial discrimination and the community cohesion on Crest Street were present. But the outline also included discussion of air and noise pollution, energy conservation and public transit, city tax-base losses due to suburbanization, and negative impacts of the expressway on middle-income White neighborhoods adjacent to the expressway right-of-way.

The position paper relied on library research augmented by the results of personal interviews. More than 30 persons interviewed displaced persons and community leaders from Black Durham as well as White officials at City Hall, in corporations, in the Chamber of Commerce, and at Duke University. Interviewers were baffled by their friendly reception from the White officials, even though PA members introduced themselves as "part of a citizens' group interested in the East-West Expressway issue"; researchers concluded that PA was simply not perceived as a serious group, and that the expressway, in the officials' minds, was a "nonissue" which merited no serious concern. It apparently *was* a nonissue because both NCDOT and the Durham City Council were on record as favoring the project. The only issue for the officials was the timing and the modus operandi for the relocation of Crest Street residents.

The research team circulated a 60-page first draft to PA members, the CSC, friendly city council members, and potential allies. A final version ("A Case against the East-West Expressway: A People's Alliance Position Paper") was released to the full 13-member council and the city media in June 1978. One PA activist recalled that "the position paper was a great success, because, as a quasi-scientific advocacy document which had eight appendices and was a thick, 60-page report, it convinced even those who didn't want to read it that there might be another *legitimate* way to look at the expressway issue" (emphasis added). In short, PA showed that citizen views regarding the highway issue deserved consideration alongside the conclusions of professional highway planners. Nelkin (1979) suggests that such challenges to opponents' experts have become a critical part of the campaigns of citizen movements across the United States today. PA members brought research skills to the movement which they had learned in college and which their allies on Crest Street did not possess. As Freeman (1979) has noted for the women's movement, the generation of campus activists was using its talents in a new political setting.

BUILDING THE BROAD-BASED COALITION

Interaction with Potential Allies. The anti-expressway position paper summarized the message that PA and CSC wanted to give to potential allies; i.e., the expressway was a mistake for the city of Durham from all important viewpoints: racial, economic, and environmental. Crest Street residents, both young and old, contrary to the literature's dominant view of poor people's skills (Marullo 1980; Taylor and Potter 1978; Piven 1966; Lazar 1970), were able to articulate their anti-expressway stance, and willingly met with any potential ally in Durham. Assuredly one reason for CSC's high level of participation—in marked contrast to other groups' low turnout in earlier "War on Poverty" community participation programs— was the tangible goal of saving the neighborhood from destruction. A second reason appeared to be the enthusiasm of PA members, whose example of participation in public meetings encouraged CSC during the crucial summer of 1978.

Interaction with CSC also had a major impact on PA. As an underdog facing city and state governments that sought to destroy its neighborhood, CSC came to symbolize the struggle for racial justice which had dominated the civil rights movement in Durham a decade earlier. Solidarity, both between PA and CSC and within each group, increased with each of the harmonious meetings at the neighborhood New Bethel Baptist Church, which inevitably ended with the singing of "freedom songs." Unquestionably, PA members contributed their skills to the building of the anti-expressway movement in part as "conscience constituents" inspired by the impressive example of Crest Street residents, who had declared that they would fight to the end to save the neighborhood. CSC's impassioned defense of its homes must be seen as an important psychological resource which motivated PA. CSC's neighborhood pride also led members to invite the entire city council—whether pro, anti, or uncommitted on the expressway—to visit members' houses, especially those that absentee landlords had ignored. Half of the council, including four members who were uncommitted on the issue, toured the neighborhood, and acknowledged publicly that the homes were impressive on the inside, and that media pictures of the rental housing had been an unfair criticism of Crest Street residents. CSC's ability to conduct the neighborhood tours constituted an organizational resource that the prevailing literature cited above assumes is absent among low-income citizens.

PA and CSC recognized that their crucial allies would be those organizations with contacts to the moderate "swing votes" on city council. The targets were the three Blacks, all influenced by the DCABP, and four upper-middle-class Whites especially sympathetic to the pro-neighborhood views of better-educated Whites.

PA sought out White middle-class leaders from neighborhoods within a mile of the proposed expressway right-of-way, and found positive reaction from both the Watts Hospital and Trinity Park areas. The PA position paper's arguments about pollution, suburban sprawl, and interstate through-traffic convinced many homeowners there who had opted for the central city instead of the suburbs and who were nurturing their $50,000 to $75,000 investments. The two neighborhoods differed, however, in the level of their sympathy for the Crest Street community. Watts Hospital, whose leaders were racial liberals who had been fighting Jim Crow segregation in North Carolina before many PA members were born, worked closely with both PA and CSC in promoting the citywide Black-White coalition. Trinity Park's leaders had not been civil rights activists and opposed the highway more narrowly; "Crest Street has to fight its own battles," said one Trinity Park member. Watts Hospital constituents, despite large age differences, shared with PA a dual self-interest and sympathy-for-the-underdog (beneficiary and conscience) perspective on the expressway.

CSC renewed its conversations with DCABP leaders, using its longstanding arguments about NCDOT racism as well as some of PA's position paper analysis. Committee leaders were receptive to the notions that Durham Blacks would not benefit from suburban sprawl, and would be disproportionately burdened by a declining city tax base (see Frey 1979; Marshall 1979). However, DCABP leaders questioned the wisdom of challenging the city's White business-political elite (see Luebke 1980; Burgess 1962) if CSC's case was "just but futile." At this point CSC once again demonstrated its organizational resources first by reminding the DCABP leaders at a general membership meeting that CSC had supported Black candidates in numerous past elections for city council, county commissioner, and state representative, and now was ready to collect political favors. Second, CSC used its professional legal assistance to reassure the DCABP that city and state officials could not deny Crest Street residents their relocation funding in retaliation against CSC's vigorous anti-expressway position.

Crest Street's lawyers viewed their responsibilities as twofold: ensuring the rights of residents against pro-highway city and state officials; and building a case against relocation by stressing the importance of existing neighborhood cohesion (Schewel 1979). The lawyers' work contributed substantially to the DCABP's decision in October 1978 to oppose the expressway publicly. First, they filed a civil rights complaint with the USDOT to establish a legal record of all interaction between the CSC and city and state officials, and to argue that the expressway and relocation plans constituted racial discrimination. Second, they worked with anthropologists and sociologists who, in the style of *Urban Villagers* (Gans 1962), completed a community study (Friedman 1978) of the Crest Street area which demonstrated the strength of neighborhood kinship and friendship ties. The study concluded that these ties would be broken in a typical relocation project (see Stack 1974; Kasarda and Janowitz 1974; Erickson 1976). This community study, plus the CSC-led neighborhood tours, forced city officials in the "Crest Street Task Force," who had hoped to focus on technical details of relocation, to acknowledge in a final report that relocation would be deleterious to Crest Street residents. Their conclusion, published in December 1978, reinforced the anti-expressway sentiments of undecided council members, and strengthened the neighborhood's legal case against the expressway.

By October 1978, PA and CSC had constructed a citywide coalition that exceeded the expectations of early summer. The DCABP plus the Watts Hospital and Trinity Park neighborhood groups were lobbying the city council. Established progressive groups like the Voters Alliance and Carolina Action had joined the coalition, and, as icing on the cake, PA and CSC added environmentalist groups like Sierra Club and Audubon Society, Black associations like the NAACP and the Black Ministerial Alliance, and conscience groups such as the Friends Meeting and the Duke University Faculty Group.

Interaction with City Council. The PA decision to approach the city council in a low-key, polite manner may have been critical. PA leaders, both native and transplanted Southerners, understood the liability of confrontation tactics before a group of mostly middle-aged White and Black Southerners. "Presentation of self" (Goffman 1959) was always civil, rational, and articulate, so that even pro-expressway opponents on the city council came to respect PA's determination and sense of fair play. An anti-expressway council member told PA that it was often compared favorably to Carolina Action, which had opted for more confrontationist tactics at City Hall. PA's activity appears to have neutralized labeling by the pro-expressway faction of the city council.

The observation of positive effects of civility in Durham differs with a recent analysis of Black political protest in nearby Greensboro (N.C.), which concluded that civility was a tactic of benefit only to the White power structure (Chafe 1980). In Durham, politeness toward council members was a Southern folkway that legitimized both the groups and the anti-expressway arguments inside council chambers. The anti-expressway coalition was already strong and interracial; civility as a tactic maximized the coalition's strength. This experience is similar to that of the Association of Southern (White) Women for the Prevention of Lynching in the 1930s, whose members used "Southern institutions and folkways" skillfully to pressure sheriffs to oppose vigilante groups (Reed 1968). By contrast, civility on the part of a relatively weak Black protest movement in Greensboro convinced neither the city council nor the business-political elite to support the movement's political goals. Indeed, the Greensboro movement wrested its best concessions from the elite when sit-ins and demonstrations were its major tactics (Chafe 1980).

A comparison of the Durham and Greensboro cases suggests that civility is an important tactic for movements that are seeking to win votes at city halls or state legislatures in the South. Failure of movement constituents to act civilly may give elected officials an excuse to vote against the movement's goals. However, if the movement is too weak to gain majority support from legislative bodies, Southern-style civility creates little or no advantage. In short, civility at city hall may be necessary in some cases, but is not a sufficient feature of a Southern movement's planning.

Interaction with the Media. It was essential that the media take note of the PA position paper, of the breadth of the anti-expressway coalition, and of the continuing expressway debate before city council. Despite widespread conviction among PA members that the media, especially the daily press, would bias the coverage of the expressway issue (see Tuchman 1978; Molotch 1979), PA's media committee called a formal press conference to highlight the position paper, and individual reporters and editorial writers met and interviewed committee members. In the opinion of media committee members, it was the good personal relationships with the press (see Molotch 1979:84) that were primarily responsible for two extremely favorable items: a banner headline and long story on the local page of the *Durham Morning Herald* (June 13, 1978) reporting the contents of the position paper, followed by a lead editorial in the July 29 *Herald* endorsing PA's call for a city council study of alternatives. One PA member analyzed the interaction with the media this way:

> *We were directly trying the convince the City Council that our idea that alternatives would work was legitimate. But by persuading the editorial page editor that our ideas were okay, we gained an indirect ally. The Council was being told by the Herald that the expressway was still worthy of public debate.*

Prominent coverage in the two daily papers was complemented by extensive stories on television news. Unquestionably, media coverage turned a nonissue into an issue (see Tuchman 1978; Molotch 1979; Gitlin 1980). Once the coalition testimony before city council was reported as news, the pro-expressway council members who considered the expressway a nonissue could not limit public debate. During this period of expanding media coverage of the anti-expressway coalition, the city's business-political elite remained unruffled, still convinced that the pro-expressway majority at city council would prevail. Anti-expressway activists, on the other hand, was favorable media coverage as important "morale boosters" for themselves and other movement adherents (Molotch 1979:77), and were eager to accommodate themselves to the media, especially television news, which wanted to tour the neighborhoods affected by the expressway.

Why did the anti-expressway movement receive extensive sympathetic news coverage, contrary to the findings of Tuchman and Molotch in other social movement cases? First, PA members cultivated the media, "explaining the issue" patiently and cordially to any reporter who would listen. PA recognized the "legitimation function" (Molotch 1979) of the media, and succeeded in convincing reporters that opposing the expressway was a rational strategy. Reporters who considered themselves "realistic" and "hard-nosed" (Tuchman 1978) usually replied to PA members that the highway could not be stopped. The reporters' attitudes suggest a second reason why news coverage was good: PA and CSC were seen by the press as underdogs fighting a valiant but hopeless battle against the "White power structure." The story made "good copy," especially during the slow news days of summer. In February 1979, when the city council shocked the business-political elite and the media by voting against the expressway, the *Durham Morning Herald* used the largest banner headline in recent years to report the news.

MOBILIZING PUBLIC SUPPORT

The Citywide Petition Drive. To demonstrate public support beyond the anti-expressway coalition, PA launched a petition drive in which movement activists solicited signatures from Durham city residents "urging the City Council to endorse less destructive and less costly alternatives." Five thousand five hundred signatures were gathered, mostly on two weekends in September 1978, in time to be presented to city council at the October public hearing. Of the 18 organizations publicly opposed to the expressway, and the 6 committed to active lobbying at city council, only 3 (PA, CSC, and the White middle-class Watts Hospital neighborhood group) made a major commitment, involving members in going door-to-door or soliciting signatures at shopping centers. As had become the norm for the movement, PA members did most of the coordinating work: they wrote a petitioner's handbook which summarized the issues and recounted the history; mobilized workers from CSC and the Watts Hospital group; gathered about two-thirds of the signatures; and organized a press conference, six days before the October hearing, at which coalition representatives discussed the petition drive with reporters from print and electronic media.

Generating Popular Presence for the Anti-Expressway Movement. PA also produced T-shirts and bright buttons that exclaimed: "Stop the Expressway." The buttons were used at every public hearing and city council meeting at which PA members spoke and were special favorites with television cameramen. Both buttons and t-shirts, it was hoped, would interest more of the "bystander public" (Turner 1969) in the issue, and especially help to recruit constituents who would either become active workers, attend a public hearing, or, at least, write letters to the uncommitted council members.

Organizing Crowds. A final task was to generate a "noticeably large crowd" at every public event, and the size of the crowd depended on the tactical importance of the event and the meeting room in which it was held. Thus, when public meetings on alternatives to the expressway were held at night and in the regular council chambers, the coalition sought—and attained— participation at each meeting of about 75 adherents, who reflected the racial and age mix of the movement. For similar meetings scheduled during the day, a dozen participants was viewed as an acceptable number. Such decisions on "necessary numbers" were usually made by PA leaders, after consultation with Watts Hospital activists and CSC leaders and lawyers. The cumulative effect of the petition drive, the T-shirts, and the crowds was to manifest publicly, especially before the city council, what was in fact true: that a sizable proportion of Durham residents, perhaps a majority, opposed the expressway. . . .

REFERENCES

Blumer, Herbert. 1939. Collective Behavior. *In* An Outline of the Principles of Sociology. Robert E. Park, ed. Pp. 65–121. New York: Barnes and Noble.

Braungart, Richard G., and Margaret M. Braungart. 1980. Political Career Patterns of Radical Activists in the 1960s and 1970s: Some Historical Comparisons. Sociological Focus 13(3):237–54.

Burgess, M. Elaine. 1962. Negro Leadership in a Southern City. Chapel Hill: University of North Carolina Press.

Chafe, William H. 1980. Civilities and Civil Rights: Greensboro, North Carolina and the Black Struggle for Freedom. New York: Oxford University Press.

Davidson, Chandler. 1972. Biracial Politics: Conflict and Coalition in the Metropolitan South. Baton Rouge: Louisiana State University Press.

Davidson, Jeffrey L. 1979. Political Partnerships: Neighborhood Residents and Their Council Members. Beverly Hills, California: Sage Publications.

Erikson, Kai T. 1976. Everything in its Path: Destruction of Community in the Buffalo Creek Flood. New York: Simon and Schuster.

Fendrich, James M., and Ellis Krauss. 1978. Student Activism and Adult Left-Wing Politics: A Causal Model of Political Socialization for Black, White and Japanese Students of the 1960s Generation. *In* Research in Social Movements, Conflicts, and

Change, Vol. I. Louis Kriesberg. ed. Pp. 231–55. Greenwich, Conn.: JAI Press.

Fendrich, James M.; and Alison T. Tarleau. 1973. Marching to a Different Drummer: Occupational and Political Correlates of Former Student Activists. Social Forces 52(2):245–53.

Fireman, Bruce, and William A. Gamson. 1979. Utilitarian Logic in the Resource Mobilization Perspective. *In* The Dynamics of Social Movements. Mayer N. Zald and John D. McCarthy, eds. Pp. 8–44. Cambridge, Mass.: Winthrop Publishers.

Frazier, E. Franklin. 1925. Durham: Capital of the Black Middle Class. *In* The New Negro. Alain Locke, ed. Pp. 333–40. New York: Albert and Charles Boni.

Freeman, Jo. 1979. Resource Mobilization and Strategy: A Model for Analyzing Social Movement Organization Actions. *In* Dynamics of Social Movements. Mayer N. Zald and John D. McCarthy, eds. Pp. 167–89. Cambridge: Winthrop Publishers.

Frey, William H. 1979. Central City White Flight. American Sociological Review 44(3):425–48.

Friedman, Elizabeth. 1978. Crest Street: A Family/Community Impact Statement. Center for the Study of the Family and the State. Institute of Policy Sciences and Public Affairs. Duke University.

Gamson, William A. 1975. The Strategy of Social Protest. Homewood, Ill.: Dorsey.

Gans, Herbert. 1962. The Urban Villagers. New York: Free Press.

Gitlin, Todd. 1980. The Whole World Is Watching: The Mass Media in the Making and Unmaking of the New Left. Berkeley: University of California Press.

Goffman, Erving. 1959. The Presentation of Self in Everyday Life. Garden City, N.J.: Doubleday.

Heberle, Rudolf. 1951. Social Movements. New York: Appleton.

Howard, John. 1974. The Cutting Edge: Social Movements and Social Change in America. Philadelphia: Lippincott.

Inglehart, Ronald. 1977. The Silent Revolution: Changing Values and Political Styles Among Western Publics. Princeton: Princeton University Press.

Jenkins, J. Craig, and Charles Perrow. 1977. Insurgency of the Powerless: Farm Worker Movements (1946–1972). American Sociological Review 42(2):249–67.

Kasarda, John D. 1978. Industry, Community, and the Metropolitan Problem. *In* Handbook of Contemporary Urban Life. David Street, ed. Pp. 27–57. San Francisco: Jossey-Bass.

Kasarda, John, and Morris Janowitz. 1974. Community Attachment in Mass Society. American Sociological Review 39(7):328–39.

Kopkind, Andrew. 1975. Arkansas Winning With ACORN. Working Papers for a New Society 3 (Summer):13–20.

Lazar, Irving. 1970. Which Citizens Participate in What? *In* Citizen Participation: A Case Book In Democracy. Edgar Cahn and Barry A. Passet, eds. Pp. 278–95. Trenton, N.J.: New Jersey Community Action Training Institute.

Leites, Nathan, and Charles Wolf, Jr. 1970. Rebellion and Authority. Chicago: Markham.

Lorence, Jon, and Jeyland T. Mortimer. 1979. Work Experience and Political Orientation. A Panel Study. Social Forces 58(12):651–76.

Luebke, Paul. 1979. The Social and Political Bases of a Black Candidate's Coalition: Race, Class, and Ideology in the 1976 North Carolina Primary Election. Politics and Society 9 (Fall):239–61.

Luebke, Paul, 1980. Neighborhood Groups Versus Business Developers in the New South: Expressway Politics in the Scarce-Energy Era. Paper presented at the 6th Annual Conference on the Urban South, Norfolk, VA.

Mannheim, Karl. 1973. The Problem of Generations. *In* Essays on the Sociology of Knowledge. Paul Kecksckmeti, ed. Pp. 276–320. New York: Oxford University Press.

Marshall, Harvey. 1979. White Movement to the Suburbs. American Sociological Review 44 (6):975–94.

Marullo, Sam. 1980. The National Welfare Rights Organization. A Case Study of the Dual Nature of Mobilization. The Human Factor 14:1–27.

McCarthy, John D., and Mayer N. Zald. 1973. The Trend of Social Movements in America: Professionalization and Resource Mobilization. Morristown, N.J.: General Learning Press.

McCarthy, John D., and Mayer N. Zald. 1977. Resource Mobilization and Social Movements. American Journal of Sociology 82 (5):1212–41.

Molotch, Harvey. 1979. Media and Movements. *In* The Dynamics of Social Movements. Mayer N. Zald and John D. McCarthy, eds. Pp. 71–93. Cambridge: Winthrop Publishers.

Murray, Richard, and Arthur Vedlitz. 1978. Racial Voting Patterns in the South: An Analysis of Major Elections in Five Cities. The Annals of the American Academy of Political and Social Science 439:29–39.

Nelkin, Dorothy. 1979. Controversy: Politics of Technical Decisions. Beverly Hills, California: Sage.

Oberschall, Anthony. 1973. Social Conflict and Social Movements. Englewood Cliffs: Prentice-Hall.

Piven, Frances Fox. 1966. Participation of Residents in Neighborhood Community Action Programs. Social Work 7:73–80.

Reed, John Shelton. 1968. An Evaluation of an Anti-Lynching Organization. Social Problems 16:172–82.

Schewel, Stephen. 1979. Positively Ninth Street (A Tale of Durham Politics). School of Education. Duke University.

Stack, Carol. 1974. All Our Kin: Strategies for Survival in a Black Community. New York: Harper & Row.

Taylor, Anne K., and Harry R. Potter. 1978. Citizen Participation: A Comparison of Differences in the Poverty and Environmental Movements. Institute for the Study of Social Change. Lafayette, Ind.: Purdue University.

Tilly, Charles. 1978. From Mobilization to Revolution. Reading, Mass.: Addison-Wesley.

Tuchman, Gaye. 1978. Making News: A Study in the Construction of Reality. New York: Free Press.

Turner, Ralph H. 1969. The Public Perception of Protest. American Sociological Review 34:815–31.

Turner, Ralph H., and Lewis Killian. 1972. Collective Behavior. Englewood Cliffs: Prentice-Hall.

Walsh, Edward J. 1978. On the Interaction Between a Movement and It s Environment. American Sociological Review 43 (1):110–12.

Walsh, Edward and Charles Carypo. 1979. Union Oligarchy and the Grass Roots: The Case of the Teamsters' Defeat in Farmworker Organizing. Sociology and Social Research 63 (3):269–93.

Weissman, Harold H. 1969. Problems in Maintaining Stability in Low-Income Social Action Organizations. *In* Community Development in the Mobilization for Youth Experience. Harold H. Weissman, ed. Pp. 163–77. New York: Association Press.

Wilson, John. 1973. Introduction to Social Movements. New York: Basic Books.

PART SIX

Outcomes of Collective Behavior and Movements

The traditional view of the effects of social movements and collective behavior, extending at least as far back as G. LeBon's treatises on the crowd, reflects a dual emphasis on effects. On the one hand, collective action and social movements are seen as agents of social change, as constituting, to paraphrase Robert E. Park, the origins of social institutions. On the other hand, they are seen as impacting the lives of people, freeing them from established routine and conceptions of selves. In short, the effects of collective behavior and social movements have been studied at various units of aggregation and analysis, from the individual to the societal. Various types of outcomes have been identified, including cooptation, success, defeat, abeyance, and goal replacement. Complicating the analysis of outcomes in that any given instance of collective behavior or social movement may have important albeit quite different effects in different units of aggregation, and such effects, if they exist, may be temporary.

In this section three distinct outcomes are presented. B. E. Aguirre's analysis is couched at the societal level (Article 33). It uses Lofland's concept of dominant emotion to identify the main forms of collective behavior in post-1959 Cuba: the joyful crowd, the celebration of death and martyrs, the mass political gathering, the testimonial of solidarity, and the ceremonial of reception. The article discusses the cultural background of the forms, the ecological context in which the forms occur, the interrelationships among them, and the way they are structured and used by the institutions of the socialist state.

Article 34, couched at the individual level of analysis, is by James Max Fendrich and Kenneth L. Lovoy. It documents the lasting effects of participation in student political activism on the adult political behavior of activists. The results support Mannheim's theory that intragenerational units in some cases become active social change units. They also document the occurrence of remarkable continuity in the style of political participation of people throughout their lives. Very few studies in the collective behavior and social movement literature use a longitudinal design to understand sociocultural dynamics.

Article 35, by Verta Taylor, is an excellent exception to this general pattern. Using data from the women's movement from 1945 to the 1960s, it presents and documents the important concept of movement abeyance structure. Five characteristics of these structures are discussed: temporality, purposive commitment, exclusiveness, centralization, and culture. Another of the important features of this article is its recognition of the importance of movement abeyance for subsequent movement activism. Taylor's reading demonstrates how the abeyance strategy, followed by the women's movement during unfavorable time periods, had important implications for the future of the movement. The article is also important because it documents the difficulty of determining "final" clear-cut outcomes such as success and failure.

ARTICLE 33

The Conventionalization of Collective Behavior in Cuba

B. E. AGUIRRE

This paper focuses on how collective behavior becomes conventionalized. It describes the social setting for certain collective behaviors in Cuba and shows how the revolutionary government has partially conventionalized them. These Cuban data, collected from a kind of social organization different from that of the United States, can enlighten us about frequently neglected questions. I propose to identify the prevailing forms of collective behavior occurring in Cuba and to offer a sociological analysis of the collective behaviors produced by the institutions of the Cuban revolution. . . .

THE SETTING

In revolutionary Cuba, politics is characterized by the political mobilization of the masses, a system directed by the Cuban Communist party and by the mass organizations which requires the constant, direct, nonvoting participation of the people in government programs. The dynamics of this system of political mass mobilization are not well understood; the social organization of one of its constituents, the collective behavior of the people, has not received much attention. Scholars of the Cuban revolution have emphasized the historical antecedents of the revolution, the actions of the revolutionary elite, and the broader aspects of social change brought about by the revolution, such as the emergence of new institutions and the setting of public policy (but see Domínguez 1978, 1982; Leogrande 1978; Fagen 1972).

My focus in this paper is on the actual instances of collective behavior occurring in Cuba, their social organization, and their relationships to the institutions of the revolution. The four parts of the paper are (1) a discussion of the procedures used in the analysis; (2) a description of the institutional context of collective behavior in Cuba, showing the importance of two mass organizations, the Committees for the Defense of the Revolution and the Central Organization of Cuban Trade Unions; (3) descriptions of five forms of collective behavior abstracted from the data: political gatherings, testimonials of solidarity, ceremonials of reception, celebrations of death, and joyful crowds; and (4) an assessment of the implications of these findings for theories of collective behavior. . . .

THE INSTITUTIONAL CONTEXT

It is not productive to try to understand instances of collective behavior in Cuba during 1966–81 as autonomous from and in opposition to the established institutions. The opposite is more nearly true: instances of collective behavior are the result of purposeful, goal-oriented, rational, mani-

Aguirre, B. E. (1984, November). The conventionalization of collective behavior in Cuba. *American Journal of Sociology, 90,* 541–566. Reprinted with permission of The University of Chicago Press.

fest, and institutionalized activities. In Cuba, collective behavior—the scheduling of events; the resources needed to carry them out; the logistics of their displacement, concentration, and dispersal; the ideological justification and approval of the acts—is the product of established mass organizations and state agencies under the control of revolutionary elites (Gonzalez 1974, pp. 153–76; Thomas 1983).

Two mass organizations are important for structuring and controlling collective behavior events: the Committees for the Defense of the Revolution (CDR) and the Central Organization of Cuban Trade Unions (CTC). Other mass organizations—such as the Federation of Cuban Women (FMC) (Randall 1981, pp. 132–35; Azicri 1981), the National Association of Small Peasants (Mesa-Lago 1978, pp. 97–101), and People's Power (Kenworthy 1983)—cooperate with the CDR and the CTC and often take a leading role in the production of collective behavior events (e.g., for FMC rallies: August 28, 1966; August 31, 1968). In many cases, however, the pivotal mass organizations are the CDR and the CTC (Lewis, Lewis, and Rigdon 1978, p. 534); the CDR's domain is the neighborhood, the CTC's, the workplace.

The Committees for the Defense of the Revolution

The CDR is permanently engaged in a number of activities, the importance of which, since CDR's founding in September 1960, have changed from an initial emphasis on armed struggle against terrorism, sabotage, and violent counterrevolution to a present-day ubiquitous social mechanism of revolutionary socialization. (For a history of the CDR see Domínguez [1978], pp. 261–67.)

The CDR maintains close organizational ties with the Committee of Revolutionary Orientation of the Central Committee (CC) of the PCC, the Ministry of Interior, the National Police, the CTC, the FMC, other mass organizations, and other ministries and institutes of the government. The CDR could not be as effective as it is without their support.

The CDR is an exceptional mass organization with a membership of 6 million (about 80% of the adult population of Cuba). It is organized pyramidically (Salas 1979, pp. 296–329), with a national directorate headed by a coordinator and vice-coordinator at the top. At the next level are the CDR provincial committees. Each province is divided into regions or sections made up of CDR zones or municipalities, each with its own regional CDR committee. At the bottom, each zone CDR supervises city block or base CDRs, the most numerous subunits of the CDR (Butterworth 1980, pp. 110–11).

Each city block CDR has a president, secretary, and treasurer who are elected annually by the members of the committee. Base CDRs are made up of subcommittees (*frentes)* in charge of different organizational functions among the neighbors. Thus there are *frentes* in charge of vigilance, finances and savings, education, voluntary work, upkeep of public places, public health, recreation, collection of reusable material, and ideological work and study.

The internal division of labor in the other higher levels of the CDR organization could not be determined either in this study or from the available literature (Butterworth 1974, p. 188), although it possibly reflects the major organizational concerns identified so far (Salas 1979, p. 304; Leogrande 1979, p. 53).

Zonal jurisdictions are purposely kept small, usually encompassing a score or fewer base CDRs (Butterworth 1980, p. 110) to make it possible for zone and city block leaders and members to know each other personally and in order to assign responsibility to specific individuals for carrying out the numerous activities of the organization.

The jurisdictions of zone CDR committees overlap the jurisdictions of the lowest organization level of the National Police, the zone police substations (Salas 1979, p. 278). This interorganizational overlap facilitates efficient social control, for once the residence of someone suspected by the police or internal security is known, the authorities can activate their agents in that person's zone; the agents, in turn, can contact the proper CDR committee members for current, authenticated information on the suspect's friends, visitors, family, biography, work history, present-day activities, participation in revolutionary programs, and overall moral revolutionary character (Lewis et al. 1978, p. 553). This can be done retrospectively as well since the official identification card of every adult gives the person's residential history. The CDRs made 180,000 reports to the police from 1977 to 1981 (Domínguez 1982, p. 47).

The CDRs are of enormous importance in many other aspects of the daily life of the people (Yglesias 1969, pp. 283–93). For example, in order to change residence, permission must be secured from the appropriate base CDR to transfer the family food identification card to the new address. Repairing or remodeling a house requires a certificate from the CDR to request the necessary (and scarce) building materials from People's Power, the organization in charge of their distribution (Harnecker 1980, pp. 209–17; Leogrande 1979, pp. 53–60). Or, to give another example, letters from base committees vouching for the correct revolutionary orientation of individuals help in gaining access to membership in the Union of Cuban Communist Youth (UJC) and to professional university programs and other avenues of upward social mobility (Butterworth 1980, pp. 100–101; Salas 1979, p. 52; Lewis et al. 1978, p. 534).

The CDR, centered in the place of residence, will be shown to be an important force in structuring some types of collective behavior in Cuba. There is another key spatiotemporal dimension which is also closely regulated: the workplace.

The Central Organization of Cuban Trade Unions

Almost every Cuban in the labor force is a member of the CTC (Mesa-Lago and Zephirin 1971, pp. 160–68; Domínguez 1978, pp. 271–79). Usually in work places there are a manager for the enterprise; technical cadres; member(s) of the PCC; secretaries of the CTC, UJC, and FMC; and industrial security personnel or members of the Committee for Physical Protection (Salas 1979, p. 279) who are in charge of labor safety, the control of theft, and the physical protection of the plant (Mesa-Lago 1978, pp. 82–97; 1982; Salas 1979, pp. 330–66).

Work discipline is enforced through several practices. The major problems are loafers, absenteeism, negligence, fraud, carelessness, inferior product quality, disobedience, and other matters adversely affecting productivity (Loney 1973). Serious episodes of indiscipline involve the Ministry of the Interior and the local security personnel or "economic police" (Policia Economica). Workers have individual files or work records (Salas 1979, p. 339) which contain information on their work history, level of technical training and proficiency, frequency of voluntary labor contributions, absences, and number of merits nad demerits. Every place of work has production assemblies in which the workers analyze production problems (Domínguez 1982, p. 39). In these assemblies, there is discussion of absenteeism, lateness, mistreatment of consumers, lack of respect toward superiors, relative fulfillment of productive norms, and future production goals allocated by central planning personnel. Decisions based on labor merits are made about which of the workers in the work unit will receive the right to purchase television sets and other permanent consumer goods allocated to the unit.

Labor merits are earned by voluntary work, participation in revolutionary acts, passing educational courses, and acting as a voluntary teacher. Lack of discipline, wastefulness, inefficiency, and having been punished or admonished at work are considered demerits (Mesa-Lago 1973, p. 32). The CTC selects advance (model) workers annually on the basis of labor merits accumulated during the preceding years (Harnecker 1980, p. 18). Exemplary work centers have the privilege of flying the Banner of the Heroes of Moncada, and workers from these centers have special benefits (MacEwan 1975, pp. 89–93).

The CDR and the CTC help create instances of collective behavior in Cuba. Encouraging participation in mass mobilizations is an important responsibility of these mass organizations. Their roles will be shown following a discussion of the major types of collective behavior.

TYPES OF COLLECTIVE BEHAVIOR

The variety of forms of collective behavior present in a society at any given time is limited (Tilly 1978, p. 151). Only five major forms of collective behavior could be identified in this study: the joyful crowd, the celebration of death and martyrs, the mass political gathering, the testimonial of solidarity, and the ceremonial of reception.

Each form stands in a different relationship to the established traditions of the culture and to the revolutionary organisms of social control (Sales 1979). Joyful crowds and celebrations of death and martyrs have rich traditional roots in the Cuban culture antedating the revolutionary triumph and are occasions of preferential behavior reflecting attachment to a line of behavior which has an overwhelming expressive meaning to the individual (Goffman 1961, pp. 88–90). The other three forms of collective behavior (the political gathering, the testimonial of solidarity, and the ceremonial of reception) are new to the cultural landscape. They represent, in comparison with the other two forms, occasions of deferential behavior or commitment in which the persistent participation of persons over time is predominantly for instrumental reasons. These are the three forms in which the coercive nature of the revolutionary institutions that structure collective behavior is strongest.

The Stranger: The Choreography of Political Gatherings

Mass political gatherings are either stationary or mobile, as in parades. They are carefully structured events in which the CDR and the CTC have considerable influence. The revolutionary institutions' successes in the orderly production of political gatherings result from their ambitious use of space and, to a lesser extent, of time. In conjunction with their control of the social organizations of the neighborhoods and the places of work, their control of the space and time dimensions of the gatherings are the key factors. Most gatherings occur during the daytime, and persons participate in them as members of residential, school, or work-related groups which have their preassigned specific physical locations in the pattern of the gathering. What may appear to the untrained eye as an immense sea of anonymous faces of persons temporarily detached from their customary social relations to participate in the *jornadas* of the revolutionary calendar is instead a publicly acknowledged, carefully rehearsed, and studied choreographic exercise of groups who are firmly attached to existing institutions and occupy clearly specified and lasting niches.

La Plaza de la Revolution. The most massive examples of political gatherings occur in Revolution Square, Havana's civic center. The square is approximately 4.6 million square feet, too small to hold the stationary gatherings of close to 1.5 million people which occasionally are held there. On such occasions the open areas of surrounding government buildings are pressed into service, adding approximately another 2 million square feet of space. Towering over the square is the statue of the apostle José Martí y Perez, a 426-foot-high monument overlaid with 10,000 tons of white marble. The square was used first on May Day 1959, four months after Castro's victory.

The successful execution of political gatherings is a complex exercise in interorganizational coordination. In each city block, CDR members canvass the residents to ascertain whether they intend to participate in the upcoming gathering. There are legitimate reasons for not participating. For example, the elderly, the sick or infirm, mothers (or other child-care providers) in charge of infants and very young children, members of mass organizations or of agencies assigned to vigilance and other services, and workers involved in production are not expected to attend. Persons in these categories who rearrange their affairs so that they may attend nonetheless are given special recognition as committed revolutionaries.

Neighbors without these bona fide reasons face unmitigated pressure to conform. No one is required by law to attend the gatherings but everyone finds it advantageous to do so. For individuals attendance builds up a certain amount of moral capital in their relations with the CDR and other mass organizations and government agencies. This capital is exchanged later on for relative advantages in other areas of life (Salas 1979, p. 305). A few days after a gathering, diplomas are distributed among the participants as symbolic reminders of the promissory exchange nexus.

The list of names of would-be participants collected by the block CDR members is passed on to the zone CDR committee, which arranges for transportation. Neighbors meet at a prearranged time and place, usually in front of the zone CRD's office, travel together as a group with their CDR leaders to a preassigned point located on streets near the square and return there to go home after the gathering. Zone CDR groups (and groups from other organizations) carry placards with their identifying names nad numbers and this information is used for assembling them in the square. Apparently, on-site coordinating units direct the movement of the participants from their points of disembarkment to their preassigned locations in the square. This implies the existence of an official plan which divides the square into smaller spaces. These spaces are then assigned to specific groups on the bases of certain commonalities; FMC groups, CDR groups from the same municipality, and CTC groups from the same industry or occupational or professional categories occupy adjacent spaces in the square.

A similar mobilization, paralleling that of the CDR, occurs in all work centers. Under the direction of the CTC, and as part of a regional mobilization plan in which the various representatives of the different mass organizations and the party serve as coordinating links, a segment of the labor force (participation is limited by the labor needs of ongoing production) goes to the gatherings. Workers and their local organizers leave their work centers in groups and return to work after the gathering is over.

These arrangements lead logically to the characteristics of mass political gatherings in Cuba: their enormous size, the control of emotion, and the fact that mechanisms of social control continue to regulate individuals' behavior. Anonymity in the political gathering is reduced. *Granma* (May 8, 1966) describes the 1966 May Day celebration in which approximately 1 million people participated. The article speaks of an old man, poorly shaved, retired, who reportedly entered the parade lines, passed by the reviewing stand at the base of the José Martí Monument, and then asked a militiaman for permission to leave because he was too old to continue with the rest. The union members with whom he joined in the parade recognized him immediately as a stranger; he was not a member of their group! The intent of the *Granma* article is to celebrate the man's patriotism, but the unintended message—and from my viewpoint the more important one—is that a stranger can be recognized among a million faces.

Multiplied untold numbers of time through whole provinces, the impact of the mobilization efforts of the CDR, CTC, and other mass organizations on daily patterns of social ordering is overwhelming. Again, *Granma* (May 11, 1980) documents the effects, this time with photographs. On May Day 1980 in the midst of the incidents in the Peruvian Embassy and the subsequent Mariel-Key West sealift, 1.5 million people from Havana Province went to Revolution Square to listen to Fidel Castro's speech. They began to assemble in the morning, the stationary rally started at 5 P.M., and Castro began his hour-and-a-half speech three hours later. The pictures in *Granma* show well-known main thoroughfares of Metropolitan Havana (Linea Street, intersections of L, and Twenty-third Street and Twelfth and Twenty-third Streets in Vedado, Thirty-first Avenue in Marianao) completely deserted during that day, and the article calls this "yet another indication of the fact that everybody was in the Square on May Day" (May 11, 1980). That this was true is doubtful. Total surveillance and control and perfect interorganizational coordination and linkages are not possible. Nevertheless, the empty streets are ample proof of the exceptional effectiveness of the mobilization apparatus.

Castro recognized this accomplishment in his speech that evening:

> *On the way to this meeting this afternoon, I could see, once again, the incredible sight of absolutely empty streets. How could I have imagined the size of this meeting? I thought it would be very big. I thought it would be the biggest in all the 21 years of the revolution; but it was really impossible to imagine its magnitude. . . . They say that I am organizing the march. They say that I am organizing it. They say, that was organized by Castro. It was really the mass organizations that organized it. . . . The Party can't organize the march; it simply can't; the march can be organized only by the mass organizations, this rally can be organized only by the mass organizations. [May 11, 1980].*

The Twenty-Sixth of July. The twenty-sixth of July commemoration is the best-known example of the recurrent, scheduled, stationary political gathering. It marks the date of the 1953 attack on Moncada Garrison in the city of Santiago de Cuba by a group of revolutionaries led by Fidel Castro, and the emergence of Castro as a national leader. Information reported in *Granma* expands and confirms our knowledge of the political gathering as an analyzable form of collective behavior.

The historic Twenty-sixth of July cannot be encompassed by the construct, political gathering. It is a collective effervescence, the apex of the revolutionary calendar, and a date of quasi-magical significance, a combination of Thanksgiving, Fourth of July, and Christmas. It includes almost three weeks of festivals, dances, caravans, and assemblies throughout the island; it is a period of collective reflection, reverence, inspiration and reaffirmation, sober record taking, and proud public recognition of work well done.

The preparations for the Twenty-sixth of July are detailed and all-encompassing; for example, in 1978 the main rally to celebrate the twenty-fifth Anniversary of the attack on Moncada Garrison was held in the twenty-sixth of July School City (the garrison itself) in Santiago de Cuba (August 6, 1978). A national committee and provincial organizing committees were set up; the national committee was made up of subcommittees in charge of supplies, transportation, cultural and recreational activities, rallies, meetings and exhibits, and agitation and propaganda.

There were also two working groups, one to look after both the foreign delegations invited to the main rally and the diplomatic corps accredited in Cuba, and the other to look after the surviving men who had fought in the attack and the relatives of those who had died (April 9, 1978).

Even as far back as 1966 the various provinces had their own slogans (e.g., that of the Province of Matanzas, "all canefields cleaned and fertilized by the twenty-sixth") and special activities (e.g., in the Province of Havana, discussion of the "History Will Absolve Me" speech made by Castro during his trial in the aftermath of the Moncada Garrison attack); CDR members adopted new goals to which they pledged themselves; work centers met in assemblies to discuss the meaning of the twenty-sixth of July (July 17, 1966); and local governments held municipal assemblies in every municipality in the country to report their activities to their neighbors and to honor the twenty-sixth (July 10, 1966).

In 1968 the twenty-sixth of July was celebrated in Revolution Square, Santa Clara, Las Villas Province. The gathering started at 9 A.M. (July 21, 1968). Castro and other dignitaries on the speakers' platform were joined by over 2,000 vanguard workers and other outstanding youth; students; farmers; women; members of the armed forces, CDR, FMC, and other organizations; and winners of special emulations (June 2, 1968).

In conjunction with this event *Granma* reports the major tasks of the mass organizations which show that the twenty-sixth of July as a political gathering—that is, as the assembling of hundreds of thousands of people at a given place and time to listen to the revolution's leaders—is deeply enmeshed in the larger, established pattern of the social organization of the country. The symbol of the "twenty-sixth" justifies the leaders' demands on the people to perform meritorious acts at work and elsewhere. Moreover, the claims of this quasi-magical, vital myth have been redirected and reexpressed, not in the form of a political gathering but in agricultural work. In 1969, there was no mass political gathering; instead, people were mobilized to honor the twenty-sixth of July through work in the sugarcane fields to fulfill Castro's goal of 10 million tons of sugar cane for that year (August 3, 1969). The attempt failed (Leogrande 1979, pp. 49–50), but the remarkable powers of the mass organizations were shown once again.

Parades. The May Day Parade is the most recurrent and massive example of a scheduled nonstationary political gathering. Although parades differ from stationary gatherings, the preplanning and control by organs of state power also operate here.

The CTC is the mass organization primarily responsible for the May Day Parades. In 1966 Lázaro Peña, a member of the Central Committee (CC) of the PCC and secretary general of the CTC, presided over the CTC organizing committee of the May Day Parade. Peña's organizing committee stressed the need for uniformity among the participants, warning against a "desire for individual distinction that might exist within the [various] unions." Preparations involved flash meetings in work centers of Havana to urge workers to participate, the issuance of slogans for the occasion, the decoration of work centers, and trial parades to achieve maximum efficiency.

Trial parades complete with standard bearers, Pioneers, militia members, students, teachers, members of the CDR and FMC, and workers were held in regional units of the CTC and in municipalities throughout the province. The minister of labor and other government officials presided over these trial parades.

The 1966 parade began at 3 P.M. with 25 unions, separated into blocks of workers from the same labor union, participating. Each block was made up of forward-facing lines of 25 participants. Other mass organizations participated, but only residents of the western provinces of Havana, Pinar del Rio, and Matanzas marched in the celebrations in Revolution Square.

The 1974 May Day Parade started at 4 P.M. with the playing of the national anthem and a 21-gun salute and lasted three hours. Castro, other dignitaries, and invited guests paraded to their seats in the presiding stand at the base of the José Martí Monument. Hundreds of vanguard workers sat on bleachers in front of the reviewing stand. Other workers occupied their assigned places along the parade's route. Roberto Veiga, general secretary of the CTC, and Ramiro Valdés, member of the Political Bureau of the PCC, spoke; the parade started immediately afterward. More than 140,000 workers (organized into 23 unions), students, a gymnastic tableau of 2,340 workers, and other persons paraded past the reviewing stand. A military band concluded the proceedings (May 12, 1974).

In subsequent years the descriptions in *Granma* of the structural features of the May Day Parade do not vary appreciably, although they detail an increasing elaboration of the ornamental features of the event. Thus, by 1976 the parade began at 3 P.M. with the singing of the national anthem by a 2,000-voice choir of the Havana provincial branch of the CTC, accompanied by a 400-piece band from the National Trade Union of Arts and Entertainment Workers (May 9, 1976).

The organizational principles established by the mid-1980s endure to this day: the scheduling of participation during the daytime, structuring of the parade and rally in groups of people who know one another, the careful use of the sideline space of the parade route, the use of vanguard workers and committed revolutionaries as human barriers in front of the reviewing stand to add to the security of the persons in it, and the use of the parade to recognize meritorious work toward the goals of the revolution.

Participation in the May Day Parade, either as invited guests in the receiving stand or in front of it, or as participants in the parade itself, is an honor—a means to encourage moral rather than material motivation among the people. Not only are Vanguard Workers and Heroes and Heroines of Labor recognized in such events, but work centers which have won various emulations are also invited to participate. These uses of parades (and stationary gatherings) for recognition of revolutionary merit indicate how collective behavior is manipulated by the Cuban state.

With appropriate modifications, these general principles of organization are used repeatedly in other unscheduled parades. Such evolving traditions illustrate a process of elite tactical learning or cultural accumulation: the use of normative and material resources developed through trial and error by such organs of state power as the CDR and the CTC in subsequent mobilizations of the masses in support of state policy.

The March of the Fighting People is a recent example of nonrecurrent and nonstationary political gatherings. It occurred during the period in which, on removal of the Peruvian Embassy's guards by the Cuban government, thousands of Cubans entered that embassy's grounds soliciting political asylum (Domínguez 1981, pp. 56–57). The march was organized by the CDR and made to coincide with the celebration of the anniversary of the Victory at the Bay of Pigs, April 17, 1961.

More than 1.5 million people marched by the Peruvian Embassy on Quinta Avenida (Fifth Avenue), Havana. The march lasted 13 hours. People from 15 *municipios* throughout the city and from municipalities throughout the province of Havana participated in blocks. There were areas of concentration, where people from these different political entities assembled prior to marching, and areas of mobilization (the route of the parade itself) (April 27, 1980). *Granma* refers to the Municipio of Tenth of October, which had gathered more than 100,000 people but could not enter the area of mobilization because of the lack of space. This was so despite estimates that the march moved so rapidly that over 100,000 participants passed in front of the embassy every hour (April 27, 1980).

Almost a month later, on May 17, a second March of the Fighting People, again organized on the same principles, occurred in Havana to protest the May 2 incidents in front of the U.S. Interest Section (in which disaffected Cubans had protested the long wait to obtain U.S. visas). This second march began at 10 A.M. Almost 2 million Cubans marched down the Malecon (seafront drive), passing by the building which houses the U.S. delegation in Havana.

The control of emotion evinced in these two occasions is noteworthy. Hundreds of thousands of people were showing strong feelings against the American and Peruvian diplomats, encouraged to express such feelings by their revolutionary leaders, and yet the marchers were uniformly capable of limiting their acts to respect the property and person of these foreigners. During the march, 2,400 unarmed militia personnel guarded the Embassy of Peru (April 27, 1980).

In addition to the recurrent scheduled parades, previous embassy incidents are another source of systemic learning which undoubtedly helps explain the effectiveness of the social control mechanisms in these two marches. For example, in 1970 two Swiss diplomats were kept inside the hostile crowd surrounded the building, demanding the release of 11 Cuban fishermen who had been apprehended by U.S. Navy personnel off the coast of the Bahamas (May 24, 31, 1970).

The Testimonial of Solidarity

The testimonial, a variety of collective hostility (Lofland 1981, p. 428), is another form of collective behavior that occurs in Cuba. Testimonials are organized by the CDR, CTC, and other mass organizations to mobilize the Cuban people in support of the government's foreign policy. They offer opportunities for citizens to prove their revolutionary identifications to their fellows and to participate, however symbolically and vicariously, in the drama of international politics. They serve as a vehicle for socializing the people into the Marxist eschatology of the international class struggle.

Testimonials are frequently part of a complex of activities associated with official national declarations of solidarity, such as the weeks of solidarity with the people of the Dominican Republic (May 1, 1966) and Vietnam (March 31, 1968), the five days of solidarity with the people of Uruguay (July 6, 1975), the International Conference of Solidarity with the Independence of Puerto Rico (September 21, 1975), the month of solidarity with the Korean people (July 6, 1969), and the International Seminar on the Eradication of Apartheid (June 6, 1976).

As compared with political gatherings, testimonials are much more frequent, smaller, and more localized. They often occur in places such as parks, schools, factories, or clinics which previously have been named for the country in question, for example, Heroic Vietnam Dam, Nguyen Van Troi Park, Pedro Albizu Campos School (Puerto Rico), and Presidente Allende School for the Training of Elementary School Teachers.

Thousands of testimonials have been held, justified by various occasions. One dominant theme is the protestation of the "imperialist" actions of the U.S. government or those of its local surrogates. For example, U.S. actions in Vietnam, the Dominican Republic, Korea, Cambodia, Laos, Puerto Rico, Chile, Uruguay, Nicaragua, El Salvador, Angola, and Mozambique have occasioned testimonials of solidarity.

The subjugation of racial and other minorities in the United States has also occasioned testimonials: thousands gathered at the monument to the *Maine* in Havana to express their solidarity with the struggling "Afro–North American people" in their fight against racism (August 27, 1967); three years later the killing of Kent State University students brought about a similar response (May 10, 1970).

Testimonials are more than acts of protest. Protest is juxtaposed with the belief in the inevitability of the revolutionary victory in the ongoing worldwide struggle against the United States and its capitalist allies. The CTC organized flash rallies of workers to celebrate the downing of the three-thousandth American warplane over North Vietnam, and students held similar rallies (July 7, 1968). Revolutionaries throughout the world who die in the struggle or who suffer political imprisonment and revolutionary organizations that are participating in national liberation struggles are also the subjects of testimonials.

The largest testimonial of solidarity was occasioned by the death of Chilean president Salvador Allende. Five massive political gatherings took place; moreover, from the morning of September 14 to the evening of September 19 a continuous line of mourners passed by the José Martí Monument in Revolution Square to sign a book of condolences (September 23, 1973).

I could not obtain detailed information on the organization of testimonials. Probably they are organized the same way as political gatherings with groups from various mass organizations used as building blocks. In contrast to political gatherings, testimonials occur in changing physical settings, so that the location of the various groups in the testimonials is much less certain; this probably masks the social control of the participants more problematic. Whether this is the case must await further investigations of collective behavior in Cuba. My notes show that the frequency of testimonials has decreased during the late 1970s. However, because of the limitations of my sources, this is only an impression.

The Ceremonial of Reception

As with political gatherings and testimonials of solidarity, the ceremonial of reception, which began in the late 1960s, is a relatively new form of collective behavior in Cuba. Like these other forms, it is a culturally developed pattern for mobilizing people in support of the goals of the state.

Like excited crowds, ceremonials are a marginal type of collective behavior (Lofland 1981, p. 441). They are welcoming acts that begin with the arrival of an invited guest, usually a head of state, at the José Martí International Airport. In contrast to testimonials, ceremonials have recurrently stable physical locations: the airport itself, the known routes from it to the diplomatic protocol residences of the government in Miramar (a subdivision of the city of Havana), and the routes on which Fidel Castro subsequently takes the foreign dignitaries to a few well-chosen agricultural and industrial projects located in most instances in the province of Havana (e. g., Genetic Cattle Project) and in the cities of Cienfuegos, Santa Clara, and Santiago de Cuba.

Ceremonials have their rituals and orderly sequence of events, understood by everyone but perhaps the strangers for whom the occasion has been organized. They take place in the late morning or early afternoon and vary in their complexity in accordance with the statuses of the foreigners and the subtle symbolic elements of foreign policy.

In its most developed form, the ceremonial of reception includes diplomatic rituals offered to the honored guest at the time of arrival at the airport, that is, the greeting by Fidel Castro and other leaders, the 21-gun salute, the playing of the national anthems of the two countries by the Band of the General Staff of the Revolutionary Armed Forces (FAR), and a review of ceremonial honor troops. The occasion also includes a large and enthusiastic assemblage at the airport itself and on both sides of the streets on the route driven on by the open motorcade carrying Fidel Castro and his guests, with the people waving a sea of flags of the visitors' country and cheering the guests wildly. All of this takes place on streets lined with posters and banners of welcome.

As with political gatherings in Revolution Square, the space along each side of the streets on the route from the airport to the protocol residences is carefully allocated to specific subunits of such mass organizations as the CTC, the CDR, the FMC, and the UJC. The same mobilization strategy used in political gatherings is used in the ceremonials of reception. The overall effect on the visitors must be quite pleasant, for the route is almost 24 kilometers long. Apparently, the invited guests are welcomed by a mass of individuals disconnected from the activities of their daily lives, but, in reality, these individuals are surrounded by their neighbors, workers, loved ones, and associates. Therefore, their presence (or absence) in the ceremonial is noted by significant others and is a meaningful act in the broader contexts of their lives.

Ceremonials of reception are associated with other forms of collective behavior. Usually the visitor is taken on tours of the countryside and of industrial projects in Cienfuegos, Santa Clara, and, most often, Santiago de Cuba. Receptions and political gatherings are organized in these locations, and the visiting dignitary has the opportunity to speak to a Cuban audience. In a very few occasions a giant political gathering to honor the visiting dignitary is conducted in Revolution Square, Havana.

At times ceremonials of reception establish the locales for future testimonials of solidarity. Thus, Marien Ngouabi, president of the People's Republic of the Congo, inaugurated a senior high school (Repblica Popular del Congo High School) in Artemisa, Havana Province, during his visit to Cuba in September 1975 (September 28, 1975). Similarly, Erich Honecker, president of the German Democratic Republic, formally opened a cement plant (the Karl Marx Cement Plant) in Cienfuegos which had been partly funded by his country (June 8, 1980). And, of course, the political gatherings that are a part of a reception also at times occur in these allegorically names places. For example, during his recent official stay in Cuba, Angolan president José Eduardo dos Santos spoke at a rally held in the

President Agostinho Neto School in the Isle of Youth (March 30, 1980). Finally, some empirical instances of collective behavior straddle the line between ceremonials and testimonials. On November 5, 1979, a huge throng of people congregated on Salvador Allende Avenue in response to a call issued by the CTC for them to express their solidarity with the Puerto Rican people, and Lolita Lebrón, Oscar Collazo, and other Puerto Rican political prisoners who recently had been released from prisons in the United States and welcomed to Cuba were present and honored during the afternoon's proceedings (November 18, 1979).

The Celebration of Death and Martyrs

Celebrations of death and martyrs and joyful crowds represent traditional instances of collective behavior in Cuba in which people get together to act out their internalized expectations. These two forms existed prior to the revolution. In comparison with the testimonials of solidarity and the ceremonials of reception, and even perhaps with most political gatherings, the existential justifications of these forms are closer to the historical experiences and daily lives of the people. They represent continuity of cultural forms in the ever-changing social organization of the revolutionary society. The government uses these two traditional forms of collective behavior to lend legitimacy to the newer forms of collective behavior used in mass mobilizations, and they too are regulated by the agencies of state power.

The theme of death and martyrs, so much a part of Hispanic culture, occasions instances of collective behavior in Cuba. The revolutionary government has adapted this traditional aspect of the culture, linking its own struggles with this deeply felt need of the Cubans to remember their honorable dead. The ongoing redirection of cultural patterns can be detected in the makeup of the contemporary pantheon of martyrs deemed worthy of remembrance. Not all honorable dead are included; history is rewritten anew, at least partly, by every generation, and the dead are affected by these reinterpretations; they, too, have their own cycles of popularity (Kearl and Rinaldi 1983).

The number of celebrated heroes who died in the struggle for Cuban independence from Spain has diminished: José Martí, Antonio Maceo, Carlos Manuel de Céspedes, and the eight medical students from the University of Havana who were executed by Spanish authorities on November 27, 1871, make up the short list of persons whose deaths are currently remembered and honored (December 14, 1975; March 10, 1974; December 9, 16, 1973; February 15, 1970; December 3, 17, 1967; February 3, 1980.

Martyrs of political struggles in this century can be divided into those who died before Fidel Castro's rise to political prominence and those who died afterward. The first category includes persons whose intellectual positions could be easily integrated into the contemporary revolutionary ideology. Again, it is a relatively short list of names: Julio Antonio Mella, Jesus Menendez, Eduardo Chibás, and Antonio Quiteras (August 21, 1966; May 15, 1966; February 1, 1973; August 24, 1969; February 3, 1974). Most martyrs honored today are in the second category, they died either during the struggle against Fulgencio Batista's government or in defense of the present-day government.

The latter, the most recent dead in the pantheon, died while occupying social positions in the revolutionary society: as members of Cuba's diplomatic corps in Portugal (May 2, 1976) and Canada (April 16, 1972); as internationalist teachers in Nicaragua (November 1, 1981; December 13, 1981); as acting members of the CDR (May 11, 1980); as military personnel defending the coasts (April 26, 1970) or the land area surrounding the U.S. Naval Base in Guantanamo (May 29, 1966); as casualties in the Battle of Giron; and as victims of sabotage in Cuba (March 10, 1968), of attacks on the fishing fleet, or of traffic accidents (April 9, 1972). Other martyrs in this group are the young men and women who died October 6, 1976, in the bomb explosion aboard a Cuban Airways plane off the coast of Barbados while on their way to represent Cuba in a regional sports meet (October 24, 1976). However, in spite of some brief recognition (September 23, 1979), those who died in the recent military campaigns in Africa (Gonzalez 1977, pp. 9–10; Domínguez 1981) are excluded from the status of martyrs.

The most famous of the current heroes is Camilo Cienfuegos, the popular commander who disappeared at sea in 1959 and around whose memory a cult has emerged. Every year thousands of meetings and marches to the sea occur throughout Cuba, and young children throw flowers into the gulf in homage to him (November 4, 1979; October 16, 1965; November 7, 1971; November 2, 1969). Ernesto (Che) Guevara (who died in Bolivia in 1967) is also an important figure in this group, as is his lieutenant, Haydee Tamara Bunke Bider (Tania). With time, of course, even old soldiers (e.g., Celia Sanchez, Lázaro Peña) die of illnesses and infirmities, and this natural process of attrition continues to add revolutionary heroes to the pantheon.

Celebrations of death have their characteristic structure and rituals. An ongoing practice is the intensification through rituals of the collective memory of the martyrs of the pantheon. There are various types of intensification ceremonies, from the solemn annual commemorations of the dates of the ultimate sacrifice of specific individuals, usually in the form of pilgrimages to their tomb, to the collective remembrance that occurs every year on the Day of the Martyrs of the Revolution, July 10 (August 7, 1966). The rededication of the ashes is the most culturally complex manifestation of these occasions of intensification; the remains are exhumed and subjected to physical manipulations which invest them with higher social prestige and status, such as the urn's being carried in a procession and made the focus of a solemn public ceremony attended by the leaders of the revolution. After these ceremonies, the ashes are then housed in a more fitting permanent resting place (September 7, 1975; January 11, 1976; August 7, 1977; March 26, 1978).

The other important social-processing ritual of death is the funeral procession. The official funeral processions for the revolutionary elect reflect the customs of the general population (August 14, 1977; October 8, 1965), among whom, because the dead are still very much part of their social lives, the handling of the funeral processions retains the unspecialized character of an earlier America. What has changed in these official funerals has been the trappings of power available to the state.

The social organization of martyred death grants legitimacy to the revolutionary government, thus supporting its claims to be the true depositor and guardian of the nation's patriotic honor. The dead live and, recognized by the revolution, continue to work on its behalf. Thus, the solemnity of the Twenty-sixth of July derives from the remembrance of those who died in the attack on the Moncada Garrison. Guevara died in Bolivia and in Cuba Fidel inaugurated the Land Clearing Trailblazers Brigade in his honor (November 5, 1967; December 31, 1967), and nationwide work drives (October 12, 1969) and month-long ideological campaigns are carried out to pay homage to Guevara and Cienfuegos (November 4, 1979). The observance of the memory of the dead solidifies the relationship of the revolutionary government to the Cuban nation.

. . . Collective joys (Lofland 1982) are the other form of collective behavior identified in this study. People have fun together in Cuba as elsewhere, and their fun is not necessarily in accordance with the relevant officially approved definitions of what feelings and activities are appropriate for given occasions. Much collective euphoria in Cuba occurs in such official secular acts not solely devoted to fun as the inauguration of industries and other plants and projects (December 16, 1979).

The enormous size of most political gatherings and the fact that crowd polarization is at a minimum, with only a small proportion of the participants close to the speakers' platform (Milgram and Toch 1969; Marx and Wood 1975), ensure the existence of tangential, interstitial social definitions of the situation and accompanying activities which may include merriment and entertainment; the very structure of these collective occasions allows the existence of micro social worlds, fleeting yet enjoyable moments of relaxation and disassociation from the more serious business at hand.

The massive parades also permit joyful occurrences. Perhaps they are even more conducive to merriment than stationary gatherings because in them the spatiotemporal dimensions of the relevant enforceable and enforced official definition of reality are quite limited; most of the time the participants are not performing in front of the reviewing stand (or other central focus of the event) and are left to their own devices in the company of their fellows.

Ceremonials of reception are also conducive to collective joy, for presumably people participate to show their happiness in and appreciation of their guests. Moreover, they are similar to parades in that the participants' performance is quite short; most of the time they must wait for their moment to cheer the moving focus of collective adulation. Under these conditions merriment is encouraged, and the culturally appropriate gestures of merriment occur. It is not known whether the cause of the merriment is the relatively unknown strangers or the more immediate and personal relationships of group members. My guess, however, is that most participants enjoy their outings mostly for the second reason.

Secular collective joys also occur during occasions designed for gaiety and jubilation. However, the business of revolutionary politics is never fully disassociated from collective proletarian joys (May 9, 1976); the latter is preamble to the former.

Street dances and other joyful events, such as Children's Day (July 15), (August 12, 1979) and the International Pioneers' Camp in Varadero (August 7, 1977; August 19, 1973), occur throughout the country prior to the twenty-sixth of July and the May first anniversaries. National and international art festivals usually occur prior to political occasions (July 22, 1979; July 23, 1967). Humor festivals also occur at these times (July 16, 1978); Santiago de Cuba hosts the twenty-sixth of July main ceremony even as its carnival winds down (July 15, 1973; July 23, 1967). The same is true of Havana's carnival, which in 1967 was moved from February and March to the weekends prior to July 26 (March 12, 1966; July 10, 1966). Similarly, carnivals of music (December 13, 1981) and festivals of cinematography (December 16, 1979) occur prior to the January 1 celebration of the end of the Batista regime.

The information in *Granma* on the social organization of carnivals is scanty. Apparently people participate with their unions. Each union has its group of dancers, float, and candidate for the carnival queen contest (February 27, 1966). A carnival commission, as well as the Commission of Revolutionary Orientation of the CC of the CPC, organizes the proceedings. The latter is the same party unit that is in charge of synchronizing the activities of the various mass organizations in other types of collective behavior; thus, perhaps the same procedures developed for these other occasions are used in carnivals as well (July 5, 1970). In 1970, the work of these bodies included the scheduling of activities and the designation of the areas of the city of Havana that were to be used for the festivities. These areas were assigned to "production and service agencies" (unions?), which were responsible for the festive activities that occurred in them. The agencies prepared stands, band platforms, dances, and entertainment programs (July 5, 1970).

Carnival queens are elected every year (July 5, 1970; July 18, 1971; July 16, 1972; July 15, 1973), and outstanding workers are chosen to escort the star and starlets during the inauguration balls (July 15, 1973). In 1971 Georgette, the star of the Carnival of Havana, was escorted by a fisherman who recently had been released from prison in the United States (July 18, 1971).

One of the most massive occasions of collective joy was the Eleventh Festival of Youth and Students. The festival was preceded, in 1977, by a National Youth and Student Festival which honored the twenty-sixth of July (July 24, 1977).

It took place in Havana during July 28–August 5, 1978 (August 5, 1978). The festival consisted of political debates and seminars, parades, gymnastic displays involving almost 15,000 performers (May 21, 1978), ceremonies, street dances, and a huge rally on Revolution Square (February 12, 1978). More than 18,000 young foreigners were in attendance. On July 31 these youngsters met FMC and base CDR members who had earlier rehearsed their welcome. The hosts had cleaned and decorated the streets and had prepared food and amateur theatrical performances for the foreign delegates (July 2, 1978).

The five centers for political debate in the festival had "prearranged topics revolving around anti-imperialist solidarity, peace and friendship, the Festival's watchwords" (July 2, 1978). Commissions, debates, parades, and public forums were also carefully organized by at least four committees: the Permanent Commission of the International Preparatory Committee; the National Preparatory Committee (NPC), chaired by Fidel Castro; the Organizing Committee of the NPC; and the Support Committee of the Organizing Committee of the NPC (May 21, 1978).

CONCLUSION

The various forms of collective behavior in Cuba are conventionalized and used by the institutions of the revolution. The forms are interrelated. Joyful crowds create the background for massive political gatherings, celebrations of death solemnize them, and testimonials of solidarity and ceremonials of reception socialize the people in the symbolism of the international class struggle and the communist ideology. Instances of collective behavior represent important instrumentalities of the socialist state.

The conventionalization and manipulation of collective behavior are central to the purposes and goals of the revolutionary government. Collective behavior keeps alive the political ideology of the elite; maintains gemeinschaft linkages among the Cuban people and the elite; and, by encouraging the people to participate in revolutionary programs, provides the basis for identifying the lukewarm, the potentially deviant, and the true believer. The participation expands the amount of time the average person must devote to matters of concern to the government and consequently contracts his or her private life; it serves to maintain hatred of the United States while preserving ingroup-outgroup boundaries and a sense that Cuba is an embattled country, thereby strengthening the people's solidarity and loyalty to the ruling elite.

The conventionalization of collective behavior in Cuba has implications for our understanding of social control. Instead of using internalized social standards, the government manipulates the behavior of masses of people to channel individuals' behaviors (Janowitz 1978; Troyer 1983). Particularly in the new forms of collective behavior established by the revolutionary movement, social behavior is not regulated through the presence of legitimate standards of social conduct in the individual's conscience. Instead, the structures of social domination make it profitable for people to conform to the expectations of the state. The hope of the revolutionary movement is that these practices of social manipulation will eventually create a new socialist man. Such a prototypical human represents, however, a drastic departure from the cultural ideal of anarchic individualism.

That collective behavior might be subservient to state policy should not be surprising; it is an illustration of how some kinds of social organization can focus collective behavior more effectively than other kinds of social organizations. Indeed, it may be that in the modern world with its emphasis on planning and social control conventionalized collective behavior may become more prominent than in the past. And it might not only become so in communist states. Zurcher (1979, pp. 21–22) refers to the "business of collective behavior," lucrative enterprises devoted to the generation of fads, spontaneous crowds, political support, mass hysteria, and the manipulation of public opinion and tastes through propaganda and advertising. Clearly, planned collective behavior is often functionally equivalent to more spontaneous incidents, for instance, in the generation of solidarity in social organizations. Such planned events may preclude the disruptions which often accompany the latter.

Even as cross-cultural comparative studies come to characterize the social science specialty of collective behavior, increasing attention needs to be devoted to the study of the conventionalization of collective behavior and its manipulation by revolutionary movements in power throughout the world. The link between this specialty and the field of comparative politics is long overdue, for such intellectual cross-fertilization would be instrumental in developing knowledge from which to derive generalizations and testable hypotheses about the topic.

However tentative the findings of this research, I believe that future research will underscore a basic premise revealed by it: it is theoretically and empirically unfruitful to think of collective behavior in Cuba as spontaneous, irrational, unplanned, or without lasting consequences. Nor is it fruitful to think of it as the behavior of alienated and isolated persons. On the contrary, the integration of individuals into the process of revolutionary reconstruction increases their participation in instances of collective behavior and ensures that their participation is controlled (Zurcher and Snow 1981, pp. 451–53; Waldman 1976).

REFERENCES

Azicri, Max. 1981. "Women's Development through Revolutionary Mobilization: A Study of the Federation of Cuban Women." Pp. 276–308 in *Cuban Communism,* edited by Irving Louis Horowitz. New Brunswick, N.J.: Transaction.

Bennett, Gordon. 1976. *Mass Campaigns in Chinese Communist Leadership*. Berkeley: Center for Chinese Studies, University of California.

Blumer, Herbert. 1951. "Collective Behavior." Pp. 67–121 in *Principles of Sociology,* edited by Alfred McLung Lee. New York: Barnes & Noble.

Butterworth, Douglas. 1974. "Grass-Roots Political Organization in Cuba: A Case of the Committees for the Defense of the Revolution." Pp. 183–206 in *Anthropological Perspectives on Latin American Urbanization,* edited by Wayne A. Cornelius and Felicity M. Trueblood. Beverly Hills, Calif.: Sage.

———. 1980. *The People of Buena Ventura: Relocation of Slum Dwellers in Post-Revolutionary Cuba*. Urbana: University of Illinois Press.

Domínguez, Jorge I. 1978. *Cuba: Order and Revolution*. Cambridge, Mass.: Harvard University Press, Belknap Press.

———. 1981. "Cuba in the 1980's." *Problems of Communism* (March-April), pp. 48–59.

———. 1982. "Revolutionary Politics: The New Demands for Orderliness." Pp. 19–70 in *Cuba: Internal and International Politics,* edited by Jorge I. Domínguez. Beverly Hills, Calif.: Sage.

Fagen, Richard R. 1972. "Mass Mobilization in Cuba: The Symbolism of Struggle." Pp. 201–24 in *Cuba in Revolution,* edited by Rolando E. Bonachea and Nelson P. Valdés. Garden City, N.Y.: Doubleday.

Goffman, Erving. 1961. *Encounters*. Indianapolis: Bobbs-Merrill.

Gonzalez, Edward. 1974. *Cuba under Castro: The Limits of Charisma*. Boston Houghton Mifflin.

———. 1977. "Complexities of Cuban Foreign Policy." *Problems of Communism* (November-December), pp. 1–15.

Harnecker, Marta. 1980. *Cuba: Dictatorship or Democracy?* Westport, Conn.: Hill.

Janowitz, Morris. 1978. "The Intellectual History of Social Control." Pp. 20–45 in *Social Control for the 1980s: A Handbook for Order in a Democratic Society,* edited by J. S. Roucek. Westport, Conn.: Greenwood.

Kearl, Michael C., and Anoel Rinaldi. 1983. "The Political Uses of the Dead as Symbols in Contemporary Civil Religions." *Social Forces* 61 (3): 693–708.

Kenworthy, Eldon. 1983. "Dilemmas of Participation in Latin America." *Democracy* 3 (1): 72–83.

Lane, Christel. 1981. *The Rites of Rulers: Ritual in Industrial Study—the Soviet Case*. Cambridge: Cambridge University Press.

Leogrande, William M. 1978. "Mass Political Participation in Socialist Cuba." Pp. 114–28 in *Political*

Participation in Latin America, edited by J. S. Booth and M. A. Seligson. New York: Holmes & Meier.

———. 1979."The Theory and Practice of Socialist Democracy in Cuba: Mechanisms of Elite Accountability." *Studies in Comparative Communism* 12 (1): 39–62.

Lewis, Oscar, Ruth M. Lewis, and Susan M. Rigdon. 1978. *Neighbors: Living the Revolution*. Urbana: University of Illinois Press.

Lofland, John. 1981. "Collective Behavior: The Elementary Forms." Pp. 411–46 in *Social Psychology: Sociological Perspectives,* edited by Morris Rosenberg and Ralph Turner. New York: Basic.

———. 1982. "Crowd Joys." *Urban Life* 10 (4): 355–81.

Loney, Martin. 1973. "Social Control in Cuba." Pp. 42–60 in *Politics and Deviance*. edited by Ian Taylor and Laurie Taylor. Baltimore: Penguin.

MacEwan, Arthur. 1975. "Incentives, Equality and Power in Revolutionary Cuba." Pp. 74–101 in *The New Cuba: Paradoxes and Potentials,* edited by R. Radosh. New York: Morrow.

McPhail, Clark. 1969. "Student Walkout: A Fortuitous Examination of Elementary Collective Behavior." *Social Problems* 16 (4): 441–55.

Marx, Gary T. 1980. "Conceptual Problems in the Field of Collective Behavior." Pp. 258–74 in *Sociological Theory and Research: A Critical Appraisal,* edited by H. M. Blalock, Jr. New York: Free Press.

Marx, Gary T., and James L. Wood. 1975. "Strands of Theory and Research in Collective Behavior." *Annual Review of Sociology* 1:353–428.

Mesa-Lago, Carmelo. 1973. "Castro's Domestic Course." *Problems of Communism* (September), pp. 27–38.

———. 1978. *Cuba in the 1970s: Pragmatism and Institutionalization.* Albuquerque University of New Mexico Press.

Mesa-Lago, Carmelo, and Luc Zephirin. 1971. "Central Planning." Pp. 145–84 in *Revolutionary Change in Cuba.* edited by Carmelo Mesa-Lago. Pittsburgh: University of Pittsburgh Press.

Milgram, Stanley, and Hans Toch. 1969. "Collective Behavior: Crowds and Social Movements." Pp. 507–609 in *The Handbook of Social Psychology,* edited by G. Lindzey and E. Aronson. Reading, Mass.: Addison-Wesley.

Montaner, Carlos A. 1981. *Secret Report on the Cuban Revolution.* New Brunswick, N.J.: Transaction.

Nichols, John Spicer. 1982. "The Mass Media: Their Functions in Social Conflict." Pp. 71–112 in *Cuba: Internal and International Affairs,* edited by Jorge I. Domínguez. Beverly Hills, Calif.: Sage.

Park, Robert E., and Ernest Burgess. 1924. *Introduction to the Science of Sociology.* Chicago: University of Chicago Press.

Randall, Margaret. 1981. *Women in Cuba: Thirty Years Later*. New York: Smyrna.

Salas, Luis. 1979. *Social Control and Deviance in Cuba.* New York: Praeger.

Smelser, Neil J. 1963. *Theory of Collective Behavior*. Glencoe, Ill.: Free Press.

Smith, Thomas S. 1968. "Conventionalization and Control: An Examination of Adolescent Crowds." *American Journal of Sociology* 74:172–83.

Thomas, Hugh. 1983. *The Revolution on Balance.* Washington, D.C.: Cuban-American National Foundation.

Tilly, Charles. 1978. *From Mobilization to Revolution.* Reading, Mass.: Addison-Wesley.

Troyer, Ronald J. 1983. "Social Control in the People's Republic of China." Unpublished manuscript, available from author on request.

Turner, Ralph H., and Lewis M. Killian. 1957. *Collective Behavior*. Englewood Cliffs, N.J.: Prentice-Hall.

Waldman, Loren K. 1976. "Mass Society Theory and Religion: The Case of the Nazis." *American Journal of Political Science* 20 (2): 319–26.

Weller, Jack, and Enrico Quarantelli. 1973. "Neglected Characteristics of Collective Behavior." *American Journal of Sociology* 79 (November): 665–85.

Yglesias, José. 1969. *In the Fist of the Revolution: Life in a Cuban Country Town.* New York: Random House.

Zurcher, Louis A. 1979. "Collective Behavior: From Static Psychology to Static Sociology." Unpublished manuscript, available from author on request.

Zurcher, Louis Al, and David A. Snow. 1981. "Collective Behavior: Social Movements." Pp. 447–82 in *Social Psychology: Sociological Perspectives,* edited by M. Rosenberg and R. H. Turner. New York: Basic.

ARTICLE 34

Back to the Future: Adult Political Behavior of Former Student Activists

JAMES MAX FENDRICH
KENNETH L. LOVOY

INTRODUCTION

The research objective is to study the long-term consequences of student protest. The question is whether early patterns of student political behavior are good predictors of adult politics. Former radical civil rights activists are compared to institutional activists (former student government leaders) and a random sample of noninvolved undergraduates. An earlier 10-year follow-up study showed that former radical activists in their thirties were significantly more politically active on a five-item scale than either of the control groups (Fendrich and Tarleau 1973).

Twenty-five years after leaving college, this cohort is beginning to reach the chronological age of maximum political participation (Verba and Nie 1972). Contrary to the "Big Chill" syndrome, some scholars believe that the critical mass of three million radicals from the 1960s will be major political actors during the 1990s (e.g., Harrington 1872; Lerner 1988). They will be the political leaders of one of the largest identified voting blocks (*Times Mirror* 1988). A longitudinal study provides an excellent opportunity to explore this prediction.

This research builds on Mannheim's theory of political generations ([1928] 1972). Mannheim argues that generational differences are not a direct function of age or biology but of major political and social events occurring during young adulthood (ages 18–25). He contends that there can be different intragenerational units within the same age cohort. Subgroups within the same age cohort cultivate the materials of their common experiences in different yet specific ways, constituting separate intragenerational units. Generational replacement becomes one of the major engines of social and political change (Jennings 1987) as distinctive intragenerational units mature.

Empirical studies (Fendrich and Tarleau 1973; Jennings 1987; Marwell, Aiken, and Demerath 1987) support Mannheim's theory that distinctive generational units form out of intense youthful politics. However, previous research has not focused on the dimensions and levels of adult political involvement.

Conceptual and methodological advancements by Verba, Nie, and Kim (1971) and by Milbrath and Goel (1977) since our 10-year longitudinal study make it possible to measure the multidimensionality of political behavior. These researchers recognized the importance of analyzing patterns of political behavior beyond voting studies. Using cluster and factor analysis, they

Fendrich, James Max, & Lovoy, Kenneth L. (1988, October). Back to the future: Adult political behavior of former student activists. *American Sociological Review, 53,* 780–784. Reprinted by permission of the American Sociological Association.

discovered that political participation is multidimensional. Moreover, political behaviors can be arranged hierarchically according to the threshold or difficulty of behavior and the resources and talents political participants have at their disposal.

Subsequent work by Milbrath and Goel (1977) verified six dimensions of political behavior. The first, voting and patriotic activity, reflects activities that political sociologists define as "passive support" for the political system. The remaining five dimensions are *active* forms aimed at influencing the polity. In their analysis, Milbrath and Goel found that active respondents have higher SES backgrounds, particularly on measures of education. They also claim there is a small number of political activists who score high on all the dimensions. These are the complete activists.

There are three advantages of the data set we use in this analysis. First, student politics occurred during the early 1960s, providing the longest time span between student and adult politics. Compared to previous research, the data provide a more rigorous test of student politics' effect on adult politics. Second, no other data set has a comparison group of institutional activists. This group provides a means of comparing radical activists with a different intragenerational unit of political activists who were not involved in protests. Third, the research provides a unique opportunity to explore the level of political involvement among the groups on established multidimensional measures of political behavior.

DATA AND VARIABLES

The research design is partially determined by our first follow-up study. Data were gathered using an after-only design with the three groups selected on the basis of previous student political involvement. The research subjects are former students of Florida State University in Tallahassee, Florida, one of the major centers of the civil rights movement in the early 1960s (Matthews and Prothro 1966; Rabby 1984).

Three groups occupy positions along a continuum of student political activism. At one extreme are the radical civil rights activists, who engaged in noninstitutional protest politics, using the tacts of political confrontation to radically change the racial practices of Southern institutions. At the other extreme are the noninvolved undergraduates. Between these two groups are the institutional activists whose political expression followed a consensual, cooperative model of adult institutional politics. As student government leaders, they are playing anticipatory socialization roles for adult politics, which was not unusual for the South at that time (e.g., one former student body president at Florida State University eventually became governor). Student government leaders did not approve of segregation; however, they strongly disapproved of student protest tactics. Like their adult counterparts, student government leaders felt the civil rights movement was going too far, too fast.

In 1971 we mailed a total of 150 questionnaires (50 for each group); 95 people (63 percent) returned the questionnaires. In 1986, we used the addresses of the 10-year follow-up study, current addresses from the alumni office, phone directories, and phone calls, to locate 101 of the original 150 subjects. Eighty-five returned questionnaires.

The dependent variable is a modified 20-item scale measuring different dimensions of political behavior: (1) Protest; (2) Community Activism; (3) Party and Campaign Participation; (4) Political Communication; (5) Parochial Interest; and (6) Voting and Patriotism. There were four responses for each item: regularly, occasionally, seldom, and never. Respondents were asked, "During the past two years, have you. . . ."

A confirmatory factor analysis was used to discover whether the same factor structure existed for our data set as in the previous research by Milbrath and Goel (1977). The results are a five-factor solution. The one separate dimension that was not confirmed was Parochial Interest; this item loaded on the Community Activism factor instead of Party and Campaign

Participation. Otherwise, the other five factors are comparable.

ANALYSIS

Table 1 reports the percentage of active political participation by student politics. Each item is listed under the appropriate factor. The percentages reported are sums of those who expressed some level of activity, i.e., everyone who did not answer "never."

All three groups of college graduates are more active than reported findings for national samples (Verba et al. 1971; Milbrath and Goel 1977). This is not surprising given the high levels of education and the fact that the respondents are in the age group of prime political activity. The

TABLE 1 Active Participation by Student Politics

FACTOR ITEM	RADICAL ACTIVISTS (%)	INSTITUTIONAL ACTIVISTS (%)	NONINVOLVED (%)
Protest			
Join in a protest march	61	7	9
Attend protest meetings	74	37	25
Participate in any form of political activity that could lead to arrest	61	7	6
Community Activism			
Be a candidate for office	17	20	9
Work with others on local problems	83	83	63
Form a group to work on a local problem	61	53	34
Contact local officials on social issues	87	60	59
Contact a local, state, or federal official about a particular personal problem	74	67	66
Go with a group to protest to a public official	83	37	13
Party and Campaign Work			
Join and support a political party	87	77	69
Take an active part in political campaign	87	80	59
Participate in a political party between elections as well as at election time	70	70	38
Political Communication			
Keep informed about politics	100	100	100
Engage in political discussions	100	100	97
Send messages to a political leader when they are doing well or poorly	83	80	63
Inform others in my community about politics	91	87	69
Try to persuade others how to vote	91	83	81
Voting and Patriotism			
Vote in elections	96	100	96
Have a feeling of love for my country	87	100	100
Show my patriotism by flying the flag or in some other way	52	97	91
N=	23	30	32

noninvolved college students have a level of political participation closest to national participation rates.

The ex-student radicals and institutional activists are very active in adult politics. They participate in a wide range of local activities. They are more active in political parties and campaign work. They work harder at keeping informed and informing others about politics. In addition, the former radical activists continue to engage in political protest, and they score substantially lower on the two items measuring patriotism.

Table 2 reports the analysis of variance for the dimensions of political participation by student politics. In addition to the dimensions in Table 1, a sixth, Complete Activist, is added. It is the sum of the four active dimensions of political behavior. The higher the scores, the higher the political participation.

The findings are quite clear. The radicals are more politically active on every dimension except Voting and Patriotism, the most passive form of political behavior. They are especially more active in political protest. They also are more active on the three institutional dimensions of political behavior: local community politics, party and political campaign work, communicating and trying to persuade others to vote. Finally, they score significantly higher on the complete-activism measure.

TABLE 2 Analysis of Variance for Dimensions of Political Participation by Student Politics

STUDENT POLITICS	$\bar{X}$	S.D.	CASES	D.F.	MEAN SQUARES	*F*
Protest						
Radical activists	5.61	1.99	23	2	33.72	13.03***
Institutional activists	3.80	1.85	30			
Noninvolved	3.47	.92	32			
Community Activism						
Radical activists	13.04	4.43	23	2	82.00	4.67**
Institutional activists	12.20	4.89	30			
Noninvolved	9.78	3.18	32			
Party and Campaign Work						
Radical activists	8.00	2.95	23	2	27.06	3.12*
Institutional activists	7.87	3.08	30			
Noninvolved	6.28	2.80	32			
Political Communicators						
Radical activists	16.39	3.33	23	2	80.55	6.19***
Institutional activists	15.63	3.78	30			
Noninvolved	13.19	3.63	32			
Voting and Patriotism						
Radical activists	8.87	2.32	23	2	43.63	17.71***
Institutional activists	11.33	1.12	30			
Noninvolved	10.91	1.22	32			
Complete Activism						
Radical activists	43.04	10.19	23	2	772.16	7.70***
Institutional activists	39.50	11.27	30			
Noninvolved	32.72	8.53	32			

* Significant at .05.
** Significant at .01.
*** Significant at .001.

The institutional activists are the second most active group. On the conventional forms of political activity, the institutional activists have mean scores closer to the radicals. On the unconventional-protest measure, their mean score is closer to the noninvolved. They are also the most patriotic.

Although ex-radicals and institutional activists are very active as adults, the content of their politics differs. Unreported data show that 40 percent of the institutional activists are involved in the Republican party, but none of the radicals. In contrast, 61 percent of the radicals, compared to 33 percent of the institutional activists, are involved in the Democratic party. On a measure of political self-identification and two measures of political attitudes—one measuring radical conservatism and the other measuring attitudes toward the Reagan administration—the two groups are statistically different beyond the .0001 level. Open-ended responses to questions revealed praise for the Reagan administration from institutional activists and contempt from radicals. The groups' participation in voluntary organizations also differs. Radicals now belong to progressive political and humanitarian organizations, whereas the institutional activists are in conservative organizations. Both belonged to professional organizations. In political arenas, these two groups continue to be on opposite sides.

SUMMARY AND CONCLUSIONS

This 25-year longitudinal study of early 1960s college students supports Mannheim's theory of distinctive intragenerational units. It confirms distinctive types of adult political behavior and the existence of complete activists. Political behavior in college was formative and an excellent predictor of adult politics.

Although our research design has the merits of being able to compare three different intragenerational units form the 1960s, it is difficult to generalize the findings. However, independent research does report similar findings for political activists from the late 1960s (Jennings 1987; Marwell et al. 1987; Whalen and Flacks 1980). Both radicals and institutional activists represent only a small minority of the massive college cohort of the 60s. However, their contemporary significance should not be underestimated. Given the low levels of active political participation in the general population, these two distinctive groups are likely to have an influence on political institutions that extends beyond their sheer numbers.

The significance of the 1960s social movements and their participants has been trivialized (Bell 1976; Gitlin 1987). Empirical investigations suggest this characterization is in error. A different standard for evaluating the significance of the 60s activists is whether their adult behavior is consistent with the democratic ideal. The democratic ideal expects citizens to be interested and informed about politics, actively participating in political parties and election campaigns and trying every way possible (including protest) to make their voices heard as political decisions are being made (Milbrath and Goel 1977). Our findings reveal that 1960s radicals and, to a lesser extent, institutional activists are the ideal citizens in the 1980s.

REFERENCES

Bell, Daniel. 1976. *The Cultural Contradictions of Capitalism*. New York: Basic Books.

Fendrich, James M. and Alison T. Tarleau. 1973. "Marching to a Different Drummer: The Occupational and Political Orientations of Former Student Activists." *Social Forces* 52:245–53.

Gitlin, Todd. 1987. *The Sixties: Years of Hope, Days of Rage*. New York: Bantam Books.

Harrington, Michael. 1872. *Fragments of the Century*. New York: E. P. Dutton.

Lerner, Michael. 1988. "The Legacy of the Sixties for the Politics of the Nineties." *Tikkun* 3:44–48.

Jennings, M. Kent. 1987. "Residues of a Movement: The Aging of the American Protest Generation." *American Political Science Review* 81:367–82.

Mannheim, Karl. [1928] 1972. "The Problem of Generations." In *The New Pilgrims,* edited by Phillip G. Altbach and Robert S. Lauffer. New York: David McKay.

Marwell, Gerald, Michael Aiken, and N.J. Demerath. 1987. "The Persistence of Political Attitudes Among 1960s Civil Rights Activists." *Public Opinion Quarterly* 51:359–75.

Matthews, Donald and James Prothro. 1966. *Negroes and the New Southern Politics*. New York: Harcourt, Brace & World.

Milbrath, Lester and M.L. Goel. 1977. *Political Participation,* 2nd ed. Boston: Rand McNally.

Rabby, Glenda. 1984. *Out of the Past: The Civil Rights Movement in Tallahassee, Florida*. Ph.D. Diss., Florida State University.

Times Mirror Survey. 1988. *New York Times* 137:E21, February 14.

Verba, Sidney and Norman Nie. 1972. *Participation in America: Political Democracy and Social Equality*. New York Harper and Row.

Verba, Sidney, Norman Nie, and Jae-on Kim. 1971. *Modes of Democratic Participation: A Cross-National Comparison*. Beverly Hills, CA: Sage Publications.

Whalen, John and Richard Flacks. 1980. "The Isla Vista 'Bank Burners' Ten Years Later: Notes on the Fate of Student Activists." *Sociological Focus* 13:215–36.

ARTICLE 35

Social Movement Continuity: The Women's Movement in Abeyance

VERTA TAYLOR

INTRODUCTION

Scholars of the social movements of the 1960s have by and large held an "immaculate conception" view of their origins. These "new social movements" (Klandermans 1986) seemingly emerged out of nowhere and represented a sudden shift from the quiescent 1940s and 1950s (Flacks 1971; Touraine 1971; McCarthy and Zald 1973; Jenkins 1987). Recent empirical work, however, challenges this view, suggesting that the break between the sixties movements and earlier waves of political activism was not as sharp as previously assumed (e.g., Isserman 1987; McAdam 1988). The overemphasis on movement origins and on new elements in the sixties movements has blinded students of social movements to the "carry-overs and carry-ons" between movements (Gusfield 1981, p. 324). What scholars have taken for "births" were in fact breakthroughs or turning points in movement mobilization.

This paper develops a framework that specifies the processes of movement continuity. The framework is grounded in research on the American women's rights movement from 1945 to the mid-1960s. . . .

ABEYANCE PROCESSES IN SOCIAL MOVEMENTS

The term "abeyance" is borrowed from Mizruchi (1983) and is central to a theory of social control. Abeyance structures emerge when society lacks sufficient status vacancies to integrate surpluses of marginal and dissident people. The structures that absorb marginal groups are abeyance organizations. They temporarily retain potential challengers to the status quo, thereby reducing threats to the larger social systems. Abeyance organizations have certain properties that allow them to absorb, control, and expel personnel according to the number of status positions available in the larger society (Mizruchi 1983, p. 17).

Although Mizruchi recognizes the social change potential of abeyance organizations, he does not address this aspect systematically (Kimmel 1984). I both challenge and extend Mizruchi's thesis to hypothesize that social movement abeyance organizations, by providing a measure of continuity for challenging groups, also contribute to social change. I hold that the abeyance process characterizes mass movements that succeed in building a support base and achieving a measure of influence, but are con-

Taylor, Verta. (1989, October). Social movement continuity: The women's movement in abeyance. *American Sociological Review, 54,* 761–775. Reprinted by permission of the American Sociological Association.

fronted with a nonreceptive political and social environment. A central tenet of resource mobilization theory concerns the role that changing opportunity structures play in the emergence and the attenuation of collective action (McCarthy and Zald 1973; Barkan 1984; Jenkins 1983). As a movement loses support, activists who had been most intensely committed to its aims become increasingly marginal and socially isolated. If insufficient opportunities exist to channel their commitment into routine statuses, then alternative structures emerge to absorb the surplus of people. These structures both restrain them from potentially more disruptive activities and channel them into certain forms of activism. In short, a movement in abeyance becomes a cadre of activists who create or find a niche for themselves. Such groups may have little impact in their own time and may contribute, however unwillingly, to maintenance of the status quo. But, by providing a legitimating base to challenge the status quo, such groups can be sources of protest and change.

The following factors are relevant to the abeyance process. First, certain factors external to a movement create a pool of marginal potential activists. These include *changes in opportunity structures* that support and constrain the movement and an *absence of status vacancies* to absorb dissident and excluded groups. Second, there are internal factors or organizational *dimensions of social movement abeyance structures: temporality, commitment, exclusiveness, centralization, and culture*. Since these dimensions were inductively derived, I elaborate them with the case at hand. The significance of abeyance lies in its linkages between one upsurge in activism and another. I delineate three ways that social movement abeyance structures perform this linkage function: through promoting the survival of *activist networks*, sustaining a repertoire of *goals and tactics*, and promoting a *collective identity* that offers participants a sense of mission and moral purpose. . . .

The data for this study comes from documentary material in public and private archival collections and interviews with women who were activists from 1945 to the 1960s. Fuller description of the movement in this period and complete documentation are available in Rupp and Taylor (1987).

1. Archival data included the papers of the National Woman's Party and the League of Women Voters, the two major factions of the suffrage movement, and the papers of the President's Commission on the Status of Women (1961–63), whose activities facilitated the resurgence of the contemporary women's movement. Other material examined were unofficial and official organizational documents, publications, personal letters, and memos in public and private collections, most of which are housed at the Schlesinger Library at Radcliff College or the Library of Congress. The papers of individual women provided an important source of information, not only about their organizational careers, but also about the activities of diverse women's organizations.

2. The second source of data was 57 open-ended, semistructured, tape-recorded interviews, conducted between 1979 and 1983, with leaders and core members of the most central groups involved in women's rights activities. Twelve of the women were active at the national level and thirty-three at the local level. Twelve other transcribed interviews conducted by other researchers and available in archival collections were used.

THE WOMEN'S MOVEMENT IN THE POSTSUFFRAGE DECADES: THE TRANSFORMATION OF FEMINIST ACTIVISM

Feminism activism continued in the years after the suffrage victory but was transformed as a result of organizational success, internal conflict, and social changes that altered women's common interests (Lemons 1973; Becker 1981; Buechler 1986; Cott 1987). Deradicalization and decline of the women's movement left militant feminists limited avenues through which to pursue their political philosophy.

In 1920, with the vote won, the women's movement was left with no unifying goal. Moreover, tactical and ideological differences divided militant from moderate suffragists and those who saw winning the vote as a means from those who viewed it as an end. As a result, the major social movement organizations of the suffrage movement evolved in two opposing directions.

The militant branch of the movement, the National Woman's Party (NWP), launched a relentless campaign to pass an Equal Rights Amendment (ERA) to the constitution. The NWP was never a mass organization but saw itself as a feminist vanguard or elite (Lunardini 1986). Hoping to enlist the support of former suffragists, NWP leader Alice Paul instead alienated both socialists and moderate feminists by her dictatorial style and the decision to focus on the ERA. The vast majority of suffragists feared that the ERA would eliminate the protective labor legislation that women reformers had earlier struggled to achieve (Balser 1987).

The mainstream branch of the movement, the National American Woman Suffrage Association, formed the nonpartisan League of Women Voters. It spearheaded the opposition to the ERA, educated women for their new citizenship responsibilities, and advocated a broad range of reforms. Other activist in the suffrage campaign channeled their efforts into new or growing organizations that did not have an explicitly feminist agenda but promoted a vast range of specific causes that, in part, grew out of the expanded role options available to women (Cott 1987). Thus, even though the women's movement was rapidly fragmenting, feminist activism continued throughout the 1920s and 1930s. But in the face of increasing hostility between the two camps of the suffrage movement, cooperation developed on only a few issues.

In addition to goal attainment and internal conflict, a third factor contributed to the dissipation of the mass base of the women's movement. Ironically, the role expansion for which the movement had fought fractured the bonds on which the solidarity of the movement had been built. As women's lives grew increasingly diverse, the definition of what would benefit women grew less clear.

As a result, the NWP—which alone continued to claim the title "feminist"—had become increasingly isolated from the main stream of American women and even from women's organizations. With the demise of the large mass-based organizations that propelled the suffrage movement, the more radical feminists sought out the NWP. When the NWP captured the feminist agenda, however, the broad program of emancipation narrowed to limited goals and tactics pursued by an elite group of women (Cott 1987). This spelled the final demise of feminism as a mass movement.

FEMINIST ACTIVISM FROM 1945 TO THE 1960'S; THE WOMEN'S MOVEMENT IN ABEYANCE

From 1945 to the 1960s, women's rights activists confronted an inhospitable political and social environment. Women who advocated equality found few outlets for their activism and became increasingly marginal and isolated from the mainstream of American women. Two social processes had this effect; First, advocates of women's rights lacked access to and support from the established political system; and, second, the cultural ideal of "the feminine mystique" that emerged after World War II affirmed the restoration of "normal family life" and discredited women who protested gender inequality. . . .

Dimensions of Social Movement Abeyance Structures

The abeyance process functions through organizations capable of sustaining collective challenges under circumstances unfavorable to mass mobilization. Properties of abeyance organizations help an organizational pattern to retain potentially dissident populations. My analysis of the women's rights movement in the postwar period suggests that the most relevant variables with respect to the abeyance process are: temporality, purposive commitment, exclusiveness, centralization, and culture. Since these variables are derived from a single case, each dimension is treated as a hypothetical continuum with respect to other cases.

Temporality. By definition, of course, an abeyance structure persists throughout time, but temporality refers to the length of time that a movement organization is able to hold personnel. Activism provides a community that is an alternative source of integration and, thus, can have an enduring effect beyond a particular period in an individual's life (Coser 1974; White 1988).

During the 70-odd years of the first wave of the women's movement, a number of women's rights groups emerged and provided alternative status vacancies for large numbers of mainly white and middle-class women (Flexner 1959; Buechler 1986; Chafetz and Dworkin 1986). Among the 55 leaders and core activists of the NWP, 53 percent had been recruited at least four decades earlier during the suffrage campaign.

For NWP members, early participation in high-risk activism (McAdam 1986), including picketing the White House, engaging in hunger strikes while imprisoned, and burning President Wilson's speeches, kept them involved long after the suffrage victory. Lamenting the passage of that period, Florence Kitchelt asked a fellow suffragist in 1959 whether she ever felt "as I do that the modern woman is missing something very thrilling, uplifting as well as unifying in not being able to take part in a suffrage campaign? Those were the days!" Katharine Hepburn, mother of the actress, in a speech to women's rights activists, described her experiences in the suffrage struggle. "That whole period in my life I remember with the greatest delight," she said. "We had no doubts. Life was a great thrill from morning until night." Involvement in the suffrage movement had a powerful and enduring effect on participants, so much so that they continued even into the 1950s to promote women's rights in a society antagonistic to the idea. The strong and lasting effects of participation in high-risk activism is supported by McAdam's (1988) study of participants in the 1964 Freedom Summer Project.

By the 1940s and 1950s, a core of women in the NWP had devoted a major portion of their lives to feminist activity. Typical participation patterns are reflected in the comments of two members. In 1952, one woman wrote, "Since 1917 I have devoted all my spare time to feminism." Another woman asked in 1950 for a "cure for giving too much of one's time to one thing," although she still continued to devote herself to passage of the ERA. Not surprisingly, the most striking characteristic of the NWP membership was advanced age. Isserman (1987, p. 24) found a similar age structure in another organization that provided continuity between two stages of mass mobilization, the American Communist Party in the 1940s and 1950s. Constant numbers—even if small— are better for morale than steady turnover, so temporality enhances the likelihood that an organization will continue to endure.

Purposive Commitment. Commitment refers to the willingness of people to do what must be done, regardless of personal rewards and sacrifices, to maintain a collective challenge and is essential for holding an organizational pattern alive between stages of mass mobilization. Research on social movement involvement has focused primarily on the types of incentives that induce activists to make an initial commitment to a movement (e.g., Pinard 1971; Fireman and Gamson 1979; Oliver 1983; McAdam 1986). In exploring movement continuity, we must pose a different question: why do individuals maintain radical or unpopular convictions over time?

The few studies that have explored this question suggest that the nature of and incentives for commitment depend on a movement's stage in the mobilization process. Kanter's (1972) research on American communes concludes that groups characterized by high commitment are more likely to retain participants and to endure. Other research suggests that, although individuals may become activists through solidary or material incentives, continued participation depends upon high levels of commitment to group beliefs, goals, and tactics (Hirsch 1986; White 1988).

From its inception, the NWP appealed to women with strong feminist sympathies. By the 1950s, continued participation depended largely on the singleness of members' devotion to the principle of sexual equality embodied in the Equal Rights Amendment. Rejecting all other proposals for a feminist program, NWP leaders insisted that ideological integrity and the dogged pursuit of legal equality, not membership gain, would guarantee triumph.

A dedicated core of NWP members worked for the ERA by lobbying Congress and the President, seeking endorsements from candidates for political office and from other organizations establishing coalitions to support the amendment, and educating the public through newspaper and magazine articles, letters to the editor, and radio and television appearances. Commenting on the persistence of feminists' lobbying efforts, one Representative from Connecticut wondered in 1945 "whether or not the Congress meets for any other purpose but to consider the Equal Rights Amendment." Since the NWP depended entirely on the volunteer work of members, commitment was built on sacrifices of time, energy, and financial resources. Recognizing the impact of such high levels of commitment, one new recruit commented that "the secret of the ability of the group to do so much in the face of such odds is that it can attract just such devotion and loyalty."

Commitment, then, contributes to the abeyance process by ensuring that individuals continue to do what is necessary to maintain the group and its purpose even when the odds are against immediate success. Moreover, such intense commitment functions as an obstacle to participation in alternative roles and organizations.

Exclusiveness. Organizations vary according to their openness to members, some having more stringent criteria than others. Mizruchi (1983, p. 44) hypothesizes that the expansion-contraction of an abeyance organization's personnel occurs in response to changes in the larger social system's requirements for absorption, mobility, or expulsion of marginal populations. To absorb large numbers of people who are unattached to other structures requires organizations to be inclusive, as happens during the peak mobilization of social movement organizations. In cycles of decline, however, when challenging groups lack widespread attitudinal support, organizations become exclusive and attempt to expel or hold constant their membership. Zald and Ash (1966) contend that exclusive movement organizations are more likely to endure than inclusive ones.

At the peak of the suffrage struggle, the NWP was inclusive across the class and political spectrum (Cott 1987, pp. 53–55). It attracted wage-earning women from a variety of occupations as well as elite women social activists. Its members had ties to political parties, government, and industry, as well as to the socialist, peace, labor, and anti-lynching movements. But when the NWP launched its ERA campaign, many bodies organized on occupational, religious, and racial grounds and devoted to other policy issues began to absorb women from mainstream suffrage groups and siphon off NWP members. This left the NWP with a small and relatively homogeneous permanent core of feminists.

By the end of World War II, the NWP had lost most of its members and was not attracting new ones. Compared to its 60,000 members in the last years of the suffrage campaign, the NWP had about 4000 "general" members by 1945 and only 1400 by 1952. More revealing, it listed 627 "active" members in 1947 and 200 by 1952. Although the NWP also lost members as a result of an internal conflict over whether to expand membership in 1947 and again in 1953, the leadership preferred to keep the organization a small elite vanguard. As one member put it, "no mass appeal will ever bring into the Party that type of woman who can best carry forward our particular aims. We are an 'elect body' with a single point of agreement."

Just as important, the membership of the NWP also grew increasingly homogeneous and socially advantaged over the decades. Of 55 core activist, 90 percent of the employed held professional, managerial, or technical positions. Several researchers have noted that intellectuals and other privileged groups are likely to be overrepresented among the leadership and supporters of neo-liberal and communal movements. Some have attributed this to the risks and resources that participation entails (Lenin 1970; McCarthy and Zald 1973; Oberschall 1973, p. 161), while others look to the unique political culture of intellectuals and professionals (Pinard and Hamilton 1988).

Despite the fact that the NWP leaders preferred a small homogeneous membership, they recognized the significance of size and diversity for public impact. In order to give the appearance of a mass constituency, the NWP devised certain strategies. Members maintained multiple memberships in women's organizations in order to win endorsements for the ERA; they established coalitions to give the impression of a large membership; they financed a "front" organization to give the appearance of cooperation between feminists and labor women; and they recruited leaders of the National Association of Colored Women in order to obtain its endorsement of the ERA. Yet, despite attempts to appear inclusive, the NWP did not seriously try to build an indigenous base of support.

Organization exclusivity is closely related to the commitment variable. Organizations that insist upon high levels of purposive commitment and make stringent demands of time and financial resources cannot absorb large numbers of people. They are, however, good at holding constant those members that they have. Thus, exclusiveness is an important characteristic of abeyance organizations because it ensures a relatively homogeneous cadre of activists suited to the limited activism undertaken.

Centralization. Organizations vary in their centralization of power. Some operate through a "single center of power," whereas decentralized groups distribute power among subunits (Gamson 1975, p. 93). Although centralization contributes to a decline in direct-action tactics (Piven and Cloward 1977; Jenkins and Eckert 1986), it has the advantage of producing the organizational stability, coordination, and technical expertise necessary for movement survival (Gamson 1975; Wehr 1986; Staggenborg 1989).

By the end of World War II, the NWP functioned almost entirely on the national level with a federated structure in which local and state chapters had little control. State branches, which had been active in the 1920s, consisted in most cases of little more than a chairman and served the organization primarily as letterheads to use in lobbying senators and representatives.

A national chairman headed the NWP. The Party's founder and leading light, Alice Paul, however, directed and kept a tight reign on its activities, even though she formally occupied the chair for only a brief period from 1942 to 1945. As one member described it, Paul "gave the chairman all deference. But if you were a wise chairman, you did what Alice Paul wanted, because she knew what was needed." The chairman headed a national council that met periodically at the Washington headquarters. There was also a national advisory council composed of prominent women who lent their names to the group's work.

Paul, reputedly a charismatic leader committed to the point of fanaticism, maintained tight control over the ERA campaign. She decided when it was time to press Congress and when to maintain a low profile and, according to members' reports, worked from six in the morning until midnight. On at least two occasions serious conflict erupted over the lack of democratic procedures in the Party. It focused specifically on Alice Paul's autocratic leadership style and on the refusal of the national leadership to allow state branches to expand membership. A letter, circulated in 1947, contained charges typical of those directed against Paul: "You have made it clear that you consider yourself and the small group around you an elite with superabundant intellect and talents, and consider us, in contrast, the commonfolk." Thus centralization of leadership, like exclusiveness, had the potential to provoke conflict among members. But it also had advantages in a nonreceptive political environment.

Paul used her influence to direct a small group of activists with highly specialized skills—lobbying and researching, testifying, and writing about policy issues—who viewed themselves as an embattled feminist minority. The NWP was able to finance its activities with some invested funds, dues, contributions from members, and revenue from the rental of rooms in its Washington property. As a result, activists did not have to expend energy generating resources to maintain the organization.

This kind of central direction allowed the NWP to sustain the feminist challenge through the years by concentrating on a single strategy that could be carried out by a dedicated band of activists with highly specialized skills. Thus, centralization contributes to the abeyance process by ensuring the maintenance of organization and at least minimal activity during periods when conditions do not favor mass mobilization.

Culture. The culture of a social movement organization is embodied in its collective emotions, beliefs, and actions. Although all social movements create and bear culture, movement organizations vary in the character and complexity of their cultures (Lofland 1985).

The effectiveness of an organization with respect to its abeyance function depends, in part, on its capacity to motivate persons to assume certain positions. As the larger political and cultural atmosphere becomes less hospitable to the social movement, recruitment of personnel becomes difficult. In order to make participation more attractive, organizations must elaborate alternative cultural frameworks to provide security and meaning for those who reject the established order and remain in the group. Previous research suggests that the more highly developed an organization's culture, the more it offers members the satisfaction and other resources necessary for its survival (Kanter 1972; Lofland 1985).

The NWP developed an elaborate and expressive culture through activities at the Alva Belmont House, its national headquarters in Washington, D.C. Belmont House served not only as an office for national council meetings, but also as a center where lobbying efforts were coordinated and where the monthly newsletter was published. It also created the kind of female world essential to the maintenance of feminism (Freedman 1979; Rupp 1985). A few women lived at Belmont House and in two other Party-owned houses, while lobbyists stayed there from a few days to several months. In addition, Belmont House was the site of feminist events and celebrations: teas to honor women politicians or sponsors of the ERA, victory celebrations, and parties on Susan B. Anthony's birthday or on the anniversary of the suffrage victory. The activities and relationships women formed at Belmont House provided both ideological and affective support for participation in women's rights work.

Although NWP members believed in the pervasiveness of discrimination against women, the Party did not develop and advance a well-articulated ideological and theoretical position. Rather, feminism was defined principally through a culture that promoted a feminist worldview. One member expressed her world view, complaining of "Masculinity running rampant *all over the earth!*" and rebelling at the "utter manmindedness" she saw all around her. Alice Paul characterized women's rights advocates as sharing a "feeling of loyalty to our own sex and an enthusiasm to have every degradation that was put upon our sex removed." Despite occasional conflict over whether men should be brought into the movement, the NWP retained a separatist strategy. To ensure that the Party remain committed to its original vision—collective action by women for women—wealthy benefactor Alva Belmont included a clause in her bequest revoking her legacy if men ever joined or participated in the organization.

In addition to reinforcing feminist beliefs, the culture harbored at Belmont House fulfilled expressive and symbolic functions that contributed to the survival of feminism. Women who lived and worked at the house become for some, the "Women's Party family." Many who could not live at the house, because of family, work, and financial constraints, made regular pilgrimages in order to remain a part of the women's community. One member wrote that she was "looking forward with joy to my return home, and Home to me now, means the dear Alva Belmont House." In fact, bringing friends to Belmont House was the primary way that women recruited new members.

Personal ties of love and friendship among members were an important cultural ideal. A willingness to shape personal relationships around the cause was, in large measure, what made possible the intense commitment of members. NWP members described their ties as mother-daughter or sororal relationships, and members' letters to one another were filled with expressions of intimacy and friendship. Ties among members took the form of close friendships, intense devotion to Alice Paul, and couple relationships. Having another woman as life partner seemed to facilitate feminist work because these women's personal lives meshed well with their political commitments.

Movement organizations that cultivate and sustain rich symbolic lives, then, enhance the abeyance function by helping to hold members. This finding is consistent with other research the demonstrates that commitment to peer and to a shared political community promotes sustained involvement in social movements (Rosenthal and Schwartz forthcoming; McAdam 1988; White 1988).

In summary, I have described the NWP in the post-1945 period as an organizational pattern characterized by high longevity of attachment; intense levels of individual commitment to movement goals and tactics; high exclusiveness in terms of membership; high centralization that ensures a relatively advanced level of specialized skills among core activists; and a rich political culture that promotes continued involvement in the movement. This appears to be the ideal combination of factors necessary to hold a movement in abeyance until the external forces make it possible to resume a more mass-based challenge.

CONCLUSION

This paper presents new data that challenge the traditional view that no organized feminist challenge survived in the 1940s and 1950s. I have used the NWP case to highlight the processes by which social movements maintain continuity between different cycles of peak activity. I analyze the factors associated with adaptations of Mizruchi's (1983) abeyance process. Abeyance is essentially a holding pattern of a group which continues to mount some type of challenge even in a nonreceptive political environment. Factors that contribute to abeyance are both external and internal to the movement. Externally, a discrepancy between a surplus of activists and a lack of status opportunities for integrating them into the mainstream creates conditions for abeyance. Internally, structures arise that permit organizations to absorb and hold a committed cadre of activists. These abeyance structures, in turn, promote movement continuity and are employed in later rounds of mass mobilization.

Although any theory based on a single case is open to challenge, recent research points to the utility of the abeyance model for understand other movements of the 1960s, particularly the civil rights (McAdam 1988), New Left (Gittlin 1987; Isserman 1987; Hayden 1988), and gay rights (D'Emilio 1983) movements. But this work has not yet had major impact on revising theory about the sixties movements or on social movement theory in general.

Why have scholars of social movements neglected sources of continuity between cycles of movement activity and, instead, preferred an "immaculate conception" interpretation of social movements? First, scholars generally are more interested in movements undergoing cycles of mass mobilization and have done little research on movements in decline and equilibrium. Second, the limited conceptualization of movement organization in the literature has perpetuated classical conceptions of social movements as numerically large and mass-based. Research on a variety of organizational forms, including becalmed movements (Zald and Ash 1966), professional movements (McCarthy and Zald 1973), movement halfway houses (Morris 1984), elite-sustained movements (Rupp and Taylor 1987), and consensus movements (McCarthy and Wolfson unpublished), is now challenging the classical view by suggesting that these types of movements are capable of sustained activism in nonreceptive political climates (Staggenborg 1988). Third, existing approaches overlook social movement continuity by neglecting to think about outcomes (Gamson 1975). Focusing on short-term gains ignores the possibility that social reform proceeds in a ratchetlike fashion, where the gains of one struggle become the resources for later challenges by the same aggrieved group (Tarrow 1983).

The research presented above specifies the ways that organizational and ideological bridges span different stages of mobilization. Most movements have thresholds or turning points in mobilization which scholars have taken for "births" and "deaths." This research suggests that movements do not die, but scale down and retrench to adapt to changes in the political climate. Perhaps movements are never really born anew. Rather, they contract and hibernate, sustaining the totally dedicated and devising strategies appropriate to the external environment. If this is the case, our task as sociologists shifts from refining theories of movement emergence to accounting for fluctuations in the nature and scope of omnipresent challenges....

REFERENCES

Balser, Diane. 1987. *Sisterhood and Solidarity: Feminism and Labor in Modern Times.* Boston: South End.

Barkan, Steven E. 1979. "Strategic, Tactical and Organizational Dilemmas of the Protest Movement against Nuclear Power." *Social Problems* 27: 19–37.

———. 1984. "Legal Control of the Southern Civil Rights Movement." *American Sociological Review* 49:552–69.

Becker, Susan. 1981. *The Origins of the Equal Rights Amendment: American Feminism between the Wars.* Westport, CT: Greenwood.

Breines, Wini. 1985. "Domineering others in the 1950s: Image and Reality." *Women's Studies International Forum* 8:601–8.

Buechler, Steven M. 1986. *The Transformation of the Woman Suffrage Movement: The Case of Illinois.* 1850–1920. New Brunswick, NJ: Rutgers University Press.

Carden, Maren Lockwood. 1974. *The New Feminist Movement.* New York: Russell Sage.

Chafe, William H. 1972. *The American Woman: Her Changing Social, Economic, and Political Roles.* 1920–1970, New York: Oxford University Press.

Chafetz, Janet Saltzman and Anthony Gary Dworkin. 1986. *Female Revolt: Women's Movements in World and Historical Perspective.* Totowa, NJ: Rowan and Allanheld.

Cohen, Jean L. 1985. "Strategy or Identity: New Theoretical Paradigms and Contemporary Social Movements." *Social Research* 52:663–716.

Coser, Lewis. 1974. *Greedy Institutions.* New York: Free Press.

Cott, Nancy F. 1987. *The Grounding of Modern Feminism.* New Haven: Yale University Press.

D'Emilio, John. 1983. *Sexual Politics, Sexual communities.* Chicago: University of Chicago Press.

Erskine, Hazel. 1971. "The Polls: Women's Role." *Public Opinion Quarterly* 35: 287–87.

Evans, Sara. 1979. *Personal Politics: The Roots of Women's Liberation in the Civil Rights Movement and the New Left.* New York: Knopf.

Ferree, Myra Marx and Beth B. Hess. 1985. *Controversy and Coalition: The New Feminist Movement*. Boston: Twayne.

Fireman, Bruce and William A. Gamson. 1979. "Utilitarian Logic in the Resource Mobilization Perspective." Pp. 8–44 in *The Dynamics of Social Movements*. edited by M. Zald and J. McCarthy. Cambridge, MA: Winthrop.

Flacks, Richard. 1971. *Youth and Social Change*. Chicago: Markham.

Flexner, Eleanor. 1959. *Century of Struggle*. Cambridge: Harvard University Press.

Freedman, Estelle. 1979. "Separatism as Strategy: Female Institution Building and American Feminism. 1870–1930." *Feminist Studies*. 5: 512–29.

Freeman, Jo. 1975. *The Politics of Women's Liberation*. New York: David McKay.

———. 1979. "Resource Mobilization and Strategy: A Model for Analyzing Social Movement Organization Actions." Pp. 167–89 in *The Dynamics of Social Movements*, edited by M. Zald and J. McCarthy. Cambridge, MA: Winthrop.

———. 1983. *Social Movements of the Sixties and Seventies*, New York: Longman.

———. 1987. "Whom You Know versus Whom You Represent: Feminist Influence in the Democratic and Republican Parties." Pp. 215–44 in *The Women's Movements of the United States and Western Europe*. edited by M. Katzenstein and C. Mueller. Philadelphia: Temple University Press.

Friedan, Betty. 1963. *The Feminine Mystique*. New York: Dell.

———. 1976. *It Changed My Life*. New York: Dell.

Gamson, William A. 1975. *The Strategy of Social Protest*. Homewood, IL: Dorsey.

Gelb, Joyce and Marian Lief Palley. 1982. *Women and Public Policy*. Princeton: Princeton University Press.

Giddings, Paula. 1984. *When and Where I Enter: The Impact of Black Women on Race and Sex in America*. New York: Bantam.

Gittlin, Tod. 1987. *The Sixties*. New York: Bantam.

Gusfield, Joseph R. 1970. *Protest, Reform, and Revolt*. New York: Wiley.

———. 1981. "Social Movements and Social Change: Perspectives of Linearity and Fluidity." Pp. 317–39 in *Research in Social Movements, Conflict and Change*. Vol. 4, edited by Louis Kriesberg. Greenwich, CT: JAI Press.

Harrison, Cynthia. 1988. *On Account of Sex*. Berkeley: University of California Press.

Hayden, Tom. 1988. *Reunion*. New York: Random House.

Hirsch, Eric L. 1986. "The Creation of Political Solidarity in Social Movement Organizations." *Sociological Quarterly* 27:373–87.

Isserman, Maurice. 1987. *If I Hand a Hammer: The Death of the Old Left and the Birth of the New Left*. New York: Basic.

Jenkins, J. Craig. 1983. "Resource Mobilization Theory and the Study of Social Movements." *Annual Review of Sociology* 9:527–53.

———. 1987. "Interpreting the Stormy 1960s: Three Theories in Search of a Political Age." *Research in Political Sociology* 3:269–303.

Jenkins. J. Craig and Craig M. Eckert. 1986. "Channeling Black Insurgency: Elite Patronage and Professional Social Movement Organizations in the Development of the Black Movement." *American Sociological Review* 51:812–29.

Jenkins. J. Craig and Charles Perrow. 1977. "Insurgency of the Powerless: Farmworkers Movement (1946–1972)." *American Sociological Review* 42:249–68.

Kanter, Rosabeth Moss. 1972. *Commitment and Community*. Cambridge, MA: Harvard University Press.

Kimmel, Michael. 1984. *Review of Regulating Society* by Ephraim H. Mizruchi. *Society*, July/August:90–92.

Klandermans, Bert. 1986. "New Social Movements and Resource Mobilization: The European and the American Approach." *Mass Emergencies and Disasters* 4:13–38.

Klein, Ethel. 1984. *Gender Politics: From Consciousness to Mass Politics*. Cambridge, MA: Harvard University Press.

Lemons, J. Stanley. 1973. *The Woman Citizen: Social Feminism in the 1920s*. Urbana: University of Illinois Press.

Lenin, V. I. 1970. "What is to be Done?" Pp. 458–72 in *Protest, Reform, and Revolt*, edited by Joseph R. Gusfield. New York: Wiley.

Lofland, John. 1985. "Social Movement Culture." Pp. 219–39 in *Protest: Studies of Collective Behavior and Social Movements,* edited by John Lofland. New Brunswick. NJ: Transaction.

Lunardini, Christine A. 1986. *From Equal Suffrage to Equal Rights*. New York: New York University Press.

Lundberg, Ferdinand and Marynia F. Farnham. 1947. *Modern Woman: The Lost Sex*. New York: Harper.

May, Elaine Tyler. 1988. *Homeward Bound: American Families in the Cold War Era*. New York: Basic.

McAdam, Douglas. 1982. *Political Process and the Development of Black Insurgency,* 1930–1970. Chicago: University of Chicago Press.

———. 1986. "Recruitment to High-Risk Activism: The Case of Freedom Summer." *American Journal of Sociology* 92:64–90.

———. 1988. *Freedom Summer*. New York: Oxford University Press.

McCarthy, John D. and Mayer N. Zald. 1973. *The Trend of Social Movements in America: Professionalization and Resource Mobilization*. Morristown, NJ: General Learning.

———. 1977. "Resource Mobilization and Social Movements: A Partial Theory." *American Journal of Sociology* 82: 1212–41.

McCarthy, John D. and Mark Wolfson. Unpublished. "Exploring Sources of Rapid Social Movement Growth: The Role of Organizational Form, Consensus Support, and Elements of the American State." Paper presented at the Workshop on Frontiers in Social Movement Theory, June 1988, Ann Arbor, MI.

Melucci, Alberto. 1985. "The Symbolic Challenge of Contemporary Movements." *Social Research* 52:789–816.

Mizruchi, Ephraim H. 1983. *Regulating Society*. New York: Free Press

Morris, Aldon. 1984. *The Origins of the Civil Rights Movement: Black Communities Organizing for Change*. New York: Free Press.

Mueller, Carol McClurg. 1987. "Collective Consciousness. Identity Transformation, and the Rise of Women in Public Office in the United States." Pp. 89–108 in *The Women's Movements of the United States and Western Europe,* edited by M.F. Katzenstein and C.M. Mueller. Philadelphia: Temple University Press.

———. Unpublished. "The Life Cycle of Equal Rights Feminism: Resource Mobilization, Political Process, and Dramaturgical Explanations." Paper presented at the 1987 Annual Meetings of the American Sociological Association, Chicago.

Oberschall, Anthony. 1973. *Social Conflict and Social Movements*. Englewood Cliffs, NJ: Prentice-Hall.

Oliver, Pamela. 1983. "The Mobilization of Paid and Volunteer Activists in the Neighborhood Movement." Pp. 133–70 in *Research in Social Movements, Conflict and Change*. Vol. 5. Greenwich, CT: JAI Press.

Oliver, Pamela E. and Gerald Marwell. 1988. "The Paradox of Group Size in Collective Action: A Theory of the Critical Mass. II." *American Sociological Review* 53:1–8.

Pinard, Maurice. 1971. *The Rise of a Third Party: A Study in Crisis Politics*. Englewood Cliffs, NJ: Prentice-Hall.

Pinard, Maurice and Richard Hamilton. 1988. "Intellectuals and the Leadership of Social Movements: Some Comparative Perspectives." *McGill Working Papers on Social Behavior*.

Piven, Frances Fox and R.A. Cloward. 1977. *Poor People's Movements*. New York: Pantheon.

Pizzorno, Allessandro. 1978. "Political Science and Collective Identity in Industrial Conflict." Pp. 277–98 in *The Resurgence of Class Conflict in Western Europe since 1968,* edited by C. Crouch and A. Pizzorno. New York: Holmes and Meier.

Rosenthal, Naomi, M. Fingrutd, M. Ethier, R. Karant, and D. McDonald. 1985. "Social Movements and Network Analysis: A Case of Nineteenth Century Women's Reform in New York State." *American Journal of Sociology* 90:1022–54.

Rosenthal, Naomi and Michael Schwartz. Forthcoming. "Spontaneity and Democracy in Social Protest." In *Organizing for Change: Social Movement Organizations in Europe and the U.S. Vol. 5*. Greenwich, CT: JAI Press.

Rupp, Leila J. 1982. "The Survival of American Feminism." Pp. 33—65 in *Reshaping America,* edited by R.H. Bremner and G.W. Richard. Columbus: Ohio State University Press.

———. 1985. "The Women's Community in the National Woman's Party, 1945 to the 1960's." *Signs* 10:715–40.

Rupp, Leila J. and Verta Taylor. 1987. *Survival in the Doldrums: The American Women's Rights Move-*

ment, 1945 to the 1960s. New York: Oxford University Press.

Snow, David A., Lewis A. Zurcher, and Sheldon Eckland-Olson. 1980. "Social Networks and Social Movements: A Microstructural Approach to Differential Recruitment." *American Sociological Review* 45:787–801.

Staggenborg, Suzanne. 1988. "Consequences of Professionalization and Formalization in the Pro-Choice Movement." *American Sociological Review* 53:585–606.

———. 1989. "Stability and Innovation in the Women's Movement: A Comparison of Two Movement Organizations." *Social Problems* 36:75–92.

Tarrow, Sidney. 1983. *Struggling to Reform: Social Movements and Policy Change during Cycles of Protest*. Center for International Studies, Western Societies Occasional Paper no. 15. Ithaca, NY: Cornell University.

Taylor, Verta. 1989. "The Future of Feminism: A Social Movement Analysis." Pp. 473–90 in *Feminist Frontiers II*, edited by Laurel Richardson and Verta Taylor. New York: Random House.

Tilly, Charles. 1979. "Repertoires of Contention in America and Britain, 1750–1830." Pp. 126–55 in *The Dynamics of Social Movements*, edited by M. Zald and J. McCarthy. Cambridge, MA: Winthrop.

Touraine, Alain. 1971. *The Post-Industrial Society*. New York: Random House.

Wehr, Paul. 1986. "Nuclear Pacifism as Collective Action." *Journal of Peace Research* 22:103–13.

White, Robert. 1988. "Commitment, Efficacy, and Personal Sacrifice Among Irish Republicans." *Journal of Political and Military Sociology* 16:77–90.

Zald, Mayer and Roberta Ash. 1966. "Social Movement Organizations: Growth, Decay, and Change. *Social Forces* 44:327–41.